CLAUDE VINCENT

*This book is dedicated to the memory of Claude Vincent,
who stayed in Laos when many people fled, and who
tragically died near Kasi on 11 September 1996.*

Laos
Handbook

Joshua Eliot and Jane Bickersteth

Footprint Handbooks

The day does not exist when we shall forget
A Laotian poet and refugee from the Plain of Jars

Footprint Handbooks

6 Riverside Court, Lower Bristol Road
Bath BA2 3DZ England
T 01225 469141 F 01225 469461
E mail handbooks@footprint.cix.co.uk
www.fooprint-handbooks.co.uk

ISBN 0 900751 89 4 ISSN 1363-7452
CIP DATA: A catalogue record for this book is
available from the British Library

In North America, published by

a division of *NTC Publishing Group*

4255 West Touhy Avenue, Lincolnwood
(Chicago), Illinois 60646-1975, USA
T 847 679 5500 F 847 679 24941
E mail NTCPUB2@AOL.COM

ISBN 0-8442-4921-1
Library of Congress Catalog Card
Number: 96-72528
Passport Books and colophon are registered
trademarks of NTC Publishing group

©Footprint Handbooks Limited
January 1997

First published in 1992 as part of *Thailand,
Indochina & Burma Handbook* by Trade &
Travel Publications Ltd

Every effort has been made to ensure that
the facts in this Handbook are accurate.
However travellers should still obtain
advice from consulates, airlines etc about
current travel and visa requirements and
conditions before travelling. The authors
and publishers cannot accept responsibility
for any loss, injury or inconvenience,
however caused.

The maps are not intended to have any
political significance.

Cover design by Newell and Sorrell; cover
photography by Life File/Richard Powers

Production: Design by Mytton Williams;
Typesetting by Jo Morgan, Ann Griffiths and
Melanie Mason-Fayon; Maps by Sebastian
Ballard, Alasdair Dawson and Kevin Feeney;
Charts by Ann Griffiths; Original line drawings
by Andrew Newton; Proofread by Rod Gray
and David Cotterell.

Printed and bound in Great Britain by
Clays Ltd., Bungay, Suffolk

Contents

The Editors

Joshua Eliot

Joshua has a long-standing interest in Southeast Asia. He was born in Calcutta and grew up in Hong Kong. Southeast Asian Studies was his obvious choice for a degree course and during this time he lived and travelled widely throughout the region, conducting research in Thailand, Sumatra and Laos. The travelling has continued for over 15 years. He speaks Thai, Lao and Indonesian. Joshua lives and works in the North of England and continues to make regular visits to all the Southeast Asian countries.

Jane Bickersteth

Jane has worked on the Southeast Asia guidebooks since 1992. She has been visiting the region for over 10 years, spending a year there with her young son whilst she researched the first edition of the Footprint Handbook on Southeast Asia. Jane is an artist by training and is particularly inspired by the Khmer ruins of Thailand and the candis of Java and Bali.

Acknowledgements

Much help has been received from friends, colleagues, researchers and fellow travellers during the preparation of this edition. All contributors have been tremendously helpful and are acknowledged on page 303. However, there are a number of people we would particularly like to thank for their assistance. Gillian Henson, in Vientiane, was enormously hospitable, informative and helpful and did much to make our last trip to Laos such a ball. Angus McDonald and Frederic Dionne-Vachon, based in Vientiane, did an excellent job helping with the updating of much of the northern section of the book, travelling to all the towns that we were unable to cover during our visit. In the United States, Kenneth Thompson – aka Raven 58 – provided a wealth of detailed comment on his experiences during the secret war in Laos. His recollections are reproduced as separate 'boxes' through the text. Rocio Helena Venegas and Mélanie Pinard, both at the School of Architecture in the University of Montréal, provided the detailed architectural information on Lao and French-colonial houses in Luang Prabang. They also provided the drawings reproduced in the section and devised the suggested walking tour of the city. Carol Cassidy of *Lao Textiles* commented on the textile section.

Other people who have provided assistance or encouragement include, in no particular order: Bob Hardy of the School of Architecture at the University of Montréal in Québec, and Roche-Hardy; Patrick and Nicole Millischer; Pierre Mainetti of the *Phou Vao Hotel* in Luang Prabang; Mr Boonliep Konechane of *Sodetour* in Pakse; Mr Yoi Soumpholphakdy of the *Auberge Sala Done Khong* in Muang Khong; Mr Khamphat Boua of the *Hotel Residence du Champa* in Pakse; Mr Leng Samthavilai of the *Savannakhet Tourism Company*; Mrs Vayakone Bodhisane of *Diethelm Travel* in Vientiane; Mr Medsanh Inthavilay of the *Lane Xang Travel and Tour Co Ltd* in Luang Prabang; and Santi of the *Villa Santi* in Vientiane. Finally we would like to record our thanks to Claude Vincent of *Sodetour*, in many ways the architect of modern tourism in Laos, who tragically died near Kasi on 11 September 1996.

Writing to us

Many people write to us - with corrections, new information, or simply comments. If you want to let us know something, we would be delighted to hear from you. Please give us as precise information as possible, quoting the edition and page number of the Handbook you are using and send as early in the year as you can. Your help will be greatly appreciated, especially by other travellers. In return we will send you details about our special guidebook offer.

For hotels and restaurants, please let us know:

- each establishment's name, address, phone and fax number
- number of rooms, whether a/c or air-cooled, attached (clean?) bathroom
- location - how far from the station or bus stand, or distance (walking time) from a prominent landmark
- if it's not already on one of our maps, can you place it?
- your comments - either good or bad - as to why it is distinctive
- tariff cards
- local transport used

For places of interest:

- location
- entry, camera charge
- access - by whatever means of transport is most approriate, eg time of main buses or trains to and from the site, journey time, fare
- facilities - nearby drinks stalls, restaurants, for the disabled
- any problems, eg steep climb, wildlife, unofficial guides
- opening hours
- site guides

Introduction and hints

L AOS is the 'forgotten country' of Southeast Asia. A country where, it is sometimes said, farmers lie back and 'watch the rice grow'. It is one of the poorest nations on earth with an income per person of just US$320 and total exports valued at a mere US$300mn. There are only 2,000 km of surfaced road in a country the size of New Zealand, and most of that is in a terrible state. The average Lao is a farmer who posts one letter a year, shares a television with 150 other people, and stands a one in 500 chance of having visited a cinema during the previous 12 months. In villages in the north, infant mortality rates sometimes approach 50%, and just one person in four people has access to safe water.

The image that figures like these conjure up is one of grinding poverty and unremitting struggle. It comes as a surprise, then, to find Laos to be one of the most civilized countries in Southeast Asia. The towns are elegant and refined, largely untrammelled – so far – by the scourge of thoughtless redevelopment that has so scarred the other cities of the region. The pace of life is leisurely; the food is sophisticated; the Lao are welcoming and relaxed; and there is a sense of style that is absent elsewhere. Foreign residents of Vientiane, Luang Prabang and Pakse revel in the thought that expats in cities like Bangkok and Singapore regard living in Laos as the equivalent of being sent to Mars. They treasure the anonymity of their secret paradise. On paper Laos may, in UN parlance, be a least developed country. In fact, it is rich way beyond the scope of statistics to record.

But for the visitor, notching up 'sights' in Laos is difficult. There just aren't many in the traditional sense. Certainly, the old royal capital of Luang Prabang, set on the banks of the Mekong and tucked into a fertile upland rice valley, is a city without peer and justifiably a UNESCO World Heritage Site. Wat Phou in the south, a remnant of the ancient Khmer kingdom based at Angkor in neighbouring Cambodia, is also a notable destination. Vientiane is a charming capital city, while other lesser towns like Thakhek and Savannakhet are also atmospheric places to spend a day or two. The Mekong islands of the south are enchanting, and the Plain of Jars, with its giant and ancient stone jars, is also interesting in a rather arid way. But there are certainly not the sights in Laos – at least in terms of number – to compete with other countries of Southeast Asia. What is so priceless and unique about Laos has to be felt and experienced through the skin, as a slow process of osmosis. And when Laos gets under your skin, you are hooked!

Where to go

LAOS is a large country with a small population: some 5 million people inhabit an area of 237,000 sq km – roughly the size of the United Kingdom. It is also very poor and has been ravaged by a terrible war, experiencing, in the process, some of the heaviest bombing the world has ever witnessed. Couple this with the mountainous terrain and a tropical climate of seasonal torrential rains, and it is no wonder that road construction poses a considerable challenge in many areas. The government of the Lao People's Democratic Republic was also cut off from the West from 1975 – when the Lao People's Revolutionary Party finally ousted the Royal Lao Government – until the mid-1980s, when it hesitatingly embraced a programme of economic reform and international integration. All this means that roads in Laos are not good and travel is rarely easy. Of course there are also large areas of the country where there simply are no roads.

TRANSPORT AND TRAVELLING

As the introduction to this section has already emphasized, road transport in Laos is not well developed. To illustrate: many Lao making the overland journey between the N and S hop over the border to Thailand, catch a Thai bus, and then hop back again. Even with two border crossings and a substantial detour, using Thai roads and vehicles still makes for a much faster, and a more comfortable journey. For foreign visitors such international agility is not usually possible as

unlike the Lao (and Thais) visas do not allow multiple entry.

On page 323 we provide a table of **road conditions**, travel times and road speeds – on **public buses** – for mid 1996. As the table indicates, average speeds of 20-40 km/hr are the norm. The poor roads, ancient buses – many no more than converted Soviet trucks – innumerable stops for snacks and passengers, breakdowns, and mud and wet during the rainy season, mean that exploring the country by bus is a slow and at times gruelling experience. Those who have done it, of course, will also say that it is the only way to see the country and meet its people. On the country's main roads, there is a fairly regular bus service, and this is improving as each year passes. The roads are being upgraded, and the Soviet trucks gradually replaced with Japanese vehicles. However, most buses leave early in the morning and it is not unusual to find yourself stranded in a town that you had hoped to skip through. In the rainy season the problems tend to be amplified still further. On some roads, bus services are suspended altogether, and on others journey times increase as speeds descend to single figures.

Nor are the problems of overland travel just linked to the quality of the roads and the vehicles that ply them. There are some stretches which are still plagued by sometimes fatal attacks by bandits. This is particularly true of the road between Vientiane and Luang Prabang, and particularly the northern stretch from Van Vieng to Luang Prabang. In the few months before this book went to press there had been several killings on this road and embassy staff and residents in Vientiane were strongly advising against travelling by road.

There is no rail network in Laos, but **river transport** remains an important means of communication. The Mekong, and its tributaries, carry goods and passengers between many of the country's main cities and towns. For foreign visitors the most popular route is between Ban Houei Xai (on the Thai border) and Luang Prabang, and from Luang Prabang to Vientiane. However,

there are also boats that continue downriver from Vientiane all the way to Pakse, and some from Pakse to close to the Cambodian border. During the dry season smaller rivers may be too low for large boats to pass and services are either suspended or smaller (and less comfortable) vessels used.

Lao Aviation, the country's **domestic airline**, has a modest domestic network servicing the main towns and cities. On the primary routes, the airline uses fairly modern Boeing 737s. The ageing Yaks and Antonovs – not exactly the last word in aviation technology – are being gradually replaced by modern French-built

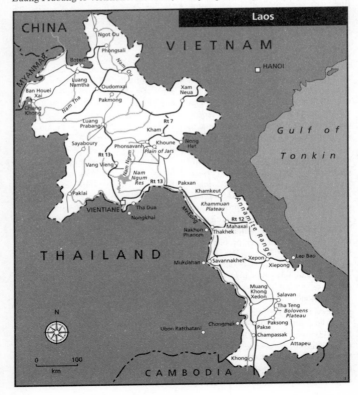

ATR 72s on the shorter and more minor sectors. Given the length of time it takes to travel by road, and the discomfort involved, flying has great advantages and attractions. Domestic tickets are also comparably cheap by western standards. The difficulty is that *Lao Aviation* offices are not 'on line' and so it is not possible, after buying a ticket from Vientiane to Luang Prabang, to at the same time book seats on additional legs from, say, Luang Prabang to Phonsavanh and from there back to Vientiane. At each stage in the journey a flight and seat has to be booked, and even then there is no guarantee that the flight will ever arrive. Or, for that matter, that a party of VIPs will not come along and claim all the seats.

TIMETABLING A VISIT

Given the transport glitches noted above, allowing some leeway in a schedule is strongly recommended. Assuming, for example, that it will be possible to catch a flight from Phonsavanh to Vientiane to connect with another from Vientiane to Bangkok, and from there to the US or Europe, is – to say the least – risky. The same goes for road transport, especially during the wet season. Those on organized tours have some distinct advantages in this regard. They will have the services of a local tour guide to apply pressure and perhaps supply gifts to free seats on overbooked planes. Local guides are also much more aware of when problems are likely to arise. A lone traveller, with no Lao, will find it hard to do the same deals and are likely to be left floundering on the tarmac.

Nonetheless, a 2-3 week visit to Laos is sufficient to see much of the country – or at least that fraction of the country that it is possible to see. The main issue, perhaps, is how to couple a visit to the N with a trip to the S where Pakse, Champassak, Wat Phou and the Mekong Islands are to be found. Vientiane to Pakse is a journey of around 750 km and many people, because they have booked a flight into and out of Vientiane, have then to retrace those 750 km to catch their plane out. By air this is bearable; by road it may be testing one's patience. The alternative, now that visas no longer need to stipulate where a visitor has to arrive and depart, is to enter and exit at different ends of the country. Thus it is possible to enter at Chiang Khong/Ban Houei Xai in the far N, travel S, and then exit at Pakse/Chongmek. There is also the option of entering or departing from Vietnam using the road that links Danang and Savannakhet (by far the most popular route across the Annamite mountains); or from China using the crossing at Boten (see the box on border crossings on page 290).

HIGHLIGHTS

River trips and hiking
Rivers remain important arteries of communication in Laos, and the Mekong and its major tributaries can be used to explore the country.

The North: Laos' trekking industry is not well developed compared with Thailand. However, there are several towns in the N where it is possible to visit minority villages, including Udom Xai, Muang Khua, Phongsali, Luang Namtha and Muang Sing.

The South: Tad Lo, a resort on the Bolovens Plateau, is a good base from which to hike.

Natural (and unnatural) features
Luang Prabang: the former royal capital's position on the Mekong, set in an upland valley, is particularly beautiful.

The North: the Nam Ngum Dam is a lakeside retreat. Van Vieng, en route to Luang Prabang, has good caves with swimming. Vieng Xai has a series of caves although their interest is linked to their use as underground redoubts against the American bombing onslaught.

The Centre: the limestone region of Mahaxai, E of Thakhek, is locally renowned for its beauty and its caves.

The South: the Bolovens Plateau and Tad Lo; the latter is the best place to relax in this beautiful and fertile area of the country. The Mekong islands of the S are another beautiful place to visit with spectacular cascades, freshwater dolphins and a relaxed atmosphere.

Historical sites and ancient cities

Vientiane: That Luang, the country's most holy site; Wat Sisaket, a beautiful cloistered monastery; Wat Phra Kaeo, which has been turned into a museum of Buddhist art; the Garden of the Buddhas outside the city with its zany sculptures drawn from Buddhism and Hinduism.

Luang Prabang: the whole central portion of the city is a historical site and has been recognized as such by UNESCO which has awarded Luang Prabang World Heritage status. Of particular note are Wat Xieng Thong and Wat May.

The North: the Pak Ou Caves, 25 km N of Luang Prabang, contain literally thousands of wooden Buddha images. The Plain of Jars is famous for its eponymous and enigmatic giant jars; it is also the area of the country where the effects of the American bombing campaign are most clearly in evidence. Vieng Xai has numerous caves which were used and extended by the Pathet Lao to protect the leadership against American air attack.

The Centre: That Sikhot, outside Thakhek, is one of the holiest thats (stupas) in the country; it also enjoys a wonderful position on the banks of the Mekong.

The South: Wat Phou near Champassak is a Khmer temple dating from the 5th-6th centuries AD and the finest archaeological site in the country; Oup Moung, not far away, is also worth visiting at the same time.

Culture

Laos has a rich and diverse culture including many different hill peoples. Unlike Thailand the trekking industry is poorly developed.

Vientiane: Boun That Luang is celebrated throughout the country over a week in Nov but most enthusiastically and colourfully at That Luang in Vientiane.

Luang Prabang: Pimay or 'New Year', celebrated in April, is best experienced in Luang Prabang where the festivities and processions extend over more than a week. Minority villages are accessible from Luang Prabang.

The North: Minority villages are accessible from several towns in the N, including: Udom Xai, Muang Khua, Phongsali, Luang Namtha and Muang Sing.

The South: hiking to a few minority villages is possible from Tad Lo on the Bolovens Plateau.

Shopping and handicrafts

Vientiane: for traditional Lao textiles, silverware and handicrafts.

Luang Prabang: not as good a selection of handicrafts, textiles and silverware as in Vientiane, but it is possible to pick up odd 'antiques' – old loom parts and baskets, for example.

The North: Xam Neua and the surrounding area has the finest weaving tradition, although many of the best pieces are now being produced in Vientiane.

Cuisine and night life

Vientiane: Vientiane has a surprisingly wide selection of good restaurants; European food is particularly recommended. There are also more than a few good bars in the capital, some with passable live music.

Museums

Vientiane: Wat Phra Kaeo is a monastery which has been converted into a museum of Buddhist art; Wat Sisaket is also officially a museum. The Revolutionary Museum displays lots of photographs of stiff-backed workers and HEP schemes as well as some ethnographic and other pieces.

Luang Prabang: the former Royal Palace and National Museum has a good collection of Buddhist art as well as momentos from more recent history – photographs and various state gifts, for example.

The South: the newly opened Champassak Museum in Pakse has a mixed collection from the somewhat interesting to the decidedly wacky.

NB The above is only a selection of places of interest and is not exhaustive. It is designed to assist in planning a trip to the region. Any 'highlight' list is inevitably subjective.

How to go

BEST TIME TO VISIT

The best time to visit Laos is during the dry and comparatively cool months between Nov and Mar. After Mar, although it can remain dry (meaning that road transport is still relatively easy), it can also be extremely hot. As the wet season wears on, so unsurfaced roads begin to suffer and overland transport becomes slow or impossible in some areas. For more information on climate see the section in the introduction on page 23, and the monthly climate graphs for the following towns: Vientiane (page 89), Luang Prabang (page 118), Savannakhet (page 173), and Pakse (page 188).

HEALTH

Health care in Laos is poor and most foreign residents go to Thailand or Singapore for treatment beyond simple illnesses and injuries. For a more comprehensive roundup of health related issues, see page 314.

WHAT TO TAKE

Travellers usually tend to take too much, even to a place like Laos which is not noted as a shopping Mecca. In Vientiane it is possible to buy most toiletries as well as things like photographic supplies and peanut butter. Luang Prabang, Savannakhet and Pakse also stock most basic items. Outside these cities little is available beyond items like soap, washing powder, batteries, shampoo, and the like.

Suitcases are not appropriate if you are intending to travel overland by bus. A backpack, or even better a travelpack (where the straps can be zipped out of sight), is recommended. Travelpacks have the advantage of being hybrid backpacks-suitcases; they can be carried on the back for easy porterage, but they can also be taken into hotels without the owner being labelled a 'hippy'.

In terms of clothing, dress in Laos is relatively casual – even at formal functions. Suits are not necessary. However, though formal attire may be the exception, dressing tidily is the norm. There is a tendency, rather than to take inappropriate articles of clothing, to take too many of the same article. Laundry services are cheap, and the turn-around rapid.

Checklist
Bumbag
Earplugs
First aid kit
Insect repellent and/or electric mosquito mats, coils
International driving licence
Passports (valid for at least 6 months)
Photocopies of essential documents
Short wave radio
Spare passport photographs
Sun protection
Sunglasses
Swiss Army knife
Torch
Umbrella
Wet wipes
Zip-lock bags

Those intending to stay in budget accommodation might also include:
Cotton sheet sleeping bag
Money belt
Padlock (for hotel room and pack)
Soap
Student card
Toilet paper
Towel
Travel wash

MONEY

Travellers cheques denominated in US$ can be changed in major centres. Though it may be possible to change other currencies, like French Francs and pounds sterling, some banks are reluctant to give anything but kip in exchange. US$ and Thai baht can be used as cash in most shops, restaurants and hotels. A certain amount of cash (in US$ or Thai baht) can also be useful in an emergency. Keep it separate from your TCs. In Dec 1996, US$1 was worth 920 kip.

● ISIC

Anyone in full-time education is entitled to an International Student Identity Card (ISIC). These are issued by student travel offices and travel agencies across the world and offer special rates on all forms of transport and other concessions and services. The ISIC head office is: ISIC Association, Box 9048, 1000 Copenhagen, Denmark, T (45) 33 93 93 03.

GETTING THERE

AIR

Most people arrive in Laos via Bangkok which has become a transport hub for the whole Indochina region. There are several flights a day between Bangkok and Vientiane. Many airlines offer non-stop or direct flights to Bangkok from Europe, North America and other cities within the Asian region. There are also air direct connections with Vientiane from the following cities: Hanoi and Ho Chi Minh City (Vietnam), Kunming and

Guangzhou (China), Phnom Penh (Cambodia), Yangon/Rangoon (Myanmar/Burma), Chiang Mai (Thailand), and Singapore.

Discounts

It is possible to obtain significant discounts on flights to Bangkok, especially outside European holiday times, most notably in London. Shop around and book early. It is also possible to get discounts from Australasia, South Asia and Japan. Note that 'peak season' varies from airline to airline – many using 8-10 bands. This means one airline's high season may not be another's.

OVERLAND

Most international visitors arrive in Laos by air through Wattay Airport in Vientiane. However, as overland entry becomes easier so more and more visitors are opting to arrive overland. The most popular overland border crossing is via the Friendship Bridge which crosses the Mekong and links the Thai town of Nong Khai the Lao capital, with Vientiane. There are rail and bus services between Bangkok and Nong Khai. The nearest Thai airport to Nong Khai is Udon Thani.

In addition to the Nong Khai crossing, it is possible to enter Laos from Thailand at the following places: Chongmek near Ubon Ratchathani, to Pakse; Mukdahan to Savannakhet; Nakhon Phanom to Thakhek; and Chiang Khong to Ban Houei Xai. The latter three crossings involve fording the Mekong by ferry or boat. It is also possible to enter Laos from Vietnam by way of Lao Bao to Xiepong and onto Savannakhet; and from China via Boten in the N.

THAILAND SECTIONS IN THIS GUIDE

Because so many people enter Laos through Thailand we have included information on a handful of relevant Thai towns as well as Bangkok. Those towns are: Nong Khai, Udon Thani, Ubon Ratchathani, Mukdahan, Nakhon Phanom, and Chiang Khong. The information is arranged towards the end of the book.

SAFETY

Laos still attracts relatively few tourists and possibly as a result the confidence tricksters and thieves that plague Thailand are not present in any great number. We have yet to receive a single letter warning of thieves. Nonetheless, simple common sense when it comes to safeguarding your possessions is required: Laos is extremely poor and all foreigners, on no matter how low a budget, are infinitely richer than the average Laotian.

Banditry

Far more serious is banditry. On some roads, especially that between Vientiane and Luang Prabang, as well as the Luang Prabang to Phonsavanh stretch, the holding up of vehicles, sometimes with fatal results, has become so common that overland travel along these two stretches is not recommended as this book goes to press. Elsewhere in the country, however, there are no current dangers of this nature.

WOMEN TRAVELLING ALONE

Women travelling alone face greater difficulties than men or couples although in Laos these problems are less pronounced than in many other countries. Women are nonetheless advised to dress modestly.

WHERE TO STAY

Laos lacks hotels and guesthouses at the very top and the very bottom of the range. There are no luxury hotels in the country and budget accommodation is also very limited. However, there are comfortable places to stay in the main towns that have rooms with air conditioning and attached hot water bathrooms, restaurants, perhaps a swimming pool, and other facilities. Though hotels may lack the amenities that have become the norm across the Mekong in Thailand, many more than make up for this in terms of charm. Old colonial villas have been converted into small 'auberge' in several towns and service, although it might not be slick, is generally warm and friendly.

Because many people still visit Laos on a tour, budget accommodation for independent travellers is scarce and prices, perhaps surprisingly, are higher than they are in (richer) Thailand.

FOOD AND DRINK

Food

Food in Laos is surprisingly good. One is tempted to think that this is a legacy of the French presence in the country. All towns of any size will have the requisite Chinese/Vietnamese restaurant as well as stalls selling simple single dish meals. In most towns it will also be possible to buy freshly baked baguettes and to order fresh and strong Lao coffee. In Luang Prabang there are also restaurants serving good French food, while Vientiane is very well provided for with a range of good restaurants.

Water

Bottled water is easily obtainable in Laos. It is not advisable to drink water straight from the tap. Imported soft drinks are also widely sold (though comparatively expensive), as well as locally brewed beer.

GETTING AROUND

AIR

Lao Aviation serves major towns flying a range of new (737s and ATR 72s) and not so new (Antonovs and Yaks) planes. Fares are cheap but the airline is wonderfully chaotic in terms of schedules and booking.

ROAD

Buses and converted trucks are the main form of transport between towns. Roads, on the whole, are very poor and journey times are long. The wet season presents particular transport difficulties. Local transport is by a variety of means from *tuk tuks* (motorized three-wheelers) to *saamlors* (human powered three-wheelers).

CAR HIRE

Cars for self-drive hire are not widely available although it is sometimes possible to negotiate an informal arrangement. More common is to hire a driver as well as the car. As roads in Laos are so poor and road sense is merely nascent it is best to pay a local to negotiate the human and physical obstacles. In towns it is easiest just to charter a *tuk-tuk* for the day or half-day.

HITCHHIKING AND CYCLING

Hitchhiking is not common in Laos although travellers have reported considerable success hitching lifts. Because public transport can be very limited in more out of the way spots and at certain border crossings, it is sometimes necessary to resort to hitching a lift on a truck. A small payment is usually expected.

Long-distance bicycle touring is not common. However it is possible to hire bicycles in many towns and because traffic is comparatively light and speeds slow, exploring local areas by bicycle is an attractive option.

BOAT

Rivers remain important arteries of communication and the Mekong and its tributaries represent significant transport links for both cargo and passengers.

LANGUAGE

English is not widely spoken. There are rather more French speakers, but even they are small in number and confined to the main towns. Lao, like Thai, is a tonal language and is hard to pick up.

Horizons

LAOS is strategically sandwiched between China, Vietnam, Cambodia, Thailand and Myanmar (Burma). It has always been the landlocked, mountainous, under-developed backwater of Indochina. But its rich history, magnificent scenery, fragile culture and its years of isolation have left Laos an unexplored jewel in Southeast Asia. More than three-quarters of the population are subsistence farmers and only a tenth of its villages are anywhere near a road. One child in five dies before its fifth birthday and cars seem to have a longer life expectancy than people. The diet is inadequate, sanitation poor, and only a quarter of the population has access to safe drinking water. Dehabilitating and fatal diseases from malaria to bilharzia, are endemic in rural Laos while the health and education systems are limited. In northern provinces the opium addiction rate is double the literacy rate. With per capita income of US$220, Laos is one of the poorest countries in the world.

Laos has also earned the distinction of being the most heavily-bombed nation on earth, per head of population – a record which even Iraq cannot match. During a 9-year secret war against the Communists, the United States dropped 6,300,000 tonnes of bombs on Indochina. About a third of them fell on Laos. In the 1960s and early-70s, more bombs rained on Laos than were dropped during WW2 – the equivalent of a plane load of bombs every 8 mins around the clock for 9 years. This cost American tax-payers more than US$2mn a day – but the cost to Laos was incalculable. But the B-52s were merely the climax of the final chapter in a centuries-long catalogue of warfare in which Laos has suffered from successive incursions by the Vietnamese, Siamese, Chinese, French and Japanese.

Now, after more than a decade of Soviet-inspired Marxism-Leninism, Laos is finally at peace and the septogenarian ex-guerrillas who head the Lao People's Revolutionary Party are tacitly conceding that their revolution has been an economic disaster. Communism's bamboo curtain has proved more resilient than its iron counterpart in Europe, but Party rhetoric is now deeply unfashionable. Just 15 years after the Marxists moved from their mountain caves to the capital's corridors of power, the capitalists began their advance on Vientiane. This time there is little doubt who will win.

While shying away from too much in the way of *glasnost*, the leadership has rubber-stamped the move from a centrally planned economy and embarked on a rapid transition to capitalism, known as *Chin Thanakaan Mai* or 'New Thinking'. The hammer and sickle were discreetly painted out of the state emblem in 1991. Having watched the Eastern bloc crumble, the Politburo's Old Guard wants to go down looking good. President Kaysone Phomvihane, who died in Nov 1992, redeemed his regime's reputation by spearheading a series of economic reforms. With the demise of Soviet Communism, there will be no more handouts from Moscow or its erstwhile allies. As Vientiane turns to the W for investment, there is concern that the impoverished country, with no industrial infrastructure, could become a casualty of capitalism. Three-quarters of its intellectuals fled the country in advance of the Communist takeover in 1975 and thousands disappeared to jungle re-education camps, so Laos has few people experienced in managing a market economy.

At first the pace of change was what Laos call *koi koi bai* – slowly, slowly – but the momentum picked up in 1991 and now everything, it seems, is viable for privatization – from state enterprises to entire economic sectors. One of the first to fall to the capitalist onslaught has been tourism; as an easy foreign exchange earner it was an obvious target. In May 1991, the government began contracting out its regional tourism monopolies to private operators. An unwelcome invasion of backpackers in 1987 convinced the government that the Thai model for tourism development was not worth emulating. Laos began effectively to means-test its visitors: tours to Laos did not – and still do not – come cheap. This attempt to control tourism and accept only high value added visitors is now changing – to a small degree. Inter-provincial travel restrictions have been lifted, visitors can enter and exit at will at any border post provided they have a valid visa, and obtaining visas without booking a tour is also becoming easier. Given the clamp down in 1987, though, this process could conceivably be reversed – there are still powerful voices in the party and government who oppose unrestrained tourism. In addition it is worth remembering that Laos' tourist infrastructure is woefully inadequate to meet any sudden increase in flows. Indeed, there are already some provincial officials who are complaining to central government about 'scruffy' travellers spending too little. This may be viewed as a harsh indictment of independent travel and travellers but in the case of Laos it carries force and has significant resonance.

The allure of capitalism, consumerism and westernism to many Lao is obvious. They do not want to be cultural artefacts forever, but with rapid change, it is easy to question the price of progress. At present rates, tourism alone will not destroy the gentle Lao spirit or the cultural treasure-trove which has remained intact despite years of war. But in downtown Vientiane, expectations are running high: Thai television, with its brash, materialist message, is beamed across the Mekong into front rooms in Vientiane, Thakhek, Savannakhet and Paksé and has already proved too much for party ideologues. Young Lao know what they want: stereos and motorbikes from Japan, rock music from Thailand, and Levi 501s from the USA.

Meanwhile, a steady stream of Thai businessmen has arrived to test the water on the other side of the Mekong. They have unleashed a capitalists' jamboree, rousing the Land of a Million Elephants from a long siesta and reintroducing corruption to Vientiane's legions of underpaid bureaucrats. Vientiane, although sleepy by the standards of other Southeast Asian capitals, is bustling with new businesses setting up every day.

The cycle of wet rice cultivation

There are an estimated 120,000 rice varieties. Rice seed – either selected from the previous harvest or, more commonly, purchased from a dealer or agricultural extension office – is soaked overnight before being sown into a carefully prepared nursery bed. Today farmers are likely to plant one of the Modern Varieties or MVs bred for their high yields.

The nursery bed into which the seeds are broadcast (scattered) is often a farmer's best land, with the most stable water supply. After a month the seedlings are up-rooted and taken out to the paddy fields. These will also have been ploughed, puddled and harrowed, turning the heavy clay soil into a saturated slime. Traditionally buffalo and cattle would have performed the task; today rotavators, and even tractors are becoming more common. The seedlings are transplanted into the mud in clumps. Before transplanting the tops of the seedlings are twisted off (this helps to increase yield) and then they are pushed in to the soil in neat rows. The work is back-breaking and it is not unusual to find labourers – both men and women – receiving a premium – either a bonus on top of the usual daily wage or a free meal at midday, to which marijuana is sometimes added to ease the pain.

After transplanting, it is essential that the water supply is carefully controlled. The key to high yields is a constant flow of water, regulated to take account of the growth of the rice plant. In 'rain-fed' systems where the farmer relies on rainfall to water the crop, he has to hope that it will be neither too much nor too little. Elaborate ceremonies are performed to appease the rice goddess and to ensure bountiful rainfall.

In areas where rice is grown in irrigated conditions, farmers need not concern themselves with the day-to-day pattern of rainfall, and in such areas 2 or even 3 crops can be grown each year. But such systems need to be carefully managed, and it is usual for one man to be in charge of irrigation. In Bali he is known as the *klian subak*, in North Thailand as the *hua naa muang fai*. He decides when water should be released, organizes labour to repair dykes and dams and to clear channels, and decides which fields should receive the water first.

Traditionally, while waiting for the rice to mature, a farmer would do little except weed the crop from time to time. He and his family might move out of the village and live in a field hut to keep a close eye on the maturing rice. Today, farmers also apply chemical fertilisers and pesticides to protect the crop and ensure maximum yield. After 90-130 days, the crop should be ready for harvesting.

Harvesting also demands intensive labour. Traditionally, farmers in a village would secure their harvesters through systems of reciprocal labour exchange; now it is more likely for a harvester to be paid in cash. After harvesting, the rice is threshed, sometimes out in the field, and then brought back to the village to be stored in a rice barn or sold. It is only at the end of the harvest, with the rice safely stored in the barn, that the festivals begin. As farmers say, having rice in the barn is like having money in the bank.

LAND

THE REGIONS OF LAOS

Laos is dominated by the Mekong River and the Annamite chain of mountains which both run SE towards the South China Sea. 1,865 km of the 4,000 km-long **Mekong River** flows along the borders of Laos and is the country's main thoroughfare. The lowlands of the Mekong valley form the principal agricultural areas, especially around Vientiane and Savannakhet, and these are home to the lowland Lao – sometimes argued to be the 'true' Lao. The Mekong has three main tributaries: the Nam Ou and Nam Tha from the N, and the Nam Ngum, which flows into Vientiane province.

Much of the N half of Laos is 1,500m or more above sea-level and its karst limestone outcrops are deeply dissected by steep-sided river valleys. Further S, the **Annamite chain** has an average height of 1,200m. Heavily forested, rugged mountains form a natural barrier between Laos and Vietnam. Most of the country is a mixture of mountains and high plateau. There are four main plateau: the **Xieng Khouang plateau**,

Provinces & Provincial Capitals

CHINA

MYANMAR

VIETNAM

N

Gulf of Tonkin

THAILAND

CAMBODIA

PROVINCES:
1. Phongsali
2. Luang Namtha
3. Bokeo
4. Oudomxai
5. Luang Prabang
6. Houa Phan
7. Sayaboury
8. Vientiane
9. Préfecture de Vientiane
10. Xieng Khouang
11. Bolikhamxai
12. Khammouane
13. Savannakhet
14. Salavan
15. Sekong
16. Champassak
17. Attapeu

Phongsali
Luang Namtha
Oudomxai
Ban Houei Xai
SPECIAL REGION
Luang Prabang
Sayaboury
Phonhong
VIENTIANE
Phonsavanh
Pakxan
Xam Neua
Thakhek
Khanthabouli
Salavan
Sekong
Pakse
Attapeu

0   100
km

Laos: population density			
Province	**Population ('000s)**	**Area km² ('000s)**	**Population Density/km²)**
Attapeu	80	10,320	8
Bokeo	64	4,970	13
Bolikhamxai	145	16,470	9
Champassak	469	15,415	30
Houa Phan	243	16,500	15
Khammouan	249	16,315	15
Luang NamTha	114	9,325	12
Luang Phrabang	339	16,875	20
Udom Xai	291	21,190	14
Phongsali	142	16,270	9
Salavan	211	10,385	20
Savannakhet	640	22,080	29
Sayaboury	182	11,795	15
Sekong	58	7,665	8
Vientiane (municipality)	442	3,920	113
Vientiane (province)	312	19,990	16
Xieng Khouang	189	17,315	11

Source: Ministry of Agriculture and Forestry

better known as the **Plain of Jars**, in the N, the **Nakai** and the limestone **Khammuan plateau** in the centre and the 10,000 sq km **Bolovens Plateau** to the S. The highest peak is the 2,800m Bia Mountain, which rises above the Xieng Khouang plateau to the NE.

GEOGRAPHY

Laos stretches about 1,000 km from N to S, while distances from E to W range from 140 to 500 km. The country covers an area of 236,800 sq km – less than half the size of France and just a third of the size of Texas. Only 15% of the population live in towns and the country has the lowest population density in Asia with 17 people/sq km. The population is 4.6 million (1995) and is growing at 2.9% a year.

Rugged mountains cover more than three-quarters of the country and with few all-weather roads (there are just 2,000 km of sealed roads in the entire country), rivers are important communication routes. Historically, the Mekong River has been the country's economic artery. On its banks nestle

Laos' most important cities: in the N the small, colourful former royal capital of Luang Prabang, further S the administrative and political capital of Vientiane, and farther S still the regional centres of Thakhek, Savannakhet and Paksé.

CLIMATE

The rainy season is from May through to Sep/Oct; the tropical lowlands receive an annual average rainfall of 1,250 mm a year. Temperatures during these months are in the 30s°C. In mountainous Xieng Khoung Province, it is cooler and temperatures can drop to freezing point in Dec and Jan. The first half of the dry season, from Nov to Apr, is cool, with temperatures between 10° and 20°C. This gives way to a hot, dry season from Mar to Jun when temperatures soar and are often in excess of 35°C. Average rainfall in Vientiane is 1,700 mm, although in N Laos and the highlands it is much wetter, with more than 3,000 mm each year. For the best time to visit, see page 288. There are monthly temperature and rainfall graphs for the following centres:

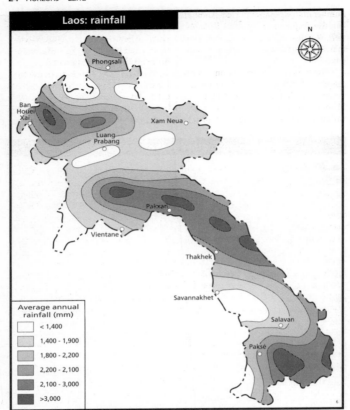

Laos: rainfall

Average annual
rainfall (mm)

- < 1,400
- 1,400 - 1,900
- 1,800 - 2,200
- 2,200 - 2,100
- 2,100 - 3,000
- >3,000

Vientiane (see page 89), Luang Prabang (see page 118), Savannakhet (see page 173 and Pakse (see page 188).

FLORA AND FAUNA

Much of Laos is forested. The vegetation is rich and diverse: a mix of tropical and sub-tropical species. Grassy savanna predominates on plateau areas such as the Plain of Jars. In the forests, some hardwoods tower to over 30m in height, while tropical palms and mango are found in the settled lowlands and large stands of pine in the remote N hills.

About half the country is still covered in primary forest but this is being seriously threatened by logging which provides Laos with more than two-thirds of its export earnings. Officially, around 450,000m³ are felled each year for commercial purposes, although in reality this is probably an under-estimate owing to the voracious activities of illegal loggers – many of whom are Thai. A ban on the export of logs in 1988 caused official timber export earnings to slump 30% – but environmentalists claim that the ban has had little impact on the number of logs being exported. Another ban was imposed in late 1991. In addition, shifting cultivators clear an estimated 100,000 ha of forest a year (see page 28).

Government reforestation programmes far from compensate for the destruction. In Oct 1989 the Council of Ministers issued a decree on the preservation of forests of which the people appear to be blissfully unaware. There was a half-hearted propaganda campaign to 'teach every Lao citizen to love nature and develop a sense of responsibility for the preservation of forests'.

Mammals include everything from wildcats, leopards and tigers to bears, wild cattle and small barking deer. Laos is also home to the large Asian elk, rhinoceros, elephants, monkeys, gibbons and ubiqui-

The Mekong: mother river of Southeast Asia

The Mekong River is one of the 12 great rivers of the world. It stretches 4,500 km from its source on the Tibet Plateau in China to its mouth (or mouths) in the Mekong Delta of Vietnam. (On 11 April 1995 a Franco-British expedition announced that they had discovered the source of the Mekong – 5,000m-high, at the head of the Rup-Sa Pass, and miles from anywhere.) Each year, the river empties 475 billion m^3 of water into the South China Sea. Along its course it flows through Burma, Laos, Thailand, Cambodia and Vietnam – all of the countries that constitute mainland Southeast Asia – as well as China. In both a symbolic and a physical sense then, it links the region. Bringing fertile silt to the land along its banks, but particularly to the Mekong Delta, the river contributes to Southeast Asia's agricultural wealth. In former times, a tributary of the Mekong which drains the Tonle Sap (the Great Lake of Angkor and Cambodia), provided the rice surplus on which that fabulous empire was founded. The Tonle Sap acts like a great regulator, storing water in time of flood and then releasing it when levels recede.

The first European to explore the Mekong River was the French naval officer Francis Garnier. His Mekong Expedition (1866-1868), followed the great river upstream from its delta in Cochin China. Of the 9,960 km that the expedition covered, 5,060 km were 'discovered' for the first time. The motivation for the trip was to find a southern route into the Heavenly Kingdom – China. But they failed. The river is navigable only as far as the Lao-Cambodian border where the Khone rapids make it impassable. Nonetheless, the report of the expedition is one of the finest of its genre.

Today the Mekong itself is perceived as a source of potential economic wealth – not just as a path to riches. The Mekong Secretariat was established in 1957 to harness the waters of the river for hydropower and irrigation. The Secretariat devised a grandiose plan incorporating a succession of seven huge dams which would store 142 billion m^3 of water, irrigate 4.3 million hectares of riceland, and generate 24,200MW of power. But the Vietnam War intervened to disrupt construction. Only Laos' Nam Ngum Dam on a tributary of the Mekong was ever built – and even though this generates only 150MW of power, electricity exports to Thailand are one of Laos' largest export earners. Now that the countries of mainland Southeast Asia are on friendly terms once more, the Secretariat and its scheme have been given a new lease of life. But in the intervening years, fears about the environmental consequences of big dams have raised new questions. The Mekong Secretariat has moderated its plans and is now looking at less ambitious, and less contentious, ways to harness the Mekong River.

Forest protection propaganda by post

tous rabbits and squirrels. Ornithological life encompasses pheasants, partridges, many songbirds, ducks and some hawks and eagles – although in rural areas many birds (and other animals) have been killed for food. There is an abundant reptilian population, including cobras, kraits, crocodiles and lizards. The lower reaches of the Mekong River, marking the border between Cambodia and Laos, is the last place in Indochina where the rare Irrawaddy dolphin is to be found. However dynamite fishing is deminating the population, and today there are probably just 100 or 200 left. Another rare denizen of the Mekong, but one that stands a greater chance of survival, is the *pa buk* catfish (*Pangasianodon gigas*) which weighs upto 340 kg. This riverbed-dwelling fish was first described by western science only in 1930, although Lao fishermen and their Thai counterparts had been catching it for many years – as James McCarthy notes in the account of his travels through Siam and Laos published in 1900. The fish is a delicacy, and

clearly has been for many years – its roe was paid as tribute to China in the late 19th century. Because of over-fishing, by the 1980s the numbers of *pa buk* had become severly depleted. However a breeding programme is having some success and young *pa buk* fingerlings are now being released into the Mekong.

There is an enormous problem of smuggling rare animals out of Laos, mainly to S Korea and China. In 1978, the gall bladder of a black bear from Laos was auctioned in Seoul for US$55,000. Teeth and bones of cats from Laos are in demand for Chinese medicine. In 1992 the English-language daily, *Khao San Pathet Lao*, published a report estimating that in 1992 more than 10 tonnes of protected wild animals had been slaughtered for export in the north-eastern province of Hona Phan alone.

HISTORY

Scholars of Lao history, before they even begin, need to decide whether they are writing a history a Laos; a history of the Lao ethnic group; or histories of the various kingdoms and principalities that have, through time, been encompassed by the present boundaries of the Lao People's Democratic Repubublic. Historians have tended to confront this problem in different ways without, often, acknowledging on what basis their 'history' is built. It is common to see 1365, the date of the foundation of the kingdom of Lane Xang, as marking the beginning of Lao history. But, as Martin Stuart-Fox points out, prior to Lane Xang the principality of Muang Swa, occupying the same geographical space, was headed by a Lao. The following account provides a brief overview of the histories of those peoples who have occupied what is now the territory of the Lao PDR.

Archaeological and historical evidence indicates that most Lao originally migrated S from China. This was followed by an influx of ideas and culture

The universal stimulant – the betel nut

Throughout the countryside in Southeast Asia, and in more remote towns, it is common to meet men and women whose teeth are stained black, and gums red, by continuous chewing of the 'betel nut'. This, though, is a misnomer. The betel 'nut' is not chewed at all: the three crucial ingredients that make up a betel 'wad' are the nut of the areca palm (*Areca catechu*), the leaf or catkin of the betel vine (*Piper betel*), and lime. When these three ingredients are combined with saliva they act as a mild stimulant. Other ingredients (people have their own recipes) are tobacco, gambier, various spices and the gum of *Acacia catechu*. The habit, though also common in South Asia and parts of China, seems to have evolved in Southeast Asia and it is mentioned in the very earliest chronicles. The lacquer betel boxes of Myanmar and Thailand, and the brass and silver ones of Indonesia, illustrate the importance of chewing betel in social intercourse. Galvao in his journal of 1544 noted: "They use it so continuously that they never take it from their mouths; therefore these people can be said to go around always ruminating". Among Westernized Southeast Asians the habit is frowned upon: the disfigurement and ageing that it causes, and the stained walls and floors that result from the constant spitting, are regarded as distasteful products of an earlier age. But beyond the elite it is still widely practised.

from the Indian subcontinent via Burma/Myanmar, Thailand and Cambodia – something which is reflected in the state religion, Theravada Buddhism.

Being surrounded by large, powerful neighbours, Laos has been repeatedly invaded over the centuries by the Thais (or Siamese) and the Vietnamese – who both thought of Laos as their buffer zone and backyard. They too have both left their mark on Lao culture. In recent history, Laos has been influenced by the French during the colonial era, the Japanese during WW2, the Americans during the Indochinese wars and, between 1975 and the early 1990s, by Marxism-Leninism.

THE FIRST KINGDOM OF LAOS

Myth, archaeology and history all point to a number of early feudal Lao kingdoms in what is now S China and N Vietnam. External pressures from the Mongols under Kublai Khan and the Han Chinese forced the Tai tribes to migrate S into what had been part of the Khmer Empire. The mountains to the N and E served as a cultural barrier to Vietnam and China, leaving the Lao exposed to influences from India and the W. There are no documentary records of early Lao history, although it seems probable that parts of present-day Laos were annexed by Lannathai (Chiang Mai) in the 11th century and by the Khmer Empire during the 12th century. But neither of these states held sway over the entire area of Laos. Xieng Khouang, for example, was probably never under Khmer domination. This was followed by strong Siamese influence over the cities of Luang Prabang and Vientiane under the Siamese Sukhothai Dynasty. Laos (the country), in effect did not exist; although the Laos (the people) certainly did.

The downfall of the kingdom of Sukhothai in 1345 and its submission to the new Siamese Dynasty at Ayutthaya (founded in 1349) was the catalyst for the foundation of what is commonly regarded as the first truly independent Lao Kingdom – although there were smaller semi-independent Lao *muang* (city states) existing prior to that date.

FA NGOUM AND LANE XANG

The **kingdom of Lane Xang** (Lan

Fields in the forest – shifting cultivation

Shifting cultivation, also known as slash-and-burn agriculture or swidden-ing, as well as by a variety of local terms, is one of the characteristic farming systems of Southeast Asia. It is a low-intensity form of agriculture, in which land is cleared from the forest through burning, cultivated for a few years, and then left to regenerate over 10-30 years. It takes many forms, but an important distinction can be made between shifting field systems where field systems are rotated but the settlement remains permanently sited, and migratory systems where the shifting cultivators shift both field (swidden) and settlement. The land is usually only rudimentarily cleared, tree stumps being left in the ground, and seeds sown in holes made by punching the soil with a dibble stick.

For many years, shifting cultivators were regarded as 'primitives' who followed an essentially primitive form of agriculture and their methods were contrasted unfavourably with 'advanced' settled rice farmers. There are still many government officials in Southeast Asia who continue to adhere to this mistaken belief, arguing that shifting cultivators are the principal cause of forest loss and soil erosion. They are, therefore, painted as the villains in the region's environmental crisis, neatly sidestepping the considerably more detrimental impact that commercial logging has had on Southeast Asia's forest resources.

Shifting cultivators have an intimate knowledge of the land, plants and animals on which they depend. One study of a Dayak tribe, the Kantu' of Kalimantan (Borneo), discovered that households were cultivating an average of 17 rice varieties and 21 other food crops each year in a highly complex system. Even more remarkably, Harold Conklin's classic 1957 study of the Hanunóo of the Philippines – a study which is a benchmark for such work even today – found that the Hanunóo identified 40 types and subtypes of rocks and minerals when classifying different soils. The shifting agricultural systems are usually also highly productive in labour terms, allowing far more leisure time than farmers using permanent field systems.

But shifting cultivation contains the seeds of its own extinction. Extensive, and geared to low population densities and abundant land, it is coming under pressure in a region where land is becoming an increasingly scarce resource, where patterns of life are dictated by an urban-based élite, and where populations are pressing on the means of subsistence.

Chang) emerged in 1353 under Fa Ngoum, a Lao prince who had grown up in the Khmer court of Angkor. He was reputedly born with 33 teeth and was banished to Angkor after his father, Prince Yakfah, was convicted of having an incestuous affair with a wife of King Suvarna Kamphong. In 1353 Fa Ngoum led an army to Luang Prabang and confronted his grandfather, King Suvarna Kamphong. Unable to defeat his grandson on the battlefield, the aged king is said to have hanged himself and Fa Ngoum was invited to take the throne. 3 years later, in 1356, Fa Ngoum marched on Vientiane which he took with ease and then on Vienkam which proved more of a challenge (see box). Lane Xang – the land of a million elephants (or, if not accented, the valley of Elephants) – is portrayed in some accounts as stretching from China to Cambodia, and from the Khorat Plateau in present-day NE Thailand to the Annamite mountains in the E. But it would be entirely wrong to envisage the kingdom controlling all

Cunning Fa Ngoum takes Vienkam

ML Manich in his *History of Laos* relates a slightly fanciful but nonetheless entertaining story of how Fa Ngoum took Vienkam in 1356. The town was surrounded by an impenetrable thicket of bamboo and defended by a skilled commander, Phya Pao. Unable to take the town, he ordered his three generals to shoot arrows of gold and silver into the thicket for 3 days. Then he withdrew. The townspeople, scarcely believing their luck, cut down the bamboo to recover the precious arrow heads and in so doing opened their city up to attack by Fa Ngoum. But rather than taking the city he invited Phya Pao to fight him in a single-handed elephant duel. They fought for so long without either one gaining an advantage that Fa Ngoum reinstated Phya Pao as governor of Vienkam. In the ensuing celebrations in Vientiane 10 elephants, 1,000 cows and 2,000 buffalo were slaughtered for the feast.

these regions. Lane Xang probably only had total control over a comparatively small area of present-day Laos, and parts of NE Thailand; the bulk of this grand empire would have been contested with other surrounding kingdoms. In addition, the smaller *muang* and principalities would themselves have played competing powers off, one against another, in an attempt to maximize their own autonomy. It is this 'messiness' which led scholars of Southeast Asian history to suggest that territories as such did not exist, but rather zones of variable control, termed *mandalas* by OW Wolters (see the box on page 30).

Legend relates that Fa Ngoum was a descendant of Khoum Borom, "a king who came out of the sky from S China". He is said to have succeeded to the throne of Nanchao in 729, aged 31 and died 20 years later, although this historical record is, as they say, exceedingly thin. Khoum Borom is credited with giving birth to the Lao people by slicing open a gourd in Muong Taeng (Dien Bien Phu, Vietnam) and his seven sons established the great Tai kingdoms. He returned to his country with a detachment of Khmer soldiers and united several scattered Lao fiefdoms. In those days, conquered lands were usually razed and the people taken as slaves to build up the population of the conquering group.

(This largely explains why, today, there are far more Lao in Northeastern Thailand than in Laos – they were forcibly settled there after King Anou was defeated by King Rama III of Siam in 1827 – see page 32.) The kings of Lane Xang were less philistine, demanding only subordination and allegiance as one part of a larger *mandala*.

Luang Prabang became the capital of the kingdom of Lane Xang. The unruly highland tribes of the NE did not come under the kingdom's control at that time. Fa Ngoum made Theravada Buddhism the official religion. He married the Cambodian king's daughter, Princess Keo Kaengkanya, and was given the gold **Phra Bang** (a golden statue and the most revered religious symbol of Laos) by the Khmer court.

It is common to read of Lane Xang as the first kingdom of Laos; as encompassing the territory of present-day Laos; and as marking the introduction of Theravada Buddhism to the country. On all counts this portait is, if not false, then deeply flawed. As noted above, there were Lao states that predated Lane Xang; Lane Xang never controlled Laos as it currently exists; and Buddhism had made an impact on the Lao people before 1365. Fa Ngoum did not create a kingdom; rather he brought together various pre-existing *muang* (city states)

Making space

Western historians like to think of kingdoms 'controlling' territory. In Southeast Asia such cut-and-dried spatial categorization made little sense until the early 20th centuries. This led the historian OW Wolters to suggest the word *mandala* to describe the manner in which Southeast Asian kingdoms controlled territory:

A *mandala* "...represented a particular and often unstable political situation in a vaguely defined geographical area without fixed boundaries and where smaller centres tended to look in all directions for security. *Mandalas* would expand and contract in concertina-like fashion. Each one contained several tributary rulers, some of whom would repudiate their vassal status when the opportunity arose and try to build up their own network of vassals."

into a powerful *mandala*. As Martin Stuart-Fox writes, "From this derives his [Fa Ngoum's] historical claim to hero status as the founder of the Lao Kingdom". But, as Stuart-Fox goes on to explain, there was no central authority and rulers of individual *muang* were permitted considerable autonomy. As a result the "potential for disintegration was always present ..."

After Fa Ngoum's wife died in 1368, he became so debauched, it is said, that he was deposed in favour of his son, **Samsenthai (1373-1416)** who was barely 18 when he acceded the throne. He was named after the 1376 census, which concluded that he ruled over 300,000 Tais living in Laos: *samsen* means, literally 300,000. He set up a new administrative system based on the existing *muang*, nominating governors to each, that lasted until it was abolished by the Communist government in 1975. Samsenthai's death was followed by a period of unrest. Under **King Chaiyachakkapat-Phaenphaeo (1441-1478)**, the kingdom came under increasing threat from the Vietnamese. How the Vietnamese came to be peeved with the Lao is another story which smacks of fable than fact. King Chaiyachakkapat's eldest son, the Prince of Chienglaw, secured a holy white elephant. The emperor of Vietnam, learning of this momentous discovery, asked to be sent some of the beast's hairs. Disliking the Vietnamese,

the Prince dispatched a box of its excrement instead, whereupon the Emperor formed an army of an improbably large 550,000 men. The Prince's army numbered 200,000 and 2,000 elephants. (Considering that the population of Lane Xang under Samsenthai was said to be 300,000 this beggars statistical belief. Still, it is a good story.) The massive Vietnamese army finally prevailed – two Lao generals were so tired they fell of their elephants and were hacked to pieces – and entered and sacked Luang Prabang. But shortly thereafter they were driven out by Chaiyachakkapat-Phaenphaeo's son, **King Suvarna Banlang (1478-1485)**. Peace was only fully restored under **King Visunarat (1500-1520)**, who built Wat Visoun in Luang Prabang (see page 126).

Increasing prominence and Burmese incursions

Under **King Pothisarath (1520-1548)** Vientiane became prominent as a trading and religious centre. He married a Lanna (Chiang Mai) princess, Queen Yotkamtip, and when the Siamese King Ketklao was put to death in 1545, Pothisarath's son claimed the throne at Lanna. He returned to Lane Xang when his father died in 1548. Once again an elephant figured as a prime mover in the event: Pothisarath was demonstrating his prowess in the manly art of elephant lassoing when he was flung from his mount and fatally crushed. Asserting his right as successor to the throne, he was crowned **Setthathirat** in 1548 and ruled until 1571 – the last of the great kings of Lane Xang.

At the same time, the Burmese were expanding E and in 1556 Lanna fell into their hands. Setthathirat gave up his claim to that throne, to a Siamese prince, who ruled under Burmese authority. (He also took the Phra Kaeo – Thailand's famous 'Emerald' Buddha and its most sacred and revered image – with him to Luang Prabang and then to Vientiane. The residents of Chiang Mai are reputed to have pleaded that he leave it in the city, but these cries fell on death ears. The Phra Kaeo stayed in Vientiane until 1778 when the Thai general Phya Chakri 'repatriated' it to Thailand.) In 1563 Setthathirat pronounced Vieng Chan (Vientiane) the principal capital of Lane Xang. 7 years later, the Burmese King Bayinnaung launched an unsuccessful attack on Vieng Chan itself.

Setthathirat is revered as one of the great Lao kings, having protected the country from foreign domination. He built Wat Phra Kaeo (see page 95) in Vientiane, in which he placed the famous Emerald Buddha brought from Lanna. Setthathirat mysteriously disappeared during a campaign in the S province of Attapeu in 1574, which threw the kingdom into crisis (see page 186). Vientiane fell to invading Burmese the following year and remained under Burmese control for 7 years. Finally the anarchic kingdoms of Luang Prabang and Vientiane were reunified under Nokeo Koumane (1591-96) and Thammikarath (1596-1622).

DISPUTED TERRITORY

From the time of the formation of the kingdom of Lane Xang to the arrival of the French, the history of Laos was dominated by the struggle to retain the lands it had conquered. Following King Setthathirat's death, a series of kings came to the throne in quick succession. King Souligna Vongsa, crowned in 1633,

Kings of Lane Xang	
Fa Ngoum	1353-1373
Samsenthai	1373-1416
Lan Kamdaeng	1417-1428
Phommathat	1428-1429
Mun Sai	1429-1430
Fa Khai	1430-1433
Khong Kham	1433-1434
Yukhon	1434-1435
Kham Keut	1435-1441
Chaiyachakkapat-Phaenphaeo (aka Sao Tiakaphat)	1441-1478
Suvarna Banlang (aka Theng Kham)	1478-1485
Lahsaenthai Puvanart	1485-1495
Sompou	1497-1500
Visunarat	1500-1520
Pothisarath	1520-1548
Setthathirat	1548-1571
Saensurin	1572-1574
Mahaupahat (under Burmese control)	1574-1580
Saensurin	1580-1582
Nakhon Noi (under Burmese control)	1582-1583
Interregnum	1583-1591
Nokeo Koumone	1591-1596
Thammikarath	1596-1622
Upanyuvarat	1622-1623
Pothisarat	1623-1627
Mon Keo	1627
Period of confusion	1627-1637
Sulinya Vongsa	1637-1694

brought long awaited peace to Laos. The 61 years he was on the throne are regarded as Lane Xang's golden age. Under him, the kingdom's influence spread to Yunnan in S China, the Burmese Shan States, Isan in NE Thailand and areas of Vietnam and Cambodia.

Souligna Vongsa was even on friendly terms with the Vietnamese: he married Emperor Le Thanh Ton's daughter, and he and the Emperor agreed the borders between the two countries. The frontier was settled in a deterministic – but nonetheless amicable – fashion: those living in houses built on stilts with verandahs were considered Lao subjects and those living in houses without piles and verandahs owed allegiance to Vietnam.

During his reign, foreigners first visited the country – the Dutch merchant Gerrit van Wuysthoff arrived in 1641 to assess trading prospects – and Jesuit missionaries too. But other than a handful of adventurers, Laos remained on the outer periphery of European concerns and influence in the region.

The three kingdoms

After Souligna Vongsa died in 1694, leaving no heir, dynastic quarrels and feudal rivalries once again erupted, undermining the kingdom's cohesion. In 1700 Lane Xang split into three: Luang Prabang under Souligna's grandson, Vientiane under Souligna's nephew and the new kingdom of Champassak was founded in the S 'panhandle'. This weakened the country and allowed the Siamese and Vietnamese to encroach on Lao lands. *Muang* which previously owed clear allegiance to Lane Xang began to look towards Vietnam or Siam. Isan *muang* in present-day NE Thailand, for example, paid tribute to Bangkok; while Xieng Khouang did the same to Hanoi and, later, to Hué. The three main kingdoms that emerged with the disintegration of Lane Xang leant in different directions: Luang Prabang had close links with China, Vientiane with Vietnam's Hanoi/Hué and Champassak with Siam.

By the mid-1760s **Burmese influence** once again held sway in Vientiane and Luang Prabang, and before the turn of the decade, they sacked Ayutthaya, the capital of Siam. Somehow the Siamese managed to pull themselves together, and only 2 years later in 1778 successfully rampaged through Vientiane. The two sacred Buddhas, the Phra Bang and the Phra Kaeo (Emerald Buddha) were taken as booty back to Bangkok. The Emerald Buddha was never returned and now sits in Bangkok's Wat Phra Kaeo (see page 214).

King Anou (an abbreviation of Anurutha) was placed on the Vientiane throne by the Siamese. With the death of King Rama II of Siam, King Anou saw his chance of rebellion, asked Vietnam for assistance, formed an army, and marched on Bangkok in 1827. In mounting this brave – some would say foolhardy – assault, Anou was apparently trying to emulate the great Fa Ngum. Unfortunately, he got no further than the NE Thai town of Korat where his forces suffered a defeat and were driven back. Nonetheless, Anou's rebellion is considered one of the most daring and ruthless rebellions in Siamese history and he was lauded as a war hero back home.

King Anou's brief stab at regional power was to result in catastrophe for Laos – and tragedy for King Anou. The first US arms shipment to Siam allowed the Siamese to **sack Vientiane**, a task to which they had grown accustomed over the years. (For those who are interested in such things, this marks America's first intervention in Southeast Asia.) Lao artisans were frog-marched to Bangkok and many of the inhabitants were resettled in NE Siam. Rama III had Chao Anou locked in a cage where he was taunted and abused by the population of Bangkok. He died soon afterwards. The cause of his death has been variously linked to poison and shame. One of his supporters is said to have taken pity on the king and bought him poison. Other explanations simply say that he wished himself dead. Whatever the cause, the disconsolate Anou, before he died, put a curse on Siam's monarchy, promising that the next time a Thai king set foot on Lao soil, he would die. To this day no Thai king has crossed the Mekong River. When the agreement for the supply of hydro-electric power was signed with Thailand in the 1970s, the Thai king was invited officially to open the Nam Ngum Dam, a feat he managed from a sandbank in the middle of the Mekong.

Disintegration of the kingdom

Over the next 50 years, Anou's Kingdom was destroyed. By the time the French arrived in the late 19th century, the virtually unoccupied city was subsumed into the Siamese sphere of influence. Luang Prabang also became a Siamese vassal state, while Xieng Khouang province was invaded by Chinese rebels – to the chagrin of the Vietnamese, who had always considered the Hmong mountain kingdom (they called it Tran Ninh) to be their exclusive source of slaves. The Chinese had designs on Luang Prabang too, and in order to quash their expansionist instincts, Bangkok dispatched an army there in 1885 to pacify the region and ensure the N remained firmly within the Siamese sphere of influence. This period was clearly one of confusion and rapidly shifting allegiances. In James McCarthy's book of his travels in Siam and Laos, *Surveying and exploring in Siam* (1900), he states that an old chief of Luang Prabang remarked to him that the city had never been a tributary state of Annam (N Vietnam) but had formerly paid tribute to China. He writes:

"The tribute had consisted of 4 elephants, 41 mules, 533 lbs of nok (metal composed of gold and copper), 25 lbs of rhinoceros' horns, 100 lbs of ivory, 250 pieces of home-spun cloth, 1 horn, 150 bundles of areca-palm nuts [for betel 'nut' chewing], 150 cocoanuts [sic], and 33 bags of roe of the fish pla buk [the giant Mekong cat fish, see page 26]."

The history of Laos during this period becomes, essentially, the history of only a small part of the current territory of the country: namely, the history of Luang Prabang. And because Luang Prabang was a suzerain state of Bangkok, the history of that kingdom is, in turn, sometimes relegated to a mere footnote in the history of Siam.

THE FRENCH AND INDEPENDENCE

Following King Anou's death, Laos became the centre of Southeast Asian rivalry between Britain, expanding E from Burma, and France, pushing W through Vietnam. In 1868, following the French annexation of S Vietnam and the establishment of a protectorate in Cambodia, an expedition set out to explore the Mekong trade route to China. Once central and N Vietnam had come under the influence of the Quai d'Orsay in Paris, the French became increasingly curious about Vietnamese claims to chunks of Laos. Unlike the Siamese, the French – like the British – were concerned with demarcating borders and establishing explicit areas of sovereignty. This seemed extraordinary to most Southeast Asians at the time who could not see the point of spending so much time and effort mapping space when land was so abundant. However, it did not take long for the Siamese king to realize the importance of maintaining his claim to Siamese territories if the French in the E and the British in the S (Malaya) and W (Burma) were not to squeeze Siam to nothingness.

However, King Chulalongkorn was not in a position to confront the French militarily and instead he had to play a clever diplomatic game if his Kingdom was to survive. The French, for their part, were anxious to continue to press westwards from Vietnam into the Lao lands over which Siam held suzerainty. Martin Stuart-Fox argues that there were four main reasons underlying France's desire to expand W: the lingering hope that the Mekong might still offer a 'backdoor' into China; the consolidation of Vietnam against attack; the 'rounding out' of their Indochina possessions; and a means of further pressuring Bangkok. In 1886, the French received reluctant Siamese permission to post a vice consul to Luang Prabang and a year later he persuaded the Thais to leave. However, even greater humiliation was to come in 1893 when the French, through crude gunboat diplomacy – the so-called Paknam incident – forced King Chulalongkorn to give up all claim to Laos on the flimsiest of historical pretexts. Despite attempts by Prince Devawongse to manufacture a compromise, the French forced Siam to cede Laos to France and, what's more, to pay compensation. It is said that after this humiliation, King Chulalongkorn retired from public life, broken in spirit and health. So the French colonial era in Laos began.

What is notable about this spat between France and Siam is that Laos – the country over which they were fighting – scarcely figures. As was to happen again in Laos' history, the country was caught between two competing powers who used Laos as a stage on which to fight a wider, and to them, more important, conflict.

Union of Indochina

In 1893 France occupied the left bank of the Mekong and forced Thailand to recognize the river as the boundary. The French Union of Indochina denied Laos the area which is now Isan, NE Thailand, and was the start of 50 years of colonial rule. Laos became a protectorate with a *resident-superieur* in Vientiane and a vice-consul in Luang Prabang. However, as Martin Stuart-Fox points out, Laos could hardly be construed as a 'country' during the colonial period. "Laos existed again", he writes, "but not yet as a political entity in its own right, for no independent centre of Lao political power existed. Laos was but a territorial entity within French Indochina." The French were not interested in establishing an identifiable Lao state; they saw Laos as a part, and a subservient part at that, of Vietnam, serving as a resource-rich appendage to Vietnam. Though they had grand plans for the development of Laos, these were only airly expressed and none of them came to anything. "The French were never sure what to do with Laos", Stuart-Fox writes, "either the parts or the whole". Unlike Cambodia to the S, the French did not perceive Laos to have any historical unity or coherence and therefore it could be hacked about, and developed or otherwise, according to their whim, as if it were a piece of brie.

In 1904 the Franco-British convention delimited respective zones of influence. Only a few hundred French civil servants were ever in Vientiane at any one time and their attitude to colonial administration – described as 'benign neglect' – was as relaxed as the people they governed. To the displeasure of the Lao, France brought in Vietnamese to run the civil service (in the way the British used Indian bureaucrats in Burma). But for the most part, the French colonial period was a 50-year siesta for Laos. The king was allowed to stay in Luang Prabang, but had little say in administration. Trade and commerce was left to the omnipresent Chinese and the Vietnamese. A small, French-educated Lao élite did grow up, and by the 1940s they had become the core of a typically laid-back Lao nationalist movement.

Japanese coup

Towards the end of WW2, Japan ousted the French administration in Laos in a coup in Mar 1945. The eventual surrender of the Japanese in Aug that year gave impetus to the Lao independence movement. Prince Phetsarath, hereditary viceroy and premier of the Luang Prabang Kingdom, took over the leadership of the **Lao Issara**, the Free Laos Movement (originally a resistance movement against the Japanese). They prevented the French from seizing power again and declared Lao independence on 1 September 1945. 2 weeks later, the N and S provinces were reunified and in Oct, Phetsarath formed a Lao Issara government headed by Prince Phaya Khammao, the governor of Vientiane.

France refused to recognize the new state and crushed the Lao resistance. King Sisavang Vong, unimpressed by Prince Phetsarath's move, sided with

Wars of the roses?

Post WW2 politics in Laos have been compared with the English Wars of the Roses: rival elements within one royal family, representing different political opinions, were backed by different foreign powers. By the early 1960s King Savang Vatthana was convinced that his centuries-old kingdom, now a pawn of conflicting superpower interests, was doomed to extinction. A speech made to the nation in 1961 reflects his despondency:

"Our country is the most peaceful in the world... At no time has there ever arisen in the minds of the Lao people the idea of coveting another's wealth, of quarrelling with their neighbours, much less of fighting them. And yet, during the past 20 years, our country has known neither peace nor security... Enemies of all sorts have tried to cross our frontiers, to destroy our people and to destroy our religion and our nation's aura of peace and concord... Foreign countries do not care either about our interests or peace; they are concerned only with their own interests."

the French, who had their colony handed back by British forces. He was crowned the constitutional monarch of the new protectorate in 1946.

The rebel government took refuge in Bangkok. Historians believe the Issara movement was aided in their resistance to the French by the Viet Minh – Hanoi's Communists.

Independence

In response to nationalist pressures, France was obliged to grant Laos ever greater self government and, eventually, formal independence within the framework of the newly reconstructed French Union in Jul 1949. Meanwhile, in Bangkok, the Issara movement had formed a government-in-exile, headed by Phetsarath and his half-brothers: **Prince Souvanna Phouma** and **Prince Souphanouvong**. Both were refined, French-educated men, with a taste for good wine and cigars. The Issara's military wing was led by Souphanouvong who, even at that stage, was known for his Communist sympathies. Within just a few months the so-called Red Prince had been ousted by his half-brothers and joined the Viet Minh where he is said to have been the moving force behind the declaration of the Democratic Republic of Laos by the newly-formed Lao National Assembly. The Lao People's

Democratic Republic emerged – albeit in name only – somewhere inside Vietnam, in Aug 1949. Soon afterwards, the **Pathet Lao** – literally, 'the Lao nation' was born. The Issara movement quickly folded and Souvanna Phouma went back to Vientiane and joined the newly-formed Royal Lao Government.

By 1953, Prince Souphanouvong had managed to move his Pathet Lao headquarters inside Laos, and with the French losing their grip on the N provinces, the weary colonizers granted the country full independence. Retreating honourably, France signed a treaty of friendship and association with the new royalist government and made the country a French protectorate.

THE RISE OF COMMUNISM

French defeat

While all this was going on, the king sat tight in Luang Prabang instead of moving to Vientiane. But within a few months of independence, the ancient royal capital was under threat from the Communist Viet Minh and Pathet Lao. Honouring the terms of the new treaty, French commander General Henri Navarre determined in late 1953 to take the pressure off Luang Prabang by confronting the Viet Minh who controlled the strategic approach to the city at Dien

Prince Souvanna Phouma: architect of independence and helmsman of catastrophe

Prince Souvanna Phouma was Laos' greatest statesman. He was Prime Minister on no less than eight occasions between 1951 and 1975 for a total of 20 years. He dominated mainstream politics during the turbulent years from independence until the victory of the Pathet Lao in 1975. But in the last analysis he was never able to preserve the integrity of Laos in the face of much stronger external forces. "Souvanna stands as a tragic figure in modern Lao history", Martin Stuart-Fox writes, a "stubborn symbol of an alternative, neutral, 'middle way'".

He was born in 1901 into a branch of the Luang Prabang royal family. Like many of the Lao élite he was educated abroad, in Hanoi, Paris and Grenoble, and when he returned to Laos he married a woman of mixed French-Lao blood. He was urbane, educated and, by all accounts, arrogant. He enjoyed fine wines and cigars, spoke French better than he spoke Lao, and was a Francophile – as well as a nationalist – to the end. In 1950 Souvanna became a co-founder of the Progressive Party and in the elections of 1951 he headed his first government which negotiated and secured full independence from France.

Souvanna made two key errors of judgement during these early years. First, he ignored the need for 'nation building' in Laos. And second, he underestimated the threat that the Communists posed to the country. With regard to the first of these misjudgements, he seemed to believe – and it is perhaps no accident that he trained as an engineer and architect – that Laos just needed to be administered efficiently to become a modern state. The belief that the government first had to try and inculcate a sense of Lao nationhood he either appeared to reject, or to ignore. The second misjudgement was his long held belief – until it was too late – that the Pathet Lao was a nationalist and not a communist organization. He let the Pathet Lao grow in strength and this, in turn, brought the US into Lao affairs.

By the time the US began to intervene in Lao affairs, during the late 1950s, the country already – with hindsight – seemed to be heading for catastrophe. But in his struggle to maintain some semblance of neutrality and independence for his tiny country, he ignored the degree to which Laos was being sucked into the quagmire of Indochina. As Martin Stuart-Fox writes:

"He [Souvanna] knew he was being used, and that he had no power to protect his country from the war that increasingly engulfed it. But he was too proud meekly to submit to US demands – even as Laos was subjected to the heaviest bombing in the history of warfare. At least a form of independence had to be maintained...".

When the Pathet Lao entered Vientiane in victory in 1975, Souvanna did not flee into exile. He remained to help in the transfer of power. The Pathet Lao, of course, gave him a title and then largely ignored him as they pursued their Communist manifesto. Again, Martin Stuart-Fox writes:

"Souvanna ended his days beside the Mekong. He was to the end a Lao patriot, refusing to go into exile in France. The leaders of the new regime did consult him on occasions. Friends came to play bridge. Journalists continued to seek him out, although he said little and interviews were taped in the presence of Pathet Lao minions. When he died in January 1984, he was accorded a state funeral."

The above is a summary of the discussion of Souvanna Phouma in "Suvanna Phuma and the quest for Lao neutrality", in *Buddhist kingdom, Marxist state: the making of modern Laos* (Bangkok: White Lotus, 1996).

Bien Phu. The French suffered a stunning defeat which prestaged their withdrawal from Indochina. The subsequent occupation of two N Lao provinces by the Vietnam-backed Pathet Lao forces, meant the kingdom's days as a western buffer state were numbered.

With the **Geneva Accord** in Jul 1954, following the fall of Dien Bien Phu in May, Ho Chi Minh's government gained control of all territory N of the 17th parallel in neighbouring Vietnam. The Accord guaranteed Laos' freedom and neutrality, but with the Communists on the threshold, the US was not prepared to be a passive spectator: the demise of the French sparked an increasing US involvement. In an operation that was to mirror the much more famous war with Vietnam to the E, Washington soon found itself supplying and paying the salaries of 50,000 royalist troops and their corrupt officers. Clandestine military assistance grew, undercover special forces were mobilized and the CIA began meddling in Lao politics. In 1960 a consignment of weapons was dispatched by the CIA to a major in the Royal Lao Army called Vang Pao – or VP, as he became known – who was destined to become the leader of the Hmong.

US involvement and the domino effect

Laos had become the dreaded 'first domino', which, using the scheme of US President Dwight D Eisenhower's famous analogy, would trigger the rapid spread of Communism if ever it fell. The time-trapped little kingdom rapidly became the focus of superpower brinkmanship. At a press conference in Mar 1961, President Kennedy is said to have been too abashed to announce to the American people that US forces might soon become embroiled in conflict in a far-away flashpoint that went by the inglorious name of 'Louse'. For three decades Americans have unwittingly mis-pronounced the country's name as Kennedy decided, euphemistically, to label it 'Lay-os' throughout his national television broadcast.

Coalitions, coups and counter-coups

The US-backed **Royal Lao Government** of independent Laos – even though it was headed by the neutralist, Prince Souvanna Phouma – ruled over a divided country from 1951 to 1954. The Communist Pathet Lao, headed by Prince Souphanouvong, emerged as the only strong opposition. The growth of the Pathet Lao had been overseen and sponsored by N Vietnam's Lao Dong party since 1949. By the mid-1950s, **Kaysone Phomvihane**, later Prime Minister of the Lao PDR, began to make a name for himself in the Indochinese Communist Party. Indeed the close association between Laos and Vietnam went deeper than just ideology. Kaysone's father was Vietnamese, while Prince Souphanouvong, and Nouhak Phounsavanh both married Vietnamese women. Entrenched in the N provinces, Pathet Lao troops – supported by the Communist Viet Minh forces – made several incursions into central Laos and civil war erupted.

Government of National Union

Unable to secure cooperation with the Communists, elections were held in Vientiane in Jul 1955 but were boycotted by the Pathet Lao. **Souvanna Phouma** became Prime Minister in Mar 1956. He aimed to try to negotiate the integration of his half-brother's Pathet Lao provinces into a unified administration and coax the Communists into a coalition government. In 1957 the disputed provinces were returned to royal government control and in May 1958 elections were held. This time the Communists' Lao Patriotic Front clinched nine of the 21 seats in the Government of National Union. The Red Prince, **Souphanouvong**, and one of his aides were included in a coalition cabinet and former Pathet Lao members were elected deputies of the National Assembly.

Almost immediately problems which

had been beneath the surface emerged to plague the government. The American-backed rightists were rather shaken by the result, and the much-vaunted coalition lasted just 2 months. The National Union fell apart in Jul 1958. Pathet Lao leaders were jailed and the right-wing Phoui Sananikone came to power. With anti-Communists in control, Pathet Lao forces withdrew to the Plain of Jars in Xieng Khouang province. A three-way civil war ensued, between the rightists, the Communists and the neutralists.

Civil war

CIA-backed strongman General Phoumi Nosavan thought Phoui's politics rather tame, and with a nod from Washington he stepped into the breech in Jan 1959, eventually overthrowing Phoui in a coup in Dec, and placing Prince Boun Oum in power. Confusion over Phoumas, Phouis and Phoumis led one American official to comment that it all "could have been a significant event or a typographical error".

Within a year, the rightist regime was overthrown by a neutralist coup d'état led by General Kong Lae, and Prince Souvanna Phouma was recalled from exile in Cambodia to become Prime Minister of the first National Union. Souvanna Phouma incurred American wrath by inviting a Soviet ambassador to Vientiane in Oct. With US support, Nosavan staged yet another armed rebellion in Dec and sparked a new civil war. Kong Lae backed down, Souvanna Phouma shuffled back to Phnom Penh and a new right-wing government was set up under Boun Oum.

Zurich talks and the Geneva Accord

The new Prime Minister, the old one and his Marxist half-brother finally sat down to talks in Zurich in Jun 1961, but any hope of an agreement was overshadowed by escalating tensions between the superpowers. A year later an international agreement on Laos was hammered out in Geneva by 14 participating nations and accords were signed, once again guaranteeing Lao neutrality.

By implication, the accords denied the Viet Minh access to the **Ho Chi Minh Trail**. But aware of the reality of constant N Vietnamese infiltration through Laos into S Vietnam, the head of the American mission concluded that the agreement was "a good bad deal".

Another coalition government of National Union was formed under the determined neutralist Prince Souvanna Phouma (as Prime Minister), with Prince Souphanouvong for the Pathet Lao and Prince Boun Oum representing the right. It was no surprise when it collapsed within a few months and fighting resumed. This time the international community just shrugged and watched Laos sink back into the vortex of civil war. Unbeknown to the outside world, the conflict was rapidly degenerating into a war between the CIA and N Vietnamese jungle guerrillas.

The war that wasn't

With the Viet Minh denying the existence of the Ho Chi Minh Trail, while at the same time enlarging it, Kennedy dispatched an undercover force of CIA-men, Green Berets and US-trained Thai mercenaries to command 9,000 Lao soldiers. To the N, the US also supplied **Vang Pao's** force of 30,000 Hmong guerrillas, dubbed 'Mobile Strike Forces'. With the cooperation of Prince Souvanna Phouma, the CIA's commercial airline, Air America, ferried men and equipment into Laos from Thailand (and opium out). Owing to the clandestine nature of the military intervention in Laos, the rest of the world – believing that the Geneva settlement had solved the foreign interventionist problem – was oblivious as to what was happening on the ground. Right up until 1970, Washington never admitted to any activity in Laos beyond 'armed reconnaissance' flights over N provinces. Richard Nixon, for example, claimed that "there are no American ground combat troops in Laos", which was stretching the truth to breaking point. Souvanna Phouma appropriately referred to it as 'the forgotten war' and it is often termed now the 'non-attributable war'. The willingness on the part of the Americans to dump millions of tonnes of ordnance on a country which was ostensibly neutral may have been made easier by the fact that some people in the administration did not believe Laos to be a country at all. Bernard Fall wrote that Laos at the time was "neither a geographical nor an ethnic or social entity, but merely a political convenience", while a Rand Corporation report written in 1970 described Laos as "hardly a country except in the legal sense". More colourfully, Secretary of State Dean Rusk described it as a 'wart on the hog of Vietnam'. Perhaps those in Washington could feel a touch better about bombing the hell out of a country which, in their view, occupied a sort of political never-never land – or which they could liken to an unfortunate skin complaint.

Not everyone agrees with this view that Laos never existed until the French wished it into existence. Dommen, for example, traces a true and coherent Lao identity back to Fa Ngoum and his creation of the kingdom of Lane Xang in 1353, writing that it was "a state in the true sense of the term, delineated by borders clearly defined and consecrated by treaty" for three and a half centuries. He goes on:

"Lao historians see a positive proof of the existence of a distinct Lao race (*sua sat Lao*), a Lao nation (*sat Lao*), a Lao country (*muong Lao*), and a Lao state (*pathet Lao*). In view of these facts, we may safely reject the notion, fashionable among apologists for a colonial enterprise of a later day, that Laos was a creation of French colonial policy and administration" (Dommen 1985:19).

American bombing of the N Vietnamese Army's supply lines through Laos to S Vietnam along the Ho Chi Minh Trail in E Laos (see page 178) started in 1964 and fuelled the conflict between the Royalist Vientiane government and the Pathet Lao. The neutralists had been forced into alliance with the Royalists to avoid defeat in Xieng Kouang province. US bombers crossed Laos on bombing runs to Hanoi from air bases in Thailand, and gradually the war in Laos escalated. In his book *The Ravens* (1987), Christopher Robbins sets the scene:

"Apparently, there was another war even nastier than the one in Vietnam, and so secret that the location of the country in which it was being fought was classified. The cognoscenti simply referred to it as 'the Other Theater'. The men who chose to fight in it were hand-picked volunteers, and anyone accepted for a tour seemed to disappear as if from the face of the earth."

The **secret war** was conducted from a one-room shack at the US base in Udon Thani, 'across the fence' in Thailand. This was the CIA's Air America operations room and in the same compound was stationed the 4802 Joint Liaison Detachment – or the CIA logistics office. In Vientiane, US pilots supporting Hmong General Vang Pao's rag-tag army, were given a new identity as rangers for the US Agency for International Development; they reported directly to the air attaché at the US embassy. Robbins writes that they "were military men, but flew into battle in civilian clothes – denim cutoffs, T-shirts, cowboy hats, and dark glasses ... Their job was to fly as the winged artillery of some fearsome warlord, who led an army of stone-age mercenaries in the pay of the CIA, and they operated out of a secret city hidden in the mountains of a jungle kingdom ..." He adds that CIA station chiefs and field agents "behaved like warlords in their own private fiefdoms."

'Over the fence' - with Raven 58

As a Raven Forward Air Controller (Raven FAC), I had the privilege of belonging to an élite group of pilots who flew covert operations in Laos in support of the Royal Lao Government. We would fly in support of the Royal Laotian Army or the CIA Special Guerrilla Units (SGUs).

Special Guerrilla Units were trained by CIA Country Team members. They were an élite fighting force designed to interdict movement of the North Vietnamese along the Ho Chi Minh Trail in the S or in areas around the Plain of Jars in the N. When they operated along the trail or in other forward locations, their supplies would be flown in by a Porter aircraft, piloted by Continental Air Service or Air America pilots. The advantage of this aircraft was that it could land and take off on a very short 'runway' – about 100 ft in length.

Normally, I would support the SGUs from the air, providing reconnaissance or fighter aircraft support. However, on one day they returned the favour. My airplane crashed in a rice paddy S of Attapeu. Nine North Vietnamese were across the paddy as I made a judicious move toward the opposite side. I knew that the SGUs were in the area near Attapeu, as I headed in that direction. As I came upon them, I recognized that they were friendly and shortly thereafter I was picked up by an Air America helicopter and flown to a nearby Lima Site (PS-38) for the night.

During the time of the Ravens, 1966 to 1975, there were only a total of 191 pilots. Very few Americans actually ever went into Laos – except along the Ho Chi Minh Trail. My time in Laos was quite enjoyable. Officially, I was a 'forest ranger' working for the Lao Government. In fact, I worked for the American Ambassador and was assigned to provide visual reconnaissance and direct air support for the Royal Laotian Army and the CIA SGUs.

And, there was much to discourage volunteers. The casualty rate was said to be 50%. The conditions were more harsh. And, then there were the drug dealers and gold dealers. (At that time it was illegal to trade in gold in the United States. One could only buy 'jewellery'. For that reason, contracted CIA pilots from Air America and Continental Air Service would be seen wearing heavy gold bracelets which were not much more than gold bars formed into a bracelet.)

But, I had volunteered to join the Air Force for the specific purpose of going to Vietnam and Laos. I had been a student at Ohio State University and was exempt from the draft. I was 26 years old when I joined the Air Force – just under the 26.5 age limit required of Air Force pilots. Having never flown before in my life I became a '90-day Wonder' as I received my commission as a 2nd Lieutenant at Lackland Air Force Base in San Antonio, Texas. From Lackland I went to Laredo, Texas for Undergraduate Pilot Training. I completed my training in 1968, followed

The most notorious of the CIA's unsavoury operatives was Anthony Posepny – known as Tony Poe, on whom the character of Kurtz, the crazy colonel played by Marlon Brando in the film *Apocalypse Now*, was based. Originally, Poe had worked as Vang Pao's case officer; he then moved to N Laos and operated for years, on his own, in Burmese and Chinese border territories, offering his tribal recruits one US dollar for each set of Communist ears they brought back. Many of the spies and pilots of this secret war have re-emerged in recent years in covert and illegal arms-smuggling rackets to Libya, Iran and the Nicaraguan Contras.

By contrast, the Royalist forces were

by 0-1 (Bird Dog) Special Operations Training, POW training and then on to the Philippines for Jungle Survival Training.

In Vietnam I was stationed at the Tuy Hoa MACV (Military Assistance Command Vietnam) compound where I flew in support of the Vietnamese Army. I volunteered for the *Steve Canyon Program* soon after arriving at Tuy Hoa. The Steve Canyon Program was named after 'Steve Canyon' – the flamboyant adventurist comic strip character. As I departed Bien Hoa Air Force Base near Saigon for Laos, I learned why it was called 'Steve Canyon'. The colonel who drove me to the airplane which would take me to my first stop in Thailand said: "Well, now all you have to look forward to is ... glory, money and medals!"

Ravens were a breed apart. They would wear what they wanted when flying – shorts and T-shirts, home-made flying suits or cowboy outfits. They would disregard the Air Force standards for flying time and clock as much as 150 to 200 hours a month.

The monetary rewards were appealing. While not the income a true 'mercenary' might receive – for example, US$50,000 or US$100,000 for flying certain cargo in Southeast Asia or the Middle East – the extra *per diem* income, free in addition to being paid for board and room, maids and cooks, and combat pay was welcome. It could amount to an extra US$1,000 per month.

Arriving at Udon Air Force Base in Northeast Thailand, I was directed to a remote area of the base called 'Det-1'. The commander did not know much about what I would be doing, but he was responsible for maintaining my Air Force records, since when I went into Laos, I would be a 'civilian'. Flying into Laos was quite different from flying into other countries. To protect my destination, when I crossed the border I would radio: "Raven 58, crossing the fence". 'Laos' would never be mentioned.

Along with the AOC (Air Operations Center) commander, a radio operator, two airplane mechanics and a medic, I lived in the town of Paksé, in a large colonial villa. The living conditions were excellent. After flying out into the war zone each day and returning, I would go down town to a movie or to the Mekong Bar for dancing and music, or to an inviting sidewalk café for dinner.

I believed that the Lao knew who I was. But, I found out that many did not. While trying to make a call to Vietnam to speak with my future Vietnamese wife, Kim Chi, a new Air Force Lieutenant received the call and became inquisitive as to why I referred to myself as "Mister Thompson" rather than "Captain". Even military personnel in Vietnam, including Air Force Forward Air Controllers, did not know about the clandestine operations of the Ravens.

reluctant warriors: despite the fact that civil war was a deeply ingrained tradition in Laos, the Lao themselves would go to great lengths to avoid fighting each other. One foreign journalist, reporting from Luang Prabang in the latter stages of the war, related how Royalist and Pathet Lao troops, encamped on opposite banks of the Nam Ou, agreed an informal cease-fire over Pimay (Lao New Year), to jointly celebrate the king's annual visit to the sacred Pak Ou Caves, upstream from the royal capital (see page 134). Correspondents who covered the war noted that without the constant goading of their respective US and N Vietnamese masters, many Lao soldiers would have happily gone home. During the war, a US commander was quoted in a newspaper as saying that the Royalist troops were "without doubt the worst army I have ever seen," adding that they made the [poorly regarded] "S Vietnamese Army look like Storm Troopers."

Air Force planes were often used to carry passengers for money – or to smuggle opium out of the Golden Triangle. In the field, soldiers of the Royal Lao Army regularly fled when faced with a frontal assault by the NVA. The officer corps was uncommitted, lazy and corrupt; many ran opium-smuggling rackets and saw the war as a ticket to get rich quick. In the S, the Americans considered Royal Lao Air Force pilots unreliable because they were loath to bomb their own people and cultural heritage.

The air war

The clandestine **bombing of the Ho Chi Minh Trail** (see page 178) caused many civilian casualties – so-called collateral damage – and displaced much of the population in Laos' E provinces. By 1973, when the bombing stopped, the US had dropped 2,093,100 tonnes of bombs on Laos – equivalent to 300 kg of explosives pp. 580,994 bombing sorties were flown. The bombing intensified during the Nixon administration: up to 1969 less than half-a-million tonnes of bombs had been dropped on Laos; from then on nearly that amount was dropped each year. The war was not restricted to bombing missions – once potential Pathet Lao strongholds had been identified, fighters, using rockets, were sent to attempt to destroy them. Such was the intensity of the bombing campaign that villagers in Pathet Lao controlled areas are said to have turned to planting and harvesting their rice at night. Few of those living in Xieng Khouang province, the Bolovens Plateau or along the Ho Chi Minh Trail had any idea of who was bombing them or why. The consequences were often tragic as in the case of Tam Phiu Cave (see page 151).

In *The Ravens*, Robbins tells of how a fighter pilot's inauspicious dream would lead the commander to cancel a mission; bomber pilots hated dropping bombs, and when they did, aluminium canisters were carefully brought back and sold as scrap. After the war, the collection and sale of war debris turned into a valuable scrap-metal industry for tribespeople in Xieng Khouang province and along the Ho Chi Minh Trail. Bomb casings, aircraft fuel tanks and other bits and pieces that were not sold to Thailand have been put to every conceivable use in rural Laos. They are used as cattle troughs, fence posts, flower pots, stilts for houses, water carriers, temple bells, knives and ploughs.

But the bombing campaign has also left a more deadly legacy – of unexploded bombs and anti-personnel mines. Today, over two decades after the air war ended, people are dying in the fields and forests of provinces like Xieng Khouang. Anthropologist Grant Evans reported in the *Far Eastern Economic Review* that in 1993 100 people were killed in Xieng Khouang province alone; 30 more in the first half of 1994. The greatest irony of all perhaps, is that most of Xieng Khouang was not even a military target – pilots would simply dump their ordnance so that they would not have to risk landing with their bomb bays packed with high explosive. Making farming in this part a Laos a highly dangerous occupation was simply one of those 'accidents' of war.

The land war

Within Laos the war largely focused on the strategic Plain of Jars, in Xieng Khouang province, and was co-ordinated from the town of Long Tieng (the secret city), tucked into the limestone hills to the SW of the plain. Known as the most secret spot on earth, it was not marked on maps and was populated by the CIA, the Ravens (the air controllers who flew spotter planes and called in air strikes)

Vietnam War

CHINA

NORTH VIETNAM

○Dien Bien Phu

HANOI □   ○Haiphong

LAOS   ○Xam Neua

Luang Prabang

Phonsavanh
Plain of Jars

Gulf of
Tonkin

CHINA

VIENTIANE □

Mekong

Ho Chi Minh Trail

**Demilitarized zone
(22-7-54)**

THAILAND

Khe Sanh ○

Hamburger Hill ○   ○Hué   ○Danang

○ Pakse

○ My Lai

○Pleiku
Ia Drang Valley   ○Qui Nhon

CAMBODIA

SOUTH VIETNAM

Mekong   *Ho Chi Minh Trail*

Cam Ranh Bay

PHNOM PENH □   ○Dalat

○Tay Ninh

○Cu Chi   ○Bien Hoa

Sihanoukville ○   SAIGON
○Ap Bac

South China Sea

Gulf of Thailand   ○Camau

N

Raven FACs: a personal view

Raven was the call sign used by Forward Air Controllers (FACs) in Laos. It came to designate, however, a special breed of FAC – someone who was highly motivated, aggressive, decisive, daring and exceptionally skilled and professional in his work. The mystique was heightened by the secrecy of the assignment. Pilots would leave Vietnam and seemingly disappear. This became clear when I read a personal advertisement in the Vietnam Veterans Newspaper requesting information about a *Raven FAC* I had known. When I called the person who placed the ad, he said that the last time he had seen the Major was at Bien Hoa. He said that he had not seen nor heard of him since. I told him that he had been 'undercover' in Laos.

The importance of the mission of the Raven is put in perspective by understanding first the mission of a FAC. Essentially, a FAC had three responsibilities: (1) to conduct air reconnaissance to obtain first-hand information concerning enemy locations, activity and threats; (2) to control and direct Air Force or Navy aircraft bombers or Army artillery on enemy targets; and (3) to control, direct and coordinate air strikes with ground troops for close air support.

The importance of the first responsibility was clearly demonstrated when I precluded an attack on Tuy Hoa by a North Vietnamese battalion. As a result of my daily flights over the mountains W of Tuy Hoa, I came upon a North Vietnamese battalion digging trench lines and bunkers, preparing for an assault on Tuy Hoa. In addition, I also observed trays of rice drying in the open down the side of the mountain and was thus able to pinpoint the enemy locations in the caves and bunkers nearby. As a result of these sightings, I declared a tactical emergency. That declaration resulted in an unlimited amount of air power being diverted for my use.

The FAC is in a position to have immediate information about troop movements and direct air power or artillery very effectively on the target. He is an on-scene commander with all the responsibilities and authority of that position. The FAC has the responsibility and right to over-rule even the orders of a general officer. I exercised

and the Hmong.

The Pathet Lao were headquartered in caves in Sam Neua province, to the N of the plain. Their base was equipped with a hotel cave (for visiting dignataries), a hospital cave and even a theatre cave.

The **Plain of Jars** (coloquially known as the PDJ, after the French Plaine de Jarres) was the scene of some of the heaviest fighting and changed hands countless times, the royalist and Hmong forces occupying it during the wet season, the Pathet Lao in the dry. During this period in the conflict the town of Long Tien, known as one of the country's 'alternate' bases to keep nosy journalists away (the word 'alternate' was meant to indicate that it was unimportant) grew to such an extent that it

became Laos' second city. James Parker in his book *Codename Mule* claims that the air base was so busy that at its peak it was handling more daily flights than Chicago's O'Hare airport. There was also fighting around Luang Prabang and the Bolovens Plateau to the S.

The end of the war

Although the origins of the war in Laos were distinct from those which fuelled the conflict in Vietnam, the two wars had effectively merged by the early 1970s and it became inevitable that the fate of the Americans to the E would determine the outcome of the secret war on the other side of the Annamite Range. By 1970 it was no longer possible for the US administration to shroud the war in secrecy: a flood of Hmong refugees had arrived in Vientiane that authority in Vietnam shortly after I was assigned to Tuy Hoa.

Personnel had been spotted in the field by a commanding officer on a mountain top overlooking the valley. He was ready to open fire when I flew over and countermanded the order. In this case after the fact I realized that the artillery fire should have been carried out, as the people were in fact enemy. However, regardless of my lack of experience at the time, my order not to fire stopped the action of a field officer who was more experienced and of much higher rank

But in time I gained the experience to differentiate clearly between 'friendlies' and the enemy. This ability was demonstrated when I directed air strikes on a 'friendly' outpost near Pakxong on the Bolovens Plateau. This time, when I spotted the troops, I knew they were enemy. However, after returning to Paksé, the CIA commander called me in and wanted to know why I had bombed one of his outposts. In fact, the outpost had been overrun, and after flying over the post at about 200 ft to confirm the identity of the troops, I did not hesitate to direct air strikes against it.

Whereas my error of judgement in Vietnam cost the life of one civilian who was killed following the infiltration of the town that evening by the troops I had saved from artillery fire, in Laos I saved the lives of many friendly troops.

Close air support was the most challenging of a FAC's responsibilities, since he had to maintain a continuing awareness of where the enemy was and where the friendlies were. In some situations, the FAC had to also consider the ordnance being delivered by the aircraft, and the reliability of the information being provided by the ground troops. In Vietnam I had to send an F-4 out to sea to drop its ordnance since the location of the friendly troops could not be clearly determined. In this case the ordnance was a 10,000 pound bomb. It was not quite appropriate for 'close air support' – especially when the location of the friendly troops was in doubt.

This box was written by Ken Thompson, or Raven 58 who flew as a FAC in Vietnam and Laos over 26 months between 1968 and 1970. He was awarded two distinguished Flying Crosses and a Bronze Star for valour.

in an effort to escape the conflict.

During the dying days of the US-backed regime in Vientiane, CIA agents and Ravens lived in quarters S of the capital, known as Silver City. On the departure of the Americans and the arrival of the new regime in 1975, the Communists' secret police made Silver City their new home. Today, Laotians still call military intelligence officers 'Silvers' – from time to time Silvers are even assigned as tour guides. Silver City however, 6 km from Vientiane, is now known just as KM-6, and its agents go by the same name – the Lao version of Britain's MI5.

A ceasefire was agreed in Feb 1973, a month after Washington and Hanoi struck a similar deal in Paris. Power was transferred in Apr 1974 to yet another coalition government set up in Vientiane under the premiership of the ever-ready Souvanna Phouma. The neutralist prince once again had a Communist deputy and foreign affairs minister. The Red Prince, Souphanouvong headed the Joint National Political Council. Foreign troops were given 2 months to leave the country. The N Vietnamese were allowed to remain along the Ho Chi Minh Trail, for although US forces had withdrawn from S Vietnam, the war there was not over.

The communist's final victories over Saigon (and Phnom Penh) in Apr 1975 were a catalyst for the Pathet Lao who advanced on the capital. As the end drew near and the Pathet Lao began to advance out of the mountains and towards the more populated areas of the Mekong valley – the heartland of the Royalist government – province after province fell with scarcely a shot being fired. The mere arrival of a small contingent of Pathet Lao soldiers was sufficient to secure victory. Rightist ministers, ranking civil servants, doctors, much of the intelligentsia and around 30,000 Hmong crossed the Mekong and escaped into Thailand as the Pathet Lao approached Vientiane. Many lived for years in squalid refugee camps, although the better connected and those with skills to sell secured US, Australian and French passports. For Laos, virtually all of its human capital drained westwards, creating a vacuum of skilled personnel that would hamper – and still does – efforts at reconstruction and development. Vientiane was declared 'officially liberated' on 23 August 1975. The coalition government was dismissed and Souvanna Phouma resigned for the last time. All communications with the outside world were cut.

LAOS UNDER COMMUNISM

The **People's Democratic Republic of Laos** was proclaimed in Dec 1975 with Prince Souphanouvong as President and Kaysone Phomvihane as Secretary-General of the Lao People's Revolutionary Party (a post he had held since its formation in 1955). The king's abdication was accepted and the ancient Lao monarchy was abolished, together with King Samsenthai's 600-year-old system of village autonomy. But instead of executing their vanquished foes, the LPRP installed Souvanna and the ex-king, Savang Vatthana, as 'special advisers' to the politburo. On Souvanna's death in 1984, he was accorded a full state funeral. The king did not fare so well: he later died ignominiously while in detention.

Surprisingly, the first actions of the new revolutionary government was not to build a new revolutionary economy and society, but to stamp out unsavory behaviour. Dress and hairstyles, dancing and singing, even the food that was served at family celebrations, was all subject to rigorous scrutiny by so-called 'Investigation Cadres'. If the person(s) concerned were found not to match up to the Party's scrupulous standards of good taste they were bundled off to re-education camps.

Relations with Thailand, which in the immediate wake of the revolution remained cordial, deteriorated in late 1976. A military coup in Bangkok led to rumours that the Thai military, backed by the CIA, was supporting Hmong and other right-wing Lao rebels. The regime feared that Thailand would be used as a spring-board for a royalist coup attempt by exiled reactionaries. This prompted the arrest of King Savang Vatthana, together with his family and Crown Prince Vongsavang, who were all dispatched to a Seminar re-education camp in Sam Neua province. They were never heard of again. In Dec 1989 Kaysone Phomvihane admitted in Paris, for the first time, that the king had died of malaria in 1984 and that the queen had also died "of natural causes" – no mention was made of Vongsavang. The Lao people have still to be officially informed of his demise.

The re-education camps

Between 30,000 and 40,000 reactionaries who had been unable to flee the country were interned in remote, disease-ridden camps for 're-education'. The reluctant scholars were forced into slave labour in squalid jungle conditions and subjected to incessant political propaganda. Old men, released back into society after more than 15 years of 're-education' are cowed and subdued, some are prepared to talk in paranoid whispers about their grim experiences in Sam Neua.

It is unclear how many died in the camps, but at least 15,000 have been freed. Officials of the old regime, ex-government ministers and former Royalist air force and army officers, together with thousands of others unlucky enough to have been on the wrong side, were released from the camps during the 1980s. Most of the surviving political prisoners have now been reintegrated into society and it is not clear whether there are any still in captivity. Some work in the tourism industry and one, a former colonel in the Royal Lao Army, jointly owns the *Asian Pavilion Hotel* (formerly the *Vieng Vilai*) on Samsenthai Rd in downtown Vientiane. After years of being force-fed Communist propaganda he now enjoys full government support as an ardent capitalist entrepreneur.

The refugee camps

A total of 300,000 Lao – 10% of the population, and mostly middle class – fled the country's increasingly totalitarian regime between 1973 and 1975. From 1988, these refugees began to head back across the Mekong from camps in Thailand, and to asylum in the US and France. More than 2,000 refugees were also repatriated from Yunnan Province in China. For those prepared to return from exile overseas, the government offered to give them back confiscated property so long as they stay at least 6 months and become Lao citizens once again. Thailand's Lao refugee camps are now part of history. One of the best accounts of this period is Lynellyn D. Long's *Ban Vinai: the refugee camp*. As a Jesuit priest who worked at the camp explained to the author: "Before they [came to the camps the refugees] had a life revolving around the seasons ... Here they cannot really work ... Here people make only dreams".

ART AND ARCHITECTURE

Lao art is well known for its wealth of ornamentation. As in other neighbouring Buddhist countries, the focus has been primarily religious in nature. Temple murals and bas-reliefs usually tell the story of the Buddha's life – the jataka tales. There has never been the range of art in Laos that there is in Thailand, as the country has been constantly dominated and influenced by foreign powers. Much of it has been destroyed over the centuries, as plundering neighbours ransacked towns and cities. The *Ramayana*, the Indian epic, has become part of the Lao cultural heritage and is known as the *Phra Lak Phra Lam* (see page 70). Many of the doors and windows of temples are engraved with scenes from this story, depicting the struggle between good and evil. Prime examples are the huge teak shutters at Wat Xieng Thong in Luang Prabang.

LAO SCULPTURE

Sculpture in Laos is more distinctive in style; the best pieces originate from the 16th to 18th centuries. Characteristic of Lao Buddha images are a nose like an eagle's beak, flat, extended earlobes and tightly curled hair. The best examples are in Wat Phra Kaeo and Wat Sisaket in Vientiane.

The 'Calling for Rain' mudra (the Buddha standing with hands pointing towards the ground, arms slightly away from the torso) is distinctively Lao (see page 98). The 'Contemplating the Tree of Enlightenment' mudra is also uniquely Lao – it depicts a standing Buddha with hands crossed in front of the body. There are many examples in the Pak Ou Caves, on the Mekong, 25 km upstream from Luang Prabang (see page 134).

That Luang showing the characteristic angular shape of the Lao *That*

The Lao wat

👣 There is no English equivalent of the Lao word *wat* or *vat*. It is usually translated as either monastery or temple, although neither is correct. It is easiest to get around this problem by calling them wats. They were, and remain to some extent, the focus of the village or town; they serve as places of worship, education, meeting and healing. Without a wat, a village cannot be viewed as a 'complete' community. The wat is a relatively new innovation. Originally, there were no wats, as monks were wandering ascetics. It seems that although the word 'wat' was in use in the 14th century, these were probably just shrines, and were not monasteries. By the late 18th century, the wat had certainly metamorphosed into a monastery, so sometime in the intervening 4 centuries, shrine and monastery had united into a whole. Although wats vary a great deal in size and complexity, there is a traditional layout to which most conform.

● Wats are usually separated from the secular world by **two walls**. Between these outer and inner walls are found the **monks' quarters** or dormitories (*kutis*), perhaps a drum or bell **tower** (*hor kong*) that is used to toll the hours and to warn of danger and, in larger complexes, schools and other administrative buildings. Traditionally the *kutis* were placed on the S side of the wat. It was believed that if the monks slept directly in front of the principal Buddha image they would die young; if they slept to the left they would become ill; and if they slept behind it there would be discord in the community of monks.

● The inner wall, which in bigger wats often takes the form of a **gallery** or cloister (*phra rabieng*) lined with Buddha images, represents the division between the worldly and the holy, the sacred and the profane. It is used as a quiet place for meditation. Within the inner courtyard, the holiest building is the **ordination hall** or **sim**, reserved for monks only. This is built on consecrated ground, and has a ring of eight stone tablets or boundary markers (*bai sema*), sometimes contained in mini-pavilions, arranged around it at the cardinal and subcardinal points and shaped like stylized leaves of the bodhi tree, often carved with representations of Vishnu, Siva, Brahma or Indra, or of nagas. Buried in the ground beneath the bai sema are stone spheres – and sometimes gold and jewellery. The bai sema mark the limit of earthly power. The ordination hall is characteristically a large, rectangular building with high walls and multiple sloping roofs (always odd in number) covered in glazed clay tiles (or wood tiles, in the N). At each end of the apex of the roof are *dok sofa*, or 'bunches of flowers', which represent garuda grasping two nagas (serpents) in its talons. *Chao faa*, flame-like protrusions are attached to the extreme edge of the downward slope of the roofs. Inside, often through elaborately carved and inlaid doors, is the main Buddha image. There may also be numerous subsidiary images. The inside walls of the sim may be decorated with murals depicting the Jataka tales or scenes from Buddhist and Hindu cosmology. Like the Buddha, these murals are meant to serve as meditation aids. It is customary for pilgrims to remove their shoes on entering any Buddhist building (or private house for that matter). Many complexes have secondary chapels, or **hor song phra** attached to the main sim.

Also found in the inner courtyard may be a number of other structures. Among the more common are *that* (chedis), tower-like **relic chambers** which in Laos and parts of Northeastern Thailand (which is also Lao in terms of culture) take the distinctive lotus bud form. These can be built on a massive scale (such as That Luang in Vientiane, see page 91), and contain holy relics of the Buddha himself. More often, thats are smaller affairs containing the ashes of royalty, monks or pious lay people.

● Another rarer feature is the **library** or scripture repository (*hau tai*), usually a small, tall-sided building where the Buddhist scriptures can be stored safely, high off the ground. *Salas* are open-sided **rest pavilions** which can be found anywhere in the wat compound; the *sala long tham* or **study hall** is the largest and most impressive of these and is almost like a sim or viharn without walls. Here the monks say their prayers at noon.

● Sometimes wats have a boat house to shelter the local boat used in the annual boat race.

● In rural villages wats often consist only of a sala, or meeting hall.

● It seems that wats are often short-lived. Even great wats, if they lose their patronage, are deserted by their monks and fall into ruin. Unlike Christian churches, they depend on constant support from the laity; the wat owns no land or wealth, and must depend on gifts of food to feed the monks and money to repair and expand the fabric of its buildings.

Generalized Plan of a Wat

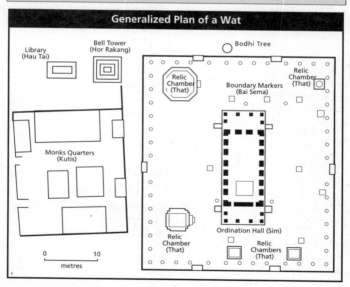

Library (Hau Tai)

Bell Tower (Hor Rakang)

Bodhi Tree

Relic Chamber (That)

Relic Chamber (That)

Boundary Markers (Bai Sema)

Monks Quarters (Kutis)

Relic Chamber (That)

Ordination Hall (Sim)

Relic Chambers (That)

0   10
metres

LAO ARCHITECTURE

The architecture of Laos reflects its turbulent history and has strong Siamese/Thai, Burmese and Khmer influences. Philip Rawson in his book *The art of Southeast Asia* (Thames & Hudson) goes so far as to state that "The art of Laos is a provincial version of the art of Siam". This is unjustified in so far as art and architecture in Laos, though it may show many links with that of Siam/Thailand (unsurprisingly as over the centuries the two countries have, at various times, held sway over parts of each other's territory), also has elements and styles which are unique to it.

A *nyak* or *naga*

Unfortunately, little has survived because many of the older structures were built of wood and were repeatedly ransacked by the Siamese/Thais, Chinese and Vietnamese and then bombed by the Americans. Religious buildings best exhibit the originality of Lao art and architecture.

Like Thailand and Myanmar (Burma), the stupa is the most dominant architectural form in Laos. In its classic Indian form, it is a voluptuous half round – a hemisphere – very like the upturned begging bowl that it is supposed to symbolize. This is surmounted by a shaft representing the Buddha's staff, and a stepped pediment symbolizing his folded cloak. In Thailand the stupa has become elongated while in Laos it is also more angular, with four distinct sides. They are referred to as *that* (rather than *chedi*, as in Thailand).

In addition to the *that*, a Lao monastery or *wat* (*vat*) will also have a number of other buildings of which the most important is the *sim* or ordination hall (in Thai, *bot* or *ubosoth*). See the box on page 48 for a short run down on the main structures found in a orthodox Lao *wat*.

Architectural styles

Lao wats are generally less ornate and grand than those in Thailand, although the temples of Luang Prabang are stunning, with their layered roofs that sweep elegantly towards the ground. There are three main styles of temple architecture in Laos: Luang Prabang, Vientiane and Xieng Khouang. The last of these was almost lost forever because of the destruction wrought on the city of Xieng Khouang during the war (see page 150). Fortunately one or two examples exist in Luang Prabang.

The **Vientiane style** is influenced by the central Thai-style, with its high, pointed and layered roofs. Most of the main sanctuaries are rectangular and some, such as Wat Phra Kaeo in Vientiane, have a verandah around the entire building – a stylistic feature imported from Bangkok. Most of the larger *sim* have a verandah at the back as well as at the front. Vientiane's wats have higher roofs than those in Luang Prabang, the buildings are taller and the entrances more prominent. The steps leading up to the main entrance are often guarded by nagas or *nyaks*, while the doorways themselves are usually flanked by pillars and topped with intricately carved porticoes. That Luang, in Vientiane, historically provided a template for most Lao stupas and its unique shape is found

The 'lost wax' process

A core of clay is moulded into the desired form and then covered in beeswax and shellac. Details are engraved into the beeswax. The waxed core is then coated with a watery mixture of clay and cow's dung, and built up into a thick layer of clay. This is then fired in a kiln, the wax running out through vents cut into the clay. Molten bronze is poured into the mould where it fills the void left by the wax and after cooling the mould is broken to reveal the image.

Traditional Lao house styles

only in Laos and some areas of N and NE Thailand. As in other Buddhist countries, many of the stupas contain sacred relics – bones or hairs of the Buddha, or the ashes of kings.

The **Luang Prabang architectural style** has been influenced by N Thai temples. The roofs of the main sanctuaries are very low, almost touching the ground – best exemplified by the magnificent Wat Xieng Thong in Luang Prabang. The pillars tend to narrow towards the top, as tree trunks were originally used for columns and this form was copied when they started to be constructed of stuccoed brick. The wats often have a verandah at the back and the front. The most famous wats in Luang Prabang and Vientiane were built with royal patronage. But most wats in Laos were, and are, constructed piece-meal with donations from the local community. Royal wats can be identified by the number of *dok sofa*: more than 10 'flowers' signifies that the wat was built by a king.

The **Xieng Khouang style** appears to be an amalgam of Vientiane and Luang Prabang influences. The *sim* is raised on a multi-level pediment, as with Vientiane-style *sim*, while the low, sweeping roofs are similar to *sim* in Luang Prabang.

LAO TEXTILES

Of all Laos' artistic traditions, perhaps none is more varied and more vital than its handwoven textiles. These inevitably show some stylistic links with Thailand, but in many respects Laos' tradition is richer and certainly the cloth being produced in Laos today is far finer, more complex and more technically accomplished than any currently being woven in Thailand (although there are those in Thailand who would dispute this, assuming – wrongly – that Thailand is more advanced than Laos in every regard).

Weaving is a craft almost entirely performed by women, and it has always been a mark of womanhood. Traditionally, a girl was not considered fit for marriage until she had mastered the art of weaving and the Lao Loum women were expected to weave a corsage for their wedding day. Today these traditions are inevitably less strictly adhered to, and there are also a handful of fine male weavers. (Indeed, it has been suggested that these few male weavers produce better – or at least more adventurous – work than their female counterparts because they are less constrained by tradition and more willing to experiment with new designs.) Even so, a skilled weaver is held in high regard and enjoys a position of respect. Cloth is woven from silk, cotton, hemp and a variety of synthetic materials (mostly polyester) – or in some combination of these.

The finest weavers and the finest weaving comes from the north. Around **Xam Neua** (and especially near Xam Tai), the **Lao Neua** produce

Weaving fundamentals	
Colours/dyes:	red, orange, indigo and yellow
Motifs, animal:	*naga/nyak* (river serpent), *hong* (mythological goose-like bird), *naak* (dragon), *to mom* (deer), *siharath* (elephant lion), *singh* (lion)
Motifs, geometric:	zig-zag, triangles, spirals
Motifs, natural:	trees, flowers
Motifs, other:	palace buildings, *that* (stupas)
Primary pieces:	*sin/phaa sin* (wrap around sarong worn by women usually finished with a separate hand woven border), *pha baeng (shoulder cloth or shawl), pha tai luuk* (shawl worn by mothers to carry their infants), pha mon (head scarf) wedding corsage, funeral outfits

NB The above is very generalized; different weaving traditions of the country use different motifs, colours, techniques and designs.

some outstanding pieces. Traditionally these were handed down through a family as heirlooms, stored in lidded stone jars to protect them from insects, moisture and sunlight, and only worn for special occasions. However the recent history of this area forced many people to sell their treasured textiles and few remain *in situ*. Indeed it was feared that the art of traditional weaving had been lost entirely in the area. Only the work of some NGOs and committed supporters has resuscitated high quality weaving in the area (and in Vientiane where some of the finest weavers now live and work). Lao Neua textiles are usually woven with a cotton warp and a silk weft and pieces include *pha sin* (sarong), *pha baeng* (shawl) and blankets. Various methods are employed including *ikat* (see the box on page 111) – where cotton is used as the Lao Neua consider that indigo dye does not take well on silk – and supplementary weft techniques. Pieces show bold bands of design and colour and the *pha sin* is usually finished with a separate handwoven border. Among the designs are swastika motifs, *hong* (geese), diamond shapes, *nyak* (snake) heads, lions and elephants.

The **Lao Loum of the Luang Prabang area** also have a fine weaving tradition, different from that of the far N and NE.

Pha sin produced here tend to have narrow vertical stripes, often alternating between dark and light. Silk tends to be used throughout on the finer pieces, although the yarn may be imported rather than locally produced and it is coloured using chemical dyes. Motifs include zig-zags, flowers, and some designs that are French in inspiration.

Around **Pakse in the south** and also in **central Laos around Savannakhet and Thakhek**, designs are influenced by the Khmer and closest to those produced in the Isan region of Northeast Thailand. *Matmii* ikat-woven cotton cloth is most characteristic. Designs are invariably geometric and today it is unusual to find a piece which has not been dyed using chemicals. Designs are handed down by mothers to their daughters and encompass a broad range from simple *sai fon* ('falling rain') designs where random sections of weft are tied, to the more complex *mee gung* and *poom som*. The less common *pha kit* is a supplementary weft ikat, although the designs are similar to those found in *matmii*. *Pha fai* is a simple cotton cloth, in blue or white and sometimes simply decorated, made for everyday use and also as part of the burial ceremony, when a white length of *pha fai* is draped over the coffin.

CULTURE AND LIFE

PEOPLE

Laos is less a nation state than a collection of different tribes and languages. The country's enormous ethnic diversity has long been an impediment to national integration. In total there are more than 60 minority tribes which are often described as living in isolated, self-sufficient communities. (A summary of the origins, economy and culture of the major groups is provided on pages 55-61.) Although communication and intercourse may have been difficult – and remains so – there has always been communication, trade and inter-marriage between the different Lao 'worlds' and today, with even greater interaction, the walls between them are becoming more permeable still.

Laos' ethnically diverse population is usually – and rather simplistically – divided by ecological zone into three groups: the wet rice cultivating, Buddhist *Lao Loum* of the lowlands, who are politically and numerically dominant, constituting over half of the total population; the *Lao Theung* who occupy the mountain slopes and make up about a quarter of the population; and the *Lao Soung*, or upland Lao, who live in the high mountains and practice shifting cultivation, and who represent less than a fifth of Laos' total population. The terms were brought into general usage by the Pathet Lao who wished to emphasize that all of Laos' inhabitants were 'Lao', and to avoid the more derogatory terms that had been used in the past – such as the Thai word *kha*, meaning 'slave', to describe the Mon-Khmer *Lao Theung* like the Khmu and Lamet. Stereotypical representations of each category are depicted on the 1,000 kip note. From left to right: *Lao Theung*, *Lao Soung* and *Lao Loum*.

The French viewed the Lao, and not to put too fine a point on it, as if they were at times an exasperating child. But, as Virginia Thompson put it in the late 1930s, "For the rare Frenchman who sees in the Laotians a silly, lazy and naive people, there are hundreds who are charmed by their gentle affability ...". It was this affability which Henri Mouhout noted in the 1860s, and which led some Frenchmen to express their concern as to what might happen to the Lao if the uncontrolled immigration and settlement of Siamese, Vietnamese and Chinese was permitted. (Norman Lewis in *A dragon apparent* said much the same about Frenchmen who had gone native: "Laos-ized Frenchmen are like the results of successful lobotomy operations – untroubled and mildly libidinous.") By the outbreak of the Second World War towns like Vientiane and

From left to right, a Lao Theung, Lao Soung and Lao Loum girl

Thakhek already had larger populations of Vietnamese than they did of Lao and had the Japanese occupation and independence not nipped French plans in the bud, Laos might well have become a country where the Lao were in a minority.

Although the words have a geographical connotation, they should be viewed more as contrasting pairs of terms: *loum* and *theung* mean 'below' and 'above' (rather than hillsides and lowland), while *soung* is paired with *tam*, meaning 'high' and 'low'. These two pairs of oppositions were then brought together by the Pathet Lao into one three-fold division. Thus, the *Lao Theung* in one area may, in practice, occupy a higher location than *Lao Soung* in another area. In addition, economic change, greater interaction between the groups, and the settlement of lowland peoples in hill areas, means that it is possible to find *Lao Loum* villages in upland areas, where the inhabitants practice swidden, not wet rice agriculture. So, although it is broadly possible to characterize the mountain slopes as inhabited by shifting cultivating *Lao Theung* of Mon-Khmer descent, in practice the neat delimitation of people into discrete spatial units breaks down, and as the years go by is becoming increasingly untenable.

It has been noted that the Lao who have reaped the rewards of reform are the *Lao Loum* of T'ai stock – not the *Lao Theung* who are of Mon-Khmer descent or the *Lao Soung* who are 'tribal' peoples, especially Hmong but also Akha and Lahu. Ing-Britt Trankell in her book *On the road in Laos: an anthropological study of road construction and rural communities* (1993) writes that the *Lao Loum's* "sense of [cultural and moral] superiority is often manifested in both a patronizing and contemptuous attitude toward the Lao Theung and Lao Sung, who are thought of as backward and less susceptible to socio-economic development because they are still governed by their

archaic cultural traditions".

During the 6th and 7th centuries the **Lao Loum** arrived from the S provinces of China. They occupied the valleys along the Mekong and its tributaries and drove the *Lao Theung* to more mountainous areas. The *Lao Loum*, who are ethnically almost indistinguishable from the Thais of the Isan region (the NE of Thailand), came under the influence of the Khmer and Indonesian cultures and sometime before the emergence of Lane Xang in the 14th century embraced Theravada Buddhism. The majority of Lao are Buddhist but retain many of their animist beliefs. Remote *Lao Loum* communities still usually have a *mor du* (a doctor who 'sees') or medium. The medium's job description is demanding: he must concoct love potions, heal the sick, devise and design protective charms and read the future.

Today, the *Lao Loum* are the principal ethnic group, accounting for just over half the population, and Lao is their mother tongue. As the lowland Lao, they occupy the ricelands of the Mekong and its main tributary valleys. Their houses are made of wood and are built on stilts with thatched roofs – although tin is far more popular these days. The extended family is usually spread throughout several houses in one compound.

There are also several tribal subgroups of this main Thai-Lao group; they are conveniently colour-coded and readily identifiable by their sartorial traits. There are, eg the Red Tai, the White Tai and the Black Tai – who live in the upland valley areas in Xieng Khouang and Hua Phan provinces. That they live in the hills suggests they are *Lao Theung*, but ethnically and culturally they are closer to the *Lao Loum*.

The **Lao Theung**, consisting of 45 different sub groups, are the descendants of the oldest inhabitants of the country and are of Mon-Khmer descent. They are sometimes called *Kha*, meaning 'slave', as they were used as labourers by the Thai and Lao kings, and are generally still poorer than the *Lao Loum*. Traditionally, the *Lao Theung* were semi-nomadic and they still live mainly on the mountain slopes of the interior – along the whole length of the Annamite Chain from S China. There are concentrations of *Akha*, *Alak* and *Ta-Oy* on the Bolovens Plateau in the S (see page 180) and *Khamu* in the N.

Most *Lao Theung* still practise slash-and-burn, or shifting, agriculture and grow dry rice, coffee and tobacco. They would burn a small area of forest, cultivate it for a few years, and then, when the soil was exhausted, abandon the land until the vegetation had regenerated to replenish the soil. Some groups merely shifted fields in a 10-15 year rotation; others not only shifted fields but also their villages, relocating in a fresh area of forest when the land had become depleted of nutrients. To obtain salt, metal implements and other goods which could not be made or found in the hills, the tribal peoples would trade forest products such as resins and animal skins with the settled lowland Lao. Some groups, mainly those living closer to towns, have converted to Buddhism but many are still animist.

The social and religious beliefs of the *Lao Theung*, and their general outlook on health and happiness, are governed by their belief in spirits. The shaman is a key personality in any village. The *Alak*, from the Bolovens Plateau (see page 182) test the prospects of a marriage by killing a chicken: the manner in which it bleeds will determine whether the marriage will be propitious. Buffalo sacrifices are also common in *Lao Theung* villages and it is not unusual for a community to slaughter all its livestock to appease the spirits.

Viet Minh guerrillas and American B-52s made life difficult for many of the *Lao Theung* tribes living in E Laos, who were forced to move away from the Ho Chi Minh Trail. By leaving their birth places the *Lao Theung* left their protecting spirits, forcing them to find new and unfamiliar ones.

The **Lao Soung** began migrating to Laos from S China, Tibet and Burma, in the early 18th century, settling high in the mountains (some up to 2,500m). The *Hmong* (formerly known as the *Meo*) and *Yao* (also called the *Mien*) are the principal *Lao Soung* groups.

The Yao (or Mien)

The **Yao** mainly live around Nam Tha – deep inside the Golden Triangle, near the borders with Thailand, Burma and China.

Population by ethnic group		
Group	**Official category**	**% of total population**
T'ai	Lao Loum	60%
Mon-Khmer	Lao Theung	25%
Tibeto-Burman	Lao Soung	15%

Papaver Somniferum: the opium of the people

The very name the Golden Triangle, is synonymous in many people's minds with the cultivation of the opium poppy (*Papaver somniferum* L). It is a favourite cash crop of the Lahu, Lisu, Yao and Hmong (the Akha only rarely grow it). The attractions of cultivating the poppy are clear: it is profitable, can be grown at high altitudes (above 1,500m), has low bulk (important when there is poor transport) and does not rot. Today, most opium is grown in Myanmar and Laos, and then often traded through Thailand to the world's drug markets.

The opium poppy is usually grown as part of a rotation, alternating with maize. It is sown in Sep/Oct (the end of the wet season) and 'harvesting' stretches from the beginning of Jan through to the end of Mar. Harvesting occurs after the petals have dropped off the seed heads. The 'pod' is then carefully scoured with a sharp knife, from top to bottom, allowing the sap to ooze through and oxidize on the surface of the pod. The next day, the brown gum is scraped off, rolled into balls, and wrapped in banana leaves. It is now ready for sale to the buyers who travel the hills.

Though a profitable crop, opium production has not benefited the hilltribes. It makes those who grow it criminals, and opium addiction is widespread – among the Hmong it is thought to be about 30% of the population. Efforts to change the ways of the hilltribes have focused upon crop substitution programmes (encouraging farmers to cultivate crops such as cabbages) and simple intimidation.

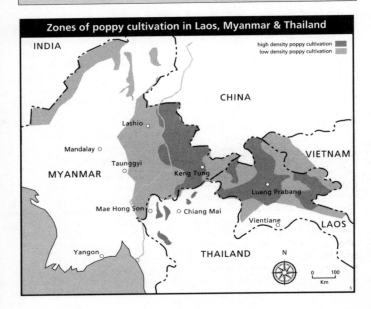

Zones of poppy cultivation in Laos, Myanmar & Thailand

The Hilltribe calendar

	Hmong	Yao (Mien)	Akha
Jan	new year festival	embroidering	weaving
Feb	scoring poppies	scoring poppies	clearing fields
Mar	clearing field	clearing field	burning field
Apr	burning field	burning field	rice spirit ceremony
May	rice planting	rice and maize planting	rice planting
Jun	weeding	weeding	weeding
Jul	weeding	weeding	weeding
Aug	weeding	harvesting	swinging ceremony
Sep	poppy seeding	poppy seeding	maize harvest
Oct	thinning poppy field	rice harvest	rice harvest
Nov	rice harvest	rice harvest	rice harvest
Dec	new year festival	rice threshing	new year festival

Source: Tribal Research Institute, Chiang Mai University

They are best-known as craftsmen – the men make knives, crossbows, rifles and high-quality, elaborately designed silver jewellery, which is worn by the women. Silver is a symbol of wealth amoung the Yao and Hmong.

The Mien or Yao, are unique among the hilltribes in that they have a tradition of writing based on Chinese characters. Mien legend has it that they came from 'across the sea' during the 14th century, although it is generally thought that their roots are in S China where they originated about 2,000 years ago.

The Mien village is not enclosed and is usually found on sloping ground. The houses are large, wooden affairs, as they need to accommodate an extended family of sometimes 20 or more members. They are built on the ground, not on stilts, and have one large living area and four or more bedrooms. As with other tribes, the construction of the house must be undertaken carefully. The house needs to be orientated appropriately, so that the spirits are not disturbed, and the ancestral altar installed on an auspicious day.

The Mien combine two religious beliefs: on the one hand they recognize and pay their dues to spirits and ancestors (informing them of family developments); and on the other, they follow Taoism as it was practised in China in the 13th and 14th centuries. The Taoist rituals are expensive, and the Mien appear to spend a great deal of their lives struggling to save enough money to afford the various life cycle ceremonies, such as weddings, and death ceremonies. The Mien economy is based upon the shifting cultivation of dry rice, maize, and small quantities of opium poppy.

Material culture The Mien women dress distinctively, with black turbans and red-ruffed tunics, making them easy to distinguish from the other hilltribes. All their clothes are made of black or indigo-dyed homespun cotton, which is then embroidered using distinctive cross-stitching. Their trousers are the most elaborate garments. Unusually, they sew from the back of the cloth and cannot see the pattern they are making. The children wear embroidered caps with red pompoms on the top and by the ears. The men's dress is a simple indigo-dyed jacket and trousers, with little embroidery. They have been dubbed "the most elegantly dressed but worst-housed people in the world".

The Akha (or Kaw)

The Akha have their origins in Yunnan, southern China, and from there spread into Burma (where there are nearly 200,000) and Laos, and rather later into Thailand.

The Akha are shifting cultivators, growing primarily dry rice on mountainsides but also a wide variety of vegetables. The cultivation of rice is bound up with myths and rituals: the rice plant is regarded as a sentient being, and the selection of the swidden, its clearance, the planting of the rice seed, the care of the growing plants, and finally the harvest of the rice, must all be done according to the Akha Way. Any offence to the rice soul must be rectified by ceremonies.

Akha villages are identified by their gates, a village swing and high-roofed houses on posts. They have no word for religion but believe in the 'Akha Way'. They are able to recite the names of all their male ancestors (60 names or more) and they keep an ancestral altar in their homes, at which food is offered up at important times in the year such as New Year, during the village swing ceremony, and after the rice harvest.

At the upper and lower ends of the village are gates which are renewed every year. Visitors should walk through them in order to rid themselves of the spirit of the jungle. The gates are sacred, and must not be defiled. Visitors must not touch the gates and should avoid going through them if they do not intend to enter a house in the village. A pair of wooden male and female carved figures are placed inside the entrance to signify that this is the realm of human beings.

The two most important Akha festivals are the 4-day Swinging Ceremony celebrated during Aug, and New Year when festivities also extend over 4 days.

Material culture Akha clothing is made of homespun blue-black cloth, which is appliquéd for decoration. Particularly characteristic of the Akha is their head-dress, which is adorned with jewellery. The basic clothing of an Akha woman is a head-dress, a jacket, a short skirt worn on the hips, with a sash and leggings worn from the ankle to below the knee. They wear their jewellery as an integral part of their clothing, mostly sewn to their head-dresses. Girls wear similar clothing to the women, except that they sport caps rather than the elaborate head-dress of the mature women. The change from girl's clothes to women's clothes occurs through four stages during adolescence. Unmarried girls can be identified by the small gourds tied to their waist and head-dress.

Men's clothing is much less elaborate. They wear loose-fitting Chinese-style black pants, and a black jacket which may be embroidered. Both men and women use cloth shoulder bags.

Today the Akha are finding it increasingly difficult to follow the 'Akha Way'. Their complex rituals set them apart from both the lowland Lao and from the other hilltribes. The conflicts and pressures which the Akha currently face, and their inability to reconcile the old with the new, is claimed by some to explain why the incidence of opium addiction among the Akha is so high.

The Hmong (or Meo)

Origins The Hmong, also known as the Meo, claim that they have their roots in the icy N. They had arrived in Laos by 1850 and by the end of the 19th century had migrated into the northern provinces of Thailand.

Economy and society The Hmong value their independence, and tend to live at high altitudes, away from other

Visiting the hilltribes: house rules

Etiquette and customs vary between the hilltribes. However, the following are general rules of good behaviour that should be adhered to whenever possible.

1. Dress modestly and avoid undressing/changing in public.
2. Ask permission before photographing anyone (old people and pregnant women often object to having their photograph taken).
3. Ask permission before entering a house.
4. Do not touch or photograph village shrines.
5. Do not smoke opium.
6. Avoid sitting or stepping on door sills.
7. Avoid excessive displays of wealth and be sensitive when giving gifts (for children, pens are better than sweets).
8. Avoid introducing western medicines.

tribes. This independence, and their association with poppy cultivation and their siding with the US during the war, has meant that of all the hilltribes it is the Hmong who have been most severely persecuted. They are perceived to be a threat to the security of the state; a tribe that needs to be controlled and carefully watched. Like most hilltribes, they practise shifting cultivation, moving their villages when the surrounding land has been exhausted. The process of moving is stretched out over two seasons: an advance party finds a suitable site, builds temporary shelters, clears the land and plants rice, and only after the harvest do the rest of the inhabitants follow in their steps.

Hmong villages tend not to be fenced, while their houses are built of wood or bamboo at ground level. Each house has a main living area, and two or three sleeping rooms. The extended family is headed by the oldest male; he settles family disputes and has supreme authority over family affairs. Like the Karen, the Hmong too are spirit worshippers and believe in household spirits. Every house has an altar, where protection for the household is sought.

The Hmong are the only tribe in Laos who make batik; indigo-dyed batik makes up the main panel of their skirts, with appliqué and embroidery added to it. The women also wear black leggings from their knees to their ankles, black jackets (with embroidery), and a black panel or 'apron', held in place with a cummerbund. Even the youngest children wear clothes of intricate design with exquisite needlework. Traditionally the cloth would have been woven by hand on a foot-treddle/back-strap loom; today it is increasingly purchased from markets.

The White Hmong tend to wear less elaborate clothing from day to day, saving it for special occasions only. Hmong men wear loose-fitting black trousers, black jackets (sometimes embroidered), and coloured or embroidered sashes.

The Hmong particularly value silver jewellery; it signifies wealth and a good life. Men, women and children wear silver – tiers of neck rings, heavy silver chains with lock-shaped pendants, earrings and pointed rings on every finger. All the family jewellery is brought out at New Year and is an impressive sight, symbolizing the wealth of the family.

The Hmong in Laos: persecution and flight

The **Hmong** are probably the best-known tribe in Laos. In the 19th century, Chinese opium farmers drove many thousands of Hmong off their poppy fields and forced them S into the mountains of Laos. The Hmong did not have a written language before contact with Europeans and Americans, and their heritage is mainly preserved through oral tradition. Hmong mythology relates how they flew in from S China on magic carpets. Village story-tellers also like to propagate the notion that the Hmong are in fact werewolves, who happily devour the livers of their victims. This warrior tribe now mainly inhabits the mountain areas of Luang Prabang, Xieng Khouang and Xam Neua provinces where they practise shifting cultivation (see page 28).

Until a few years ago, other Lao and the rest of the world knew the Hmong as the *Meo*. Unbeknown to anyone except the Hmong, 'Meo' was a Chinese insult meaning 'barbarian' – conferred on them several millennia ago by Chinese who developed an intense disliking for the tribe. Returning from university in France in the mid-1970s, the Hmong's first highly qualified academic decided it was time to educate the world. Due to his prompting, the tribe was rechristened Hmong, their word for 'mankind'. This change in nomenclature has not stopped the Hmong from continuing to refer to the Chinese as 'sons of dogs'.

Nor has it stopped the *Lao Loum* from regarding the Hmong as their cultural inferiors. But, again, the feelings are reciprocated: the Hmong have an inherent mistrust of the lowland Lao – exacerbated by years of war – and *Lao Loum* guides reluctantly enter Hmong villages.

As animists, the Hmong believe everything from mountains and opium poppies to cluster bombs, has a spirit – or *phi* – some bad, some good. Shamans – or witchdoctors – play a central role in village life and decision making. The *phi* need to be placated incessantly to ward off sickness and catastrophe. It is the shaman's job to exorcise the bad *phi* from his patients. Until modern medicine arrived in Laos along with the Americans,

opium was the Hmong's only palliative drug. Due to their lack of resistance to pharmaceuticals, the Hmong responded miraculously to the smallest doses of penicillin. Even Bandaids were revered as they were thought to contain magical powers which drew out bad *phi*.

In the dying days of the French colonial administration, thousands of Hmong were recruited to help fight the Vietnamese Communists. Vang Pao – known as VP – who would later command 30,000 Hmong mercenaries in the US-backed war against the Pathet Lao, was first picked out by a French colonel in charge of these '*maquisards*' or 'native movements'. Later, the Hmong were recruited and paid by the CIA to fight the Pathet Lao. Under General VP, remote mountain villagers with no education were trained to fly T-28 fighter-bombers. It is said that when these US aircraft first started landing in remote villages, locals would carefully examine the undercarriage to see what sex they were.

An estimated 100,000 Hmong died during the war – even after the Pathet Lao's 'liberation' of Vientiane in 1975, Hmong refugees, encamped in hills to the S of the Plain of Jars, were attacked and flushed out by Vietnamese troops. Stories of chemical weapons being used against them (most notably 'yellow rain') were found to be US propaganda as the suspected biological agents, trichothecane mycotoxins, supposedly dumped on Hmong villages by the government, were identified as bee faeces. Swarms of over-flying bees have a habit of defecating simultaneously when they get too hot, showering the countryside with a sticky, yellow substance.

When the war ended in 1975 there was a mass exodus of Hmong and today more than 100,000 live in the US – mostly on the W coast and in Minnesota. A small group of Hmong, led by Vang Pao, is still optimistically fighting the Lao government, but they have lost much credibility in recent years and are widely regarded as bandits. VP is known to have extorted funds from *Hmong* in the US and regularly lobbies Republican politicians. His rebels' biggest public relations disaster came in 1989 when they shot dead several Buddhist monks while attacking a government convoy on the road to Luang Prabang. The Lao Air Force still carries out search-and-destroy missions against VP's bandits. The little-heard of United Front for the Liberation of the Lao People, under the command of another Hmong leader, Vang Shur, claimed in 1989 that their "10,000 resistance forces had scored many successes against the Vietnamese-backed Kaysone government" and controlled many villages in remote N Laos. Today this Hmong resistance movement can be viewed as only a minor irritant to the government in Vientiane.

Following liberation, Hmong refugees continued to pour into Thailand, the exodus reaching a peak in 1979 when 3,000 a month were fleeing across the Mekong. Thousands also ended up in the US and France, fresh from the mountains of Laos: unsurprisingly they did not adapt easily. Various stress disorders were thought to have triggered heart attacks in many healthy young Hmong – a condition referred to as Sudden Unexplained Nocturnal Death Syndrome. In *The Ravens*, Robbins comments that "in a simpler age, it would have been said that the Hmong are dying of a broken heart".

There are three main groups of Hmong living in Laos – the Black, White and the Striped – identifiable, again, by their traditional dress and dialect. All the groups practise slash-and-burn agriculture and mainly grow dry hill rice and maize. They raise animals and also hunt and forage to supplement their diet. Opium poppies is the main cash crop for the Hmong and refined opium is exported on horseback to markets in Chiang Mai. They also export their embroidery to the tourist markets in Northern Thailand. They are well known for their appliqué (and reverse appliqué work) but these days, to produce saleable items quickly, some of the original patterns have been simplified and enlarged.

Other communities

The largest non-Lao groups in Laos are the Chinese and Vietnamese communities in the main cities. Many of the Vietnamese were brought in by the French to run the country and stayed. In more recent years, Vietnam also tried to colonize parts of Laos. The Vietnamese are not well-liked: one of the few rude words in the Lao language refers to them. The Chinese have been migrating to Laos for centuries and are usually traders, restaurateurs and shop-owners. With the relaxation in Communist policies in recent years, there has been a large influx of Thais; most are involved in business. In Vientiane there is also a small community of Indians running restaurants, jewellery and tailors' shops. The majority of the Europeans in Laos are embassy staff or involved with aid projects and oil prospecting companies and live on the S and E side of Vientiane.

RELIGION

Theravada Buddhism, from the Pali word *thera* ('elders'), means the 'way of the elders' and is distinct from the dominant Buddhism practiced in India, Mahayana Buddhism or the 'Greater Vehicle'. The sacred language of Theravada Buddhism is Pali rather than Sanskrit, Bodhisattvas (future Buddhas) are not given much attention, and emphasis is placed upon a precise and 'fundamental' interpretation of the Buddha's teachings, as they were originally recorded. By the 15th century, Theravada Buddhism was the dominant religion in Laos – as it was in neighbouring Siam (Thailand), Burma (Myanmar) and Cambodia. Buddhism shares the belief, in common with Hinduism, in rebirth. A

Mudras and the Buddha image

An artist producing an image of the Buddha does not try to create an original piece of art; he is trying to be faithful to a tradition which can be traced back over centuries. It is important to appreciate that the Buddha image is not merely a work of art but an object of, and for, worship. Sanskrit poetry even sets down the characteristics of the Buddha – albeit in rather unlikely terms: legs like a deer, arms like an elephant's trunk, a chin like a mango stone and hair like the stings of scorpions. The Pali texts of Theravada Buddhism add the 108 auspicious signs; long toes and fingers of equal length, body like a banyan tree and eyelashes like a cow's. The Buddha can be represented either sitting, lying (indicating *paranirvana*), or standing, and occasionally walking. He is often represented standing on an open lotus flower: the Buddha was born into an impure world, and likewise the lotus germinates in mud but rises above the filth to flower. Each image will be represented in a particular *mudra* or 'attitude', of which there are 40. The most common are:

Abhayamudra – dispelling fear or giving protection; right hand (sometimes both hands) raised, palm outwards, usually with the Buddha in a standing position.

Varamudra – giving blessing or charity; the right hand pointing downwards, the palm facing outwards, with the Buddha either seated or standing.

Vitarkamudra – preaching mudra; the ends of the thumb and index finger of the right hand touch to form a circle, symbolizing the Wheel of Law. The Buddha can either be seated or standing.

Dharmacakramudra – 'spinning the Wheel of Law'; a preaching mudra symbolizing the teaching of the first sermon. The hands are held in front of the chest, thumbs and index fingers of both joined, one facing inwards and one outwards.

Bhumisparcamudra – 'calling the earth goddess to witness' or 'touching the earth'; the right hand rests on the right knee with the tips of the fingers 'touching ground', thus calling the earth goddess Dharani/Thoranee to witness his enlightenment and victory over Mara, the king of demons. The Buddha is always seated.

Dhyanamudra – meditation; both hands resting open, palms upwards, in the lap, right over left.

Buddha calling for rain – a common image in Laos but very rare elsewhere; the Buddha is depicted standing, both arms held stiffly at the side of the body, fingers pointing downwards.

Other points of note:

Vajrasana – yogic posture of meditation; cross-legged, both soles of the feet visible.

Virasana – yogic posture of meditation; cross-legged, but with the right leg on top of the left, covering the left foot (also known as *paryankasana*).

Buddha under Naga – a common image in Khmer art; the Buddha is shown seated in an attitude of meditation with a cobra rearing up over his head. This refers to an episode in the Buddha's life when he was meditating; a rain storm broke and Nagaraja, the king of the nagas (snakes), curled up under the Buddha (seven coils) and then used his seven-headed hood to protect the Holy One from the falling rain.

Bhumisparcamudra – calling the earth goddess to witness. Sukhothai period, 13th-14th century.

Dhyanamudra – meditation. Sukhothai period, 13th-14th century.

Abhayamudra – dispelling fear or giving protection. Lopburi Buddha, Khmer style 12th century.

Vitarkamudra – preaching, "spinning the Wheel of Law". Dvaravati Buddha, 7th-8th century, seated in the "European" manner.

Abhayamudra – dispelling fear or giving protection; subduing Mara position. Lopburi Buddha, Khmer style 13th century.

ZTB 201

person goes through countless lives and the experience of one life is conditioned by the acts in a previous one. This is the Law of Karma (act or deed, from Pali *kamma*), the law of cause and effect. But, it is not, as commonly thought in the West, equivalent to fate.

For most people, nirvana is a distant goal, and they merely aim to accumulate merit by living good lives and performing good deeds such as giving alms to monks. In this way the layman embarks on the Path to Heaven. It is also common for a layman to become ordained, at some point in his life (usually as a young man), for a 3 month period during the Buddhist Rains Retreat.

Monks should endeavour to lead stringently ascetic lives. They must refrain from murder, theft, sexual intercourse, untruths, eating after noon, alcohol, entertainment, ornament, comfortable beds and wealth. They are allowed to own only a begging bowl, three pieces of clothing, a razor, needle, belt and water filter. They can only eat food that they have received through begging. Anyone who is male, over 20, and not a criminal can become a monk.

The 'Way of the Elders', is believed to be closest to Buddhist as it originally developed in India. It is often referred to by the term 'Hinayana' (Lesser Vehicle), a disparaging name foisted onto Theravadans by Mahayanists. This form of Buddhism is the dominant contemporary religion in the mainland Southeast Asian countries of Laos, Thailand, Cambodia, and Myanmar.

In Theravadan Buddhism, the historic Buddha, Sakyamuni, is revered above all else and most images of the Buddha are of Sakyamuni. Importantly, and unlike Mahayana Buddhism, the Buddha image is only meant to serve as a meditation aid. In theory, it does not embody supernatural powers, and it is not supposed to be worshipped. But, the popular need for objects of veneration has meant that most images *are* worshipped. Pilgrims bring flowers and incense, and prostrate themselves in front of the image. This is a Mahayanist influence which has been embraced by Theravadans.

Buddhism in Laos

The Lao often maintain that the Vientiane area converted to Buddhism at the time of the Moghul emperor Asoka. This seems suspiciously early and is probably untrue. The original stupa at That Luang, so it is claimed, was built to encase a piece of the Buddha's breastbone provided by Asoka. Buddhism was undoubtedly practised before Fa Ngoum united Lane Xang and created a Buddhist Kingdom in the mid-14th century. He was known as the Great Protector of the Faith and brought the Phra Bang, the famous golden statue – the symbol of Buddhism in Laos – from Angkor in Cambodia to Laos.

Buddhism was gradually accepted among the lowland Lao but many of the highland tribes remain animist. Even where Buddhism has been practised for centuries, it is usually interwoven with the superstitions and rituals of animist beliefs. Appeasing the spirits and gaining merit are both integral features of life. Most highlanders are animists and the worship of *phi* or spirits has remained central to village life throughout the revolutionary years, despite the fact that it was officially banned by the government. Similarly, the *baci* ceremony – when strings representing guardian spirits are tied around the wrists of guests – is still practised throughout Laos.

In the late 1500s, King Setthathirat promoted Buddhism and built many monasteries or *wats*. Buddhism was first taught in schools in the 17th century and prospered until the Thai and Ho invasions of the 18th and 19th centuries when many of the wats were destroyed. With the introduction of socialism in 1975 Buddhism was banned from pri-

Punishments in the eight Buddhist hells commonly found on murals behind the principal Buddha image in the *sim*.

Adapted from Hallet, Holt (1890) *A thousand miles on an elephant* in the Shan States, William Blackwood: Edinburgh

In Siddhartha's footsteps: a short history of Buddhism

Buddhism was founded by Siddhartha Gautama, a prince of the Sakya tribe of Nepal, who probably lived between 563 and 483 BC. He achieved enlightenment and the word *buddha* means 'fully enlightened one', or 'one who has woken up'. Siddhartha Gautama is known by a number of titles. In the W, he is usually referred to as *The Buddha*, ie the historic Buddha (but not just Buddha); more common in Southeast Asia is the title *Sakyamuni*, or Sage of the Sakyas (referring to his tribal origins).

Over the centuries, the life of the Buddha has become part legend, and the Jataka tales which recount his various lives are colourful and convoluted. But, central to any Buddhist's belief is that he was born under a *sal* tree (*Shorea robusta*), that he achieved enlightenment under a bodhi tree (*Ficus religiosa*) in the Bodh Gaya Gardens, that he preached the First Sermon at Sarnath, and that he died at Kusinagara (all in India or Nepal).

The Buddda was born at Lumbini (in present-day Nepal), as Queen Maya was on her way to her parents' home. She had had a very auspicious dream before the child's birth of being impregnated by an elephant, whereupon a sage prophesied that Siddhartha would become either a great king or a great spiritual leader. His father, being keen that the first option of the prophesy be fulfilled, brought him up in all the princely skills (at which Siddhartha excelled) and ensured that he only saw beautiful things, not the harsher elements of life.

Despite his father's efforts Siddhartha saw four things while travelling between palaces – a helpless old man, a very sick man, a corpse being carried by lamenting relatives, and an ascetic, calm and serene as he begged for food. These episodes made an enormous impact on the young prince, and he renounced his princely origins and left home to study under a series of spiritual teachers. He finally discovered the path to enlightenment at the Bodh Gaya Gardens in India. He then proclaimed his thoughts to a small group of disciples at Sarnath, near Benares, and continued to preach and attract followers until he died at the age of 81 at Kusinagara.

mary schools and people prohibited from giving alms to monks. With the increasing religious tolerance of the regime it is now undergoing a revival and many of the wats are being rebuilt and redecorated. Males are expected to become monks for 3 months or so before marriage, usually during Buddhist Lent. All members of the priesthood are placed under the authority of a superior – the *Phra Sangharaja*– whose seat was traditionally in the capital of the kingdom.

In line with Buddhist tradition, materialism and the accumulation of personal wealth is generally frowned-on in Laos. Poverty is admired as a form of spirituality. This belief proved rather convenient for the Communist regime, when it was taken to extremes. Today, in the new capitalist climate, the traditional attributes of spirituality sit uncomfortably with Laos' increasingly bourgeois aspirations.

Buddhism, as it is practised in Laos, is not the 'other-worldly' religion of western conception. Ultimate salvation – enlightenment, or *nirvana* – is a distant goal for most people. Lao Buddhists pursue the Law of Karma, the reduction of suffering. Meritorious acts are undertaken and demeritorious ones avoided so that life, and more particularly future life, might be improved. 'Karma' is often thought of in the W as 'fate'. It is not. It is true that previous karma determines a person's position in society, but there is still room for individual action – and a person is ultimately responsible for

In the First Sermon at the deer park in Sarnath, the Buddha preached the Four Truths, which are still considered the root of Buddhist belief and practical experience. These are the 'Noble Truth' that suffering exists, the 'Noble Truth' that there is a cause of suffering, the 'Noble Truth' that suffering can be ended, and the 'Noble Truth' that to end suffering it is necessary to follow the 'Noble Eightfold Path' – namely, right speech, livelihood, action, effort, mindfulness, concentration, opinion and intention.

Soon after the Buddha began preaching, a monastic order – the *Sangha* – was established. As the monkhood evolved in India, it also began to fragment as different sects developed different interpretations of the life of the Buddha. An important change was the belief that the Buddha was transcendent: he had never been born, nor had he died; he had always existed and his life on earth had been mere illusion. The emergence of these new concepts helped to turn what up until then was an ethical code of conduct, into a religion. It eventually led to the appearance of a new Buddhist movement, Mahayana Buddhism which split from the more traditional Theravada 'sect'.

Despite the division of Buddhism into two sects, the central tenets of the religion are common to both. Specifically, the principles pertaining to the Four Noble Truths, the Noble Eightfold Path, the Dependent Origination, the Law of Karma and nirvana. In addition, the principles of non-violence and tolerance are also embraced by both sects. In essence, the differences between the two are of emphasis and interpretation. Theravada Buddhism is strictly based on the original Pali Canon, while the Mahayana tradition stems from later Sanskrit texts. Mahayana Buddhism also allows a broader and more varied interpretation of the doctrine. Other important differences are that while the Thervada tradition is more 'intellectual' and self-obsessed, with an emphasis upon the attaining of wisdom and insight for oneself, Mahayana Buddhism stresses devotion and compassion towards others.

that action. It is the law of cause and effect.

It is important to draw a distinction between 'academic' Buddhism, as it tends to be understood in the W, and 'popular' Buddhism, as it is practiced in Laos. In Laos, Buddhism is a 'syncretic' religion: it incorporates elements of Brahmanism, animism and ancestor worship. Amulets are worn to protect against harm and are often sold in temple compounds. In the countryside, farmers have what they consider to be a healthy regard for the spirits (*phi*) and demons that inhabit the rivers, trees and forests. Astrologers are widely consulted by urban and rural dwellers alike. It is these aspects of Lao Buddhism which help to provide worldly assurance, and they are perceived to be complementary, not in contradiction, with Buddhist teachings.

Most Lao villages will contain a 'temple', 'monastery' or *wat* (the word does not translate accurately). The wat represents the mental heart of each community, and most young men at some point in their lives will become ordained as monks, usually during the Buddhist Rains Retreat, which stretches from Jul to Oct. Previously this period represented the only opportunity for a young man to gain an education and to learn how to read. An equally important reason for a man to become ordained is so that he can accumulate merit for his family, particularly for his mother, who as a woman cannot become ordained.

Monks receiving alms from the laity

As in Thailand, Laos has adopted the Indian epic the *Ramayana* (see page 70), which has been the inspiration for much Lao art and sculpture. Complete manuscripts of the Lao *Ramayana* – known as the *Phra Lak Phra Lam*, used to be kept at Wat Phra Kaeo and Wat Sisaket.

Buddhism under Communism

Buddhism's relationship with Communism has been complex and usually ambivalent. As the Pathet Lao began their revolutionary mission they saw in the country's monks a useful means by which to spread their message. Many monks, though they may themselves have renounced material possessions and all desires, were conscious of the inequalities in society and the impoverished conditions that many people lived their lives. Indeed most of them came from poor, rural backgrounds. In addition many monks saw themselves as the guardians of Lao culture, and as the US became more closely involved in the country so they increasingly felt that it was their job to protect the people against the spread of an alien culture and mores. Therefore, right from the start, monks had a natural sympathy with the ideals of the Pathet Lao. Indeed, significant numbers renounced their vows and joined the revolution. Others stayed on in their monasteries, but used their positions and the teachings of the Buddha to further the revolutionary cause. The Pathet Lao, for their part, saw the monks as a legitimizing force which would assist in their revolutionary efforts. Monks were often the most respected individuals in society and if the Pathet Lao could somehow piggy-back on this respect then they too, it was reasoned, would gain in credibility and respect. The Rightist government also tried to do the same, but with notably less success.

With the victory of the Pathet Lao in 1975, their view of the *sangha* (monkhood) changed. No longer were monks a useful vehicle in building revolution; overnight they became a potential threat. Monks were forced to attend re-education seminars where they were instructed that they could no longer teach about merit or *karma*, two central pillars of Buddhism. Their sermons were taped by Pathet Lao cadres to be scrutinized for subversive propaganda and a stream of disillusioned monks began to flee to Thailand. So the *sangha* was emasculated as an independent force. Monks were forced to follow the directives of the Lao People's Revolutionary Party and the *sangha* came under strict Party control. Monasteries were expected to become mini-cooperatives so that they did not have to depend on the laity for alms, and they were paid a small salary by the State for undertaking teaching and health work. In short, the LPDR seemed intent on undermining the *sangha* as an independent force in Lao society, making it dependent on the State for its survival and largely irrelevant to wider society. The success of the Pathet Lao's policy of marginalization can be seen in the number of monks in the country. In 1975 there were around 20,000 monks. By 1979 this had shrunk to just 1,700.

However before the *sangha* could sink into obscurity and irrelevance, the government eased its policy in 1979, and began to allow monks and the *sangha* greater latitude. In addition, and perhaps more importantly, the leadership embraced certain aspects of Lao culture, one of which was Theravada Buddhism. The memorial to the revolutionary struggle in Vientiane, for example, was designed as a Buddhist *that* (stupa) and government ministers enthusiastically join in the celebration of Buddhist festivals.

Christianity in post-1975 Laos

Growing religious tolerance has also rekindled Christianity. While many churches in provincial towns were turned into community centres and meeting halls after the revolution, Vientiane's Evangelical Church has held a Sun service ever since 1979. But Christians have only felt free to worship openly in recent years. In 1989 the first consultation between the country's Christian leaders (Protestant and Roman Catholic) was authorized by the government – it was the first such meeting since 'liberation'. Government representatives and two leaders of the Buddhist Federation were also invited to attend – ironically both were Hmong.

Foreign missionaries were ejected from Laos in 1975. But with indigenous priests and missionaries now operating in the countryside (many under the guise of non-governmental aid organizations), church leaders predict the rapid growth of Christianity – they say there are around 17,000 Christians in the country. Not many Buddhists have converted to Christianity but it seems to be growing among the animist hilltribes. The US Bible Society is currently working on a modern translation of the Bible into Lao, but tribal language editions do not yet exist. The shortage of bibles and other literature has prompted Christian leaders to 'offer unsolicited gifts' to the department of religious affairs to ease restrictions on the import of hymn books and bibles from Thailand.

LANGUAGE AND LITERATURE

Language

The official language is Lao, the language of the ethnic majority. Lao is basically a monosyllabic, tonal language. It contains many polysyllabic words borrowed from Pali and Sanskrit (ancient Indian dialects) as well as words borrowed from Khmer. It has 6 tones, 33 consonants and 28 vowels. Lao is also spoken in NE Thailand and N Cambodia, which was originally part of the kingdom of Lane Xang. Lao and Thai, particularly the NE dialect, are mutually intelligible. Differences have mainly developed since French colonial days when Laos was insulated from developments of the Thai language. French is still spoken in towns – particularly by the older generation – and is often used in government but English is being increasingly used. Significant numbers of Lao have been to universities and colleges in the former Soviet Union and Eastern Europe, so Eastern European languages and Russian are spoken.

Many of the tribal groups have no system of writing and the Lao script is similar to Thai, to which it is closely related. One of the kings of the Sukhothai Dynasty, Ramkhamhaeng, devised the Thai alphabet in 1283 and introduced the Thai system of writing. Lao script is modelled on the early Thai script and is written from left to right with no spacing between the words.

Literature

Lao literature is similar to Thai and is likewise also influenced by the Indian epic *Ramayana*, which in Laos is known as the *Phra Lak Phra Lam* (see page 70). Scenes from the Phra Lak Phram Lam can often be seen depicted in temple murals. The first 10 **jataka tales**, recounting the last 10 lives of the Gautama Buddha (the historic Buddha), have also been a major inspiration for Lao literature. The versions that are in use in Laos are thought to have been introduced from Lanna Thai (northern Thailand, Chiang Mai) in the 16th century, or perhaps from the Mon area of present day Myanmar and Thailand. In these 10 tales, known as the *Vesantara Jataka*, the Buddha renounces all his earthly possessions, even his wife and

The Lao Ramayana: the Phra Lak Phra Lam

The *Phra Lak Phra Lam* is an adaptation of the Indian Hindu classic, the Ramayana, which was written by the poet Valmiki about 2,000 years ago. This 48,000 line epic odyssey – often likened to the works of Homer – was introduced into mainland Southeast Asia in the early centuries of the first millennium. The heroes were simply transposed into a mythical, ancient, Southeast Asian landscape.

In Laos, as in Thailand, the *Phra Lak Phra Lam* quickly became highly influential. In Thailand this is reflected in the name of the former capital of Siam, Ayutthaya, taken from the legendary hero's city of Ayodhia. Unfortunately, these early Thai translations of the Ramayana, which also filtered into Laos, were destroyed following the sacking of Ayutthaya by the Burmese in 1767. The earliest extant version was written by Thai King Taksin in about 1775.

The Lao, and Thai, versions of the Ramayana, closely follow that of the original Indian story. They tell of the life of Ram (Rama), the King of Ayodhia. In the first part of the story, Ram renounces his throne following a long and convoluted court intrigue, and flees into exile. With his wife Seeda (Sita) and trusted companion Hanuman (the monkey god), they undertake a long and arduous journey. In the second part, his wife Seeda is abducted by the evil king Ravana, forcing Ram to wage battle against the demons of Langka Island (Sri Lanka). He defeats the demons with the help of Hanuman and his monkey army, and recovers his wife. In the third and final part of the story – and here it diverges sharply from the Indian original – Seeda and Ram are reunited and reconciled with the help of the gods (in the Indian version there is no such reconciliation). Another difference to the Indian version is the significant role played by Hanuman – here an amorous adventurer who dominates much of the third part of the epic.

Hanuman
Adapted from Hallet, Holt (1890) *A thousand miles on an elephant in the Shan*

There are also numerous sub-plots which are original to the *Phra Lak Phra Lam*, many building upon local myth and folklore. In tone and issues of morality, the Lao and Thai versions are less puritanical than the Indian original. There are also, of course, difference in dress, ecology, location and custom.

children. Although the jataka tales in Laos are clearly linked – in religious terms – with Buddhism and therefore with India, the stories have little in common with the Indian originals. They draw heavily on local legends and folklore and have merely been incorporated within a religious literary milieu. They are essentially animist tales provided with a Buddhist gloss.

Traditionally, as in other parts of Southeast Asia, texts were recorded on palm leaves. The letters were inscribed with a stylus and the grooves darkened with oil. A **palm leaf manuscript** kept under good conditions in a well-maintained *hau tai* or library can last 100 years or more.

With the incorporation of Laos into French Indochina at the end of the 19th century, the Lao élite effectively renounced traditional **Lao literature** in

Transcribing Lao: playing with words

How to transcribe the Lao language is a vexed issue which even the French never really worked out in some 50 years of trying. It is common to find 3 or 4 transcriptions of a town's name – Salavan, Saravane and Saravan; or Muang Khammouane, Mouang Khammouan and Muang Khammuan, for example. Generally in this book we have used the French 'x' instead of the English 's' as this is more widely accepted in the country. So we use Xekong instead of Sekong. But where an 'English' spelling has gained acceptance – for example in the case of Paksé rather than Pakxé – we have kept the 's'. In either instance we provide alternative spellings where appropriate.

favour of the French language and French artistic traditions. Many of the Lao élite were educated in France, and those that were not still enjoyed a French-style education. The upshot was that Lao literature came to be looked down upon as primitive and simplistic and most scholars wrote instead in French.

As with traditional songs, much **Lao poetry** has been passed down the generations and remains popular. *Sin Xay* is one of the great Lao poems, and has been written down (although many have not) and is found in many temples.

In 1778 the Thais plundered Laos and along with the two most sacred Buddha images – the Phra Bang and the Phra Kaeo (Emerald Buddha) – they pillaged a great deal of Lao religious literature and historical documents. Most Lao manuscripts – or *kampi* – are engraved on palm leaves and are between 40 and 50 cm long, pierced with two holes and threaded together with cord. A bundle of 20 leaves forms a *phuk*, and these are grouped together into *mat*, which are wrapped in a piece of cloth.

DANCE, DRAMA AND MUSIC

Lao music, songs and dances have much in common with those of the Thai. Instruments include bamboo flutes, drums, gongs, cymbals and pinched or bowed string instruments shaped like banjos. The national instrument is the *kaen*, a hand-held pipe organ. It is made from bamboo and is similar in appearance to the South American pan pipes. Percussion is an important part of a Lao orchestra and two of the most commonly used instruments are the *nang nat*, a xylophone, and the *knong vony*, a series of bronze cymbals suspended from a wooden frame. The *seb noi* orchestra – a consortium of all these instruments – is used to introduce or conclude vocal recitals. The *seb gnai* orchestra includes two big drums and a Lao-style clarinet as well; it was used in royal processions and still accompanies certain religious ceremonies.

Despite the lack of written notation, many epic poems and legends have survived to the present day as songs, passed, with the composition itself, from generation to generation. Early minstrels took their inspiration from folklore, enriched by Indian myths. Traditional Lao music can now only be heard during performances of the *Phra Lak Phra Lam*, the Lao version of the Indian epic the Ramayana. Many of the monasteries have experts on percussion who play every Buddhist sabbath. There is also a strong tradition of Lao folk music, which differs between tribal groups.

Secular songs, drawing largely on Lao literature for inspiration, are known as *mau lam* and can be heard at festival time not just in Laos but also in NE Thailand (where they are known as *mor lam*), which is also, culturally, 'Lao'. Indeed, there has been something of a Lao cultural revival in NE Thailand and some of the best performers are based there. It is also the best place to pick up cassette tapes of famous *mor lam/mau lam* singers.

Musicians commemorating the
20th anniversary of the
World Tourism Organization

In Vientiane and the provincial capitals, younger Lao tend to opt for western-style pop. To the raucous strains of the likes of *Joan Jett and the Blackhearts* – with the lyrics roughly translated into Lao – local bands entertain Levi-clad dancers well into the early hours in Vientiane's discos and nightclubs. The Communist leadership have become increasingly concerned at this invasion of western and Thai culture, and there has been an attempt to limit the quantity of non-Lao music that is played in clubs and karaoke bars. The authorities have dictated that only a certain proportion of songs can be non-Lao and there are cultural police who occasionally check that these rules are being observed.

Classical Lao theatre and dance have Indian origins and were probably imported from the Cambodian royal courts in the 14th century. Thai influence has also crept in over the years.

MODERN LAOS

POLITICS

Laos underwent the political equivalent of an earth tremor in Mar 1991 at the Fifth Congress of the Lao People's Revolutionary Party (LPRP). **Pro-market reforms** were embraced and the politburo and central committee got a much-needed transfusion of new blood. At the same time, the hammer and sickle motif was quietly removed from the state emblem and enlightened sub-editors set to work on the national credo, which is emblazoned on all official documents.

This shift in economic policy and ideology can be traced back to the Party Congress of 1986, making Laos one of the very first countries to embrace 'perestroika'. As late General Secretary Kaysone Phomvihane stated at the Fourth Party Congress in 1986:

"In all economic activities, we must know how to apply objective laws and take into account socio-economic efficiency. At the present time, our country is still at the first stage of the transition period. Hence the system of economic laws now being applied to our country is very complicated. It includes not only the specific laws of socialism but also the laws of commodity production. Reality indicates that if we only apply the specific economic laws of socialism alone and defy the general laws pertaining to commodity production, or vice versa, we will make serious mistakes in our economic undertaking during this transition period" (General Secretary Kaysone Phomvihane, Fouth Party Congress 1986; quoted in Lao PDR 1989:9).

Under the horrified gaze of Marx and Lenin – their portraits still dominate the plenary hall – it was announced that the state motto had changed from "Peace, Independence, Unity and Socialism" to "Peace, Independence, Democracy, Unity and Prosperity". The last part is wishful thinking for the poorest country in Southeast Asia, but it reflects the realization that unless Laos turns off the socialist road fast, it will have great difficulty digging itself out of the economic quagmire that 15 years' adherence to Marxism has created. In Aug 1991, at the opening of the People's Supreme Assembly, Kaysone Phomvihane, the late President, said: "Socialism is still our objective, but it is a distant one. Very distant." Now that the 'New Thinking' – or *Chin Thanakan Mai* – has begun to

Bun Bang Fai: the Lao Sky Rocket Festival

Perhaps Laos' best known festival is the *bun bang fai* or skyrocket festival. This is celebrated across Laos and in Thailand's northeastern region (which is also Lao) between May and June – the end of the dry season. The festival was originally linked to animist beliefs, but through time it also became closely associated with Buddhism. The climax of the festival involves the firing of massive rockets into the air to ensure bountiful rain by propiating the rain god Vassakarn (or, as some people maintain, Phya Thaen), who also has a penchant for fire. The rockets can be 4m or more long and contain as much as 500 kg of gunpowder. As well as these *bang jut* rockets, there are also *bang eh* – rockets which are heavily and extravagently decorated and which are not fired, and just for show. Traditionally the rockets were made of bamboo; now steel and plastic storm pipes are more commonly used in Thailand such is the size of *bang jut*. Specialist rocket-makers commissioned months before hand have taken over from the amateurs of the past. The rockets are mounted on a bamboo scaffold and fired into the air with much cheering and shouting – and exchanging of money as gambling has become part and parcel of the event.

Traditionally, *bun bang fai* were local festivals when neighbouring villages would take it in turns to bear the cost. The rockets were made by Buddhist monks who were the only people with the time and knowledge to build the gunpowder-packed rockets. It was far more lewd and wild than today. Men wearing phallic symbols would parade through the village, drunken groups would dance wildly imitating sexual intercourse, and young men and women would take the opportunity to meet and court. At the same time, young boys would be ordained and monks blessed.

permeate, the floodgates have swung open.

President Kaysone Phomvihane died in Nov 1992, aged 71. (His right hand man, Prince Souphanouvong – the so-called Red Prince – died just over 3 years later on 9 January 1985.) As one obituary put it, Kaysone was older than he seemed, both historically and ideologically. He had been chairman of the LPRP since the mid-1950s and had been a prodigé and comrade of Ho Chi Minh, who led the Vietnamese struggle for independence from the French. After leading the Lao Resistance Government – or Pathet Lao – from caves in Sam Neua province in the N, Kaysone assumed the premiership on the abolition of the monarchy in 1975. But under his leadership – and following the example of his mentors in Hanoi – Kaysone became the driving force behind the market-orientated

reforms. The year before he died, he gave up the post of Prime Minister for that of President. His death didn't change things much, as other members of the old guard stepped into the breach. Nouhak Phounsavanh – a spritely 78-year-old former truck driver and hardline Communist – succeeded him as President. General Khamtai Siphandon – who had become Prime Minister the previous year – took over as head of the LPRP. Parliamentary elections were held the month after Kaysone's death. 154 officially recruited candidates stood for 85 seats and most of the country's 2 million voters prudently voted. Before the election, Party leaders said there would be no change after the election and the electorate got what they voted for.

In 1986, before *perestroika* had caught on in the former USSR, the

Party introduced a New Economic Mechanism (or NEM, see 'Economy', below) and embarked on the transition from a centrally planned economy to what is sometimes rather quaintly termed 'market socialism' (the equivalent of China's 'capitalism with Chinese characteristics'). Expectations have been running high, but as in neighbouring Vietnam, economic liberalization has not really been matched by political *glasnost*. So far, the **monolithic Party** shows few signs of equating capitalism with democracy. While the Lao brand of Communism has always been seen as relatively tame, it remains a far-cry from political pluralism. Laos' first constitution since the Communists came to power in 1975, was approved in 1991. The country's political system is referred to as a 'popular democracy', yet it rejected any move towards multi-party reforms.

On the dreamy streets of Vientiane, the chances of a Tiananmen-style uprising are remote, but the events of the late 1980s and early 1990s in Eastern Europe and Moscow have doubtless alarmed hard-liners – just as they did in Beijing and Hanoi. They can be reasonably confident, however, that in their impoverished nation, most people are more worried about where their next meal is going to come from than they are about the allure of multi-party democracy.

The greatest concern for the Lao leadership, and in this sense the country mirrors developments in many other countries of Asia, is what effect 'westernization' is having upon the population. The economic reforms, or so the authorities would seem to believe, have brought not only foreign investment and new consumer goods, but also greed, corruption, consumerism and various social ills from drugs to prostitution. This was starkly illustrated at the most recent party congress held in Mar 1996. Observers were expecting to find the congress reaffirm the policy of economic

reform and rubber stamp it 'business as usual'. Instead one of the architects of the reform programme, Deputy Prime Minister Khamphoui Keoboualapha, was unceremoniously dumped. The reason? It was thought that he had become too close to Thailand, and in particular to influential Thai investors. He was blamed more than most for the development of the various social ills that the leadership are so desperate to stem. So although there is no evidence that the economic reforms will be pegged back, it does seem that uncontrolled capitalism is beyond the pale, particularly if it is perceived to promote cultural erosion. That the leadership want to keep a firm hand on the tiller is reflected in the composition of the 9-man politburo: 6 are generals, another a colonel, leaving just two members outside the military. Reports during 1996 indicated that the leadership see Myanmar's State Law and Order Restoration Council as a form of government worth emulating.

Foreign relations

The government has taken steps to improve its foreign relations – and **Thailand** is the main beneficiary. Historically, Thailand has always been the main route for international access to landlocked Laos. Survival instincts told the Vientiane regime that reopening its front door was of paramount importance. The 1990s began with an unprecedented visit by a member of the Thai royal family, Crown Princess Sirindhorn and in 1994 the Friendship Bridge officially opened (see page 90) linking Laos and Thailand. The border disputes with Thailand have now been settled, and the bloody clashes of 1987/88, when thousands on both sides lost their lives, are history. Thailand is Laos' largest investor, and the success of the market reforms depend more on Thailand than any other country. Economic pragmatism, then, has forced the leadership in Vientiane to cosy up to Bangkok. This does not mean, though, that relations are warm. Indeed, Vientiane is irredeemably suspicious of Thai intentions, a suspicion born of a history of conflict.

Laos is rapidly becoming a 'keystone' in mainland Southeast Asia (see the economy section, below) and sees its future in linking in with its more powerful, and richer, neighbours. To this end Laos has applied for membership of the Association of Southeast Asian Nations (ASEAN), and if all goes according to plan it will join the Association in 1997, becoming the group's second Communist member (Vietnam joined in July 1995). By joining, Vientiane is hoping to be in a better position to trade-off the interests of the various powers in the region, thereby giving it greater room for manoeuvre.

The Golden Triangle – the Lao connection

Since 1990, attempts have been made to combat the production and trafficking of illicit drugs – sizeable industries in Laos and one in which its mountain tribespeople excel. They contribute to the Golden Triangle's hard drugs output, providing at least 60% of the world's heroin supply. Laos is the third largest producer of opium after Burma and Afghanistan – 375 tonnes of it were produced in 1989 according to US figures. The opium trade was legal in Laos until US pressure forced the government to outlaw it in 1971. The French quietly bought and sold the Hmong opium crop to finance their war efforts against Vietnam's Communists and the Americans turned a blind eye to the trade and allegedly fostered it too. During the 1960s, the drugs trade was run by a handful of high-ranking Royalist officers who became very rich.

Today, in Laos' N provinces, the opium addiction rate of 50% in some villages is more than twice the literacy rate, and small *parakeets* (sachets) of opium have become an unofficial currency. A recent livestock survey in Luang Prabang province was an interesting pointer: most villages listed a few water buffalo, and a few hundred pigs and chickens. One Hmong village had none of these, but listed 214 ponies, which had just left for Chiang Mai when the survey team arrived.

In October 1990, following accusations from the US State Department that the Lao government and military authorities were actively involved in the narcotics trade network, Laos agreed to co-operate with the US in narcotics control and US aid is providing US$20mn to substitute cash crops – such as sesame, coffee and mulberry trees (for silk) – for *Papaver somnifera* (opium poppies) in the mountainous NE Houa Phan province. By signing up for the war against drugs, Laos has opened its empty coffers to a welcome flow of funds. Seizures of raw opium and heroin have increased and there have been reports of opium confiscated from traffickers being ceremonially burned. Traffickers are also being convicted in the Lao courts. The deputy foreign minister, Souban Salitthilat, who heads the National Committee for Narcotic Drugs Supression has been stressing to foreign governments that Laos is a signatory of the UN's Vienna Convention which proscribes production and trafficking.

But in the Golden Triangle area, bordering Burma and Thailand, anti-government insurgents finance their activities with opium smuggling and Vientiane reportedly wants to keep Washington's tendrils well away. There is also widespread suspicion that smuggled opium and heroin are countertraded for Thai consumer goods – everything from toothpaste to televisions have flooded the bustling markets of Vientiane and Luang Prabang.

Relations have also thawed with **China**. Laos and China have set up a bilateral trade agreement and the previous president, Kaysone, paid an official visit to Beijing in Oct 1991, returning a visit by Chinese Premier Li Peng to Vientiane in 1990. In 1993 the Lao and Chinese governments signed a defence cooperation agreement, and the Chinese are now important suppliers of military hardware to the Lao. This is causing some worries in **Vietnam**, which shares a 1,300 km-long border with Laos and historically has had poor relations with China. As the old men of the Lao Communist Party, who owed so much to the Vietnamese, die off so their replacements are looking elsewhere for investment and political support. They do not have such deep fraternal links with their brothers in Hanoi and are keen to diversify their international relations.

Laos is also the only country in Indochina to have maintained relations with the **US** since 1975 – despite the fact that they never offered reparations or aid to the country. Washington even expected the Lao government to allocate funds to help locate the bodies of US pilots shot down in the war. When Vientiane pledged to co-operate with the US over the narcotics trade during Foreign Affairs Minister General Phoune Sipaseuth's meeting with US Secretary of State James Baker in Oct 1990, it agreed to step up the search for the 530 **American MIAs** still listed as missing in the Lao jungle. In mid-1993, tri-lateral talks between Laos, Vietnam and the US allowed for greater cooperation in the search for MIAs. Many of the unaccounted-for servicemen are thought to have been airmen, shot down over the Ho Chi Minh trail which ran through Lao territory along the border with Vietnam. The MIA charity, based in Vientiane, has assumed quite a high profile and, in the absence of other US aid organizations, has become a major conduit for humanitarian assistance to the Lao government. In Oct 1992, America's diplomatic presence in Laos was upgraded to ambassadorial status from chargé d'affaires. But, unwilling to put all its eggs in the basket of the superpower, Vientiane has also courted smaller western countries, particularly Sweden (a long time friend), France, Germany and Australia.

Japan is now Laos' biggest aid donor, although Australia and Sweden are also very significant in this regard. These days Washington and Tokyo offer more in the way of hope for the embattled regime than Moscow: in 1991, 100 Soviet economic and technical advisers were pulled out of the dilapidated flats they occupied on the outskirts of Vientiane. There will be no more Soviet/Russian aid, although Laos has been given a few years' leeway before it has to pay back its 750-million rouble debt (three-quarters of Laos' total foreign debt). All purchases of military hardware from Russia now have to be paid for in hard currency.

As Laos turned to the W, Japan and Thailand for economic help, the government became more critical of its closest Communist ally, **Vietnam**. Following Vietnam's invasion of Cambodia in Dec 1978, thousands of N Vietnamese moved into N Laos as permanent colonizers and by 1978 there were an estimated 40,000 Vietnamese regulars in Laos. In 1987, 50,000 Vietnamese troops withdrew. With the death of President Kaysone Phomvihane in Nov 1992, another historical link with Vietnam was cut. He was half-Vietnamese and most of his cabinet owed their education and their posts to Hanoi's succour during the war years. In 1990 a Vientiane census found 15,000 Vietnamese living illegally in the capital, most of whom were promptly deported.

Laos is the only landlocked country in Southeast Asia and Vientiane is keen to pursue a cooperative 'equilibrium policy' with its neighbours. There is a widely held view that Laos – a small, poor, weak and land-locked country – is best served by having multiple friends in international circles. The leadership in Vientiane are in the tricky situation of having to play off China's military might, Thailand's commercial aggressiveness, and Vietnam's population pressures, while keeping everyone happy. The answer, in many people's minds, is to promote a policy of inter-dependence in mainland Southeast Asia. In 1993 a western diplomat quoted by the French newspaper *Le Monde* said: "This country's only hope is to become, within the next 10 or 20 years, a bridge between its powerful neighbours, while at the same time managing to avoid being engulfed by either of them".

ECONOMY

Until just a few years ago, if the world's financial markets crashed and international trade and commerce collapsed overnight, Laos would have been blissfully immune from the catastrophe. It would be 'farming as usual' the next morning. Since the mid-1980s, though, the government has gradually begun to tread the free-market path, veering off the old command system. Farms have been privatized and the state has to compete for produce with market traders at market prices. Many of the unprofitable state-owned business and factories have been leased or sold-off. Cutting credit to those old monoliths has helped bring the annual inflation rate down from nearly 80% in 1989 to less than 7% in 1994, although it has since risen again, to around 19% in 1996. Aid and other grants from international donors are still needed to fund nearly a third of the government's budget and in 1995 the government in sleepy Vientiane was forced to devalue the national currency, the appropriately named kip.

But foreign investment is coming in, after a slow start – most in the garment and textiles sector. Economists say the country's greatest economic potential lies in its mineral resources – gold, precious stones, coal and iron – and hydro-power. It has been estimated that only 1% of the country's hydo-power potential of some 18,000 MW has so far been exploited and myriad schemes are being discussed (see below). Timber is another considerable source of foreign exchange. Malaysian, Taiwanese, Chinese and Thai firms have been awarded timber concessions in the country, many of them working in collaboration with the Lao army which has become an important economic player. (Strict reafforestation commitments were written into the contracts although there are grave doubts how far the agreements are honoured.)

But though Laos may be reforming its economy and attracting large sums (for it) of foreign investment, there is no getting away from the fact that Laos is still – in economic terms – an extraordinarily poor place. In 1995 the government published its first ever **survey of consumption**, undertaken with the help of the UNDP. It showed what most people already knew: that people don't have much surplus income. On average, the survey showed, 62% of household income is spent on food. By some international standards, if food accounts for 60% or more of total household consumption then a household should be regarded as poor. In other words, according to this definition, nearly two-thirds of households in Laos live in poverty. The survey also showed that Laos does not have the deep disparities that are so painfully visible in neighbouring countries like Thailand (but see the section below on 'Emerging inequalities'). Although two-thirds of households may be 'poor', two-thirds also have an income that lies within 50% of the median. Laos, then, is a fine example of 'shared poverty' – we are poor, but at least we are all poor.

Economic reform

Laos made the jump from a sleepy agrarian economy hidden behind a façade of

AIDS in Laos

Like the other countries of Southeast Asia, Laos is thought to have the potential for 'rapid increase' in the HIV/AIDS epidemic. As of the end of Jun 1994, there were only 14 reported AIDS cases in Laos. However, a study undertaken in 1993 showed that 0.8% of blood donors were HIV-infected, and the low number of cases to date probably reflects a lack of research and the fact that the country is at a comparatively 'early' stage in the epidemic.

socialism to a reforming economy like China and Vietnam's in the 1980s. In English this change in direction is rather blandly named the **New Economic Mechanism** (NEM). Locally, the more evocative terms *chin thanakaan mai*, or 'new thinking', and *kanpatihup setthakit*, or the 'reform economy', are used. The origins of the NEM can be traced back to 1982 when the possibility of fundamental reform of the economy was first entertained by a small group within the leadership. For the next 3 or 4 years the debate continued within this small circle, and it was not until 1985 that the NEM was actually pilot-tested in the Vientiane area. The success of the reforms there led to the NEM being presented at – and adopted by – the critical Fourth Party Congress of 1986. The NEM encompasses a range of reformist policies, much like those adopted in other countries from Russia to Vietnam:

● a move to a market determination of prices and resource allocation.

● a shift away from central planning to 'guidance' planning.

● a decentralization of control to industries and lower levels of government, and the encouragement of the private sector.

● the encouragement of foreign investment and the promulgation of a new investment law allowing 100% foreign ownership.

● a lifting of barriers to internal and external trade.

(Source: Rigg, Jonathan [1997] 'Uneven development and the re-engagement of Laos')

Former President Kaysone Phomvihane

shouldered much of the blame for the miserable state of the economy, admitting that the Party had made mistakes. At the Congress in 1991 he set the new national agenda: Laos had to step up its exports, encourage more foreign investment, promote tourism and rural development, entice its shifting cultivators into proper jobs and revamp the financial system. In doing so he prioritized the problems but offered no solutions bar the loosening of state control and the promotion of private enterprise.

Since 1986, when economic reforms were first introduced, Laos has eliminated six of its seven official exchange rates to create a unified market-related rate and the kip has stabilized at around 700 to the dollar. The once-booming black market has all but disappeared. Although a non-convertable currency, the kip is now in as much demand in Laos as the US dollar and Thai baht. This helped put Laos on a more commercially-competitive footing. Now market forces are firmly in place as the central plank of economic planning, old-fashioned capitalism has taken root again.

What Laos was able to achieve was a very rapid reorientation of its economy. This, as some economists have pointed out, was because when you get down to it there was remarkably little in Laos to reform. The great majority of the population were poor farmers (and they still are), and the country's industrial base was almost non-existent. There were no communes to break up; and there was no large state industrial sector to dismember. It all meant that the task of the

Landmarks of economic reform, 1975-1994

1975	**December:** full and final victory of the communist Pathet Lao.
1982	Reforms first touted.
1985	Pilot studies of financial autonomy in selected state-run industries.
1986	Decentralization of decision-making to the provinces including provincial tax administration. Freeing-up the market in rice and other staples. **November:** NEM endorsed by the Party Congress.
1987	Restrictions on the cross-provincial movement of agricultural produce abolished; barriers to external trade reduced. **June:** prices of most essentials market-determined.
1988	Forced procurement of strategic goods at below market price abolished; reduction in public sector employment; tax reforms introduced; private sector involvement in sectors previously resvered as state monopolies permitted; introduction of new investment law. **March:** prices of fuel, cement, machinery and vehicles freed; tax reforms enacted; state and commercial banking sectors separated; state enterprises made self-reliant and autonomous; explicit recognition of the rights of households and the private sector to use land and private property. **June:** nationwide elections held for 2,410 positions at the district level. **July:** multiple exchange rates abolished; liberal foreign investment code introduced; payment of wages in kind abolished.
1989	**June:** second tax reform enacted. **October:** first joint venture bank with a foreign bank begins operation, the Joint Development Bank.
1990	**March:** privatization ('disengagement') law introduced. **June:** key economic laws covering contracts, property, banking and inheritance discussed by National Assembly. **July:** State Bank (Central Bank) of the Lao PDR established and fiscal management of the economy formally handed over to the new bank.
1992	Thai Military Bank begins operating a full branch in Vientiane. **January:** Commercial Bank and Financial Institutions Act introduced.
1993	Accelerated privatization programme announced. **December:** removal of last quantitative restrictions and licensing requirements for imports.
1994	**March:** new investment and labour laws passed in March by the National Assembly, to be enforced within 60 days. As an incentive to foreign investors, the investment law lowers some import taxes and the tax on net profit, streamlines the approval process, and ends the foreign investment period limit of 15 years.

Source: Rigg, Jonathan (1997) *Southeast Asia: the human landscape of modernization and development*, London: Routledge.

Lao leadership has been comparatively easy when compared with, say, Vietnam. In a sense, Laos was never socialist except in name and so the shift to a market economy involved not a move from socialism to capitalism, but from subsistence to capitalism.

This doesn't mean that reform has been a doddle, because although Laos may not have had to undo years of socialist reconstruction and development, there was also little that the leadership could build on to promote modernization. There are few skilled workers, there is a great dearth of engineers and graduates, the stock of roads is woefully thin, large slices of the country are almost impossible to reach, there is little domestic demand to fuel industrialization, there are few entrepreneurs, and there are even fewer people with the money to invest in new ventures. In other words, Laos is short of most of the elements that constitute a modern economy and most of the people that make it tick.

Agriculture

Rice is the staple food crop – it is cultivated by 75% of the population – and nearly three-quarters of Laos' farmers grow enough to sell or barter some of their crop. Output has risen by 30% since 1985 and the country now produces 1.7 million tonnes of rice a year from nearly 600,000 ha of paddy land. More than half the rice is grown in the hills. In N Laos maize and cassava are often grown as substitutes. Northern provinces suffered a serious drought in 1992/93 however, prompting the UN's World Food Programme to provide about US$1mn in emergency assistance. The drought, followed by a long cold spell in the provinces of Luang Nam Tha, Phongsaly, Houa Phan and Xieng Khouang, cut rice production in some districts by 80%.

The main agricultural areas are on the Mekong's floodplains, especially around Vientiane and Savannakhet.

The government has been successful in expanding the area capable of producing two rice crops a year by upgrading and developing the country's irrigation infrastructure. Cotton, coffee, maize and tobacco are the other main crops and the production of these and other 'industrial' crops such as soya and mung beans has increased in recent years. On the Bolovens Plateau in the S, rice, coffee and cardamom – 500 tonnes of the latter is produced a year – are grown. Fisheries and livestock resources are being developed – the cattle population has grown by about 30% in the past decade, as has the number of pigs.

While shifting cultivators continue to pose a problem in Laos, their numbers have dropped by about a third since 1985. This is reflected by the fact that they cut down 100,000 ha of forest a year now, compared with 300,000 in the early 1980s. The situation has improved dramatically since the mid-1970s when Hmong General Vang Pao complained to a *National Geographic* reporter that "In one year a single family will chop down and burn trees worth US$6,000 and grow a rice crop worth US$240". He demanded the Hmong get their share of fertile, irrigated land – a share they are still waiting for.

Centuries of war and 15 years of Communism had little impact on the self-reliant villages of rural Laos. The government's attempts at co-operativization proved unpopular and unworkable. Just before the cooperativization programme was abruptly suspended in mid-1979 there were 2,800 cooperatives accounting for perhaps 25% of farming families. But even these figures over-estimate the role of cooperatives at that time, for many were scarcely functioning and those that were were doing so with considerable foot-dragging on the part of the farmers who ostensibly belonged to them. The reasons why cooperatives were such a failure are numerous. To begin with, and unlike

China and Vietnam, there were almost no large landlords, there was little tenancy, and there was abundant land. The inequalities that were so obvious in neighbouring countries simply did not exist in Laos. Second, most farmers were subsistence cultivators; capitalism had barely made inroads into the Lao countryside and the forces of commercialization were largely absent. Further, and third, the LPDP provided little support either of a technical or financial kind. As a result, farmers – largely uneducated and bound to their traditional methods of production – saw little incentive to change. In some areas it was not so much a lack of interest in cooperatives, but a positive dislike of them. There were reports of farmers slaughtering their cattle, burning their fields, and eating their poultry, rather than handing their livestock or crops over to the Party. By mid-1979, when the policy was suspended, the leadership in Vientiane had concluded that their attempts at cooperativization had been a disaster.

Since the suspension of the policy, the government has effectively returned to a free enterprise system in the countryside. Farmers now own their land, they can produce whatever crops they like, and they can sell these on what has become virtually a 'free market'. Lao farmers, though they may be poor and though technology may be antiquated, are in essence no different in terms of the ways they work than the kinsfolk over the Mekong in Thailand.

Building up the economy

Tens of thousands of people work for the government in a top-heavy and often corrupt **bureaucracy**. Civil servants are doing well if they make US$15-20 a month and life is difficult for Laos' underpaid teachers, doctors, soldiers and civil servants. Junior government ministers earn around US$50 a month (far less than the US$100 a Vientiane trishaw pedlar can earn). Not surprisingly, official corruption and profiteering are on the increase – there is little else to explain the new houses and cars in the capital.

Major **development constraints** are the shortage of skilled workers and capital, an undeveloped communication system (10,000 km of road, only 20% of which are sealed), poor educational and health resources, rugged terrain and low population density. A piece in the *New Yorker* magazine, published in Aug 1990 and entitled 'Forgotten country', reported the experience of two aid workers as they struggled to travel to Phong Saly Province in the far N where they worked: "When David Merchant and Lois Fochringer [two aid workers] visit Phong Saly Province – the northernmost province of Laos, on the China border – they have to travel for $3\frac{1}{2}$ days by boat and are then met by provincial authorities and given a jolting ride up the side of a mountain in a 4WD truck. The truck itself arrived by boat, having been cut into two pieces for the voyage. For 8 months or so of each year, Phong Saly Province is accessible only by helicopter, because the water level is too low for boat traffic" (Sesser 1990).

Traditionally, one of Laos' most important sources of foreign exchange has been receipts from **over-flight rights**, as the Bolovens Plateau lies on the flight path from Bangkok to Hong Kong and Tokyo. Nearly 100 international flights traverse Lao airspace every day, and the government receives US$300 for each one: a total of almost US$11mn a year. One of the country's biggest foreign exchange earners is **hydro-power**. Much of this comes from the Nam Ngum Dam, N of Vientiane and from the Xeset Dam in southern Laos. These generate not only electricity (the country's potential is estimated to be more than 18,000 MW), but more than US$20mn a year in exports to Thailand.

Plans are underway to further exploit the potential of the Mekong and its

The First Five Year Plan (1981-1985)
brings prosperity to all

tributaries and a raft of over 60 projects has been slated for development over the next decade. The biggest proposed project is the Pa Mong Dam, 20 km upstream from the capital. If built, the resultant flooding would require the relocation of more than 6,000 people and the price tag is an estimated US$2.8bn, a vast sum for a country with a GDP of around US$1 billion. The decision to build the dam rests with the Mekong Committee, whose members include Laos, Thailand, Cambodia, Myanmar and Vietnam. Laos has been variously dubbed the 'battery' or 'Kuwait' of Southeast Asia and the government has signed various deals with Thailand and Vietnam to sell electricity. A few years ago this all seemed eminently sensible. But the Lao leadership did not count on the influence of the international environmental lobby. The US$1.2 bn Nam Theun 2 Dam, for example, has been delayed by discoveries of rare bats and birds and it is still not certain whether it will receive financial backing from multi-lateral loan agencies such as the Asian Development Bank.

Most of the new enterprise has been in the **service sector** – there is little evidence that the reforms have prompted a significant increase in manufacturing activity. Most industry in Laos is small scale – rubber shoes, matches, tobacco processing, brewing, and soft drinks and ice manufacturing. Saw-milling and timber processing account for the majority of factories – a toothpick plant is still a large source of manufactured export earnings. Pottery is produced at the cottage industry level. Altogether, industry employs only a few thousand people and accounts for a tiny fraction of the gross domestic product. However, this is gradually changing, albeit from an extremely low base: textile manufacturers have set up shop in the country and garments are now one of Laos' most valuable export (see below).

With the odds stacked against it, the government cannot afford to be choosy when it comes to investment. No international bank will guarantee companies operating in Laos, which has a high risk rating. Nearly 300 foreign investment contracts have been approved since the government adopted a more liberal investment code in 1988, many of them textile factories and enterprises in the tourism sector. By the end of 1992 the latter had absorbed more than a fifth of all foreign investment in Laos. Unlike

Number of tourist arrivals (1990-1995)	
1990	14,400
1991	37,613
1992	87,571
1993	102,946
1994	146,155
1995	208,271

most of its Southeast Asian neighbours, Laos' embryonic garment industry is not subject to quotas from markets in the US and the European Community. The supposed 'flood' of foreign investment in this sector has been nothing more than blue-jeans and T-shirt manufacturers from Thailand, Hong Kong, Macao and France, relocating to avoid export restrictions. In 1993 garments became Laos' leading foreign exchange earner (US$35mn in 1993), although in the following year they were pushed into second place by wood products, a traditionally strong source of foreign exchange.

In an effort to make the business climate more attractive, the state bank now supplies credit to all sectors of the economy. Provincial banks have been told to operate as autonomous commercial banks. State enterprises have been warned that if their bottom line does not show a profit, they are out of business. Provinces are free to conclude their own trading agreements with private companies and neighbouring countries – which generally means Thailand.

Fears of dependency on Thailand

Thailand is Vientiane's lifeline to the outside world. Just 3 years after their last bloody border dispute in 1987/88, the old enemies patched up their differences and agreed to build the Mittaphab – or Friendship – bridge across the Mekong linking Vientiane with Nong Khai in NE Thailand. The bridge was built with Australian assistance and opened in 1994 (see page 90). However, fears of Laos becoming a Thai commercial colony has led the government to extend an extremely cautious welcome to Thai proposals to build another bridge at Savannakhet in the southern 'panhandle', which would link NE Thailand with southern Vietnam. There is also talk of a bridge linking Chiang Khong in Thailand's N with Ban Houai Xai, allowing Thailand easier access to the rich market of Yunnan in southern China.

Following the visit of Thai Crown Princess Sirindhorn in early 1990 – the first visit by a member of the Thai royal family for 15 years – Thailand lifted a ban of the export on 200 'strategic goods' to Laos, which had been in place since 1975 and which covered everything from military equipment to food and bicycles. Most of these goods now go through the ports of Keng Kabao (near Savannakhet) and Tha Dua.

Thais have emerged as the biggest foreign investors in Laos. Two way trade grew to US$233.4mn in 1993, with the balance heavily in Thailand's favour. Between 1988 (when a new foreign investment code was promulgated) and 1995 Thailand's investment in Laos totalled US$1.94bn, 43% of total investment.

Six Thai commercial banks have set up in Laos, along with businessmen, consultants and loggers. The warming of relations between Bangkok and Vientiane has raised some eyebrows: sceptics say Laos' wealth of unexploited natural resources is a tempting reward for patching things up. Laos has about 2 million ha of forest – 400,000 ha of which is teak and other high quality timber – and it is disappearing fast. But to its credit, Thailand has prioritized aid to Laos and has signed joint ventures in almost every sector – from science and technology to trade, banking and agriculture. Thai businessmen have partially taken over the state beer and brewery, and the Thai conglomerate Shinawatra have been given telecommunications concessions. Nonetheless, Thai diplomats are only too aware of the poor reputation that their businessmen have in Vientiane. They are regarded as over-bearing and superior in their attitude to the Lao, and rapacious, predatory and mercenary in their business dealings. The Thai government has even run courses to try and improve business behaviour. But Thai perceptions of their neighbours are deeply entrenched. As one Thai critic remarked in 1995: "Thai cultural diplomacy starts with the assumption that Thai culture is superior."

In the early 1990s Thailand proposed, before the UN General Assembly, that Laos be admitted to the Association of Southeast Asian Nations (ASEAN), along with Vietnam and Myanmar (Burma). Vietnam is already an ASEAN member and Laos is due to join in 1997. Since this process of rapprochement began trade between the two countries has boomed and Thai investment blossomed. Young Lao who previously attended universities in the Soviet bloc are now being dispatched to Thai universities. The Vientiane government is acutely aware that skilled workers remain the country's number one limitation – three-quarters of its intellectuals left in 1975.

To understand Laos' **fears of Thailand** it is necessary to look back in history. Until the French absorbed Laos into Indochina, Laos came under Thai suzerainty, and indeed the Siamese saw Laos as a junior, rather primitive, colony of theirs. When the foolhardy King Anou of Vientiane tried to recreate the great 14th century Lao kingdom of Fa Ngoum and invaded Siam he was soundly thrashed in a battle at Korat, in NE Thailand, and then saw his capital Vientiane plundered, sacked and razed by Siamese forces – a fact which explains why today this ancient city is so devoid of architecture pre-dating the French period. Anou was captured and later died in captivity. Needless to say, Thai and Lao history is at odds on this period

of history: Thai accounts paint Anou as a rebel; those written by Lao historians characterize him as a national hero.

It is only with this background in mind that Lao fears of Thai commercial hegemony can be fully appreciated. When, in 1988, former Thai Prime Minister Chatichai Choonhaven expressed a desire to turn Indochina 'from a battlefield into a market place', this was viewed by many Lao – and some more thoughtful Thais – as tantamount to a threat of commercial invasion. (The theme was returned to in 1995 when a senior Thai diplomat, Suridhya Simaskul, remarked to the journalist Michael Vatikiotis, "We have passed the stage of turning battlefields into markets; now the market itself has become the battlefield.") Thailand, its own natural resources denuded through years of thoughtless exploitation, was hoping to pillage Laos' resource-rich larder. In Jul 1989, state run Radio Vientiane broadcast a commentary, presumably officially sanctioned, stating: "Having failed to destroy our country through their military might [referring to the Ban Rom Klao border conflict of 1987-88], the enemy has now employed a new strategy in attacking us through the so-called attempt to turn the Indochinese battlefield into a marketplace..." It is this fear of Thailand, and of over-dependence on Thailand, which has prompted the Lao government to do its utmost to try and diversify its commercial links. In a rather novel departure from the usual state of affairs, the Lao are also more scared of Thai cultural pollution, than western cultural pollution. The similarities between the two countries, and the fact that many Lao households watch Thai television, makes Thailand seem more of a risk. In 1993, former president and Pathet Lao veteran Phoumi Vongvichit warned against the dangers of prostitution, 'depraved' dancing and gambling. The source of these threats to pristine Lao culture was Thailand.

Facing up to reality

In Mar 1995, the *Bangkok Post* reported the story of a new Lao face cream and the television commercial used to promote it. In the commercial, a woman using the cream is regarded by her friend with the exclamation "Wongdevan, you look so beautiful!", and then asked confidentially about the secret of her physical transformation. Laos subsequently began to greet friends looking rather the worse for wear with the stock phrase "My, Wongdevan, you look so beautiful!". Unfortunately, the actress in the commercial happened to be the girlfriend of an influential Lao, and in a fit of pique, no doubt believing the joke cast aspersions on his own taste in women, he had a new law introduced banning satirical jokes based on Lao TV commercials – with offenders liable to a fine of 2,500 kip or US$3.50. Latest reports are that the joke is more popular than ever, and sales of the face cream are sluggish.

Newspaper reports even dubbed the Mittaphaap Bridge the AIDS Bridge, because it is thought that it will bring prostitution and AIDS to the country.

Dependency on aid, and development aims

Laos depends heavily on imports – everything from agricultural machinery and cars to petrol products, textiles and pharmaceuticals – 75% of which are financed by foreign aid. Western bilateral donors are enthusiastically filling the aid gap left by the Socialist bloc. Countries and private donors are falling over each other to fund projects; NGOs are homing in and multi-lateral development banks are offering soft loans and structural adjustment programmes. As Laos' US$500mn foreign debt is mostly on highly concessional terms, it is not crippled by repayment schedules. But with development banks accelerating their project-funding, fears are mounting that Laos is teetering on the edge of a debt trap.

At more than US$170mn a year, or US$39/head, external assistance now accounts for nearly one fifth of Laos' gross domestic product – over double the country's export earnings and a third of the government's budget. By 1990, Vientiane's capacity to absorb this aid was swamped, its ministries overwhelmed by one of the highest per capita aid inflows in the developing world.

While western economic advisers have been touting investment strategies, project co-ordination and quality have suffered in the rush.

The country and its foreign strategists are looking to four distinct areas for future income. The first concentrates on mining and energy. Laos already has two HEP dams that generate power for export to Thailand and others are planned. South Korea's Daewoo group signed a contract for an HEP scheme in southern Laos which is nearing completion (see page 111). Mining rights to some of Laos' huge lignite reserves have been sold to Thai investors. Other untapped mineral resources include reserves of gold, gemstones and iron ore, while foreign companies have undertaken preliminary search for oil. The second area of interest is agriculture and forestry. Investors are looking at growing feed grains like soyabeans and maize for export to Thailand. Raw timber exports will be ended and replaced by processed wood industries. The third potential is tourism but the government is wary of Laos going the same way as Thailand. The fourth strategy – and the most ambitious – is for Laos to become the 'service centre' between China, Vietnam, Cambodia and Thailand (see the section titled, Laos as the 'keystone' of mainland Southeast Asia, below).

Laos: fact file

Geographic

Land area	236,800 sq km
Arable land as % of total	3.8%
Average annual deforestation rate	1.0%
Highest mountain, Bia	2,800m
Average rainfall in Vientiane	1,720mm
Average temperature in Vientiane	27°C

Economic

GNP/person (1994)	US$320
GDP/person (PPP*, 1992)	US$1,760
GNP growth (/capita, 1980-1990)	0.7%
% labour force in agriculture	78%
Total debt (% GNP)	136%
Debt service ratio (% exports)	7.7%
Military expenditure (% GDP) (1992)	6.1%

Social

Population	4.7 million
Population growth rate (1960-92)	2.3%
Population growth rate (1990-1994)	3.1%
Adult literacy rate	43%
Mean years of schooling	2.9 years
Tertiary graduate as % of age group	2%
Population in absolute poverty	n.a.
Rural population as % of total	79%
Growth of urban population/year (1960-92)	5.1%
(1990-94)	6.4%
Urban population in largest city (%)	48%
Televisions per 1,000 people	7

Health

Life expectancy at birth	52 years
Population with access to clean water	28%
Calorie intake as % of requirements	111%
Malnourished children under 5 years old	0.25 million
Infant mortality rate (per 1,000 live births, 1994)	92
Contraceptive prevalence rate†	n.a.

* PPP = Purchasing Power Parity (based on what it costs to buy a similar basket of goods and services in different countries).

† % of women of childbearing age using contraception.

Source: United Nations Development Programme (1995) *Human development report 1995*, OUP: New York; World Bank (1996) *World Development Report 1996*, OUP: New York; and other sources.

The government claims its "programme for the basic elimination of illiteracy among the masses", launched in 1984 was "an outstanding success". Literacy rates are still low – 35% for women, 65% for men. Adult education has been expanded, schools upgraded and 62 classrooms built "for 1,600 tribal youths". But while the government has been busy building schools, the quality of education has slipped further: they cannot afford to pay teachers or buy textbooks.

Health care has suffered for the same reasons. Infant and under-five mortality rates are some of the highest in the world, the latter estimated at 193 per 1,000 live births. Half of those who do survive suffer malnutrition, nearly all contract malaria, diarrhoea, respiratory and intestinal diseases and few live beyond 50.

Emerging inequalities

As in neighbouring Vietnam, the economic reforms are beginning to widen inequalities in society. Most of those who are doing well live in towns or at least close to one of the country's main roads. This means that off-road communities, and especially those in highland areas, are finding that – at least in relative terms – they are becoming poorer. In addition, because it is mostly minority Lao Soung and Lao Theung who live in these marginal areas, the economic reforms are widening inequalities between ethnic groups. One foreign aid worker was quoted in the *Far Eastern Economic Review* at the beginning of 1996 saying: "When they come down to Vientiane, where the lowland Lao [the Lao Loum] live, it's like Hong Kong to them. Here's money, here's development. In their own villages, there's nothing". As in Vietnam, the need to ensure that the economic reforms bring benefits to all, and not just a few, is a key political question. The leadership are acutely aware that widening inequalities could fuel political discontent.

Laos as the 'keystone' of Mainland Southeast Asia

"From the air-conditioned offices of Bangkok, Laos is peripheral, lying on the very edge of the global economy. But from the moulding colonial buildings of Vientiane, the vision is of creating a country which lies at the very heart of a dynamic sub-regional economic grouping including some of the fastest-growing economies in the world" (Rigg, 1997).

In what sceptics might view as an ultimately futile effort, the leadership in Vientiane have chanced upon an economic future for their country: as the 'keystone' or 'crossroads' of Southeast Asia. Nor is it just Lao leaders who are drumming up enthusiasm for this notion. The Asian Development Bank (the Asian arm of the World Bank) is at the forefront of developing – and funding – what has become known as the Greater Mekong Sub-region or GMS. This will link southwest China, Thailand, Myanmar, Cambodia, Vietnam and Laos. And within this scenario, Laos is the crucial pivotal country through which most road and rail links will have to go. There is talk of a 'Golden Quadrangle' (as opposed to the infamous Golden Triangle) – even of a Golden Land. This reference draws on ancient Indian texts which talked of *Suvarnaphum* – a Golden Land – which encompassed modern day Thailand, Laos, Myanmar and probably Malaya and Indonesia too. Deputy Prime Minister Khamphoui Keoboualapha remarked in an interview in 1995 for the *Far Eastern Economic Review* that "We [Laos] want to become the link between Vietnam, China, Thailand, Burma and Cambodia".

Vientiane

IN 1563, King Setthathirat made the riverine city of Vientiane the capital of Laos. Or, to be more historically accurate, Vieng Chan – the 'City of the Moon' – became the capital of Lane Xang. In those days it was a small fortified city on the banks of the Mekong with a palace and two wats, That Luang and Wat Phra Kaeo (built to house the Emerald Buddha). The city had grown prosperous from the surrounding fertile plains and taxes levied from trade going upriver. As Francis Garnier put it, this was the "former metropolis of the kingdom of Laos".

Vieng Chan remained intact until 1827 when it was ransacked by the Siamese – explaining why many of its wats are of recent construction. Francis Garnier in 1860 wrote of 'a heap of ruins', and having surveyed the 'relics of antiquity' decided that the "absolute silence reigning within the precincts of a city formerly so rich and populous, was ... much more impressive than any of its monuments ...". A few years later, Louis de Carne wrote of the vegetation that it was like "a veil drawn by nature over the weakness of man and the vanity of his works ...". The city was abandoned for decades and only reconstructed by the French at the end of the 19th century, who built rambling colonial villas and wide tree-lined boulevards, befitting their new administrative capital, Vientiane. At the height of American influence it was renowned for its opium dens and sex shows.

Today Vientiane is a quiet capital city with a population of over 450,000 – about 10% of the population of Laos (it has grown from 70,000 in 1960). Before 1970 there was only one set of traffic lights in the whole city and even with

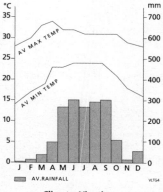

Climate: Vientiane

Thai stamp commerorating the official opening of the Friendship Bridge in 1994

Bridging the Mekong

In April 1994, King Bhumibol of Thailand and the President of Laos, accompanied by Prime Ministers Chuan Leekpai of Thailand and Australia's Prime Minister Keating opened the first bridge to span the lower reaches of the Mekong River, linking Nong Khai in Northeast Thailand with Vientiane in Laos. The bridge has been a long time in coming. It was first mooted in the 1950s, but war in Indochina and hostility between Laos and Thailand scuppered plans until the late 1980s. Then, with the cold war ending and growing rapprochement between the countries of Indochina and Asean, the bridge, as they say, became an idea whose time had come.

The 1.2 km-long Friendship Bridge, or Mittaphab has been financed with US$30 million of aid from Australia. It is a key link in a planned road network that will eventually stretch from Singapore to Beijing. For land-locked Laos, it offers an easier route to Thailand and through Thailand to the sea. For Thailand, it offers an entrée into one of the least developed countries in the world, rich in natural resources and potential. While for Australia, it demonstrated the country's Asian credentials. The Thais would like to build two further bridges. One will probably link Savannakhet and Mukdahan, although it is not expected to be completed much before 2002. The Lao and Thai governments have also signed a memorandum of understanding to build a bridge between Thakhek and Nakhon Phanom although Vientiane is decidedly cool about the prospect. They worry that bridges not only bolster trade, but also bring consumerism, crime, prostitution and environmental degradation.

the arrival of cars and motorbikes from Thailand in recent years, the streets are a far-cry from the congestion of Bangkok. There are only scattered traces of French town planning – unlike Phnom Penh and Saigon – and the architecture is a mixture of E and W, with French colonial villas and traditional wooden Lao buildings intermingled with Chinese shop-houses and more contemporary buildings. Some locals worry that foreign investment and re-development will ruin the city. Already some remarkably grotesque buildings are going up although officials do seem aware that there is little to be gained from creating a Bangkok in microcosm.

The capital is divided into *ban* or villages, mainly centred around their local wats, and larger *muang* or districts: **Muang Sikhottabong** lies to the W, **Muang Chanthabouli** to the N, **Muang Xaisettha** to the E and **Muang Sisattanak** to the S. Vientiane can be rather confusing for the first-time visitor as there are few street signs and most streets have two names – pre- and post-revolutionary. The names of major streets – or *thanon* – usually correspond to the nearest wat. Traffic lights and wats serve as directional landmarks. But because Vientiane is so small and compact it doesn't take long to get to grips with the town and the best way to do this is either on foot or by bicycle.

PLACES OF INTEREST

Most of the interesting buildings in Vientiane are of religious significance. **That Luang**, on Thanon That Luang, is considered Vientiane's most important site. The golden spire looks impressive at the top of the hill, 3 km NE of the city. According to legend, a stupa was first built here in the 3rd century AD by emissaries of the Moghul Emperor Asoka and it is supposed to have contained a relic of the Buddha. But excavations on the site have only located the remains of a 11th-13th century Khmer temple. It was built in its present form, encompassing the previous buildings, in 1566 by King Settathirat (his statue stands outside). Plundered by the Thais and the Chinese Ho in the 18th century, it was restored by King (Chao) Anou at the beginning of the 19th century. He added the cloister and the Burmese-style pavilion containing the That Sithamma Hay Sok.

It was again carefully restored by

That Luang by post

l'Ecole Francaise d'Extreme-Orient – whose conservators also restored parts of Angkor Wat – at the beginning of this century. The stupa was rebuilt yet again in 1930, as many Lao disapproved of the French restoration. The reliquary is surrounded by a square cloister, with an entrance on each side, the most famous on the E. There is a small collection of statues in the cloisters including one of the Khmer king Jayavarman VII. The cloisters are used as lodgings by monks who travel to Vientiane for religious reasons and especially for the annual That Luang festival (see page 102).

The base of the stupa is a mixture of styles, Khmer, Indian and Lao, and each side has a *hor vay* or small offering temple. The second tier is surrounded by a lotus wall and 30 smaller stupas, representing the 30 Buddhist perfections. Each of these originally contained smaller golden stupas but they were stolen by Chinese raiders in the 19th century. The 30m-high spire dominates the skyline and resembles an elongated lotus bud, crowned by a stylized banana flower and parasol. It was designed so that pilgrims could climb up to the stupa with walkways around each level. There was originally a wat on each side of the stupa but only two remain: **Wat Luang Nua** to the N and **Wat Luang Tai** to the S. That Luang is disappointing compared with Wat Sisaket and Wat Phra Kaeo (see below) largely because it seems to have been constructed out of concrete, but it is an important historical monument nonetheless and revered by the Lao. The *that* is also the prototype for the distinctive Lao-style angular chedi which can be seen in NE Thailand – which is also populated by ethnic Lao – as well as across Laos. A booklet with more detail about the wat is on sale at

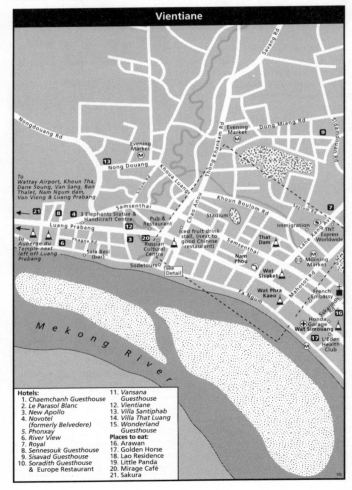

Vientiane

To Wattay Airport, Khoun Tha, Dane Soung, Van Sang, Ban Thalet, Nam Ngum dam, Van Vieng & Luang Prabang

To Auberge du Temple next left off Luang Prabang

Nongdouang Rd

Sisou Rd

Nong Douang

Evening Market

Khoua Luang

Thong Khantam Rd

Evening Market

Dong Miang Rd

Sidamdouan Rd

Samsenthai

3 Elephants Statue & Handicraft Centre

Luang Prabang

Phagna Rd

Sala Basi (bar)

Chao Anou

Khoun Boulom Rd

Stadium

Iced fruit drink stall, (next to good Chinese restaurant)

Russian Cultural Centre

Sodetours

see Detail

Samsenthai

Nam Phou

Saylom Rd

Immigration

Lane Xang Ave

That Dam

Wat Sisaket

Fa Ngum

Wat Phra Kaeo

Mahosot Rd

Morning Market

French Embassy

Honda Garage

Wat Simouang

L'Eden Health Club

Pub & Restaurant

M e k o n g   R i v e r

Hotels:
1. Chaemchanh Guesthouse
2. Le Parasol Blanc
3. New Apollo
4. Novotel (formerly Belvedere)
5. Phonxay
6. River View
7. Royal
8. Sennesouk Guesthouse
9. Sisavad Guesthouse
10. Soradith Guesthouse & Europe Restaurant
11. Vansana Guesthouse
12. Vientiane
13. Villa Santiphab
14. Villa That Luang
15. Wonderland Guesthouse

Places to eat:
16. Arawan
17. Golden Horse
18. Lao Residence
19. Little Panda
20. Mirage Café
21. Sakura

the entrance. Admission 200 kip. Open 0800-1130, 1400-1630 Tues-Sun (except 'special' holidays).

The **Revolutionary Monument** on Phon Kheng is visible from the parade ground, which resembles a disused parking lot, in front of That Luang. This spectacularly dull monument, a landmark on top of the hill, was built in memory of those who died during the revolution in 1975. The **Pathet Lao Museum**, to the NW of Wat That Luang, is only open to VIPs and never to the public. But there are a few tanks, trucks,

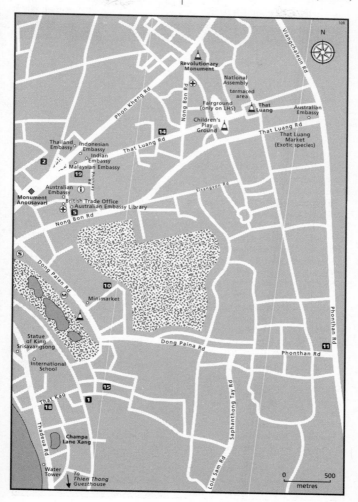

Wat Sisaket in Vientiane

McCarthy, James (1900) *Surveying and exploring in Siam with descriptions of Lao dependencies and of battles against the Chinese Haws*, John Murray: London. The pen and ink sketches are by H Warrington Smyth.

guns and aircraft used in the war lying in the grounds, which can be seen from the other side of the fence.

At the end of Thanon That Luang and the top of Lane Xang is the Oriental answer to Paris' Arc de Triomphe and Vientiane's best known landmark, the monstrous **Monument Anousavari**. It is called the Anou Savali, officially renamed the Pratuxai or Victory Gate, but is affectionately known as 'the vertical runway'. It was built by the former regime in memory of those who died in the wars before the Communist takeover, but the cement ran out before its completion. Refusing to be beaten, hundreds of tonnes of cement – part of a US aid package to help with the construction of runways at Vientiane's new Wattay Airport – were diverted up Thanon Lane Xang to finish off the monument in 1969. The top affords a birds-eye view of the leafy capital. The glittering golden dome in the distance is the expensive, Russian-built opera house, which is now only used during National Day celebrations.

The interior of the Monument Anousavari is reminiscent of a multi-storey car park (presumably as a counterpoint to the parade ground by the Revolutionary Monument), sporadically decorated with graffiti daubed on top of unfinished Buddhist bas-reliefs in reinforced concrete. The frescoes under the arches at the bottom represent mythological stories from the Lao version of the Ramayana, the Phra Lak Pralam. Until 1990 there was a bar on the bottom floor; today Vientiane's young hang out on the parapet, listening to the *Lambada* in Lao. Admission 200 kip (30 kip to park a bike). Souvenir shops at ground level and up the monument charge exorbitant rates; bargain hard.

Further down Thanon Lane Xang is the **morning market** (see below under markets) and beyond, where Thanon Setthathirat meets Thanon Lane Xang, is one of Vientiane's two national museums, **Wat Sisaket**. Built in 1818 during the reign of King Anou, it is one of the most important buildings in the capital. A traditional Lao monastery, the buildings survived the Thai sacking of the town in 1827 (perhaps out of deference to its having been completed only 10 years before the invasion), making it the

Imagine

Library, Wat Sisaket

oldest wat complex in Vientiane. The main sanctuary, or sim, with its sweeping roof has many stylistic similarities with Wat Phra Kaeo (see below): window surrounds, lotus shaped pillars and carvings of deities held up by giants on the rear door. The **sim** contains 2,052 Buddha statues (mainly terracotta, bronze and wood) in small niches in the top half of the wall. There is little left of the Thai-style jataka murals on the lower walls but the depth and colour of the originals can be seen from the few remaining pieces. The ceiling was copied from temples King Anou had seen on a visit to Bangkok. The standing image to the left of the altar is believed to have been cast in the same proportions as King Anou.

The sim is surrounded by a large courtyard, which originally had four entrance gates (3 are now blocked). The cloisters shelter 120 large Buddhas in the attitude of subduing Mara (see page 62) and thousands of small figures in niches, although many of the most interesting Buddha figures are now in Wat Phra Kaeo. The pile of broken Buddhas in the gateway were found during the French colonial period when they were reconstructing many of the local wats. Most of the statues are 16th-19th century, but there are some earlier images. The cloister walls were originally decorated with murals. Behind the sim is a large trough, in the shape of a naga, used for washing the Buddha images during the water festival (see page 300). An attractive Burmese-style library, or *hau tai*, stands on Thanon Lane Xang outside the courtyard. The large casket inside used to contain important Buddhist manuscripts but they have now been moved to protect them against vermin. Wat Sisaket is the home of the head of the Buddhist community in Laos, Phra Sangka Nagnok. Sadly Wat Sisaket is badly in need of restoration. Admission 200 kip. Open 0800-1130, 1400-1630 Tues-Sun.

Just behind Wat Sisaket is an entire complex of superbly preserved colonial houses in a well maintained garden, where the French ambassador resides. The cathedral was built in 1928.

Almost opposite Wat Sisaket on Thanon Setthathirat is the other national museum, **Wat Phra Kaeo** (entrance on Thanon Mahosot). It was

The cloister of Wat Sisaket with its many niches
each containing an image of the Buddha
The French in Indochina (1884, reprinted in 1995 by White Lotus, Bangkok)

originally built by King Setthathirat in 1565 to house the Emerald Buddha (or *Phra Kaeo*), now in Bangkok. He brought the image from Chiang Mai where he had previously been king. Wat Phra Kaeo was never a monastery but was kept for royal worship. The Emerald Buddha was removed by the Thais in 1778 and Wat Phra Kaeo was destroyed by them in the sacking of Vientiane in 1827. Francis Garnier, the French explorer, who wandered the ruins of Vieng Chan in 1860 describes Wat Phra Kaeo "shin[ing] forth in the midst of the forest, gracefully framed with blooming lianas, and profusely garlanded with foliage". Louis de Carne in his journal, *Travels in Indochina and the Chinese Empire* (1872), was also enchanted, writing when he came upon the vegetation-choked ruin that it "made one feel something of that awe which filled men of old at the threshold of a sacred wood". The building was expertly reconstructed in the 1940s and 1950s and is now surrounded by a garden.

The **sim** stands on three tiers of galleries, the top one surrounded by majestic, lotus-shaped columns. The tiers are joined by several flights of steps and guarded by nagas. The main door is an exquisite example of Lao wood sculpture with carved Buddhas surrounded by flowers and birds. This door, and the one at the rear, are the only notable remnants of the original wat. The sim now houses a superb assortment of Lao and Khmer art and some pieces of Burmese and Khmer influence, mostly collected from other wats in Vientiane.

Notable pieces: *3, 4, 17*: bronze Buddhas in typical Lao style; *294, 295*: Buddhas influenced by Sukhothai-style (Thailand), where the attitude of the walking Buddha was first created (see page 62); *354*: Buddha meditating – made of lacquered wood shows Burmese influence, 18th century; *372*: wooden, Indian-style door with erotic sculpture, dating back to the 16th century, originally from

The Buddha 'Calling for Rain'
a mudra unique to Laos

the Savannakhet region; *388*: copy of the Phra Bang, the revered statue associated with the origins of Buddhism in Laos (see page 29); *416*: a Khmer diety with 4 arms; *412, 414, 450*: also Khmer pieces; *415*: is a hybrid of Vishnu and Buddha; *430, 431*: are 18th century copies of the famous Khmer apsaras, the celestial nymphs of Angkor; *698*: this stone Buddha is the oldest piece of Buddhist art in Laos, 6th-9th century; *collection of stelae*: inscribed in Lao and Thai script, including one with a treaty delineating a 16th century agreement between Siam and Lane Xane. An unusual exhibit is the "Atom Struck Tile" found on the site of Sairenji Temple, Hiroshima.

A short description of each exhibit is given in French and Lao. The garden has

The story of Quan Am

Quan Am was turned onto the streets by her husband for some unspecified wrong doing and, dressed as monk, took refuge in a monastery. There, a woman accused her of fathering, and then abandoning, her child. Accepting the blame (why, no one knows), she was again turned out onto the streets, only to return to the monastery much later when she was on the point of death – to confess her true identity. When the Emperor of China heard the tale, he made Quan Am the Guardian Spirit of Mother and Child, and couples with a son now pray to her. Quan Am's husband is sometimes depicted as a parakeet, with the Goddess usually holding her adopted son in one arm and standing on a lotus leaf (the symbol of purity).

a small jar from the Plain of Jars (see page 147), which was helicoptered down to Vientiane. Admission 200 kip. Open 0800-1130, 1400-1630 Tues-Sat.

Adjacent to the museum is the **old royal palace**, today the presidential palace, closed to the public.

Travelling N on Chanta Koummane, the distinctive brick stupa of **That Dam** can be seen. It is renowned for the legend of the 7-headed dragon, which is supposed to have helped protect the city from Thai invaders. In the centre of town, on Samsenthai near the stadium, is the musty **Revolutionary Museum**. This distinctive white building houses a fascinating collection of artefacts and photographs depicting the 'fall' of the colonialists and their 'brutal ways'. Ironically it is housed in a French Colonial building, the Résidence Supérienre, the office of the highest-ranking French official in Laos. In Oct 1945, the Lao Issara government took it over and renamed it the Présidence du Conseil. Downstairs there is an exhibition of historic sights in Laos and Achievements of Communism. There are also some mini jars from the Plain of Jars in the museum's grounds. Admission 200 kip. Open 0800-1130, 1400-1630 Tues-Sun.

Parallel to Samsenthai is Setthathirat and Wat Ong Teu (with bright orange monks' quarters). Constructed by King Setthathirat, it houses one of the biggest Buddhas in Vientiane, which weighs several tons. The wat is also noted for its magnificent *sofa* and ornately carved wooden doors and windows with motifs from the Phra Lak Pralam (the Ramayana). The monastery runs one of the larger Buddhist schools in Laos and the Deputy Patriarch, Hawng Sangkharat, of the Lao monastic order lives here. The wat comes alive every year for the That Luang festival – originally a ceremony where nobles swore allegiance to the king and constitution, which amazingly has survived the Communist era (see page 102). Admission 100 kip.

A short walk away, on the banks of the Mekong (junction of Chao Anou and Fa Ngoum) is **Wat Chan**. Unfortunately, it was wrecked by the marauding Thais in 1827 – only the base of a single stupa remains in front of the sim. The stupa originally had Buddha images in the 'Calling for Rain' attitude on each side (see page 62); only one remains. Inside the reconstructed sim is a remarkable bronze Buddha from the original temple on this site. The wat is also renowned for its panels of sculpted wood on the doors and windows.

For those who have had their fill of Theravada Buddhist wats, there is a fine Mahayana Buddhist *chua* (pagoda) just off Khoun Boulom. The **Chua Bang-Long** is tucked away down a narrow lane and was established by Vientiane's large and active Vietnamese population. Before the outbreak of WW2 it was said that Vientiane had more Vietnamese residents than it did Lao. A statue of the Chinese goddess Quan Am (see box, page 98) stands in front of a Lao-style *that* which, in turn, fronts a large pagoda – almost Cao Dai in style. In 1996 the pagoda was undergoing extensive renovations and embellishment. Not far away, at the intersection of Samsenthai and Khoun Boulom is another, much smaller and more intimate, pagoda.

Further E of town on Simoung is **Wat Simoung**. It contains the town foundation pillar (*lak muang*), which was erected in 1563 when King Settathirat established Vientiane as the capital of the kingdom of Lane Xang. It is believed to be an ancient Khmer boundary stone, which marked the edge of the old Lao capital. The sim was reconstructed in 1915 around the foundation pillar, which forms the centre of the altar. In front of the altar is a Buddha, which is thought to have magical powers, and is often consulted by worshippers. Wat Simouang may not be charming, refined or architecturally significant but in some senses it is the most important monastery in the capital. Street hawkers selling offerings of fruit, flowers, candles and incense line the surrounding streets, supplying the scores of people who come here hoping for good fortune. In the grounds of the wat are the ruins of what appears to be a Khmer laterite chedi. Admission: 200 kip. 50 kip to leave a bike.

Just beyond Wat Simoung, where Settathirat and Samsenthai meet, is the **statue of King Settathirat**, the founder of Vientiane. The original statue was carved by a Lao sculptor, which apparently made the king look like a dwarf. Consequently it was destroyed. It was replaced by the present statue (there's a copy of it in Luang Prabang) which was, peculiarly, donated by the Russians. Just as strangely, the statue survived the revolution.

Buses, trucks and pick-ups to destinations around Vientiane all leave from the station next to the Morning Market; it is also possible to hire a car (around US$45/day). Taxis can be hired for the day from the Morning Market or outside one of the main hotels and cost around 21,000 kip/day for excursions outside Vientiane. Also see **car hire**, page 112.

EAST/SOUTH

The Garden of the Buddhas (Xieng Khonane) is a few kilometres beyond **Tha Deua** and 25 km E of Vientiane (on Route 2), close to the frontier with Thailand. It has been described as a Laotian Tiger Balm Gardens with reinforced concrete Buddhist and Hindu sculptures of Vishnu, Buddha, Siva etc. There's also a bulbous-style building with three levels containing smaller sculptures of the same gods. The garden was built in the late 1950s by a priest called Luang Pu, who combined the Buddhist and Hindu philosophies. He is very popular in Laos and N Thailand, where he now lives. He also built Wat Khaek in Nong Khai, just over the border in Thailand. Open Mon-Sun 0800-1700. Admission 200 kip. *Getting there*: 1 hr by bus (200 kip), the bus stops first at the border and then at Xieng Khonane (1.5 km on). For returning to Vientiane, there is a bus stop in front of the Garden.

555 Park (Saam Haa Yai) are extensive, but rather uninspiring, gardens, with Chinese pavilions, a lake and a small zoo, 14 km down the Thanon Tha Deua (Route 2) from Vientiane. In the 1980s, a white elephant was captured in S Laos. Revered in this part of the world for their religious significance, it had to be painted to ensure it was not stolen on the way to the capital. Formerly kept in the Saam Haa gardens, it has since been moved to a secret location somewhere in Vientiane and is paraded in front of the crowds to marvel at during the That

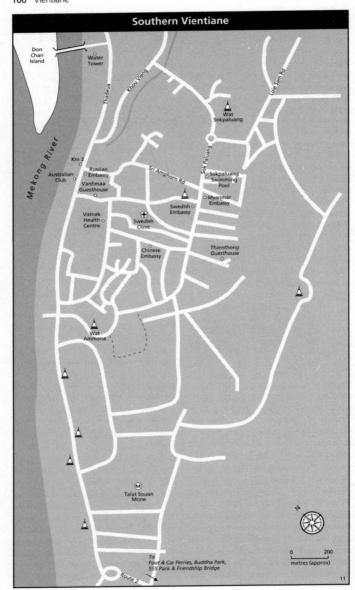

Southern Vientiane

Don Chan Island

Mekong River

Water Tower

Thadeua

Khou Vieng

Loïe Sam Rd

Wat Sokpaluang

Km 3

Russian Embassy

Australian Club

Vanhmaa Guesthouse

Sri Amphorn Rd

Sok Paluang

Sokpaluang Swimming Pool

Myanmar Embassy

Swedish Embassy

Vatnak Health Centre

Swedish Clinic

Chinese Embassy

Thienthong Guesthouse

Wat Ammona

Talat Souan Mone

To Foot & Car Ferries, Buddha Park, 555 Park & Friendship Bridge

Route 2

N

0   200
metres (approx)

11

Luang festival. White elephants are not really white, but pink.

Lao Pako lies 50 km NE of Vientiane, on the banks of the Nam Ngum (off route 13). There is a 'nature lodge' here, with river trips, treks, walks to Lao villages etc. **Accommodation** is in a Lao style longhouse **B-D** (**E** dorms) or in single bungalows overlooking the river, 3-star restaurant serves excellent Lao and European food. The owners have 50 ha of land, through which they have cut paths and planted trees. A lovely place to retreat to, for swimming, walking and rafting; reasonably priced. Can be crowded at weekends. For further information, contact Walter Pfabigan, c/o Burapha, 14 Fa Ngoum (close to *Pornthip Guesthouse*), Vientiane, T 312234. *Getting there*: take bus No 19 from the Morning Market (they leave at 0630, 1100 and 1500) towards Pakxap along route 13 and get off at Som Sa Mai, 1 hr. From Som Sa Mai take a local boat to Lao Pako (another 25 mins).

Tad Leuk waterfall is a 2 hr drive E in the direction of Pakxan. There's a tarmaced road to Thabok (the waterfall sign is easily seen on the left) and then a dirt track for 1 hr. A good picnic spot, and it is possible to swim in the lake behind the waterfall.

Prabat Phonsanh, 80 km down the Pakxan road, is built on a plug of volcanic rock, in the middle of a coconut plantation. It is known for its footprint of the Buddha and has a statue of a reclining Buddha – a mudra rarely seen in Laos. Houei Nhang Forest Reserve, on route 13 South, has a nature trail through lowland semi-evergreen forest. Mouse deer, porcupines and civet cats have been spotted here.

Friendship Bridge The observation area by the Mekong River makes a good picnic spot, or it would be possible to take lunch in Thailand for visitors with multi-entry visas. Forms need to be filled in and travel across the bridge is by minibus. Tuk-tuks wait at the other end.

NORTH

Dane Soung is 30 km from Vientiane, on the Luang Prabang road. Turn left at the 22 km mark towards Ban Houa Khoua. Dane Soung is 6 km down the track, and is only accessible in the dry season. Large fallen rocks form a cave with Buddhist sculptures inside. On the left of the entrance is a footprint of the Buddha.

Nam Suong rapids and waterfall are 40 km N on Route 13. Turn left at the Lao-Australian Livestock Project Centre and right before the bridge: there is an absurdly out-of-place, Surrey-style picnic spot by the lake. For the rapids and waterfall, turn left before the bridge along a precipitously narrow track – they are only impressive during the rainy season.

Ban Keun is about 50 km N of Vientiane on Route 10. There's a zoo here and a café and picnic area. Admission 1,000 kip for adults, free for children, pleasant trip.

Vang Sang, near the village of Houei Thone, 63 km up the road to Luang Prabang is home to the remains of the 11th century Mon sanctuary of Vang Sang. Five Buddha statues stand on what is said to be an old elephants' graveyard.

Ban Thalat and **Nam Ngum Dam** are 90 km from Vientiane on Route 13 to Luang Prabang (see page 114).

Vang Vieng is about 150 km N on the road to Luang Prabang, Route 13 (see page 115).

LOCAL FESTIVALS

Oct: *Freedom of the French Day* (12th: public holiday) see page 300. *Boun Souang Heua* (Water Festival and boat races), full moon, end of Buddhist Lent. A beautiful event, with candles in all the homes and the landing of thousands of banana-leaf boats holding flowers, tapers and candles, after candle-lit processions around the wats and through the streets to the river. On the second day, boat races take place, with 50 or so men in each boat; they power up the river in perfect unison. An exuberant event, with plenty of merry-making.

Nov: *Boun That Luang* (movable), is celebrated in all of Vientiane's *thats* – but most of all at That Luang (the national shrine). Pilgrims pay homage to the Buddha, and there is a candlelit procession around the stupa. A week-long carnival surrounds the festival with fireworks, music and dancing. The entertainments range from dodgems to 'freak' shows, a fascinating cavalcade of people and events.

TOURS

All tour companies and many hotels and guesthouses will arrange city tours and excursions to surrounding sights.

LOCAL INFORMATION

Price guide

A+	US$100-200	D	US$8-15
A	US$50-100	E	US$4-8
B	US$25-50	F	under US$4
C	US$15-25		

● **Accommodation**

Vientiane has just one hotel (the *Novotel Vientiane*) which could really be considered international grade – a second the *Lao Hotel Plaza* should open in Jan 1997 – but a large number of very well run, and elegant, converted former colonial villas. There is also a dearth of places at the lower end of the market reflecting the fact that comparatively few backpackers make it here, although this seems to be changing as independent travel becomes easier.

A+ *Lao Hotel Plaza*, Samsenthai, T 213511, F 213512 (or Bangkok T (662) 2553410, F (662) 2553457), 3 restaurants, fitness centre, pool, nightclub, conference centre, monstrosity that Vientiane could do without; **A** *Lane Xang*, Fa Ngoum, T 214106/214102, F 214108, a/c, international restaurant, pool, small suites available on the 3rd flr, payment in US dollars only, Government run, to many this is a monstrosity of Soviet architecture married to lime green murals and gauche bed spreads – it has heavy furniture and clocks

showing the time in cities around the world (who wants to know?), to others, it lies at the cutting edge of fashion – hip in the hippest sense, rooms are OK and it also has a swimming pool, tennis court, sauna, snooker and topiary, take your pick; **A** *River View*, Luang Prabang, T 216244, F 216231, a/c, restaurant, this hotel sounds as though it might be attractive: don't be deluded, painted lurid pink on the exterior, the lobby is filled with brightly painted umbrellas, glass knick-knacks, uncomfortable furniture and mouse droppings, the rooms, at this price, are pretty dismal too, in short, it's a lot to endure for a river view; **A** *Royal Dokmaideng*, Lane Xang, T 214455, F 214454, a/c, restaurant, pool, slightly out of centre, not far from the Anousavari Monument, this is a refurbished hotel of 80 rooms with a Chinese feel to it – heavy furniture, marble and high pressure Karaoke Bar, they also do a good line in blurb: 'brilliantly greets guests, sincerity broadcast thousand miles', at this price there are several other places which offer more ambience and a better location – a placeless place; **A** *The Novotel Vientiane*, Samsenthai, nr the junction with Luang Prabang, T 213570, F 213572, a/c, restaurant, pool, price incl breakfast, but tax is on top, large international style hotel, best in town, gym, tennis court, sauna, Lao massage, disco etc, for tourists it suffers from a poor location on the edge of town towards Wattay Airport, the building itself is also so characterless as to be virtually DOA, this is the place where many business people stay because it works; **A** *Tai-Pan*, 22/3 François Ngin Rd, T 216907, F 216223, a/c, restaurant, new hotel with that 'could be anywhere' international feel, hard to fault in terms of service and facilities (for Laos anyway), 36 well equipped rooms with IDD telephones, satellite TV and an increasingly popular bar, it also has a good central location.

B *Auberge du Temple*, 184/1 Ban Khounta (off road to Wattay Airport down towards the river, 100m W of *Novotel*), T/F 214844, a/c, this is a really stylish new auberge owned by a Frenchman, converted villa in a large compound, verandahs, large rooms, relaxed and sophisticated, a kilometre or two out of the town centre, but worth it, rec; **B** *Le Parasol Blanc*, behind National Assembly, close to Anousavari Monument (not very well marked), T 216091, F 215444, a/c, restaurant (see below), good sized pool, very attractive leafy haven, 45 spacious rooms with wooden floors

Vientiane Centre

Hotels:
1. Anou
2. Asian Pavilion
3. Day Inn
4. Douang Deuane
5. Ekkalath Metropole
6. Inter
7. Lani I
8. Lani II
9. Lao International Guesthouse
10. Mixai House
11. Phornthip Guesthouse
12. Plaza
13. Samsenthai
14. Santisouk Guesthouse
15. Saysana
16. Settha & Hong Kong Restaurant
17. Syri Guesthouse
18. Tai-Pan
19. Vannasinh Guesthouse

Places to eat:
20. Ban Hay Sok
21. Dao Vieng
22. Kua Lao
23. Le Bayou
24. Le Bistrot
25. Le Santal & Samlo Pub
26. Le Vendôme
27. Malibu Bar
28. Mixai
29. Nang Chazy
30. Seoul
31. Shanghai
32. Sweet Home & Bakery
33. Vanh Mixay
34. Vientiane No 2

Lanatours
Morning market - uncovered
To Anousavari monument
TNT Express Worldwide
Lane Xang Ave
Talat Sao Rd
Talat Sao (Morning market) - covered
Taxis for Tha Deua
Vietnam Airlines
Immigration
Khou Vieng
Phai Nam
That Dam
Khoun Boulom
Pang Kham
Champa Gallery
Kanchana Boutique (bicycles)
To Wat Simuong & Srisavangvong monument
Nangxuan Antiques & Silverware
Phimphone Market
Bartolini Rd
Embassy
Konica Foto Express
Samsenthai
Wat Sisaket
To Wat Phra Kaeo
Setthathirath
Presidential Palace
Swimming Pool
Kodak Express
Textile Shop
Chanta Khoumane
see detail
Nam Phou
Pang Kham
Quai Fa Ngoum
Ky Huong
National Stadium
Tennis Club
Revolutionary Museum
Anglican Episcopal Church
Hero Snooker Club & Joint
Lao Gallery
Lao Textiles
Lao Theatre
Minimarket
Mixay Massage
Wat Xieng Khoune
Manthatirath
Boats to Luang Prabang
Saigon
Hai Phong
Touran Rd
Rajah Tours
Pinom Penh
Samsenthai
Laundry
Mixay Arcade & Yanis
Nokeo Koummane
Wat Mixay
Francois Nginn Rd
Phai Nam
Du Puits
Hanoi
Chao Anou
Kodak Express
Wat Ong Teu
Wat Chan
Mekong River
Evening Snack Foodstalls
Supermarket
Fuji Express
Foodstalls
Samsenthai
Khoun Boulom
Sertthathirath
Wat Inpeng
Chao Anou
Heng Rd
Wat Chan
Buapha Consultants
To Luang Prabang

0   150
metres

N

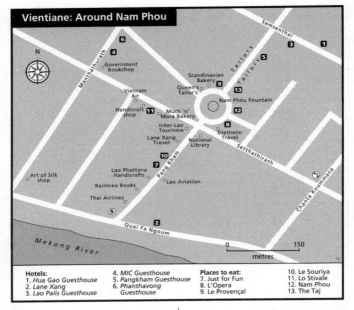

Vientiane: Around Nam Phou

Hotels:
1. Hua Gao Guesthouse
2. Lane Xang
3. Lao Palis Guesthouse
4. MIC Guesthouse
5. Pangkham Guesthouse
6. Phanthavong Guesthouse

Places to eat:
7. Just for Fun
8. L'Opera
9. Le Provençal
10. Le Souriya
11. Lo Stivale
12. Nam Phou
13. The Taj

and sizeable bathrooms, some look onto garden, with sitting area in front, charming place, well run, rec; **B** *New Apollo*, 69A Luang Prabang, T/F 213244, a/c, restaurant with live music every night, rather a monstrous hotel in terms of its architecture, also suffers from being on the main road out to the airport; **B** *Asian Pavilion*, 379 Samsenthai, T 213430, F 213432, a/c, restaurant, 50 very average rooms in a very average hotel, it is possible to do much better at this price; **B** *Lani I*, 281 Setthathirat (set back from the road next to Wat Hay Sok), T 214919/216103, F 216103, a/c, restaurant (excellent Chinese, cooked by Lani's father on request), outside bar, clean and well run, set in a quiet garden, telex and fax service, used by long-term visitors and very popular (book in advance), the rooms on the ground floor can be dark, this is an elegant almost urbane place, with a good central position yet set back from the road in a quiet compound next to a wat, perhaps a little overpriced; **B-C** *Lao Paris*, 100 Samsenthai, T 216382, F 222229, a/c, private bathrooms with hot water, TV in room, clean but uninspired, ugly town hotel; **C-D** *Samsenthai*, 15

Manthathurath, T 212116, a/c, restaurant attached, some private bathrooms, some h/w, a bit of a mixed bag, cheaper rooms are grubby and depressing, top end rooms large and reasonably clean, but the whole hideous block smells fusty, central location; **B** *Saysana*, Chao Anou, T 213580, a/c, restaurant, not as smart as it looks from the outside, *Victory disco* opens 2100-2330, the hotel blurb sells Vientiane as 'the land of virginal valuable outstanding artistic culture', which is quite a string of words; **B-C** *Anou*, 1-3 Heng Boun, T 213630, F 213635, some a/c, restaurant being redeveloped, large and impersonal, ugly, poorly maintained block, overpriced; **B-C** *Douang Deuane*, Nokeo Koummane Rd, T 222301, F 222300, a/c, restaurant, opened in 1996, from the exterior this looks an unremarkable place, but the rooms are very good: parquet wood floors, excellent bathrooms, satellite TV and a decent size, central position, the room rates, for the moment at least, are also very competitive, rec; **B-C** *Hotel Day Inn*, Pang Kham, T 214792, F 222984, a/c, restaurant, bike hire, new hotel that opened in 1996, good position in quiet part of town just to the N of the main concentration of bars and restaurants, oldish converted villa, large rooms, excellent bathrooms, perhaps all a little bare but excellent value; **B-C Villa That Luang**, 307 That Luang, T 413370, F 412953, a/c, restaurant ('*snake bar*' [sic]), another converted villa with large and attractively furnished rooms (sitting area), laundry is included in the room rate, about 1½ km N of town centre almost at That Luang itself, bicycles available for hire, well run; **B-E Ekkalath Metropole**, Samsenthai (not far from That Dam), T 213420, F 215628, some a/c, restaurant (European and Vietnamese), some up-market rooms with breakfast incl, lower priced rooms in guesthouse attached to hotel – very basic with no hot water but fairly clean, popular budget hotel, rooms in main block are very large, some with attached sitting area ('suite' would be too grand a word for these spartan affairs).

C Chaemchanh Guesthouse, 78 Khou Vieng, T 312700, a/c, airy, rather run down villa, large rooms with bathrooms, extensive garden compound, it is about 1.5 km from the town centre just off the raised, tree-lined Khou Vieng but is accessible by bicycle, a peaceful and attractive place to relax; **C Lani II**, 268 Saylom (set back from the road, entrance opp T junction), T 213022, F 215639, a/c, private bathrooms, hot water, food available if ordered in advance, clean, quiet and friendly, nice garden, just as good as *Lani I*, quite a few long-term visitors, so booking advisable, rec; **C Panghar**, Pang Har Rd, nr fountain, some a/c, hot water, clean, larger rooms are more expensive and have the luxury of a window, rec; **C Sisavad**, 93/12 Sisavad Neua, N of town, nr the Monument, T/F 212719, some a/c, restaurant, pool, ensuite bathrooms, characterless bedrooms, adequate hotel, mostly caters to Asian tourists; **C Soradith**, 150 Ban Dong Palan, 15 mins walk from Morning Market, T/F 413651, a/c, hot water, TV, fridge, 10% discount for longer stays, welcoming owner, 10 rooms in well kept garden, clean but boring rooms, quiet spot down side street, 8 new rm under construction, which will have an Asian restaurant on the ground floor, the excellent *Europe* restaurant is also in this compound, mountain bikes for hire here at US$3/day; **C Syri**, Quartier Chao Anou (nr the stadium), T 212682, F 217251, a/c, restaurant for breakfast and drinks only, some ensuite bathrooms, very hot water, clean sheets daily, average, unexciting rooms, old building looking rather run-down, family run and friendly, leafy entrance, quiet

street, first floor sitting area, bikes for hire, cheapest option is a triple room (US$8) but no private bathroom; **C Vientiane**, Luang Prabang, T 212928, some a/c, restaurant (downstairs from hotel), situated on the busy main road out to the airport, not a place noted for its style or ambience, just somewhere to sleep; **C Wonderland Guesthouse**, Phonesavan Tai (off Khou Vieng, S of town), T 314682, a/c, restaurant, small guesthouse in private villa down quiet lane some way from the centre of town. Attractive garden, birds, verandahs and clean and good sized rooms and bathrooms, consider staying here if you don't mind (or prefer) being out of the town centre – easily accessible by bicycle along attractive, tree-lined Khou Vieng; **C-D Lao International Guesthouse (LIG)**, 015/2 François Ngin Rd, T/F 216571, some a/c, just a handful of rooms here, rather dark, downstairs is a Vietnamese restaurant, French and English spoken; **C-D Pangkham Guesthouse**, 72/6 Pang Kham, T 217053, more expensive rooms have a/c, all rooms have hot showers, cheaper rooms have no windows, basic, clean rooms in featureless block; **C-D Settha Guesthouse**, 80/4 Samsenthai, T 213241, F 215995, a/c, restaurant, Chinese-run guesthouse attached to the *Hong Kong Restaurant*, 9 rooms, central location, good sized rooms with clean bathrooms and hot water, efficiently managed.

D Inter, 24-25 Fa Ngoum/Chou Anou (next to Wat Chan), T 213582, a/c, restaurant, recently refurbished and Thai-owned, the 20 rooms may not win any local character prizes but they are clean with good hot water showers, the hotel also enjoys a central location and is competitively priced; **D Mixai House**, 30/1 Fa Ngoum, T 216213, a/c, restaurant, 2 rm overlook the river, rest a bit dark and pokey, shared bath, good value for a/c rooms, poor value for a shared bathroom (same owners as the *Mekong*); **D Phornthip**, 72 Inpeng Rd, T 217239, some a/c, a quiet, family-run, very friendly guesthouse, almost always full (pre-booking is rec), perhaps a trifle overpriced (a function, no doubt, of its popularity), there's a courtyard at the back, but no garden, large rooms, attached bathrooms, rec; **D Santisouk**, 77/79 Nokeo Koummane (above *Santisouk Restaurant*), T 215303, a/c, some rooms with shared facilities, others with attached showers, all are clean but also small, those over the popular restaurant below can be noisy too, but good value at this rate, no English spoken; **D Villa Santiphab**, Nong Douang, a/c, restaurant (order meals, no menu), friendly and small hotel in an old villa, 1 room with attached bathroom (**C**), rec; **C-D** *Vannasinh Guesthouse*, 051 Phnom Penh Rd (off Samsenthai), clean, big rooms and well managed, with friendly staff, bicycles for hire, rec; **D-E** *Hua Guo*, 359 Samsenthai, T 216612, some a/c, some private bathrooms and hot water, basic, unfriendly, Chinese guesthouse, bikes and motorbikes for rent, bargaining possible; **D-E** *Minister of Information and Culture (M.I.C.) Guesthouse*, 67/11 Manthathurath, T 212362, fan rooms, some with bathroom attached, good value for money, dingy lobby and stairwell and dirty rooms, very popular with budget travellers; **D-E** *Phanthavong Guesthouse*, Manthathurath, T 214738, rather semi-detached service, rooms are on the grubby side but quite well priced, central location, restaurant serving travellers food; **D-E** *Sennesouk*, 100 Luang Prabang, T 215567, F 217449, some a/c, just W of *Novotel Hotel* on airport side, some Western bathrooms, restaurant, clean, comfortable and friendly, if a little out of town, can be noisy when the restaurant is in full swing.

E *Phonxay*, Nong Bon Rd, large, very ugly, very run down and looks like it can't exist for much longer, only for the hardened traveller.

Further out: **B** *Vansana*, Phonthan, T 413171, F 414189, a/c, h/w, restaurant (Western and Lao), pool, reception room, quiet, garden, cars for hire, well out of town to the E but free bikes for guests, rec.

C *Thien Thong*, Sokpaluang, T 313782, F 312125, a/c, good food, h/w and fridge, 13 clean rooms with tiled showers attached, in attractive leafy compound, about 1.5 km from town centre, so bicycles needed, rec.

● **Accommodation in wats (monasteries)**
It is possible to stay in monks' quarters at Wat Sisaket, Lane Xang, in exchange for informal English lessons.

● **Places to eat**

Price guide			
♦♦♦♦	over US$10	♦♦♦	US$5-10
♦♦	US$2-5	♦	under US$2

Lao: ♦♦♦*Dao Vieng*, Heng Boun, large menu, good reputation, popular at lunchtime; ♦♦♦*Kua Lao*, 111 Samsenthai, T 215777, tastefully refurbished colonial house provides sophisticated atmosphere for quality Lao and Thai food, avoid set menu, good Lao music accompaniment, good value food, rec; ♦♦♦*Lane Xang Restaurant*, Quai Fa Ngoum, overlooks the river and produces Lao Specials such as baked moose, grilled eel, baked turtle, some international dishes, see Entertainment; ♦♦♦*Lao Residence*, That Luang, just beyond Anousavari Monument, classy Lao restaurant, though not as good as *Kua Lao*. Patrons can drink in the garden of this converted private house and then eat in the a/c restaurant. Locals maintain the food here is good; ♦♦♦*Mekong*, Tha Deua, not far from the Australian Club, in bridge direction, T 312480, good food overlooking the Mekong, drinks on the balcony at sunset, Lao and international cuisine; ♦♦*Just for Fun*, 57/2 Phang Kham, opp *Lao Aviation*, good Lao food, selection of coffees and soft drinks and the largest selection of teas in Laos, if not SE Asia, a/c, with newspapers and comfy chairs (also sells textiles), rec; ♦♦*Mixai* (also known as the 'Russia Club'), Fa Ngoum, wooden restaurant overlooking the Mekong, selection of mainly Lao dishes, some international food, popular with expats, slow, inefficient and grumpy service (this is the *Aeroflot* of Fa Ngoum), mediocre food and noisy but a good place to watch the sunset; ♦♦*Restaurant Vientiane No 2*, Heng Boun, this is a throw back to revolutionary days when Restaurant Vientiane No 2 would be visited by the heroes of Cooperative No 12 or Tractor Plant No 16. Lao dishes including frog, eel, wild birds and other delicacies are served in a restaurant of stunning characterlessness.

Chinese: there are a number of noodle shops in Chinatown along Khoun Boulom, Heng Boun and Chao Anou which all have a palatable array of vermicelli, *muu daeng* (red pork), duck and chicken. ♦♦♦♦-♦♦♦*Little Si Chuan*, Setthathirat; ♦♦♦*Ban Hay Sok*, Heng Boun, excellent Lao and Chinese cuisine in a/c splendour including abalone, shark's fin and other speciality dishes, the chef is reputed to have formerly worked for the Laotian royal family, rec; ♦♦♦*Shanghai*, 2 blocks W of museum on Samsenthai, sophisticated Chinese restaurant; ♦♦♦*Hong Kong*, Samsenthai, behind what must once have been a petrol station is an ostentatious and quite smart Chinese restaurant.

Korean: ♦♦♦*Seoul*, Chao Anou, the only Korean restaurant in town, a/c with good food although pricey for Vientiane.

Indian: ♦♦♦*The Taj*, 75/4 Pang Kham, a/c, good food.

Japanese: ◆◆◆-◆◆◆◆*Sakura*, Luang Prabang, Km 2/Soi 3, T 212274 (see map), regarded as the best Japanese food in town, expensive for Vientiane but good value for Japanese food anywhere else, restaurant in converted private house.

Vietnamese: served in many of the stalls in the 'Chinatown' area. ◆*Nang Chazy*, 54/2 Chao Anou/Heng Boun, good Vietnamese stall food.

International: ◆◆◆◆*L'Opera*, Nam Phou Circle, T 215099, a/c Italian restaurant, with delicious ice-cream, wide range of pizza and pasta dishes, also barbecue steaks, expensive for Vientiane, same ownership as restaurants of same name in Bangkok and Manila; ◆◆◆-◆◆◆*Lo Stivale* (formerly *Deli Café*), Setthathirat, just W of Nam Phou, extensive Italian menu with good pizzas, pastas, steaks and desserts, attentive service in airy stuccoed a/c restaurant; ◆◆◆*Europe*, Dong Palan, left just before Wat Dong Palan, T 413651. Run by Swiss, serving Swiss, French, Italian and local food, classiest restaurant in town for quality of food, but not particularly attractive surroundings, open 1200-1400, 1800-2300, closed Mon; ◆◆◆*Le Provençal*, Nam Phou Circle, T 217251, quite new, large French restaurant, with beamed ceiling, attempting (unsuccessfully) to recreate rural France. However, food is good, especially salad and steaks, good value, open 1130-1400, 1830-2230, closed Sun; ◆◆◆*Le Souriya*, 31/2 Pang Kham (opp *Lao Aviation*), T 215887, French, tasty menu with fillets and frogs' legs in sauces one dreams about, fine wines, Lao cuisine on request, owned by Hmong princess from Xieng Khouang and named after her son, closed Mon, rec; ◆◆◆*Le Vendôme*, Soi Inpeng, run by a young Frenchman, as good as any 1* Michelin restaurant in France, a/c inside and an outside terrace, one of the best in town, good ambience, mouth-watering menu of fish, deer, rabbit, steaks, pizzas, soufflés, salads and a self-service salad bar, choice of wines, rec; ◆◆◆*Le Parasol Blanc*, behind National Assembly building, extensive (and good) French menu and some Lao dishes, incl Mekong fish, reasonably priced, attractive leafy environment, some a/c tables too; ◆◆◆*Nam Phou*, 20 Nam Phou Circle, T 216248, French, Lao food on request, upmarket and quietly sophisticated, rec; ◆◆◆*Scandinavian Bakery*, 74/1 Pang Kham, on Nam Phou Circle, delicious pastries, bread, cakes and sandwiches, one table outside and several more inside (a/c),

friendly *farang* chef/baker, who made the cake for the President of Tanzania's daughter's wedding (photo to prove it), open 0700-1900 daily, rec; ◆◆◆*Pub and Restaurant* (formerly *Win West*), opp Russian Cultural Centre by traffic lights, Luang Prabang Rd, quite good food, live music in Western-style surroundings, buffet lunch, happy hour; ◆◆◆-◆◆*Le Bayou*, Setthathirath, popular brasserie and bar, generous helpings of pizza, sandwiches, French desserts and fruit drinks, good for late evening coffee and drinking (the draft beer is well priced), also open for breakfast, children's menu available, the live bird is a little unnerving, French speaking (same owner as *Le Vendôme*), good value, rec; ◆◆◆-◆◆*Golden Horse*, Fa Ngum Rd, nr Wat Simuang, best fish restaurant in town, evenings only; ◆◆*La Santal*, 101 Setthathirath, Lao, Thai, French and Italian food including fish, steaks and pizzas in a/c restaurant; ◆◆*Arawan*, 472-480 Samsenthai (not far from Wat Simoung/statue of king), the oldest French restaurant in Vientiane, run by a Corsican, good selection of cheeses ('flomages' [sic]) and wines – but short on atmosphere and clientele, bar; ◆◆*Inter*, Chao Anou (part of hotel), renowned for its steaks, Lao food on advance order; ◆◆*Le Bistrot*, 10/3 François Ngin, opp *Tai-pan Hotel*, Bistro-food and breakfast in friendly atmosphere, French-Lao run; ◆◆*Santi-souk*, entrance to stadium just off Samsenthai, extensive French menu, reasonably priced steaks, rec.

Vegetarian: see the *Just for Fun* entry in Lao food. Although not a vegetarian restaurant it produces excellent vegetarian food.

Breakfast and snack food: ◆◆-◆*Bakery House (Liang Xiang Bakery)* and *Sweet Home* are two pavement cafes; *Much 'n' More*, Setthathirath, good bread, cookies, pastries and lunches. ◆*Fresh fruit iced drinks* (safe ice), Chao Anon Rd. Also on this road, close to here are coffee shops and bakeries. For a low cost 'travellers' breakfast, the *Phanthavong Guesthouse* on Manthathurath has a good selection of fruit shakes, offering freshly baked pastries, croissants, pain au chocolat, doughnuts and ice creams – open every day from about 0700 until 2330. *Scandinavian Bakery*, 74/1 Pang Kham, great place for a leisurely breakfast of coffee and pastries, with English-language newspapers provided, pricey for Laos but a necessary European fix for many expats.

Stalls: food stalls in the evening along Quai Fa Ngoum (the river road), comparable food in an incomparable setting.

● **Bars**

The bars of the debauched pre-revolutionary days have faded into legend: *The Purple Porpoise*, the *White Rose* pick-up joint and the renowned *Les Rendezvous des Amis*, run by Madame Lulu, which reportedly offered patrons "warm beer and oral sex".

There are a number of bars-cum-stalls which set up in the evening along Quai Fa Ngoum (the river road), a good place for a cold beer as the sun sets and the evening breeze picks up. *Belle-Ile Creperie and Pub*, 21 Lane Xang, open Thur-Sun 1700-2400 (or later unofficially), good music, very popular after 2200; *Lane Xang Restaurant* (part of *Lane Xang Hotel*), almost opp the hotel on Quai Fa Ngoum, garden bar; *Malibu*, Samsenthai, a new night spot opened by a Frenchman, clean, attractive decor; *Mirage*, 010 Thanon Luang Prabang, T 512830, nr Russian Cultural Centre (corner of Khoun Boloum), opened a few months back, popular pub for expats, BBQ, garden, friendly owner; *Nam Phou Circle*, enter through the gate in the hedge around the fountain and drink in Vientiane's version of Piccadilly Circus: the fountain started spouting again in 1991 thanks to a Swedish joint venture (pricey drinks), serves Indian food and snacks – remains popular with expats, and has probably the only loos in Laos decorated with graffiti (in English); *Sala Basi*, river road downstream from *River View Hotel*, a simple bar built on a wooden platform above the Mekong, cane chairs and cold beer, a great place to drink, read and otherwise chill out; *Sala Beer Lao* (Beer Lao House), opp Evening Market at Thong Khankam, saloon bar featuring occasional performances by Lao band Sapphire, and other live acts, the closest thing in Vientiane to a rock 'n' roll pub – as opposed to discos with live bands; *Samlo Pub*, Setthathirat, owned by a Belgian, good ambience, popular meeting place for expats (good place for coffee after dinner), snooker, darts, pizza-type food; *Sunset Bar* (aka *The End of the World*), end of Fa Ngoum, open wooden house overlooking the Mekong with good atmosphere, favourite meeting place of expats to watch the sunset; *Tai-pan Hotel*, 2-12 François Nguin Rd, lively bar; *Win West Bar*, opp *Mirage* on Luang Prabang, cowboy bar with appropriate decor, live band.

● **Airline offices**

Lao Aviation, 2 Pang Kham (Fa Ngoum end) T 212051, F 212056 for international flights and T 212057 for domestic connections. Lao Aviation also have an office at Wattay Airport, T 512000, open 0800-1200, 1400-1700 Mon-Fri, 0800-1200 Sat. Lao Aviation operate as agents for **Air France**. **Thai**, Pang Kham (in front of Lao Aviation), T 216143, open 0800-1200, 1400-1700 Mon-Fri, 0800-1200 Sat. **Vietnam Airlines**, booking offices 225 Saylom Rd, T 222370, F 222370 and on Setthathirath.

● **Banks & money changers**

See **Money** (page 289) in Information for travellers for more details on changing money in Laos. There are more than half a dozen money changers at the covered market, some open 7 days a week. The exchange office on Samsenthai, opp *Ekkaleth Hotel*, is open 7 days a week. **Banque Pour le Commerce Exterieur**, 1 Pang Kham. **Joint Development Bank**, 33 Lane Xang (opp market); **Setthathirat Bank**, Setthathirat Rd. With the loosening of banking regulations a number of Thai banks have set up in Vientiane. They all offer efficient and competitive exchange facilities: **Thai Military Bank**, 69 Khoun Boulom; **Siam Commercial Bank**, Lane Xang; **Thipphachanh Vongxay Exchange**, nr Phimphone Minimart offer an efficient service and the best rate in town for German marks; **Bank of Ayudhya**, Lane Xang (past the Morning Market travelling towards the Anousavari Monument); **Krung Thai**, Lane Xang. **Mini Mart** on Samsenthai also changes cash, as do many shopkeepers in the capital.

● **Embassies & consulates**

Australia, Nehru, Quartier Phone Xay, T 413610. **NB** The British operate through the Australian Embassy; **Myanmar (Burma)**, Sok Paluang, T 312439; **Cambodia**, Saphantong Neua, T 314952, F 312584; **China**, Wat Nak, T 315103; **Czechoslovakia**, Tha Deua, T 315291; **France**, Setthathirat, T 215258, F 215250; **Germany**, 26 Sok Paluang, T 312111; **India**, That Luang Rd, T 413802; **Indonesia**, Phon Kheng, T 413910; **Japan**, Sisavangvong, T 414400, F 414403; **Malaysia**, That Luang, T 414205; **Russia**, T 312219; **Sweden**, Sok Paluang, T 315018, F 315001; **Thailand**, Phon Kheng, T 214582 (consular section on That Luang): 2 month Thai visa costs ¢300 (only baht acceptable), it takes 2 days to process; **USA**, That Dam (off Samsenthai), T 212580, F 212584; **Vietnam**, That Luang, T 413400.

● **Entertainment**

Bands and discos: many of the discos in town, both in hotels and independent setups feature live bands usually playing a mixture of Lao and Thai music and cover versions of Western rock classics. Unless otherwise stated, the bands play 7 nights a week, 2000 until midnight. *Anou Cabaret*, Heng Boun, very popular, friendly but crowded and loud, one of the best live bands in town; *Dao Vieng*, 40 Heng Boun, disco above restaurant; *Saysana Club*, Saysana Hotel (ground floor), Chao Anou; *Viengratry May*, Lane Xang, live music, quite expensive; *Olympia*, Lane Xang Hotel, operates at the weekends; *Blue Star Disco*, Luang Prabang, on the airport side of the Novotel, popular with the Lao, good live band playing Lao, Thai and western; *Apollo Nightclub*, New Apollo Hotel, Luang Prabang, live music, popular; *Friendship Disco*, Mekong Hotel, Luang Prabang, opp the Regent Centre, Chinese run nightclub with live music; *Sprite Club*, Samsenthai, between Khoun Boloum and the creek, large disco with live band; *Melody Club*, Ekkalath Hotel, Samsenthai, live band; *Muang Lao*, Muang Lao Hotel, Tha Deua, good band.

Cinema: Vientiane has a number of **Theatres de Spectacles** which are enthusiastically attended. Before 1975, Bruce Lee was in; now it's Indian idol Shashi Kapoor. Hindi epics are screened nightly. Lao voice-overs are dubbed in live every night by a team of skilled local dubbers who handle up to three voices each and try to put everything in the local context. There are considerable variations in the script from one show to another. During the screening of a western, eg one cowboy inquired of another "Wher've you ridden fram boy?" Reply: "Ah've come fram the Morning Market". For western films, the **Odeon**, off Talat Nong Douane (nr the evening market) shows occasional western films; the **American Embassy**, That Dam, shows a movie every Wed at 1930, US$3. The **Australia Club**, on Tha Deua, shows a laser video every fortnight. The **Centre de Langue Francaise** (CLF), Lane Xang, T 215764, shows French movies each Thur, 1930, 700 kip.

Saunas and massage: many **local wats** have herbal saunas, which can be used by prior arrangement. After each session in the sauna one can sit on the verandha and sip tea provided by nuns. Donation in region of 1000 kip would be appreciated. Avoid washing for 4-5 hrs afterwards, to allow the herbs to soak in:

Wat Sok Paluang, Sok Paluang, to get there, go through the small stupas to left of Wat, the sauna is a rickety building on stilts on right-hand side, recognizable by blackened store underneath, herbal sauna, followed by herb tea, peaceful leafy setting in the compound of Wat Sok Paluang, nuns attend your needs, very relaxing experience; *Wat Sri Amphorn*, Sri Amphorn; *Mixay Massage*, Nokeo Koummane, Lao massage ($5/hr), facials, manicure, pedicure, sauna, 1700-2100; *L'Eden Health Centre*, off Setthathirat, on RHS just after big Honda Garage on left, sauna, massage (4,000 kip/1 hr), facials, exercise class etc, T 213528, open 1630-2100; *Vatnak Health Centre*, S of town, beyond Australia Club, T 312628. Good for a hard Thai massage.

Traditional dance: *Lane Xang Restaurant* provide excellent traditional dancers, accompanied by Lao musicians, while you eat every night 1900-2145; *Natasin Lao School*, Phoun Hang, nr the stadium, traditional dance.

Videos: in the bar of the *Ekkalath Metropole*, 1900.

● **Hospitals & medical services**

Clinics: *Australian Clinic*, Australian Embassy, T 413603, open Mon, Tues, Thur and Fri 0800-1200 and 1400-1700, Wed 0830-1200; *Swedish Clinic*, Sok Paluang (nr Swedish Embassy), T 315015, open Mon, Tues, Wed and Fri 0800-1200, 1400-1600, Thur 0800-1200. *International Clinic*, Mahosot Hospital, Setthathirat (see general Vientiane map), T 214018, open Mon-Sun, 24 hrs a day.

Hospitals: *Clinique Setthathirat*, next to That Luang. **NB** The Australian embassies have clinics for emergencies.

Pharmacies: Khoun Boulom and Samsenthai.

● **Places of worship**
Churches: *Vientiane Evangelical Church*, Luang Prabang, on way to airport. Sun services in Lao, 1000.

● **Laundry & dry cleaning**
101/3 Samsenthai, 1-day service.

● **Post & telecommunications**
Area code: 021.

International telephone office: Setthathirat, nr Nam Phou, telephone service open 24 hrs a day, fax service open 0730-2130. Dial 170 for international operator.

Packers & shippers: *DHL*, Nokeo Khoummane; *Transpack Lao*, That Luang Tai; *State*

Enterprise for Construction and Shipping, 105 Khoun. **Couriers**: *DHL*, 52 Nokeo Khoummane Rd.

Post Office: Khou Viang/Lane Xang (opp market). Poste restante, local and international telephone calls, and fax services (see page 298 for more detailed information). They also offer a good packing service and a philately counter where any stamp collecting desires can be quenched.

● **Shopping**

The Chinese quarter is around Chao Anou, Heng Boun and Khoun Boulom and is a lively spot in the evenings.

Books (also see **Maps**): *Government Bookshop*, Setthathirath, mainly Lao books but some English research books, plus a few maps. Also small selection of maps and books on Laos in the *Lane Xang Hotel* and at *Lani I*. *Raintree Books*, Pang Kham, opp Lao Aviation, first English-language bookshop in Laos, selection of coffee-table books, book exchange welcomed, glossy magazines and maps also available here. Books can also be found in some of the handicraft shops listed below.

Clothing: *Yani*, Mixay Arcade, Setthathirath, French designed fashion using local fabrics, good quality and good value (by European standards), small selection of handicrafts.

Galleries: *Kuanming Art Gallery*, 265 Samsenthai; *Lao Gallery*, 108/2 Samsenthai, exhibits local artists; *Champa Gallery*, by That Dam (next to US Embassy), T 216299, an attractive French colonial house, mostly the work of Canadian artist Monique Mottahedeh and her family (who own the gallery) but some local work and a few handicrafts.

Handicrafts and antiques: the main shops are along Setthathirath, Samsenthai and Pang Kham, the morning market is certainly worth a browse, with artefacts such as appliquéd panels, decorated hats, decorated sashes, basketwork – both old and new, small and large, wooden tobacco boxes, sticky-rice lidded baskets, axe pillows, embroidered cushions and a big range of silver work. There is a new custom built **handicraft village** in the triangle where Luang Prabang and Samsenthai roads meet – there are also some sterilized food stalls here. *Bouacham* (but no name outside), Setthathirat; *Lao Handicrafts*, 43/2 Setthathirath, mostly cloths and cotton goods like bags and wallets; *Mai Phuong*, 43/3 Setthathirath, old handicrafts and also some antiques; *Vanxay*

Art Handicraft, Samsenthai, antique and modern materials; *Phattana Handicraft*, 29/3 Pang Kham, mainly fabric, both made up and on the roll, some handicrafts; *Somsri Handicrafts*, 20 Setthathirath with a fair selection of crafts and antiques upstairs; *Lao Handicraft*, 72/5 Pang Kham, mainly wood carvings; *Union des Entreprises d'Artisanat Lao Export-Import*, Phon Kheng (about 500m N of the Monument Anousavari), large selection of materials from the N and the S; *Namsin Handicrafts*, Setthathirat, wooden objects; *Nang Xuan*, 385 Samsenthai, selection of opium pipes, silver boxes, Lao jewellery and Vietnamese trinkets; *Lao Culture and Antiquity Gallery*, 397 Samsenthai; *Nguyen Ti Selto*, 350 Samsenthai, Lao and Vietnamese antiques; *Phonethip Handicrafts and Ceramics*, 55 Saylom.

Jewellery and silverware: many of the stones sold in Vientiane are of dubious quality, but silver and gold are more reliable. Gold is always 24 carat, so darker in colour and softer, but is good value. Silver is cheap but not necessarily silver, nevertheless, the selection is interesting, with amusing animals, decorated boxes, old coins, ear-rings, silver belts. Big selection in *Morning Market*. Silver and gold shops on Samsenthai. For better quality jewellery, *Yani*, in Mixay Arcade, has some choice. *Lane Xang* at Carol Cassidy for top of the range silver designer-ware.

Maps: (also see **Books**) government produced tourist/town maps available from *Venus*, Samsenthai (opp *Asian Pavilion Hotel*). The best tourist map is the map of Vientiane produced by the Womens International Group (WIG). Available from *Raintree Books* (see Books) and elsewhere.

Markets: Vientiane has several excellent markets: the *Morning Market* (*Talat Sao*) off Lane Xang is the biggest and the best – it's busiest in the mornings, but it runs all day. It sells imported Thai goods, electrical goods, watches, stationery, cosmetics, a selection of handicrafts (see above), an enormous choice of Lao fabrics, and upstairs there is a large clothing section, silverware, some gems and gold and a few handicraft stalls . There is also an interesting produce section (*Talat Khua-Din*) the other side of the bus stop. *Talat Thong Thum*, on the corner of Khoun Khum and Dong Miang, is the largest produce market. It is sometimes known as the evening market as it was built to replace the evening market in

Nong Douang but is busiest in the mornings. **Other markets**: *Talat Simuang*, Fa Ngoum/Simuang, *Talat That Luang*, S of parade ground, *Talat Dong Palane*, Dong Palane (nr the cinema).

Photographs: *Konica Plaza*, 110/5 Samsenthai; *Kodak Express*, Samsenthai and two on Heng Boun.

Silver: see Jewellery and silverware.

Tailors: many Vietnamese tailors along Samsenthai and Pang Kham, about 4200-7000 kip/article depending on complexity, good at copying; *Queen's Beauty Tailor*, by the fountain, is quite good for ladies clothes, but allow at least a week; *Adam Tailleurs*, 72 Pang Kham; *La Fantasie*, 55 Pang Kham; *Nova*, 64 Samsenthai; *TV Chuong*, 395 Samsenthai. A few tailors in the Morning Market.

Textiles: *Lao Women's Union Projects*, Nam Phou Place, handwoven cottons with traditional designs some made up into cushion covers, bags, dressing gowns; *Kanchana*, Chanta Koummane, handwoven silks and cottons; *The Textile Centre* (*Lao Handicraft and Garment Co*), Luang Prabang (next to the statue of the three elephants), pottery and textile, Government run and tends to be the stop off point for tour groups; *Lao Cotton*, on Luang Prabang, out towards Wattay airport, approximately ¼ mile on right from *Novotel Hotel*, good range of material, shirts, handbags and housecoats, good to see the looms; *Lao Textiles* by Carol Cassidy, Nokeo Koummane, T 212123, F 216205, exquisite silk fabrics, including ikat (see box) and traditional Lao designs, run by an American, from a beautifully renovated colonial property, pricey, but many of the weavings are really museum pieces, dyeing, spinning, designing and weaving all done on premises (and can be viewed), custom made pieces available on request, exclusive silver jewellery from *Lane Xang* also available, rec; *The Art of Silk*, Manthathurath, opp *Samsenthai Hotel*, large selection of old and new weaving, small museum of old pieces of weaving, baskets and a loom, not cheap, but worth a visit; every hue and design available in

Ikat production

🦶 In the handicraft shops and at the morning market in Vientiane, it is possible to buy distinctively patterned cotton and silk ikat. Ikat is a technique of patterning cloth characteristic of Southeast Asia and is produced from the hills of Burma to the islands of Eastern Indonesia. The word comes from the Malay word *mengikat* which means to bind or tie. Very simply, bundles of warp or weft fibres, and in one Balinese case both, are tied with material or fibre (or more often plastic string these days) so that they resist the action of the dye. Hence the technique's name – resist dyeing. By dyeing, retieing and dyeing again through a number of cycles it is possible to build up complex patterns. This initial pre-weaving process can take anything from 2-10 days, depending on the complexity of the design. Ikat is distinguishable by the bleeding of the dye which inevitably occurs no matter how carefully the threads are tied; this gives the finished cloth a blurred finish. The earliest ikats so far found date from the 14th-15th centuries.

To prepare the cloth for dyeing, the warp or weft is strung tight on a frame. Individual threads, or groups of threads are then tied together with fibre and leaves. In some areas wax is then smeared on top to help in the resist process. The main colour is usually dyed first, secondary colours later. With complex patterns (which are done from memory, plans are only required for new designs) and using natural dyes, it may take up to 6 months to produce a piece of cloth. Today, the pressures of the market place mean that it is more likely that cloth is produced using chemical dyes (which need only one short soaking, not multiple long ones – 6 hrs or so – as with some natural dyes), and design motifs have generally become larger and less complex. Traditionally, warp ikat used cotton (rarely silk) and weft ikat, silk. Silk in many areas has given way to cotton, and cotton sometimes to synthetic yarns.

the **Morning Market** (Lao silk for 1,800 kip a metre). Hmong appliquéd quilts, bedspreads and cushion covers from unmarked shop opp *Asian Pavilion Hotel* on Samsenthai.

Western goods Charcuterie: *Arawan*, Samsenthai, next to restaurant, just before Wat Simuang on RHS. Good choice of French cheese, salamis and patés, olives, French wine, pasta, chocolate and coffee. **Supermarkets**: *Phimphone Minimarket*, Samsenthai, next to *Ekkalath Metropole Hotel*, good choice of bread, cheese, wine and other European food, as well as Russian caviar and almost opp on Samsenthai. *Simuang Minimarket*, Samsenthai, E end of Wat Simuang. Small *minimarket* next to bakeries on Chao Anou sells western goods; *Friendship Intershop*, 92/3 Samsenthai, alcohol and soft drinks; *Foodland Minimarket*, 117 Chou Anou; *Lao Phanit Supermaket*, 104 Khoun Boulom; *Yoghurt Shop*, Heng Boun, makes fresh yoghurt daily. The vast supermarket in Morning Market building sells everything from pastries to Chinese bicycles.

● **Sports**
Golf: Km 6, Road 13 South, T 130261, open Mon-Sun 0630-Sunset, clubs for rent. To get there: right at Peugeot showroom (6 km S of town), left after bridge, right at fork, right at top of hill.

Snooker: *Kaonhot*, Sakarin; three full size snooker tables, also tables on Heng Boun.

Swimming: *Lane Xang Hotel*, Fa Ngoum, 3,000 kip/day. *Australia Club*, Km 4 Tha Deua Rd, members only (monthly membership available, US$40), attractive, large pool in lovely position next to the river, western food available, rec; *Sokpaluang Swimming Pool*, Sokpaluang, S of centre (see South Vientiane map), admission: 1,000 kip for the day, open 0800-2000 Mon-Sun, costumes for hire, good sized pool for serious swimmers, paddling pool for children, restaurant and bar.

Tennis: *Vientiane Tennis Club*, next to the stadium. Equipment for hire, 2,000 kip/hr, floodlit courts stay open until 2100, bar.

● **Tour companies & travel agents**
14 April (*Sip-sii Mesa*), 29/3 Pang Kham (opp Lao Aviation), T 212979; *Diethelm Travel*, Nam Phou Circle, Setthathirath, T 213833, F 217151; *Inter-Lao Tourisme*, Setthathirath, Nam Phou Circle, T 214832, F 216306; *Lane Xang Travel and Tour*, Pang Kham, T 213469, F 215804; *Lao National Tourism*

(Lanatour), 8/2 Lane Xang Ave, T 216671, F 212013 (at least 2 weeks notice required); *Mixay Travel Service*, Fa Ngoum, T 216213, F 215445; *Phatana Khet Phoudoi*, 118/2 Luang Prabang, T 214673, F 216131; *Raja Tour*, 3 Heng Boun, T 213633, F 213635; *Mekhong Guesthouse*, Km 3 Tha Deua, T 215975, the Lao end of the Bangkok-based *Inter-Companion Group*; *Sodetour*, 114 Fa Ngoum, T 216314, F 215123, upmarket travel agent; *That Luang Tour*, 28 Kham Khong, T 215809, F 215346.

● **Tourist offices**
Lao National Tourism and *Vientiane Tourist Office*, Lane Xang Ave, T 212251, F 212769, 2nd floor offices, very little information except for a few brochures and some postcards.

● **Useful addresses**
Immigration: Phai Nam (Morning Market end). Open 0730-1130, 1400-1700 Mon, Tues and Thur-Sat, 0730-1130, 1400-1500 Wed, unfriendly place – easier to extend visa at Lao National Tourism, who will process it within the day.

Police Station: Setthathirat, in emergency, T 212707 or 190.

University: *Dong-Dok*, 10 km N on Route 10.

● **Transport**
Local Bicycle hire: for those energetic enough in the hot season, bikes are the best way to get around town. Many hotels have bikes for hotel guests (eg *Lani I*, *Syri*, *Hotel Day Inn*, Samsenthai, *Lao-Paris*, *Mekong Guesthouse*). There are also bike hire shops springing up eg attached to *Kanchana Boutique*, the handicraft shop opp the *Ekkalath Hotel*, on Chantha Koummane (the road going up to That Dam); the *Raintree Bookshop*, Pang Kham, and *Minimart*, Samsenthai, expect to pay about 1-2,000 kip/day depending on the state of the machine. Markets, post offices and government offices usually have 'bike parks' where it is advisable to leave your bike, pay 50 kip for it to be 'minded'. **Buses**: round central Vientiane and to outlying areas, most leave from the bus station by the Morning Market. Destinations, distances and fares are listed on a board in English and Lao. **Car hire**: it is not essential to hire a driver but in the event of an accident it is always the foreigner's fault. Rates vary according to state and model of vehicle and also whether out-of-town trips are planned. Expect to pay about US$40-50/day. **Burapha**, 14 Quai Fa Ngoum, T 216600; **Jo**

Rumble Asia Vehicle Hire, 08/3 Lane Xang Ave, T 217310, F 212933; **Lane Xang Hotel**, Fa Ngoum, T 214100; **Mr Seuth**, T 412785; **Samsenthai Hotel**, T 212116; **Phimphone Minimart**, 110/1 Samsenthai, T 216963. Many hotels will also have cars for hire. **Motorbike hire**: about US$10/day. **Vientiane Motors**, 35/1-3 Setthathirat. **Phimphone Minimart**, Samsenthai, T 216963. **Taxis**: mostly found at the Morning Market or around the main hotels. Newer vehicles have meters but are ageing jalopies. A taxi to Tha Deua from the Morning Market costs 3,000 kip, and about 1,500 kip to the airport. **Tuk-tuks**: available around the fountain area until 2330 but quite difficult to hire after dark in other areas of town.

Air Wattay Airport lies 6 km W of town centre. Vientiane is the hub of Laos' domestic airline system and to travel from the N, S or vice versa it is necessary to change planes here. See timetable and domestic route map on page 324 for full list of destinations and departure days and times. **Transport to town**: no buses, except from the main road outside the airport (200 kip, every 45 mins), only taxis are allowed to pick up (1,000-2,000 kip to the centre of town) although tuk-tuks can drop off. But tuk-tuks can be taken from the main road and sometimes lurk at the far side of the airport parking area, nr the exit (1,000 kip). The dual carriageway into town is one of only a handful of such stretches of road in the country.

Road Many roads from Vientiane are under construction at present. **Bus/truck**: most leave from the Morning Market on the E edge of the town centre, usually in the morning. There is a useful map here and bus times and fares are usually listed clearly in Lao and English. The road S to Savannakhet and Pakse is OK to Savannakhet and then deteriorates (see the transport section in Information for travellers for more details, page 297). 8 hrs to Thakhek, 12-15 hrs to Savannakhet, 20-24 hrs to Pakse. There are also buses/trucks which make the trip to Luang Prabang via Vang Vieng (no direct connections). This 600 km stretch of road has recently been upgraded (work finished at the end of 1996) but rather than being plagued by pot holes the road is plagued by bandits who pose a very real danger. If travelling overland to Luang Prabang check with locals beforehand and allot at least 24 hrs. **NB** In Nov 1995 two French tourists were injured in an attack by anti-government Hmong tribesmen

and in Sep 1996 Claude Vincent, a respected and knowledgeable tour operator, and his Sodetour colleagues were murdered on this road by bandits (probably also Hmong). At the end of 1996, as this book went to press, residents in Vientiane were advising against travelling by road to Luang Prabang and the French Embassy were effectively barring their nationals from travelling on some stretches. There are also buses for **Tha Deua** and the **Friendship Bridge**. **Taxis**: taxis for **Tha Deua** and the **Friendship Bridge** (for Thailand) leave from outside the front of the covered Morning Market. Taxis for other destinations and for charter are also available here. **Saamlor**: most leave from Morning Market, also outlying markets.

Boat To the S leave from S jetty near the Mekong Restaurant (big restaurant lit with fairy lights) and boats to the N leave from N jetty. The journey upriver to Luang Prabang takes 4 days, with a change of boat at Paklai (it is possible to shorten the journey by taking a speedboat from Paklai – 5 hrs instead of 2 days and nights), 9,000 kip. The large boats for the first leg leave Luang Prabang most days, carrying passengers and cargo. Wooden boats are preferable to corrugated iron, as it gets very hot during the day. Take a blanket, warm clothes (cold at night) and *plenty* of food and drink. There are shops in Paklai to restock (and some very basic guesthouses). Note that women travellers may not sit on top of the boat, and the trip is not comfortable. There do not appear to be any boats travelling the entire distance from Vientiane to Luang Prabang at present.

The stretch from Paklai to Luang Prabang is quite rough and passengers are asked to walk along the bank for the particularly dangerous bits. The **speedboat** option is a noisy one (and for the fearless – everyone wears motorcycle helmets and life jackets). It carries about 6 people and not much baggage, and costs ¢11,000. The slow boat costs 5,200 kip for the first leg and 5,000 kip for the second leg. **NB** The boat navigator will take passports for stamping or just checking, in Vientiane and Paklai; there is usually a charge of 500 kip. There are buses from the small port to Luang Prabang, but they're not that frequent, 2-3 hrs (1,200 kip), or hitch a ride.

Travelling S downstream, there are 2 boats/week to Savannakhet, 2 days and 1 night (7,000 kip). There are also more regular commercial vessels making the journey S – ask at the harbour S of Vientiane on Tha Deua Rd,

ບະມາຄານເຂື່ອນ້ຳງຸ່ມ

The Nam Ngum dam on the 50 kip (US$0.05) note

just past *Mekong Restaurant*, travelling out of town.

International connections with Thailand via the Friendship Bridge: see bus and taxi above for details on transport to the bridge, and page 291 for crossing into Thailand.

BAN THALAT AND NAM NGUM DAM

The Nam Ngum dam is the pride of Laos and figures prominently in picture postcards. It provides electricity for much of the country and exports to Thailand are the country's second biggest foreign exchange earner. No photographs are allowed at the dam wall or the HEP plant.

The lake is very picturesque and is dotted with hundreds of small islands. Huge semi-submerged tree-trunks pose an additional navigational hazard, as no one had the foresight to log the area before it was flooded. The untapped underwater cache of timber has been spotted by the Thais looking for alternative sources for their lucrative timber trade. Sub aqua chainsaws are used to take out the 'treasure'. For all their skills, it is necessary to bargain hard with boatmen before boarding to cross the lake. Boats from Nam Ngum Dam to Ban Pao Mo on the other side take around 2 hrs. Vang Vieng is 2 hrs ride from the dam.

Getting there: turn right at Phone Hong at the strategically-placed concrete post in the middle of the road.

Then head left to the village of Ban Thalat – where the market is worth a browse – then right across the narrow bridge to the dam, about 4 km up the road. There is an alternative route through much prettier countryside on Route 10 out of Vientiane, across the Nam Ngum by ferry. Turn right at the end of the road for the dam.

● **Accommodation** C *Japanese Bungalows*, a/c, h/w; **D** *Done Dok Khounkham Resort*, on an island in the lake, 6 rooms only, bathrooms ensuite, basic but clean, electricity after 1830, restaurant across a small bay (lim-

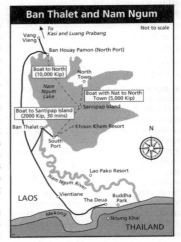

Ban Thalet and Nam Ngum

Not to scale

To Kasi and Luang Prabang

Vang Vieng

Ban Houay Pamon (North Port)

Boat to North (10,000 Kip)

North Town

Nam Ngum Lake

Boat with Nat to North Town (5,000 Kip)

Santipap Island

Boat to Santipap Island (2000 Kip, 30 mins)

Ban Thalat

South Port

Khoun Kham Resort

N

Lao Pako Resort

Nam Ngum River

Vientiane

Tha Deua

Buddha Park

LAOS

Mekong

Noung Khai

THAILAND

ited food, no alcohol – take your own), boat tours and fishing trips organized, isolated and quiet; **D** *Floating Hotel*, run by *Nam Ngum Tours*, a/c, h/w; **D** *Nam Ngum Dam Hotel* (on the right after the long bridge on the way to the dam), seafood restaurant in hotel; **E** *Santipab*, on island, rooms with bathrooms, deteriorating guesthouse with no electricity, tend to overcharge for the boat trip out there.

● **Places to eat** ♦♦*Lao Food Raft*, next to *Floating Hotel*, tasty food, friendly staff.

● **Transport Road Bus**: buses and saamlors leave every 2 hrs from the morning market in Vientiane to Ban Thalat, 3 hrs (3,500 kip), and then a taxi on to Nam Ngum (400 kip). **Taxi**: by taxi (US$30).

VANG VIENG

Vang Vieng lies 160 km N of Vientiane on the much improved Route 13. The drive follows the valley of the Nam Ngum N to Phonhong, and then climbs steeply onto the plateau where Vang Vieng is situated. The area around Vang Vieng is particularly picturesque, with its limestone caves and waterfalls, the caves are renowned in local mythology. The area is inhabited by the Hmong and Yao tribes. The best cave (Tham Cheng) goes right under the mountain and is fed by a natural spring, perfect for an early morning swim (bring a waterproof torch). Most visitors must pay at the *Vang Vieng Resort* to swim in the pools (and into the caves) although it is possible to wade across the river (during the dry season) and arrive at them from a different point.

● **Accommodation D** *Vang Vieng Resort*, a new resort close to the caves, T 222671, F 214743, bar and noodle restaurant, some chalets with bathrooms, the resort has control of Tham Chang, the cave, and has erected concrete steps and put lights inside. As a result it has lost its natural beauty and visitors are charged to get into the resort (200 kip), and then to get into the cave (2,000 kip), and then again to take pictures; **E** *Phou Bane*, close to the market and the bus station, restaurant (good), very friendly, convenient and manager speaks perfect French, nice garden to lounge in, the best guesthouse here, rec; **F** *Phabeng*, behind the Post Office; **F** *Siripanga*, nr the bus

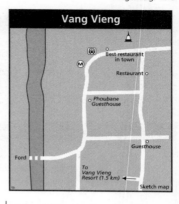

Vang Vieng

Best restaurant in town
Restaurant
Phoubane Guesthouse
Guesthouse
Ford
To Vang Vieng Resort (1.5 km)
Sketch map

station, better value than *Phou Bane* as all rooms have clean bathroom attached, but not such a good atmosphere.

● **Places to eat** Good food is available from the market. Alternatively there is a restaurant opp the *Sripanga Guesthouse* where diners are served with whatever is cooking that day – which is usually good.

● **Transport Road Bus**: buses leave from the morning market in Vientiane at 0630 and 1330, the road is new and in good condition, 3½ hrs (1,500 kip). The upgrading of the road onto Luang Prabang from Vang Vieng was finally completed at the end of 1996. **Car hire**: with driver, US$120, 3 hrs.

Route 13 continues N to Kasi (60 km on), 2 hrs 45 mins. **Accommodation** Available here at several guesthouses, eg **E** *Somchith*, 14 Main Rd, restaurant. The road from Kasi to Luang Prabang (a distance of 80 km), though it has been recently upgraded, is still slow and, more importantly, dangerous (6,000 kip). To catch the bus, wait at the *Somchith Guesthouse*, as the bus stops here for food. The bus departs every second day between 1700 and 1800. Good bus, but full and you may have to sit on the roof.

SAYABOURY (XAYABOURY)

Sayaboury is the capital of the five provinces of Laos on the right bank of the Mekong. It is not a spectacular town but an isolated, and therefore traditional, area. The village of **Ban Na La**, an ethnic Lao village, is 15 km from Sayaboury. The houses are indigenous and constructed from wood. The village is known for its weaving of scarves. **Ban Nam Phoui**, a pretty Hmong village, is next to the Mekong and not far from Sayaboury. Because of its proximity to Thailand this province is now being pillaged by Thai loggers.

● **Transport Air** Connections with Vientiane 4 times a week, 45 mins. The flights are currently on Mon, Wed, Fri and Sat, and on each occasion the plane makes a round trip (ie Vientiane-Sayaboury-Vientiane).

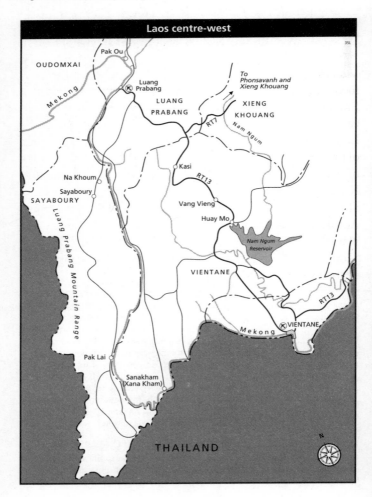

Laos centre-west

Luang Prabang

LUANG PRABANG is the town that visitors often remember with the greatest affection. Its rich history, incomparable architecture, relaxed atmosphere, good food, friendly population and stunning position mark Luang Prabang out as exceptional. It was established as the royal capital by Fa Ngoum, the first monarch of Lane Xang, the Land of a Million Elephants, in the 14th century. The name of the city refers to the holy *Pra Bang*, Laos' most sacred image of the Buddha which was given to Fa Ngoum, Laos' greatest King, by his father-in-law the King of Cambodia. The city had already been the seat of local kingdoms for about 600 years. According to legend, the site of the town was chosen by two resident hermits and was originally known as Xieng Thong – 'Copper Tree City'. Interestingly, the ancient name for Luang Prabang was Chawa, which translates as Java.

Luang Prabang lies 300m above sea-level, on the upper Mekong, at its confluence with the Nam Khan. The most popular time to visit the town is during the comparatively cool months of Nov and Dec. By Feb the weather is hotting up and the views are often shrouded by a haze produced, so it is said, by shifting cultivators using fire to clear the forest for agriculture. This does not really clear until June.

Luang Prabang is a sleepy town known for its magnificent temples, particularly the former royal Wat Xieng Thong and is dominated by Phousi – the 'marvellous mountain' – which sits in the middle of the town. In the 18th century there were more than 65 wats in the city; many have been destroyed over the years but over 30 remain intact. The continuing splendour and historical significance of the town led UNESCO to designate it a World Heritage Site at the end of 1995.

The English travel writer Norman Lewis described Luang Prabang in 1950 as: "... a tiny Manhattan, but a Manhattan with holy men in yellow robes in its avenues, with pariah dogs, and garlanded pedicabs carrying somnolent Frenchmen nowhere, and doves in its sky. Down at the lower tip, where Wall Street should have been, was a great congestion of monasteries".

In some respects even more evocative than Lewis, James McCarthy, an otherwise rather plodding recorder of events and sights, wrote of Luang Prabang at the end of the 19th century:

"In a clear afternoon, Luang Prabang stood out distinctly. At evening the pagoda spires and the gilded mouldings of the wats, glancing in the light of the setting sun, added their effect to that of the natural features of the landscape – and caused in me a feeling of irresistible melancholy. Since my visit in Feb 1887, Luang Prabang had passed through much suffering. It had been ravaged by the Haw; its people had been pillaged and murdered or driven from their homes, and the old chief had only been rescued by his sons forcing him to a place of safety. The town seemed doomed to suffer, for within 2 months last past it had again been burned, and, more recently still, about 500 of its inhabitants had died of an epidemic sickness."

Today Luang Prabang is an easy-going provincial city with about 20,000 inhabitants. Even the local attitude to crime and punishment is laid-back, as evidenced by the Nam Pha 'free-range' jail, where prisoners are reportedly reluctant to be released. Cycling or walking around town in the early evening, this royal 'city' feels more like a small, provincial town. Children play in the streets and women cook while old men lounge in wicker chairs and young boys play *takro*. The great fear, of course, is that all this will change. In the early 1990s it was suggested that a highway be constructed from Vientiane, through Luang Prabang, to the Chinese border. As Martin Stuart-Fox writes in *Buddhist Kingdom, Marxist state: the making of modern Laos* (1996): "The prospect that Luang Prabang could become a truck and tourist bus stopover on the way from Bangkok to Kunming horrifies the Lao. The fragile beauty of Luang Prabang with its delicate temples on a much smaller scale than those of Bangkok, its narrow streets and peaceful atmosphere could so easily be destroyed by heavy traffic and an influx of tourists." Fortunately, with UNESCO's designation of Luang Prabang as a World Heritage site the scope for redevelopment is much less. The old town – essentially the promontory – is fully protected while elsewhere only limited redevelopment and expansion is permitted (no building, for example, can be higher than 3 storeys).

HISTORY

The town has been successively pillaged, razed and rebuilt over the years – the last invaders were the Chinese Ho (or Haw) in the mid-1880s. Virtually all traces of older structures have disappeared as they were built of wood and susceptible to fire and the vagaries of climate.

King Setthathirat moved the capital to Vieng Chan (Vientiane) in 1563 – now the political hub of modern Laos. Luang Prabang's importance diminished in the 18th century, following the death of King Souligna Vongsa and the break-up of Lane Xang, but it remained a royal centre until the Communist takeover in

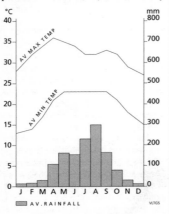

Climate: Luang Prabang

Mekong monsters, real and imagined

It is said that the *pla buk*, the giant catfish of the Mekong, was only described by western science in 1930. That may be so, but the English explorer and surveyor, James McCarthy, goes into considerable detail about the fish in his book *Surveying and exploring in Siam* which was first published in 1900 and draws upon his travels in Siam and Laos between 1881 and 1893. He writes:

"The month of June in Luang Prabang is a very busy one for fishermen. Nearly all the boats are employed on fishing, each paying a large fish for the privilege. Two kinds of large fish, *pla buk* and *pla rerm*, are principally sought after. ... A *pla buk* that I helped to take weighed 130 lbs; it was 7 ft long and 4 ft 2 ins round the body; the tail measured 1 ft 9 ins. The fish had neither scales nor teeth, and was sold for 10 rupees. The roe of this fish is considered a great delicacy. The fish is taken in...Jun, Jul and Aug, when on its upward journey. Returning in Nov, it keeps low in the river, and a few stray ones only are caught."

McCarthy also recounts the story of a mythical river-serpent of the Mekong:

"It lives only at the rapids, and my informant said he had seen it. It is 53 ft long and 20 ins thick. When a man is drowned it snaps off the tuft of hair on the head [men wore their hair in this manner], extracts the teeth, and sucks the blood; and when a body is found thus disfigured, it is known that the man has fallen victim to the nguak, or river serpent, at Luang Prabang."

1975. Despite the demise of the monarchy (King Savang Vatthana and Crown Prince Vongsavang both died in re-education camps after the Pathet Lao came to power in 1975) and years of revolutionary rhetoric on the city tannoy, its dreamy streets have somehow retained the aura of old Lane Xang. In 1926 American Harry Franck found paradise in Luang Prabang when he wrote in his book *East of Siam* that "it is not a city at all, in the crowded, noisy, Western sense, but a leisurely congregation of dwellings of simple lines, each ... with sufficient ground so that its opinions or doings need not interfere with its neighbours. In short, Luang Prabang town is in many ways what idealists picture the cities of Utopia to be ...".

PLACES OF INTEREST

The sights are conveniently close together in Luang Prabang. Most are walkable – the important ones can be covered leisurely within 2 days, but a bike is the best way to get around. When visiting the wats it is helpful to take a guide to obtain entry to all the buildings, which are often locked

for security reasons. Without a guide, your best chance of finding them open is early in the morning.

The **Royal Palace** (also called the **National Museum**) is right in the centre of the city on the main road, Phothisarath which runs along the promontory. This allowed royal guests ready access from the Mekong. Unlike its former occupants, the palace survived the 1975 revolution and was converted into a museum the following year. It replaced a smaller wooden palace on the same site. The palace is not old: building started in 1904, during the reign of Sisavang Vong, and took 20 years. Although the bulk of the construction was completed by 1909, the two front wings were extended in the 20s and a new, more Lao, roof added at the same time. These later changes also saw the planting of the avenue of palms and the filling in of one of two fish ponds. As local residents saw the ponds as representing the 'eyes' of the capital, the blinding of one eye was taken as inviting bad fortune by leaving the city unprotected. The subsequent civil war was taken as a vindication of

Luang Prabang and Phousi from the Mekong

McCarthy, James (1900) *Surveying and exploring in Siam with descriptions of Lao dependencies and of battles against the Chinese Haws*, John Murray: London. The pen and ink sketches are by H. Warrington Smyth, another chronicler of the Kingdom.

their fears. The palace is Khmer in style – cruciform in plan and mounted on a small platform of four tiers. It was built by the French for the Lao King, in an attempt to bind him and his family more tightly into the colonial system of government. The only indication of French involvement can be seen in the two French lilies represented in stucco on the entrance, beneath the symbols of Lao royalty. Indeed the palace, in many respects, is more foreign than Lao: it was designed by a French architect; built by masons from Vietnam; embellished by carpenters from Bangkok; and funded by the largesse of the colonial authorities.

The museum contains a collection of 15th-17th century Buddha statues, including the famous Golden Buddha and artefacts from many of the wats in Luang Prabang such as the Khmer bronze drums from Wat Visoun. The palace itself is modest; its contents, spectacular.

On the right wing of the palace, as you face it, is the kings' private chapel, containing a copy of the **Pra Bang** – the Golden Buddha from whence the city derived its name. The Buddha is in the attitude of Abhayamudra or 'dispelling fear' (see page 62). The original image is reportedly kept in a bank vault. It is

90% solid gold, stands 83cm high and weighs around 50 kg. Reputed to have originally come from Ceylon (and said to date from any time between the 1st and 9th centuries), the statue was brought to Cambodia in the 11th century and was then taken to Lane Xang by King Fa Ngoum, who had spent some time in the courts of Angkor and married into Khmer royalty. An alternative story has the Pra Bang following Fa Ngoum to the city: it is said that he asked his father-in-law, the King of Angkor, to send a delegation of holy men to assist him in spreading the Theravada Buddhist faith in Lane Xang. The delegation arrived bringing with them the Pra Bang as a gift from the Cambodian King. The Pra Bang's arrival heralded the capital's change of name, from Xieng Thong to Nakhon Luang Prabang – 'The great city of the big Buddha'.

In 1563 King Setthathirat took the statue to Lane Xang's new capital at Vientiane. 200 years later in 1779 the Thais captured it but it was returned to Laos in 1839 and rediscovered in the palace chapel in 1975. The Pra Bang is revered in Laos as its arrival marked the beginnings of Buddhism in Lane Xang. The **Wat Ho Prabang** – whose untidy foundations are to the right of the entrance to the Royal Palace – was designed to house the statue but it was never completed (presently being restored). The intended building was designed by the Royal Secretary of the time, paid for by small donations sent in from across the country, and begun in 1963. The chapel also contains four other Khmer Buddhas, ivories mounted in gold, bronze drums used in religious ceremonies and about 30 smaller Buddha images, surrounding the Pra Bang, which came from temples all over the city.

The main entrance hall of the palace was used for royal religious ceremonies, when the Supreme Patriarch of Lao Buddhism would oversee proceedings from his gold-painted lotus throne. The room to the immediate right of the entrance was the king's reception room, also called the Ambassadors' Room. It contains French-made busts of the last three monarchs, a model of the royal hearse (which is kept in Wat Xieng Thong) and a mural by French artist Alex de Fontereau, depicting a day in the life of Luang Prabang in the 1930s.

To the left of the entrance hall is the reception room of the king's secretary, and beyond it, the queen's reception room, which together house an eccentric miscellany of state gifts from just about every country except the UK. Of particular note are the moon rock presented to Laos by the US following the Apollo 11 and 17 lunar missions and a rifle inlaid with pearl – a present from Soviet premier Leonid Brezhnev in 1963. Also in this room are portraits of the last king, Sisavong Vattana, Queen Kham Phouy and Crown Prince Vongsavang, painted by a Soviet artist in 1967.

The coronation room, to the rear of the entrance hall, was decorated between 1960 and 1970 for Sisavong Vatthana's coronation, which was postponed because of the war. The walls are a brilliant red with Japanese glass mosaics embedded in a red lacquer base with gilded woodwork and depict scenes from Lao festivals. To one side of the carved howdah throne, with its gold 3-headed elephant insignia, a huge candle, the same height as the king, stands guard; to the other, a tall pot to hold the crown. To the right of the throne, as you face it, are the ceremonial coronation swords and a glass case containing 15th and 16th century crystal and gold Buddhas, many from inside the 'melon stupa' of Wat Visoun. Because Luang Prabang was constantly raided, many of these religious artefacts were presented to the king for safekeeping long before the palace became a national museum.

In comparison, the royal family's private apartments behind are modestly decorated. They have been left virtually untouched since the day they left for exile in Xam Neua province. The king's library backs onto the coronation room: Savang Vatthana was a well-read monarch, having studied at the *Ecôle de Science Politique* in Paris. Behind the library, built around a small inner-courtyard are the queen's modest bedroom, the king's bedchamber and the royal yellow bathroom with its two regal porcelain thrones standing side by side. The remaining rooms include a small portrait gallery, the children's bedroom, dining room and a corridor containing the royal sedan chair which carried the king to religious ceremonies. Domestic rooms, offices and library are located on the ground floor beneath the state apartments.

Just to the left of the palace is the small and very modest 'Winter Palace'. Visitors often wonder about the use and name of this building: it was built as a refuge to which women could retire in the days before and after childbirth. Finally, in the near, left hand corner (southern) of the compound, is the Luang Prabang Conference Hall. This was built for the coronation of Savang Vatthana, an event which never came to pass – the 1975 revolution interrupted preparations. **Admission**: 1,000 kip, or if you want a guided tour, *Luang Prabang Tourism* can organize this; they charge US$3. Most visitors visit in a group. Open Tues-Sun 0830-1030; they also open in the afternoon for large groups (10 plus) and pre-arranged tours.

Further down Phothisarath, next to the Royal Palace is **Wat May** (Wat Mai). This temple was officially called Wat Souvanna Phommaram and was the home of the Buddhist leader in Laos, Phra Sangkharath. The royal building, inaugurated in 1788, has a 5-tiered roof and is one of the jewels of Luang Prabang. It took more than 70 years to complete. The façade is particularly interesting: a large golden bas-relief tells the story of Phravet (one of the last reincarnations of the Gautama or historic Buddha) with several village scenes including depictions of wild animals, women pounding rice, and people at play. The interior is an exquisite amalgam of red and gold; the supporting pillars are similar to those in Wat Xieng Thong and Wat Visoun. The central beam at Wat May is carved with figures from Hindu mythology – the story of the birth of Ravanna and Hanuman. It was the home of the Pha Bang from 1894 until 1947. During *Pimay* (new year) the Pha Bang is taken from the Royal Palace and installed at Wat May for its annual ritual cleansing. It is returned to the Palace on the third day. Admission: 200 kip.

Directly opposite the Royal Palace is the start of the steep climb up Phousi. As you start the ascent, to the right is **Wat Pa Huak**, a disused wat, with lovely murals inside. 328 steps wind up to **Phousi**, a gigantic rock with sheer forested sides, in the centre of town, which affords a splendid panoramic view of Luang Prabang and its surrounding mountains. The Mekong lies to the N and W and the city to the SE. Near the anti-aircraft gun, a sign warns visitors not to point your camera towards the E; this is not for religious reasons, but because beyond the Nam Khan bridge lies Luang Prabang's secret weapon: the airport. Luang Prabang was probably sited at this point on the Mekong, in part at least, because of the presence of Phousi. Many capitals in the region are founded near sacred hills or mountains which could become local symbols of the Hindu Mount Mahameru or Mount Meru, the abode of the gods and also the abode of local tutelary spirits. Admission at western steps: 500 kip.

Apart from being a magnificent spot from which to watch the sun go down, Phousi is culturally and symbolically very important. In the 18th century it was covered in monasteries and **Wat Chom Si**, built in 1804, still sits on the summit. Its shimmering gold-spired stupa rests on a rectangular base, ornamented by small metal Bodhi trees. Next to the stupa is a little sanctuary, from which a candle-lit procession descends at the Lao New Year festival, *Pimay*, accompanied by effigies of *Nang Sang Kham*, the guardian of the new year, and *Naga*, protector of the city. The drum, kept in the small *hor kong* on the E side of the hill, is used only on ceremonial occasions. The path going down from next to the ack-ack cannon leads to **Wat Tham Phousi**, which is more like a carport than a temple, but which is home to a rotund Buddha, *Kaccayana* (also called Phra Ka Tiay). At the top of the steps leading out of the wat stand a pair of tall cacti, planted defiantly in the empty shell casings of two large US bombs – the local monks' answer to decades of war.

Down a path to the N of Wat Tham Phousi is **Wat Siphouttabath**, just off the central road running along the promontory, which contains a 3m long footprint of the Buddha. Most of Luang Prabang's important wats are dotted along this main road, Phothisarath.

Wat Sen, further up the promontory, was built in 1718 and was the first sim

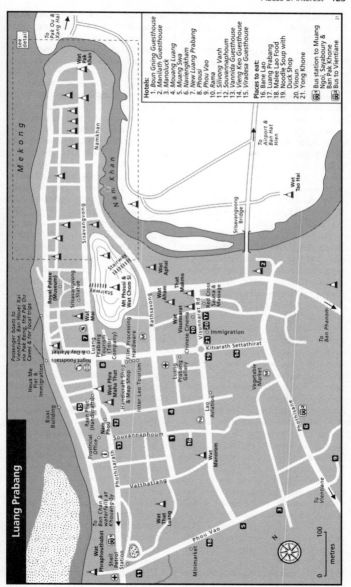

Luang Prabang

Hotels:
1. Boun Gning Guesthouse
2. Manilath Guesthouse
3. Manoluck
4. Mouang Luang
5. Muang Swa
6. Naviengkham
7. New Luang Prabang
8. Phousi
9. Phou Vao
10. Rama
11. Silivong Vanh
12. Souvannaphoum
13. Vannida Guesthouse
14. Vieng Keo Guesthouse
15. Viradesa Guesthouse

Places to eat:
16. Bane Lao
17. Luang Prabang
18. Malee Lao Food
19. Noodle Soup with Duck Shop
20. Visoun
21. Yong Khone

🚌 Bus station to Muang Ngoi, Sayaboury & Ban Pak Khone
🚌 Bus to Vientiane

in Luang Prabang to be constructed in Thai style, with a yellow and red roof, and lacks the subtlety of earlier Lao temples. Sen means 100,000 and the wat was built from a local donation of 100,000 kip. The donor is said to have discovered 'treasure' in the Khan River – quite what this was is unclear. The exterior may lack subtlety, but the interior is delicate and rather refined, painted red, with gold patterning on every conceivable surface. At the far end of the wat compound is a building containing a large, gold, albeit rather crudely modelled, image of the Buddha in the 'calling for rain' mudra (standing, arms held stiffly down). Note the torments of hell depicted on the façade of the building (top, left).

Further N on Xienthong Rd is **Wat Xieng Thong Ratsavora viharn**, usually known as just **Wat Xieng Thong**, set back from the road, and at the top of a flight of steps leading down to the Mekong. This monastery was a key element in Luang Prabang's successful submission to UNESCO for recognition as a World Heritage site. The striking buildings in the tranquil compound are decorated in gold and post-box red, with imposing tiled roofs, intricate carvings, paintings and mosaics – making this the most important and finest royal wat in Luang Prabang. It was built by King Setthathirat in 1559, and is one of the few buildings to have survived the successive Chinese raids. It retained its royal patronage until 1975 and has been embellished and well-cared for over the years – even the crown princess of Thailand, Mahachakri Sirindhorn, has donated funds for its upkeep. The sim is a perfect example of the Luang Prabang-style, with its low, sweeping roofs in complex overlapping sections. The eight central wooden pillars have stencilled motifs in gold and the façade is finely decorated. At the rear of the sim is a mosaic representation of the Thong copper tree in glass inlay. This traditional technique can also be seen on the 17th century doors of Wat Ing Hang, near Savannakhet in S Laos. The interior of Wat Xieng Thong is decorated with rich frescoes and dharma wheels on the ceiling.

Behind the sim are two red *hor song phra* (side chapels): the one on the left houses a rare Lao reclining Buddha in bronze, dating from the construction of the monastery, which was shown at the 1931 Paris Exhibition. The red exterior mosaics on the hor song phra, which relate local tales, were added in 1957 to honour the 2,500th aniversary of the Buddha's birth, death and enlightenment. The other *hor song phra* houses a standing image of the Buddha which is paraded through the streets of the city each phii mai (new year) and doused in water. A small stone chapel with an ornate roof stands to the left of the sim.

The *hor latsalot* (chapel of the funeral chariot) is diagonally across from the sim. The grand 12m-high gilded wooden hearse, with its 7-headed serpent was built for King Sisavang Vong, father of the last sovereign, and carried his urn to the stadium next to Wat That Luang (see below) where he was cremated in 1959. It was built on the chassis of a 6-wheel truck by the sculptor, Thid Tun. The mosaics inside the chapel were never finished but the exterior is decorated with scenes from the Ramakien, sculpted in enormous panels of wood and covered with gold leaf. The *hor kong* at the back of the garden was constructed relatively recently in the 1960s, and near it is the site of the copper tree after which Wat Xieng Thong took its name. Admission: 250 kip.

At the far NE end of Phothisarath is **Wat Pak Khan**, which is not particularly noteworthy other than for its scenic location overlooking the confluence of the two rivers. It is sometimes called the Dutch Pagoda as the sculptures on the S door are of figures dressed in 18th and 19th century Dutch costume.

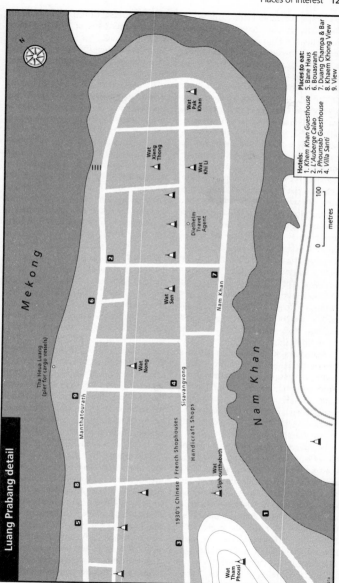

Luang Prabang detail

Mekong

Tha Heua Luang (pier for cargo vessels)

Wat Xieng Thong

Wat Pak Khan

Wat Khi Li

Wat Sen

Diethelm Travel Agent

Wat Nong

Nam Khan

Manthatourath

Sisavangvong

1930's Chinese / French Shophouses

Handicraft Shops

Wat Siphoutthabath

Nam Khan

Wat Tham Phousi

0   100
metres

Hotels:
1. Khem Khan Guesthouse
2. L'Auberge Calao
3. Phounsab Guesthouse
4. Villa Santi

Places to eat:
5. Bane Haus
6. Bouasavanh
7. Duang Champa & Bar
8. Khaem Khong View
9. View

Wat Visunnarat is on the S side of Mt Phousi, next to the *Siensavan Cinema*, an eccentric-looking Chinese-built cinema, with painted nagas climbing around the pillars. Rumour has it that the Chinese owners have gloriously renovated the interior, but that they have not received permission to re-open as a cinema. Wat Visunnarat is a replica of the original wooden building constructed in 1513. Destroyed by marauding Chinese tribes, it was rebuilt in 1898, although it is still very medieval looking. The sim is virtually a museum of religious art, with the numerous Buddha statues it exhibits: most are more than 400 years old and have been donated over the years by locals. It also contains the largest Buddha in the city and old stelae engraved with Pali scriptures (called *hiu chaluk*). The big stupa, commonly known as **That Makmo** ('melon stupa'), was built by Queen Visounalat in 1504. It is of Sinhalese influence with a smaller stupa at each corner, representing the four elements. The arch on the NW side of the sim is original and the only piece remaining of the 16th century building.

Wat Aham, next door, was built by a relative of the king in 1823. The interior has rather beautiful pillars and roof and overbearing modern murals of the torments of hell, as well as a panoramic view of Luang Prabang. Entrance to the *sim*: 250 kip. The two Bodhi trees outside are important spirit shrines.

Wat Phra Maha That, close to the *Hotel Phousi* on Phothisarath, is a typical Luang Prabang wat, built in the 1500s and restored at the beginning of this century. The ornamentation of the doors and windows of the sim merit attention with their graceful, golden figures from the *Phra lak phra lam* (the *Ramayana*). The pillars, ornamented with nagas, are also in traditional Luang Prabang style. The front of the sim was renovated in 1991.

Behind the market at the far NW end of Phothisarath is **Wat Phra Bath** (or Phraphoutthabat Tha Phralak). The original wooden temple on this site dated back to the 17th century, but most of the present structure was built in 1959 by the local Chinese and Vietnamese community. It is worth a visit for its picturesque position above the Mekong. It is renowned for its huge Buddha footprint – '*bath*' is the Pali word for footprint.

Close by, behind the stadium, is **Wat That Luang**. A royal wat, built in 1818 by King Manthaturat, it contains the ashes of the members of the royal family. Note the bars on the windows of the sim in wood and gold leaf, typical of Luang Prabang. The gold stupa at one end of the compound is the mausoleum of King Sisavang Vong, the last king. He is remembered fondly in Luang Prabang and many offerings are left at his stupa. The stone stupa contains relics of the Buddha and is the site of the Vien Thiene (candlelit) festival in May. There are also some traditional style *kuti*, or monks quarters, with carved windows and low roofs. When James McCarthy visited Wat Luang at the end of the 19th century, he was told of the ceremonies that were performed here on the accession of a new 'chief'. In his book *Surveying and exploring in Siam* (1900) he writes that the "... Kamus assembled and took the oath of allegiance, swearing to die before their chief; shot arrows over the throne to show how they would fight any of its enemies, and holding a lighted candle, prayed that their bodies might be run through with hot iron and that the sky might fall and crush them if they proved unfaithful to their oaths."

South of Wat That Luang (between Phou Vao and Kisarath Settathirat) is **Wat Manorom**. It was built by the nobles of Luang Prabang to entomb the ashes of King Samsenthai (1373-1416) and is notable for its large armless bronze Buddha statue, one of the oldest Laotian images of the Buddha, which dates back to 1372 and weighs 2 tonnes. It has an attractive weathered look and the usual carved doors and painted ceilings.

Wat Phra Phone Phao (Monastery of Phao Tree Forest Hill) is 3 km out of town to the E, near Ban Phanom. Looking as though it is made of pure gold from a distance, this wat is rather disappointing close up. The small huts to the right of the entrance are meditation cells. The wat's construction, funded by donations from Lao living abroad and overseas Buddhist Federations, was started in 1959. But the building, modelled on the octagonal Shwedagon Pagoda in Yangon (Rangoon), was only completed in 1988. The names of donors are inscribed on pillars inside. The inner walls are festooned with gaily painted gory frescoes of macabre allegories by a local equivalent of Hieronymus Bosch. Lurid illustrations depict the fate awaiting murderers, adulterers, thieves, drunks and liars who break the five golden rules of the Buddhism. The less grotesque paintings document the life of the Buddha and these extend right up to the 5th floor. On the second level, it is possible to duck through a tiny opening to admire the Blue Indra statues and the view of Luang Prabang. Open 0800-1000, 1300-1630 Mon-Sun.

A GUIDE TO LUANG PRABANG'S SECULAR BUILDINGS

Traditional Lao

The traditional Lao house is rectangular, supported on timber stilts, with a two-sided steep roof and built of bamboo, wood or daub. The stilts help to protect the occupants against wild animals at night and also help to keep the living area dry, especially during the rainy season. The underside also provides a shaded spot for working during the day, as well as area for storage. Living above ground is said to be a characteristic of the Lao and a 16th century Lao text, the *Nithan*

Khun Borom, records that the Lao and Vietnamese kingdoms of Lane Xang and Dai Viet agreed to demarcate their respective zones of influence according to house style: people living in houses raised on stilts would owe allegiance to Lane Xang, those living on the ground, to Dai Viet. Simple.

The traditional Lao house is divided into three principal sections, recognizable from the exterior: the sleeping room, the verandah, and the kitchen. Under the main roof is the sleeping area and the very characteristic verandah is contiguous to it. The kitchen is linked to the main building by an open deck commonly used for bathing and washing. Roof, gables, rafters and balustrade are ornamented with lots of *savoir-faire*. The building process of traditional Lao houses was governed by strict rules: its orientation, the date when building could commence, the setting of the wooden piles, and so on, had to conform to spiritual guidelines.

French colonial

The French introduced new technologies and materials into house construction, in particular the fired brick and the ceramic roof tile. Traditionally, these materials were reserved for wat construction – explaining why almost all buildings of pre-colonial vintage in Laos today are religious. The main characteristics of French colonial architecture are: extensive roof area to protect against sun and rain; large window openings, paned and shuttered; verandahs; arcades; a monumental entrance; a fireplace and chimney breast; brick and wooden decorative details expressing different construction systems (for instance, columns, capitals, rafters and lintels), and ceramic roof tiles.

Lao-French colonial

As French influence grew, so Lao builders began to incorporate some aspects of French design into their constructions. For example, some houses which in all other respects conform to the traditional

Traditional Lao house

French Colonial Lao house

French Colonial house

International modern house

French Colonial style

International modern 'compartment'

Lao-French Colonial 'compartment'

Contemporary Lao house

Lao house style, have French openings and a grandiose doorway leading to a flight of impressive stairs.

French colonial-Lao

In the same way as Lao builders adopted some French elements, so French architects and builders embraced Lao stylistic features. This is most evident in the use of temple-style ornamentation, on the roof for example.

International-modern

Many houses are now built of concrete and the bungalow has become common. In many cases, traditional Lao architectural motifs and designs are merely made from concrete rather than the traditional wood. But concrete has also allowed some innovations in design: cantilevers, flat roofing, pre-fabricated elements and geometric ornamentation are all linked in part to the change in building medium from wood and bamboo, to concrete. 'International modern' includes both domestic buildings and compartments (shophouses).

Lao contemporary house

Lao contemporary houses tend to fall into two categories. Either they are respectful of traditional Lao style; or they embrace modern design and construction materials wholesale. Houses in the first category can be seen to be part of an evolution of the traditional Lao house: the main entrance has shifted to the gable side, the verandah is smaller, while the open area between the piles below the main house is enclosed with brick or concrete walls and has physically become part of the house. Wood is still used for exterior facing for the first floor, but the walls of the ground level floor are made from stone and bricks. This is the most common form of house built today. The second category of Lao contemporary house is built entirely of brick and concrete and most Lao consider it to be more luxurious.

A WALKING TOUR OF LUANG PRABANG'S ARCHITECTURAL HERITAGE

This is a suggested walking tour of Luang Prabang's architectural highlights. To begin with it may be worth climbing Phousi or taking a stroll along the Mekong and Nam Khan river roads to get a better idea of the layout of the town. With a town as small as Luang Prabang it is easy enough just to set out and find your own route, following whatever appeals. The map marks some of the more significant buildings – other than the usual monasteries – and can be used to help explore the city. However, we have also provided a two-stage foot/bicycle tour. The first stage, which can be walked, concentrates on the peninsula and the streets that form the original core of the city. The second part of the tour is best undertaken by bicycle and covers the outer streets.

Walking tour: the peninsula

The tour begins on Thanon Phothisarath in front of the Royal Palace. Historically, the area to the W of the palace was considered the noble quarter of town, the E was inhabited by the middle classes, while the working class lived around the foot of Phousi.

Walking from the Royal Palace along Phothisarath SW towards the Post Office, the first building that deserves special note is the **traditional Lao house** in front of Wat Mai. This is a construction on stilts with a closed verandah. Continuing along Phothisarath, on your left, is the 'Gendarmerie', a **French colonial building** constructed of bricks with gables on the facade. On the other side of the road is the **Lao Bank**, another example of a **French colonial building**.

Turn right onto Kitsarath Setthathirat Rd and walk down towards the Mekong. Past the post office, on the right, is a Lao house showing French colonial influences – our **Lao-French colonial** classification. Take the first road on your

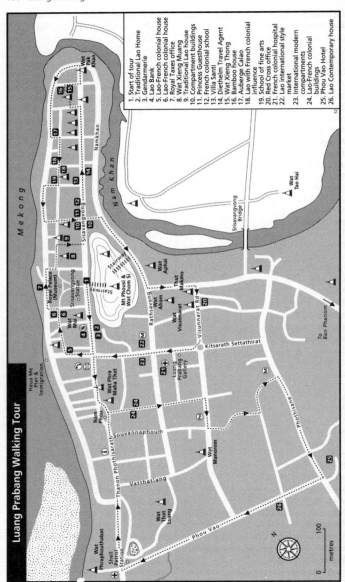

Luang Prabang Walking Tour

1. Start of tour
2. Traditional Lao Home
3. Gendarmerie
4. Lao Bank
5. Lao-French colonial house
6. Lao-French colonial house
7. Royal Taxes office
8. Wat Xieng Muang
9. Traditional Lao house
10. Compartment buildings
11. Princess Guesthouse
12. French colonial school
13. Villa Santi
14. Diethelm Travel Agent
15. Wat Xieng Thong
16. Bamboo house
17. Auberge Calao
18. Lao with French colonial influence
19. School of fine arts
20. Red Cross office
21. French colonial hospital
22. Lao international style market
23. International modern compartments
24. Lao-French colonial buildings
25. Phou Vao Hotel
26. Lao Contemporary house

right to see more examples of **traditional Lao houses**. In some cases the formerly open ground level area has been enclosed to increase the habitable space, using a variety of different materials – bricks, wood and bamboo, for example. At the very end of this street, just beside the Royal Palace, are two opulent **Lao-French colonial style houses**. Turn left to reach the Mekong river road, and then right to walk along the river bank. The **Royal Taxes office** lies behind the Royal Palace. To see some truly beautiful examples of **traditional architecture**, enter Wat Xieng Muang and take the exit into the alley behind the temple.

Continue back up to Phothisarath, turn left and take a look at the '**compartment' buildings** on both sides of the street. These skilfully combine commercial and residential functions under the same roof, much like the Chinese 'shophouse' found throughout Southeast Asia. The ground floor is usually a business, usually a shop or trading outlet, but sometimes a seamstress or even a mechanical workshop. Here the 'compartments' are built in a variety of styles, but mainly French colonial and Lao-French colonial. The Lao traditionally never lived and worked in the same building; they always ran their businesses from some other location, even if it was a streetside stall just a few yards away from their home. It is therefore safe to assume that these compartments were used by Chinese and Vietnamese immigrants.

Walking on towards the tip of the peninsula, there are several other notable buildings including the **princess guesthouse** just before the **French colonial school** on the left hand side of the road, the **Villa Santi Hotel** (also on the left) and the **Diethelm agency office** (on the right). At Wat Xieng Thong take the exit from the monastery on the E side to look at the very **modest bamboo house** down the alley.

At the tip of the peninsula, turn back along the Mekong river road. On the left

is the **Auberge Calao**, an example of a renovated colonial building and the only Portuguese building on the peninsula. Immediately after the auberge, take the first road on your left and then turn right. Along this road, at the first intersection, are two very fine **Lao houses with French colonial influences**. Past the intersection further along the same street, the School of Fine Arts, a Lao traditional style building with two adjoining roofs is one of the few structures in Luang Prabang showing this architectural design. Turn right to return to the Mekong river road along which are a number of buildings showing various degrees of international influence.

Walk across the peninsula to the Nam Khan river road and then follow the road around Phousi. Along the road are a number of examples of **Lao traditional** and **Lao-French colonial buildings**. Turn right on to Visunnarat Rd and facing Wat Visunnarat, the **Lao Red Cross Office** is worthy of note.

Turn right on to Kitsarath Setthathirat and walk back towards the market and the centre of town. Along this street is the **French colonial architecture** of the city hospital, the **Lao-international style market**, and the **international modern compartment** buildings facing the market. At the post office intersection, turn left onto Phothisarath and follow the road until it reaches the *L'Hotel Souvannaphoum* on the left. The next street on the left has a number of buildings showing **French influences on Lao architecture**.

Bicycle tour: the outer city

From here, the route is best completed by bicycle. These outer streets, away from the original core of the city, have a number of recently constructed hotels and large villas. The buildings, though perhaps not beautiful to the western eye, illustrate the way in which Lao architecture is using modern materials and incorporating modern design elements and architectural motifs.

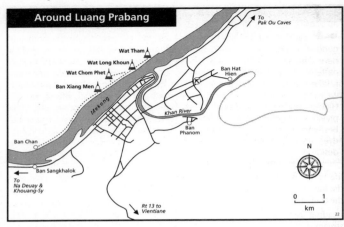

Around Luang Prabang

To Pak Ou Caves

Wat Tham

Wat Long Khoun

Wat Chom Phet

Ban Hat Hien

Ban Xiang Men

Mekong

Khan River

Ban Phanom

Ban Chan

N

Ban Sangkhalok

To Na Deuay & Khouang-Sy

Rt 13 to Vientiane

0   1
km

22

Bicycle SW out of town along Phothisane Rd to the intersection with Phou Vao Rd. Set on the top of the small hill here is one of Luang Prabang's most modern buildings, the *Phou Vao Hotel*. Turn right on to Phou Vao Rd and bicycle towards the river. Along here are a number of **Lao contemporary** buildings as well as the **French colonial slaughterhouse**. Return to town along Phothisarath Rd.

EXCURSIONS

Officially, places around Luang Prabang are not open to tourists, so it is inadvisable to travel off the beaten track, unless accompanied by a tour operator. The places mentioned below are 'in-bounds' to independent travellers. The **monasteries and villages on the right bank** (West) of the Mekong are accessible by boat from the landing areas downstream from the royal palace. For anyone who does not fancy spending 3 hrs on a boat travelling to and from the Pak Ou caves, this makes for an enchanting half day excursion. The first stop is usually **Wat Long Khoun** at the top of a flight of steps leading up from the river bank almost opposite Wat Xieng Thong. This wat was

built in two stages and was renovated by the École Française de'Extrême Orient in Jan 1994 at a cost of 400,000 FF. The oldest section is at the back and dates from the 18th century. The beautifully sculpted door was made in 1937. The *sim* on the river side of the compound is a delightful building. Small, well-proportioned and intimate it has some vibrant murals. On the exterior, either side of the main doorway, are two bearded warriors, swords slung over their backs. They would seem to be representations of Chinese soldiers (Ho/Haw?). The kings of Lane Xang are said to have come on 3-day retreats to this spot, to prepare for coronation. Admission 200 kip. **Wat Tham**, literally 'cave monastery', is 100m or so upstream from Wat Long Khoun, above a delapidated *sala*. A well-trodden path leads there. The wat is a limestone cave temple with stairs and ballustrades cut out of the stone. The interior is very dark but is worth exploring, as it is stacked with ancient, rotting Buddha images. A resident monk, with the aid of dim torches, will lead visitors down into the airless cavern pointing out rock formations and Buddha images. Fearful that the torches may not be powered by long

Weaving

Women can distinguish themselves through excellence in weaving – a good weaver never has much problem finding a husband. Different ethnic groups have different styles of weaving, usually in strong, bold colours with striped patterns. Many of the northern groups embroider cloth, similar to some of the northern Thai tribal fabrics. In the NE, around Xam Neua where many of the best weaving is done, the patterns are intricate and the designs often symbolic. High-quality cloth is also produced in the Luang Prabang area because of the previous royal patronage of weavers in this region. Central and southern Laos are best-known for their *mat mi* (ikat – see page 111) designs and the use of indigo dyes. The ikat-style silks produced in southern Laos are influenced by Cambodian designs.

life batteries, visitors may emerge into the light with a degree of relief. Not for the claustrophobic. Admission: 500 kip.

Leading from Wat Long Khoun downstream is another well trodden track. A plaque incongruously announces that the route was repaired with a contribution from Condé Nast publications. Before reaching Ban Xiang Men a stairway leads up to **Wat Chom Phet**, a hilltop *sim* offering fine views over the Mekong and Luang Prabang. The site has been apparently abandoned as a religious edifice although the mouldering *sim* and kiltering chedis give the place a rather attractive 'lost wat in the forest' feel. This place, like elsewhere hereabouts, also has a profusion of apricot-coloured lilies. Walking on downstream the track passes through **Ban Xiang Men**, a peaceful village where households cultivate the exposed river banks during the dry season, taking advantage of the annual deposition of silt. **Wat Xiang Men** dates from the last century and stands at the foot of a bamboo-clad slope near the centre of the village.

About 1 km downstream, in a clearing in the middle of the forest, is the **royal cemetery**. There are sculptures depicting members of the royal family who could not be cremated for religious reasons, eg children who died as infants, and victims of contagious diseases. It is hard to find a local guide willing to take

you there as most are terrified of ghosts. Also on the right bank are two hills – **Phou Thao** and **Phou Nang**, named after the legend of two lovers. Thao Phouthasene and Nang Kang Hi died tragically and romantically only to find themselves transformed into rock and incorporated in the local landscape. The hills are said to look like a man and woman sleeping next to each other.

Ban Chan is a few kilometres downstream from Luang Prabang (about 1,500-2,000 kip by boat) or 4 km on the road beyond the evening market to Ban Sangkhalok and a short crossing by boat (villagers will paddle you across). The village is known for its pottery industry and mostly produces *thongs* (large water storage jars) and salt pots. *Getting there*: boats regularly cross the river – anywhere from 100-1,000 kip, depending on the number of passengers. Alternatively charter a boat for a couple of hours (about 3-4,000 kip). It is possible to cross over to Wat Long Khoun, walk downstream and catch another boat back to the Luang Prabang bank of the river either at Ban Xiang Men or Ban Chan. Or the circuit could be completed in the reverse direction. There are a couple of food stalls in Ban Xiang Men.

Ban Phanom (Tit Cliff Village) is 3 km E of Luang Prabang. This is a 300-year-old weaving village where shawls (*pha biang*) and sarongs (*pha sin*) are made from silk and cotton. The 100-odd families in Ban Phanom are members of the Lu minority who originated from Yunnan in S China. They were traditionally the king's weavers, soldiers and palace servants. Because they have integrated with modern Lao society, they do not take kindly to being referred to as tribals. Although best known for its weaving, the village's main economic activity is rice cultivation. A few years ago cloth was sold from a street market in the middle of the village. Now some of the larger producers have turned their houses into small shops.

Henri Mouhot's tomb lies about 2 km beyond Ban Phanom, at the top of a bank looking down into the Nam Khan, a tributary of the Mekong. The French explorer Henri Mouhot stumbled across Angkor Wat in 1860 but succumbed to a malarial attack in Luang Prabang on 10 Nov the following year. Resident foreign aid workers spent months searching for the grave before rediscovering it in 1990. The tomb was not constructed until 6 years after his death, in 1867, and was designed by another French explorer, Doudart de Lagrée. In 1990 the town of Mouhot's birth, Montbéliard, donated a plaque inscribed, simply, 'Proud of Our Son'. The French government has granted an allowance for its upkeep (it is still overgrown). *Getting there*: by saamlor to Ban Phanom and a bit beyond (400 kip) or by bicycle. Ask villagers in Ban Phanom for directions; small boys will sometimes show visitors the way.

Ban Hat Hien is on the airport road, fork right before the terminal and at the end of the road is Luang Prabang's knife-making village. Residents beat scrap metal over hot stoves to make blades and tools. The flames are fanned by bellows, originally made from teak tubes and operated with plungers – but several craftsmen use old 155 mm Howitzer propellants and say their "little presents from the US come in very handy". One shed is stacked with hundreds of old car batteries from which the lead is extracted and poured into moulds for ball bearings and gunshot. The results of their labours can be seen in the markets in town. From the nearby Nam Khan, villagers harvest 'seaweed' – which is dried and eaten with sesame. *Khai pehn* from Luang Prabang is sold all over the country. *Getting there*: saamlor (500 kip).

Pak Ou Caves (the lower caves are called Tham Thing, the upper, Tham Phum) are 25 km upstream, in the side of a limestone cliff and opposite the mouth of the Mekong's Nam Ou tributary (Pak Ou means 'Mouth of the Ou'). This is a popular outing and it is very easy to organize, as almost anyone will take you. Ensure you tell the driver you only want to see the caves and come back, otherwise village visits will be added, and the cost will rise. Alternatively, go by boat – see the end of the entry for details. The two sacred caves, supposedly discovered by King Setthathirat in the 16th century, are studded with thousands – the official figure is 4,000, 2,500 in the lower cave and 1,500 in the upper – of wood and gold Buddha statues; some are thought to be more than 300 years old. It is likely, though, that these caverns were associated with spirit (*phi*) worship before the arrival of Buddhism in Laos. Many of the images are in the distinctive attitude of the Buddha calling for rain (with arms by his side, palms turned inwards). For years the caves, which locals still believe to be the home of guardian spirits, were inhabited by monks. The king visited them every new year and stayed at Pak Ou village on the opposite bank of the Mekong, where there is a royal wat with beautiful old murals on the front gable. The caves are one of the main venues for Pimay in Apr, when hundreds make the pilgrimage upriver from Luang Prabang. During the dry season the river shrinks, exposing huge sandbanks, which are improbable gold fields. Families camp out on the banks of the Mekong and pan for gold, most of which is sold to Thailand. Bring a torch. *Getting there*: charter a boat from Tha Heua Me (see map). The going rate for the journey – about 2 hrs upstream and 1 hr down with stops en route – is US$20. Boats vary in size, but the larger ones can take up to 8 people. Note that many restaurants, hotels, guesthouses and tour companies will arrange this trip and it is probably better to do it this way. **NB** Take water.

Xang Hai is 20 km upstream, on the way to Pak Ou caves. The name of this village literally translates as 'making wine pots' and on the beach villagers brew *lau-lao*, a moonshine whisky. In the rainy season they grow glutinous rice and in the dry season they ferment it in water and yeast. The distilled 'wine' is sold illegally for 300 kip/litre in Luang Prabang. Villagers are delighted to give visitors a tasting sample. **NB** Lao for 'Cheers': *Seung Dium*. *Getting there*: see Pak Ou Caves (above).

The **Waterfalls at Khouang-Sy** are 30 km S on a tributary of the Mekong. These falls, though not high, are spectacular and really quite beautiful. The coating of deposits and the lush vegetation makes them appear almost organic from a distance. The UNDP has cleared a path to the falls and there are usually vendors selling snacks and drinks. If that sounds commercialized, don't be put off. The pools below the falls are sheltered and comparatively private and make a wonderful spot for a swim. Entrance fee: 700 kip. *Getting there*: travel agents run tours here, US$50 (incl lunch). Alternatively, negotiate the charter of a tuk-tuk, about 15,000 kip there and back. Buses do run to Khouang Sy from the bus terminal by the stadium, but the journey takes up to 2 hrs.

There are several **Hmong villages** within a shortish motorcycle ride of

Luang Prabang. **Ban Longlan** is E of town. To get there, take the main road upstream. At Ban Pak Xuang, just before the bridge over the River Xuang (Pak Xuang = Mouth of the Xuang), turn right to follow this tributary of the Mekong. Just before reaching Ban Kokvan turn right onto a track. This leads to Ban Natan. From here an even smaller track leads off to the left. It follows the Houai Hia, a small stream, between two mountains, and works its way upwards to the mountain village of Ban Longlan. Allow 2 hrs to get there. Few tourists visit this village so dress modestly and be especially sensitive. Another Hmong village downstream from Luang Prabang is **Ban Long Lao**. Take the road SW from town and after about 8 km turn left (after Ban Lekpet and before Ban Naxao). At the radio transmitter carry straight ahead rather than turning right – which leads to a waterfall. The road climbs steeply, passing a small dam, and ends at the village of Long Lao. Again this is a village visited rarely by tourists.

TOURS

Many hotels and restaurants will organize 'tours' to surrounding places; this is not officially allowed, but it happens. Visitors may find travelling around much simpler with a tour operator, as roads remain unmarked and Lao people outside Luang Prabang are not used to tourists.

FESTIVALS

Apr: *Pimay* (movable: public holiday) is celebrated in Laos around 14 Apr. This festival has special significance in Luang Prabang, as it was the royal capital; certain traditions are celebrated in the city which are no longer observed in Vientiane. People from all over the province, and even further afield, descend on the city. The newly crowned Miss New Year (*Nang Sang Khan*) is paraded through town, riding on the back of the auspicious animal of the year. Pimay is the time when the tutelary spirits of the old year are replaced by those of the new. In the past the King and Queen would symbolically clean the principal Buddha images in the city's main wats – like Wat Xieng Thong and Wat May – while masked dancers would prance through the streets re-enacting the founding of the city by two mythical beasts. **Day 1**: bazaar market trade fair in streets around the post office; sprinkling of Buddha statues with water; release of small fish into Mekong from pier behind Royal Palace – a symbolic gesture, hoping for good luck in the New Year; construction of sand stupas on western bank of Mekong, at Mong Khoum, next to Wat Xiang Men; fireworks in the evening. **Day 2**: first procession from Wat That to Wat Xieng Thong; dance of the masks of Pou Nheu Nha Nheu and Sing Kaeo Sing Kham; fireworks and festivities in the evening. **Day 3**: second procession from Wat Xieng Thong to Wat That; procession of bronzes; baci celebrations across town (see page 299, **festivals**); fireworks in evening. **Day 4**: The Royal Palace Pha Bang is moved to Wat May. **Day 5**: all day traditional washing of Pha Bang at Wat May. **Day 7**: Pha Bang Buddha returned to Wat May. **Days 9-11**: Wat Xieng Thong Phraman image brought outside temple for ritual washing. **May**: *Vien Thiene* festival (movable) is the candlelit festival. **Aug**: *Boat races* (movable) celebrated in Luang Prabang in Aug unlike other parts of the country, where they take place in Sep. Boats are raced by the people living in the vicinity of each wat.

LOCAL INFORMATION

● Accommodation

Price guide

A+	US$100-200	D	US$8-15
A	US$50-100	E	US$4-8
B	US$25-50	F	under US$4
C	US$15-25		

For Laos' most important tourist destination after Vientiane, accommodation remains limited. In early 1995, there were only 204 rooms. Since then, several new guesthouses and hotels have opened, of variable quality. The restored colonial villas on the peninsular and the *Phou Vao* tend to get booked up, so for the upper range it is advisable to arrange accommodation in advance. **NB** Road names are not widely used, and there seems to be some confusion over precisely what some of the roads are called.

A *L'hotel Souvannaphoum*, Phothisarath, T 212200, F 212577, a/c, restaurant (see places to eat), hot water, 2 restored villas, owned by Inter-Lao Tourism, full of interesting objects d'arts, set in attractive, large garden; *La Residence* (or *tuk mai* to the staff), has 20 twin rooms in French colonial style with balconies, cool wooden floors, marble bathrooms and attractive decor; *La Villa* (more expensive) has two exceptionally stylish, very large rooms but the other rooms are not so good, no credit cards accepted; **A** *Mouang Luang*, Boun Khong Rd, T/F 212790, a/c, restaurant, pool. New, rather grandiose and lavish re-interpretation of traditional Lao architecture in cement. 35 unexpectional but very functional rooms, with enthusiastic staff endeavouring to make their mark on the Luang Prabang hotel scene, Lao and European food in the restaurant, small kidney-shaped pool, which has, the local rumour mill reports, been built without any cleaning system; **A** *Phou Vao*, Phou Vao, T 212194, F 212534, a/c, restaurant, pool, recently renovated hotel set on a hill slightly out of town, with good views, foreign management and 59 modern rm with attached bathrooms, the restaurant here serves Lao and Continental cuisine and provides the only buffet breakfast in town, rooms are on the small side but well fitted out with good bathrooms and some local touches, credit cards accepted; **A-B** *L'Auberge Calao*, river road, T 212100, F 212100, a/c, restaurant (see below), 5 twin rooms in this new beautifully restored 1902 building, with an incomparable position overlooking the Mekong, 4 are on the first floor with verandahs above the river, clean, relaxing and very well run by French Canadians with a passion for Luang Prabang.

B *Manoluck* (sometimes *Manoruck*), 121/3 Phou Vao Rd, T 212250, F 212508, a/c, restaurant, new, quasi-classical hotel, rooms are OK with polished wooden floors but a surfeit of ostentatious furnishings in the lobby, slightly over done but comfortable; **B** *New Luang*

Prabang, Sisavangvong Rd, T 212076, a/c, restaurant (good value), 4 flrs and 15 rm in a rather ugly building, central position, all rooms have hot water and a balcony, management is keen and friendly, rooms are clean, if a little sterile, restaurant serves Lao, Chinese and western food, boat available for trips; **B Villa Santi**, Sisavangvong, T 212267, F 212267, a/c, restaurant (see below), restored early 20th century private house of Princess Khampha. 11 rooms in old building and 14 rooms in second stylishly-built 'annexe'. The newer rooms have baths and showers, the older rooms are more traditional, charming place, full of character, efficiently run, attractive seating areas both in the garden, lobby or on the balcony, rec, free pick-up from airport if you call in advance. On departure, the staff will also arrange for your luggage and passports to be taken to the airport 2 hrs ahead (as requested by Lao Aviation); **B-C Naviengkham**, 4 Phothisane Rd, T 212439, F 212739, a/c, restaurant, new hotel which opened in 1996; **B-C Phousi**, Kitsarath Setthathirat, T 213633, F 213635, some a/c, restaurant, recently upgraded and expanded, OK, twin rooms with wooden floors and decent shower rooms, extensive garden with seating area, good central location, bikes for hire at US$2/day.

C Muang Swa, Phou Vao, T 212263, some a/c, restaurant, bathrooms attached, new but rooms are rather small and a trifle dingy for the price, rather dodgy nightclub here – beware of being ripped off by the girls; **C Silivong Vanh**, Phou Vao, should be open when this book is on the shelves.

D Khem Khan Guesthouse, Nam Khan Rd, some a/c, small guesthouse with just 3 bamboo bungalows overlooking the Khan River, pleasant owner with some French, undergoing expansion in mid-1996; **D Phounsab Guesthouse**, 6/7 Sisavangvong Rd, T 212595, 11 rooms in this town guesthouse, friendly owner with adequate English, 3 rooms with a/c, clean and adequate, breakfast provided, bikes for hire; **D Rama**, nr Wat Visunnarat, Visunnarat Rd, T 212247, hot water (of sorts), basic, fan rooms, adequate but bare, friendly owner without English; **D Vannida Guesthouse**, T 212374, 10 rooms in rambling old house, kept cool by balcony, basic fan cooled rooms, outside bathrooms, garden with seating, characterful, one of the better cheaper places to stay, rec; **D-E Boun Gning Guesthouse**, 109/4 Ban That Luang, T 212274, attractive

balcony, cold drinking water gratis, bicycles for hire, friendly and helpful English-speaking management, very clean, the UNDP office is next door, so there are often UN workers staying here – interesting if you want to find out more about Laos.

E Manilath Guesthouse, nr bridge to airport, T 212371, some attached bathrooms, pleasant guesthouse down quiet lane in village close to river, friendly staff, decent clean rooms; **E Vieng Keo**, Kitsarath Setthathirat (just round the corner from the *Rama*), T 212271, attractive old building but scruffy, fan rooms with concrete floors, some rooms with mosquito nets (very necessary), rather basic. Some private, some shared bathrooms downstairs in courtyard (cold water and klong jars only), comfortable beds with two blankets each. Balcony with plenty of comfy chairs and water on the table all day, good place to recover and meet other travellers, friendly (if rather giggly) management. Also known as the 'Chinese Guesthouse', as it's a big old Chinese house; **E Viradesa**, off river road (see map), hot water, portable fans, some rooms with bathrooms, quiet street with eager owners and over-the-top touches in decent size bedrooms, good value.

● **Places to eat**

Price guide			
◆◆◆◆	over US$10	◆◆◆	US$5-10
◆◆	US$2-5	◆	under US$2

Luang Prabang produces a number of culinary specialities which make good souvenirs. They are, however, more likely to be found in the local market than in the restaurants. The most famous is *khai pehn*, dried 'seaweed', mainly from the Nam Khan, which is mixed with sesame and eaten nationwide. *Chao bong* – a mildly hot pimento purée is also popular throughout the country. Other delicacies incl: *phak nam*, a watercress which grows around waterfalls and is commonly used in soups and salads; *mak kham kuan* (tamarind jam) and *mak nat kuan* (pineapple jam). Baguettes can be bought at many roadside stalls.

Perhaps the best – at least in terms of ambience – places to eat are the cafés and restaurants along the Mekong River, where the procession of boats and people make for fascinating viewing. The food can also be pretty good.

◆◆◆◆–◆◆◆*L'Hotel Souvannaphoum*, Phothisarath, Lao dishes with French influence, good selection of wine, quite smart restaurant in a beautiful setting – covered verandah looking out over the garden, fish, duck and quail all on menu; ♦♦♦*L'Auberge Calao*, light American lunch – hamburgers, open sandwiches, ice-cream etc, Lao food only provided for groups in advance (set menu), restaurant open 0630-2100, good breakfasts, the manager promises to initiate a tuk-tuk burger delivery service which should shake up the Luang Prabang restaurant scene; ♦♦♦*Phousi* (in *Phousi Hotel*), Kitsarath Setthathirat, set menu, also bar food; ♦♦♦*Phou Vao* (hotel), Phou Vao Rd, good Lao and Continental a la carte menu, buffet breakfast, hotel set on hill with great views over the town; ♦♦♦*Villa Santi*, Sisavangvong, attractive first floor restaurant in this airy villa, providing good choice of French and Lao food, the chef is the daughter of Phia Sing (chef to the Royal Family), his recipes have been translated and published (see Food in Information for travellers for publication details); ♦♦♦–♦♦*Duang Champa*, Nam Khan, open 0900-2300, Lao and French food in a trendy restaurant, produce flown in (good range of cheeses), salads, sorbets, adapted Lao dishes, bar downstairs, surly service on our last visit, but the food is good and it also overlooks the Khan River; ♦♦*Bouasavanh*, Manthatourath, Lao and Thai food, overlooking the river; ♦♦*Luang Prabang*, opp Wat Visunnarat, extensive menu of Lao, Thai and Vietnamese food, and an East German cuckoo clock, good vegetarian food, rec spring rolls as well as specialities such as deer, clean, efficient and friendly, with tasteful decor – no neon lights and plenty of attractive Lao weaving, traditional music performed, locals maintain this is the best restaurant in town for Lao food, rec; ♦♦*Khaem Khong*, Manthatourath, one of the better river restaurants; ♦♦*Ban Hous*, Manthatourath, another good sunset spot; ♦♦*Bane Lao*, behind Wat Manorom, big purpose-built restaurant, mostly Lao and some French cuisine, catering for tour groups; ♦♦*View*, Manthatourath, tasty food, particularly rec vegetables; ♦♦*Malee Lao Food Restaurant*, Phou Vao, Lao food, including Luang Prabang specialities, the *laap* is particularly rec here, good food but a little overpriced; ♦*Noodle Soup With Duck Shop*, corner of Kitsarath Setthathirath and Vissunarat, established noodle house, popular with locals; ♦*Khem Khan Food Garden*, on bank of Khan River, under renovation at present, pleasant spot to eat; ♦*Visoun*, opp Rama Hotel, good Chinese food; ♦*Yong Khoune*, diagonally across from Rama, run by Cantonese family, Chinese dishes, Thai food,

excellent fish dishes, good breakfasts (hot baguette with real butter and jam), omelettes and salads, popular with helpful management (one of the daughters, Tina, speaks English and is a good source of information on the city and environs), rec.

● **Bars**

There are several anonymous wooden platforms built over the bank of the Mekong on Manthatourath, which makes for an incomparable place to have a beer at sunset. *La Villa* (*L'Hotel Souvannaphoum*) has a very attractive bar area, with colonial rattan chairs and lovely decor, dress reasonably smart; *Visun Bar*, opp *Rama*, good selection of beer, Chinese and local wines and spirits; *Villa Santi* and *L'Auberge Calao* both provide attractive settings for a drink, as do the restaurants along the river road; *The Duang Champa* provides an extensive choice of spirits.

● **Airline offices**

Lao Aviation, nr *Rama Hotel*.

● **Banks & money changers**

Lane Xang Bank, nr Wat May, changes US$ TCs into dollars or kip, open 0830-1200, 1330-1530 Mon-Fri. Many of the jewellery stalls in the old market will change US$ and Thai baht – although this is strictly black market and, given the fiscal reforms, may not be worth the effort.

● **Entertainment**

Disco: Occasional disco at *Rama Hotel*.

Sauna: *Red Cross Sauna* or massage, opp Wat Visunnarat, 2,000 kip/hr, Wed-Sun 1700-1900 and Sun 0900-1100. Traditional Lao herbal sauna.

● **Post & telecommunications:**

Area code: 071.

Post Office and Telephone Office: Phothisarath. Express mail service, fax and international telephone facilities, philately section.

● **Shopping**

Baskets: the best collection can be found in several shops along Sisavangvong, nr *Villa Santi*.

Handicrafts: *Raan Phat*, opp Wat Phra Maha That, eclectic assortment of dusty rice baskets, spoons, bird traps, weaving paraphernalia, textiles and some clothing. Next door, on a balcony is an '*Antique Shop*', with similar goods; *Luang Prabang Gallery*, Kitsarath Setthathirath, quirky collection of handicrafts/antiques.

Hardware: shops sell chopping blocks, buffalo bells, watering cans. Also some available in Central Market.

Maps: the best city map is one of a series of five, compiled by the National Geographic Department of Lao. It can be bought in the shop next to the handicraft shop, along from the *Phousi Hotel* and almost opp the Central Market.

Markets: *Central Market* in concrete market building in the middle of town (see map), mostly imported goods on sale here, but there are a few stalls selling silver boxes and belts and a handful with textiles. A couple of stalls sell loom parts and yarns for weaving, the busiest time of day is 0900-1100, but it is still open up to 1700 or 1800, depending on shopkeepers. The *New Market* on Phothisane sells mostly fruit and vegetables. The *Street Market* by the Post Office on Kitsarath Setthathirat sells fruit, wild honey, roots and tubers, fresh and dried fish, and knives and other ironmongery made by the smiths of Ban Hat Hien. In the evening, food stalls also set up shop here. Continuing towards the river, this area bustles with activity; it seems to be an important trading and trans-shipment area. Boats dock at Heua Me pier to unload their goods. There is a *Morning Market* (talat sao) at the downstream side of town, nr the stadium.

Silver: one of Luang Prabang's traditional crafts is silversmithing. During the Communist era between 1975 and 1989 many silversmiths turned to other occupations, such was the lack of demand. However, with the rise in tourism and the economic reforms demand has increased and many silversmiths have returned to their craft. Most tourists buy their silver – and other crafts – from the main market in Luang Prabang. However, almost none of the pieces on sale here is from the Luang Prabang area – despite what the marketeers might say. Most are made instead in Vientiane and trucked to the royal capital. Expert silversmiths like Thithpeng Maniphone maintain that these Vientiane-made pieces are inferior, and certainly the finer engraving and silverwork does appear ruder. *Thit Peng*, signposted almost opp Wat That, workshop and small shop with jewellery and pots. The silversmith along the river, nr the rear of the Royal Palace, produces good workmanship. His father made one of the King's crowns.

Weaving: opp Wat Phra Maha That, Central Market. Tribal peoples come into town to sell their wares from the roadside nr the Central Market. The best collection of shops selling local textiles, both new and old, is along Sisavangvong.

Woodcarving: *Art Gallery*, opp Wat May, makes coffins as well as traditional woodcarvings which are for sale.

● **Tour companies & travel agents**
Diethelm Travel, Phothisarath, T 212277; *Inter-Lao Tourism*, Kitsarath Settathirath; *Luang Prabang Tourism*, Phothisarath, this is a government-run tour company; *Sodetour* will open a Luang Prabang office soon and *Lane Xang Tourism* are upgrading their presence here, T 212198; *Yong Khoune*, the restaurant on Visunnarat Rd, organizes daily tours to all the local sights, considerably cheaper than many of the travel agents or hotels.

● **Tourist offices**
Luang Prabang Tourism, on the corner opp the Post Office may appear to be a tourist office, but in fact it is just a state-owned tour company, providing little information, except a map for sale. The **official tourist office** is next to the provincial office on Phothisarath Rd (not far from the *Souvannaphoum Hotel*) but there are only 2 people here who are useful to non-Lao speaking visitors (one speaks French, the other some English), and they are rarely available. There is also an **Information and Cultural Service** almost opp Wat Mai. As 90% of visitors arrive on tours there is considered to be little need for a tourist information service.

● **Useful addresses**
Immigration office: opp *Rama Hotel* on Visunnarat Rd. For people arriving by road, passports must be stamped here on day of arrival (100 kip), and register again on day of departure (100 kip). Open Mon-Fri 0800-1200, 1400-1630. For those arriving by air – there is an immigration desk at the airport. For boat arrivals, there is a place at the ticket office at the pier where passports can be stamped.

● **Transport**
NB It is important to get passports stamped upon arrival in Luang Prabang (100 kip charge), otherwise a fine is incurred upon departure of 3,500 kip/day. Note that visitors with business or 'visit' visas (as opposed to tourist visas) also need to have their passports checked at the immigration office opp the *Rama Hotel*.

Local Bicycle hire: from most hotels and guesthouses, also from the *Yong Khoune Restaurant* and from a couple of places near the

Boats to/from Luang Prabang		
	FAST BOAT	**SLOW BOAT**
Luang Prabang upriver on the Mekong to:		
Pak Beng	13,500 kip	6,000 kip
Ban Houei Xai	27,000 kip	12,000 kip
Luang Prabang downriver on the Mekong to:		
Tha Deua	6,000 kip	3,600 kip
Pak Lay	15,700 kip	9,000 kip
Vientiane	47,250 kip	18,000 kip
Luang Prabang upriver on the Nam Ou to:		
Muang Ngoy/Nong Khiaw	7,000 kip	3,500 kip
Muang Khua (for Phongsali)	18,000 kip	

NB During the dry season (roughly Jan-Jul) the river may be too low for larger passenger vessels to travel downstream from Luang Prabang to Vientiane. Travel on the upstream stretch from Luang Prabang to Ban Houei Xai via Pak Beng is usually navigable year round. It takes 2-3 days downriver to Vientiane and 2 days (with a night in Pak Beng) upstream to Ban Houei Xai.

Mid-1996 prices quoted.

Kodak Shop opp the Central Market. Expect to pay about 2-3,000 kip/day depending on the state of the machine. **Boats**: can be hired from the bottom of the steps below the royal palace, but prices should be negotiated first. A boat to the Pak Ou caves (2 hrs upstream, 1 hr down) should cost about US$20. **Bus**: buses leave from the market and go to other nearby towns. **Minibus with driver**: US$60/day around Luang Prabang, US$80/day if travelling further afield, available from several hotels. **Motorbike hire**: from the *Phou Vao*. **Saamlor and tuk-tuk**: lots around town, which can be hired to see the sights or to go to nearby villages.

Air The airport is about 2 km NE of town; there is a standard 1,000 kip charge to take passengers into town although it is possible to walk. In 1997 a new airport terminal – funded by the Thai government – should open, replacing the collection of shacks that currently serve this purpose. There are plans to begin an international service between Luang Prabang and Chiang Mai (Thailand) in 1997, and Silk Air are reputedly negotiating for rights to operate between Singapore and Luang Prabang. Daily connections with Vientiane, 40 mins, US$46. Early morning departures are often delayed during the rainy season, as dense cloud makes Luang Prabang airport inoperable until about 1100. Flights to Phonsavanh on

Wed and Fri, 1030, 30 mins (US$31), and connections with Ban Houei Xai, Udom Xai, Xieng Khouang and Luang Nam Tha. See timetable on page 324.

Boat Most boats leave from the two docking areas just down stream from the Royal Palace. (Cargo vessels tend to dock at Tha Heua Luang, the palace pier.) Boats travel downriver to Vientiane and upstream to Ban Houei Xai via Pak Beng. Boats for local charter, whether to the Pak Ou caves (see **Excursions**) or just to the other bank of the Mekong, are available here too. The trip to Vientiane takes 2-3 days (longer travelling upriver). Larger boats only go in the rainy season but try local boatmen as most boats making the journey take passengers even if they are commercial. It may be helpful to use a translator in order to negotiate the price. It can take several days of hanging around, whilst the freight is loaded. From Ban Pak Khone (see **Bus**) there are plenty of boats travelling S, but few people speak English and negotiating a fare is a tough business. The boat captains wait to get enough passengers on board and if they don't get enough, they increase the price. The price to Pak Lai should be about 5,200 kip, so do not let the ticket office overcharge you. This stretch of river is quite hazardous, with a fair number of rapids, and there will probably be an overnight stop, sleeping on board. **Accommodation**

in Pak Lai One government guesthouse, **E** Savang, 20 mins' walk from ticket office at the end of the village, next to a timber factory, friendly and helpful staff, meal for 1,000 kip, remember to pay immigration fee at ticket office first. From Pak Lai, there are (dangerous) speedboats and some slower boats to Sanakham and onto Vientiane. It is possible to see working elephants on the strip between Pak Lai and Sanakham. **Sanakham** is quite an interesting place to stop, it contains three wats, one with a ruined stupa and another wat with an unusual Buddha image. There are a few restaurants here and one government guesthouse (**E**) but no-one living there, so you need to ask around, and are left to your own devices, once established. There is a river border crossing here to Chiang Khan in Thailand, but it is doubtful that foreigners can cross here – frequent boats ply the Mekong and no-one asks for your passport. From Sanakham to Vientiane, it is not advisable travelling overland (bad road and insurgency activities). Boats from here are intermittent, and they take about 8 hrs (3,000 kip), arriving at the northern jetty. Bring enough food and water (see page 113 for more details). There are also boats going upriver to Ban Houei Xai via Pak Beng (very slow overnight trip – US$7). Speedboats on to Ban Houei Xai take 3 hrs (US$15), no slow boats on Sun (see page 167) or in the other direction up the Nam Ou to Muang Ngoi. Boats depart at 0830 and take up to 9 hrs. Hazardous and uncomfortable but exhilerating travelling. The boat continues on to Muang Khua. **NB** No boats run between Luang Prabang and Vientiane on Sun.

Road Bus: buses to Vientiane leave from the station on Phothisane Rd (see map) at 0900 and (should) arrive in Vientiane at 0300 (18 hrs travelling but allot 24 hrs). The journey between Luang Prabang and Vientiane is **not entirely safe**. In Nov 1995 two French tourists were injured and four Laotians killed in an attack by Hmong bandits and in 1996 there were several more ambushes, with fatalities. (These Hmong are sometimes characterized as 'freedom fighters' but it seems from their modus operandi – attacking trucks and stealing goods – that they are just thieves with firearms.) By the time this book is published the stretch from Luang Prabang to Vang Vieng should be surfaced (the Vang Vieng to Vientiane portion is so already). Buses to Phonsavanh go via Muang Ngoi, from the bus station on the junction of Phothisarath and Phou Vao roads. No fixed departure time, but usually it's early morning. 8 hrs to Muang Ngoi (accommodation here **F** basic). (There are also boats to Muang Ngoi, on the Nam Khong and Nam Ou, see above.) From here there are pick-ups to Pakxeng and on to Phonsavanh via Muang Xiem. It might be possible to travel from Muang Ngoi to Phonsavanh in one day, if pick-ups (or lifts) are available. If not, there are basic places to stay in both Pakxeng (near the bridge) and in Muang Xiem. The road from Luang Prabang to Phonsavanh is adequate; the journey may seem arduous but the scenery is very rewarding, passing through many hilltribe villages. There are also buses to Sayaboury from the same bus station, leaving early morning and to Ban Pak Khone, on the Mekong (from where it is possible to get boats S), 3 hrs 45 mins (see Boat). **NB** There have been periodic attacks on vehicles by bandits on the Phonsavanh road; check on safety before departing.

Plain of Jars, Phonsavanh and Xam Neua

X IENG KHOUANG province has a murky history. This remote area was incorporated into the kingdom of Lane Xang by King Fa Ngoum in the 14th century but was often ruled by the Vietnamese (who called it Tran Ninh) because of its proximity to the border.

Apart from the historic Plain of Jars, Xieng Khouang province is best-known for the pounding it took during the war. Many of the sights are battered monuments to the plateau's violent recent history. Given the cost of the return trip and the fact that the jars themselves aren't that spectacular, some consider the destination oversold. Indeed, any straw poll of visitors to the region will probably reveal a majority who feel disappointed by what they have seen – and doubtless slightly shell-shocked too at the sheer scale of devastation. However, for those interested in modern military history, it's fascinating, and the countryside – particularly towards the Vietnam frontier – is beautiful. The jars, too, are interesting by dint of their very oddness: as if a band of giants' carousing had been suddenly interrupted, casting the jars across the plain in their hurry to leave.

As the Lao Aviation Y-12 turbo-prop begins its descent towards the plateau, the meaning of the term 'carpet bombing' becomes clear. On the final approach to the main town of **Phonsavanh**, the plane banks low over the cratered paddy fields, affording a T-28 fighter-bomber pilot's view of his target, which in places has been pummelled into little more than a moonscape. Some of the craters are 15m across and 7m deep. During the secret war against the North Vietnamese Army and the Pathet Lao, Xieng Khouang province received some of the heaviest bombing. The Plain of Jars was hit by B-52s returning from abortive bombing runs to Hanoi as bombloads were jettisoned before heading back to the US air base at Udon Thani in Thailand.

Tens of thousands of cluster bomb units (CBUs) were dumped on Xieng Khouang province in the 1960s and 1970s – as testified by the scrap metal trade in CBU casings. Each unit was armed with 150 anti-personnel plastic 'pineapple' bomblets, which still regularly kill children and cripple adults. Hundreds of thousands of these bomblets – and their equally lethal cousins, impact mines, which the Lao call *bombis* – remain buried in Xieng Khouang's grassy meadows. One aid worker relates how in the mid-1980s, a specially

Laos centre-east

designed, armour-plated tractor was terminally disabled by *bombis* while attempting to clear them from the fields. The UK-based Mines Advisory Group (MAG) is currently engaged in clearing the land of UXO (Unexploded Ordnance). They are beginning with schools and hospitals and then moving on to clear areas where fatalities are greatest.

Villagers can also put requests in to have their back gardens cleared of ordnance. The fact that the MAG found a 500lb bomb close to their own HQ in Phonsavanh recently illustrates the scale of the problem. Because the war was 'secret' there are few records of what was dropped and where – until someone is maimed. Often even the workings of the

20-Alternate

'20-Alternate' was the clandestine CIA headquarters near the Plain of Jars in northern Laos. It was so named to discourage journalists from going there, since it was but an 'alternate' air base, one of little importance. Also it was not shown on any maps. 20-Alternate was the staging base for General Vang Pao, the leader of the Hmong who fought the N Vietnamese for the Americans. At one time, during the height of the fighting, the 20-Alternate airfield was the busiest airport in the world with a landing or take-off every minute.

mines when they are uncovered is uncharted territory – the Americans used Laos as a testing ground for new ordnance and blueprints are unavailable. Note that the MAG do not welcome tourists and their work should not be viewed as an 'attraction'.

Uncle Sam has, however, bequeathed to local people an almost unlimited supply of twisted metal. Bombshells and flare casings can frequently be seen in Xieng Khouang's villages where they are used for everything from cattle troughs and fences, to stilts for houses and watercarriers. In Phonsavanh steel runway sheets make handy walls while plants are potted out in shell casings. Research has shown that many villagers no longer see UXO as a problem. They have lived with it for over 20 years and more people die from malaria and in childbirth than they do from UXO.

At 1,000m, the plateau area can be cold from Dec to Mar. The chief activity here is cattle rearing, although this has been much reduced by the after effects of the war. Xieng Khouang also supported tea plantations before the war and many French colonial settlers took to the temperate climate. Like the Bolovens Plateau to the S, the French colonial administration had visions of populating the Plain of Jars with thousands of hard working French families. Only in this way, it was reasoned, could Laos be made to pay for itself. And only to the Plain of Jars and the Bolovens Plateau could French men and women be enticed to settle.

In the surrounding hills, the Hmong grew opium, which they traded to western pedlars in Xieng Khouang town. Phonsavanh is the main town of the province today – old Xieng Khouang having been flattened and its small airstrip is a crucial transport link in this mountainous region. The old town of Xieng Khouang – now rebuilt and renamed Muang Khoune – has a population of just a few thousand and Phonsavanh 25,000. The whole province has a population of only around 200,000, a mix of different ethnic groups, predominantly Hmong, Lao and a handful of Khmu.

The province of Xieng Khouang is one of the poorest in an already wretchedly poor country. Government attempts to curtail shifting cultivation and encourage the Hmong to settle have been unsuccessful partly because there are no alternative livelihoods available that might induce the Hmong to change their swiddening ways. Travelling through the province there is a sense not just that the American air war caused enormous suffering and destruction, but that the following decades have not provided much in the way of economic opportunities.

PHONSAVANH

The town offers little of interest other than the daily market, which is busy but rather undistinguished with the usual assortment of cheap Chinese bric-a-brac. The food market, behind the Post Office, is more lively and worth a wander. Infact the town is notable mainly for its sheer

A
journey of
1000 miles
begins with
your first
footprint...

With apologies to
Lao Tzu c.604 - 531 BC

Win two Iberia flights to Latin America

Welcome to Footprint Handbooks - the most exciting new development in travel guides since the original South American Handbook from Trade & Travel.

We want to hear your ideas for further improvements as well as a few details about yourself so that we can better serve your needs as a traveller.

We are offering you the chance to win two Iberia flights to Latin America. Iberia is the leading airline for Latin America, currently flying to 34 destinations. Every reader who sends in their completed questionnaire will be entered in the Footprint Prize Draw. 10 runners up will win an exclusive Footprint T-shirt!

Complete in a ball-point pen and return this tear-off questionnaire as soon as possible.

1 **Title of this Handbook**_____

2 **Age** Under 21 ☐ 21 - 30 ☐ 31 - 40 ☐
41 - 50 ☐ over 50 ☐

3 **Occupation** _____

4 **Which region do you intend visiting next?**
North America ☐ India/S. Asia ☐ Africa ☐
Latin America ☐ S.E. Asia ☐ Europe ☐
Australia ☐

5 **Which country(ies) do you intend visiting next?**
_____

6 **There is a complete list of Footprint Handbooks at the back of this book. Which other countries would you like to see us cover?**
_____

Please enter your name and permanent address:
Name_____
Address_____
_____
_____
E-mail_____

Offer ends 30 November 1997. Prize Draw winners will be notified by 30 January 1998. Flights are subject to availability.

IBERIA Win two Iberia flights to Latin America

Footprint Handbooks
6 Riverside Court
Lower Bristol Road
Bath
BA2 3DZ
England

Affix
Stamp
Here

Footprint Handbooks

6 Riverside Court
Lower Bristol Road
Bath BA2 3DZ
T 01225 469141
F 01225 469461
handbooks@footprint.cix.co.uk

Andalucia Handbook

Zimbabwe & Malawi Handbook with Botswana, Mozambique, Zambia

Caribbean Islands Handbook with the Bahamas

Morocco Handbook with Mauritania

Indonesia Handbook

Chile Handbook

Cambodia Handbook

India Handbook

Vietnam Handbook

Thailand Handbook

East Africa Handbook with Kenya, Tanzania, Uganda and Ethiopia

South Africa Handbook

Tibet Handbook with Bhutan

Peru Handbook

Malaysia & Singapore Handbook

Namibia Handbook

Myanmar (Burma) Handbook

Egypt Handbook

Ecuador & Galápagos Handbook

Mexico & Central America Handbook

Laos Handbook

South American Handbook

Tunisia Handbook with Libya

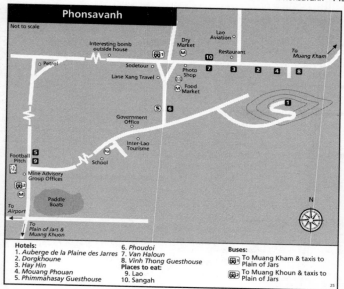

Phonsavanh

Not to scale

Interesting bomb outside house

Dry Market

Lao Aviation

Restaurant

To Muang Kham

Petrol

Sodetour

Lane Xang Travel

Photo Shop

Food Market

Government Office

Inter-Lao Tourisme

Football Pitch

School

Mine Advisory Group Offices

Paddle Boats

To Airport

To Plain of Jars & Muang Khuon

N

Hotels:
1. *Auberge de la Plaine des Jarres*
2. *Dorgkhoune*
3. *Hay Hin*
4. *Mouang Phouan*
5. *Phimmahasay Guesthouse*
6. *Phoudoi*
7. *Van Haloun*
8. *Vinh Thong Guesthouse*

Places to eat:
9. *Lao*
10. *Sangah*

Buses:
To Muang Kham & taxis to Plain of Jars
To Muang Khoun & taxis to Plain of Jars

25

ugliness. It was only established in the mid-1970s and sprawls out from a heartless centre with no sense of plan, direction or pattern. Nonetheless, there are a fair number of hotels and guesthouses in Phonsavanh for this is the only base available from which to explore the Plain of Jars.

NB It is cold here from Nov-Mar; several jumpers and a thick jacket are required. Also note that travel agents and airlines tend to refer to Phonsavanh as Xieng Khouang, while Xieng Khouang is usually referred to locally as Muang Khoune, which leads to a good deal of confusion.

Tours

Hotels, guesthouses and tour companies in town run tours to the Plain of Jars, Muang Khoune (Xieng Khouang), and to Hmong villages to the NE of Phonsavanh. A full day tour for 4 people, travelling about 30 km into the countryside, should cost about 8,000 kip. *Sodetour*

seems to be the most switched on company here, with 5 members of staff speaking some English and French.

Excursions

Plain of Jars lies 10 km SE of Phonsavanh (see page 147). Further SE is the old city of **Muang Khoune** (**Xieng Khouang**) (see page 150). To the NE, route 7 runs to **Muang Kham** and the Vietnamese border (see page 151). Along this route are numerous Hmong villages; tour companies in town run trips out here. *Getting there*: public transport is limited and sporadic (see the entries for Muang Khoune, Plain of Jars and Muang Kham for more details). Taxis and tuk-tuks can be chartered from the market in the centre of town. Expect to pay 8-20,000 kip depending on distance and length (time) of charter.

Festivals

Dec: *National Day* (2nd), horse-drawn drag-cart racing festival in Phonsavanh.

Dec/Jan: *Hmong New Year* (movable) is celebrated in a big way in this area. Festivities centre around the killing of a pig and offering the head to the spirits. Cloth balls, *makoi*, are given by boys to girls they've taken a fancy to.

Local information
● Accommodation

B *Auberge de la Plaine des Jarres*, T/F (Vientiane) 212613, 1 km from centre in spectacular position, on a hill overlooking town, restaurant, 16 attractive stone and wood-built chalets with living room and fireplace, shower-room with hot water (sometimes), clean and comfortable, good food, lovely views, roses, geraniums and petunias planted around the chalets, the friendly owner speaks French; **B-E** *Phoudoi* (formerly the *Mittaphap*), restaurant (with considerable array of loudspeakers for karaoke), hot water shower, **B** is a suite with lurid blue satin bedcovers, clean enough, cheapest rooms have shared bathrooms, own generator provides power 1800-2300, functional block.

D-E *Dorgkhoune*, clean rooms with bare concrete floors and some with attached clean bathrooms, 10 rooms, sitting area, small balcony, substantial house with Russian shell casings in lobby, some used as plantpots. One of the better places to stay; **D-E** *Mouang Phoun*, 12 rooms in motel style with well kept garden in front, annexe down side street, so very quiet, bungalow with partitioned rooms and sitting area looking onto a little garden, shared squat loos and wash area for annexe rooms, own toilets and washbasin in main hotel rooms, hot water in thermos flasks provided, price incl breakfast, blankets offered in cold season; **D-E** *Phimmahasay*, attached bathrooms, large rooms but rather out of town, clean and quite good value for lower range rooms. Lao restaurant next door; **D-E** *Van Haloun*, some with bathroom, ugly Chinese concrete house, clean enough and friendly.

E *Vinhthong*, T 212622, some attached bathrooms with squat loos, raffia partitions to rooms, last place in town, quite good, also organize tours to surrounding countryside; **E-F** *Hay Hin*, basic, but toilet paper and soap is provided, rooms partitioned with hardboard, all a bit of a warren, upstairs where there is a balcony and a communal sitting area the rooms are slightly better, tea provided, the manager does not speak English but is extremely enthusiastic.

● Places to eat

♦♦♦*Auberge de Plaine de Jarres*, reasonable menu of Lao dishes and some French food; **♦♦♦***Mouang Phou*, also nr market, marginally better than the *Hay Hin*.

♦♦*Daokham*, on road to airport, 500m past Chinese market, right going out of town, good local restaurant, but it's a long wait (or order food 1 hr in advance).

♦*Hay Hin*, nr market, restaurant, basic; **♦***Phonsavanh Service*, next to the airport, serves whisky, beer, nibblies and good noodle soup if you can avoid swallowing the flies too; **♦***Sangah*, opp *Van Haloun Hotel*, according to locals, best in town.

● Banks & money changers

Arun May Bank, opp *Phoudoi Hotel*, is unlikely to change TCs; it does change US$, 0800-1600.

● Post & telecommunications

Opposite dry market. International telephone service available, no fax service.

Area code: 071.

● Tour companies & travel agents

Lane Xang, on road S from the market, helpful but no English-spoken (other people in neighbouring shops may help interpret – eg the pharmacy); *Inter-Lao Tourisme*, slightly out of town, opp the government office (see map); *Sodetour*, opp bus station (see map). *Vinhthong Guesthouse*, organizes cheap daily tours to Plain of Jars and Hmong villages.

● Useful information

Electricity available 1830-2130.

● Useful addresses

Police station: for entry and exit stamp is 2 km out of town on the road to the airport, opp the Red Cross Hospital. Open 0700-1200, 1400-1630.

● Transport

NB Visitors with tourist visas must have their passports stamped on arrival. Those with visitors or business visas must also have their passports checked and stamped at the Police Station (see **Useful addresses** and map). Fee: 500 kip.

Local Jeep hire: from *Hay Hin*, US$20-30/day. **Tuk tuk and taxi:** 5,000 kip return fare to Plain of Jars. Taxis and tuk-tuks wait at both bus terminals. **NB** It is not possible to walk from the airport to the Plain, as there is a military base in between.

Air The airport, or rather air-shack (although a new shack is under construction), is about 5 km from town. 500 kip exit fee, 300 kip airport tax. Tuk tuk to town, 500 kip pp, airport tax 300 kip. Daily connections with Vientiane, 40 mins and 3 a week with Luang Prabang, on Sun, Wed and Fri, 25 mins. Airport tax on arrival 500 kip.

Road Regular buses and trucks to Muang Kham where there are connections to Xam Neua via Nam Nouan. There is one direct Phonsavanh-Xam Neua bus a week, 12 hrs. From Nam Nouan there are also buses westwards to Nam Bak and Udom Xai. However, travelling overland between Udom Xai and Phonsavanh it is usually necessary to stopover enroute. There are guesthouses in Nam Bak (see entry) and Nam Nouan. The road to Luang Prabang (Route 7, W and then Route 13, N) is open, but is periodically attacked by anti-government tribespeople, probably just bandits. The route is: Phonsavanh-Muang Xiem-Pakxeng-Muang Ngoi (see page 141 for more details). An alternative, and safer, route to Luang Prabang is to take a bus to Nam Bak (changing at Nam Nouan) and then catch a boat from Nam Bak to Luang Prabang; or, from Luang Prabang, take a boat to Nam Bak and then catch a bus to Phonsavanh via Nam Nouan. It is also possible to take a bus along route 7 to route 13 and then run S to Vientiane via Vang Vieng, although this route, like that to Luang Prabang, is not considered safe. There are plans to upgrade Route 22 S to Pakxan which would greatly improve access with Vientiane. In mid-1996, though, it was still in a terrible state with no bus services. Locals are not optimistic about it being upgraded in the near future.

PLAIN OF JARS

The 1,000m-high, 1,000 sq km undulating plateau of the Plain of Jars (also known as Plaine de Jarres, or Thong Hai Hin) is about 50 km E to W. More than 300 jars survive, mainly (286, apparently) scattered on one slope – so-called 'site 1'. This site is closest to Phonsavanh (about 10 km) and has the largest jar – along with a small restaurant. For true jar lovers, sites 2 (68 jars) and 3 (88 jars) are about 30-40 km away, past Muang Khoune. A car is required to get there. Most of the jars are 1m to 2.5m high, around 1m in diameter and weigh about the same as three small cars. The jars have long presented an archaeological conundrum – leaving generations of theorists nonplussed by how they got there and what they were used for. Local legend relates that King Khoon Chuong and his troops from S China threw a stupendous party after their victory over the wicked Chao Angka and had the jars made to brew outrageous quantities of *lau-lao*.

However attractive the alcohol thesis, it is more likely that they are in fact 2,000 year-old stone funeral urns. The larger jars are believed to have been for the local aristocracy and the smaller jars for their minions. Some archaeologists speculate that the cave below the main site was hewn from the rock at about the same time as the jars themselves and that the hole in the roof possibly means the cave was used for cremation or that the jars were made and fired in the cave. But it's all speculation and their origins and function remain a mystery: the stone from which they are hewn doesn't even seem to come from the region. Closer to sites 2 and 3 are some half-hewn jars and archaeologists have postulated that they were carved here and then transported to site 1. The rock, apparently, is the same. Tools, bronze ornaments, ceramics and other objects have been found in the jars indicating that a civilized society was responsible for them – but no one has a clue which one, as the artefacts bear no relation to those left behind by other ancient Indo-chinese civilizations. Some of the jars were once covered with round lids and there is one jar with a rough carving of a dancing figure in the group facing the entrance to the cave.

Over the years a few jars have been stolen and a number have been helicoptered down to Vientiane's Wat Phra Kaeo and the back yard of the Revolutionary Museum. Local guides claim that despite four or five B-52 bombing

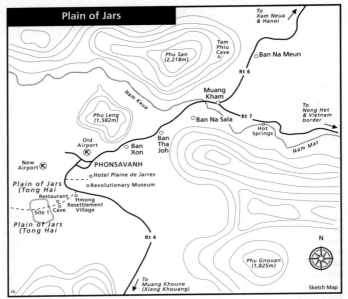

raids every day for 5 years, the jars remained mysteriously unscathed; however, at the main site, several bomb craters and damaged jars show this to be a fanciful myth. During the heavy fighting on the Plain in the early 1970s, the Pathet Lao command set up their headquarters in the 'cave' next to the jars and then posed among the jars for photographs (which can be seen in the Revolutionary Museum in Vientiane). Around the entrance to the cave are numerous bomb craters as the US targetted the sanctuary in a futile attempt to dislodge the communists.

The Plain occupies an important niche in modern Lao history as it became one of the most strategic battlegrounds of the war. For General Vang Pao's Hmong, it was the hearthstone of their mountain kingdom; for the royalist government and the Americans it was the Armageddon of the Orient; for Hanoi it was their back garden, which

had to be secured to protect their rear flank. It was also the Pathet Lao's staging post in their march on the capital.

From the mid-1960s, neutralist forces were encamped on the Plain (dubbed 'the PDJ' during the war). They were supported by Hmong, based at the secret city of Long Tieng, to the SW. US-backed and North Vietnamese-backed forces fought a bitter war of attrition on the PDJ; each time royalist and Hmong forces were defeated on the ground, US air power was called in to pummel from above. In mid-Feb 1970, American Strategic Air Command, on Presidential orders, directed that B-52 Stratofortress bombers should be used over the PDJ for the first time. Capable of silently dumping more than 100 500-pound bombs from 40,000 ft, they had a devastating effect on the towns and villages. Half-a-million tonnes of bombs had been dropped on the PDJ by the end of the war – not including the thousands

Plain of Jars, Xieng Khouang

of tonnes jettisoned by bombers returning to bases in Thailand from Hanoi. But they had minimal effect on Communist morale. Even if the B-52s had managed to wipe out North Vietnamese and Pathet Lao forces, the US-backed troops were unable to reach, let alone hold, the territory. Hanoi had garrisons of reinforcements waiting in the wings.

On the Plain, the B-52 proved as inappropriate and ineffective a weapon as it later would on the Ho Chi Minh Trail. As the US bomber command increasingly turned its attention to the Trail, the Pathet Lao quickly seized the upper hand and retook the PDJ. The Communists were beaten back onto the surrounding hills and ridges a few more times by Vang Pao's forces and American bombers, but they kept swarming back. By Mar 1972, the North Vietnamese Army had seven divisions in Laos supporting the Pathet Lao. **Phu Kheng** ('Mountain of Courage' – the hill behind the new airport to the NW), was the scene of some particularly hard fighting. It was here that the royalists, encamped on Phu Kheng, were trapped on two fronts by the Communists. When the Pathet Lao retook Xieng Khouang for the last time in 1973, they consolidated their position and then began their march on Vientiane.

A vast aviation fuel depot was built next to the jars, early in the 1990s, to supply the huge new airbase just to the W. The base, designed by Soviet technicians, is the new headquarters for the Lao Air Force – which amounts to a grand total of 9 Migs. Admission fee to Plain of Jars: 1,000 kip. Restaurant here for drinks etc.

Along with the bomb craters that scar the landscape there are also patches of bare earth that have nothing to do with the Indochina conflict. These are avine free-fire zones. Local people clear the land of grass over an area of about 10m x 10m and build a small hide. They then put sticky rice down and wait for the poor creatures to alight for a leisurely lunch before being blasted. The main season is after the first rains.

On the grasslands around the Jars are stumpy little flowers, known as '*Baa*' by the Hmong and '*dok waan*' by the Lao; they are eaten by local people – the stem is cooked in soup, the red buds are fried. Once the flower has bloomed (turning yellow), they are no longer tasty. En route to the Plain, the road passes through a **Hmong resettlement village**; distinctive for its style of housing – their homes are not built on stilts and there is no separate kitchen area on the side.

• **Transport** Only accessible by taxi or tuk tuk from Phonsavanh (see local transport, page 146). It should be possible to drive to the PDJ, see the Jars, and return to town in 2 hrs. A chartered tuk-tuk should cost about 5,000 kip.

MUANG KHOUNE (XIENG KHOUANG)

The original, old town of Xieng Khouang was destroyed during the war along with the civilization that went with it. The town was founded by Chao Noi Muang and was a stronghold for the Xieng Khouang royal family. In 1832 the Hmong mountain state of Xieng Khouang was annexed by Vietnam and renamed Tran Ninh. The king was marched off to Vietnam and publicly executed in Hué while the population of Xieng Khouang was forced to wear Vietnamese dress.

Many important temples were built here in the distinctive Xieng Khouang-style but these were completely obliterated by the American bombing. The religious architectural style of the province was one of the three main styles of Laos (Luang Prabang and Vientiane styles being the other 2). The town was also the main centre for the French in this area during the colonial period and remnants of French colonial architecture are still in evidence.

Xieng Khouang was most heavily bombed during 1969 and 1970 when US air power was called in to reverse the success of the Communists' dry season offensive on the Plain of Jars. In his book *The Ravens*, Christopher Robins interviews several former US pilots who describe the annihilation of the town in which 1,500 buildings were razed, together with another 2,000 across the plain. Three towns, he says, "were wiped from the map. By the end of the year [1970] there would not be a building left standing". During this time most villagers left their homes and lived in caves or in the forest. They subsisted on rice from China and Vietnam. So incessant was the bombing and strafing that peasants took to planting their rice fields at night.

The town (little more than a village really) was rebuilt after 1975 and renamed Muang Khoune, but today it holds nothing in the way of aesthetic charm and a sense of impermanence pervades; it consists of a row of wooden Lao houses and a market area. This, at least in the dry season, is Xieng Khouang province's equivalent of Dry Gulch. Its position, however, is quite impressive, as it is surrounded by mountains.

Places of interest

Those excited about the prospect of visiting a unique collection of 500-year old wats must, for the most part, be content with piles of 16th century bricks. There is virtually nothing left of the 16th century **Wat Phia Wat** (far end of town on right hand side by the road), except the basement and several shrapnel-pocked Buddha statues.

A half-hearted attempt at renovation remains barely noticeable. Walking up the hill, the French colonial remains of the Governor's house can be seen, with some old tile floors still in place and a hospital, patched together Lao-style. Next door to the Governor's house is a weaving school set up with UNDP money, teaching up to 60 students. Two stupas perch on a pair of hills above the town. **That Chompet** – also known as That Dam – dates from the 16th century and is quite sizeable. The *that* is said to contain relics of the Indian emperor Asoka but this should be taken with a large drop of *nam pa*. But it does explain, perhaps, why the heart of the stupa has been hollowed out as thieves have searched – apparently in vain – for buried treasure. It is possible to scramble through the middle of the stupa. **That Phuane**, on the further hill, is smaller, with a square base. The centre of the stupa has also been dug out by treasure hunters. **Wat Si Phoum** (opposite the market below the main road) was also destroyed by the war. A new inelegant wat has been built next to the ruined *that*. There is a small monastery attached to the wat. The market here holds little interest for the tourist, with nothing on sale but the bare essentials.

● **Accommodation** None.

● **Places to eat** Good *feu* opp market in marked restaurant.

● **Transport Road** The road is unsurfaced between Muang Khoune and Phonsavanh (35 km). **Bus**: daily bus connections with Phonsavanh from the Morning Market. There are also trucks running between the two towns. **Tuk-tuk or taxi**: possible in the dry season (about 15,000 kip)/1 hr journey. **NB** The bus leaves Phonsavanh from the station next to the Morning Market, 1-2 km out of town (towards Highway 4), **not** the one by the market; take a tuk-tuk.

ROUTE 7 AND MUANG KHAM

Route 7 heads E from Phonsavanh towards Muang Kham and the border with Vietnam. Attractive rolling hills and grassy meadows in the wet season, but very barren in the dry season, especially where the bomb craters have pockmarked the landscape. 12 km E of Phonsavanh is the village of **Ban Xon** which lays claim to two famous daughters, Baoua Kham and Baoua Xi. These two heroines of the revolution are feted for having shot down a US B-52 with small arms fire. War historians are very sceptical about this claim, but a Lao popular song was nonetheless written about them. The ballad is said to characterize the women of Xieng Khouang, extolling their beauty and courage. On a roadside cutting just before the village did lie a large unexploded US bomb – given a wide berth by passing buses. It should have been defused and removed by now. For the agriculturally-minded, the drive is an abject lesson in the potentially destructive nature of (some forms of) shifting cultivators. The figures are of dubious accuracy, but some authorities estimate that 100,000 ha of forest is destroyed each year in Laos by shifting cultivation. The government has had some success in reducing this from an estimated 300,000 ha in the 1970s, but it has been difficult to control. The difficulty in apportioning blame is that the Lao authorities would like to blame the minority shifting cultivators – especially the Hmong. Often swidden agriculturalists will cultivate land already logged-over by commercial timber firms for the simple reason that it is easier to cultivate. They then find themselves blamed for the destruction. Route 7 winds its way down off the plateau along the **Nam Keua**, a fertile area where Hmong villagers grow rice and maize.

About 30 km E of Phonsavanh is the roadside Hmong village of **Ban Tha Joh**. For those wishing to visit a more traditional Hmong village, **Ban Na Sala** is 3 km up the road. Leave your vehicle at Ban Na Sala Mai on the road, and walk S, up a very pleasant valley to the village. It is one of the best places to see the creative architectural and household application of war debris.

Muang Kham, 53 km E of Phonsavanh, is a small trading town in the centre of a large open valley on the route to Vietnam and China. It was devastated during the war, but now has a thriving economy dealing in Vietnamese and Chinese goods. The valley is an important fruit and rice growing area. There's a market early every morning in the centre of town.

More evidence of the dirty war can be seen. The intensity of the US bombing campaign under the command of the late General Curtis Le May was such that entire villages were forced to take refuge in caves. (Curtis Le May is infamously associated with bragging that he wanted to bomb the Communists 'back into the Stone Age'.) If discovered, fighter bombers were called in to destroy them. In the **Tam Phiu (Phiu Cave)**, overlooking the fertile valley near Muang Kham, 365 villagers from nearby Ban Na Meun built a 2-storey bomb shelter and concealed its entrance with a high stone wall. They lived there for a year, working in their rice fields at night and taking cover during the day from the relentless bombing raids which killed thousands in the area. On the morning of 8 March 1968 2 T-28 fighter-bombers took off from Udon Thani air base in neighbouring Thailand and located the cave mouth which had been exposed on previous sorties. It is likely that the US forces suspected that the cave contained a Pathet Lao hospital complex.

The first rocket destroyed the wall, the second, fired as the planes swept across the valley, carried the full length of the chamber before exploding. There were no survivors and 11 families were completely wiped out. Local rescuers claim they were unable to enter the cave for 3 days, but eventually the dead were buried in a bomb crater on the hillside next to the cave mouth. Remains of their skulls, bones and teeth still litter the orange earth covering their makeshift grave. The interior of the cave was completely dug up by the rescue parties and relatives looking for their belongings and today there is nothing but rubble inside. It makes for a poignant lesson in military history, and locally it is considered a war memorial. *Getting there*: the cave is to the W of the Muang Kham-Xam Neua road, just after the 183 km post. A taxi from Muang Kham should cost about 2,500 kip. A rough track leads down to an irrigation dam, built in 1981. An unexploded bomb lies embedded in the stream by the dam and the cave mouth is directly above.

Not far from Muang Kham, off the Vietnam road are some **hot springs** (*bor nam lawn*), on the Nam Mat. They are said to have enormous potential for geothermal power but this is hard to believe as they do not appear to be particularly active. The murky water is distinctly uninviting but it is piped to showers, which is quite pleasant. Locally they are known for their curative properties. **Accommodation** See below. *Getting there*: no buses go to the Hot Springs from Muang Kham, **taxis** may take you there for about 20,000 kip.

Excursions

Nong Het is approximately 60 km from Muang Kham on the Vietnamese border. It is deep in Hmong country and is an important trading post with Vietnam, which is just a few kilometres down the road.

● **Accommodation** E *Hot Spring Guesthouse*, at the big hot spring, 2 bungalows, 4 rooms, bathroom in each bungalow. There is no accommodation at Muang Kham.

● **Transport Road** This area is accessible by truck, bus and sometimes songthaew. The only way to visit the minority villages en route to Muang Kham is by hiring a taxi. **Bus**: from Phonsavanh, buses to Muang Kham leave from the bus station near the market in the centre of town. **Taxi**: costs about 35,000 kip to hire a taxi to visit the minority villages around Muang Kham.

XAM NEUA (SAM NEUA)

Xam Neua is the capital of Hua Phan Province which had a total population in 1995 of 250,000. Hua Phan is known in Laos as a 'revolutionary province'. One of the poorest and most isolated areas of the country, it has been sheltered from the free market ethos that has spilled into towns along the Thai and Chinese borders, and memories of the period when it was the base for the revolutionary struggle in the 1950s, 60s and 70s are still close to the surface. The Lao Communist Party was formed in Xam Neua in 1955 and the Pathet Lao had their headquarters in the area as they confronted the Rightist government in Vientiane and the US. American planes tried to dislodge the Communists from their mountain redoubt, but protected in their caves they survived the onslaught. After the war, senior members of the Royal Lao Government were sent to re-education camps in the province. Archways throughout the town – many of them painted for the 20th anniversary celebrations in 1995 – commemorate the final victory of the Pathet Lao in 1975. Loudspeakers in the market area blast music and propaganda from 0600 in the morning, and there is a strong military presence. A camp in the middle of town is off limits to foreigners, and the largest construction site – at present little more than a scar on a hillside overlooking Xam Neua from the SE – is also to be accommodation for the army.

Places of interest

As the town was obliterated during the war and has been rebuilt since 1973, it is not terribly surprising that it offers little in the way of sights. Indeed Xam Neua's chief attraction is as a staging point for the caves at Vieng Xai. However the town's setting, at 1,200m amid forested hills and rice fields, is pleasant enough. Walking a kilometre or 2 up Highway 6 which leads to Nam Bak and Phonsavanh – the dirt road which runs down one side of the *Laohung Hotel* – affords excellent views of the town and an adjoining valley. The area is at its most picturesque in Oct, when the rice is almost ripe.

There is much evidence of swidden agriculture on the hillsides; indeed families practising slash-and-burn can be found within a few minutes' walk of the central market. The **market** itself is good for hilltribe spotting – Hmong, Yao, Thai Dam (Black Thai), Thai Khao (White Thai), Thai Neua (Northern Thai) and other hill peoples can all be found buying and selling various commodities. There is also a strong Chinese and Vietnamese presence in the town. In the adjoining dry market, examples of the distinctive weaving of Xam Neua and Xam Tai can be found at reasonable prices.

The province is known for its **weaving** and many houses have looms set up on their verandahs. There are several workshops with four or five looms each; some of these use traditional vegetable dyes rather than the aniline (chemical) dyes which are the norm in most other areas. As far as is known from the somewhat sketchy evidence, Hua Phan was one of the 'cradle' areas for Lao weaving. This, combined with its remoteness, means that the diversity of designs produced in the province is second to none, as techniques that have become rare elsewhere are still practised here. The premier centre for weaving is at Xam Tai (local pronunciation, Xam Teua), 100 km to the SE (see Excursions).

Best time to visit: summer is pleasant in Xam Neua but temperatures at night reach freezing in winter. Bring a pullover even in summer. The mosquitoes are monstrous, precautions against malaria advised.

Excursions

NB Tourists should exercise caution when travelling independently in Hua Phan, as some of the authorities harbour a residual suspicion of westerners. It is a very good idea to register with the Tourism Authority – Room 107 in the 3-storey grey office block over the road from the *Laohung Hotel* – and tell its director, Mr Lamphan, how long you plan to stay and where you intend to go. For a fee of 2,000 kip he will write a letter of permission which local officials will probably ask to see if you travel outside Xam Neua. He will suggest that you be accompanied by a Lao person wherever you go, although it is possible to travel around the province on your own using local transport. Mr Lamphan doesn't speak English but he knows what tourists want, so sign language and a phrase book should suffice if your Lao isn't up to scratch. He will also organize transport around the province if you wish.

Nam Tok Dat Salari is an excellent waterfall which zig-zags 100m down a rock face, 36 km along Highway 6 to

Nam Neun, visible on the left 3 km after the village of Ban Doan. This might sound rather convoluted, but the falls are difficult to miss as there are numerous empty houses and stalls by the road, used once a year by much of the population of Xam Neua when it decamps en masse to celebrate Pimai (Lao New Year) at the site. A track leads through the jungle on the right of the falls right to the top – a very good swimming and picnic spot.

Xam Tai lies 100 km to the SE of Xam Neua, close to the Vietnamese border. It is the most famous weaving centre in the area, and is also said to be scenically beautiful. The road is bad and there is no guesthouse at Xam Tai. *Getting there*: arrange transport through Mr Lamphan at the *Laohung Hotel*.

Sop Hao, 60 km E on the Vietnam border, features a trade fair each Sat. However, the town and the fair are currently barred to foreigners and the border is also closed although there is some talk in Vientiane of this border crossing being the next to open.

Local information
● **Accommodation**
D-E *Laohung*, name not marked in English, next to the bridge over the Nam Xam facing the market, formerly the *Sam Neua* or *No 1 Guesthouse*, now privately run and gradually improving, doubles with or without attached bath, rooms vary from grubby downstairs to semiclean upstairs, ensuite bathrooms are filthy, communal bathrooms a little better, squat toilets and baths using bucket-and-scoop technology, pleasant view of the town and hills from upstairs, friendly staff, restaurant (not operating at time of writing), watch out for rats.

F *Dok Dai Mieng Guesthouse*, on the main road facing the market area, 2 and 3-bed dormitory accommodation, priced per bed, shared bath and squat loo, basic; **F** *Phanxay*, on the main road just after it turns half left away from the market area, dormitory accommodation, rooms with 2 to 4 beds are priced per bed, rooms have attached bath, moderately clean, light, more spacious than the other dormitory options, restaurant; **F** *Phoulong Guesthouse*, up the road from the *Dok Dai Mieng*, doubles

and one single, 1,500 kip a bed, shared bath and squat toilet, accommodation cramped.

● **Places to eat**
◆◆◆Mr Lamphan of the Tourist Office and his wife operate a small restaurant serving Xam Neua food at their house immediately behind the *Laohung Hotel* on Highway 6, homely atmosphere, reasonable food, place dinner orders in the afternoon.

◆◆*Phanxay Hotel Restaurant*, fair Lao and Chinese food, none too clean.

◆Many noodle shops in the market area along the street adjacent to the river, of which *Joy's Place* (sign in English) is the best.

● **Banks & money changers**
Arounmay Bank, halfway along the main street, changes US$.

● **Post & telecommunications**
There is a **post office** on the main street and a new **telephone exchange** behind it offering long distance facilities.

● **Useful addresses**
Police station: next to the telephone exchange – follow the dirt road that leads off the main street beside the post office, registration is advisable and costs 100 kip at the Immigration section.

● **Transport**
Air Thrice weekly flights from Vientiane, 1 hr 15 mins, US$71 one way. The airport is 3 km from the centre of town on the road that leads to Vieng Xai and Vietnam, 300 kip in a tuk-tuk. All flights are subject to delay or cancellation due to the area's susceptibility to fog, especially during winter. An ancient Antonov II biplane designed for paratroopers but operated commercially by Air Lao makes irregular runs into Xam Neua from Vientiane and will occasionally fly passengers out to other towns depending on how many fares it can gather; prices negotiable (which tells you what sort of operation they run). The tyres are flat and oil leaks from the engine. Not for nervous fliers.

Road Passenger trucks leave daily for Nam Neun, where there are daily connections to Phonsavanh and, less regularly, to Nam Bak. 6-8 hrs Xam Neua-Nam Neun, 3,500 kip, depart 0530 opp the post office; 6 hrs Nam Neun-Phonsavanh, 4,000 kip. It's difficult to avoid staying overnight in Nam Neun, 3,500 kip for a room, take some food as only noodles are available at the town.

VIENG XAI (VIENGSAY)

Hua Phan and Phongsali Provinces were the base areas for left wing insurgency from the late 1940s until the final victory of the Pathet Lao over the royalist forces in 1975. From 1964 onwards operations were directed from the cave systems at Vieng Xai, which proved an effective refuge from furious bombing attacks. At the height of the war, thousands of soldiers, government officials and their families occupied the valley at Vieng Xai, and more operated from the surrounding region. The spectacular limestone karsts of the area are riddled with natural caves. Many were enlarged to create living quarters, offices, garages, supply depots, hospitals, schools and ammunition dumps. In the runup to the fall of Vientiane there was even talk among the Pathet Lao leadership of making Vieng Xai an alternative capital, but this idea was dropped after 1975.

Members of the Lao Issara who had fled to Vietnam after French forces smashed the movement in 1946 infiltrated areas of NE Laos in 1947-49 under the sponsorship of the Viet Minh. The movement coalesced when Prince Souphanouvong, who had fled to Thailand, arrived in Hanoi and organized a conference in Aug 1950 at which the Free Lao Front and the Lao Resistance Government were formed. Thereafter, the Pathet Lao adopted strategies developed by the Viet Minh in Vietnam, who in turn drew on the strategies of Mao Zedong and the Chinese Communists: the establishment of bases in remote mountain areas, use of guerrilla tactics, exploitation of the dissatisfactions of tribal minorities, and mobilization of the entire populations of liberated areas in support of the revolutionary struggle.

By the time of the Geneva Agreement of 1954 following the French defeat at Dien Bien Phu, Communist forces effectively controlled Hua Phan and Phongsali, a fact acknowledged in the terms of the settlement, which called for their regroupment inside these provinces pending a political settlement. The Pathet Lao used the breathing space afforded by this and the succession of coalition governments in the late 1950s and early 60s to reorganize their operations. The Lao People's Revolutionary Party was formed at Xam Neua in 1955, and the Neo Lao Hak Sat, or National Front was established in 1956. While Party President Prince Souphanouvong spent a good deal of time in Vientiane participating in successive coalition governments between 1958 and 1964, Secretary-General Kaysone Phomvihane remained in Hua Phan overseeing the political and military organization of the liberated zone.

The beginning of the American bombing campaign in 1964 forced the Pathet Lao leadership to find a safe haven from which to direct the war. Vieng Xai was chosen because its numerous limestone karsts contained many natural caves which could be used for quarters, while their proximity to each other inhibited attack from the air. Nevertheless, phosphorous rockets and napalm caused many casualties in the less fortified caves.

Previously, the valley had been home only to two small villages, Ban Bac and Nakay. The Pathet Lao leadership renamed the area Vieng Xai, meaning 'City of Victory', and it became the administrative and military hub of the revolutionary struggle. The first bombing raid on the area took place in 1965, and the caves were enlarged and reinforced with concrete during 1965, 1966 and 1967.

Places of interest

Five **caves**, those formerly occupied by senior Pathet Lao leaders Prince Souphanouvong, Kaysone Phomvihan, Nouhak Phounsavanh, Khamtai Siphandon and Phoumi Vongvichit, are officially open to tourists, and the valley contains many other poignant reminders of the struggle. There is less war debris around than in Xieng Khouang, with the ubiquitous cluster bomb casings the most obvious example. The setting is a delight, with crags jutting vertically from fields of snooker-table green, and it is worth spending more time there than the one day required to see the caves. At present the site is rundown, having had virtually no maintenance since 1976, but moves have been underway to restore it since Kaysone's death in 1992, and some preliminary work has been done.

The **village of Vieng Xai** is 31 km E of Xam Neua on a road that branches off Route 6 to Sop Hao on the Vietnam border. The turnoff to the right is at Km 20. Built in 1973 when the bombing finally stopped and the short-lived Provisional Government of National Union was negotiated, the former capital of the liberated zone is an unlikely sight. Surrounded by rice fields at the dead end of a potholed road, it features street lighting, power lines, sealed and kerbed streets and substantial public buildings – all in varying stages of decay. In the display window of an abandoned department store, a single manequin still models a dusty sin and blouse. Just before the market and truckstop, a wonderful socialist-realist statue in gold-painted concrete pays tribute to those three pillars of the revolution: the farmer, the soldier and the worker. The worker has one boot firmly planted on a bomb inscribed 'USA'.

The main street divides as it reaches the top of the village to form a town 'square' which is in fact a triangle. At the apex is a war monument topped by a red star, and along the base, a yellow 2-storey building houses government offices. The road that forms the southern side of the triangle leads past this building to the caves of Kaysone and Nouhak, while the road along the northern edge leads to the caves of Souphanouvong and Phoumi. Go right on the road along the base of the triangle to reach Khamtai's cave and what was once a recreation area, behind a sports ground featuring a derelict grandstand.

All the caves are within walking distance of the village, but you must be accompanied by the attendant, who can be found at the government office on the square. Admission is 2,000 kip per cave. Kaysone's, Souphanouvong's and Khamtai's are the most impressive, but it is worth seeing all five. The attendant carries a kerosene lamp but it's a good idea to bring your own torch.

Each cave burrows deep into the mountainside and all of them feature 60 cm-thick concrete walls, living quarters, meeting rooms, offices, dining and storage areas. All but Khamtai's include an outside kitchen and at least two exits. Each cave also contains a centrally-located 'emergency room', installed in case of a gas attack or similar eventuality. This consists of a fully sealed concrete bunker with room for 10 to 20 people, in the corner of which can be found the remains of a hand-cranked oxygen pump of Soviet manufacture. Below and outside the entrance to each cave, buildings house additional accommodation and meeting rooms. The occupants of the caves slept in these buildings, as raids rarely took place at night.

Until recently the original furniture and other items including books, maps and papers remained in the caves. The site is now slated for restoration under the the auspices of the Kaysone Memorial Fund and almost all the furniture has been removed, leaving the caves bare. Restoration work is due to begin in 1997, although some work has already been done on Nouhak's cave, which suffers extensively from seepage.

To the right of the path leading to **Souphanouvong's cave** stands a pink stupa, the tomb of the prince's son, who was captured and beaten to death by infiltrators a few kilometres away in 1967 at the age of 28. Inside the room used by the attendant below the cave, an ancient black and white photograph of Souphanouvong with Khruschev is stuck to the wall, while the next building contains a makeshift memorial to the prince decorated with a few dusty souvenirs of the USSR. Souphanouvong and Phoumi's caves both feature a 'garage cave' at the base of the karst, a cavity in the limestone large enough to accommodate a car. An interesting feature of Kaysone's cave is a long, narrow passage which connects the living quarters to a large meeting area which includes emergency accommodation for dozens of guests.

Khamtai's cave is slightly different from the others. The first thing the visitor notices is a set of three bomb craters within metres of the entrance to the cave. The craters, now overgrown, are so close together they almost touch. Possibly inspired by their arrival, the entrance is shielded by an enormous, tapering slab of concrete, 4.5m high and nearly 2m wide at the base. Inside, the cave is darker and more claustrophobic than the others, with no outside areas. The attendant may or may not lead you through a thick steel door at the bottom of some stairs well inside the cave. It gives access to a staircase which descends steeply before ending in a sheer drop of several metres to the floor of an underground theatrette.

A small distance from Khamtai's cave, and included in its entry price, is the large and obvious entrance to what is known as **Tam Xang Lot**, or 'cave that an elephant can walk through'. This natural cavern was used as a theatre, complete with stage, arch, orchestra pit and a concrete floor with space for an audience of several hundred. At the opposite end from the stage, a long passage featuring a number of stalactites and lit by daylight connects to the theatrette below Khamtai's cave.

There is also a **small museum** in Vieng Xai village, behind the gold statue, which contains some interesting old photographs, many of them unlabelled. Ask the attendant to show it to you if he doesn't offer of his own accord.

There are many abandoned caves around Vieng Xai which were obviously used during the war and at least one, on the left past Phoumi's cave, is quite extensive. The wisdom of fossicking about in them, given the attitude of local authorities, is debatable; unexploded bombs must also be assumed to be a risk whenever walking off the beaten track.

A conservation survey of the area in 1982 identified 95 caves of historical significance. Included in these was a former hospital complex approximately 15 km from Vieng Xai, and a cave housing a school for children of government officials at Ban Bac. A separate cave complex at Hang Long, 25 km from Xam Neua, housed the provincial government during the war years, but is now completely abandoned.

Excursions

There is a fairly spectacular **waterfall** 8 km before Vieng Xai. 3 km after the turnoff from Route 6, a swift stream passes under a steel and concrete bridge. A path just before the bridge leads off to the left, following the river downstream. It takes just a few minutes to reach the top of the waterfall, but the path leads all the way to the bottom, about 20 mins' walk. Swimming is not advised.

Local information
● **Accommodation**

If you stay overnight at Vieng Xai the only accommodation is at the *Viengsay Guesthouse*, which is as atmospheric as many of the other sites in the valley. Following the road that leads to Khamtai's cave but turning left at the football field, the hotel is the first building on the left. The guesthouse is the mouldering remnant of what were once comfortable quarters for visiting dignitaries, and has been slated for renovation in anticipation of more tourist arrivals.

E *Viengsay Guesthouse* (see above), extremely rundown but offers a few threadbare comforts, silk bedspreads and teasets in some rooms evoke past splendour, superb setting amid eucalypt and Norfolk Island pines with views of surrounding karsts, doubles and triples 5,000 kip, ask for an upstairs room, common bath, food, beer and cigarettes available, no electricity.

● **Places to eat**
♦♦*Viengsay Guesthouse*, will prepare breakfast, lunch and dinner if you ask them far enough in advance, fare plentiful but unexciting, vegetarians be prepared for lots of steamed choko and boiled eggs.

♦Basic noodles at the market.

● **Useful addresses**
Police station: behind the disused department store on the town square.

● **Transport**
31 km from Xam Neua.

Road Pickups and passenger trucks shuttle all day between Xam Neua and Vieng Xai, ask around the market, 700 kip one way, 60-90 mins. Alternatively, Mr Lamphan in Xam Neua will organize a car and driver for US$40 return.

NAM OU ROUTE

MUANG NGOY (NONG KHIAW)

Muang Ngoy lies NE of Nam Bak and is a delightful little village on the banks of the Nam Ou, surrounded by limestone peaks. It is possible to swim in the river (women should wear sarongs) or walk around the town or up the cliffs. The bridge across the Nam Ou offers fine views and photo opportunities.

● **Accommodation F** Very basic hotel by the river, where the boats leave and songthaews stop, food available, one dormitory room is the sum total of the accommodation, the toilet is a hole in the floor of an outside hut, the bath is the river, small mattress on the floor, mosquito nets; **F** *Siamphai Guesthouse*, comparable to the preceding, but with proper squat toilets, mosquito nets, disinterested service, poor food.

● **Useful addresses Immigration**: by the boat station, registration 100 kip.

● **Useful information Electricity**: 1800-2200.

● **Transport** It is far more convenient and pleasant to travel between Luang Prabang and Muang Ngoy by boat, than by bus. The river passes mountains, teak plantations, dry rice fields and a movable water wheel mounted on a boat, which moves from village to village and is used for milling. **Road Songthaew**: to Nam Bak and on to Udom Xai, it may be necessary to change pick-ups in Pak Mong, 1 hr (500 kip) – there is a small noodle shop here – from Pak Mong to Udom Xai takes 2½ hrs (2,000 kip). **Truck**: it is possible (but it isn't easy) to travel E from Muang Ngoy on Highway 1 to Nam Nuan and from there either turn S down Highway 6 or continue E to Xam Neua. Trucks are infrequent and the road is

very poor, so be prepared to wait a long time. **Boat** To Luang Prabang (0730-0800), 5-6 hrs (3,500 kip for locals) for the slow boat, 4 hrs (7,000 kip) for the fast boat. To Muang Khua, slow boats leave between 0700-0800 and 1500-1700, 6,000 kip for a slow boat, 4-5 hrs, if you take the afternoon boat be prepared to sleep in the boat. There are usually a few fast boats available, prices negotiable depending on the number of passengers, starting at 10,000 kip/head. Note that many boat owners expect foreigners to pay more; if you wish to pay the local rate be very patient and calm.

NAM BAK

The town of Nam Bak lies on the banks of the Nam Bak. It is a rather beautiful place and is worth an overnight stop, on the route N. The market is interesting in the very early morning, when hill people including Blue Hmong converge to sell exotic birds, insects, bats, and other forest species. There is a small wat on the left at the end of town as you come from Muang Ngoy, called Wat Tiom Tian.

The road on to Udom Xai is particularly beautiful, passing Blue Hmong villages.

● **Accommodation F** Big blue house with shutters, set on a hill in the centre of town, (the bus/truck driver will point it out), shared toilets, beautiful views, all Lao and Chinese customers, hardly used by tourists as there are better options now for the same price; **F** *Boun Thieme Guesthouse*, at opp end of town from the market, double and triple rooms, mosquito nets provided, not as clean or friendly as *Vanmisay*; **F** *Vanmisay Guesthouse*, doubles and triples, basic service, clean, mosquito nets provided, toilet and bathrooms outside, bath uses bucket and scoop.

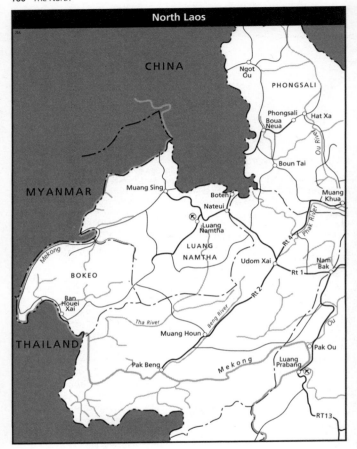

North Laos

- **Places to eat** Noodle shops.

- **Useful addresses Immigration**: in front of *Vanmisay Guesthouse*, 100 kip registration.

- **Useful information Electricity**: 1800-2300.

- **Transport** 94 km from Udom Xai. **Road Bus/truck**: 1 hr from Muang Ngoy by truck, good road. The trucks wait for the boats to arrive from Luang Prabang and Muang Khua, 1,000 kip. Trucks leave Nam Bak for Muang Ngoy around 0700, otherwise during the day when they're full, be prepared to wait around for a few hours. Regular connections with Luang Prabang; the bus leaves from Luang Prabang when full (0700-0800) from just before the Srisavangvong Bridge, outside Wat Munna, 8 hrs (3,000 kip). The road runs parallel with the river for most of the journey; a dusty ride. Buses to Udom Xai leave throughout the day; be prepared to wait a couple of hours, 3,000 kip. From the intersection in Udom Xai, take a pick-up truck to Muang Khua

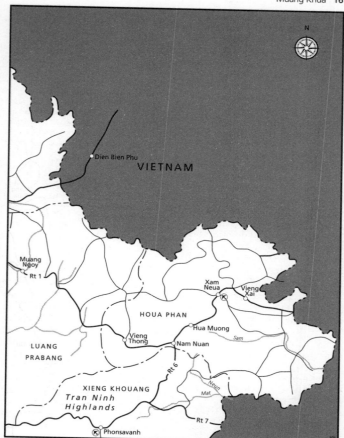

(90 km), 4 hrs (2,000 kip). Very few people use the road between Nam Bak and Xam Neua; it is very rough and vehicles are infrequent.

MUANG KHUA

Muang Khua is situated in the southern part of the province of Phongsali. Being at the junction of the Nam Ou and Nam Phak, the town has long been a crossroads between Vietnam and Laos. A French garrison was based in Muang Khua until 1954, when it was ousted by Vietnamese troops in the aftermath of the battle at Dien Bien Phu. For a brief period from 1958, Polish and Canadian officials of the Comite International de Controle were quartered in the town to monitor the ceasefire between the Pathet Lao and the Royal Lao government. Nowadays, Muang Khua is home to a burgeoning market in Vietnamese goods, trucked in from Dien Bien Phu.

It's a small town with two 'hotels' and very few restaurants. What it lacks in restaurants, it makes up for in pool tables; very small children show a frightening aptitude. Be prepared to have an instant audience if you try your hand. There is usually a box in which you are expected to make a donation.

There is a 30m wood and iron pedestrian suspension bridge across the Nam Phak to a small village on the other side. Excellent views up and down the river but as the bridge tends to wobble, it is not for the vertiginous.

It is an attractive town to walk about, but be prepared for a group of children to join you on your saunter. The morning market sells fresh vegetables and meat, some Akha women come to the market. The goldsmith just off the main square is usually surrounded by a small group watching his very delicate work. There is a small new wat.

Excursions The Akha are the main hilltribe in the area. The nearest villages are 20 km out of town; you will need a guide if you want to visit them.

● **Accommodation F** *Chinese hotel*, up the hill from the boat station, on the left, 3 to 4 beds per room, mosquito nets, dirty, no food, shared bathroom with squat toilets and showers, the building looks like it's been under construction for 20 years; **F** *Muang Khua Guesthouse*, up the hill from the boat station at the intersection with the main street, attached bathrooms and toilets, not very clean.

● **Places to eat** Baguettes can be bought for a few hours in the morning from an old lady in the market, and again in the evening half way down the steep road to the Nam Ou. Next to this is the only place that sells hot coffee. Noodles in the market.

● **Useful addresses Immigration**: in a little hut on the main square, registration 200 kip. On arrival, officials will want to see your passport.

● **Transport Road** The road that parallels the river N to Phongsali is very rough and should be avoided. Another little used road which goes NW is also rough, but is rather beautiful as it goes through the mountains, at least 3 hrs (1,500 kip). To Udom Xai about 4 hrs, a beautiful ride on a reasonably good road, pickups leave 0700-0800 from the Police Immigration office and later in the day if you're prepared to wait around, 3,000 kip. **Boat** Ferry boats travel N and S, leaving 0700-0800. To Phongsali in the N, approx 6 hrs (8,000 kip for a slow boat; 9,000-15,000 kip pp for a fast boat, depending on number of passengers and your bargaining skills); a beautiful journey, especially for bird-watching, with kingfishers everywhere. It is quite shallow in places, and there is also quite a lot of white water. Take a blanket. Boats stop at Hat Xa, just to the NE of Phongsali. A jeep or truck transports travellers to town, 20 km but 1½-2 hrs along a very bad road, especially in the rainy season. Try to get to Hat Xa before mid-afternoon, as the villagers are getting sick of having to put up foreigners who have missed the last truck to Phongsali, the road is OK (1,500 kip). For boats to Muang Ngoy – travel time is 4-5 hrs and the whole boat would cost 30,000 kip, if there are not enough passengers.

PHONGSALI

High up in the mountains, this northern provincial capital provides beautiful views. Phongsali was one of the first areas to be liberated by the Pathet Lao in the late 1940s. The old post office (just in front of the new one) is the sole physical reminder of French rule. The architecture is a strange mix of the Chinese post-revolutionary concrete style, Lao houses of wood and brick with tin roofs, and bamboo or mud huts with straw roofs. The Chinese influence is very prominent here, mainly since the new road network linked the town with the border. The town has a very different feel to the southern towns, new Chinese shophouses are under construction and the roofs are mainly corrugated iron. It is possible to buy apples, pears and even potatoes here – the few restaurants along the only tarmaced road sell chips; a welcome relief after days of *feu*. The rice is steamed rather than sticky.

The area is a potpourri of ethnicities, with between 22 and 26 minorities inhabiting the area, depending on how you define them. The principal groups are the Phou Noi, Akha, Lu, Yunnanese and Lao Seng. A small museum in front of the *Seang Fa Hotel* displays hilltribe costumes and photographs. Opening hours are erratic, but if you go there during the week and ask around, someone will probably open it for you. The town itself is home to about 20,000 people, mostly Lao, Phou Noi and Chinese. Anyone wishing to visit hilltribe villages is well advised to enlist a guide in Luang Prabang, as there are no travel agencies in Phongsali and transport options are very limited – the town boasts only one taxi.

Phongsali is especially beautiful from Jan to Mar, when wildflowers and opium poppies bloom in the surrounding hills. The town is at an altitude of 1,628m, and can be cold at any time of the year – take some warm clothes. Mornings tend to be foggy.

Many paths lead out of town over the hills; the walking is easy and the views are spectacular. It is not possible to hire bikes, tuk-tuks or even ponies; there is little to do other than walk. There are a few pool tables in town and a basketball pitch in the centre of town (play commences around 1700).

• **Accommodation** D-E *Seang Fa*, Chinese monstrosity, very nr the *Phou Fa*, price negotiable for longer stays, dormitory beds (**F**), all rooms have shared bathroom, mosquito nets provided, no English or Lao spoken, only Chinese, good restaurant; **F** *Lucksoon*, through town opp the new 3-storey Chinese shophouses, it is a 2-floored wooden house, with a good restaurant downstairs (groups of men come here to eat and drink every night – it is best to arrange dinner for earlier in the day, ask for chips in advance – they are worth it), 4 rm with 3 beds in each. Shared bathroom, no electricity, small balcony overlooks the street, the best of the 3, despite the mice and rats, just in front of the *Seang Fa*, very friendly people who will ply you with lau lao and beer, otherwise extremely basic; **F** *Phou Fa*, just past *Seang Fa* on left, up on the hill, overlooking town, good views but it looks and feels like a concentration camp, very dirty, unwelcoming atmosphere.

• **Places to eat** The restaurant at the **Seang Fa** has good food, french fries, stuffed crepes, omelettes etc, no menu. The **Lucksoon** also has a restaurant, cheap and good.

• **Post & telecommunications Post Office**: red roofed building at the end of the main road in town (heading towards China), no sign, but it is just past the new shophouses, on the other side of the road. Only a radio phone is available so international calls are not possible.

• **Useful addresses Immigration**: in a grey and blue concrete building to the right after the *Seang Fa Hotel* as you go uphill away from the road to Hat Xa, closed Sat and Sun.

• **Useful information Electricity**: from 1800-2200.

• **Transport** The Chinese border on the road W from Phongsali is only open for Lao and Chinese; this does not appear likely to change in the near future. **Air**: there is no passenger service to Phongsali, as the airport is solely for military helicopters. **Road Bus**: all buses leave early (0730-0800), from next to the *Lucksoon Hotel*. Buses to Hat Xa leave 0700-0730 from in front of the *Seang Fa Hotel*, if you miss them you may have to wait another day. The road to Udom Xai is in very bad condition, especially the first third from Phongsali to Boun Tai, and is closed from the beginning of rainy season until Nov. About 7 hrs to Udom Xai. There is an elephant farm near, Km 14; elephants can sometimes be seen from the road. **Boat** Take a truck to Hat Xa, boats leave in the morning for Muang Khua, 4-5 hrs (5,000 kip). It can be cold and wet – wear waterproofs if you have them.

THE WESTERN ROUTE

PAK BENG

This long thin strip of village is perched half way up a hill, with fine views over the Mekong. There is not much to do here but it makes a stop-over point for the journey to Ban Houei Xai from Luang Prabang; the village is worth a visit for its traditional atmosphere and the friendliness of the locals. There's a good place to swim in the dry season, just downstream from the port – but be careful as the current is strong.

● **Accommodation** **E** *Soukchareun Sarika*, a wooden hotel on the steep cliff overlooking the river, basic facilities, but rooms are clean, mosquito nets provided, great toilet and shower area on the edge of the cliff – probably the best view from a bathroom in the whole of Laos; **F** *Phuvieng*, a little further up the road, basic, half wooden, half concrete house with shared bathrooms.

● **Places to eat** 4 or 5 places opp the hotel serving a good selection of Lao food (and a good range of beers and whiskys).

● **Entertainment** 3 pool tables, one small 'cinema' – more a television really, showing Lao and Thai movies.

● **Useful addresses Immigration**: it is important to get entry and exit stamps at the police station. The police station is open Mon-Fri 0730-1200, 1400-1630.

● **Useful information Electricity**: available from 1800-2300.

● **Transport Road Bus/songthaew**: buses leave from the jetty or the hotel for the route northwards to Muang Houn and Udom Xai in the mornings, 5-7 hrs (3,500 kip). There is no road between Pak Beng and Ban Houei Xai. **Boat** Slow boat to Ban Houei Xai leaves at 0800 sharp from the port and takes all day (4,000 kip). Fast boats to Luang Prabang and to Ban Houei Xai.

MUANG HOUN

This is a new town (although it looks as old as any other), built in 1986 by the government to entice hill people down from the hills, in an attempt to stop them growing opium. There are a lot of Blue Hmong in town.

● **Accommodation** **F** A 2-storey concrete house, with a little balcony upstairs, electricity in the evenings until 2200 (the hotel is rather proud of its electricity and there are fairy lights all over the place), no restaurant but good indoor bathroom to share, good value.

● **Places to eat** Two places in town, selling noodles, eggs and sticky rice.

● **Transport Road Bus**: regular buses to Pak Beng, 2 hrs (1,000 kip) from opp the main restaurant past the market.

UDOM XAI (MUANG XAI, OUDOM XAI)

Udom Xai is a hot and dusty town, but it makes a good stop off point N or S. This provincial capital was razed during the war and the inhabitants fled to live in the surrounding hills; what is there now has been built since 1975. Since the early 1990s the town has been experiencing an economic boom as a result of its position on the intersection of roads linking China, Vietnam, Luang Prabang and Pak Beng, and commerce and construction are thriving. The **market** here is second to none, with a huge variety of fresh goods – honeycombs, limes, lots of *kanom*, papayas etc. A good place to stock up on food and have lunch. The village of **Ban Ting**, behind Udom Xai is interesting to wander through and the wat just the other side of the stream has a ruined monastery. The wat at Ban Ting now includes quite a bizarre attraction – a life-size tree made of concrete featuring tin leaves, concrete animals in the fiolage and two concrete reclining Buddhas on the topmost branches. The wat also includes a Buddhist high school for monks, and offers a good view of the town and surrounding mountains.

Excursions Ban Mok Kho is a Hmong village 16 km along Route 1 to Nam Bak where the inhabitants wear traditional dress and live in longhouses. Catch a ride on a pickup going to Nam Bak, or negotiate a price with a taxi or tuk-tuk.

● **Accommodation** **C** *Sing Tong*, reservations: T (071) 212813, T/F in Vientiane (021) 412686, opp the market on the main street, attached bath and western toilet, towels and soap provided, no hot water yet but promised, restaurant serves European breakfast, hotel has its own generator which is turned on whenever the disco is in use, so electricity sometimes goes beyond 2200; **D** *Sai Xi*, by the market, some rooms with bathroom attached, a basic Chinese establishment with good views of the town and hills beyond from the roof, **F** for dormitory beds, shared bathroom and toilet; **E** *Phet Muang Nuan Guesthouse*, downhill from the market on the main road, turn left before the bridge, attached toilet and bathroom, ask for a room with a balcony, the owner is a friendly old woman who speaks no English; **E** *Saithivong*, attached bathroom, currently undergoing extensions, friendly people; **E** *Vong Prachith*, attached bathroom, friendly, good restaurant here; **F** *Chienxaip-ingkouane*, the ugliest hotel in town, only Chinese spoken, shared bath, extremely dirty; **F** *Phouxai*, downhill on the main street from the market and across the bridge, turn right after the petrol station, there is a sign at the petrol station, attached shower and toilet, nice garden with sitting area, there is a monkey in a cage but at least the cage is quite big, friendly service, good food, clean rooms, quietest part of town, probably the best of the budget options; **F** *Yang Lou Guesthouse*, in the centre of town on the main street, some with attached bathrooms, friendly service. **F** There are two cheaper guesthouses on the same street, just before the *Phouxai Hotel*.

- **Places to eat** ♦♦*Thanoonsin*, friendly service, menu in English, good basic Lao food; ♦*Si Muang* and *San Souk* both offer good Lao food, no menu but you can request dishes. All restaurants are in front of the market. *The Sing Tong Hotel* restuarant serves proper European breakfast incl eggs, bread, orange juice, cheese, jam (expensive). Stalls in front of the market sell beer and snacks from nightfall.

- **Banks & money changers** Lane Xang Bank, downhill from the market on the main street on the left after 5 mins walk, changes US$ cash.

- **Post & telecommunications** Opposite the *Sai Xi Hotel*, uphill from the market. International calls available.

- **Useful addresses Immigration**: in front of Lane Xang Bank, registration is free.

- **Useful information Electricity**: from 1800 to 2200, but is expected to run 24 hrs as of Dec 1996 when the town is connected to the grid.

- **Transport Air** Connections 5 days a week to Vientiane and Luang Prabang. A larger airport is under construction, due for completion by the end of 1996. Some connections a week with Luang Prabang. Some flights go via Ban Houei Xai. From Luang Prabang there are multiple daily flights to Vientiane. Two direct connections between Udom Xai and Vientiane

each week, currently on Wed and Sat. **Road Bus/truck/songthaew**: buses for the S to Muang Houn and Pak Beng (6 hrs) leave from the main crossroads, nr the market at about 1400 (2,000 kip). Attractive journey through a valley with paddy fields and many villages, on a good road. From here, there are boat connections on to Ban Houei Sai west or Luang Prabang east (8 hrs). Pickups to Nateui, Boten and Luang Namtha depart 0700-0800, 5 hrs, 8,000 kip. The road passes Lao Su and Hmong villages. Buses depart fairly frequently for Muang Ngoy and Nam Bak, 3,000 kip. **International connections with China**: buses leave for the border at Boten (2,500 kip). For information on crossing into China, see page 291.

NATEUI

Stopover town for truck drivers making the drive from Luang Prabang to Mengla (in China). At the weekend, the border handles no commercial traffic, so truck-drivers sleep in their cars, or in one of the two simple guesthouses.

- **Accommodation F** Guesthouse on the main road, no traffic in the evening – so it is quiet, quite good food.

- **Transport** 80 km from Udom Xai, 18 km from Boten. Pick-ups infrequent to Namtha and Udom Xai. **International connections**: the border with China is open for international traffic, but no Chinese visas can be obtained here. Coming from China, it might be possible to acquire a Lao visa at immigration here.

LUANG NAMTHA

Luang Namtha is yet another town that was obliterated during the war, and the concrete structures erected since 1975 have little charm. The main attraction is the food market, where members of the many minorities which inhabit the area can be found trading exotic species. Principal minorities include Thai Lu, Thai Dam, Lang Ten, Hmong and Khamu.

Excursions Ban Nam Chang is a Lang Ten village 3 km walk along a footpath outside town. Ask your way. The Lang Ten women are easily recognized – they wear their hair back, and pluck their eyebrows when they turn 15, keeping them plucked from then on. Their clothes are black with coloured borders, and they wear a lot of delicate silver jewellery.

Ban Lak Khamay is quite a large Akha village 27 km from Luang Namtha on the road to Muang Sing. It was resettled from a nearby location higher in the hills in 1994 as part of government policy to protect upland forests. The community now grows teak and rubber trees commercially. The village chief speaks Lao. The settlement features a traditional Akha entrance; if you pass through this entrance you must visit a house in the village, or you are considered an enemy. Otherwise you can simply pass to one side of the gate. Other features of interest in Akha villages are the swing, at the highest point in the village and used in the annual swing festival, and the meeting house, where unmarried couples go to meet, and where newly married couples live until they have their own house. There is another, smaller Akha village a few kilometres towards Muang Sing.

● **Accommodation D** *Hongtha Xaysonboun*, toilet and bath attached, nice garden area, nightclub attached so it can be noisy at night, friendly people, own generator providing power until midnight, good restaurant but quite pricey; **F** *Big Chinese hotel*, nr the market, you might get a room if the staff aren't busy playing GO when you arrive; **F** *Hanbao Restaurant and Guesthouse*, nr the market on the same side of the street, dormitory accommodation, shared smelly toilet and bucket and scoop bath; **F** *Small Chinese hotel*, in front of the market by the bus stop, shared bathroom, dirty, good restaurant.

● **Places to eat** The ♦♦*Hongtha Xaysonboun Hotel* has a restaurant with English menu, good Lao and Chinese food. The ♦*small Chinese hotel* in front of the market by the bus stop has a restaurant with good, cheap Chinese food, French bread and croissants are available in the food market behind the main market. *Feu* stalls by the main market and the bus stop.

● **Airline offices** Lao Aviation office, in-

side departure hall at the airport, 7 km from town. Book flights 1 day in advance.

● **Banks & money changers** Lane Xang Bank, in the centre of town takes TCs but at a sizeable commission, and will change US$ cash, Chinese yuan and Thai baht. An exchange in the market changes US$, yuan and baht.

● **Tour companies & travel agents** *Luang Namtha Travel Service*, on main road.

● **Useful addresses Immigration**: in front of Lao Aviation at the opp end of town from the highway, in a military barracks. You must wear long trousers when you go for registration, neither men or women are permitted to enter if they are wearing shorts. Registration is free.

● **Useful information Electricity**: 1800-2200.

● **Transport Air** Small planes fly twice a week to Vientiane, Luang Prabang and Ban Houei Xai, Wed and Sat, 33,800 kip to Ban Houei Xai, 31,300 kip to Luang Prabang, 73,600 kip to Vientiane via Luang Prabang. There are no direct flights to Vientiane. The airport is 7 km from town – 3,000 kip by tuk-tuk. **Road** Pickups leave frequently for Boten on the Chinese border via Nateui, 1½ hrs, you need a Chinese visa to cross into China. This stretch of road is one of the more enjoyable bits of travelling in Laos. To Muang Sing, 2 hrs (2,000 kip), pickups depart throughout the day. To Udom Xai (4,000 kip), 4-5 hrs, departures throughout the day. The road to Ban Houei Xai is unpaved and potholed. 15 hrs by pick-up in dry season almost impossible during rainy season. **Boat** It is said to be possible to catch a fast boat from a point on the Namtha 7 km from Luang Namtha, to the Mekong. There you have to change boats in order to travel N to Ban Houei Xai. The boats are quite expensive at about 50,000 kip for a boat just to the Mekong.

MUANG SING

Many visitors consider this peaceful valley to be one of the highlights of the N. Lying at the terminus of the highway in the far NW corner of Laos, it is a natural point to stop and spend a few days recovering from the rigours of the road, before either heading S or moving on to China.

NB There is a road that leads directly from Muang Sing to the Chinese border – but it is closed to foreigners. Boten is still the only point where people who are neither Lao nor Chinese may cross.

Muang Sing itself is little more than a village, situated on a picturesque plateau at an elevation of about 1,200m. The town features some interesting old wooden buildings; an old French fort is now off limits to visitors, as it is occupied by the army. The market is worth a look early in the morning (it starts about 0545), for Akha and other hilltribes. It is definitely worth getting there before 0730, as it starts to wind down after that. Most Buddhist temples in the vicinity are Thai Lu style. The town is predominantly Thai Lu but the population of the district is 50% Akha, a further 10% are Thai Nua. The area around Muang Sing is home to many minorities who have been resettled, either from refugee camps in Thailand or from highland areas of Laos; the population of the district trebled between 1992 and 1996. As a result, it is one of the few places in northern Laos where hilltribe villages are readily accessible. The main activity for visitors is to hire bicycles and visit the villages which surround the town in all directions. There are several international projects working there – there is a German Centre (GTZ) in town, where displays of the project's aims are on view.

Excursions At Km 103, turn right into a dirt-road, after 1½ km, you'll come to a Yao village and on the other hill, after another 10-min walk, there is an Akha village. Back on the main road, at Km 106, there is a boundary post/checkpoint – Pangthong Checkpoint – which is 10 km from Muang Sing. The border is only open for Lao and Chinese. It is sometimes possible to go by pick-up the 4 km to the Chinese border. Advice for visiting hilltribe villages: it is better not to visit in late afternoon; this seems to be a private time and should be respected.

● **Accommodation**   E *Singxai Guest-*

house, just behind the market, doubles and triples, attached bath with squat toilet and shower, mosquito nets, slow service but rooms fairly clean, in a beautiful spot by paddy fields; **F** *Sangdaeone*, at the far end of town from the bus stop, shared bathroom outside, rooms have iron doors which make the place resemble a dungeon, nice view from the roof; **F** *Seng Thong Guesthouse* and *Viengxai Guesthouse* are both central and clean, shared bathroom, both have restaurants, both quite clean, both have paper-thin walls, and rent bicycles for 2,000 kip/day; **F** *Vieng Phone Guesthouse*, shared bathroom, large restaurant.

● **Places to eat** ◆ *Viengxai Guesthouse* has a restaurant with a menu in English, friendly service, good chips, reasonable prices, *Vieng Phone Guesthouse* has a restaurant downstairs. Fried fruits, baguettes, freshly made cookies, at the market in the morning.

● **Banks & money changers** *Viengxai Guesthouse* will exchange limited amounts of baht and US$.

● **Useful addresses Immigration**: just before the market as you enter town, on the opp side of the street, registration free.

● **Transport Local Bicycles**: for rent from some of the guesthouses, 800 kip for half day. **Car hire**: is possible (10,000 kip for a full day) and may be a good idea for visiting nearby hilltribes, with a driver who can act as translator. **Road** The road from Muang Sing to Luang Namtha is asphalt but is sometimes broken – the terrain on this route is mountainous and dense forest. The only way to get to Muang Sing is by truck or pick-up from Luang Namtha, nr the market. Vehicles leave throughout the day, 2 hrs (2,000 kip).

BAN HOUEI XAI (HOUEI XAI)

Ban Houei Xai is in the heart of the Golden Triangle (see page 75) and is known for its poppy fields. The town has a large ethnic mix of different minorities. The surrounding regions are very traditional and the way of life here cannot have changed much in the past few millennia. Ban Houei Xai has long been a wealthy town as it was on the heroin route to Chiang Mai in Thailand. Sapphires are also mined in this area. The town now mostly lives on timber exports to Thailand. **Wat Chom Kha Out Mani-rath**, in the centre of town, is worth a visit if only for its views. There is also a large former French fort here called **Fort Car-not** now used by the Lao army (and consequently out of bounds). **Ban Nam Keun**, a small traditional village on the high plateau not far from the main town, is worth a visit for its natural beauty. Ban Houei Xai is quite a good place to shop for Lao weaving and gems, as it is cheaper than Vientiane. Though the town is growing rapidly as links with Thailand intensify it is still small and easy enough to get around on foot. Most passengers dock close to the centre of town at the passenger ferry pier. The vehicle ferry pier is around 750m further N (upstream) while the post office is about 500m S, at the edge of town.

Excursions The sapphire mine is S of the town, near the fast boat terminal. The miners pan in the morning and clean the stones in the afternoon, so afternoon is the best time to visit.

● **Accommodation D** *Arimid Guesthouse*, at the NW end of the town, new guesthouse, extremely friendly service, the owners M and Mme Chitaly, speak excellent French and a little English, comfortable individual bungalows, bathroom attached, no hot water, nice garden area, Mme Chitaly will cook tasty Luang Prabang food, and serve it to you at your bungalow, at least three dishes for 4,000 kip pp; **D** *Hotel Sai*, in the centre of town, with attached bathroom incl toilet and hot shower, lounge area on the first floor with pleasant view over the Mekong, basic but clean hotel, and friendly staff; **D-E** *Manirath*, in the middle of town, with attached bathroom incl toilet and hot shower, restaurant serving only breakfast; **E** *Bokeo*, outside washing facilites; **E** *Manirath*, basic, but clean rooms with own bathroom, better than the *Houei Sai*; **F** *Muang Da*, a few doors along from *Houei Sai*, Chinese guesthouse with good food.

● **Places to eat** **♦♦**_Lao Zhang Sheng Co Ltd_, good Chinese, Lao and Thai food in a restaurant run by a Taiwanese man and his Thai wife. Noodle stalls everywhere.

● **Banks & money changers** Lane Xang Bank, in the middle of town changes TCs, US$ cash and baht, and offers a slightly better rate than the Lane Xang Bank beside the terminal where boats depart for Chiang Khong.

● **Tour companies & travel agents** *Bokeo Travel*, next to *Bokeo Hotel*. English and French speaking, very helpful company with information on tours to villages and sapphire mines; *Lane Xang Travel* have international telephone service; *Phatthana Phoudoi Travel and Tours*, arranges tours to the mines and hilltribe villages, and offers an international phone service, helpful people.

● **Useful addresses Immigration**: at the boat terminal and the airport. Open 0800-1200, 1400-1630 Mon-Fri.

● **Transport Air** Daily flights to Luang Prabang, 38,700 kip, connecting to Vientiane. Flights to Udom Xai, Mon and Thurs, 31,300 kip. Flights to Luang Namtha, Wed and Sat, 33,800 kip. **Boat** Daily boats to Pakbeng (half way to Luang Prabang) and connections on to Luang Prabang – 2 days travel. The slow boat leaves between 0800 and 1100 from jetty 1½ km N of town (a charming journey through lovely scenery – worth sitting on the roof for), 6-7 hrs (US$6). Speedboats are a noisy, unrelaxing alternative, they leave from the jetty S of town, 2-3 hrs (US$12). There are also boats that make the journey all the way from Ban Houei Xai to Luang Prabang – 2 days and 1 night, with the night spent in a simple guesthouse at the village where the vessel moors. **International connections: Boat** To Chiang Khong, small boats ferry passengers to and from Chiang Khong throughout the day, 700 kip/฿20. Thailand Immigration open 0800-1200, 1400-1630 Mon-Fri. **NB** It is important to get an exit stamp from the Immigration office before leaving town, otherwise a fine of US$5/day is charged. **Road** Route 3 to Luang Namtha is being upgraded at the time of writing but the northern part is still very rough. Russian army trucks depart 0500-0800 but not every day, will take passengers, 10-12 hrs about 10,000 kip. It is possible to break the journey halfway along, in Viengphoukha.

The South

PAKXAN (PAKSAN)

There is almost no reason to stop in Pakxan – a provincial capital without any attitude – except to break the journey N or S. Even this reason has almost become redundant as road upgrading has shortened journey times (Vientiane-Thakhek takes about 7-9 hrs now). There is, though, an acceptable hotel here, should anyone get stranded.

Indulging in some futurology, there is also the possibility that Pakxan will find itself on the map in more than just the cartographic sense when – and if – proposed Route 22 is upgraded making it possible to reach Xieng Khouang, Phonsavanh and the Plain of Jars from Pakxan.

● **Accommodation** E *Pakxan Phattana Hotel* (better known as the *Phou Doi*), Route 13, T 102, rather overpriced but then there's no competition, simple rooms with shared bathrooms (clean though), electricity 1830-2230.

● **Banks & money changers** Setthathirat Bank, Route 13 (by the bus stop and market – incongruously new building in this setting).

● **Transport** 155 km from Vientiane, 190 km from Thakhek. **Road Bus**: the bus stop is on Route 13. Connections with Vientiane 2-3 hrs (1,300 kip), Thakhek 5-6 hrs (2,500 kip) and Savannakhet.

THAKHEK (MUANG KHAMMOUAN)

Founded in 1911-12, Thakhek is also known by its old name, **Muang Khammouan**; Khammouan is the province of which the town is the capital. Thakhek is sometimes translated as Indian (*Khek* or *Khaek*) Port (*Tha*), although it probably means Guest (*Khaek*) Port after the large number of people who settled here from the N.

The recovery of commercial traffic has brought some life back to this small settlement, although Thakhek remains a quiet town, set in beautiful countryside. As in Savannakhet and Pakse, the locals are hoping that their town will be blessed by a bridge over the Mekong linking it with the Thai city of Nakhon Phanom. In Jun 1996 Vientiane and Bangkok signed a memorandum of understanding but the Lao are noticeably less enthusiastic than the Thai. Transport and Construction Minister, Phao Bounaphon, frantically hedged his bets when he stated: "The bridge comes under the national plan of Laos, but the question of when it will be built depends on further study and financial factors". If it comes to fruition, Thakhek will be quiet no longer. To the NE the impressive karst landscape of the Mahaxai area is visible (see **Excursions**).

Places of interest

There are few officially designated 'places of interest' in town but it is a gem of a settlement. Quiet and elegant it has a fine collection of **colonial-era shophouses**, a breezy riverside position, and a relaxed ambience. What locals must regard as the Central Business District at the river end of Kouvoravong Rd is wonderful for its peeling buildings.

Laos South

There are three **markets** in Thakhek. The largest, Talat Souk Somboun (Talat Lak Saam [3]) is out at the bus terminal, 2-3 km E of town. Tuk-tuks constantly ferry market-goers to and fro (300 kip). Talat Lak Song [2] is at the E end of Kouvoravong Rd, about 1½-2 km from the town centre. It is a mixed, largely dry goods market. Finally, N on Chaoanou Rd is the Talat Nabo.

Excursions

Visible from town is the karst landscape of the **Mahaxai area** to the N and E. **Mahaxai** itself is a beautiful small town 50 km E of Thakhek on Route 12. But even more beautiful is the scenery here: exquisite valleys and imposing limestone bluffs. **Xiang Lieb (Chiang Rieb) cave** close to Mahaxai is at the foot of a limestone cliff. The **Houai Xiang Lieb** flows from the cave and there are some prehistoric paintings on the cliff face. The cave is reportedly only accessible during the dry season. Rather further away from Mahaxai is **Tham Pha Ban Tham**, a cave containing Buddha images. A local festival is held here during the 5th month of the Buddhist calendar. Again the cave itself is said to be inaccessible during the wet season. There is reportedly a third cave near Mahaxai: **Tham Nang Ang**. **Accommodation** None in Mahaxai although this may change if this incomparable area opens up to visitors. *Getting there*: by songthaew from the Thakhek bus terminal. Alternatively, charter a tuk-tuk which makes it easier to reach the caves (about 10,000 kip).

That Sikhot or **Sikhotaboun** is one of Laos' holiest sites and lies about 6 km S of Thakhet. The *that* is thought to have been built by Chao Anou at the beginning of the 15th century. It overlooks the Mekong and was restored in 1956. The *that* houses the relics of Chao Sikhot, a local hero, founder of the old town of Thakhek, and Chou Anou's son-in-law. According to local legend, Sikhot was an ordinary man who cooked some rice which he stirred with dirt – but as it turned out magic – sticks. When the local people understandably refused to eat the dirt-ridden rice he did so instead – and as a result was bestowed with Herculean strength. He conquered most of the surrounding area and took Vientiane whereupon he married the King of Vientiane's daughter. (The legend does not mention Chao Anou's name, but who wants to spoil a good story?) The king asked his daughter to discover whether Sikhot had any weakness. This she did, her husband foolishly revealing that he could only be killed through the anus. The King of Vientiane placed an archer at the bottom of Sikhot's pit latrine (a messy business that does not bear contemplating) and when the unfortunate Oriental Hercules came to relieve himself, was killed by an arrow up

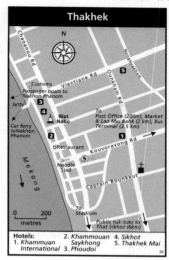

Thakhek

Hotels:
1. Khammuan International
2. Khammuan Saykhong
3. Phoudoi
4. Sikhot
5. Thakhek Mai

his anus. That Sikhot consists of a large gold *that* raised on a plinth (note the reliefs of the Buddha in various mudras along the base), with a viharn upstream built in 1970 by the last King of Laos. The whole is part surrounded by a high wall. Stalls selling drinks and some food are to be found under the trees to the left. The gate here is always open. Admission by donation (there is a wooden monk with alms bowl in front of the *that*). A further reason to come here is simply for the journey downstream along a quiet country road: bucolic Laos at its best. *Getting there*: by hired tuk-tuk (3,000 kip there and back) or by regular public tuk-tuk (stand at the intersection of Ounkham and Kouvoravong roads).

Local information
● **Accommodation**

B *Phou Doi II*, Vientiane Rd (facing the pier), new hotel under construction in 1996, will doubtless be the most luxurious in town, 4 storeys and 50-odd rooms, same management as the *Phou Doi Hotel* out nr the market.

C-D *Khammouane Saykhong*, Setthathirath Rd (or Mekong Rd), T 212216, F 212370, a/c, restaurant, large 50s hotel with 50-odd rooms in central location, had they designed the place with windows facing the Mekong, rather than the doors, it would be possible to write 'river view' – but they didn't, large, plain rooms with rather run-down, though clean, bathrooms, fine, although service is a tad dismal; **C-D** *Phou Doi I*, Route 13, T 212048, F 212510, a/c, restaurant, inconvenient location 2 km E of town, not far from bus station, OK rooms but little character as this was only built a few years ago; **C-D** *Sikhot*, Setthathirath Rd, a/c, restaurant, attractive villa facing the Mekong and the most characterful place to stay in Thakhek, the a/c rooms in the main house are best, attached bathrooms, the motel-esque annex is, well, motel-esque.

D-E *Khammuan International* (known as *Hotel Inter*), Kouvoravong Rd, T 212171, a/c, restaurant, oldish villa with potential, but for some inconceivable reason the management decided that what guests really desire is rooms without windows – so some of the a/c rooms are like caves, attached bathrooms are OK with hot water showers and the hotel has a large courtyard, a/c restaurant attached.

E *Thakhek Mai*, Vientiane Rd, on the edge of town, T 212043, some a/c, large rooms albeit showing their age, very good value at this price and friendly.

● **Places to eat**
Thakhek is not a place to come to for its cuisine. There are the usual array of noodle stalls – try the one in the town 'square' with good fruit shakes. Most restaurants are attached to hotels (of which the best, despite appearances, is that at the *Khammuan International* ◆◆◆), but an exception is the small place downstream from the *Khammouane Saykhong Hotel* on the river road (only open in the evening), simple dishes and good fish. More sophisticated (◆◆-◆◆◆) is the *Nam Thot Thip* about 1 km out of town on Kouvoravong Rd (left hand side going out) – Thai, Chinese and Lao dishes.

● **Banks & money changers**
Lao Mai Bank, Kouvoravong Rd (E end, opp Talat Lak Song and about 1½-2 km from town centre), will change cash and TCs. There is also an exchange counter at the bus terminal – cash only.

● **Post & telecommunications**
Area code: 051.

Post Office: Kouvoravong Rd (at crossroads with Nongbuakham Rd).

Telephone: international calls can be made from the *Khammuan International* and *Khammouane Saykhong* hotels.

● **Shopping**
Nothing geared to the weird predilections of visiting *farang* but functional basketry available in Talat Lak Song and such oddities as hand crafted buffalo bells.

● **Transport**
190 km from Pakxan. 139 km from Savannakhet, 346 km from Vientiane. **Air** Weekly connection with Vientiane, 1 hr. Also flights to 'Km 20'.

Road Bus/truck: the main bus terminal is 2-3 km E of town on Route 13 at Talat (market) Souk Somboun, also known as Talat Lak Saam. Tuk-tuks charge about 300 kip to ferry passengers townwards. Note that some Vientiane-bound buses leave from the extension of Kouvoravong Rd, past the *Phou-doi Hotel*. Connection with Vientiane twice a day, 8 hrs (3,100 kip). Daily connection with Savannakhet, 3-4 hrs (1,700 kip).

Boat Irregular connections with Vientiane in rainy season, 10 hrs. Boats here are becoming less common as the road to Vientiane improves.

International connections: Thakhek is across the river from Nakhon Phanom in Thailand. Customs/Immigration Office by the pier open 0800-1230, 1330-1630 Mon-Sun. Boats regularly cross between the two towns (1,000 kip).

SAVANNAKHET

On the banks of the Mekong, Savannakhet (pop 30,000) – or Savan as it is usually known – is an important river port and the gateway to the S. At the starting point of the road to Danang in Vietnam (Route 9) and an important trading centre with Thailand, it is very commercial with a large Chinese and Vietnamese population. Indeed, it is one of the only towns in Laos where there is still a sizeable Chinese population – most decided Communism did not sit well with their entrepreneurial instincts, and left. Across the Mekong, high-rise Mukdahan in Thailand may be cocking a snook at its poorer neighbour to the E, but Savannakhet has got a lot to offer that Mukdahan has bull-dozed away in the name of modernization. It feels as though the country never left Savan: cows, buffalos, goats and chickens graze and wander around the urban area and a large portion of the town's French colonial roots still stand, moulding gently in the tropical climate. Whether this will last long is questionable. Local rumour is that construction of a bridge across the Mekong to Mukdahan will commence in 1997 while the road E to Vietnam will also be upgraded. However, it is not likely to be completed before 2002.

In 1989 US servicemen arrived in Savannakhet in their search for the remains of men missing in action (MIAs) and the whole town turned out to watch their arrival at the airport. Not realizing that the Lao bear absolutely no animosity towards Americans, the men kept their heads down and refused to disembark until the crowds dispersed. During the war against the Pathet Lao, Savannakhet was the headquarters of the Royal Lao Air Force.

Places of interest

Like any town of this size, Savan has quite a number of wats, but none is particularly notable unless 'watting' is a new and novel experience. **Wat Sounantha** on Nalao Rd has a 3-dimensional raised relief on the

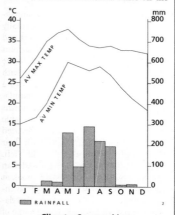

Climate: Savannakhet

outside of the front of the *sim* showing the Buddha, in the mudra of bestowing peace, separating two warring armies. **Wat Sayaphum** on the Mekong is rather more attractive and has several early 20th century monastery buildings, while the monks of **Wat Sayamungkhun**, two of whom speak some English are also pleased to talk about their 50-year-old monastery. There is a large temple school here, and arriving during lessons can mean some impromptu English teaching.

Savan's **colonial heritage** can be seen throughout the central part of town. Perhaps the most attractive area is the square E of the Immigration office between Khanthabouli and Phetsalath roads. Simuang Rd, near the Catholic church, is also rewarding in this regard. Evidence of Savan's diverse population is reflected in the **Chua Dieu Giac**, a Mahayana Buddhist pagoda at the intersection of Southanu and Phetsalath roads which serves the town's Vietnamese population, and the Chinese school close to the Catholic church. In deference to Theravada tradition, the *chua* also has a *that* in the courtyard. The **central market** sandwiched between Oudomsinh and Chaimeuang roads is the regular sort of affair: mostly dry goods, fruit and vegetables, and meat although there are also some baskets and other handicrafts for sale. For those unable to get to the Ho Chi Minh Trail, there is some rusting war scrap in the grounds of the **Provincial Museum** on the Khanthabouli Rd and a tank just to the N (see map). The museum offers little terribly enlightening or interesting. Open Tues-Sun.

Excursions

That Inheng is a holy 16th century *that* or stupa, 12 km NE of Savannakhet. It was built at the same time as That Luang in Vientiane although local guides may try to convince you it was founded by the Indian emperor Asoka over 2,000 years ago. Needless to say, there is no historical evidence to substantiate this claim. The

Savannakhet

Hotels:
1. Auberge de Paradis
2. Hoong Thip & Restaurant
3. Mekong
4. Nanhai
5. Phonepasut
6. Phonevilay
7. Savanbanhao
8. Santyphab
9. Sayamungkhun

Places to eat:
10. French Food
11. Friendship
12. Mekong Riverside
13. Savanbanhao Restaurant & Night Club
14. Savanhlaty Food Garden

wat is the site of an annual festival akin to the one celebrated at Wat Phou, Champassak (see page 194). *Getting there*: any of the regular tuk-tuks which ferry people between Savannakhet and Xeno go past the turn-off for That Inheng (500 kip). It is a 3 km walk from the road.

Kengkok is a village 60 km from Savan. The main reason to come here is to experience the beautiful surrounding countryside. *Getting there*: Kengkok is 35 km S along Route 13 and then 25 km off the road (turn left – 'inland'). There is one bus a day from Savan but no return bus until the next day (guesthouse accommodation available). Alternatively hire a car or tuk-tuk.

Ban Houan Hine is a lesser-known

Khmer site 75 km S of Savan. Built between the 6th and end of the 7th centuries it does not begin to compare with the better-known Wat Phou outside Champassak. However a visit here can be combined with a visit to **That Phone**, a hilly Buddhist *that* en route. It is also possible to travel by boat down the Mekong. The difficulty is in getting there without having to charter a car and driver. *Getting there*: as yet there are no public buses to Ban Houan Hine – it lies 15 km off Route 13 (take Route 13 S, 60 km from Savan, and then turn right onto a track for a further 15 km – it is signposted from the main road 'Stone House Pillars'). Really the only alternative is to hire a car and driver (see **Transport**, **Local**). A boat to Ban Houan Hine should cost US$50-100 depending on size.

The Ho Chi Minh Trail is an enticing prospect for some visitors but once again getting here is not easy from Savan and certainly is only possible as a day trip with a hired car, US$200 (see Ho Chi Minh Trail entry page 178 for details on doing it by public transport).

Local festivals
Feb: *Than Ing Hang* (movable) similar to the festival at Wat Phou, Champassak (see page 197).

Local information
● **Accommodation**
Savannakhet has a good selection of mid-range places to stay at US$10-20. There is no good cheaper accommodation though – at least there wasn't in mid-1996. However, Mr Leng Samthavilai is hoping to open a dedicated travellers' guesthouse with services like bicycle and motorbike hire.

B *Auberge de Paradis (Sala Savan)*, by old market, T 212445, a/c, new hotel run by *Sode-tour*, converted colonial villa, judging by their other hotels should be refined and tasteful with good food, but we have not had a chance to see it; **B** *Nanhai*, Santisouk Rd (their postal address, though, is 313RM Lasavong Rd), T 212371, F 212381, a/c, restaurant, pool, opened in 1994 and mainland Chinese-owned, this white block of a hotel has over 40 rooms with most facilities, it works and even

boasts the only lift in town but it was clearly designed by someone with sensory deprivation – it shouldn't have been allowed and at our last visit the pool was not even full; **B-C** *Hoong Thip*, Phetsalath Rd, T 212262, F 212860, a/c, restaurant, this hotel is deceptively good, from outside it looks like another over-designed place but the rooms are spotless, with satellite TV and good hot water showers, it may not fit the description 'charming' but it is good value, well run and centrally positioned – they have a car and driver for hire too.

C *Phonepasut*, Santisouk Rd, T 212158/212190, a/c, hot water, restaurant, pool (700 kip for visitors), motel-like place with 2 courtyards, rooms are clean with OK bathrooms, satellite TV, friendly and well run with support services like fax and international telephone, situated 1 km from town centre in quiet street; **C-D** *No Name Guesthouse*, on the banks of the Mekong right by the stadium and Wat Chomkeo (5 mins' walk from the *Mekong Riverside Restaurant*), this guesthouse has been warmly rec, although we have not had the opportunity to inspect it, spacious and very clean rooms, managed by the friendly Mr and Mrs Sithimolada; **C-E** *Saya-mungkhun* (in English the sign just reads 'Guest House'), 85 Ratsavong Seuk Rd, T 212426, some a/c, an excellent little hotel with 16 rooms in an airy colonial-era villa, rooms are clean and characterful, bathrooms with hot water showers, friendly owners, centrally positioned, largish compound, rec.

D *Mekong*, Tha He Rd, some a/c, this hotel, in some regards, is one of the best in Savan: it is housed in an attractive colonial villa on the Mekong, the rooms are large, generally clean, with good attached bathrooms and some character, they are also good value, the downside is that the Vietnamese management are diffident to the point of rudeness: ignore them and its great; **D** *Savanbanhao*, Senna Rd, T 212202, F 212944, some a/c, centrally located hotel with range of rooms, most expensive with attached showers and hot water, large balcony, quiet compound and *Savanbanhao Tourism Co*, a tour firm, attached; **D-E** *Phonevilay*, 137 Phetsarath Rd, S of town centre, T 212284, some a/c, more expensive rooms with attached hot water showers, small rooms but clean; **D-E** *Santyphab*, off Tha He Rd, 100m from passenger pier to Thailand, some a/c, basic and dirty but cheap rooms with attached toilet and shower available.

F Guesthouse at the bus station, basic dorm

rooms but useful for catching the Vietnam bus which leaves at 0200.

● **Places to eat**

Restaurant on riverside serving good food and beer. The market also has stalls serving good, fresh food including excellent Mekong River fish dishes.

◆◆◆-◆◆*Friendship Restaurant*, Tha He Rd (nr intersection with Phagnapul Rd), Vietnamese restaurant with acceptable food – on the 'wrong' side of the Mekong River road.

◆◆*French Food Restaurant*, between the *Santyphab Hotel* and the Customs/Immigration Office, as the name implies, French food served including good steaks, also produces Vietnamese dishes, only open in evening; ◆◆*Mekong Riverside*, Tha He Rd, T 212522, at the northern end of the riverside road, this is the most attractively positioned place to eat, a restaurant built above the Mekong with an outside terrace, food is not bad as well – great place for a beer as the sun sets to the W, rec.

◆◆-◆*Savanhlaty Food Garden* (E of Immigration Office – see map), a mini 'hawker centre' in one of the most attractive colonial squares in Savan, awnings shield diners from the sun and a handful of stalls serve good and cheap single dish Lao, Vietnamese and Thai food, rec.

● **Bars**

Savanbanhao Night Club, across street from hotel of same name, open 2000-2400.

● **Airline offices**

Lao Aviation, at the airport.

● **Banks & money changers**

Lao Mai Bank, Khanthabouli Rd, open 0800-1200, 1300-1530 Mon-Fri, branch in the Post Office. **Banque pour le Commerce Exterieur Lao**, Oudomsinh Rd. Exchange counters around the market, any currency accepted, and at pier (bad rate). The shop on the corner of Chaimeuang and Senna roads will also accept TCs, and is open on Sun too.

● **Post & telecommunications**

Area code: 041.

Post Office: Khanthabouli Rd.

Telephone and fax service (domestic and international): in Post Office, open Mon-Sun 0800-2200.

● **Shopping**

Handicrafts: baskets available from the central market.

● **Tour companies & travel agents**

Savannakhet Tourism Co, Senna Rd, T 212202, F 212944, run tours and can arrange trips to most sights in the area incl overnight trips to a local village. Mr Leng Samthavilai can also help arrange a Vietnamese visa for a service charge of US$5 (on top of the visa charge of US$70). Although it has links with the government, this is a commercial tour company.

● **Useful addresses**

Vietnam Consulate: Sisavangvong Rd, open 0830-1200, 1400-1700, provides Vietnamese visas in 3 to 5 days, 2 photos and US$70 needed (see **Tour companies** for alternative way to acquire a visa).

Immigration office: for exit to Thailand at passenger pier. Open 0830-1130, 1400-1600.

● **Transport**

487 km from Vientiane, 139 km from Thakhek.

Local Bicycle hire: from the *French Food Restaurant* opp the Immigration Office. **Car hire**: car and driver available from the *Hoongthip Hotel* (US$50/day), the *Nanhai Hotel* and from *Savannakhet Tourism Co*. **Tuk-tuk**: tuk-tuks of various shapes and sizes criss-cross town. They are locally known as *Sakaylab* (as in Skylab) because they are said to resemble that piece of space hardware. They may be more resilient and practical but certainly don't go as fast. 300 kip for a local journey.

Air Daily connections with Vientiane – ATRs, Y-7s and Y-12s. The ATRs fly straight to Vientiane through Thai airspace. The Chinese-built Y-12s, as they are not certified airworthy, have to stick to Lao airspace, following the dog-leg of the Mekong. Also twice weekly connection with Pakse and Salavan – some planes fly S to Paksé before turning N for Vientiane; don't worry!

Road Truck/bus: the bus terminal is on the N edge of town. A tuk-tuk to the centre should cost about 300 kip. There is an information desk (some English) in the Station Office. Daily connections with Vientiane, departing Vientiane in the morning, partly rough road, 10-24 hrs depending on weather conditions, 2 buses a day, one at 0730 (7,000 kip), new road under construction. Daily connections with Pakse departing Savannakhet at 0500 and 0600, 6-9 hrs (4,000 kip), along a dusty and potholed track; be prepared to get very dirty and extremely shaken. The Vientiane-bound buses drop incoming passengers off at Xeno. From there, share tuk-tuks take people into Savannakhet

(500 kip to bus terminal). Also connections with Thakhek, 4½ hrs (1,700 kip) and E to the Vietnamese border (see below).

Boat Because the road S from Vientiane was traditionally so bad, many people resorted to the river instead – especially during the rainy season. There were two or more boats each week taking over 2 days. Sadly this mode of transport is becoming increasingly less frequent as the road is improved and journey times come down. In the 1995 wet season there was just one boat a week (3 days, 2 nights, 8,000 kip with passengers either sleeping on board or in the local guesthouse in the town where the boat moored). Locals wonder whether there will be any passenger boats soon. There will, though, probably still be cargo boats making the journey.

International connections to Thailand & Vietnam Bus: daily connections with Lao Bao in Vietnam. Buses to different destinations leave on different days. Times, destinations and fares are all on a board outside the station office (tickets for sale in office). 5 hr trip to border (236 km away) on a rough track (2,800 kip). See the next entry for more details on crossing the border. Buses to Danang (508 km) 17,500 kip, Hué (409 km), 14,200 kip, Dong Ha (329 km). Exit fee 1,000 kip. **Boat**: to Thailand (Mukdahan) through the day, ฿30/850 kip (or cheaper, apparently, if you purchase the ticket once on board ship). Only one time on Sat, at 0930, but several ferries. Exit fee 1,000 kip. The new Customs and Immigration Office is near to town centre on Tha He Rd. Open 0730-1130, 1330-1630 Mon-Sun.

ROUTE-WISE: Savannakhet to Pakse This 250 km stretch of road is still unsurfaced and rough going. The journey takes anywhere between 6 and 9 hrs, perhaps 10-12 hrs in the wet season. Surfacing is occurring, from Xeno, S and Pakse, N but when they will meet in the middle is anyone's guess. The landscape is not very varied. The natural vegetation is dry dipterocarp savanna forest although this has been largely cleared along the road and converted to rain-fed rice paddies. Few people stop en route S or N: there is nowhere to stay in any case. Until the road is surfaced, passengers alight from their buses shaken and extremely stirred.

XEPON (SEPON) AND THE BORDER WITH VIETNAM

It is now possible to cross into Vietnam by taking Route 9 E over the Annamite

Around Savannakhet

The Ho Chi Minh Trail

Throughout the Vietnam War, Hanoi denied the existence of the Ho Chi Minh Trail and for most of it, Washington denied dropping 1,100,000 tonnes of bombs on it – the biggest tonnage dropped per square kilometre in history. The North Vietnamese Army (NVA) used the Trail, really a network of paths (trodden and cycled down by tens of thousands of men) and roads – some 2-lane carriageways, capable of carrying tanks and truck convoys – to ferry food, fuel and ammunition to South Vietnam. Bunkers beneath the trail housed cavernous mechanical workshops and barracks. Washington tried everything in the book to stem the flow of supplies down the trail.

By 1966, 90,000 troops were pouring down the 7,000 kilometres of Trail each year, and 4 years later, 150,000 infiltrators were surging southwards using the jungle network. Between 1966 and 1971, the Trail was used by 630,000 communist troops; over the same period, it was also the conduit for 100,000 tonnes of provisions, 400,000 weapons and 50,000 tonnes of ordnance. It was guarded by 25,000 troops and studded with artillery positions, anti-aircraft emplacements and SAM missiles.

The Trail wound its way through the Annamite mountains, entering Laos at the NE end of the 'Panhandle', and heading SE, with several access points into Cambodia and South Vietnam. The Viet Minh had used it as far back as the 1950s in their war against the French. The US airforce started bombing the Trail as early as 1964 in Operation Steel Tiger and B-52s first hit the Mu Gia pass on the Ho Chi Minh Trail in December 1965.

Carpet-bombing by B-52s was not admitted to by Lao Prime Minister Prince Souvanna Phouma until 1969, by which time the US was dispatching 900 sorties a day to hit the Trail. It is estimated that it took 300 bombs for each NVA soldier

chain of mountains to **Lao Bao** (just over the border) and from there to the Vietnamese town of Dong Ha and the city of Danang. The largest place on the Lao side of the frontier is **Xepon**. There is not much to see and do but as there is a government hotel here travellers tend to use it as a stopping place en route to Vietnam.

● **Accommodation** There is talk of guesthouses opening in Xiepong as more tourists use this route to and from Vietnam. **F** *No name hotel*, the only place to stay here, or anywhere hereabouts (although there is accommodation available just over the border in Lao Bao). A very basic government-run 'hotel'.

● **Transport Road Bus**: buses (converted trucks) leave for Xiepong from Savannakhet daily at 0500, 6 hrs (2,800 kip), and return to Savannakhet the same day. The distance between the two immigration posts is about 1 km and motorbike taxis are available (a new

immigration post is under construction which will reduce the distance to 500m). From the Vietnamese immigration post to Lao Bao is another 3 km or so. Again, motorcycle taxis available to carry weary travellers.

XEPON AND THE HO CHI MINH TRAIL

Despite the herbicides, the mountainous region around the trail is still blanketed in dense tropical forest – much of it remarkably undisturbed. Because of its inaccessibility the forest has not been raided by the timber merchants. Many of the rare birds and animals found in the markets at Saravan are caught in this area. The Vietnam border area was more heavily populated before the war. Many of the tribal groups (mainly Lao Theung) were forced to move onto the Bolovens Plateau because of the heavy bombing of killed on the trail. The B-52 air strikes proved ineffective; they never succeeded in disrupting NVA supply lines for long.

In an effort to monitor NVA troop movements, the US wired the trail with tiny electronic listening devices, infra-red scopes, heat and smell-sensitive sensors, and locational beacons to guide fighter-bombers and B-52s to their target. The NVA carefully removed these devices to unused lengths of trail, urinated on them and retreated, while preparing to shoot down the bombers, which predictably arrived, on cue, from Clarke Field Air Base in the Philippines.

Creative US military technicians hatched countless schemes to disrupt life on the trail: they bombed it with everything from Agent Orange (toxic defoliant) to Budweiser beer (intoxicating inebriant) and dish-washing detergent (to make it into a frothing skid-track). In 1982 Washington finally admitted to dumping 200,000 gallons of chemical herbicides over the Trail between 1965 and 1966. The US also dropped chemical concoctions designed to turn soil into grease and plane-loads of Dragonseed – miniature bomblets which blew the feet off soldiers and the tyres off trucks. Nothing worked.

The US invasion of Cambodia in May 1970 forced Hanoi to further upgrade the Trail. This prompted the Pentagon to finally rubberstamp a ground assault on it, codenamed Lamson 719, in which South Vietnamese and US forces planned to capture the Trail-town of Tchepone, directly E of Savannakhet, and inside Laos. The plans for the invasion were drawn up using maps without topographical features.

In Feb 1971, while traversing the Annamite range in heavy rain, the South Vietnamese forces were routed, despite massive air support. They retreated leaving the Trail intact, 5,000 dead and millions of dollars-worth of equipment behind.

the Ho Chi Minh Trail.

It is necessary to hire a Soviet jeep in order to cross the rivers because many of the bridges are broken and rivers are often impassable using other vehicles, especially during the rainy season. The trip can only be made in the dry season, Nov to Mar being the ideal time. The easiest access point to the Ho Chi Minh Trail is from Ban Tapung.

NB Warning nobody should go near the Trail without a guide – unexploded bombs abound.

Local information
● **Accommodation**
Xepon has a simple guesthouse (**F**). Basic but rock-bottom price charged per bed rather than per room.

● **Getting to the trail**
The local police discourage people visiting the trail without a guide because of the risk posed

by unexploded ordnance. A guide will charge US$10-20/day including meals and accommodation if required. (For example, from Savan it is possible to travel with a guide on public buses, staying overnight in Xepon.)

● **Transport**
Road Bus: Xepon is the nearest town (well, really a large village) to the trail. Buses for Xepon leave from Savannakhet in the morning, 5 hrs (2,800 kip). It would be possible to continue E from here and cross the border into Vietnam.

THE BOLOVENS PLATEAU

Exploring the Bolovens Plateau As tourism expands in Laos, so areas like the Bolovens are sure to become more accessible. For the moment though the tourist infrastructure is limited. Tour companies, especially in Pakse (see page 191), can organize trips. Alternatively, the best base is Tad Lo (see page 182). Other places near or on the Bolovens are Salavan, Attapeu, and Sekong (see the respective entries), and guesthouses in these towns can also offer assistance and information. Note that it is not possible to drive across the Bolovens Plateau from Salavan to Attapeu. Even the new road just constructed from Paksong comes off the plateau.

The fertile farmland of the Bolovens Plateau has given Salavan province a strong agricultural base, supporting coffee and cardamom plantations. The road from Paksong to Pakse is known as the Coffee Rd.

Coffee was introduced to the area by French settlers in the 1920s and 30s who made a quick exit as the bombing escalated in the 1960s. It is mainly exported via Pakse to Thailand, Singapore and, formerly, the USSR. Tea grown in this area is for local use. The Bolovens also has the perfect climate for durians, and villages (particularly on the road from Paksong to Pakse) are liberally dotted with durian trees. The fruit is exceptionally rich and creamy and in the peak season, between May and Jul, can be bought from roadside stalls for as little as 200 kip.

Given its fertility, the plateau is now rapidly repopulating and new farms are springing up everywhere. To claim land, settlers need only erect a territorial fence.

During the bombing of the Ho Chi Minh Trail (see box, page 178), to the E, many hilltribes and other ethnic minority groups migrated to the Bolovens, which consequently has become an ethnographic goldmine with more than 12 obscure minority groups, including the Katou, Alak, Ta-Oy, Ya Houne, Ngai and Suk, living in the area. Most of the tribes are of Indonesian (or Proto-Malay) stock and have very different facial characteristics to the Lao; they are mainly animist (see page 55).

About 40 km S from Salavan on the Bolovens Plateau is **Tha Teng**, a village that was levelled during the war. Before that it was the home of Jean Dauplay, the Frenchman who introduced coffee to Laos from Vietnam in 1920. Today the UNDP, in a joint venture with a private sector businessman, has set up a small wild-honey processing factory. Villagers are paid for the combs they collect from jungled hills around Tha Teng. The carefully labelled 'Wild honey from Laos' is exported to European health food shops. There are several ethnic minority villages in the area.

The Ta-Oy village of **Ban Paleng**, not far from Tha Teng, is also fascinating – more so in Feb/Mar, when the animist Ta-Oy have their annual 3-day sacrificial festival. A water buffalo is donated by each family in the village – built in a circle around the *kuan* (the house of sacrifice). The buffalo have their throats cut and the blood is collected and drunk. The raw meat is divided among the families and surrounding villages are invited to come and feast on it. The head of each family throws a slab of meat into the *lak khai* – a basket hanging from a pole in front of the *kuan* – so that the spirits can partake too. The sacrifice is performed by the village shaman, then dancers throw spears at the buffalo until it dies. The villagers moved from the Vietnam border area to escape the war, yet Ban Paleng was bombed repeatedly: the village is still littered with shells and unexploded bombs. Ban Khan Nam Xiep on the Coffee Rd is also a Ta-Oy village.

Note that it is not possible to drive across the Bolovens Plateau from Saravan to Attapeu. Even the new road just constructed from Paksong comes off the plateau.

The Katou villages such as **Ban Houei Houne** (on the Salavan-Pakse road) are famous for their weaving of a bright cloth used locally as *pha sin* – or sarongs. This village also has an original contraption to pound rice: on the river below the village are several water-wheels which power the rice pounders. The idea originally came from Sam Neua and was brought to this village by a man who had fought with the Pathet Lao.

PAKSONG (PAKXONG)

The main town on the Bolovens Plateau is **Paksong**, a small market town 50 km E of Pakse. It was originally a French agricultural centre, popular during the

---

The fall of Tha Teng: a personal view

In 1968, I read about the fall of Tha Teng to the Pathet Lao. The small article was buried in a back page of the newspaper. Not many Americans really cared about this loss or even knew where Laos was let alone Tha Teng.

In 1969 I was flying over Tha Teng in my Bird Dog – a Cessna 170 – which was used in my work as a Forward Air Controller (Code name, Raven 58) for the United States Air Force. All that was left of this town was about 20 homes lining a road on the northern edge of the Bolovens Plateau. The homes were gradually being overrun by heavy vegetation.

What was so important about this town that its loss would be reported in the United States? Tha Teng is strategically located on the northern edge of the Bolovens Plateau. Used as a military outpost, intelligence about enemy activity could be obtained. So, by occupying Tha Teng, the 'friendlies' – the Royal Lao Government – could, to a certain extent, control the gateway to the Bolovens. With its loss, the Pathet Lao and North Vietnamese could move more easily in their efforts to control the plateau.

The significance of the location of Tha Teng was well-known to the Pathet Lao. It was rumoured that there was a cave NE of Tha Teng which could hold a battalion of troops and whose entrance was large enough to walk an elephant through. Elephants were used to haul heavy equipment, ammunition and supplies into the cave. But, from the air, the terrain looked flat. Even the military topological maps did not indicate the possibility of a cave.

However, on Thanksgiving Day 1969, I confirmed in fact the existence of that cave by 'clearing' away the 200-ft trees which protected its entrance. Further, it exposed a large permanent bivouac area in front of the cave entrance which provided facilities for at least a battalion-size unit. This staging area proved successful as the Pathet Lao captured the Bolovens during their campaign of 1970.

The war-that-wasn't in Laos was odd in more than just the sense that it wasn't a war. In Vientiane it was a common sight to see Pathet Lao soldiers coming down out of the mountains in full combat gear, including weapons, to obtain their daily rations. They could shop without concern of being captured, and would then return to the mountains to join their combat units. These were the same soldiers that the Royal Lao army, who were also at the market, might be fighting later that same day.

Three days each year, the war would stop in southern Laos. Officials from Salavan would get in a truck and head S toward the plateau. At the edge of the Bolovens they would stop to let armed Pathet Lao (PL) get on their truck so they could continue to each village on the plateau. These PL guards would make certain that the officials would only go to the villages. As the officials visited each village, they would record the births, deaths and weddings which had taken place during the previous year. War, or no war, official government records had to be maintained. Following the 3-day yearly truce, the war would resume.

Source: Ken Thompson, Raven 58, who flew as a FAC over Laos and Vietnam for over 2 years between 1968 and 1970.

colonial era for its cooler temperature. Paksong was yet another catastrophe of the war and was virtually destroyed. The area is famous for its fruit and vegetables, even strawberries and raspberries can be cultivated here.

Excursions Not far from Paksong, 1 km off the road to Pakse, is **Tad Phan**, a dramatic 130m-high waterfall. Take a track to the left off the main road at Ban Pak Kud, Km 38, and at the end of the track a path leads down to a good view point half way down the horse-shoe shaped gorge. This, like many waterfalls in southern Laos, is really spectacular. Salavan province also has a large hydro-electric power generating capacity – the Xe Xet barrage, next to the largest of the river's three magnificent waterfalls, supplies power to Pakse and some is exported to Thailand.

● **Accommodation** A new hotel is being built in Paksong, which should open in 1997. **E** *Paksong Guesthouse*, originally built to house workers on a German development project. There are just 6 basic but passable rooms.

● **Transport** 50 km from Pakse. **Road Bus/truck**: regular connections with Pakse, 1½-2 hrs. Some Salavan-bound buses also travel via Paksong although most now take the faster Route 20.

TAD LO

Tad Lo is a popular 'resort' on the edge of the Bolovens Plateau, 30 km from Salavan. There are two places to stay here, good hiking, an exhilarating river to frolic in (especially in the wet season), and elephant trekking. In the vicinity of Tad Lo there are also hill 'tribe' villages and both resorts can arrange visits. The Xe Xet (or Houai Set) flows past Tad Lo and there are two sets of cascades nearby. Tad Hang, the lower series, are overlooked by the *Tad Lo Resort* and *Saise Guesthouse* while Tad Lo, the upper, are a short hike away. The Xe Xet is yet another river being dammed in the area to produce hydropower for export to Thailand.

Excursions

There are two Alak villages, **Ban Khian** and **Tad Soung**, close to Tad Lo. The Alak are an Austro-Indonesian ethno-linguistic group and their grass-thatched huts with rounded roofs are not at all Lao in style and are distinct from those in neighbouring Lao Theung villages. But most fascinating is the Alaks' seeming obsession with death. The head of each household carves coffins out of hollowed logs for himself and his whole family (even babies), then stacks them, ready for use, under their rice storage huts. This tradition serves as a reminder

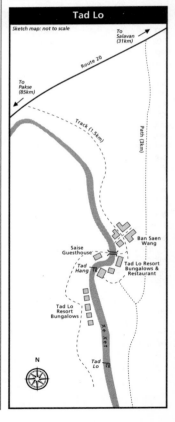

Tad Lo

that life expectancy in these remote rural areas is around 40 (the national average is a little over 50) and infant mortality upwards of 120 per 1,000 live births; the number one killer is malaria. Both guesthouses can arrange treks to visit Ban Khian and Tad Soung.

Tours

Elephant trekking can be organized by either guesthouse. This is an excellent way to see the area as there are few roads on the plateau and elephants can go where jeeps cannot. It is also a thrill being on the back of an elephant.

Local information
● Accommodation

B-D *Tad Lo Resort*, T 031 (Pakse) 212725, T 021 (Vientiane) 213478, F 021-216313, reception is at the restaurant (not at the bungalows), good restaurant producing plenty of Lao food, chalet-style accommodation (15 rooms) built right on top of the waterfalls, it is an attractive location (during the wet season) and the accommodation is comfortable – cane rocking chairs on the balconies overlook the cascades on the left bank, elephant rides available, rec, room availability can be checked by visiting *Sodetour* in Pakse.

D-E *Saise Guesthouse* (also *Sasay Guesthouse*), well designed and run resort-style accommodation (6 rooms) in raised chalet, not as atmospheric as the *Tad Lo Resort* but a slightly cheaper option.

● Transport
31 km from Salavan, 85 km from Pakse.

Road Bus: the turning for Tad Lo is on Route 20, the recently upgraded road linking Pakse with Salavan. To get there, board a morning bus in Pakse bound for Salavan or vice versa. Ensure that the bus is taking Route 20 and not the alternative Route 23 via Paksong. Most drivers know Tad Lo and will stop at Ban Houak Houa Set. There is a blue sign here indicating the way to Tad Lo – a 1½ km walk along a dirt track and through the village of Ban Saen Wang. The bus takes about 2½ hrs.

SALAVAN (SARAVAN)

The old French town of Salavan – also spelt Saravan and Saravane – was all but obliterated during the American war in Indochina. It lies at the northern edge of the Bolovens Plateau and acts as a transport hub and trading centre for the agricultural commodities produced on the plateau. The Xe Don which enters the Mekong at Pakse flows along the NE edge of town. During the war, Salavan changed hands several times as the Pathet Lao and forces of the Royal Lao Government fought for control of this critical town located on a strategic flank of the Ho Chi Minh Trail. The two sides, with the RLG supported by American air power, bombed and shelled the town in turn as they tried to dislodge one another. (There is a crude painting of the battle in

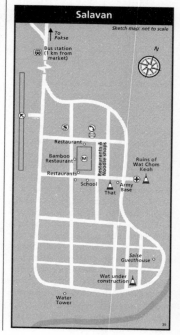

Salavan

Sketch map: not to scale

To Pakse

Bus station (1 km from market)

N

Restaurant

Bamboo Restaurant

Restaurants

Restaurants & Noodle shops

School

That

Army Base

Ruins of Wat Chom Keoh

Saise Guesthouse

Wat under construction

Water Tower

the Champassak Museum in Pakse.) A few years ago there were piles of war scrap – including unexploded bombs, shells and mortars – now cleared away leaving the memory of the war largely in the minds of older residents (most are under 30) and the pages of books. But looking carefully can yield evidence: the awnings and umbrellas in the market are often made from parachute silk. The result of the shelling and bombing, today, though, is that Salavan is a provincial capital with scarcely an ounce of physical beauty and almost no evidence of its French-era origins.

When US airforce pilots mounted bombing runs in Vietnam, their rules of engagement stated that airstrikes within 500m of a temple were illegal; in Cambodia, the margins were increased to 1 km; in Laos, rules did not apply. Like Xieng Khouang, another critical town to the N, Salavan had one of the most beautiful temples in the country, **Wat Chom Keoh**, which was destroyed in an air raid in 1968. (Philatelists should note that the wat was commemorated on a postage stamp in the 1950s.) Today all that remains of the wat are two forlorn and shell-pocked corner posts, one ruined chedi, and a dilapidated wat building decaying still further in the grounds of the Salavan general hospital.

The **daily market** in the centre of town is worth a visit, mainly, admittedly, because there is nothing else to see. In past years the market was an environmentalist's nightmare: all manner of wild creatures, some listed as endangered, would end up here, either for the cooking pot or for the trade in live wild animals (see the Flora and fauna introduction, page 24). Today the frisson of such sights is, fortunately, not on offer. The usual array of frogs and fish, and perhaps a wild bird or two but not much else.

Salavan is a town with no pretensions. Pigs and buffalo wander along the roads, children play in the streets, and shops sell such practical goods as anvils, bicycle tyres, lengths of wire, transmission parts and brightly coloured functional plastic objects. Not a handicraft (at least in the touristic sense) or postcard in sight. Wandering through the town in the cool of the evening when people are at rest, talking, cooking and playing, it seems – despite the legacy of the war – to epitomise a more innocent past.

Excursions

Ban Nong Boua, a beautiful lake near the source of the Xe Don, lies 15 km E of Salavan town. It is famed for its crocodiles which move into the river in the dry season (but remain out of sight). *Getting there*: the road to Ban Nong Boua is too rough to be negotiated by tuk-tuk, which means it is necessary to charter a jeep or other sturdier vehicle.

Local information

● **Accommodation**

Just one place to stay in Salavan which means it is sometimes booked up with government officials.

D-E *Saise Guesthouse*, 2 km from the bus station at the other side of town (get there by tuk-tuk), some a/c, attractive guesthouse in a large garden compound, a/c rooms are of a good standard, fan rooms clean enough with large attached bathrooms (tank of water and dipper), restaurant with limited menu, friendly management speak English and French and can advise on surrounding area.

● **Places to eat**

Most restaurants are situated around the market and there is little to choose between them. Perhaps the best is the bamboo clad place on the airstrip side of the market (see map). A close second is the restaurant on the opposite side of the market where the food is slightly worse but the service brighter. All restaurants serve much the same range of dishes.

● **Banks & money changers**

Phak Tai Bank, nr the market (see map) will exchange cash and TCs.

● **Post & telecommunications**

Post Office: in modern yellow building opp the market. Local calls only from telephone exchange in same building.

● **Transport**

116 km from Pakse, 31 km from Tad Lo, 76 km from Muang Khong Xedon, 98 km from Sekong.

Air The airstrip is right at the edge of town. Connections twice a week with Vientiane via Savannakhet.

Road Bus/truck: the bus terminal is 2-3 km W of the town centre. A share tuk-tuk in costs about 200-300 kip. Morning connections with Pakse, 3-4 hrs (1,500 kip). Most buses turn off Route 23 at Ban Houayhe and travel to Salavan via Route 20 which goes past Tad Lo (see page 182). Before passing Tad Lo most buses stop for a while at the small market town of Ban Lao Ngam on the Houai Tapoung (46 km from Salavan, 79 km from Pakse). Route 20 is a new and comparatively fast road. Some buses, though, take the longer and rougher route via Paksong (Route 23). There are also daily connections with Sekong via Tha Teng, 4 hrs (1,300 kip). As of 1996 the road was being surfaced so journey times should come down. Until then the bus from Salavan arrives in Sekong too late to get a connection to Attapeu. There are also bus connections between Salavan and Muang Khong Xedon on Route 16 (4 hrs) and from there N to Savannakhet.

ROUTE-WISE: Salavan-Sekong In 1996 this section of road was being widened and surfaced – a good thing as the 98 km journey took 4 hrs in its prior state. The road turns off Route 20 and onto Route 23 at Ban Beng and then climbs up to the lower slopes of the Bolovens Plateau. The area is still largely forested with a sparse population concentrated along the road and mainly cultivating coffee. The route is sometimes called the 'Coffee Road'. Buses and trucks usually stop at the local market centre of Ban Tha Teng (see Bolovens introduction for information on some of the minority groups in the area around Tha Teng). Towards Sekong the land is more intensively cultivated; there is even some irrigated rice. This is also an area of resettlement with a number of new villages carving out a small area of civilized space in the forest. But the large logging yard and saw mill at Ban Phon, about 12 km N of Sekong, demonstrates what the local economy depends upon other than coffee: timber.

SEKONG (XEKONG)

Sekong – or Xekong – is a new town and capital of the province of the same name at the eastern edge of the Bolovens Plateau about 100 km S of Salavan and a similar distance N of Attapeu. It is situated on the Kong River – hence its name Xe (River) Kong – and was created comparatively recently when Attapeu province was divided. For the present anyone travelling between Salavan and Attapeu (but probably not vice versa) must overnight here as the first bus from Salavan does not arrive until the last for Attapeu has already departed (in fact a Pakse-bound bus, see Transport). However, the road is being widened and surfaced so this should change.

Those hoping to chance upon an unknown gem of a town should be prepared to be disappointed. In theory it would be a good base to explore the peoples and scenery of the Bolovens Plateau but there is simply no tourist infrastructure to make that possible. The market is centered on the bus terminal, or vice versa, and there is a wat behind the market. The market does have some rather pathetic wild animals – giant flying squirrels for example – for sale, more so than Salavan which has a more infamous reputation in this regard. The only reason to come here, other than out of sheer perversity, is to take a boat down the Xe Kong to the much more attractive town of Attapeu (see Transport, below).

Local information
● **Accommodation**

Only one place in town to stay.

D *Sekong*, newish hotel with 10 or so rooms with attached bathrooms, very functional and already looking worn and dusty – fine for an overnight stop but the roaches are moving in in numbers, the best rooms are upstairs which have a balcony and get the breeze, the large satellite dish on the front of the building does not mean you have chanced upon a long-lost Hilton, electricity from 1800-approx 2100, one of the upstairs rooms is reputedly haunted, some Malaysian UN officials drowned taking a boat downriver to Attapeu: they left their bags in their room and presumably come back every so often to try and retrieve them.

● **Places to eat**
◆◆◆**Vietnamese Restaurant**, opp the *Sekong Hotel*, huge plates of fare, incl good Vietnamese dishes (excellent deer), Ho Chi Minh and numerous moulding calendars of Vietnamese beauties and beauty spots surround diners, the owner left Vietnam for Laos in 1990 and speaks some French.

● **Electricity**
No mains electricity; some places have generators (which means no cold beers – ice required) and there is also a municipal generator which some places are wired-up to.

● **Post & telecommunications**
Post Office: yellow building not far from victory *that*.

● **Shopping**
Basketry: the *Sekong Hotel* sells woven basket 'backpacks'. They sell for about 17,000 kip.

● **Transport**
98 km from Salavan.

Road Bus/truck: morning connections with Salavan, 4 hrs (1,300 kip), and Pakse. No regular direct connections with Attapeu – it is necessary to take a Pakse bound bus to the junction of the new road and then pick up a bus from Pakse bound for Attapeu, 4 hrs plus (but see **Boat**).

Boat To Attapeu down the Xe Kong, about 60,000 kip (4 people), 3-4 hrs.

ATTAPEU

Attapeu has an altogether different character from the Bolovens Plateau as the region is predominantly Lao Loum rather than tribal. Attapeu is an attractive, leafy town positioned on a bend of the Xe Khong, at the confluence of the Xe Kaman. It is an attractive place to walk around, with traditional wooden Lao houses with verandahs and some French buildings. It was fought over by the Pathet Lao and RLG so in many respects it is a surprise the town is as attractive as it is. The people are friendly and traffic is limited. Vegetables are grown on the banks of the Xe Khong. A ferry takes passengers across the river.

According to ML Manich in his *History of Laos*, Attapeu should really be Itkapü. If so, then a translation of the town's name is Buffalo Shit. The non-Lao local people used to raise buffalo here and when asked what the place was called by the Lao, thought they were gesturing at a pile of buffalo excrement. The French, in their turn, transliterated Itkapü as Attapeu in a sort of Lao version of Chinese whispers. For a pile of dung the town, though, is remarkably picturesque.

Outside Attapeu to the NW is a clearing on the hilltop which marks the spot where a new hydropower scheme – the Houai Ho – is under construction (it is due for completion in 1997). The Korean firm Daewoo is the contractor but the

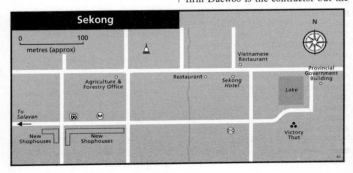

Sekong

0   100
metres (approx)

N

To Salavan →

Agriculture & Forestry Office

New Shophouses

New Shophouses

Restaurant

Vietnamese Restaurant

Sekong Hotel

Lake

Provincial Government Building

Victory That

actual work was done by South Africans. In 1996 and 1997 Pakse and Attapeu found themselves visited by black (and white) South Africans – a pretty rare event in this corner of the world. The South Africans were specifically employed to dig a 740m vertical shaft 4m in diameter. Water will be diverted down this shaft from a reservoir on the Bolovens Plateau at the rate of $22m^3$/sec with a velocity of 1.7m/sec – all to produce electricity for Thailand's booming industries. Needless to say, the timber from the area due to be flooded was removed by Vietnamese workers employed by a Thai logging firm.

Local information
● **Accommodation**
A new hotel with 100 rooms is being constructed in Attapeu – however, it is a government project so locals are not optimistic about the results.

D *Saise Guesthouse*, simple, government-run place down by the river and a 15-min walk from the bus station, some rooms with attached bathrooms, serviceable.

E *Attapeu Guesthouse*, 6-7 rooms, dusty and basic, with mosquito nets, there is a restaurant next door.

● **Banks & money changers**
Phak Tai Bank, will change cash only.

● **Post & telecommunications**
Post Office: in town centre.

● **Transport**
Air Occasional flights to Salavan from Pakse, but they are not scheduled.

Road Truck/bus: daily connections with Pakse, leaves from the market early morning (0700-0730), 7 hrs (4,000 kip). For Sekong and Salavan get off the bus at the junction with the new road and wait for a Pakse-Sekong bus. Most arrive too late to catch a connection on to Salavan the same day. The road is poor, but it's an experience. From Sekong, there may be occasional trucks – it's a good journey, with excellent views of the Bolovens Plateau to the W. During the dry season (roughly Feb-Apr) there are bus links to Attapeu along Route 18 – which links up with Route 13 between Pakse and Muang Khong.

Boat From Sekong downriver (wet season only).

Sethathirat's mysterious disappearance

The last great king of Lane Xang, Sethathirat (1548-1571), see page 31, was reputedly murdered in a dastardly plot hatched in the town of Ongkaan – thought to be old Attapeu. He was enticed to the town by the prospect of two beautiful princesses, Nang Tapkaya and Nang Utumporn who wished to 'live with him'. (Whether this was a euphemism for more than a loose bed and breakfast arrangement is not clear.) There he was ambushed in the forest and, so it is said, murdered – although his body was never recovered. Locals believed that the King never died: his magical powers permitted him to survive and live at the bottom of the river from where he would, from time to time, emerge to perform great deeds.

PAKSE (PAKXE)

The largest town in the S is strategically located at the junction of the Mekong and Xe Don rivers, and has a population of 25,000. It is a busy commercial town, built by the French early this century as an administrative centre for the S.

According to ML Manich in his *History of Laos* (which, it must be said, is a liberal mixture of fact, fiction, fable and fantasy) the French decided to make Pakse the local administrative capital rather than Champassak because they wanted to rule the country without interference from the royal house of Champassak.

Two bridges span the Xe Don River here. The single lane bridge downstream was built by the French in 1925 while the upstream structure was built by the Soviet Union and was not completed until about 1990.

The town has seen better days but the tatty colonial buildings lend an air of old world charm. Pakse is known locally for its large market. It is also the jumping-off point for visiting the old royal capital of Champassak, famed for its pre-Angkor, 7th century Khmer ruins of Wat Phou (see page 194). Presumably overcome with poetic inspiration, someone decided to name the town's roads as if they were highways: No 1 Rd through to No 46 Rd. The result, of course, is that no one knows where they live and tuk-tuk drivers are oblivious to road names. Even some hotel managers have no idea of the road outside their establishment.

Pakse, by anyone's standards, is not a seething metropolis – which, of course, gives it much of its charm. But it may be that this will change. Construction of a new bridge over the Mekong River, financed by the Japanese, is due to begin in 1997 (reportedly the feeder road will run close to the stadium on Route 13 SE of the town centre) and will take 2 years. By the end of the century, then, Pakse will be firmly linked into the Thai economy and this, without question, will bring untold change. Locals, probably, will welcome and love it; romantic *farang* tourists will move on to some quieter corner of Laos.

Places of interest

Frankly, there's not that much to see in Pakse – at least so far as official sites are concerned. Locals tend to mention the **morning market**, slap bang in the centre of town. Even for Southeast Asia this is a major agglomeration of stalls and traders and it seems that Pakse exists for little else. It is best to get here between 0730 and 0800 when the place is in full swing. Although it continues to function throughout the day, it does so in a rather semi-detached fashion.

A new 'sight' to grace Pakse is the **Champassak Museum** on No 13 Rd (the main highway) running E out of town, close to the stadium. It opened in 1995 and displays pieces recovered from Wat Phou, handicrafts from the *Lao Heung* of the Bolovens Plateau, weaponry, musical instruments and a seemingly endless array of photographs of plenums, congresses and assemblies and of prominent Lao dignatories opening hydropower stations and widget factories. Visitors are shown around by charming Lao guides who speak only limited English and nor are there any labels in English but it's still a treat for museum aficionados. Open 0830-1130, 1400-1600, Tues-Sun. Admission: 500 kip. Opposite the museum is the thatlike **Heroes Monument**.

There are two score wats in town but none figures particularly high in the wat hall of fame. **Wat Luang**, in the centre of town, is the oldest. It was built in 1830, but the sim sports a kitsch pink and yellow exterior complete with gaudy relief work, since it was reconstructed and redecorated in 1990 at the cost of 27 million kip. (For most Western visitors this might seem like 27 million kip wasted, or worse. But contributing to the construction or renovation of a monastery brings merit to the contributor, accelerating their progression through the Buddhist cycle of birth and re-birth.) The hefty doors were carved locally. The compound was originally much larger, but in the 1940s, the chief of Champassak province requisitioned the land to

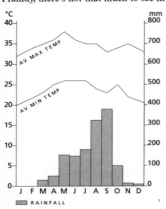

Climate: Pakse

Pakse

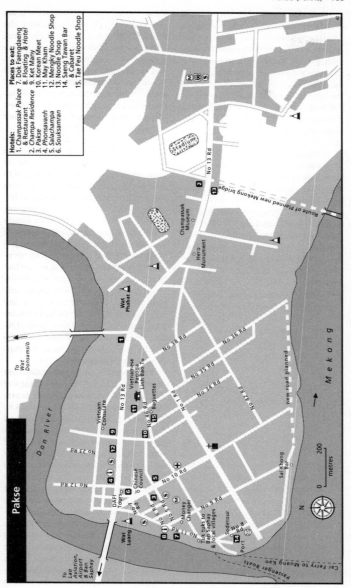

Hotels:
1. Champassak Palace & Restaurant
2. Champa Residence
3. Pakse
4. Phonsavanh
5. Salachampa
6. Souksamran

Places to eat:
7. Dok Faengdaeng Floating & Hotel
8. Ket Many
9. Korean Meat
10. May Khan
11. Mengky Noodle Shop
12. Noodle Shop
13. Saeng Tawan Bar & Cabaret
14. Tae Feu Noodle Shop
15.

To Wat Donsamsib

Don River

Mekong

To Lao Aviation, Airport & Ban Saphay

Wat Luang

DAFI Tours

Vietnam Consulate

Chinese Council

Money Changer

Vietnamese Pagoda Linh Bao Tu

Baguettes

Sodetour

Sai Khong Bar

Champassak Museum

Hero Monument

Wat Phabat

Stadium

Route of planned new Mekong bridge

new road planned

Tuk tuks to Ban Saphay & local villages

Cat Ferry to Muang Kao
Passenger Boats

No 13 Rd
No 28 Rd
No 36 Rd
No 35 Rd
No 34 Rd
No 1 Rd
No 46 Rd
No 23 Rd
No 12 Rd
No 5 Rd
No 3 Rd
No 11 Rd
No 10 Rd
No 9 Rd
No 8 Rd
No 24 Rd

0   200
metres

N

accommodate a new road. To the right of the main entrance stands a stupa containing the remains of Khatai Loun Sasothith, a former Prime Minister who died in 1959. To the right of the sim is the monks' dormitory, which dates from the 1930s; the wooden building behind the sim is the monastic school – the biggest in S Laos – and on the left of the entrance is the library, built in 1943. These earlier structures are, needless to say, the finest – at least for Western sensitivities. The compound backs on to the Xe Don River. There are many more Lao monasteries in town. For those who desire a change there is also a Vietnamese/Chinese Mahayana Buddhist pagoda on No 46 Rd, the **Linh Bao Tu Pagoda** and a **Church** on No 1 Rd.

Boun Oum Palace, on the road N towards Paksong, is now a hotel: the *Champassak Palace Hotel*. Before Thai hotel interests bought the place it was the half-finished palace of the late Prince Boun Oum of Champassak, the colourful overlord of S Laos and a great collector of objets d'art. He began constructing the house of his dreams in 1968 with the intention, so it is said, of creating a monument with more than a thousand rooms. However, the Prince was exiled to France, before his dream was realized. Looking at the hotel it is hard not to conclude that his exile was wholly for the best, at least architecturally. Even so, the hotel is by far the largest structure in town, whether it has 1,000 rooms or not.

Excursions

Wat Phou and Champassak See page 194. *Getting there*: regular bus connections with Champassak – stay on the bus if travelling to Wat Phou. There are also public boats to Champassak, 2 hrs; if taking this – more popular – option it is best to remain on board at Champassak for Wat Phou and alight at the stop downstream from the town (about 4 km). Note that if chartering a boat, which makes

sense in a larger group, a trip to Wat Phou can be combined with a visit to Um Muang (see below). Expect to pay about US$50 for boat hire for maximum of 15 people.

Um Muang, also known as **Muang Tomo** and **Oup Moung**, is a lesser-known temple complex built at about the same time as Wat Phou on the opposite bank (the left bank) of the Mekong (see page 197). It lies 40 km from Pakse and is accessible by boat from town – access by bus is more difficult. *Getting there*: unlike Wat Phou, there are no public boats to Um Muang so it is necessary to charter one from the jetty at the end of No 11 Rd. This makes sense in a big group of 10-15 so the cost of about US$50 can be split. Note that a trip to Um Muang can easily be combined with visits to Wat Phou and Champassak.

Muang Khao lies on the opposite bank of the Mekong to Pakse and, as the name suggests – it means 'Old Town' – was established before its larger brother. Most people come here en route to the Lao-Thai border at Chongmek but it does have some attractive buildings. *Getting there*: hire boats from the pier (2,000 kip return) also a ferry (100 kip) and public passenger boats (200 kip).

Ban Saphay is a specialist silk weaving village 20 km N of town on the banks of the Mekong River. Here about 200 women weave (weaving is still women's work) traditional Lao textiles on hand looms. The designs, like the classic Lao *mut mee*, show clear similarities with those of northeastern Thailand, where the population are also Lao. However, there are also some unique designs. Prices obviously vary according to quality and intricacy but a sarong length (1½m) costs about 8,000 kip. There is also an unusual statue of Indra, Ganesh and Parvati at the local wat. *Getting there*: the village is 5 km off Route No 13, 20 km in total from Pakse. Public tuk-tuks travel from the 'terminal' on No 11 Rd near the port, especially in the morning (500 kip).

Weft *ikat* textile designs from Pakse,
southern Laos (after Fraser-Lu)

Ban Pha Pho is 27 km from Ban Thang Beng on the road to Attapeu. Pha Pho is known of its working elephants. There are more than 90 in the area used to move hardwoods and to transport rice. *Getting there*: by jeep from Pakse.

Tours

There are a number of tour agencies in town. All will arrange tours to local sites like Um Muang, Wat Phou, Khong Island and Champassak. *Sodetour*, No 11 Rd, T 212122, F 212765 arrange more adventurous tours to the Bolovens Plateau, for example. Costs vary considerably according to numbers. A 4-day/3-night tour for a single person might cost over US$500; for 10 people, just US$200 per person. Other tour agencies include: *Lane Xang Travel and Tour*

Company, Souksamran Hotel, No 10 Rd, T 212281; *Champassak Palace Hotel Tours*, No 13 Rd, T 212263; *Inter-Lao Tourisme*, No 13 Rd, T 212226; *DAFI Travel and Tour*, No 13 Rd.

Tour companies and some hotels in town (eg *Souksam Lane* and *Champassak Palace*) will arrange day tours to Wat Phou (between 30,000 and 60,000 kip depending on company and the state of the vehicle) and Khong Phapheng Falls (about 80,000 kip).

A cruiser-cum-houseboat, sometimes named the *Wat Phou* and sometimes the *Croisieres du Mekong*, journeys between Pakse and Don Khong (see page 193) via Wat Phou (see page 194). The 4-day/3-night cruise includes all food and board and is priced at about US$550/person. The boat is well fitted out and the cuisine reportedly good – certainly the most civilized way to journey downstream. For booking, telephone or fax *Mekong Land* in Thailand, T (662) 7128445, F (662) 391 7212.

Local information
● **Accommodation**

B *Champa Residence (Residence du Champa)*, No 13 Rd (on the main road E of town nr the stadium and museum), T 212120, F 212765, a/c, pool planned for 1997, 25 rooms (soon to be 40), in a new colonial style house, hot water and satellite TV, very clean and with some character, attractive terrace and lush garden, credit cards accepted and tours arranged – it is run by *Sodetour* and the manager, Mr Kamphat Boua, is one of Pakse's 'Mr fixits', rec; **B** *Champassak Palace*, No 13 Rd, T 212263, F 212781, a/c, restaurant, this massive chocolate box of a hotel with 60 rooms (looks like it should have 160) was conceived as a palace (see Bak Oum Palace in **Places of interest**), now operated by a Thai firm, it has large rooms, friendly staff, a good terrace, and the best facilities in town, incl a fitness centre and karaoke bar and a great position above the Xe Don River, family rooms are a good deal but the place just can't seem to shake off the notion that it's a palace masquerading as a hotel; **B-C** *Salachampa*, No 10 Rd, T 212273, a/c, small hotel with just 15 rm, although expansion is planned, the most characterful rooms are in the 1920s main building: wooden floors, large, attached bathrooms with hot water showers – the upstairs room with balconies is best, there are also some additional rooms in a new extension, the hotel is run by Mr Outavong Nhouyvanisuong who returned from Paris in 1995 to help his father who originally bought the place in 1946; he speaks excellent French and reasonable English and this place is rec for those looking for a touch of colonial elegance and friendly service.

C *Souksamran*, No 10 Rd, T 212002, some a/c, good restaurant, own bathrooms with hot water, clean small rooms, friendly staff although this is not a place where words like 'ambience' and 'character' spring to mind: functional; tours and car hire available.

D-E *Lao Services Tourism Guesthouse*, nr the hospital, best of the cheaper places to stay, the upstairs rooms are best: one has a/c, one has a large attached bathroom, and one is big but you don't get all three in one, downstairs rooms are cheaper but still clean and serviceable; **D-E** *Pakse*, No 5 Rd (facing the market), T 212131, a range of rooms in this ugly block, some a/c, some with attached bathrooms, none with hot water, friendly enough but rooms can be noisy and check for cleanliness beforehand; **D-E** *Phonsavanh Hotel*, No 13 Rd, this is the only place in town with backpacker prices but it has nothing else going for it except a central location, rooms are grubby and basic, shared facilities, dismal feel and over-priced at that.

● **Places to eat**
Lao/Vietnamese/Thai/Chinese: ♦♦♦-♦♦*May Kham*, No 35 Rd, many locals maintain this serves the best Vietnamese and Lao food in town, a/c restaurant but no pretensions, superb steamed duck and sweet and sour fish although the intestine salad, baked scaly anteater (presumably Pangolin) and baked moose (this far east?) went untasted; ♦♦*Dok Faengdaeng Restaurant*, No 11 Rd, overlooks the Xe Don River but the food here (Thai/Lao/Chinese) is only mediocre – it is mostly used for government functions and big parties, which just about says it all; ♦♦*Ket Many Restaurant*, 227 No 13 Rd, Chinese and Lao food in a/c restaurant, the deep fried frog and Mekong River fish have both been rec, also serves ice-cream; ♦♦-♦*Xuan Mai*, open-air restaurant serving Vietnamese and Lao dishes, excellent value and very good;
Korean: ♦♦♦-♦♦*Korean Grilled Meat Res-*

taurant, No 46 Rd (nr corner with No 24 Rd), classic Korean cook-it-yourself restaurant, how it came to get here may be linked to the presence of Daewoo who are building an HEP station nr Attapeu and have an office in town, food's OK too.

Noodles: ♦*Mengky Noodle Shop*, No 13 Rd (close to Phak Tai Bank), serves bowls of tasty duck and beef noodle soup; ♦*Tae Feu Noodle Shop*, corner of 46 and 34 roads, good Vietnamese noodle shop, clean and tasty.

Bakeries: crusty baguettes are available across town; great for breakfast with wild honey and fresh Bolovens' coffee.

● **Bars**
The liveliest places in town are two bars with karaoke and music situated above the Mekong River. The *Saeng Tawan* is nr the jetty at the end of No 11 Rd while the *Sai Khong* is at the end of No 9 Rd. There is little to choose between them and Pakse's hippest dudes circulate between them. Some nights they are really jumping, at other times they are empty. Girls sit with clients but it all seems in the best possible revolutionary taste.

● **Banks & money changers**
Phak Tai Bank, No 13 Rd, changes US$, pound sterling and French franc TCs as well as most currencies (cash), open Mon-Fri 0800-1630, Sat 0800-1130. There is a branch of the Phak Tai Bank close to the bus station on Route 13, they will only change cash, however. There are money changers in the market area (see map). **Banque Pour le Commerce Exterier Lao**, nr the market (see map), open Mon-Fri 0830-1530, Sat 0930-1000.

● **Embassies & consulates**
Vietnamese consulate, just off No 24 Rd (see map), it is possible to secure visas for Vietnam here. There is also a consulate in Savannakhet, they take 1 day and cost US$30.

● **Post & telecommunications**
Area code: 031.

Post Office: No 8 Rd, overseas telephone calls can also be made from here. Express mail service available. Note the ashtrays made from defused (one hopes) unexploded shells.

● **Shopping**
Morning Market: good for loads of unnecessary plastic and metal objects. Most people come here just to look but there are also some fun things to buy: tin watering cans, clay pots, textiles and sarongs, for instance.

Textiles: traditional handwoven silk cloth is available in the Morning Market. Many people, though, prefer to visit Ban Saphay where it is produced and buy lengths there – about 8,000 kip for a sarong length (1½m) – see **Excursions**. The *mut mee* ikat designs are similar to those produced across the border in the northeastern or Isan region of Thailand. However, here in Laos it is more likely that the cloth will be produced from home-produced silk (in Thailand, silk yarn is often interwoven with imported thread) and coloured using natural rather than aniline dyes.

● **Tour companies & travel agents**
The best sources of information remain the tour companies in town, although it is obviously in their interest to convince visitors that taking a tour is the best, possibly even the only option. *Sodetour's* local manager, Mr Booliep, is a mine of information.

● **Tourist offices**
In 1995 the **Office of Tourism Champassak** opened its doors for the first time on No 11 Rd (see map), T 212021, open 0730-1130, 1400-1500 Mon-Sat. It is really a one man show – namely Mr Vixith Xatakoune – and though he has produced a brochure of sorts, the information is limited and English poor.

● **Transport**
130 km from Muang Khong, 50 km from Paksong, 85 km from Tad Lo, 40 km from Chongmek (Thailand), 38 km from Champassak, 116 km from Salavan, 250 km from Savannakhet.

Local The main modes of local transport are the tuk-tuk and saamlor. Expect to pay about 200-300 kip for a short trip. Share tuk-tuks to local villages leave from the Morning Market and from the stop on No 11 Rd nr the jetty. Tuk-tuks can also be chartered by the hour. Boats are available for charter from the jetty at the end of No 11 Rd (see map). For longer out-of-town journeys, hotels (eg *Souksam Lane* and *Champassak Palace*) and tour companies (eg *Sodetour*) have cars and minibuses (with driver) for charter. Expect to pay 50-80,000 kip/day.

Air Daily connections with Vientiane (US$170 return). **NB** We have been told that only kip is accepted here at present.

Road Bus/truck: Pakse is the local transport hub and while it is easy enough to get to local centres like Salavan and Attapeu, to travel between local centres is more difficult and may require a journey back to Pakse. The main bus terminal is 2 km SE of town on national Route 13. Tuk-tuks wait to transport passengers to the town centre (300 kip). Most departures are in the morning beginning at about 0500. There are connections N with Vientiane (10,000 kip) and Savannakhet, 6-7 hrs (4,000 kip). The road to Savannakhet is poor but improves between Savannakhet and Vientiane. There are regular connections on a bad road with Champassak (2-3 hrs) – stay on the bus for Wat Phou; it stops in a village 2 km from the ruins. Morning departures for Don Khong, 4-5 hrs (2,200 kip) on a poor road; with Salavan, 3 hrs (1,500 kip) on a good road (the quickest route is Route 20, but some buses continue on Route 13 to Paksong and then turn onto Route 23).

Boat Boats for Champassak and Wat Phou depart from the harbour nr the Mekong ferry, 2 hrs (US$25 for a boat). If going to Wat Phou it is better to get off the vessel at the stop past Champassak (about 4 km on). See Wat Phou entry below for more details.

International connections with Thailand
It is possible to cross the border to Ubon Ratchathani in Thailand via Chongmek, from Pakse. Obtain a departure permit from Pakse Police Station, stating date you intend to cross the border (100 kip for permit). Take one of the long-distance passenger boats (200 kip) or the car ferry (100 kip for passengers) from the 'port' at the end of Rd No 11 across the Mekong to the village of Muang Kao. (Literally 'Old Town', and it does have a qaintness largely absent from Pakse. As the name suggests, Muang Kao is more venerable than its larger neighbour on the opp bank but failed to take off when the French concentrated their attentions on Pakse.) From Muang Kao, large songthaews (converted trucks) and ancient share taxis like Chevrolet Belairs wait to ferry passengers to the border post at Chongmek, 1½ hrs (600 kip). This route is also an important exit point for Lao timber, and timber trucks rumble their way towards the border while lorries carrying consumer goods and tankers laden with gasoline travel in the opp direction. There is a sizeable timber yard at Chongmek, in Thailand. At the border there is a post office and duty free shop. Customs formalities are very relaxed. Converted trucks wait to transport passengers to Phibun Mangsahan in Thailand, 1½ hrs (฿13) and from there to Warin Chamrap, 1 hr (฿12), just S of the city of Ubon Ratchathani and about 90 km from the border.

Future road to Vietnam: a new highway linking Pakse with Danang in Vietnam via the Bolovens Plateau and Attapeu is due to be started in 1997. It is being financed by the Asian Development Bank. Completion, though, is still some way off.

CHAMPASSAK AND WAT PHOU

The agricultural town of Champassak with a population of less than 50,000, stretches along the right bank of the Mekong for 4 km. In 1970 Chao Boun Oum began work on yet another rambling palace on the outskirts of Champassak, but it was never finished as he was exiled to France in 1975. It is now the official residence of Champassak's squatter community. The Prince's brothers owned the two French-style houses along the main road running S. Champassak is the nearest town to the fantastic archaeological sight of Wat Phou, although most visitors choose to stay in the much larger settlement of Pakse.

Excursions

The archaeological site of **Wat Phou** is at the foot of the Phou Passak, 8 km SW of Champassak. With its teetering, weathered masonry, it conforms exactly to the Western ideal of the lost city. The mountain behind Wat Phou is also called **Linga Parvata** as the Hindu Khmers thought it resembled a lingam – albeit a strangely proportioned one. The original Hindu temple complex is thought to have been built on this site 800 years ago because of the sacred phallic mountain symbol of Siva, the Hindu deity.

Today, Linga Parvata provides an imposing backdrop to the crumbling temple ruins, most of which date from the 5th and 6th centuries, making them at least 200 years older than Angkor Wat. At that time the Champassak area was the centre of power on the lower Mekong. The Hindu temple only became a Buddhist shrine in later centuries. The French explorer, Francis Garnier, discovered Wat Phou in 1866 and local villagers told him the temple had been built by "another race". Unfortunately, not much is known about Wat Phou's history. Ruins of a palace have been found next to the Mekong at Cesthapoura (half way between Wat Phou and Champassak – now an army camp) and it is thought the 6th century Chenla capital was based there. The old city wall crosses the main road just before the ravine on the return to Champassak. Archaeologists and historians believe most of the building was the work of the Khmer king, Suryavarman II (1131-1150) who was also responsible for starting work on Angkor Wat, Cambodia. The temple remained important for Khmer kings even after they had moved

Wat Phou

their capital to Angkor. They continued to appoint priests to serve at Wat Phou and sent money to maintain the temple until the last days of the Angkor Empire.

The king and dignitaries would originally have sat on the platform above the 'tanks' or baray and presided over official ceremonies or watched aquatic games. In 1959 a palace was built on the platform so the king had somewhere to stay during the annual Wat Phou festival (see below). The smaller house was for the king's entourage. A long avenue leads from the platform to the pavilions. The **processional causeway** was probably built by Khmer King Jayavarman VI (1080-1107), and may have been the inspiration for a similar causeway at Angkor Wat. The grand approach would originally have been flanked by statues of lions and mythical animals, but few traces remain.

The sandstone **pavilions**, on either side of the processional causeway, were added after the main temple and thought to date from the 12th century (most likely in the reign of Suryavarman II). Although crumbling, with great slabs of laterite and collapsed lintels lying artistically around, both pavilions are remarkably intact, and as such are the most-photographed part of the temple complex. The pavilions were probably used for segregated worship for pilgrims, one for women (left) and the other for men (right). The porticoes of the two huge buildings face each other. The roofs were thought originally to have been poorly constructed with thin stone slabs on a wooden beam-frame and later replaced by Khmer tiles.

Only the outer walls now remain but there is enough still standing to fire the imagination – the detailed carving around the window frames and porticos is particularly well-preserved. The laterite used to build the complex was brought from Oup Moung, another smaller Khmer temple complex a few kilometres down river (see below), but the

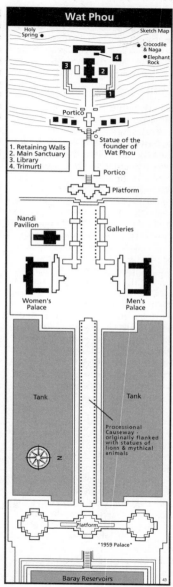

Wat Phou

Holy Spring
Sketch Map
Crocodile & Naga
Elephant Rock

Portico

1. Retaining Walls
2. Main Sanctuary
3. Library
4. Trimurti

Statue of the founder of Wat Phou

Portico

Platform

Nandi Pavilion
Galleries

Women's Palace
Men's Palace

Tank
Tank

Processional Causeway – originally flanked with statues of lions & mythical animals

N

Platform

'1959 Palace'

Baray Reservoirs

carving is in sandstone. The interiors were without partitions but it is thought they used rush matting. The furniture was limited, reliefs only depict low stools and couches. At the rear of the women's pavilion are the remains of a brick construction, believed to have been the queen's quarters. Brick buildings were very costly at that time. The original partitions were probably made of rush matting.

Above the pavilions is a small temple, the **Nandi Pavilion**, with entrances on two sides. It is dedicated to Nandi, the bull (Siva's vehicle) and is a common feature in Hindu temple complexes. There are three chambers, and each would originally have contained statues – but they have been stolen. As the hill begins to rise above the Nandi temple, the remains of six **brick temples** follow the contours, with three on each side of the pathway. All six are completely ruined and their function is unclear. Archaeologists and Khmer historians speculate that they may have been Trimurti temples. At the bottom of the steps is a **portico** and statue of the founder of Wat Phou, Pranga Khommatha. Many of the laterite paving stones and blocks used to build the steps have holes notched down each side – these would have been used to help transport the slabs to the site and drag them into position.

The **main sanctuary**, 90m up the hillside and orientated E-W, was originally dedicated to Siva. The rear section (behind the Buddha statue) is part of the original 6th century brick building. Sacred spring water was channelled through the hole in the back wall of this section and used to wash the sacred linga. The water was then thrown out, down a shute in the right wall, where it was collected in a receptacle. Pilgrims would then wash in the holy water. The front of the temple is later – probably 8th-9th century – and has some fantastic carving: asparas, dancing Vishnu, Indra on a 3-headed elephant (the former emblem of the kingdom of Lane Xang).

Above the portico of the left entrance there is a carving of Siva, the destroyer, tearing a woman in two. The Hindu temple was converted into a Buddhist shrine (either in the 13th century during the reign of the Khmer king Jayavarman VII or when the Lao conquered the area in the 14th century), and a large Buddha statue now presides over its interior. Local legend has it that the Emerald Buddha – now in Bangkok – is a fake and the authentic one is hidden in Wat Phou; archaeologists are highly sceptical. There is also a modern Buddhist monastery complex on the site.

To the left of the sanctuary is what is thought to be the remains of a **small library**. To the right and to the rear of the main sanctuary is the **Trimurti**, the Hindu statues of Vishnu (right), Siva (central) and Brahma (left). Behind the Trimurti is the **holy spring**, believed by the Khmers to have possessed purificatory powers. Some of the rocks beyond the monks' quarters (to the right of the temple) have been carved with the figures of an elephant, a crocodile and a naga. They are likely to have been associated with human sacrifices carried out at the Wat Phou festival. It is said the sacrifice took place on the crocodile and the blood was given to the naga. Visitors in Feb (during the Wat Phou festival) should note that this practice has now stopped.

The UNDP and UNESCO have agreed to finance and assist the renovation of Wat Phou and to establish a museum to hold some of its more vulnerable artefacts. A team of archaeologists is based at the site. Admission to temple complex: 300 kip (goes towards restoration). Camera: 700 kip; video: 3,000 kip. Open 0800-1630 Mon-Sun. Foodstall on the gate. *Getting there*: catch a local bus from the terminal, tell the driver your destination and he should drop you close to the entrance. Alternatively, charter a tuk-tuk in Champassak (7,000 kip, round trip). Bags can be left with the helpful (English-speaking) staff, whilst exploring the ruins. If travelling from Pakse by boat it is better to get off at the stop past Champassak – it is closer to the temple.

Oup Moung (Um Muang) is 1 km from Ban Noy on the Mekong or 2 km from Ban Phia Phay. It is accessible from the main road S from Pakse at Ban Thang Beng, Km 30, and can also be reached by jungle trail – it is about a ½-hr walk from the river. In colonial days, Oup Moung was a stopping point for ships travelling up river from Cambodia. But its main treasure is a 6th century temple complex built at roughly the same time as Wat Phou. The site is little more than an assortment of ruins, surrounded by jungle. A 7-headed sandstone naga greets you on arrival from the Mekong.

Like Wat Phou, the main temple is built of laterite and its carvings are in similar style to those of the bigger complex upriver. There are also remains of a second building, more dilapidated and moss-covered making it difficult to speculate about its function. Hidden amongst the jungle are also the remains of 2 baray. Oup Moung is not on the same scale and nowhere near as impressive as Wat Phou but stumbling across an unknown 6th century Khmer temple in the middle of the jungle is nonetheless a worthwhile diversion. With great slabs of laterite protruding from the undergrowth, and ancient sandstone carvings lying around the bushes, there is no doubt that a great deal lies undiscovered. Oup Moung is believed to be where the laterite blocks, used in the construction of Wat Phou, were taken from. Open Mon-Sun 0800-1630, admission 300 kip. Camera: 700 kip, video camera: 3,000 kip. *Getting there*: by boat from Champassak (10,000 kip), or by tuk-tuk, 30 mins (5,000 kip) or by hire car (30,000 kip) or boat from Pakse (see Pakse entry).

One hour downriver from Pakse is **Hao Pa Kho island**, where Chao Boun Oum had his weekend house, which has lain abandoned since his exile to France.

Festivals

Feb: *Wat Phou festival* (movable) lasts for 3 days with pilgrims coming from far and wide to leave offerings at the temple. In the evening there are competitions – football, boat racing, bull fighting.

Local information

● **Accommodation**

There is limited accommodation in Champassak and really only one place that could be said to be 'comfortable'. Most people stay in Pakse – where there is a much better selection of accommodation – and visit Wat Phou from there.

B *Auberge Sala Wat Phou*, T (Pakse) 212725, T (Vientiane) 213478, F (Vientiane) 216313, a/c, hot water, 9 large, clean rooms, most with bathrooms, stylish and the best place to stay in Champassak, hot water, jeep for hire, friendly but could nonetheless benefit from some improvements.

D *No name resthouse*, on the Wat Phou side of the village, there is a local government resthouse straddling the road, rooms are basic but spotless, 2 local restaurants close by, early morning buses to Pakse can be hailed from outside the complex.

E *Than Bromlap*, behind the Centre de Archéologie (not easy to find).

● **Places to eat**

A reasonable noodle restaurant in the middle of town.

◆*Champassak Restaurant*, by the pier and market.

● **Transport**

Road Bus: Champassak and Wat Phou lie on the W or right bank of the Mekong River, whilst the main road is on the E bank. The turning for the ferry is 34 km from Pakse, and the bus travels on the vehicle ferry, right into town. Regular connections with Pakse, 2 hrs (700 kip) but it is just as quick and far more entertaining to go by boat (see below).

Boat Most tourists visit Wat Phou by boat from Pakse, where accommodation is better. There are regular public boats from the jetty at the end of No 11 Rd in Pakse, 2 hrs (500 kip). It is also possible to charter a boat which makes sense if travelling in a group (they can take about 10-15 people) which also allows a visit to Um Oup (Muang Moung). Expect to pay about US$50.

The Islands of the South

THIS AREA is locally known as *See Pan Done*, 'The 4,000 Islands'. Don Khong and Don Khone are two of these many islands littered across the Mekong right at the southern tip of Laos before the Cambodian border. Half are submerged when the Mekong is in flood. Just before the river enters Cambodia it divides into countless channels. The distance between the most westerly and easterly streams is 14 km – the greatest width of the river in its whole 4,200 km course. The river's volume is swelled by the Kong, San Srepok and Krieng tributaries, which join just upstream. *Pakha* or fresh water dolphins, can sometimes be spotted in this area between Dec and May when they come upsteam to give birth to their young.

ROUTE-WISE: Pakse to Don Khong The journey from Pakse to Don Khong on national Route 13 is just 120 km but, and like many overland journeys in the S of the country, is completed at the breakneck speed of 20-30 km/hr (ie 4-5 hrs) by public bus. The road is unsurfaced for just about its entire length. In the dry season passengers emerge clothed in a film of orange dust and in the wet season travel times are even longer as vehicles get bogged down in the mud. But the trip is worthwhile for the contrast it offers to conditions in Northeastern Thailand, just a few tens of kilometres W. Much of the area is still forested (large quantities of Lao timber are trucked to Thailand via Chongmek, W of Pakse) and villages are intermittent even on this road – the national artery for N-S communications. Paddy fields sometimes appear to be fighting a losing battle against the encroaching forest and most houses are roofed in thatch rather than zinc. At Ban Hat Xay Khoune a car ferry and boats wait to transport passengers across the Mekong to Don Khong and Muang Khong.

DON KHONG AND MUANG KHONG

Don Khong is the largest of the Mekong islands at 16 km long and 8 km wide, and the main village is **Muang Khong**, a small former French settlement. Muang Khong has a population of no more than 1,000 and it feels more like a village than a town. Pigs and chickens scrabble for food under the houses and just 50m inland the houses give way to paddy fields. There are two wats here. **Wat Kan Khong**

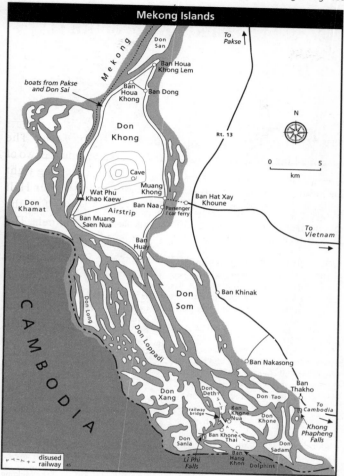

Mekong Islands

is visible from the jetty: a large gold Buddha in the mudra of subduing Mara garishly overlooks the Mekong. Much more attractive is **Wat Chom Thong** at the upstream extremity of the village which may date from the early 19th century but which was then much extended during the colonial period. The unusual Khmer-influenced sim may be gently de-

caying but it is doing so with style and the wat compound, with its carefully tended plants and elegant buildings is very peaceful. The naga heads on the roof of the main sim are craftily designed to channel water: it issues from their mouths. The old sim to the left of the main entrance is also notable – although it is usually kept locked because of its

Muang Khong

poor condition. For early risers the **morning market** in Muang Khong is also worthwhile – if only to see the fish that are served in the restaurants here before they are consigned to the cooking pot. Note that the market only really operates between 0530 and 0730. If you are getting up for the market, it is worth setting the alarm clock even earlier to get onto the banks of the Mekong before 0600 when the sun rises over the hills to the E, picking out the silhouettes of fishermen in their canoes.

Excursions

Most people come to Muang Khong as a base for visiting the **Li Phi** and **Khong Phapheng Falls** (see page 202). However the island itself is worth exploring by bicycle and deserves more time than it gets from most visitors. It is flat – except in the interior – the roads are quiet, so there is less risk of being mown down by a timber truck and the villages and countryside offer a glimpse of 'traditional' Laos. Most people take the southern 'loop' – a distance of about 25 km or 2 hrs. The villages along the section of road from **Ban Muang Saen Nua** southwards are wonderfully picturesque. Few people bicycle the northern loop – it takes a full day (0800-1600) and in any case is not so attractive as the S. But just N of Ban Muang Saen Nua is a hilltop wat which is arguably Don Khong's main claim to national fame. **Wat Phu Khao Kaew**

(Glass Hill Monastery) is built on the spot where there is an entrance leading down to the underground lair of the nagas – **Muang Nak**. This underground town lies beneath the waters of the Mekong and there are several tunnels that lead to the surface – another is at That Luang in Vientiane. Lao legend has it that the nagas will come to the surface to protect the Lao whenever the country is in danger. This means, to most Lao, whenever the Thais decide to attack. Some people believe that the Thais tricked the Lao to build *thats* over the holes to prevent the nagas coming to their rescue – the hole at Wat Phu Khao Kaew is likewise covered.

Another possible 'sight' – although rumour has it that no tourist has ever been there (or guide book writer for that matter – all are notably loose in their descriptions of how to get there) is a **holy cave** in the **Phu Khiaw** or **Green Mountains** in the centre of the island. The cave houses a number of revered and ancient wooden Buddha images. Every Lao New Year (Apr) townsfolk climb up to the cave to bathe the images. To get there employ a local as a guide and then write and tell us about it (please).

Local festivals

Dec: *Boat Racing* (early in the month). This 5-day festival with boat races on the river opposite Muang Khong coincides with National Day on the 2 Dec. A great deal of celebration, eating and drinking.

Local information
● **Accommodation**

B-C *Auberge Sala Done Khong*, a/c, this is the best place to stay on Don Khong, large rooms in traditional wooden house (it was the holiday home of the previous regime's foreign minister), the best are in the main building on the first floor where there is an attractive balcony overlooking the Mekong, attached bathrooms with hot water showers, clean and professionally run, tours arranged, bicycles for hire, good food – very relaxing, electricity 1730-2400; **B-E** *Souk Sun Bungalow and Guesthouse*, N end of town nr Wat Chom Thong, a new and expanding place with a range of rooms from well-designed a/c rooms with attached bathrooms to simple rooms with fans and shared facilities. The manageress, Mrs Khamsone, is clearly trying to cover all her options, and along with the wide array of accommodation will arrange boats to visit the falls to see the freshwater dolphins etc.

D *Done Khong Guesthouse*, opp the jetty, restaurant attached, clean rooms in raised wooden house, attractive sitting area which catches the morning and evening breeze, fans, shared toilets and showers (in fact like mandis – a barrel of water and dipper) but they were spotless on our last visit, friendly, bicycles for hire; **D** *Sala Done Khong II* (aka *Annex*), this is the cheaper annex to the *Auberge Sala Done Khong*, also well-run but without the character of its more pricey sister establishment.

● **Places to eat**

There is a growing number of simple noodle houses and a few more sophisticated places. Because there is no electricity most places only serve fish and chicken: killing a pig or cow requires a lot of hungry diners. For some reason, although many other towns and areas also make such a claim, Don Khong is renowned for the quality of its *lau-lao* (rice liquor).

♦♦♦-♦♦*Auberge Sala Done Khong*, excellent Lao food incl steamed fish in banana leaves or *mok pa* (a house speciality), ginger chicken and fish in coconut milk, note that it only operates when they have people staying in the rooms; ♦♦♦-♦♦*Souk Sun Chinese Restaurant*, attractive place built over the Mekong, only serves Chinese food incl good local fish and tasty honeyed pork; ♦♦-♦*Done Khong Guesthouse*, the restaurant attached to this guesthouse produces good food – nothing flash, just simple single dish meals.

● **Banks & money changers**

No facilities in town, although guesthouses will change cash at rates slightly lower than market rate.

● **Electricity**

Only from 1800-2000. Some hotels/guesthouses have their own generators.

● **Post & telecommunications**

Post Office: opp the jetty in centre of town.

Telephone: there are no telephones on the island.

● **Transport**

Local Bicycles for hire from the *Auberge Sala Done Khong* and the *Done Khong Guesthouse*. There are also a few tuk-tuks in town but they are hardly required around tiny Muang Khong. It is, though, possible to charter a tuk-tuk for the trip to the far side of the island, load on a bicycle or two, and then cycle back.

Air There is an airstrip W of Muang Khong, in the centre of the island. **Lao Aviation** have 3 flights a week between Muang Khong and Pakse (on Tues, Fri and Sun).

Road Don Khong is approximately 120 km S of Pakse on Route 13. **Truck/bus**: regular morning bus connections with Pakse, 4-5 hrs (2,200 kip). See 'Route-wise: Pakse to Don Khong', page 198.

Boat From Ban Hat Xay Khoune it is possible to take a motorboat (1,500 kip for the whole vessel divided by the number of passengers) or, for a cheaper crossing, take the car ferry. The ferries, which spend most of their time transporting ancient Russian Zil trucks loaded with Cambodian rosewood across the Mekong, are made from two old US pontoon boats on either side of an ageing diesel river boat with a pallet lying crossways over all 3 (100 kip). There are no public boat connections with Pakse or Champassak because of the rapids upstream from Don Khong. However, boats do occasionally take the longer route to the W of Don Khong, thus avoiding the treacherous water upstream from Muang Khong. The boats dock at Ban Muang Sen Nua, although larger vessels tend to moor at the northern tip of the island – at Ban Houa Khong Lem. Although there are no public boats between Pakse and Don Khong, there are 3-4 boats/day from Pakse to Don Sai, about ¾ of the way S. From here it is possible to charter a private boat for the final leg to Don Khong (US$50). Chartering a boat the whole way would cost about US$200.

International connections Cambodia, on paper, is easily accessible. But the border is closed to foreigners and in any case this area of Cambodia is dangerous and travel is not advisable.

THE WATERFALLS, DON KHONE AND DON DETH

For those who have travelled on the upper reaches of the Mekong, where, for much of the year it is a slow, lazy river, huge roaring waterfalls might seem rather out of character. But here, near the Cambodian border, the underlying geology changes and the river is punctuated by rapids and the Khone Falls. The name Khone is used loosely and there are in fact two impressive cascades in the area: the **Li Phi** (or **Samphamit Falls**) and **Khong Phapheng Falls** – the latter are the biggest in Southeast Asia and reputedly the widest in the world. Lt Francis Garnier was suitably impressed when he ascended the Khon cataract in 1860, his boatmen hauling their vessels "through a labyrinth of rocks, submerged trees, and prostrate trunks still clinging to earth by their many roots".

In the early 1990s environmentalists were horrified to read that there were plans afoot to build a 5-star hotel, casino and golf course at Khong Phapheng. A two-lane highway will link the resort with Pakse, and Pakse with Ubon Ratchathani. A heliport and landing strip are also planned. Fortunately the original investors pulled out of the monstrous scheme, although a memorandum of understanding was still in force in early 1996 and survey work was continuing. How such a scheme was ever considered may be linked to the fact that former Prime Minister Khamtay Siphandone was born in the area and his elder brother has links with Thai developers. Most locals like the idea: it will bring money and jobs. Most outsiders are aghast at the thought. At the party congress of 1996, Khamtay was unceremoniously ejected from his position as Prime Minister largely, it is said, because he had become too close to Thai big business. This may mean a quiet death for the project.

The closest place to take a boat to **Li Phi Falls** is from Ban Nakasang, downriver from Ban Hat Xay Khoune, the crossing point to Don Khong. The boat-trip down the fast-flowing channels between the many islands to **Don Khone** is very picturesque; the islands are covered in coconut palms, flame trees, stands of bamboo, kapok trees and hardwoods. The river is riddled with eddies and rapids and it demands a skilled helmsman to negotiate them. In the distance, a few kilometres to the S, are the Khong Hai Mountains which dominate the skyline and delineate the frontier between Laos and Cambodia.

Before putting into **Ban Khone Nua**, the main settlement on Don Khone, **Don Deth** 'port' is on the right, with what remains of its steel rail jetty. In the late 19th and early 20th centuries Don Khone served as an important by-pass around the rapids for French cargo boats sailing up-river from Phnom Penh. Ports were built at the S end (Don Khone) and N end (Don Deth) of this string of rapids and cascades, and were linked by a 5 km stretch of narrow gauge **railway track**. This railway has the unique distinction of being the only line the French ever built in Laos, although whether a 5 km stretch of steel counts as a 'line' is a moot point. A colonial-style customs house still stands in the shadow of the impressive railway bridge at Ban Khone. On the S side of the bridge lie the rusted corpses of the old locomotive and boiler car.

From the bridge, follow the path through Ban Khone Thai and then wind through the paddy fields for 1½ km (20 mins walk) to **Li Phi** (also called **Somphamit** and **Khone Yai**) falls, which are more a succession of raging rapids, crashing through a narrow rocky gorge. In the wet season, when the rice is green, the area is beautiful – in the dry season, it is scorching. From the main vantage point on a jagged, rocky outcrop, the falls aren't that impressive, as a large stretch of the falls are obscured.

One of the few places in the world where it is possible to see **freshwater dolphins** is also nearby (see map), not far from the village of Ban Hang Khon. The walk across Don Khone is some 6-8 km, or 2 hrs and some guesthouses (eg *Souk Sun Bungalow and Guesthouse*) bring bicycles along on the boats for the overland journey. Canadian Ian Baird runs the Lao Community Fisheries and Dolphin Protection Project here as he has been doing since 1993 on a budget of US$60,000/year. He has enticed 44 villages in the area to help him protect the rare freshwater Irrawaddy dolphins (*Orcaella brevirostris*) – there are probably no more than 30 here, and this is thought to be the largest group in the Mekong. Posters that he had printed showing a mother and calf that 'drowned' after being caught in fishing nets, are stuck up in many restaurants and guesthouses on Don Khong. The problem for Baird is that the Lao-Cambodian border transects the dolphin pool. Not only does this mean Baird has to organize a joint approach in a famously lawless area (at least on the Cambodian side), but Cambodian fishermen seem hooked on dynamite and hand grenade fishing technology – the piscine equivalent of the scorched earth approach. The dolphins come here only during the winter months between Dec and May and the best chance of seeing them is morning (0800-0930) or late afternoon (1700-1830).

About 36 km S, the road down to **Khong Phapheng Falls** from Route 13 forks below Ban Thakho: one branch leads to a vantage point for a fantastic front-on view of the falls, the other leads down to the bank of the Mekong, 200m away, just above the lip of the falls. At this deceptively tranquil spot, the river is gathering momentum before it plunges over the edge. The 'front view' vantage point has a large wooden struc-

ture, built up on stilts, overlooking the cascades. When you see the huge volume of white water boiling and surging over the jagged rocks below, it is hard to imagine that there is another 10 km-width of river running through other channels. A perilous path leads down from the viewpoint to the edge of the water. Unsurprisingly, the river is impassable at this juncture, as an 1860s French expedition led by adventurers Doudart de Lagrée and Francis Garnier discovered. Garnier wrote:

"There, in the midst of rocks and grassy islets, an enormous sheet of water leaps headlong from a height of 70 ft, to fall back in floods of foam, again to descend from crag to crag, and finally glide away beneath the dense vegetation of the forest. As the river at this point is about 1,000 yards in width, the effect is singularly striking."

It was said that a tongue of rock once extended from the lip of the falls, and the noise of Khong Phapheng – literally 'the voice of the Mekong' – crashing over this outcrop could be heard many miles away. The rock apparently broke off during a flood surge, but the cascades still make enough noise to justify their name.

The principal settlement near Khone Falls, and the last Laotian town of any size before the Cambodian border, is Khinnak.

Getting to the falls and elsewhere: most people get to the falls or to see the dolphins by asking one of the guesthouses to arrange a trip. There is usually only time to see the dolphins and the railway, or the Li Phi Falls and the railway, or the Khong Phapheng falls. However, there is limited accommodation available for those who might wish to stay overnight (see **Accommodation**, below). For the Li Phi Falls, the dolphins and the other sights of Don Khone, most visitors take a boat from Muang Khong (Don Khong Island) to Ban Khone Nua, and walk or bicycle from there. For the Khong Phapheng Falls most take a boat to Ban Nakasong and then charter a tuk-tuk or motorcycle from there (15,000 kip return). To charter a smallish local boat for the day costs about 18-20,000 kip (0800-1600). A cheaper option is to take the ferry back to Ban Hat Xay Khoune, walk the 1 km or so to Route 13 and then hitch or catch a bus to Ban Thakho or Ban Nakasong. Note, though, that buses are very irregular.

Excursions (from Don Khone)
It is possible to hire a boat for the day, and visit the islands and go fishing (about 20,000 kip/day).

Tours
A number of companies run tours to the area, especially from Pakse (see Pakse **Tours**, page 191). There is also a cruiser which makes its way downstream to the northern tip of Don Khong during a regular 4-day/3-night cruise (see Pakse Tours for details).

Local information
● **Accommodation**
There is little accommodation in the area although Ban Khinak is a large (-ish) commercial and trading centre and has at least one hotel.

D-E *Sala Don Khone*, Ban Khone Nua, just 3 rooms, private bathroom, no electricity, good base from which to explore the area, the place is run by the *Auberge Sala Done Khong* in Muang Khong, expansion planned.

● **Places to eat**
Ban Nakasong (the jumping off point for Don Khone): there are two small thatched beachside ♦restaurants which serve good chicken noodle soup (*feu*). In the rainy season they move further up the bank.

● **Transport**
Boat From Ban Nakasong, 25 mins.

Examples of Lao sculpture on the left a snake under the feet of the portal
guardian from Wat Aham and on the right Devata (goddess) on the sanctuary
door portal at Wat May
Source: Parmentier, Henri (1988) *L'Art du Laos* École Française D'Extrême-Orient, Paris

Bangkok and the Mekong Towns

MANY people visiting Laos pass through Thailand en route. Bangkok has the greatest concentration of companies offering tours to Laos and it is also the best place to obtain a visa. There are regular air connections between Bangkok's Don Muang and Vientiane's Wattay airports and with the easing of travel restrictions to Laos many people are also opting to enter the country at one of the several overland entry points in the North and Northeastern regions of Thailand.

This section of the book provides a basic guide to Bangkok and those Mekong towns where it is possible to cross into Laos. There is also a short **Information for travellers** section providing some general practical background. The information has been condensed from the *Thailand Handbook* also published by Footprint Handbooks. Please note that the information here is not comprehensive: much of the background material, details on the more obscure sights, and practicalities have been either omitted or substantially edited. Those wishing to spend any length of time in Thailand are strongly advised to buy a dedicated guide to the country. We, naturally enough, would recommend the *Thailand Handbook*.

BANGKOK

Bangkok is not a city to be trifled with: a population of 11 million struggle to make their living in a conurbation with perhaps the worst traffic in the world; a level of pollution which causes some children, so it is (rather improbably) said, to lose four intelligence points by the time they are seven; and a climate which can take one's breath away. (The *Guinness Book of Records* credits Bangkok as the world's hottest city because of the limited seasonal and day-night temperature variations.) As journalist Hugo Gurdon wrote at the end of 1992: "One would have to describe Bangkok as unliveable were it not for the fact that more and more people live here". But, Bangkok is not just a perfect case study for academics studying the strains of rapid urban growth. There is charm and fun beneath the grime, and Bangkokians live life with a *joie de vivre* which belies the congestion. There are also numerous sights, including the spectacular Grand Palace, glittering wats (monasteries) and the breezy river, along with excellent food and good shopping.

The official name for Thailand's capital city begins Krungthep – phramaha – nakhonbawon – rathanakosin – mahinthara – yutthayaa – mahadilok –

phiphobnobpharaat – raatchathaanii – buriiromudomsantisuk. It is not hard to see why Thais prefer the shortened version – Krungthep, or the 'City of Angels'. The name used by the rest of the world – Bangkok – is derived from 17th century Western maps, which referred to the city (or town as it then was) as Bancok, the 'village of the wild plum'. This name was only superseded by Krungthep in 1782, and so the Western name has deeper historical roots.

In 1767, Ayutthaya, then the capital of Siam, fell to the marauding Burmese for the second time and it was imperative that the remnants of the court and army find a more defensible site for a new capital. Taksin, the Lord of Tak, chose Thonburi, on the western banks of the Chao Phraya River, far from the Burmese and from Phitsanulok, where a rival to the throne had become ensconced. In 3 years, Taksin had established a kingdom and crowned himself king. His reign was short-lived, however; the pressure of thwarting the Burmese over three arduous years caused him to go mad and in 1782 he was forced to abdicate. General Phraya Chakri was recalled from Cambodia and invited to accept the throne. This marked the beginning of the present Chakri Dynasty.

Bangkok highlights

Temples Bangkok's best known sight is the temple of *Wat Phra Kaeo*, situated within the grounds of the *Grand Palace* (page 214). Other notable temples include *Wat Pho* (page 212), *Wat Arun* (page 224), *Wat Suthat* (page 218) and *Wat Traimitr* (page 221).

Museums Bangkok's extensive *National Museum* houses the best collection in the country (page 216); other notable collections include those in *Jim Thompson's House* (page 226), the *Suan Pakkard Palace* (page 225) and *Vimanmek Palace* (page 225).

Markets The sprawling *Chatuchak Weekend market* (page 227), *Nakhon Kasem* or Thieves' market (page 219), *Pahurat Indian market* (page 219) and Chinatown's *Sampeng Lane* (page 221).

Boat trip On *Bangkok's canals* (page 221).

Excursions Day trips to the *floating market at Damnoen Saduak* (page 228).

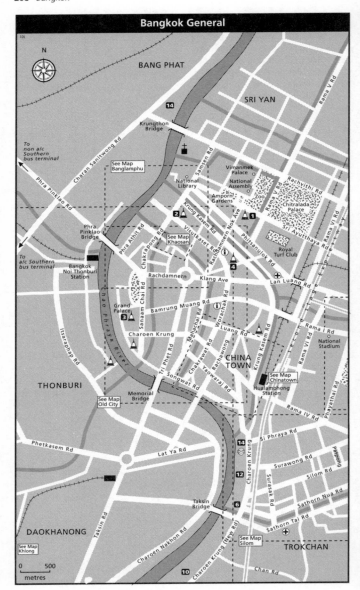

Bangkok General

BANG PHAT

SRI YAN

N

Krungthon Bridge

To non a/c Southern bus terminal

Phra Pinklao Rd

Charan Sanitwong Rd

See Map Banglamphu

National Library

Samsen Rd

Vimanmek Palace

National Assembly

Amporn Gardens

Rachvithi Rd

Zoo

Chitralada Palace

Sri Ayutthaya Rd

Krung Kasem Rd

Rachadamnern Nok Ave

Phittanulok Rd

Royal Turf Club

Phra Pinklao Bridge

Phra Athit Rd

Chakrapong Rd

Visukkatet Rd

See Map Khaosan

To a/c Southern bus terminal

Bangkok Noi Thonburi Station

Rachdamnern

Klang Ave

Lan Luang Rd

Sanaam Chai Rd

Grand Palace

Bamrung Muang Rd

Mahachai Rd

Worachak Rd

Rama I Rd

Charoen Krung

Luang Rd

Rachawong

Krung Kasem Rd

National Stadium

Tri Phet Rd

Chakrawat Rd

Yaowarai Rd

CHINA TOWN

Rama VI Rd

Phayathai Rd

Songwat Rd

See Map Chinatown

Hualamphong Station

THONBURI

Memorial Bridge

See Map Old City

Rama IV Rd

Phetkasem Rd

Lat Ya Rd

Charoen Krung

Si Phraya Rd

Surawong Rd

Surasak Rd

Silom Rd

Patpong

Taksin Bridge

Charoen Krung (New) Rd

Sathorn Nua Rd

Sathorn Tai Rd

DAOKHANONG

Taksin Rd

Charoen Nakhon Rd

See Map Silom

TROKCHAN

See Map Khlong

Chan Rd

0   500
metres

Itsaraphap Rd

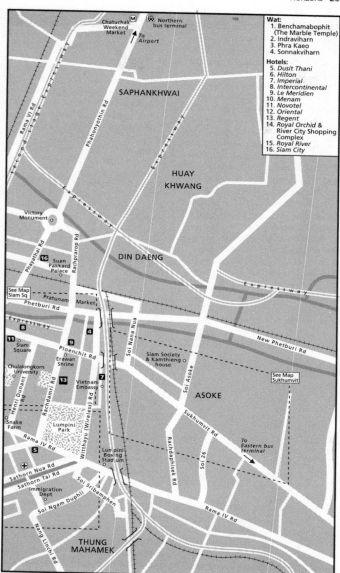

Wat:
1. Benchamabophit (The Marble Temple)
2. Indraviharn
3. Phra Kaeo
4. Sonnakviharn

Hotels:
5. *Dusit Thani*
6. *Hilton*
7. *Imperial*
8. *Intercontinental*
9. *Le Meridien*
10. *Menam*
11. *Novotel*
12. *Oriental*
13. *Regent*
14. *Royal Orchid & River City Shopping Complex*
15. *Royal River*
16. *Siam City*

In 1782, Chakri (now known as Rama I) moved his capital across the river to Bangkok (an even more defensible site) anticipating trouble from King Bodawpaya who had seized the throne of Burma. The river that flows between Thonburi and Bangkok and on which many of the luxury hotels – such as *The Oriental* – are now located, began life not as a river at all, but as a canal (or *khlong*). The canal was dug in the 16th century to reduce the distance between Ayutthaya and the sea by shortcutting a number of bends in the river. Since then, the canal has become the main channel of the Chao Phraya River. Its original course has shrunk in size, and is now represented by two khlongs, Bangkok Yai and Bangkok Noi.

This new capital of Siam grew in size and influence. Symbolically, many of the new buildings were constructed using bricks from the palaces and temples of the ruined former capital of Ayutthaya. But population growth was hardly spectacular – it appears that outbreaks of cholera sometimes reduced the population by a fifth or more in a matter of a few weeks. An almanac from 1820 records that "on the 7th month of the waxing moon, a little past 2100 in

the evening, a shining light was seen in the N-W and multitudes of people purged, vomited and died". In 1900 Bangkok had a population of approximately 200,000. By 1950 it had surpassed 1 million, and in 1992 it was, officially, 5,562,141. Most people believe that the official figure considerably understates the true population of the city – 10-11 million would be more realistic. By 2010, analysts believe Bangkok will have a population of 20 million. As the population of the city has expanded, so has the area that it encompasses: in 1900 it covered a mere 13.3 sq km; in 1958, 96.4 sq km; while today the Bangkok Metropolitan region extends over 1,600 sq km and the outskirts of the city sprawl into neighbouring provinces. Such is the physical size of the capital that analysts talk of Bangkok as an EMR or Extended Metropolitan Region.

In terms of size, Bangkok is at least 23 times larger than the country's second city, Chiang Mai – 40 times bigger, using the unofficial population estimates. It also dominates Thailand in cultural, political and economic terms. All Thai civil servants have the ambition of serving in Bangkok, while many regard a posting to the poor NE as (almost) the kiss of death. Most of the country's industry is located in and around the city (the area contributes 45% of national GDP), and Bangkok supports a far wider array of services than other towns in the country. Although the city contains only 10% of the kingdom's population, its colleges of higher education graduate 71% of degree students, it contains 83% of pharmacists, and has 69% of Thailand's telephone lines. It is because of Bangkok's dominance that people often, and inaccurately, say 'Bangkok is Thailand'.

The immediate impression of the city to a first-time visitor is bedlam. The heat, noise, traffic, pollution – the general chaos – can be overwhelming. This was obviously the impression of Somerset

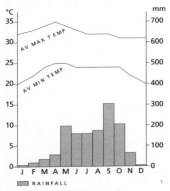

RAINFALL

Climate: Bangkok

Maugham, following his visit in 1930:

> 'I do not know why the insipid Eastern food sickened me. The heat of Bangkok was overwhelming. The wats oppressed me by their garish magnificence, making my head ache, and their fantastic ornaments filled me with malaise. All I saw looked too bright, the crowds in the street tired me, and the incessant din jangled my nerves. I felt very unwell ...'

It is estimated that over 1 million Bangkokians live in slum or squatter communities, while average traffic speeds can be less than 10 km/hour. During peak periods the traffic congestion is such that 'gridlock' seems inevitable. The figures are sometimes hard to believe: US$500mn of petrol is consumed each year while cars wait at traffic lights; one day in Jul 1992 it took 11 hrs for some motorists to get home after a monsoon storm; and the number of cars on the capital's streets increases by 800 each day (the figure for the country is 1,300); while traffic speeds are snail pace – and expected to fall further. For those in Bangkok who are concerned about their city and the environment, the worst aspect is that things will undoubtedly get worse before they get any better – despite the plethora of road building programmes the car and truck population is growing faster than the roads to accommodate them. The government of former Prime Minister Anand did give the go-ahead to a number of important infrastructural projects, but many would say a decade too late. As one analyst has observed: "Bangkok is only just beginning to happen". Even editorial writers at the *Bangkok Post* who, one might imagine, are used to the traffic find it a constant topic for comment. At the end of 1993 the newspaper stated: "Bangkok's traffic congestion and pollution are just about the worst in the world – ever. Never in history have people had to live in the conditions we endure each day".

PLACES OF INTEREST

This section is divided into five main areas: the Old City, around the Grand Palace; the Golden Mount, to the E of the Old City; Chinatown, which lies to the S of the Golden Mount; the Dusit area, which is to the N and contains the present day parliament buildings and the King's residence; and Wat Arun and the khlongs, which are to the W, on the other bank of the Chao Phraya River in Thonburi. Other miscellaneous sights, not in these areas, are at the end of the section, under Other places of interest.

GETTING AROUND THE SIGHTS

Buses, both a/c and non-a/c, travel to all city sights (see Local transport, page 249). A taxi or tuk-tuk for a centre of town trip should cost ฿50-100. Now that taxis are almost all metered visitors may find it easier, and more comfortable (they have a/c) – not to mention safer – than the venerable tuk-tuk, although a ride on one of these three-wheeled machines is a tourist experience in itself. If travelling by bus, a bus map of the city – and there are several, available from most bookshops and hotel gift shops – is an invaluable aid. The express river taxi is a far more pleasant way to get around town and is also often quicker than going by road (see map page 223 for piers, and box page 222).

THE OLD CITY

The Old City contains the largest concentration of sights in Bangkok, and for visitors with only one day in the capital, this is the area to concentrate on. It is possible to walk around all the sights mentioned below quite easily in a single day. For the energetic, it would also be possible to visit the sights in and around the Golden Mount. If intending to walk around all the sights in the old city start from Wat Pho; if you have less time or less energy, begin with the Grand Palace.

Wat Phra Chetuphon

(Temple of the Reclining Buddha) or **Wat Pho**, as it is known to Westerners (a contraction of its original name Wat Po-taram), has its entrance on Chetuphon Rd on the S side of the complex. It is 200 years old and the largest wat in Bangkok, now most famous for its 46m long, 15m high gold-plated reclining Buddha, with beautiful mother-of-pearl soles (showing the 108 auspicious signs). The reclining Buddha is contained in a large viharn built during the reign of Rama III (1832).

The grounds of the wat contain more than 1,000 bronze images, rescued from the ruins of Ayutthaya and Sukhothai

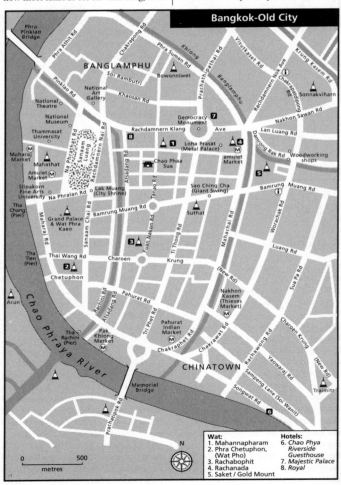

Bangkok–Old City

Wat:	Hotels:
1. Mahannapharam	6. *Chao Phya Riverside Guesthouse*
2. Phra Chetuphon, (Wat Pho)	7. *Majestic Palace*
3. Rachabophit	8. *Royal*
4. Rachanada	
5. Saket / Gold Mount	

0   500
metres

N

Wat Phra Chetuphon (Wat Pho)

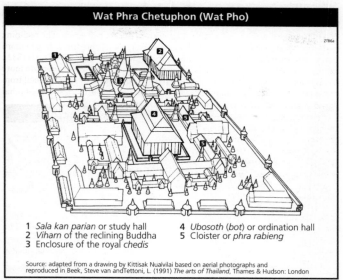

1 *Sala kan parian* or study hall
2 *Viharn* of the reclining Buddha
3 Enclosure of the royal *chedis*
4 *Ubosoth* (*bot*) or ordination hall
5 Cloister or *phra rabieng*

Source: adapted from a drawing by Kittisak Nualvilai based on aerial photographs and reproduced in Beek, Steve van andTettoni, L. (1991) *The arts of Thailand*, Thames & Hudson: London

by Rama I's brother. The bot, or ubosoth, houses a bronze Ayutthayan Buddha in an attitude of meditation and the pedestal of this image contains the ashes of Rama I. Also notable is the 11-piece altar table set in front of the Buddha, and the magnificent mother-of-pearl inlaid doors which are possibly the best examples of this art from the Bangkok Period (depicting episodes from the Ramakien). The bot is enclosed by two galleries which house 394 seated bronze Buddha images. They were brought from the N during Rama I's reign and are of assorted periods and styles. Around the exterior base of the bot are marble reliefs telling the story of the Ramakien as adapted in the Thai poem the *Maxims of King Ruang* (formerly these reliefs were much copied by making rubbings onto rice paper). The 152 panels are the finest of their type in Bangkok. They recount only the second section of the Ramakien: the abduction and recovery of Ram's wife Seeda. The

rather – to Western eyes – unsatisfactory conclusion to the story as told here has led some art historians to argue they were originally taken from Ayutthaya. Thai scholars argue otherwise.

A particular feature of the wat are the 95 chedis of various sizes which are scattered across the 20-acre complex. To the left of the bot are four large chedis, memorials to the first four Bangkok kings. The library nearby is richly decorated with broken pieces of porcelain. The large top-hatted stone figures, the stone animals and the Chinese pagodas scattered throughout the compound came to Bangkok as ballast on the royal rice boats returning from China. Rama III, whose rice barges dominated the trade, is said to have had a particular penchant for these figures, as well as for other works of Chinese art. The Chinese merchants who served the King – and who are said to have called him *Chao Sua* or millionaire – loaded the empty barges with the carvings to please their lord.

The Emerald Buddha

Wat Phra Kaeo was specifically built to house the Emerald Buddha, the most venerated Buddha image in Thailand, carved from green jade (the emerald in the name referring only to its colour), a mere 75 cm high, and seated in an attitude of meditation. It is believed to have been found in 1434 in Chiang Rai, and stylistically belongs to the Late Chiang Saen or Chiang Mai schools. Since then, it has been moved on a number of occasions – to Lampang, Chiang Mai and Laos (both Luang Prabang and Vientiane). It stayed in Vientiane for 214 years before being recaptured by the Thai army in 1778 and placed in Wat Phra Kaeo on 22 March, 1784. The image wears seasonal costumes of gold and jewellery; one each for the hot, cool and the rainy seasons. The changing ceremony occurs 3 times a year in the presence of the King.

Buddha images are often thought to have personalities. The Phra Kaeo is no exception. It is said, for example, that such is the antipathy between the Phra Bang in Luang Prabang (Laos) and the Phra Kaeo that they can never reside in the same town.

Rama III wanted Wat Pho to become known as a place of learning, a kind of exhibition of all the knowledge of the time and it is regarded as Thailand's first university. Admission ฿20. Open 0900-1700 Mon-Sun. **NB** From Tha Tien pier at the end of Tha Wang Rd, close to Wat Pho, it is possible to get boats to Wat Arun (see page 221). Wat Pho is also probably Bangkok's most respected centre of traditional Thai massage, and politicians, businessmen and military officers go there to seek relief from the tensions of modern life. Most medical texts were destroyed when the Burmese sacked the former capital, Ayutthaya, in 1776 and in 1832 Rama III had what was known about Thai massage inscribed on stone and then had those stones set into the walls of Wat Pho to guide and teach. For Westerners wishing to learn the art, special 30-hrs courses can be taken for ฿3,000, stretching over either 15 days (2 hrs/day) or 10 days (3 hrs/day). The centre is located at the back of the Wat, on the opposite side from the entrance. A massage costs ฿100 for 30 mins, ฿180 for 1 hr. With herbal treatment, the fee is ฿260 for 1.30 hr. For other centres of Thai Traditional massage see page 249.

Grand Palace and Wat Phra Kaeo
About 10-15 mins walk from Wat Pho northwards along Sanaam Chai Rd is the entrance to the **Grand Palace** and **Wat Phra Kaeo**. (**NB** The main entrance is the Viseschaisri Gate on Na Phralan Rd.) The Grand Palace is situated on the banks of the Chao Phraya River and is the most spectacular – some might say 'gaudy' – collection of buildings in Bangkok. The complex covers an area of over 1.5 sq km and the architectural plan is almost identical to that of the Royal Palace in the former capital of Ayutthaya. It was started in 1782 and was subsequently added to. Initially, the palace was the city, the seat of power, surrounded by high walls and built to be self-sufficient.

The buildings of greatest interest are clustered around **Wat Phra Kaeo**, or the 'Temple of the Emerald Buddha'. On entering the compound, the impression is one of glittering brilliance, as the outside is covered by a mosaic of coloured glass. The buildings were last restored for Bangkok's bicentenary in 1982 (the Wat Phra Kaeo Museum shows the methods used in the restoration process). Wat Phra Kaeo was built by Rama I in imitation of the royal chapel in Ayutthaya and was the first of the buildings within the Grand Palace complex

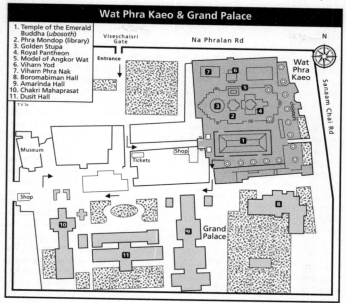

Wat Phra Kaeo & Grand Palace

1. Temple of the Emerald Buddha (*ubosoth*)
2. Phra Mondop (library)
3. Golden Stupa
4. Royal Pantheon
5. Model of Angkor Wat
6. Viharn Yod
7. Viharn Phra Nak
8. Boromabiman Hall
9. Amarinda Hall
10. Chakri Mahaprasat
11. Dusit Hall

Viseschaisri Gate

Na Phralan Rd

Wat Phra Kaeo

Sanaam Chai Rd

Entrance

Museum

Tickets

Shop

Shop

Grand Palace

to be constructed. While it was being erected the king lived in a small wooden building in one corner of the palace compound.

The ubosoth is raised on a marble platform with a frieze of gilded figures of garudas holding nagas running round the base. Bronze singhas act as door guardians. The door panels are of inlaid mother-of-pearl and date from Rama I's reign (late 18th century). Flanking the door posts are Chinese door guardians riding on lions. Inside the temple, the Emerald Buddha (see box) sits high up, illuminated above a large golden altar. In addition, there are many other gilded Buddha images, mostly in the attitude of dispelling fear, and a series of mural paintings depicting the jataka stories. Those facing the Emerald Buddha show the enlightenment of the Buddha when he subdues the evil demon Mara. Mara is underneath, wringing out his hair,

while on either side, the Buddha is surrounded by evil spirits. Those on one side have been subjugated; those on the other have not. The water from the wringing out of Mara's hair drowns the evil army, and the Buddha is shown 'touching ground' calling the earth goddess Thoranee up to witness his enlightenment. No photography is allowed inside the ubosoth.

Around the walls of the shaded cloister that encompasses Wat Phra Kaeo, is a continuous mural depicting the Ramakien – the Thai version of the Indian Ramayana. There are 178 sections in all, which were first painted during the reign of King Rama I but have since been restored on a number of occasions.

To the N of the ubosoth on a raised platform, are the Royal Pantheon, the Phra Mondop (the library), two gilt stupas, a model of Angkor Wat and the Golden Stupa. At the entrance to the

Royal Pantheon are gilded kinarees. The Royal Pantheon is only open to the public once a year on Chakri Day, 6 Apr (the anniversary of the founding of the present Royal Dynasty). On the same terrace there are two gilt stupas built by King Rama I in commemoration of his parents. The Mondop was also built by Rama I to house the first revised Buddhist scriptural canon. To the W of the mondop is the large Golden Stupa or chedi, with its circular base, in Ceylonese style. To the N of the mondop is a model of Angkor Wat constructed during the reign of King Mongkut (1851-1868) when Cambodia was under Thai suzerainty.

To the N again from the Royal Pantheon is the Supplementary Library and two viharns – Viharn Yod and Phra Nak. The former is encrusted in pieces of Chinese porcelain.

To the S of Wat Phra Kaeo are the buildings of the Grand Palace. These are interesting for the contrast that they make with those of Wat Phra Kaeo. Walk out through the cloisters. On your left can be seen Boromabiman Hall, which is French in style and was completed during the reign of Rama VI. His three successors lived here at one time or another. The Amarinda Hall has an impressive airy interior, with chunky pillars and gilded thrones. The Chakri Mahaprasart (the Palace Reception Hall) stands in front of a carefully manicured garden with topiary. It was built and lived in by Rama V shortly after he had returned from a trip to Java and Singapore in 1876, and it shows: the building is a rather unhappy amalgam of colonial and traditional Thai styles of architecture. Initially the intention was to top the structure with a Western dome, but the architects settled for a Thai-style roof. The building was completed in time for Bangkok's first centenary in 1882. King Chulalongkorn (Rama V) found the overcrowded Grand Palace oppressive and after a visit to Europe in 1897, built himself a new

home at Vimanmek (see page 225) in the area to the N, known as Dusit. The present King Bhumibol lives in the Chitralada Palace, built by Rama VI, also in the Dusit area. The Grand Palace is now only used for state occasions. Next to the Chakri Mahaprasart is the raised Dusit Hall; a cool, airy building containing mother-of-pearl thrones. Near the Dusit Hall is a museum, which has information on the restoration of the Grand Palace, models of the Palace and many Buddha statues. There is a collection of old cannon, mainly supplied by London gun foundries. Close by is a small café selling refreshing coconut drinks. All labels in Thai, but there are free guided tours in English throughout the day. Admission ฿50. Open: Mon-Sun 0900-1600.

ADMISSION to the Grand Palace complex ฿125, ticket office open 0830-1130, 1300-1530 Mon-Sun except Buddhist holidays when Wat Phra Kaeo is free but the rest of the palace is closed. The cost of the admission includes a free guidebook to the palace (with plan) as well as a ticket to the *Coin Pavilion*, with its collection of medals and 'honours' presented to members of the Royal Family and to the Vimanmek Palace in the Dusit area (see page 225). **NB** Decorum of dress is required (trousers can be hired for ฿10 near the entrance to the Grand Palace) which means no shorts, and no singlets or sleeveless shirts.

The National Museum

On the N edge of Sanamm Luang is the National Museum, reputedly the largest museum in Southeast Asia. It is an excellent place to view the full range of Thai art before visiting the ancient Thai capitals, Ayutthaya and Sukhothai.

Gallery No 1, the gallery of Thai history, is interesting and informative, as well as being air-conditioned, so it is a good place to cool-off. The gallery clearly shows Kings Mongkut and Chulalongkorn's fascination with Western technology. The other 22 galleries and 19 rooms contain a vast assortment of arts and artefacts divided according to period and style. If you are interested in Thai art, the museum alone might take a day to browse around. A shortcoming for those with no background knowledge is the lack of information in some of the galleries and it is recommended that interested visitors buy the 'Guide to the National Museum, Bangkok' for β50 or join one of the tours. Admission β20, together with a skimpy leaflet outlining the galleries. Open 0900-1600, Wed-Sun, tickets on sale until 1530. For English, French, German, Spanish and Portuguese-speaking tour information call T 2241333. They are free, and start at 0930, lasting 2 hrs (usually on Wed and Thur).

The Buddhaisawan Chapel, to the right of the ticket office for the National Museum, contains some of the finest Bangkok period murals in Thailand. The chapel was built in 1795 to house the famous Phra Sihing Buddha. Folklore has it that this image originated in Ceylon and when the boat carrying it to Thailand sank, it floated off on a plank to be washed ashore in Southern Thailand, near the town of Nakhon Si Thammarat. This, believe it or not, is probably untrue: the image is early Sukhothai in style (1250), admittedly showing Ceylonese influences, and almost certainly Northern Thai in origin. There are two other images that claim to be the magical Phra Buddha Sihing, one in Nakhon Si Thammarat and another in Chiang Mai. The chapel's magnificent murals were painted between 1795 and 1797 and depict stories from the Buddha's life. They are classical in style, without any sense of perspective, and the narrative of the Buddha's life begins to the right of the rear door behind the principal image, and progresses clockwise through 28 panels. German-speaking tours of the chapel are held on the third Tues of the month (0930).

THE GOLDEN MOUNT, GIANT SWING AND SURROUNDING WATS

From the Democracy Monument, across Mahachai Rd, at the point where Rachdamnern Klang Ave crosses Khlong Banglamphu can be seen the **Golden Mount** (also known as the Royal Mount), an impressive artificial hill nearly 80m high. The climb to the top is exhausting but worth it for the fabulous views of Bangkok. On the way up, the path passes holy trees, memorial plaques and Chinese shrines. The construction of the mount was begun during the reign of Rama III who intended to build the greatest chedi in his kingdom. The structure collapsed before completion, and Rama IV decided merely to pile up the rubble in a heap and place a far smaller golden chedi on its summit. The chedi contains a relic of the Buddha placed there by the present king after the structure had been most recently repaired in 1966. Admission β5. Open 0800-1800 Mon-Sun.

Wat Saket

This lies at the bottom of the mount, between it and Damrong Rak Rd – the mount actually lies within the wat's compound. Saket means 'washing of hair' – Rama I is reputed to have stopped here and ceremoniously washed himself before being crowned King in Thonburi (see Festivals, Nov). The only building of real note is the *library* (*hor trai*) which is Ayutthayan in style. The door panels and lower windows are decorated with woodcarvings depicting everyday Ayutthayan life, while the window panels show Persian and French soldiers from Louis XIV's reign. Open 0800-1800 Mon-Sun.

Also in the shadow of the Golden Mount but to the W and on the corner of Rachdamnern Klang Ave and Mahachai Rd lies Wat Rachanada and the Loha Prasat. Until 1989 these buildings were obscured by the Chalerm Thai movie theatre, a landmark which Bangkok's taxi and tuk-tuk drivers still refer to. In the place of the theatre there is now a neat garden, with an elaborate gilded **sala**, which is used to receive visiting dignitaries. Behind the garden the strange looking **Loha Prasat** or Metal Palace, with its 37 spires, is easily recognizable. This palace was built by Rama III in 1846, and is said to be modelled on the first Loha Prasat built in India 2,500 years ago. A second was constructed in Ceylon in 160 BC, although Bangkok's Loha Prasat is the only one still standing. The palace was built by Rama III as a memorial to his beloved niece Princess Soammanas Vadhanavadi. The 37 spires represent the 37 Dharma of the Bodhipakya. The building, which contains Buddha images and numerous meditation cells, has been closed to visitors for many years, although it is possible to walk around the outside.

Next to the Loha Prasat is the much more traditional **Wat Rachanada**. Wat Rachanada was built by Rama III for his niece who later became Rama IV's queen. The main Buddha image is made of copper mined in Nakhon Ratchasima province to the NE of Bangkok, and the ordination hall also has some fine doors. Open 0600-1800 Mon-Sun. What makes the wat particularly worth visiting is the **Amulet market** to be found close by, between the Golden Mount and the wat. The sign, in English, below the covered part of the market reads 'Buddha and Antiques Centre'. The market also contains Buddha images and other religious artefacts and is open every day.

Wat Suthat

A 5 min walk S of Wat Rachanada, on Bamrung Muang Rd, is the **Sao Ching Cha** or **Giant Swing**, consisting of two tall red pillars linked by an elaborate cross piece, set in the centre of a square. The Giant Swing was the original centre for a Brahmanic festival in honour of Siva. Young men, on a giant 'raft', would be swung high into the air to grab pouches of coins, hung from bamboo poles, between their teeth. Because the swinging was from E to W, it has been said that it symbolized the rising and setting of the sun. The festival was banned in the 1930s because of the injuries that occurred; prior to its banning, thousands would congregate around the Giant Swing for 2 days of dancing and music. The magnificent **Wat Suthat** faces the Giant Swing. The wat was begun by Rama I in 1807, and his intention was to build a temple that would equal the most glorious in Ayutthaya. The wat was not finished until the end of the reign of Rama III in 1851.

The viharn is in early-Bangkok style and is surrounded by Chinese pagodas. Its six pairs of doors, each made from a single piece of teak, are deeply carved with animals and celestial beings from the Himavanta forest. The central doors are said to have been carved by Rama II himself, and are considered some of the most important works of art of the period. Inside the viharn is the bronze Phra Sri Sakyamuni Buddha in an attitude of subduing Mara. This image was previously contained in Wat Mahathat in Sukhothai, established in 1362. Behind the Buddha is a very fine gilded stone carving from the Dvaravati Period (2nd-11th centuries AD), 2.5m in height and showing the miracle at Sravasti and the Buddha preaching in the Tavatimsa heaven.

The bot is the tallest in Bangkok and one of the largest in Thailand. The murals in the bot painted during the reign of Rama III are interesting in that they are traditional Thai in style, largely unaffected by Western artistic influences. They use flat colours and lack perspective. The bot also contains a particularly large cast Buddha image. Open 0900-1700; the viharn is only open on weekends and Buddhist holidays 0900-1700.

Wat Rachabophit

The little visited Wat Rachabophit is

close to the Ministry of the Interior on Rachabophit Rd, a few minutes walk S of Wat Suthat down Ti Thong Rd. It is recognizable by its distinctive doors carved in high relief with jaunty looking soldiers wearing European-style uniforms. The temple was started in 1869, took 20 years to complete, and is a rich blend of Western and Thai art forms (carried further in Wat Benchamabophit 40 years later, see page 225). Wat Rachabophit is peculiar in that it follows the ancient temple plan of placing the Phra Chedi in the centre of the complex, surrounded by the other buildings. It later became the fashion to place the ordination hall at the centre.

The 43m high gilded chedi's most striking feature are the five-coloured Chinese glass tiles which richly encrust the lower section. The ordination hall has 10 door panels and 28 window panels each decorated with gilded black lacquer on the inside and mother-of-pearl inlay on the outside showing the various royal insignia. They are felt to be among the masterpieces of the Rattanakosin Period (1782-present). The principal Buddha image in the ordination hall, in an attitude of meditation, sits on a base of Italian marble and is covered by the umbrella that protected the urn and ashes of Rama V. It also has a surprising interior – an oriental version of Italian Gothic, more like Versailles than Bangkok. Admission ฿10. Open 0800-1700 Mon-Sun.

From Wat Rachabophit, it is only a short distance to the **Pahurat Indian Market** on Pahurat Rd, where Indian, Malaysian and Thai textiles are sold. To get there, walk S on Ti Thong Rd which quickly becomes Tri Phet Rd. After a few blocks, Pahurat Rd crosses Tri Phet Rd. **Pak Khlong Market** is to be found a little further S on Tri Phet Rd at the foot of the Memorial Bridge. It is a huge wholesale market for fresh produce, and a photographer's paradise. It begins very early in the morning and has ended by

1000. The closest pier to the Pak Khlong Market is Tha Rachini, which is remembered for a particularly nasty episode in Thai history. It is said that in the 1840s a troublemaking upcountry *chao* or lord was brought to Bangkok and sentenced to death. His eyes were burnt out with heated irons and then the unfortunate man was suspended above the river at Tha Rachini in a cage. The cage was so positioned that the *chao* could touch the water with his finger tips but could not cup water to drink. He died of thirst and sunstroke after 3 days and for years afterwards people would not live near the spot where he died.

CHINATOWN AND THE GOLDEN BUDDHA

Chinatown covers the area from Charoen Krung (or New Rd) down to the river and leads on from Pahurat Rd Market; cross over Chakraphet Rd and immediately opposite is the entrance to Sampeng Lane. A trip through **Chinatown** can either begin with the Thieves Market to the NW, or at Wat Traimitr, the Golden Buddha, to the SE. An easy stroll between the two should not take more than 2 hrs. This part of Bangkok has a different atmosphere from elsewhere. Roads become narrower, buildings smaller, and there is a continuous bustle of activity. There remain some attractive, weathered examples of early 20th century shophouses. The industrious Sino-Thais of the area make everything from offertory candles and gold jewellery to metalwork, gravestones and light machinery.

Nakhon Kasem, or the Thieves Market, lies between Charoen Krung and Yaowaraj Rd, to the E of the khlong that runs parallel to Mahachai Rd. Its boundaries are marked by archways. As its name suggests, this market used to be the centre for the fencing of stolen goods. It is not quite so colourful today, but there remain a number of second-hand and antique shops which are worth a browse – such as the *Good Luck Antique*

Shop. Amongst other things, musical instruments, brass ornaments, antique (and not so antique) coffee grinders are all on sale here.

Just to the SE of the Thieves Market are two interesting roads that run next to and parallel with one another: Yaowaraj Road and Sampeng Lane. **Yaowaraj Road**, a busy thoroughfare, is the centre of the country's gold trade. The trade is run by a cartel of seven shops, the Gold Traders Association, and the price is fixed by the government. Sino-Thais often convert their cash into

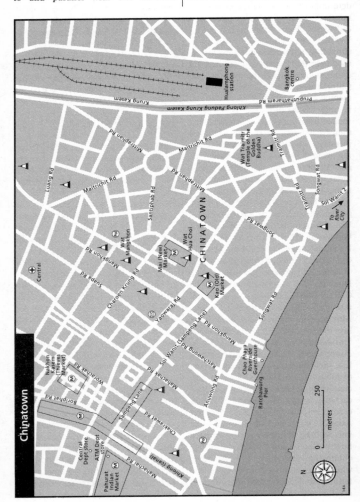

gold jewellery, usually bracelets and necklaces. The jewellery is bought by its 'baht weight' which fluctuates daily with the price of gold (most shops post the price daily). Should the owner need to convert their necklace or bracelet back into cash it is again weighed to determine its value. The narrower, almost pedestrian **Sampeng Lane**, also called **Soi Wanit**, is just to the S of Yaowaraj Rd. This road's history is shrouded in murder and intrigue. It used to be populated by prostitutes and opium addicts and was fought over by Chinese gangs. Today, it remains a commercial centre, but rather less illicit. It is still interesting (and cool, being shaded by awnings) to walk down, but there is not much to buy here – it is primarily a wholesale centre specializing in cloth and textiles although it is a good place to go for odd lengths of material, buttons of any shape and size, and things like costume jewellery.

The most celebrated example of the goldsmiths' art in Thailand sits within **Wat Traimitr**, or the **Temple of the Golden Buddha**, which is located at the E edge of Chinatown, squashed between Charoen Krung, Yaowaraj Rd and Traimitr Rd (just to the S of Bangkok's Hualamphong railway station). The Golden Buddha is housed in a small, rather gaudy and unimpressive room. Although the leaflet offered to visitors says the 3m-high, 700 year-old image is 'unrivalled in beauty', be prepared to be disappointed. It is in fact rather featureless, showing the Buddha in an attitude of subduing Mara. What makes it special, drawing large numbers of visitors each day, is that it is made of 5.5 tonnes of solid gold. Apparently, when the East Asiatic Company was extending the port of Bangkok, they came across a huge stucco Buddha image which they obtained permission to move. However, whilst being moved by crane in 1957, it fell and the stucco cracked open to reveal a solid gold image. During the Ayut-

thayan Period it was the custom to cover valuable Buddha images in plaster to protect them from the Burmese, and this particular example stayed that way for several 100 years. In the grounds of the wat there is a school, crematorium, food-stalls and, inappropriately, a money changer. Admission ฿10. Open 0900-1700 Mon-Sun. Gold beaters can still be seen at work behind Suksaphan store.

Between the river and Soi Wanit 2 there is a warren of lanes, too small for traffic – this is the Chinatown of old. From here it is possible to thread your way through to the River City shopping complex which is air-conditioned and a good place to cool-off.

RECOMMENDED READING Visitors wishing to explore the wonders of Chinatown more thoroughly, should buy Nancy Chandler's *Map of Bangkok*, a lively, detailed (but not altogether accurate) map of all the shops, restaurants and out of the way wats and shrines. ฿70 from most bookstores.

WAT ARUN AND THE KHLONGS

One of the most enjoyable ways to see Bangkok is by boat – and particularly by the fast and noisy *hang yaaws* (long-tailed boats). You will know them when you see them; these powerful, lean machines roar around the river and the khlongs at break-neck speed, as though they are involved in a race to the death. There are innumerable tours around the khlongs of Thonburi taking in a number of sights which include the floating market, snake farm and Wat Arun. Boats go from the various piers located along the E banks of the Chao Phraya River. The journey begins by travelling downstream along the Chao Phraya, before turning 'inland' after passing underneath the Krungthep Bridge. The route skirts past laden rice-barges, squatter communities on public land and houses overhanging the canals. This is a very popular route with tourists, and boats are intercepted by salesmen and women marketing everything from cold beer to straw hats. You may also get caught in a boat jam; traffic snarl-ups are not confined to the capital's roads. Nevertheless, the trip is a fascinating insight into what Bangkok must have been like when it was still the 'Venice of the East', and around every bend there seems to be yet another wat – some of them very beautiful. On private tours the first stop is usually the **Floating market** (*Talaat Nam*). This is now an artificial, ersatz gathering which exists purely for the tourist industry. It is worth only a brief visit – unless the so-called 'post-tourist' is looking for just this sort of sight. The nearest functioning floating market is at Damnoen Saduak (see excursions from Bangkok, page 228). The

The Chao Phraya River Express

One of the most relaxing – and one of the cheapest – ways to see Bangkok is by taking the Chao Phraya River Express. These boats (or *rua duan*) link almost 40 piers (or *tha*) along the Chao Phraya River from Tha Wat Rajsingkorn in the S to Tha Nonthaburi in the N. The entire route entails a journey of about 1¼-1½ hr, and fares are ฿4, ฿6 or ฿8. Adjacent to many of the piers are excellent riverside restaurants. At peak periods, boats leave every 10 mins, off-peak about every 15-25 mins. Note that boats flying red or green pennants do not stop at every pier; they also exact a ฿1 surcharge. Also, boats will only stop if passengers wish to board or alight, so make your destination known.

Selected piers and places of interest, travelling upstream

Tha Orienten By the *Oriental Hotel*; access to *Silom Road*.

Tha River City In the shadow of the *Royal Orchid Hotel*, on the S side and close to *River City* shopping centre.

Tha Ratchawong *Rabieng Ratchawong Restaurant*; access to *Chinatown* and *Sampeng Lane*.

Tha Saphan Phut Under the *Memorial Bridge* and close to *Pahurat Indian market*.

Tha Rachini *Pak Khlong Market*; just upstream, the *Catholic seminary* surrounded by high walls.

Tha Tien Close to *Wat Pho*; *Wat Arun* on the opposite bank; and just downstream from Wat Arun the *Vichaiprasit fort* headquarters of the Thai navy), lurking behind crenellated ramparts.

Tha Chang Just downstream is the *Grand Palace* peeking out above white-washed walls; *Wat Rakhang* with its white corn-cob prang lies opposite.

Tha Maharat *Lan The Restaurant*; access to *Wat Mahathat* and *Sanaam Luang*.

Tha Phra Arthit *Yen Jai Restaurant*; access to *Khaosan Road*.

Tha Visutkasat *Yok Yor Restaurant*; just upstream the elegant central *Bank of Thailand*.

Tha Thewes *Son Ngen Restaurant*; just upstream are *boatsheds* with royal barges; close to the *National Library*.

Tha Wat Chan Just upstream is the *Singha Beer* Samoson brewery.

Tha Wat Khema *Wat Khema* in large, tree-filled compound.

Tha Wat Khian *Wat Kien*, semi-submerged.

Tha Nonthaburi Last stop on the express boat route .

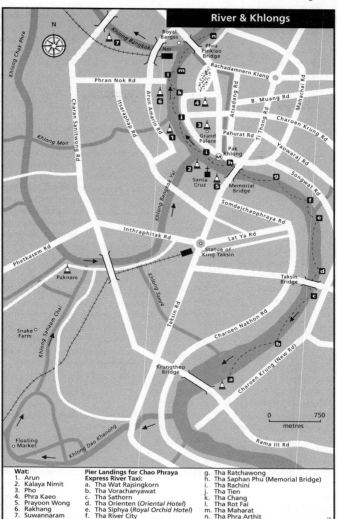

River & Khlongs

Wat:
1. Arun
2. Kalaya Nimit
3. Pho
4. Phra Kaeo
5. Prayoon Wong
6. Rakhang
7. Suwannaram

Pier Landings for Chao Phraya Express River Taxi:
a. Tha Wat Rajsingkorn
b. Tha Vorachanyawat
c. Tha Sathorn
d. Tha Orienten (*Oriental Hotel*)
e. Tha Siphya (*Royal Orchid Hotel*)
f. Tha River City

g. Tha Ratchawong
h. Tha Saphan Phu (Memorial Bridge)
i. Tha Rachini
j. Tha Tien
k. Tha Chang
l. Tha Rot Fai
m. Tha Maharat
n. Tha Phra Arthit

Snake Farm is the next stop where man fights snake in an epic battle of wills. Visitors can even pose with a python. The poisonous snakes are incited, to burst balloon with their fangs, 'proving' how dangerous they are. There is also a rather motley zoo with a collection of crocodiles and sad-looking animals in small cages.

The other snake farm in Central Bangkok is (appropriately) attached to the Thai Red Cross and is more professional and cheaper (see page 227). Admission ฿70, shows every 20 mins. Refreshments available. On leaving the snake farm, the boat will join up with Khlong Bangkok Yai at the site of the large **Wat Paknam**. Just before re-entering the Chao Phraya itself, the route passes by the impressive **Wat Kalaya Nimit**.

Wat Arun

North on the Chao Phraya River is the famous Wat Arun, or the Temple of the Dawn, facing Wat Pho across the river. Wat Arun stands 81m high, making it the highest prang (tower) in Thailand. It was built in the early 19th century on the site of Wat Chaeng, the Royal Palace complex when Thonburi was briefly the capital of Thailand. The wat housed the Emerald Buddha before the image was transferred to Bangkok and it is said that King Taksin vowed to restore the wat after passing it one dawn. The prang is completely covered with pieces of Chinese porcelain and includes some delicate gold and black lacquered doors. The temple is really meant to be viewed from across the river; its scale and beauty can only be appreciated from a distance. Young, a European visitor to the capital, wrote in 1898: 'Thousands upon thousands of pieces of cheap china must have been smashed to bits in order to furnish sufficient material to decorate this curious structure ... though the material is tawdry, the effect is indescribably wonderful'.

Energetic visitors can climb up to the halfway point and view the city. This is not recommended for people suffering from vertigo; the steps are very steep – be prepared for jelly-like legs after descending. Admission ฿10. Open 0830-1730 Mon-Sun. The men at the pier may demand ฿10 to help 'in the maintenance of the pier'. **NB** It is possible to get to Wat Arun by water-taxi from Tha Tien pier (at the end of Thai Wang Rd near Wat Pho), or from Tha Chang (at the end of Na Phralan near Wat Phra Kaeo) (฿1). The best view of Wat Arun is in the evening from the Bangkok side of the river when the sun sets behind the prang.

After visiting Wat Arun, some tours then go further upstream to the mouth of Khlong Bangkok Noi where the **Royal Barges** are housed in a hangar-like boathouse. These ornately carved boats, winched out of the water in cradles, were used by the king at 'krathin' (see OK Phansa festival, page 283) to present robes to the monks in Wat Arun at the end of the rainy season. The ceremony ceased in 1967 but the Royal Thai Navy restored the barges for the revival of the spectacle, as part of the Chakri Dynasty's bicentennial celebrations in 1982. The oldest and most beautiful barge is the Sri Supannahong, built during the reign of Rama I (1782-1809) and repaired during that of Rama VI (1910-1925). It measures 45m long and 3m wide, weighs 15 tonnes and was created from a single piece of teak. It required a crew of 50 oarsmen, and two coxwains, along with such assorted crew members as a flagman, a rhythm-keeper and singer. Its gilded prow was carved in the form of a *hamsa* (or goose) and its stern, in the shape of a *naga*. Admission ฿10. Open 0830-1630 Mon-Sun (see Festivals, Sep, page 229).

Arranging a boat tour

Either book a tour at your hotel, or go to one of the piers and organize your own customized trip. The most frequented piers are located between the Oriental Hotel and the Grand Palace (see map, or ask at your hotel). The pier just to the S of the Royal Orchid Sheraton Hotel is recommended. Organizing your own trip gives greater freedom to stop and start when the mood takes you. It is best to go in the morning (0700). For the trip given above (excluding Wat Rakhang and Wat Suwannaram), the cost for a hang yaaw which can sit 10 people should be about ฿600 for the boat for a half-day. If visiting Rakhang and Suwannaram as well as the other sights, expect to pay about another ฿200-300 for the hire of a boat. Be sure to settle the route and cost before setting out.

THE DUSIT AREA

The Dusit area of Bangkok lies N of the Old City. The area is intersected by wide tree-lined avenues, and has an almost European flavour. The **Vimanmek Palace** lies off Rachvithi Rd, just to the N of the National Assembly. Vimanmek is the largest golden teakwood mansion in the world. It was built by Rama V in 1901 and designed by one of his brothers. The palace makes an interesting contrast to Jim Thompson's House (see page 226) or Suan Pakkard (page 225). While Jim Thompson was enchanted by Thai arts, King Rama V was clearly taken with Western arts. It seems like a large Victorian hunting lodge – but raised off the ground – and is filled with china, silver and paintings from all over the world (as well as some gruesome hunting trophies). The photographs are fascinating – one shows the last time elephants were used in warfare in Thailand. Behind the palace is the Audience Hall which houses a fine exhibition of crafts made by the Support Foundation, an organization set up and funded by Queen Sirikit. Support, rather clumsily perhaps, is the acronym for the Foundation for the Promotion of Supplementary Occupations and Related Techniques. Also worth seeing is the exhibition of the king's own photographs, and the clock museum. Dance shows are held twice a day. Visitors are not free to wander, but must be shown around by one of the charming guides who demonstrate the continued deep reverence for King Rama V (tour approx 1hr). Admission ฿50, ฿20 for children. Note that tickets to the Grand Palace include entrance to Vimanmek Palace. Open 0930-1600 (last tickets sold at 1500) Mon-Sun. Refreshments available. **NB** Visitors to the palace are required to wear long trousers or a skirt; sarongs available for hire (฿100,

refundable). Buses do go past the palace, but from the centre of town it is easier to get a tuk-tuk or taxi (฿50-60).

Wat Benchamabophit

Or the **Marble Temple**, is the most modern of the royal temples and was only finished in 1911. It is of unusual architectural design (the architect was the king's half brother, Prince Naris), with carrara marble pillars, a marble courtyard and two large singhas guarding the entrance to the bot. Rama V was so pleased with the marble-faced ordination hall that he wrote to his brother: 'I never flatter anyone but I cannot help saying that you have captured my heart in accomplishing such beauty as this'. The interior is magnificently decorated with crossbeams of lacquer and gold, and in shallow niches in the walls are paintings of important stupas from all over the kingdom. The door panels are faced with bronze sculptures and the windows are of stained-glass, painted with angels. The cloisters around the assembly hall house 52 figures (both original and imitation) – a display of the evolution of the Buddha image in India, China and Japan. The Walking Buddha from the Sukhothai Period is particularly worth a look. The rear courtyard houses a large 80-year-old bodhi tree and a pond filled with turtles, released by people hoping to gain merit. The best time to visit this temple complex is early morning, when monks can be heard chanting inside the chapel. Admission ฿10. Open 0800-1700 Mon-Sun.

OTHER PLACES OF INTEREST

In addition to the Vimanmek Palace, Bangkok also has a number of other beautiful Thai-style houses that are open to the public. **Suan Pakkard Palace** or Lettuce Garden Palace is at 352-354 Sri Ayutthaya Rd, S of the Victory Monument. The five raised traditional Thai houses (domestic rather than royal) were built by Princess Chumbhot, a great-grand-daughter of King Rama IV. They contain her fine collection of antiquities, both historic and prehistoric (the latter are particularly rare). Like the artefacts in the National Museum, those in Suan Pakkard are also poorly labelled. The rear pavilion is particularly lovely, decorated in black and gold lacquerwork panels. Prince Chumbhot discovered this temple near Ayutthaya and reassembled and restored it here for his wife's 50th birthday. The grounds are very peaceful. Admission ฿80 – including a fan to ward off the heat. Open 0900-1600, Mon-Sat. All receipts go to a fund for artists.

Jim Thompson's House is on the quiet Soi Kasemsan Song (2), opposite the National Stadium on Rama I Rd. It is an assemblage of traditional teak Northern Thai houses, some more than 200 years old, transported here and reassembled (these houses were designed to be transportable, consisting of five parts – the floor, posts, roof, walls and decorative elements constructed without the use of nails). Jim Thompson arrived in Bangkok as an intelligence officer attached to the United States' OSS (Office of Strategic Services) and then made his name by reinvigorating the Thai silk industry after WW2. He disappeared mysteriously in the Malaysian jungle on 27 March 1967, but his silk industry continues to thrive. (The *Jim Thompson Silk Company*, selling fine Thai silk, is at the NE end of Surawong Rd. This shop is a tourist attraction in itself. Shoppers can buy high-quality bolts of silk and silk clothing here – anything from a pocket handkerchief to a silk suit. Prices are top of the scale.) Jim Thompson chose this site for his house partly because a collection of silk weavers lived nearby on Khlong Saensaep. The house contains an eclectic collection of antiques from Thailand and China, with work displayed as though it was still his home. Shoes must be removed before entering; walking barefoot around the house adds to the appreciation of the cool teak floorboards. Bustling Bangkok only intrudes in the form of the stench from the khlong that runs behind the house. Compulsory guided tours around the house and no photography allowed. Admission ฿100 (profits to charity). Open 0900-1630, Mon-Sat. **Getting there**: bus along Rama I Rd, taxi or tuk-tuk.

A 10 mins' walk E along Rama I Rd is the shopping area known as **Siam Square** (or *Siam Sa-quare*). This has the greatest concentration of fast food restaurants, boutiques and cinemas in the city. Needless to say, it is patronized by young Thais sporting the latest fashions and doing the sorts of things their parents would never have dreamed of doing – girls smoking and couples holding hands, for instance. For Thais worried about the direction their country is taking, Siam Square encapsulates all their fears in just a few *rai*. This is crude materalism; this is Thais aping the West; this is the erosion of Thai values and culture with scarcely a thought to the future. Because of the tourists and wealthy Thais who congregate around Siam Square it is also a popular patch for beggars. It seems that over the last few years the number of beggars has increased – which may seem odd given Thailand's rapid economic growth. It may be that this economic expansion hasn't reached the poor in rural areas (Thailand has become a more unequal society over the last decade or so); or it maybe that with greater wealth, begging has become a more attractive – in terms of economic return – occupation.

East of Siam Square is the **Erawan Shrine** on the corner of Ploenchit and Rachdamri rds, at the Rachparasong intersection. This is Bangkok's most popular shrine, attracting not just Thais but also large numbers of other Asian visitors. The spirit of the shrine, the Hindu god Thao Maha Brahma, is reputed to grant people's wishes – it certainly has little artistic worth. In thanks, visitors offer garlands, wooden elephants and pay to have dances performed for them accompanied by the resident Thai orchestra. The popular *Thai Rath* newspaper reported in 1991 that some female devotees show their thanks by covorting naked at the shrine in the middle of the night. Others, rather more coy about exposing themselves in this way, have taken to giving the god pornographic videos instead. Although it is unlikely that visitors will be rewarded with the sight of naked bodies, the shrine is a hive of activity at most hours, incongruously set on a noisy, polluted intersection tucked into a corner, and in the shadow of the Sogo Department Store.

One other traditional house worth visiting is the home of the **Siam Society**, off Sukhumvit Rd, at 131 Soi Asoke. The Siam Society is a learned society established in 1904 and has benefited from almost continual royal patronage. The **Kamthieng House** is a 120-year-old N Thai house from Chiang Mai. It was donated to the society in 1963, transported to Bangkok and then reassembled a few years later. It now serves as an ethnological museum, devoted to preserving the traditional technologies and folk arts of Northern Thailand. It makes an interesting contrast to the fine arts displayed in Suan Pakkard Palace and Jim Thompson's house. The Siam Society houses a library, organizes lectures and tours and publishes books, magazines and pamphlets. Admission ฿25, ฿10 for children. Open 0900-1200, 1300-1700, Tues-Sat, T 2583491 for information on lectures.

For those with a penchant for snakes, the **Snake Farm** of the Thai Red Cross is very central and easy to reach from Silom or Surawong rds. It was established in 1923, and raises snakes for serum production, which is distributed worldwide. The farm also has a collection of non-venomous snakes. During showtime (which lasts 30 mins) various snakes are exhibited, and venom extracted. Visitors can fondle a python. The farm is well maintained and

professional. Admission ฿70. Open 0830-1630 Mon-Fri (shows at 1100 and 1430), 0830-1200 Sat/Sun and holidays (show at 1100). The farm is within the Science Division of the Thai Red Cross Society at the corner of Rama IV and Henri Dunant rds.

Slightly further out of the centre of Bangkok is the **Chatuchak Weekend Market** which is off Phahonyothin Rd, opposite the Northern bus terminal. Until 1982 this market was held at Sanaam Luang, but was moved because it had outgrown its original home and also because the authorities wanted to clean up the area for the Bangkok bicentenary celebrations. It is a huge conglomeration of 8,672 stallholders spread over an area of 28 acres, selling virtually

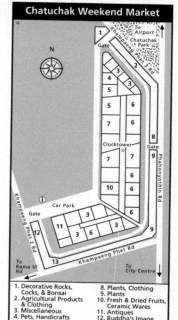

Chatuchak Weekend Market

1. Decorative Rocks, Cocks, & Bonsai
2. Agricultural Products & Clothing
3. Miscellaneous
4. Pets, Handicrafts
5. Pets
6. Clothing
7. Fresh & Dried Fruits
8. Plants, Clothing
9. Plants
10. Fresh & Dried Fruits, Ceramic Wares
11. Antiques
12. Buddha's Image, Plants & Books
13. Paintings, Plants

everything under the sun, and an estimated 200,000 people visit the market over a weekend. It is probably the best place to buy handicrafts and all things Thai in the whole Kingdom. There are antique stalls, basket stalls, textile sellers, shirt vendors, carvers, painters ... along with the usual array of fish sellers, vegetable hawkers, butchers and candlestick makers. In the last couple of years a number of bars and food stalls geared to tourists and Thai yuppies have also opened so it is possible to rest and recharge before foraging once more. Definitely worth a visit – and allocate half a day at least. In addition to the map below, Nancy Chandler's Map of Bangkok has an inset map of the market to help you get around. Believe it or not, the market is open on weekends, officially from 0900-1800 (although in fact it begins earlier around 0700). It's best to go early in the day. In 1994 plans were announced to transform the market by building a three-storey purpose-built structure with car parking and various other amenities. Such has been the outcry that the planners have retired to think again. But the fear is that this gem of shopping chaos will be re-organized, sanitized, bureaucratized and, in the process, ruined. **Beware pickpockets**. There is a tourist information centre at the entrance gate off Kamphaeng Phet 2 Rd, and the Clock tower serves as a good reference point should visitors become disoriented. Getting there: a/c buses 2 (from Silom Rd), 3, 10, 13 and 29 go past the market, and non-a/c buses 8, 24, 26, 27, 29, 34, 39, 44, 59, and 96. Or take a taxi or tuk-tuk.

EXCURSIONS

FLOATING MARKET AT DAMNOEN SADUAK

Ratchaburi Province, 109 km W of Bangkok. Sadly, it is becoming increasingly like the Floating Market in Thon-buri, although it does still function as a legitimate market. Getting there: catch an early morning bus (No 78) from the Southern bus terminal in Thonburi – aim to get to Damnoen Saduak between 0800-1000, as the market winds down after 1000, leaving only trinket stalls. The trip takes about 1½ hrs. A/c and non-a/c buses leave every 40 mins from 0600 (฿30-49) (T 4355031 for booking). The bus travels via Nakhon Pathom (where it is possible to stop on the way back and see the great chedi – see Nakhon Pathom). Ask the conductor to drop you at Thanarat Bridge in Damnoen Saduak. Then either walk down the lane (1.5 km) that leads to the market and follows the canal, or take a river taxi for ฿10, or a mini-bus (฿2). There are a number of floating markets in the maze of khlongs – Ton Khem, Hia Kui and Khun Phithak – and it is best to hire a hang yaaw to explore the back-waters and roam around the markets, about ฿300/hour (agree the price before setting out). Tour companies also visit the floating market.

TOURS

Bangkok has innumerable tour companies that can take visitors virtually anywhere. If there is not a tour to fit your bill – most run the same range of tours – many companies will organize one for you, for a price. Most top hotels have their own tour desk and it is probably easiest to book there (arrange to be picked up from your hotel as part of the deal). Prices per person are about ฿250-500 for a half day tour, ฿600-1,000 for a full day (incl lunch).

FESTIVALS AND MAJOR EVENTS

Jan: *Red Cross Fair* (movable), held in Amporn Gardens next to the Parliament. Stalls, classical dancing, folk performances etc.
Feb: *Chinese New Year* (movable), Chinatown closes down, but Chinese temples are packed. *Handicraft Fair* (mid-month), all the handicrafts are made by Thai prisoners.

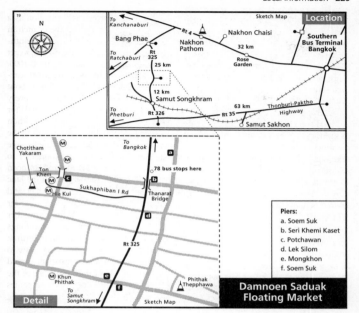

Damnoen Saduak Floating Market

Piers:
a. Soem Suk
b. Seri Khemi Kaset
c. Potchawan
d. Lek Silom
e. Mongkhon
f. Soem Suk

Mar-Apr: *Kite Flying* (movable, for 1 month), every afternoon/evening at Sanaam Luang there is kite fighting. An *International Kite Festival* is held in late Mar at Sanaam Luang when kite fighting and demonstrations by kite-flyers from across the globe take place.

May: *Royal Ploughing Ceremony* (movable), this celebrates the official start of the rice-planting season and is held at Sanaam Luang. It is an ancient Brahman ritual and is attended by the king.

Sep: *Swan-boat races* (movable), on the Chao Phraya River.

Nov: *Golden Mount Fair* (movable), stalls and theatres set-up all around the Golden Mount and Wat Saket. Candles are carried in procession to the top of the mount. *Marathon* road race, fortunately at one of the coolest times of year.

Dec: *Trooping of the Colour* (movable), the élite Royal Guards swear allegiance to the king and march past members of the Royal Family. It is held in the Royal Plaza near the equestrian statue of King Chulalongkorn.

LOCAL INFORMATION

● **Accommodation**

Bangkok offers a vast range of accommodation at all levels of luxury. There are a number of hotel areas in the city, each with its own character and locational advantages. Accommodation has been divided into five such areas with a sixth – 'other' – for the handful situated elsewhere. A new type of hotel which has emerged in Bangkok in recent years is the 'boutique' hotel. These are small, with immaculate service, and represent an attempt to emulate the philosophy of 'small is beautiful'.

For the last few years Bangkok has had a glut of hotel rooms – especially 5-star – as hotels planned during the heady days of the late 1980s and early 1990s have opened. Room rates at the top end fell around 50% between 1991 and 1996, so there are bargains to be had.

Price guide		
	US$	Baht
L	200+	5,000+
A+	100-200	2,500-5,000
A	50-100	1,250-2,500
B	25-50	625-1,250
C	15-25	375-625
D	8-15	200-375
E	4-8	100-200
F	<4	<100

NB For business women travelling alone, the *Oriental*, *Dusit Thani* and *Amari Airport* hotels allocate a floor to women travellers, with all-female staff.

Many of the more expensive places to stay are on the **Chao Phraya River** with its views, good shopping and access to the old city. Running eastwards from the river are **Silom** and **Surawong** rds, in the heart of Bangkok's business district and close to many embassies. The bars of Patpong link the two roads. This is a good area to stay for shopping and bars, but transport to the tourist sights can be problematic. A more recently developed area is along **Sukhumvit Rd** running E from Soi Nana Nua (Soi 3). The bulk of the accommodation here is in the **A-B** range, and within easy reach is a wide range of restaurants, 'girlie' bars, and reasonable shopping. But, the hotels are a long taxi or tuk-tuk ride from the sights of the old city and most of the places of interest to the tourist in Bangkok. In the vicinity of **Siam Square** are two deluxe hotels and several 'budget' class establishments (especially along Rama 1 Soi Kasemsan Nung). Siam Square is central, a good shopping area, with easy bus and taxi access to Silom and Sukhumvit rds and the sights of the old city. Guesthouses are to be found along and around **Khaosan Rd** (an area known as Banglamphu); or just to the N, at the NW end of **Sri Ayutthaya Rd** there is a small cluster of rather friendly places. **Soi Ngam Duphli**, off Rama IV Rd, is the other big area for cheap places to stay. These hotel areas encompass about 90% of Bangkok's accommodation, although there are other places to stay scattered across the city; these are listed under **Other**.

● **Silom, Surawong and the River**
L *Dusit Thani*, 946 Rama IV Rd, T 2360450, F 2366400, a/c, restaurants, pool, when it was built it was the tallest building in Bangkok, refurbished, still excellent and has been continually refurbished and upgraded, though disappointing pool, rec; **L** *Montien*, 54 Surawong Rd, T 2348060, F 2365219, a/c, restaurants, pool, one of the first high-rise hotels (opened 1967) with good location for business, shopping and bars, slick service, and continuing good reputation with loyal patrons; **L** *Oriental*, 48 Soi Oriental, Charoen Krung, T 2360400, F 2361939, a/c, restaurants, pool, one of the best hotels in the world, beautiful position overlooking the river, superb personal service despite its size (400 rm). The hotel claims that Joseph Conrad, Somerset Maugham and Noel Coward all stayed here at one time or another, although the first of these probably did not – he lived aboard his ship or, perhaps, stayed in the now defunct *Universal Hotel*. Good shopping arcade, good programme of 'cultural' events, and 6 excellent restaurants, some of the equipment and bathrooms could be said to be a little old, however it still comes highly rec; **L** *Royal Orchid Sheraton*, 2 Captain Bush Lane, Si Phraya Rd, T 2345599, F 2368320, a/c, restaurants, pool, at times strong and rather unpleasant smell from nearby khlong, lovely views over the river, close to River City shopping centre (good for antiques), rooms are average at this price but service is very slick; **L** *Shangri-La*, 89 Soi Wat Suan Plu, Charoen Krung, T 2367777, F 2368570, a/c, restaurants, lovely pool, great location overlooking river, sometimes preferred to *Oriental* but some consider it dull and impersonal, recently upgraded and extended, rec; **L** *The Western Banyan Tree*, 21/100 Sathorn Tai Rd, T 6791200, F 6791199, a/c, restaurant, pool, new hotel and the tallest in Bangkok. It is targeting the business traveller, all rooms are suites with working area, in room fax and copier, computer port and voice mail, good position for many offices; **L-A+** *Sukhothai*, 13/3 Sathorn Tai Rd, T 2870222, F 2874980, a/c, restaurants (especially good poolside Italian restaurant), pool, beautiful rooms and excellent service, in Thai postmodern style, clean and elegant, there are those who say it is even better than such established hotels as *The Regent*, even *The Oriental*, rec; **L-A+** *Holiday Inn Crowne Plaza*, 981 Silom Rd, T 2384300, F 2385289, a/c, restaurants, pool, vast, pristine marble-filled hotel, all amenities, immensely comfortable, minimum atmosphere and character.

A+ *Marriott Royal Garden Riverside Hotel*, 257/1-3 Charoen Nakorn Rd, T 4760021,

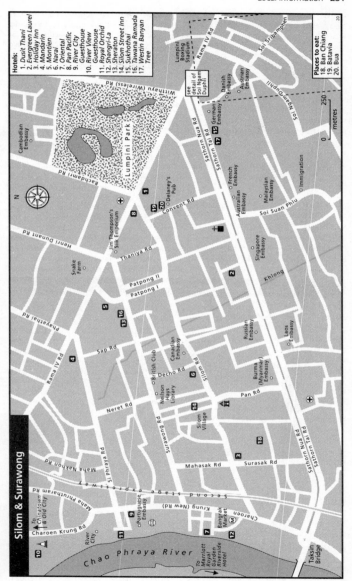

Silom & Surawong

Hotels:
1. Dusit Thani
2. Evergreen Laurel
3. Holiday Inn
4. Mandarin
5. Montien
6. Narai
7. Oriental
8. Pan Pacific
9. River City Guesthouse
10. River View Guesthouse
11. Royal Orchid
12. Shangri-La
13. Sheraton
14. Silom Street Inn
15. Sukhothai
16. Tawana Ramada
17. Westin Banyan Tree

Places to eat:
18. Ban Chiang
19. Batavia
20. Bua

Cambodian Embassy

Lumpini Park

Witthayu (Wireless) Rd

Rachdamri Rd

Rama IV Rd

Soi Sribampen

Soi Ngam Duphli

Lumpini Boxing Stadium

see detail of Soi Ngam Duphli

Danish Embassy

Austrian Embassy

Soi Suan Phlu

German Embassy

French Embassy

Australian Embassy

Malaysian Embassy

Singapore Embassy

Immigration

Sathorn Nua Rd

Sathorn Tai Rd

Delaney's Pub

Convent Rd

Jim Thompson's Silk Emporium

Henri Dunant Rd

Thaniya Rd

Snake Farm

Patpong II

Patpong I

Phayathai Rd

Rama IV Rd

Sap Rd

British Club

Canadian Embassy

Neilson Hays Library

Decho Rd

Silom Rd

Pan Rd

Burma (Myanmar) Embassy

Russian Embassy

Laos Embassy

Khlong

Surawong Rd

Silom Village

Neret Rd

Mahasak Rd

Surasak Rd

Maha Nakhon Rd

Si Phraya Rd

Maha Phruttharam Rd

Second stage expressway

Krung (New Rd)

Charoen Krung Rd

Portuguese Embassy

River City

To Chinatown & Old City

Charoen

Bangrak Market

Chao phraya River

To Marriott Royal Garden Riverside Hotel

Taksin Bridge

N

metres
0   250

F 4761120, a/c, restaurant, large pool, situated on the river but on the Thonburi bank, attractive low rise hotel with some attempt to create Thai-style and ambience; **A+** *Monarch Lee Gardens*, 188 Silom Rd, T 2381991, F 2381999, a/c, restaurants, pool, opened 1992, stark and gleaming high-tech high-rise, all facilities, still trying hard to create custom, discounts available; **A+** *Pan Pacific Hotel*, 952 Rama IV Rd, T 6329000, F 6329001, a/c, restaurant, pool, 235 rm hotel, good central position for business and shopping.

A *Mandarin*, 662 Rama IV Rd, T 2380230, F 2371620, a/c, restaurant, small pool, friendly atmosphere, comfortable rooms, popular nightclub; **A** *Silom Street Inn*, 284/11-13 Silom Rd, opp the junction with Pan Rd (between sois 22 and 24), T 2384680, F 2384689, a/c, restaurant, pool, small new hotel, small, comfortable, 30 well-equipped rm with CNN News, grubby rather seedy lobby, set back from road; **A** *Tower Inn*, 533 Silom Rd, T 2344051, F 2344051, a/c, restaurant, pool, simple but comfortable hotel, with large rooms and an excellent roof terrace, good value.

B *River City Guesthouse*, 11/4 Charoen Krung Soi Rong Nam Khang 1, T 2351429, F 2373127, a/c, not very welcoming but rooms are a good size and clean, good bathrooms, short walk to River City and the river; **B** *Rose*, 118 Surawong Rd, T 2337695, F 2346381, a/c, restaurant, pool, opp Patpong, favourite among single male visitors, but getting seedier by the month; **B** *Swan*, 31 Charoen Krung Soi 36, T 2348594, some a/c, great position, clean but scruffy rooms.

C *Chao Phya Riverside*, 1128 Songward Rd (opp the Chinese school), T 2226344, F 2231696, some a/c, old style house overlooking river, clean rooms, atmospheric, unusual location in commercial Chinatown with *sip lors* (ten-wheelers) loading rice, and metal workers fashioning steel, seems to be a little more run-down than a few years back and characteristically brusque management but worth considering for its position and character; **C** *River View Guesthouse*, 768 Songwad Soi Panurangsri, T 2345429, F 2375771, some a/c, the restaurant/bar is on the top floor and overlooks the river, food is mediocre, but

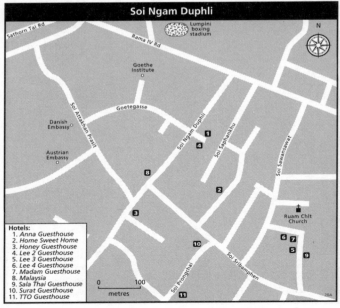

Soi Ngam Duphli

Sathorn Tai Rd

Rama IV Rd

Lumpini boxing stadium

Goethe Institute

Goetegasse

Danish Embassy

Austrian Embassy

Soi Attakhan Prasit

Soi Ngam Duphli

Soi Saphankhu

Soi Sawansawat

Ruam Chit Church

Soi Sribamphen

Soi Prongthai

Hotels:
1. *Anna Guesthouse*
2. *Home Sweet Home*
3. *Honey Guesthouse*
4. *Lee 2 Guesthouse*
5. *Lee 3 Guesthouse*
6. *Lee 4 Guesthouse*
7. *Madam Guesthouse*
8. *Malaysia*
9. *Sala Thai Guesthouse*
10. *Surat Guesthouse*
11. *TTO Guesthouse*

0   100
metres

N

the atmosphere is friendly, rooms are large, clean, some with balconies, some hot water, difficult to find but in a central position in Chinatown and overlooking (as the name suggests) the river, professional management, Khun Phi Yai, the owner, is a pharmacist, so can even prescribe pills.

● **Soi Ngam Duphli**

Soi Ngam Duphli is much the smaller of Bangkok's two centres of guesthouse accommodation. Locationally, the area is good for the shopping and bars of Silom Rd but inconvenient for most of the city's main places of interest in the old city. Guesthouses tend to be quieter and more refined than those of Khaosan Rd – and therefore more expensive too. See the Soi Ngam Duphli map for locations.

B *Malaysia*, 54 Rama IV Soi Ngam Duphli, T 2863582, F 2493120, a/c, restaurant, pool, once a Bangkok favourite for travellers.

C *TTO*, 2/48 Soi Sribamphen, T 2866783, F 2871571, a/c, well-run and popular, homely atmosphere, rooms a little small; **C-D** *Honey*, 35/2-4 Soi Ngam Duphli, T 2863460, some a/c, large rooms, in a rather rambling block, clean and good value, service can be rather surly, no hot water.

D *Sala Thai Guesthouse*, 15 Soi Sribamphen, T 2871436, at end of peaceful, almost leafy, soi, clean rooms, family run, good food, but shared bathroom, rec; **D-E** *Anna*, 21/30 Soi Ngam Duphli, clean rooms, some with bathrooms; **D-E** *Home Sweet Home*, 27/7 Soi Sribamphen (opp Boston Inn, down small soi, so relatively quiet, average rooms with attached bathrooms; **D-E** *Lee 3*, 13 Soi Saphan Khu, T 2863042, some a/c, wooden house with character, down quiet soi, rooms are clean but with shared bathrooms, rec; **D-E** *Madam*, 11 Soi Saphan Khu, T 2869289, wooden house, friendly atmosphere, attached bathrooms, no hot water, quiet, rec.

E *Lee 2*, 21/38-39 Soi Ngam Duphli, T 2862069, clean, friendly, rec; **E** *Lee 4*, 9 Soi Saphan Khu, T 2867874, spotless rooms and bathrooms, some with balconies and views over city, rec; **E** *Surat*, 2/18-20 Sribamphen Rd, T 2867919, some a/c, own bathroom, no hot water, clean and well-run, rec.

● **Siam Square, Rama I, Ploenchit and Phetburi roads**

L *Grand Hyatt Erawan*, 494 Rachadamri Rd, T 2541234, F 2535856, the replacement hotel for the much-loved old *Erawan Hotel*, towering

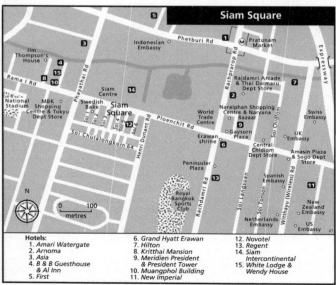

Siam Square

Hotels:
1. Amari Watergate
2. Arnoma
3. Asia
4. B & B Guesthouse & Al Inn
5. First
6. Grand Hyatt Erawan
7. Hilton
8. Kritthai Mansion
9. Meridien President & President Tower
10. Muangphol Building
11. New Imperial
12. Novotel
13. Regent
14. Siam Intercontinental
15. White Lodge & Wendy House

structure with grandiose entrance and a plastic tree-filled atrium plus sumptious rooms and every facility but has lost atmosphere in the process; **L** *Hilton*, 2 Witthayu Rd, T 2530123, F 2536509, a/c, restaurants, attractive pool, excellent hotel set in lovely grounds with a remarkable garden feel for a hotel that is so central, comparatively small for such a large plot and first class service; **L** *Novotel*, Siam Sq Soi 6, T 2556888, F 2551824, a/c, restaurant, pool, undistinguished but commendably comfortable; **L** *Siam Intercontinental*, 967 Rama I Rd, T 2530355, F 2532275, a/c, restaurants, small pool, relatively low-rise hotel, set in 26 acres of grounds, good sports facilities, excellent service; **L-A+** *Imperial*, 6-10 Witthayu Rd, (on the edge of Siam Sq area), T 2540023, F 2533190, a/c, restaurants, pool, lovely grounds but hotel seems rather jaded next to Bangkok's newer upstarts, 370 rm and numerous bars and restaurants where, apparently, it is possible to rub shoulders with the city's 'beautiful people', walls are very thin and recent visitors have been disappointed at how this hotel has declined in quality; **L-A+** *Regent Bangkok*, 155 Rachdamri Rd, T 2516127, F 2539195, a/c, restaurants (see Thai Restaurants, page 242), pool (although rather noisy, set above a busy road), excellent reputation amongst frequent visitors who insist on staying here, stylish and postmodern in atmosphere with arguably the best range of cuisine in Bangkok. It is also perhaps the most impressive piece of modern hotel architecture in Bangkok – which admittedly isn't saying much, rec.

A+ *Amari Atrium Hotel*, 1880 Phetburi Rd, T 7182000, F 7182002, a/c, restaurant, pool, Clark Hatch fitness centre, opened early 1996, 600 rm, all facilities, reasonably accessible for airport but not particularly well placed for the sights of the old city, nor for the central business district for that matter; **A+** *Amari Watergate*, 847 Phetburi Rd, T 6539000, F 6539045, a/c, restaurants, pool, fitness centre, squash court, situated close to the Pratunam market, great curvey pool (which makes swimming lengths a little tricky), but close to 600 rm makes this a hotel on a grand scale, lots of marble and plastic trees, uninspired block, good facilities; **A+** *Le Meridien President*, 971 Ploenchit Rd, T 2530444, F 2549988, pool, health club, 400 rm in this, one of the older but still excellent luxury hotels in Bangkok (it opened in 1966), tranquil atmosphere, good service, excellent French food, a new sister hotel, *The President Tower* is due for completion in late 1996 and will tower 36 storeys

skywards, the original hotel is still rec; **A+** *Siam City*, 477 Sri Ayutthaya Rd, T 2470120, F 2470178, a/c, restaurants, pool, stylish hotel with attentive staff, large rooms with in-house movies, all facilities (gym etc) and well managed, good Mediterranean restaurant and bakery, rec.

B *Florida*, 43 Phayathai Rd, T 2470990, a/c, restaurant, pool, one of Thailand's first international hotels and it shows, average even at this price.

C *A-1 Inn*, 25/13 Soi Kasemsan Nung (1), Rama I Rd, T 2153029, a/c, well run, intimate hotel, rec; **C** *Bed and Breakfast*, 36/42 Soi Kasemsan Nung (1), Rama 1 Rd, T 2153004, F 2152493, a/c, friendly efficient staff, clean but small rooms, good security, bright 'lobby', price includes breakfast, rec; **C** *Muangphol Building*, 931/9 Rama I Rd, T 2150033, F 2168053, a/c, pool, hot water, good sized rooms, reasonable rates; **C** *Wendy House*, 36/2 Soi Kasemsan Nung (1), Rama I Rd, T 2162436, F 2168053, a/c, spotless, but small rooms with eating area downstairs, hot water; **C** *White Lodge*, 36/8 Soi Kasemsan Nung (1), Rama I Rd, T 2168867, F 2168228, a/c, hot water, airy, light reasonably sized rooms, rec; **C-E** *Alternative Tour Guesthouse*, 14/1 Rachaprarop Soi Rachatapan, T 2452963, F 2467020, friendly, excellent source of information, attached to *Alternative Tour Company*, promoting culturally and environmentally sensitive tourism, clean.

● **Sukhumvit Road**

L *Imperial Queen's Park*, Sukhumvit Soi 22, T 2619000, F 2619530, massive new 37-storey hotel with a mind boggling 1,400 rm, how service can, in any sense, be personal is hard to imagine, but all possible facilities, location is away from most sights and the main business district so means guests have to battle with the traffic to do most things; **L** *Windsor Plaza Embassy Suites*, 8 Sukhumvit Soi 20, T 2580160, F 2581491, a/c, restaurants, pool, next door to the *Windsor Hotel*, 460 suites, health centre.

A+ *Delta Grand Pacific*, 259 Sukhumvit Rd, T 2544998, F 2552441, a/c, restaurants, pool, almost 400 rm in this large high-rise hotel, all facilities but characterless for the price; **A+** *Rembrandt*, 15-15/1 Sukhumvit Soi 20, T 2617040, F 2617017, a/c, restaurants, pool, new hotel with lots of marble and limited ambience; **A+-A** *Somerset*, 10 Sukhumvit Soi 15, T 2548500, F 2548534, a/c, restaurant, tiny enclosed pool, small hotel, rather ostentatious, rooms are nondescript but comfortable, baths are designed for people of small stature.

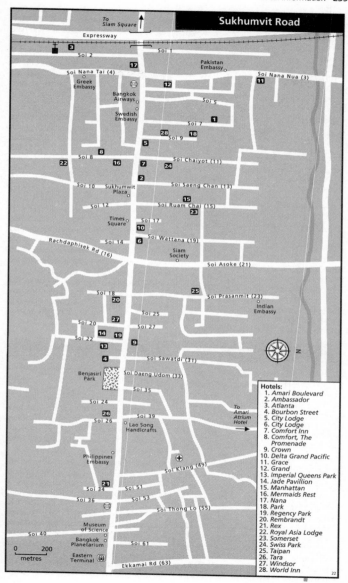

Sukhumvit Road

To Siam Square

Expressway

Soi 1
Soi 2
Soi Nana Tai (4)
Greek Embassy
Bangkok Airways
Swedish Embassy
Pakistan Embassy
Soi Nana Nua (3)
Soi 5
Soi 7
Soi 9
Soi 8
Soi Chaiyot (11)
Soi 10
Sukhumvit Plaza
Soi Saeng Chan (13)
Soi 12
Soi Ruam Chai (15)
Times Square
Soi 17
Soi 14
Soi Wattana (19)
Rachdaphisek Rd (16)
Siam Society
Soi Asoke (21)
Soi 18
Soi Prasanmit (23)
Indian Embassy
Soi 25
Soi 20
Soi 27
Soi 22
Soi Sawatdi (31)
Benjasiri Park
Soi Daeng Udom (33)
Soi 35
Soi 24
To Amari Atrium Hotel
Soi 39
Soi 26
Lao Song Handicrafts
Philippines Embassy
Soi Klang (49)
Soi 34
Soi 36
Soi 51
Soi 53
Soi Thong Lo (55)
Museum of Science
Bangkok Planetarium
Soi 40
Soi 61
Eastern Terminal
Ekkamai Rd (63)

0 200
metres

N

Hotels:
1. Amari Boulevard
2. Ambassador
3. Atlanta
4. Bourbon Street
5. City Lodge
6. City Lodge
7. Comfort Inn
8. Comfort, The Promenade
9. Crown
10. Delta Grand Pacific
11. Grace
12. Grand
13. Imperial Queens Park
14. Jade Pavillion
15. Manhattan
16. Mermaids Rest
17. Nana
18. Park
19. Regency Park
20. Rembrandt
21. Rex
22. Royal Asia Lodge
23. Somerset
24. Swiss Park
25. Taipan
26. Tara
27. Windsor
28. World Inn

A *Amari Boulevard*, 2 Sukhumvit Soi 5, T 2552930, F 2552950, a/c, restauarant, roof top, pool, good mid-range hotel, over 300 rm, fitness centre, nothing to mark it out as particularly Thai – generic tropical feel; **A** *Ambassador*, 171 Sukhumvit Rd, T 2540444, F 2534123, a/c, restaurants, pool, large, impersonal rather characterless hotel, with great food hall (see restaurants); **A** *Manhattan*, 13 Sukhumvit Soi 15, T 2550166, F 2553481, a/c, restaurant, pool, recently renovated high-rise, lacks character but rooms are comfortable and competitively priced although some are rather shabby so ask to inspect; **A** *Tai-pan*, 25 Sukhumvit Soi 23, T 2609888, F 2597908, a/c, restaurant, pool, tasteful new hotel; **A** *Windsor*, 8 Sukhumvit Soi 20, T 2580160, F 2581491, a/c, restaurant, pool, tennis.

B *Bourbon Street*, 29/4-6 Sukhumvit Soi 22 (behind Washington Theatre), T 2590328, F 2594318, a/c, small number of rooms attached to this Cajun restaurant, well run and good value, rec; **B** *China*, 19/27-28 Sukhumvit Soi 19, T 2557571, F 2541333, a/c, restaurant, a small hotel masquerading as a large one, but rooms are up to the standard of more expensive places, so good value; **B** *Comfort Inn*, 153/11 Sukhumvit Soi 11, T 2519250, F 2543562, a/c, restaurant, small hotel, friendly management, rec; **B** *Crown*, 503 Sukhumvit Soi 29, T 2580318, F 2584438, a/c, clean, good service; **B** *Grand*, 2/7-8 Sukhumvit Soi Nana Nua (Soi 3), T 2533380, F 2549020, a/c, restaurant, small hotel with friendly staff, good value.

C *Atlanta*, 78 Sukhumvit Soi 2, T 2521650, a/c, restaurant, large pool, left-luggage facility, poste restante, daily video-shows, good tour company in foyer, rec.

D *Chu's*, 35 Sukhumvit Soi 19, T 2544683, restaurant, one of the cheapest in the area, good food, rec; **D** *Happy Inn*, 20/1 Sukhumvit Soi 4, T 2526508, some a/c, basic rooms, cheerful management; **D** *SV*, 19/35-36 Sukhumvit Soi 19, T 2544724, some a/c, another cheap hotel in this area, musty rooms, shared bathrooms and poor service; **D-E** *Disra House*, 593/28 Sukhumvit Soi 33-33/1, T 2585102, some a/c, friendly and well run place which comes highly recommended, rather out-of-the-way but good value a/c rooms.

● **Banglamphu (Khaosan Road) and surrounds**

Khaosan Rd lies NE of Sanaam Luang, just off Rachdamnern Klang Ave, close to the Democracy Monument. It is continually expanding into new roads and sois, in particular the area W of Chakrapong Rd. The sois off the main road are often quieter, such as Soi Chana Songkhran or Soi Rambutri. Note that rooms facing on to Khaosan Rd tend to be very noisy.

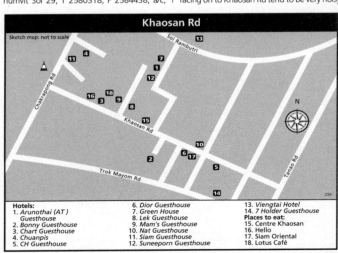

Khaosan Rd
Sketch map: not to scale

Hotels:
1. *Arunothai (AT)* Guesthouse
2. *Bonny Guesthouse*
3. *Chart Guesthouse*
4. *Chuanpis*
5. *CH Guesthouse*
6. *Dior Guesthouse*
7. *Green House*
8. *Lek Guesthouse*
9. *Mam's Guesthouse*
10. *Nat Guesthouse*
11. *Siam Guesthouse*
12. *Suneeporn Guesthouse*
13. *Viengtai Hotel*
14. *7 Holder Guesthouse*
Places to eat:
15. *Centre Khaosan*
16. *Hello*
17. *Siam Oriental*
18. *Lotus Café*

Khaosan Rd is not just a place to spend the night. Also here are multitudes of restaurants, travel and tour agents, shops, stalls, tattoo artists, bars, bus companies – almost any and every service a traveller might need. They are geared to budget visitors' needs and more than a few have dubious reputations, in general the guesthouses of Khaosan Rd itself have been eclipsed in terms of quality and cleanliness by those to the N, closer to the river. The useful little post office that used to be at the top of Khaosan Rd and operated by poste restante service and a fax facility has recently closed. Whether it will re-open is not certain.

A+ Royal Princess, 269 Lan Luang Rd, T 2813088, F 2801314, a/c, restaurants, pool, newish addition to Dusit chain of hotels, good facilities.

A Majestic Palace, 97 Rachdamnern Klang Ave (opp Democracy Monument), T 2805610, F 2800965, a/c, restaurant, pool, old hotel given half-hearted face-lift, good location but rooms overpriced and limited facilities; **A Royal**, 2 Rachdamnern Klang Ave, T 2229111, F 2242083, a/c, restaurant, pool, old (by Bangkok standards) hotel which acted as a refuge for demonstrators during the 1991 riots, rooms are dated and featureless; **A Vi-**

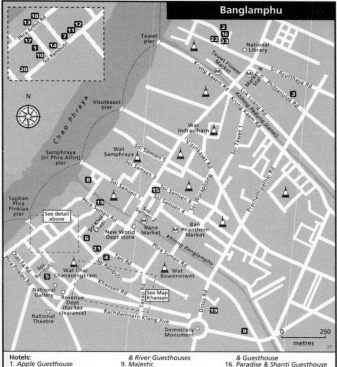

Banglamphu

Hotels:
1. Apple Guesthouse
2. Backpackers Lodge
3. Bangkok Youth Hostel
4. BK Guesthouse
5. Chai's House
6. Chusri Guesthouse
7. Green Guesthouse
8. Home & Garden

& River Guesthouses
9. Majestic
10. Mango Guesthouse
    & Roof Garden Guesthouse
11. Merry V
12. My House
13. New Merry V
14. New Siam
15. New World Apartment

& Guesthouse
16. Paradise & Shanti Guesthouse
17. Peachy Guesthouse
18. Pra Suri Guesthouse
19. PS Guesthouse
20. Rose Garden
21. Sawasdee House
22. Sawatdee Guesthouse
23. Tavee Guesthouse

engtai, 42 Tanee Rd, Banglamphu, T 2815788, a/c, restaurant, pool, rooms are very good, clean relatively spacious, with all the advantages of this area in terms of proximity to the Old City.

B *Trang Hotel*, 99/1 Visutkaset Rd, T 2811402, F 2803160, a/c, restaurant, pool, clean and friendly mid-range hotel which comes rec by regular visitors to Bangkok, discount voucher available from *Vieng Travel* in the same building.

C *New World Apartment and Guesthouse*, 2 Samsen Rd, T 2815596, F 2815596, some a/c, good location for the Old City yet away from the hurly-burly of Khaosan Rd, rooms are clean and good value even if the overall atmosphere is rather institutional; C *Pia Arthit Mansion*, 22 Phra Arthit Rd, comfortable rooms, hot water, a/c, carpeted, bath tubs, pleasant communal sitting area; C-D *7 Holder*, 216/2-3 Khaosan Rd, T 2813682, some a/c, clean, friendly, located on the narrow soi behind Khaosan Rd, so quieter than those places situated right on the street; C-D *New Siam*, Phra Athit 21 Soi Chana Songkram, T 2824554, F 2817461, some a/c, good restaurant, modern and clean, friendly helpful staff, airy rooms, but featureless block, tickets and tour information, fax facilities, lockers available, overpriced; C-E *Chart*, 58 Khaosan Rd, T 2803785, restaurant, some a/c, small but clean rooms, some have no windows; C-E *Green House*, 88/1 Khaosan Soi Rambutri, T 2819572, some a/c, ask for rooms away from street, for an extra ฿100 they will flip the switch for a/c, rec; C-E *Peachy*, 10 Phra Athit Rd, T 2816659, some a/c and more expensive rooms with hot water, recent visitors have reported a deterioration in quality and cleanliness, but still has pleasant restaurant area.

D *My House*, 37 Phra Athit Soi Chana Songkram, T 2829263, management are a little off-hand but the rooms are well maintained and loos are kept clean, remains popular; D *Pra Suri*, 85/1 Soi Pra Suri (off Dinso Rd), 5 mins E from Khaosan Rd not far from the Democracy Monument, fan, restaurant, own bathrooms (no hot water), clean and quiet, very friendly and helpful family-run guesthouse, rec; D-E *BK*, 11/1 Chakrapong Soi Sulaow, T 2815278, some a/c, in busy area of Banglamphu, but guesthouse is set back from road, so not too noisy, clean but dark rooms, shared bathrooms, good information; D-E *Buddy*, 137/1 Khaosan Rd, T 2824351, off main street, some a/c, rooms are small and dingy but it remains popular, large open restaurant area

bustles with people exchanging information; D-E *CH*, 216/1 Khaosan Rd, T 2822023, some a/c, good reputation, left luggage (฿5/day, ฿30/week); D-E *Chai's House*, 49/4-8 Chao Fa Soi Rongmai, T 2814901, F 2818686, some a/c, friendly atmosphere, clean and colourful with borgainvillea growing from the balconies and bamboos and orchids in the restaurant, last house down Soi Rambutri, so away from the others, rec; D-E *Hello*, 63-65 Khaosan Rd, T 2818579, some a/c, popular; D-E *Privacy Tourist House*, 69 Tanow Rd, T 2827028, popular, quiet, rec; D-E *Sawasdee House*, 147 Chakrapong Soi Rambutri, T 2818138, bit of a warren of a place and feels like a cross between a guesthouse and a hotel, shared loos and showers are kept clean, and rooms though box-like are fine. Out the front is a sitting area and what is rather optimistically called a beer 'garden'.

E *Apple 2*, 11 Phra Sumen Rd, T 2811219, old-time favourite, very small rooms, basic, but friendly and characterful; E *Arunothai (AT)*, 90/1, 5, 12 Khaosan Soi Rambutri, T 2826979, friendly owner, situated in a quiet little courtyard with 4 or 5 other guesthouses, good place to start looking for a room as it is easy to check them all out; E *Bonny*, 132 Khaosan Rd, T 2819877, quiet, situated down a narrow alley off Khaosan itself, reports of bed bugs; E *Chuanpis*, 86 Chakrapong Rd (nr intersection with Khaosan Rd, down small soi opp Wat Chanasongkhram), popular, geared particularly to Israeli visitors, good food, average rooms, often full; E *Democratic*, 211/8 Rachdamnern Ave, T 2826035, F 2249149, set back, opp the Democracy Monument, 4-storey concrete house with friendly management but small rooms and grubby stairwell; E *Dior*, 146-158 Khaosan Rd, T 2829142, small but clean rooms and bathrooms, quiet, set back from road, 'family' atmosphere, rec; E *Green Guesthouse*, 27 Phra Athit Soi Chana Songkram, T 2828994, not to be confused with the *Green House*, rooms are fine and competively priced; E *Home and Garden*, 16 Samphraya Rd (Samsen 3), T 2801475, away from main concentration of guesthouses, down quiet soi (quite difficult to find), good location for river taxi, rooms are small and basic but clean, well run and friendly, rec; E *Lek*, 90/9 Khaosan Soi Rambutri, T 2812775, popular; E *Mam's*, 119 Khaosan Rd, friendly, homely atmosphere, rec; E *Merry V*, 33-35 Phra Athit Soi Chana Songkram, T 2829267, some a/c, large place, some rooms with balconies although interior rooms have no outside windows and are dark, lockers available, friendly and well run with good information; **E** *Nat*, 217 Khaosan Rd, brusque management but clean, larger than average rooms with fan, rec; **E** *New Merry V*, 18-20 Phra Athit Rd, T 2803315, new guesthouse with clean but very small rooms, pleasant place to stay, friendly, with a good travel service; **E** *PS*, 9 Phra Sumen Rd, T 2823932, spotlessly clean, rooms with no windows, but satellite TV and free tea and coffee, rec; **E** *The River Guest House*, 18/1 Samphraya Rd (Samsen 3), T 2800876, next to the *Home and Garden* and very similar, good location, quiet but accessible by express boat, friendly, rec. (**NB** There is a third guesthouse on Samphraya Rd, *The Clean and Calm* about which we have received disturbing reports.) **E** *Rose Garden*, 28/6 Phra Athit Soi Trok Rongmai, T 2818366, friendly although rooms are a bit dark; **E** *Siam*, 76 Chakrapong Rd, T 2810930, rooms facing onto the street are noisy, small rooms but good clean bathrooms; **E** *Suneeporn*, 90/10 Khaosan Soi Rambutri, T 2826887, popular; **E** *Sweety*, 49 Thani Rd, clean, rec; **E-F** *Uimol Guesthouse*, Soi 2 Samsen Rd, clean relaxing and friendly guesthouse, good eating places in vicinity.

F *KC*, 60-64 Phra Sumen Rd Soi Khai Chae, T 2820618, friendly management, clean rooms, rec.

● **Sri Ayutthaya Road**

Sri Ayutthaya is emerging as an 'alternative' area for budget travellers. It is a central location with restaurants and foodstalls nearby, but does not suffer the over-crowding and sheer pandemonium of Khaosan Rd and so is considerably quieter and more peaceful. It is also close to the Tewet Pier for the express river boats (see the Banglamphu map). The guesthouses are perhaps a little more expensive but the rooms are better and the places seem to be generally better managed. One family runs four of the guesthouses which means if one is full you will probably be moved on to another.

D *Shanti Lodge*, 37 Sri Ayutthaya Rd, T 2812497, restaurant with extensive menu, very popular, rooms nicely done up, rec.

E *Backpackers Lodge*, 85 Sir Ayutthaya Rd, Soi 14, T 2823231, restaurant, rooms with fans, small patio, quiet and friendly, large python (*ngulaam*) keeps watch at the bottom of the stairs, fortunately caged, rec; **E** *Paradise*, 57 Sri Ayutthaya Rd, T 2828673, some fans, small guesthouse, rooms with no outward-looking windows, friendly management; **E** *Sawatdee*, 71 Sri Ayutthaya Rd, T 2810757, Western menu, pokey rooms, popular with

German travellers, management rather brusque and off-hand; **E** *Tavee*, 83 Sri Ayutthaya Rd, Soi 14, T 2801447, restaurant, fan, small garden, clean and pleasant, rooms and shared showers and loos are kept spotless, down a quiet little soi, has been operating since 1985 and has managed to maintain a very high standard, rec; **E-F** *Bangkok Youth Hostel*, 25/2 Phitsanulok Rd (off Samsen Rd), T 2820950, N of Khaosan Rd, away from the bustle, dorms available.

● **Others**

A+ *Central Hotel*, 1695 Phahonyothin Rd, T 5411234, F 5411087, a/c, restaurant, pool, out of town, close to w/e market, efficiently run, but inconveniently located and recently taken over by the Central Department Store group.

A+ *Marriot Royal Garden*, Riverside Resort, 257/1-3 Charoen Nakrom Rd, T 4760021, F 4761120, a/c, restaurant, excellent swimming pool, almost resort-like, very spacious surrounding, opp the *Oriental*, nr the Krung Thep Bridge, free shuttle-boat service every 30 mins between hotel and the *Oriental* and River City piers.

A *Sunroute Bangkok*, 288 Rama IX Rd, T 2480011, F 2485990, a/c, restaurants, pool, part of a Japanese chain, markets itself as the 'route to satisfaction', located away from most sights and shopping; Dusit Riverside, over Sathorn Bridge in Thonburi (opening late 1992); **A-B** *Ramada Renaissance Bridgeview*, 3999 Rama III Rd, T 2923160, F 2923164, a/c, numerous restaurants, pools, tennis, squash, new 476 room high-rise overlooking Chao Phraya River, all facilities, poor location for sights, shopping and business.

C-E *The Artists Club*, 61 Soi Tiem Boon Yang, T 4389653, some a/c, run by an artist, this is a guesthouse cum studio cum gallery in Thonburi (ie the other side of the river), clean rooms and a real alternative place to stay with concerts and drawing lessons, away from the centre of guesthouse activity.

● **Places to eat**

Bangkok has the largest and widest selection of restaurants in Thailand – everyone eats out, so the number of places is vast. Food is generally very good and cheap – this applies not just to Thai restaurants but also to places serving other Asian cuisines, and Western dishes. Roadside food is good value – many Thais eat on the street, businessmen and civil servants rubbing shoulders with factory workers and truck drivers. **NB** Most restaurants close be-

Price guide

	US$	Baht
♦♦♦♦♦	20	500+
♦♦♦♦	15+	375+
♦♦♦	5-15	125-375
♦♦	2-5	50-125
♦	under 2	under 50

tween 2200 and 2230. For a fuller listing of places to eat see *Bangkok Metro Magazine*, published monthly. The magazine is also good for bars, music venues, shopping etc.

Afternoon tea: *The Authors Lounge*, Oriental Hotel; the *Bakery Shop*, Siam Intercontinental Hotel; *The Cup*, second floor of Peninsula Plaza, Rachdamri Rd; *The Regent Hotel* lobby (music accompaniment), Rachdamri Rd; the *Dusit Thani Hotel* library, Rama IV Rd.

Bakeries: Bangkok has a large selection of fine bakeries, many attached to hotels like the *Landmark*, *Dusit Thani* and *Oriental*. There are also the generic 'donut' fast food places although few lovers of bread and pastries would want to lump the two together. *The Bakery Landmark Hotel*, 138 Sukhumvit Rd, many cakes and pastry connoisseurs argue that this is the best of the hotel places, popular with expats, wide range of breads and cakes; *Basket of Plenty*, Peninsula Plaza, Rachdamri Rd (another branch at 66-67 Sukhumvit Soi 33), bakery, deli and trendy restaurant, very good things baked and a classy (though expensive) place for lunch; *Bei Otto*, Sukhumvit Soi 20, a German bakery and deli, makes really very good pastries, breads and cakes; *Cheesecake House*, 69/2 Ekamai Soi 22, rather out of town for most tourists but patronized enthusiastically by the city's large Sukhumvit-based expat population, as the name suggests cheesecakes of all descriptions are a speciality – and are excellent; *Folies*, 309/3 Soi Nang Linchee (Yannawa), T 2869786, French expats and bake-o-philes maintain this bakery makes the most authentic pastries and breads in town, coffee available, a great place to sit, eat and read; *Jimmy*, 1270-2, nr Oriental Lane, Charoen Krung, a/c, cakes and ice creams, very little else around here, so it's a good stopping place; *La Brioche*, ground flr of Novotel Hotel, Siam Sq Soi 6, good range of French patisseries; *Sweet Corner*, Siam Intercontinental Hotel, Rama I Rd, one of the best in Bangkok; *Swedish Bake*, Siam Square Soi 2, good Danish pastries.

Chinese: most Thai restaurants sell Chinese food, but there are also many dedicated Chinese establishments. **Siam Square** has a large number, particularly those specializing in shark's fin soup. For shark's fin try the *Scala Shark's Fin* (reputed to be the best of the bunch), *Bangkok Shark's Fin*, and the *Penang Shark's Fin* all opp the Scala Cinema, Siam Square Soi 1. ♦♦♦♦-♦♦♦*Kirin*, 226/1 Siam Square Soi 2, over 20 years old, traditional Chinese decor, good atmosphere; ♦♦♦*Art House*, 87 Sukhumvit Soi 55 (Soi Thonglor), country house with traditional Chinese furnishings, surrounded by gardens, particularly good seafood; ♦♦♦*China*, 231/3 Rachdamri Soi Sarasin, Bangkok's oldest Chinese restaurant, serving full range of Chinese cuisine; ♦♦♦*Chinese Seafood Restaurant*, 33/1-5 16 Wall St Tower, Surawong Rd, Cantonese and Szechuan; ♦♦♦*Joo Long Lao*, 2/1 Sukhumvit Soi 2, spacious, with wide choice of dishes, rec; ♦♦♦*Lung Wah*, 848/3 Rama III Rd, large restaurant, with good reputation, serves shark's fin and other seafood, also serves Thai; ♦♦♦*Shangarila*, 154/4-7 Silom Rd, T 2340861, bustling Shanghai restaurant with dim sum lunch; ♦♦♦*Sunshine Noodle Square*, 392/27-30 Siam Square Soi 5, opened in 1996, clean and cool design and nouvelle Chinese cuisine – open 24 hrs; ♦♦*Tongkee*, 308-314 Sukhumvit Rd (opp Soi 19), Kwangtung food, popular with Thais.

Fast Food: Bangkok now has a large number of Western fast food outlets, such as *Pizza Hut*, *McDonalds*, *Kentucky Fried Chicken*, *Mister Donut*, *Dunkin' Donuts*, *Shakey's*, *Baskin Robbins* and *Burger King*. These are located in the main shopping and tourist areas – Siam Square, Silom/Patpong rds, and Ploenchit Rd, for example.

Foodstalls: scattered across the city for a rice or noodle dish, where a meal will cost ฿15-30 instead of a minimum of ฿75 in the restaurants. For example, on the roads between Silom and Surawong Rd, or down Soi Somkid, next to Ploenchit Rd, or opp on Soi Tonson.

Italian: ♦♦♦♦*L'Opera*, 55 Sukhumvit Soi 39, T 2585606, Italian restaurant with Italian manager, conservatory, good food (excellent salted baked fish), professional service, lively atmosphere, popular, booking essential, rec; ♦♦♦♦*Paesano*, 96/7 Soi Tonson (off Soi Langsuan), Ploenchit Rd, T 2522834, average Italian food, sometimes good, in friendly atmosphere, very popular with locals; ♦♦♦*Gino's*, 13 Sukhumvit Soi 15, Italian food in bright and airy surroundings, set lunch is good value; ***Ristorante Sorrento**, 66 North Sathorn Rd, excellent Italian food; ***Roberto's 18**, 36 Sukhumvit, Soi 18, Italian; ***Terrazzo**, *Sukhothai Hotel*, 13/3 South Sathorn Rd, T 2870222, stylish al fresco Italian restaurant overlooking the pool, wonderful Italian breads and good pasta dishes, rec; ***Trattoria Da Roberto**, 37/9 Plaza Arcade, Patpong 2 Rd, T 2336851, authentic Italian setting; ***Vito's Spaghetteria**, Basement, Gaysorn Plaza, Ploenchit Rd (next to *Le Meridien Hotel*), bright and breezy pasta bar, make up your own dish by combining 10 types of pasta with 12 sauces and 29 fresh condiments, smallish servings but good for a hurried lunch.

French: ****Beccassine**, Sukhumvit, Soi Sawatdee, English and French home cooking, rec; ****Diva**, 49 Sukhumvit Soi 49, T 2587879, excellent French restaurant, with very good Italian dishes and crepe suzette which should not be missed, friendly service, attractive surroundings, good value, rec; ****La Grenouille**, 220/4 Sukhumvit Soi 1, T 2539080, traditional French cuisine, French chef and manager, small restaurant makes booking essential, French wines and French atmosphere, rec; ****Le Banyan**, 59 Sukhumvit Soi 8, T 2535556, excellent French food; ****L'Hexagone**, 4 Sukhumvit Soi 55 (Soi Thonglor), T 3812187, French cuisine, in 'posh' surroundings; ***Brussels Restaurant**, 23/4 Sukhumvit Soi 4, small and friendly, also serves Thai dishes; ***Chez Daniel Le Normand**, 1/9 Sukhumvit Soi 24, top class French restaurant; ***Classique Cuisine**, 122 Sukhumvit Soi 49, classic French cuisine; ***Le Bordeaux**, 1/38 Sukhumvit Soi 39, T 2589766, range of French dishes; ***Le Café Français**, 22 Sukhumvit Soi 24, French seafood; ***Le Café de Paris**, Patpong 2, traditional French food, rec; ***Restaurant Des Arts Nouveaux**, 127 Soi Charoensuk, Sukhumvit Soi 55, art nouveau interior, top class French cuisine; ***Stanley's French Restaurant**, 20/20-21 Ruamrudee Village, good French food, special Sun brunch, closed Mon.

Other International: ****Neil's Tavern**, 58/4 Wittayu, Soi Ruamrudee, T 2566644, best steak in town, popular with expats; ****Wit's Oyster Bar**, 20/10 Ruamrudee Village, T 2519455, Bangkok's first and only Oyster Bar, run by eccentric Thai, one of the few places where you can eat late, good salmon fishcakes, international cuisine; ***Bei Otto**, 1 Sukhumvit Soi 20, Thailand's best known German restaurant, sausages made on the premises, good provincial food, large helpings; ***Bobby's Arms**, 2nd Flr, Car Park Bldg, 114/1-4 Patpong 2 Rd, T 2336828, British pub food; ***Bourbon Street**, 29/4-6 Sukhumvit Soi 22 (behind Washington Theatre), Cajun specialities including gumbo, jambalaya and red fish, along with steaks and Mexican dishes, served in a/c restaurant with VDOs and central bar – good for breakfast, excellent pancakes; ***Den Hvide Svane**, Sukhumvit Soi 8, Scandinavian and Thai dishes, former are good, efficient and friendly service; ***Gourmet Gallery**, 6/1 Soi Promsri 1 (between Sukhumvit Soi 39 and 40), interesting interior, with art work for sale, unusual menu of European and American food; ***Hard Rock Café**, 424/3-6 Siam Sq Soi 11, home-from-home for all burger-starved farangs, overpriced, videos, live music sometimes, and all the expected paraphernalia, a couple of Thai dishes have been included, large portions and good atmosphere. ***Haus Munchen**, 4 Sukhumvit Soi 15, T 2525776, German food in quasi-Bavarian lodge, connoisseurs maintain cuisine is authentic enough; ***Longhorn**, 120/9 Sukhumvit Soi 23, Cajun and Creole food; ***Senor Pico**, *Rembrandt Hotel*, 18 Sukhumvit Rd, Mexican, pseudo-Mexican decor, staff dressed Mexican style, large, rather uncosy restaurant, average cuisine, live music; ***Tia Maria**, 14/18 Patpong Soi 1, best Mexican restaurant in Bangkok; **Caravan Coffee House**, Siam Sq Soi 5, large range of coffee or tea, food includes pizza, curry and some Thai food; **Crazy Horse**, 5 Patpong 2 Rd, simple decor, but good French food, open until 0400; **Harmonique**, 22 Charoen Krung, small elegant coffee shop with good music, fruit drinks and coffee.

South Asian (Indian): ****Rang Mahal**, *Rembrandt Hotel*, Sukhumvit Soi 18, T 2617100, best Indian food in town, very popular with the Indian community and spectacular views from the roof top position, sophisticated, elegant and ... expensive; ***Himali Cha Cha**, 1229/11 Charoen Krung, T 2351569, good choice of Indian cuisine, mountainous meals for the very hungry, originally set up by Cha Cha and now run by his son – 'from generation to generation' as it is quaintly put; ***Moghul Room**, 1/16 Sukhumvit Soi 11, wide choice of Indian and Muslim food; ***Mrs. Balbir's**, 155/18 Sukhumvit Soi 11, T 2532281, North Indian food orchestrated by Mrs Balbir, an Indian originally from Malaysia, regular customers just keep going back, chicken dishes are succulent, Mrs Balbir also runs cookery classes; **Bangkok Brindawan**, 15 Sukhumvit Soi 35, S Indian, Sat lunch set-price buffet; **Nawab**, 64/39 Soi Wat Suan Plu, Charoen Krung, N and S Indian dishes; *Samrat*, 273-275 Chakraphet Rd, Pratuleck Lek, Indian and Pakistani food in restaurant down quiet lane off Chakraphet Rd, cheap and tasty, rec; *Tamil Nadu*, 5/1 Silom Soi (Tambisa) 11, T 2356336, good, but limited South Indian menu, cheap and filling, *dosas* are rec, there are 4 or 5 **Indian** restaurants in a row on Sukhumvit Soi 11.

Vietnamese: ****Pho**, 2F Alma Link Building, 25 Soi Chidlom, T 2518900 (another branch at 3rd floor, Sukhumvit Plaza, Sukhumvit 12, T 2525601), supporters claim this place serves the best Vietnamese in town, modern trendy setting, non-smoking area; ***Le Cam-Ly**, 2nd Flr, 1 Patpong Bldg, Surawong Rd; ***Le Dalat**, 47/1 Sukhumvit Soi 23, T 25841912, same management as Le Cam-Ly, reputed to serve the best Vietnamese food in Bangkok, arrive early or management may hassle; ***Sweet Basil**, 1 Silom Soi Srivieng (opp Bangkok Christian College), T 2383088, another branch at 5/1 Sukhumvit Soi 63 (Ekamai), T 3812834; **Saigon-Rimsai*, 413/9 Sukhumvit Soi 55, Vietnamese and some Thai dishes, friendly atmosphere.

Japanese and Korean: ***Akamon**, 233 Sukhumvit Soi 21, Japanese; ***Kobune**, 3rd Fl, Mahboonkhrong (MBK) Centre, Rama 1 Rd, Japanese, Sushi Bar or sunken tables, rec; ***Otafuku**, 484 Siam Sq Soi 6, Henry Dunant Rd, Sushi Bar or low tables, Japanese; **New Korea*, 41/1 Soi Chuam Rewang, Sukhumvit Sois 15-19, excellent Korean food in small restaurant, rec.

Indonesian and Burmese: ***Bali**, 20/11 Ruamrudee Village, Soi Ruamrudee, Ploenchit Rd, only authentic Indonesian in Bangkok, friendly proprietress; ***Batavia**, 12 Convent Rd, T 2667164, 'imported' Indonesian chefs, good classic dishes like saté, gado-gado (vegetable with peanut sauce and rice) and ayam goreng (deep fried chicken); ***Mandalay**, 23/17 Ploenchit Soi Ruamrudee, authentic Burmese food, most gastronomes of the country reckon the food is the best in the capital, rec.

Middle Eastern: ***Akbar**, 1/4 Sukhumvit Soi 3, T 2533479, Indian, Pakistani and Arabic; ***Nasir al-Masri**, 4-6 Sukhumvit Soi Nana Nua, T 2535582, reputedly the best Eastern (Egyptian) food in Bangkok, felafal, tabouli, humus, fre-

quented by large numbers of Arabs who come to Sayed Saad Qutub Nasir for a taste of home.

Asian: ***Ambassador Food Centre**, Ambassador Hotel, Sukhumvit Rd. A vast self-service, up-market hawkers' centre with a large selection of Asian foods at reasonable prices: Thai, Chinese, Japanese, Vietnamese etc, rec.

Lao/Isan food: ****La Normandie**, Oriental Hotel, 48 Oriental Ave, T 2360400, despite many competitors, La Normandie maintains extremely high standards of cuisine and service, guest chefs from around the world, jacket and tie required in the evening, very refined (and expensive); ***Bane Lao**, Naphasup Ya-ak I, off Sukhumvit Soi 36, Laotian open-air restaurant (doubles as a travel agent for Laos), Laotian band, haphazard but friendly service; ***Sarah Jane's**, 36/2 Soi Lang Suan, Ploenchit Rd, T 2526572, run by American lady, married to a Thai, best Thai salad in town and good duck, Isan food especially noteworthy, excellent value, rec; **Isn't Classic*, 154 Silom Rd, excellent BBQ, king prawns and Isan specialities like spicy papaya salad (somtam).

Vegetarian: ***Whole Earth**, 93/3 Ploenchit Soi Lang Suan, T 2525574 (another branch at 71 Sukhumvit Soi 26, T 2584900), Thailand's best known vegetarian restaurant, eclectic menu from Thai to Indian dishes, live music, ask to sit at the back downstairs, or sit Thai-style upstairs.

Thai: *****Dusit Thani Thai Restaurant**, 946 Rama IV Rd, beautiful surroundings – like an old Thai palace, exquisite Thai food, very expensive wines; *****Spice Market**, Regent Hotel, 155 Rachdamri Rd, T 2516127, Westernized Thai, typical hotel decoration, arguably the city's best Thai food – simply delectable; ****Bussaracum**, 35 Soi Phiphat off Convent Rd, T 2358915, changing menu, popular, rec; ****D'jit Pochana Oriental**, 1082 Phahonyothin Rd, T 2795000, extensive range of dishes, large and rather industrial but the food is good; ****-***there are several excellent restaurants in Silom Village, a shopping mall, on Silom Rd (N side, opp Pan Rd), excellent range of food from hundreds of stalls, all cooked in front of you, enjoyable village atmosphere, rec; ****-***Once Upon a Time**, 67 Soi Anumanrachaton, T 2338493, set in attractive traditional Thai house (between Silom and Surawong rds); ****-***Bua Restaurant**, Convent Rd (off Silom Rd), classy postmodern Thai restaurant with starched white table linen and cool, minimalist lines, the food also reflects the decor (or the other way around?):

refined and immaculately prepared; ♦♦♦*Ban Chiang*, 14 Srivdieng Rd, T 2367045, quite hard to find – ask for directions, old style Thai house, large menu of traditionally-prepared food; ♦♦♦*Ban Khun Phor*, 458/7-9 Siam Square Soi 8, T 2501732, good Thai food in stylish surroundings; ♦♦♦*Ban Krua*, 29/1 Saladaeng Soi 1, Silom Rd, simple decor, friendly atmosphere, a/c room or open-air garden, traditional Thai food; ♦♦♦*Ban Thai*, Soi 32 or Ruen Thep, Silom Village, Silom Rd, T 2585403, with classical dancing and music; ♦♦♦*Banana Leaf*, Silom complex (basement floor), Silom Rd, T 3213124, excellent and very popular Thai restaurant with some unusual dishes, including *kai manaaw* (chicken in lime sauce), *nam tok muu* (spicy pork salad, Isan style) and fresh spring rolls 'Banana Leaf', booking recommended for lunch; ♦♦♦*Garden Restaurant*, 324/1 Phahonyothin Rd, open-air restaurant or the air-conditioned comfort of a wood panelled room, also serves Chinese, Japanese and International; ♦♦♦*Kaloang*, 2 Sri Ayutthaya Rd, T 2819228. Two dining areas, one on a pier, the other on a boat on the Chao Phraya River, attractive atmosphere, delicious food, rec.; ♦♦♦*Lemon Grass*, 5/1 Sukhumvit Soi 24, T 2588637, Thai style house, rather dark interior but very stylish, one step up from Cabbages and Condoms, rec; ♦♦♦*Moon Shadow*, 145 Gaysorn Rd, good seafood, choice of dining-rooms – a/c or open-air; ♦♦♦*Seafood Market*, Sukhumvit Soi 24, this famous restaurant has recently moved to new premises, and is said to be both larger and better, "if it swims we have it", choose your seafood from the 'supermarket' and then have it cooked to your own specifications before consuming the creatures at the table, popular; ♦♦♦*Seven Seas*, Sukhumvit Soi 33, T 2597662, quirky 'nouvelle' Thai food, popular with young sophisticated and avant garde Thais; ♦♦♦*Side Walk*, 855/2 Silom Rd (opp Central Dept Store), grilled specialities, also serves French, rec; ♦♦♦*Tum Nak Thai*, 131 Rajdapisek Rd, T 2746420, 'largest' restaurant in the world, 3,000 seats, rather out of the way (฿100 by taxi from city centre), classical dancing from 2000-2130; ♦♦♦-♦♦*Ban Somrudee* 228/6-7 Siam Square Soi 2, T 2512085; ♦♦*Ban Bung*, 32/10 Mu 2 Intramara 45, Rachadapisek, well known garden restaurant of northern-style pavilions, row around the lake to build up an appetite; ♦♦*Ban Mai*, 121 Sukhumvit Soi 22, Sub-Soi 2, old Thai-style decorations in an attractive house with friendly atmosphere,

good value; ♦♦*Cabbages and Condoms*, Sukhumvit Soi 12 (around 400m down the soi), Population and Community Development Association (PDA) restaurant so all proceeds go to this charity, eat rice in the Condom Room, drink in the Vasectomy Room, good *yam kung* and honey-roast chicken, curries all rather similar, good value, rec; ♦♦*Princess Terrace*, Rama I Soi Kasemsan Nung (1), Thai and French food with BBQ specialities served in small restaurant with friendly service and open terrace down quiet lane, rec; ♦♦*Puang Kaew*, 108 Sukhumvit Soi 23, T 5238172, large, unusual menu, also serves Chinese; ♦♦*Rung Pueng*, 37 Saladaeng, Soi 2, Silom Rd, traditional Thai food at reasonable prices; ♦♦*Sanuk Nuek*, 397/1 Sukhumvit Soi 55 (Soi Thonglor), T 4935590, small restaurant with unusual decorations, live folk music, well priced; ♦♦*September*, 120/1-2 Sukhumvit Soi 23, art nouveau setting, also serves Chinese and European, good value for money; ♦♦*Suda*, 6-6/1 Sukhumvit Rd, Soi 14, rec; ♦♦*Wannakarm*, 98 Sukhumvit Soi 23, T 2596499, well established, very Thai restaurant, grim decor, no English spoken, but rated food.

Travellers' food available in the guesthouse/travellers' hotel areas (see above). *Hello* in Khaosan Rd has been recommended, the portions of food are a good size and they have a useful notice board for leaving messages. Nearly all the restaurants in Khaosan Rd show videos all afternoon and evening. If on a tight budget it is much more sensible to eat in Thai restaurants and stalls where it should be possible to have a good meal for ฿10-20.

● **Bars**

The greatest concentration of bars are in the two 'red light' districts of Bangkok – Patpong (between Silom and Surawong rds) and Soi Cowboy (Sukhumvit). Patpong was transformed from a street of 'tea houses' (brothels serving local clients) into a high-tech lane of go-go bars in 1969 when an American made a major investment. In fact there are two streets, side-by-side, Patpong 1 and Patpong 2. Patpong 1 is the larger and more active, with a host of stalls down the middle at night (see page 247); Patpong 2 supports cocktail bars and, appropriately, pharmacies and clinics for STDs, as well as a few go-go bars. The *Derby King* is one of the most popular with expats and serves what are reputed to be the best club sandwiches in Asia, if not the world. Opposite Patpong, along Convent Rd is *Delaney's* (see Silom map), an Irish pub with draft

Guinness from Malaysia (where it is brewed) and a limited menu, good atmosphere and well-patronized by Bangkok's expats – sofas for lounging and reading (upstairs). Soi Cowboy is named after the first bar here, the *Cowboy Bar*, established by a retired US Airforce officer. Although some of the bars obviously also offer other forms of entertainment (something that quickly becomes blindingly obvious), there are, believe it or not, some excellent and very reasonably priced bars in these two areas. A small beer will cost ¢45-65, with good (if loud) music and perhaps videos thrown in for free. However, if opting for a bar with a 'show', be prepared to pay considerably more.

Warning Front men will assure customers that there is no entrance charge and a beer is only ¢60, but you can be certain that they will try to fleece you on the way out and can become aggressive if you refuse to pay. Even experienced Bangkok travellers find themselves in this predicament. Massages and more can also be obtained at many places in the Patpong and Soi Cowboy areas. **NB** AIDS is a significant and growing problem in Thailand so it is strongly recommended that customers practice safe sex.

A particularly civilized place to have a beer and watch the sun go down is on the verandah of the *Oriental Hotel*, by the banks of the Chao Phraya River, expensive, but romantic; ♦♦♦*Basement Pub* (and restaurant), 946 Rama IV Rd, live music, also serves international food, open 1800-2400; ♦♦♦*Black Scene*, 120/29-30 Sukhumvit Soi 23, live jazz, also serves Thai and French food, open 1700-1300; ♦♦♦*Bobby's Arms*, 2nd Flr, Car Park Bldg, Patpong 2 Rd, English pub and grill, with jazz on Sun from 2000, open 1100-0100; *Gitanes*, 52 Soi Pasana 1, Sukhumvit Soi 63. Live music, open 1800-0100; *King's Castle*, Patpong 1 Rd, another long-standing bar with core of regulars; *Royal Salute*, Patpong 2 Rd, cocktail bar where local farangs end their working days.

Hemingway Bar and Grill, 159/5-8 Sukhumvit Soi 55, live jazz and country music at the w/e, plus Thai and American food, open 1800-0100; ♦♦*Old West Saloon*, 231/17 Rachdamri Soi Sarasin, live country music, also serves international and Thai food, open 1700-0100. ♦♦*Picasso Pub*, 1950-52 Ramkamhaeng Rd, Bangkapi. Live music, also serves Thai food, open 1800-0300; ♦♦*Round Midnight*, 106/12 Soi Langsuan, live blues and jazz, some excellent bands play here, packed at week-

ends, good atmosphere and worth the trip, also serves Thai and Italian food, open 1700-0400; *Trader Vic's*, *Royal Marriott Garden Hotel*; ♦♦*Trumpet Pub* (and restaurant), 7 Sukhumvit Soi 24, live blues and jazz, also serves Thai food, open 1900-0200. **Note** For bars with live music also see *Music*, below, under **Entertainment**, page 246.

● **Airline offices**

For airport enquiries call, T 2860190. **Aeroflot**, Regent House, 183 Rachdamri Rd, T 2510617; **Air China**, 2nd Flr, CP Bldg, 313 Silom Rd, T 6310731; **Air France**, Grd Flr, Charn Issara Tower, 942 Rama IV Rd, T 2339477; **Air India**, 16th Flr, Amarin Tower, 500 Ploenchit Rd, T 2350557; **Air Lanka**, Grd Flr, Charn Issara Tower, 942 Rama IV Rd, T 2369292; **Alitalia**, 8th Flr, Boonmitr Bldg, 138 Silom Rd, T 2334000; **American Airlines**, 518/5 Ploenchit Rd, T 2511393; **Asiana Airlines**, 14th Flr, BB Bldg, 54 Asoke Rd, T 2607700; **Bangkok Airways**, Queen Sirikit National Convention Centre, New Rajdapisek Rd, Klongtoey, T 2293434; **Bangladesh Biman**, Grd Flr, Chongkolnee Bldg, 56 Surawong Rd, T 2357643; **British Airways**, 2nd Flr, Charn Issara Tower, 942 Rama IV Rd, T 2360038; **Canadian Airlines**, 6th Flr, Maneeya Bldg, 518/5 Ploenchit Rd, T 2514521; **Cathay Pacific**, 11th Flr, Ploenchit Tower, 898 Ploenchit Rd, T 2630606; **China Airlines**, 4th Flr, Peninsula Plaza, 153 Rachdamri Rd, T 2534242; **Continental Airlines**, CP Tower, 313 Silom Rd, T 2310113; **Delta Airlines**, 7th Flr, Patpong Bldg, Surawong Rd, T 2376838; **Egyptair**, CP Tower, 313 Silom Rd, T 2310501; **Finnair**, 12 Flr, Sathorn City Tower, 175 Sathorn Tai Rd, T 6396671; **Garuda**, 27th Flr, Lumpini Tower, 1168 Rama IV Rd, T 2856470; **Gulf Air**, Grd Flr, Maneeya Bldg, 518 Ploenchit Rd, T 2547931; **Japan Airlines**, 254/1 Ratchadapisek Rd, T 2741411; **KLM**, 12th Flr, Maneeya Centre Bldg, 518/5 Ploenchit Rd, T 2548325; **Korean Air**, Grd Flr, Kong Bunma Bldg (opp *Narai Hotel*), 699 Silom Rd, T 2359220; **Kuwait Airways**, 12th Flr, RS Tower, 121/50-51 Ratchadapisek Rd, T 6412864; **Lao Aviation**, 491 17 Ground Flr, Silom Plaza, Silom Rd, T 2369822; **Lufthansa**, 18th Flr, Q-House (Asoke), Sukhumvit Rd Soi 21, T 2642400; **MAS** (*Malaysian Airlines*), 20th Flr, Ploenchit Tower, 898 Ploenchit Rd, T 2630565; **Myanmar Airways**, Charn Issara Tower, 942 Rama IV Rd, T 2342985; **Pakistan International**, 52 Surawong Rd, T 2342961; **Philippine Airlines**, Chongkolnee Bldg, 56 Surawong Rd,

T 2332350; **Qantas**, 11th Flr, Charn Issara Tower, 942 Rama IV Rd, T 2675188; **Royal Brunei**, 4th Flr, Charn Issara Tower, 942 Rama IV Rd, T 2330056; **Royal Nepal Airlines**, Sivadon Bldg, 1/4 Convent Rd, T 2333921; **Sabena**, 3rd Flr, CP Tower, 313 Silom Rd, T 2382201; **SAS**, 8th Flr, Glas Haus I, Sukhumvit Rd Soi 25, T 2600444; **Saudi**, 3rd Flr, Main Bldg, Don Muang Airport, T 5352341; **Singapore Airlines**, 12th Flr, Silom Centre, 2 Silom Rd, T 2360440; **Swissair**, 2nd Flr, 1-7 FE Zuellig Bldg, Silom Rd, T 2333810; **TWA**, 485 Silom Rd, T 2332930; **Thai**, 485 Silom Rd, T 2333810; **TWA**, 12th Flr, Charn Issara Tower, 942 Rama IV Rd, T 2337290; **Vietnam Airlines**, 584 Ploenchit Rd, T 2514242.

● **Banks & money changers**

There are countless exchange booths in all the tourist areas open 7 days a week, mostly 0800-1530, some from 0800-2100. Rates vary only marginally between banks, although if changing a large sum, it is worth shopping around.

● **Embassies**

Australia, 37 Sathorn Tai Rd, T 2872680; **Brunei**, 154 Ekamai Soi 14, Sukhumvit 63, T 3815914, F 3815921; **Cambodia**, 185 Rachdamri Rd, T 2546630; **Canada**, 12th Flr, Boonmitr Bldg, 138 Silom Rd, T 2341561/8; **Denmark**, 10 Sathorn Tai Soi Attakarnprasit, T 2132021; **Finland**, 16th Flr, Amarin Plaza, 500 Ploenchit Rd, T 2569306; **France**, 35 Customs House Lane, Charoen Krung, T 2668250. (There is also a French consulate at 29 Sathorn Tai Rd, T 2856104.) **Germany**, 9 Sathorn Tai Rd, T 2132331; **India**, Sukhumvit Rd Soi 23, T 2580300; **Indonesia**, 600-602 Phetburi Rd, T 2523135; **Israel**, 25th Flr, Ocean Tower II, 75 Soi Wattana, Sukhumvit 19, T 2604850; **Greece**, 79 Sukhumvit Soi 4, T 2542936, F 2542937; **Italy**, 399 Nang Linchi Rd, T 2854090; **Japan**, 1674 New Phetburi Rd, T 2526151; **Laos**, 502/1-3 Soi Ramkhamhaeng 39, T 5396667; **Malaysia**, 15th Flr, Regent House, 183 Rachdamri Rd, T 2541700; **Myanmar** (Burma), 132 Sathorn Nua Rd, T 2332237; **Nepal**, 189 Sukhumvit Soi 71, T 3917240; **Netherlands**, 106 Withhaya Rd, T 2547701; **New Zealand**, 93 Witthayu Rd, T 2518165; **Norway**, 1st Flr, Bank of America Bldg, Witthayu Rd, T 2530390; **People's Republic of China**, 57 Ratchadapisek Rd, Dindaeng, T 2457032; **Philippines**, 760 Sukhumvit Rd, T 2590139; **Singapore**, 129 Sathorn Tai Rd, T 2862111; **South Africa**, 6th Flr, Park Place, 231 Soi Sarasin, Rachdamri Rd, T 2538473; **Spain**, 93 Witthaya Rd, T 2526112; **Sweden**, 20th Flr, Pacific Place, 140 Sukhumvit Rd, T 2544954; **UK**, 1031 Witthayu Rd, T 2530191/9; **USA**, 95 Witthayu Rd, T 2525040; **Vietnam**, 83/1 Witthayu Rd, T 2515835.

● **Church services**

Evangelical Church, Sukhumvit Soi 10 (0930 Sun service); the *International Church* (interdenominational), 67 Sukhumvit Soi 19 (0800 Sun service); *Baptist Church*, 2172/146 Phahonyothin Soi 36 (1800 Sun service); *Holy Redeemer*, 123/19 Wittayu Soi Ruam Rudee (Catholic, 5 services on Sun); *Christ Church*, 11 Convent Rd (Anglican – Episcopalian – Ecumenical) (3 Sun services at 0730, 1000 and 1800).

● **Entertainment**

Art galleries: *The Artist's Gallery*, 60 Pan Rd, off Silom, selection of international works of art. *The Neilson Hays Library*, 195 Surawong Rd, has a changing programme of exhibitions.

Buddhism: the headquarters of the World Fellowship of Buddhists is at 33 Sukhumvit Rd (between Soi 1 and Soi 3). Meditation classes are held in English on Wed at 1700-2000; lectures on Buddhism are held on the first Wed of each month at 1800-2000.

Cinemas: most cinemas have daily showings at 1200, 1400, 1700, 1915 and 2115, with a 1300 matinee on weekends and holidays. Cinemas with English soundtracks include *Central Theatre 2*, T 5411065, *Lido*, T 2526729, *Pantip*, T 2512390, *Pata*, T 4230568, *Mackenna*, T 2517163, *Washington 1*, T 2582045, *Washington 2*, T 2582008, *Scala*, T 2512861, *Villa*, T 2589291. *The Alliance Française*, 29 Sathorn Tai Rd, T 2132122 shows French films. Remember to stand for the National Anthem, which is played before every performance. Details of showings from English language newspapers.

Cultural centres: British Council, 254 Chulalongkorn Soi 64 (Siam Square), T 6116830, F 2535311, for films, books and other Anglocentric entertainment; Check in 'What's On' section of *Sunday Bangkok Post's* magazine for programme of events; **Alliance Française**, 29 Sathorn Tai Rd; **Goethe Institute**, 18/1 Sathorn Tai Soi Atthakan Prasit; **Siam Society**, 131 Soi 21 (Asoke) Sukhumvit, T 2583494, open Tues-Sat. Promotes Thai culture and organizes trips within (and beyond) Thailand.

Meditation: *Wat Mahathat*, facing Sanaam

Luang, is Bangkok's most renowned meditation centre. Anyone interested is welcome to attend the daily classes – the centre is located in Khana 5 of the monastery. Apart from Wat Mahathat, classes are also held at *Wat Bowonniwet* in Banglamphu on Phra Sumen Rd (see the Bangkok – Old City map), and at the *Thai Meditation Centre* in the World Fellowship of Buddhists building on 33 Sukhumvit Rd, T 2511188.

Music: (see also **Bars**, page 243, for more places with live music): *Blues-Jazz*, 25 Sukhumvit Soi 53, open Mon-Sun 1900-0200, three house bands play really good blues and jazz, food available, drinks a little on the steep side. *Blue Moon*, 73 Sukhumvit 55 (Thonglor), open Mon-Sun 1800-0300, for country, rhythm, jazz and blues – particularly Fri and Sun for jazz – some food available. *Brown Sugar*, 231/20 Sarasin Rd (opp Lumpini Park), open Mon-Fri 1100-0100, Sat and Sun 1700-0200, five regular bands play excellent jazz, a place for Bangkok's trendies to hang out and be cool. *Cool Tango*, 23/51 Block F, Royal City Av (between Phetburi and Rama IX rds), open Tue-Sat 1100-0200, Sun 1800-0200, excellent resident rock band, great atmosphere, happy hour(s) 1800-2100. *Front Page*, 14/10 Soi Saladaeng 1, open Mon-Fri 1000-0100, Sat and Sun 1800-0100, populated, as the name might suggest, by journos who like to hunt in packs more than most, music is country, folk and blues, food available. *Hard Rock Café*, 424/3-6 Siam Sq Soi 11, open Mon-Sun 1100-0200, speaks for itself, burgers, beer and rock covers played by reasonable house band, food is expensive for Bangkok though. *Magic Castle*, 212/33 Sukhumvit Plaza Soi 12, open Mon-Thu 1800-0100, Fri and Sat 1800-0200, mostly blues, some rock, good place for a relaxed beer with skilfully performed covers. *Picasso Pub*, 1950-5 Ramkhomhaeng Rd (close to Soi 8), open Mon-Sun 1900-0300, house rock band, adept at playing covers. *Round Midnight*, 106/12 Soi Langsuan, open Mon-Thu 1900-0230, Fri and Sat 1900-0400, jazz, blues and rock bands.

Thai Performing Arts: classical dancing and music is often performed at restaurants after a 'traditional' Thai meal has been served. Many tour companies or travel agents organize these 'cultural evenings'. *National Theatre*, Na Phrathat Rd, (T 2214885 for programme). Thai classical dramas, dancing and music on the last Fri of each month at 1730 and periodically on other days. *Thailand Cultural Centre*, Rach-daphisek Rd, Huai Khwang, T 2470028 for programme of events. *College of Dramatic Arts*, nr National Theatre, T 2241391. *Baan Thai Restaurant*, 7 Sukhumvit Soi 32, T 2585403, 2100-2145. *Chao Phraya Restaurant*, Pinklao Bridge, Arun Amarin Rd, T 4742389; *Maneeya's Lotus Room*, Ploenchit Rd, T 2526312, 2015-2100; *Piman Restaurant*, 46 Sukhumvit Soi 49, T 2587866, 2045-2130; *Ruen Thep*, Silom Village Trade Centre, T 2339447, 2020-2120; *Suwannahong Restaurant*, Sri Ayutthaya Rd, T 2454448, 2015-2115; *Tum-Nak-Thai Restaurant*, 131 Rachdaphisek Rd, T 2773828 2030-2130.

● **Hospitals & medical services**

Bangkok Adventist Hospital, 430 Phitsanulok Rd, Dusit, T 2811422/2821100; *Bangkok General Hospital*, New Phetburi Soi 47, T 3180066; *Bangkok Nursing Home*, 9 Convent Rd, T 2332610; *St. Louis Hospital*, 215 Sathorn Tai Rd, T 2120033. **Health clinics**: *Dental Polyclinic*, New Phetburi Rd, T 3145070; *Dental Hospital*, 88/88 Sukhumvit 49, T 2605000, F 2605026, good, but expensive; *Clinic Banglamphu*, 187 Chakrapong Rd, T 2827479.

● **Immigration**

Sathorn Tai Soi Suanphlu, T 2873101.

● **Libraries**

British Council Library, 254 Chulalongkorn Soi 64 (Siam Square). Open Tue-Sat 1000-1930, membership library with good selection of English language books. **NB** In Oct 1996 Queen Elizabeth II opened the new British Council offices and it was rumoured that the library had been cut in the interests of economy; *National Library*, Samsen Rd, close to Sri Ayutthaya Rd, open Mon-Sun 0930-1930; *Neilson Hays Library*, 195 Surawong Rd, T 2331731, next door to British Club. Open: 0930-1600 Mon-Sat, 0930-1230 Sun. A small library of English-language books housed in an elegant building dating from 1922. It is a private membership library, but welcomes visitors who might want to see the building and browse; occasional exhibitions are held here. Open 0930-1600 Mon-Sat, 0930-1230 Sun; *Siam Society Library*, 131 Sukhumvit Soi 21 (Asoke), open Tue-Sat 0900-1700, membership library with excellent collection of Thai and foreign language books and periodicals (especially English) on Thailand and mainland south east Asia.

● **Meditation and Yoga**

The *Dharma Study Foundation*, 128 Soi Thonglor 4, Sukhumvit Soi 55, T 3916006, open 0900-1800 Mon-Fri and the *World Fellowship of Buddhists*, 33 Sukhumvit Rd (between sois 1 and 3), T 2511188, open 0900-1630 Mon-Fri, both offer classes in meditation and some religious discussions. Yoga classes available at *Sunee Yoga Centre*, 2nd Flr, Pratunam Centre, 78/4 Rachprarop Rd, T 2549768, open 1000-1200 and 1700-1900 Mon-Sat.

● **Post & telecommunications**

Area code: 02.

Central GPO (*Praysani Klang* for taxi drivers): 1160 Charoen Krung, opp the *Ramada Hotel*. Open 0800-2000 Mon-Fri and 0800-1300 weekend and holidays. The money and postal order service is open 0800-1700, Mon-Fri, 0800-1200 Sat. Closed on Sun and holidays. 24 hrs telegram and telephone service (phone rates are reduced 2100-0700) and a packing service.

● **Shopping**

Most shops do not open until 1000-1100. Nancy Chandler's *Map of Bangkok* is the best shopping guide. Bangkok still stocks a wonderful range of goods, but do not expect to pick up a bargain – prices are high. Stallholders, entirely understandably, are out for all they can get – so bargain hard here. The traditional street market, although not dying out, is now supplemented by other types of shopping. Given the heat, the evolution of the air conditioned shopping arcade and air conditioned department store in Bangkok was just a matter of time. Some arcades target the wealthier shopper, and are dominated by brand name goods and designer ware. Others are not much more than street side stalls transplanted to an arcade environment. Most department stores are now fixed price.

Bangkok's main shopping areas are:

1. Sukhumvit: Sukhumvit Rd, and the sois to the N are lined with shops and stalls, especially around the *Ambassador* and *Landmark* hotels. Many tailors and made-to-measure shoe shops are to be found in this area.

2. Central: 2 areas close to each other centred on Rama I and Ploenchit rds. At the intersection of Phayathai and Rama I rds there is Siam Square (for teenage trendy Western clothing, bags, belts, jewellery, bookshops, some antique shops and American fast food chains) and the massive – and highly popular – Mah Boonkhrong Centre (MBK), with countless small shops and stalls and the Tokyu Department Store. Siam Square used to be great for cheap clothes, leather goods etc, but each year it inches further up market: there are now branches of *Timberland*, the *Body Shop*, *Kookäi* and various designer outlets here. Peninsular Plaza, between the *Hyatt Erawan* and *Regent* hotels is considered the smartest shopping plaza in Bangkok. For those looking for fashion clothes and accessories, this is probably the best area. A short distance to the E, centred on Ploenchit/Rachprarop rds, are more shopping arcades and large department stores, including the World Trade Centre, Thai Daimaru, Robinsons, Gaysorn Plaza (exclusive shopping arcade), Naraiphan shopping centre (more of a market stall affair, geared to tourists, in the basement) and Central Chidlom (which burnt down in a catastrophic fire in 1995 but which should be rebuilt/renovated – although in 1996 it was still waiting for work to begin). North along Rachprasong Rd, crossing over Khlong Saensap, at the intersection with Phetburi Rd is the Pratunam market, good for fabrics and clothing.

3. Patpong/Silom: Patpong is more of a night market (opening at 2100), the streets are packed with stalls selling the usual array of stall goods which seem to stay the same from year to year (fake designer clothing, watches, bags etc). **NB** Bargain hard. The E end of Silom has a scattering of similar stalls open during the day time, and Robinsons Department Store. Surawong Rd (at the other end of Patpong) has Thai silk, antiques and a few handicraft shops.

4. West Silom/Charoen Krung (New Rd): antiques, jewellery, silk, stamps, coins and bronzeware. Stalls set up here at 2100. A 15 min walk N along Charoen Krung (close to the *Orchid Sheraton Hotel*) is the River City Shopping Plaza, specializing in art and antiques.

5. Banglamphu/Khaosan Road: vast variety of low-priced goods, such as ready-made clothes, shoes, bags, jewellery and cassette tapes.

6. Lardphrao-Phahonyothin: some distance N of town, not far from the Weekend Market (see page 227) is the huge Central Plaza shopping complex. It houses a branch of the Central Department Store and has many boutiques and gift shops.

Department Stores: *Central* is the largest chain of department stores in Bangkok, with a range of Thai and imported goods at fixed prices; credit cards are accepted. Main shops on Silom Rd, Ploenchit Rd (Chidlom Branch – which burnt down in 1995 but should be renovated), and in the Central Plaza, just N of the Northern bus terminal. Other department stores include *Thai*

Buying gems and jewellery

More people lose their money through gem and jewellery scams in Thailand than in any other way (60% of complaints to the TAT involve gem scams). **DO NOT** fall for any story about gem sales, special holidays, tax breaks – no matter how convincing. **NEVER** buy gems from people on the street (or beach) and try not to be taken to a shop by an intermediary. **ANY** unsolicited approach is likely to be a scam. The problem is perceived to be so serious that in some countries Thai embassies are handing out warning leaflets with visas.

Rules of thumb to avoid being cheated

● Choose a specialist store in a relatively prestigious part of town (the TAT will informally recommend stores).
● Note that no stores are authorized by the TAT or by the Thai government; if they claim as much they are lying.
● It is advisable to buy from shops who are members of the Thai Gem and Jewellery Traders Association.
● Avoid touts.
● Never be rushed into a purchase.
● Do not believe stories about vast profits from re-selling gems at home. They are lies.
● Do not agree to have items mailed ("for safety").
● If buying a valuable gem, a certificate of identification is a good insurance policy. The Department of Mineral Resources (Rama VI Rd, T 2461694) and the Asian Institute of Gemological Sciences (484 Rachadapisek Rd, T 5132112) will both examine stones and give such certificates.
● Compare prices; competition is stiff among the reputable shops; be suspicious of 'bargain' prices.
● Ask for a receipt detailing the stone and recording the price.

For more information (and background reading on Thailand) the *'Buyer's Guide to Thai Gems and Jewellery'*, by John Hoskin can be bought at Asia Books.

Daimaru on Rachdamri and Sukhumvit (opp Soi 71), *Robinson's* on corner of Silom and Rama IV rds, Sukhumvit (nr Soi 19) and Rachdamri rds, *Tokyu* in MBK Tower on Rama I Rd, *Sogo* in the Amarin Plaza on Ploenchit Rd, and *Zen*, World Trade Centre, corner of Rama I and Rajdamri rds.

Supermarkets: *Central Department Store* (see above), *Robinsons* – open until midnight (see above), *Villa Supermarket*, between Sois 33 and 35, Sukhumvit Rd (and branches elsewhere in town) – for everything you are unable to find anywhere else, *Isetan*, (World Trade Centre), Rachdamri Rd.

Markets: the markets in Bangkok are an excellent place to browse, take photographs and pick up bargains. They are part of the life blood of the city, and the encroachment of more organized shops and the effects of the re-developer's demolition ball are eating away at one of Bangkok's finest traditions. Nancy Chandler's map of Bangkok, available from most bookshops, is the most useful guide to the markets of the capital. The largest is the *Weekend Market* at Chatuchak Park (see page 227). The *Tewes Market*, nr the National Library, is a photographers dream; a daily market, selling flowers and plants. *Pratunam Market* is spread over a large area around Rachprarop and Phetburi rds, and is famous for clothing and fabric. Half of it was recently bulldozed for redevelopment, but there is still a multitude of stalls here. The *Bai Yoke Market* is next door and sells mostly fashion garments for teenagers – lots of lycra. A short distance S of here on Rachprarop Rd is the *Naraiphan Shopping Centre and Narayana Bazaar* an indoor stall/shopping centre affair (concentrated in the basement) geared to tourists and *farang* residents. *Nakhon Kasem* known as the *Thieves Market*, in the heart of Chinatown, houses a number of 'antique' shops selling brassware, old electric fans and woodcarvings (tough bargaining recommended, and don't expect everything to be genuine – see page 219). Close by are the stalls of *Sampeng Lane* (see page 221), specializing in toys, stationery, clothes and household goods, and the *Pahurat Cloth Market* (see page 219) – a small slice of India in Thailand, with mounds of sarongs, batiks, buttons and bows. *Bangrak Market*, S of the General Post Office, nr the river and the *Shangri-La Hotel*, sells exotic fruit, clothing, seafood and flowers. *Pak Khlong Market* is a wholesale market selling fresh produce, orchids and cut flowers and is situated nr the Memorial Bridge (see page 219). *Phahonyothin Market* is Bangkok's newest, opp the Northern bus terminal, and sells potted plants and orchids. *Banglamphu Market* is close to Khaosan Rd, the backpackers' haven, on Chakrapong and Phra Sumen rds. Stalls here sell clothing, shoes, food and household goods. The nearby *Khaosan Road Market* (if it can be called such) is much more geared to the needs and desires of the foreign tourist: CDs and cassettes, batik shirts, leather goods and so on. *Patpong Market*, arranged down the middle of Patpong Rd, linking Silom and Surawong rds, opens up about 1700 and is geared to tourists, selling handicrafts, T-shirts, leather goods, fake watches, cassettes and VDOs. *Penang Market*, Khlong Toey, situated under the expressway close to the railway line specializes in electronic equipment from hi-fis to computers, with a spattering of other goods as well. A specialist market is the *Stamp Market* next to the GPO on Charoen Krung which operates on Sun only. Collectors come here to buy or exchange stamps.

● **Tour companies & travel agents**
Travel agents abound in the tourist and hotel areas of the city – Khaosan Rd/Banglamphu, Sukhumvit, Soi Ngam Duphli, and Silom (several down Pan Rd, a soi opp Silom Village). All major hotels will have their own in-house agent. Most will book airline, bus and train tickets, arrange tours, and book hotel rooms. Because there are so many to choose from, it is worth shopping around for the best deal. For companies specialising in tours and other travel arrangements to Laos, see page309).

● **Tourist offices**
Tourist Authority of Thailand (TAT), Rachdamnern Nok Ave (at intersection with Chakrapatdipong Rd), T 2815051. There is also a smaller office at 372 Bamrung Muang Rd, T 2260060. Open Mon-Sun, 0830-1630. **NB** The main office on Rachdamnern Nok Ave opened after some delay in mid-1996. For the time being the TAT are also keeping their office on Bamrung Muang Rd open, although it may close and/or be relocated in 1997 or 1998. In addition there is a counter at Don Muang airport (in the Arrivals Hall, T 5238972) and

offices at 1 Napralarn Rd, T 2260056, and the Chatuchak Weekend Market (Kampaeng Phet Rd). The main office is very helpful and provides a great deal of information for independent travellers – certainly worth a visit.

A number of good, informative, English language magazines providing listings of what to do and where to go in Bangkok have started up recently. The best is undoubtedly *Bangkok Metro*, published monthly (฿80). It is well designed and produced and covers topics from music and nightlife, to sports and fitness, to business and children. Less independent, and with less quality information, is the oddly named *Guide of Bangkok* or GoB. Its advantage is that it is free.

● **Tourist Police**
Unico House, Ploenchit Soi Lang Suan, T 1699 or 6521721. There are also dedicated tourist police offices in the main tourist areas.

● **Traditional Thai Massage**
Many hotels offer this service; guesthouses also, although most masseuses are not trained. The most famous centre is at Wat Pho (see page 214), a Mecca for the training of masseuses. Wat Pho specializes in the more muscular Southern style. The Northern-style is less exhausting, more soothing. Other centres offering quality massages by properly trained practioners include: *Marble House*, 37/18-19 Soi Surawong Plaza (opp Montien Hotel), T 2353519, open 0100-2400 Mon-Sun, ฿300 for 2 hrs, ฿450 for 3 hrs and *Vejakorn*, 37/25 Surawong Plaza, Surawong Rd, T 2375576, open Mon-Sun 1000-2400, ฿260 for 2 hrs, ฿390 for 3 hrs.

● **Transport**
Local Bus: this is the cheapest way to get around town. A bus map marking the routes is indispensable. The *Bangkok Thailand* map and *Latest tours guide to Bangkok and Thailand* are available from most bookshops as well as many hotel and travel agents/ tour companies. Major bus stops also have maps of routes and instructions in English displayed. Standard non-a/c buses (coloured blue) cost ฿2.50. Beware of pickpockets on these often crowded buses. Red-coloured express buses are slightly more expensive (฿3.50), slightly less crowded, and do not stop at all bus stops. A/c buses cost ฿6-16 depending on distance. Travelling all the way from Silom Rd to the airport by a/c bus, for example, costs ฿14; most inner city journeys cost ฿6. There are also smaller a/c

'micro buses' (a bit of a misnomer as they are not micro at all, not even 'mini') which follow the same routes but are generally faster and less crowded because officially they are only meant to let passengers aboard if a seat is vacant. They charge a flat fare of ฿25. **NB** More people have their belongings stolen on Bangkok's city buses than almost anywhere else.

Elevated railway: an elevated railway being built by Ital-Thai is under construction and should be opened in 1997/1998.

Express boats: travel between Nonthaburi in the N and Wat Rajsingkorn (nr Krungthep bridge) in the S. Fares are calculated by zone and range from ฿4-15. At peak hours boats leave every 10 mins, off-peak about 15-25 mins (see map, page 223 for piers). The journey from one end of the route to the other takes 75 mins. Note that boats flying red or green pennants do not stop at all piers (they also exact a ฿1 express surcharge). Also, boats will only stop if passengers wish to board or alight, so make your destination known.

Ferries: small ferries take passengers across the Chao Phraya River, ฿1 (see map on page 223 for piers).

Khlong or long-tailed boats: can be rented for ฿200/hour, or more (see page 224).

Motorcycle taxi: a relatively new innovation in Bangkok (and now present in other towns in Thailand) they are the fastest, and most terrifying, way to get from A to B. Riders wear numbered vests and tend to congregate in particular areas; agree a fare, hop on the back, and hope for the best. Their 'devil may care' attitude has made them bitter enemies of many other road users. Expect to pay ฿10-20.

Taxi: most taxis are metered (they must have a/c to register) – look for the 'Taxi Meter' illuminated sign on the roof. There are a number of unmarked, unofficial taxis which are to be found around the tourist sites. Flag fall is ฿35 for a journey of 2 km or less and it should cost ฿40-100 for most trips in the city. If the travel speed is less than 6 km/hr – always a distinct possibility in the traffice choked capital – a surcharge of ฿1 per minute is automatically added. Sometimes taxis refuse to use the meter – insist they do so. Taxi drivers should not be tipped. For most tourists the arrival of the metered taxi has lowered prices as it has eliminated the need to bargain – check, though, that the meter is 'zeroed' before setting off.

Tuk-tuk: the formerly ubiquitous motorized saamlor is rapidly becoming a piece of history in Bangkok, although they can still always be found

nr tourist sites. Best for short journeys: they are uncomfortable and, being open to the elements, you are likely to be asphyxiated by car fumes. Bargaining is essential and the fare must be negotiated before boarding, most journeys cost at least ฿40. Both tuk-tuk and taxi drivers may try to take you to restaurants or shops – do not be persuaded; they are often mediocre places charging high prices.

Long distance Bangkok lies at the heart of Thailand's transport network. Virtually all trains and buses end up here and it is possible to reach anywhere in the country from the capital. Bangkok is also a regional transport hub, and there are flights to most international destinations. For international transportation, see page 275.

Air Don Muang Airport is 25 km N of the city. Regular connections on **Thai** to many of the provincial capitals. For airport details see page 277. There are a number of Thai offices in Bangkok, Head Office for domestic flights is 89 Vibhavadi Rangsit Rd, T 5130121, but this is inconveniently located N of town. Two more central offices are at 6 Lan Luang Rd (T 2800070) and 485 Silom Rd. Tickets can also be bought at most travel agents. **Bangkok Airways** flies to Koh Samui, Hua Hin, Phuket, Sukhothai, Chiang Mai, Ranong, Hat Yai, U-Tapao (Pattaya) and Mae Hong Son. They have an office in the domestic terminal at Don Muang, and two offices in town: Queen Sirikit National Convention Centre, New Rachadapisek Rd, T 2293456; and IIII Ploenchit Rd, T 2542903.

Train Bangkok has two main railway stations. The primary station, catering for most destinations, is Hualamphong, Rama IV Rd, T 2237010/2237020; condensed railway timetables in English can be picked up from the information counter in the main concourse. Trains to Nak-

Thai Airways: sample domestic routes and fares

Route	Mins	Fare (baht)*
Bangkok to:		
Chiang Mai	65	1,650
Khon Kaen	55	1,060
Korat	40	555
Ubon Ratchathani	65	1,405

* late 1996 fares quoted, one way (return fares are double)

hon Pathom and Kanchanaburi leave from the Bangkok Noi or Thonburi station on the other side of the Chao Phraya River. See page 250 for a table of fares and journey times, and page 280 for more information on Thailand's railways.

Road Bus: there are three main bus stations in Bangkok serving the N and NE, the E, and the S and W. Destinations in the Central Plains are also served from these terminals – places N of Bangkok from the northern bus terminal, SW of Bangkok from the southern terminal, and SE from the eastern bus terminal. The **Northern bus terminal** or *Mor Chit*, Phahonyothin Rd, T 2712961, serves all destinations in the N and NE as well as towns in the Central Plains that lie N of Bangkok like Ayutthaya and Lopburi. Getting to *Mor Chit* by public transport is comparatively easy as many a/c (Nos 2, 3, 9, 10, 29 and 39) and non-a/c buses travel along Phahonyothin Rd. The new non-a/c **Southern bus terminal** is on Phra Pinklao Rd (T 4110061) nr the intersection with Route 338. Buses for the W (places like Nakhon Pathom and Kanchanaburi) and the S leave from here. A/c town bus No 7 travels to the terminal. A/c buses to the S and W leave from the terminal on Charan Santiwong Rd, nr Bangkok Noi Train Station in Thonburi, T 4351199. The **Eastern bus terminal**, Sukhumvit Rd (Soi Ekamai), between Soi 40 and Soi 42, T 3912504 serves Pattaya and other destinations in the Eastern region.

Buses leave for most major destinations throughout the day, and often well into the night. There are overnight buses on the longer routes – Chiang Mai, Hat Yai, Chiang Rai, Phuket, Ubon Ratchathani. Even the smallest provincial towns such as Mahasarakham have deluxe a/c buses connecting them with Bangkok. Note that in addition to the governmentoperated buses there are many private companies which run 'tour' buses to most of the major tourist destinations. Tickets bought through travel agents will normally be for these private tour buses, which leave from offices all over the city as well as from the public bus terminals listed above. Shop around as prices may vary. Note that although passengers may be picked up from their hotel/guesthouse therefore saving on the ride (and inconvenience) of getting out to the bus terminal the private buses are generally less reliable and less safe. Many pick-up passengers at Khaosan Rd, for example.

THE MEKONG TOWNS

CHIANG KHONG

Chiang Khong is a border settlement situated on the S bank of the Mekong. It is really more a collection of villages than a town: Ban Haad Khrai, Ban Sobsom and Ban Hua Wiang were all originally individual communities – and still keep their village monasteries. For such a small town, it has had a relatively high profile in Thai history. In the 1260s, King Mengrai extended control over the area and Chiang Khong became one of the Lanna Thai Kingdom's major principalities. Later the town was captured by the Burmese.

Today, Chiang Khong owes its continued existence to legal and illicit trade with Laos: gems, agricultural products and livestock from Laos are traded for consumer goods and other luxuries. The traffic can be seen in action either at the pier end of Soi 5 or, to a greater degree, at Tha Rua Bak 1 km or so N of town. For some years, while Thais and Laos could make the crossing to trade, foreigners had to stay firmly on the Thai side of the river. This has now changed and it is easy enough to arrange a visa and cross the Mekong to another country – and another world.

There is not much here, although its position on the Mekong and the relaxed atmosphere makes it an attractive spot to unwind. **Wat Luang**, in the centre of town, dates from the 13th century. An engraved plaque maintains that two hairs of the Buddha were interred in the chedi in 704 AD – a date which would seem to owe more to poor maths or overoptimism than to historical veracity. But it was reputedly restored by the ruler of Chiang Khong in 1881. The viharn sports some rather lurid murals. **Wat Phra Kaew**, a little further N, has two fine, red guardian lions at its entrance. Otherwise it is very ordinary, save for the *kutis* (monks quarters – small huts) along the inside of the front wall which look like a row of assorted Wendy houses, and the *nagas* which curl their way up the entrance to the *viharm*, on the far side of the building.

Further S, at the track leading to the *Pla Buk Resort* at the grandly titled Economic Quadrangle Joint Development Corporation is the town's *lak muang* or foundation pillar. Like Nong Khai and the other towns that line the Mekong in the Northeastern region, the rare – and delicious – *pla buk* catfish is caught here. It is sometimes possible to watch the fishermen catching a giant catfish on the riverbank to the S of town. If that is a no go, there are some pictures of stupendous *pla buk* in the restaurant of the *Ruan Thai Sophaphan Resort*.

Trekking There are hilltribe villages within reach of Chiang Khong, but the trekking industry here is relatively undeveloped. Ask at the guesthouses to see if a guide is available.

Visas for Laos Any tour company will organize visas. *Ann Tour* in town, or *Chiang Khong Tour* and *Nam Khong Travel* near the pier N of town. A photocopy of your passport is needed. The process normally takes about 24 hrs, although visas cannot be arranged at weekends. The pier and Thai immigration are 1 km or so N of town, and long-tailed boats take people across for ฿20. The agent normally accompanies travellers and sees them through Lao immigration. At the end of 1996, all tour companies were issuing 15-day visas at the standard rate of ฿1,700.

Tours There are a growing number of tour companies in Chiang Khong. In town, *Ann Tour* is recommended. North of town, by the pier, there are the *Chiang Khong Tour* and *Nam Khong Travel*. They get most of their business arranging visas for Laos (see above) but can also provide transport and organize boat trips. *Ann Tour*, 6/1 Sai Klang Rd, T/F 791218.

● **Accommodation C** *Plabuk Resort*, Tambon 122/1 Wiang Rd, T/F 791281, a/c, restaurant open in the high season, hot water, this place is situated on the S edge of town on a large plot overlooking the Mekong. Rooms are bare but clean and large with small verandahs and attached bathrooms. There could have been more of an effort to create some sense of ambience, but it is quiet and peaceful; **C-D** *Baan Golden Triangle*, T 791350, positioned on top of a hill to the N of town, this is a stab at a 'back-to-nature' resort: wooden bungalows, garden, cart wheels, that sort of thing. The rooms are fine with attached bathrooms and hot water, great views too over a tiny rice valley to the Mekong and Laos; **C-D** *Ruan Thai Sophaphan Resort*, Tambon Wiang Rd, T 791023, restaurant, big clean rooms with own bathroom and hot water in a big wooden house with a large raised verandah. The upstairs rooms are better – down below is a little dark. There are also bungalows for 2 to 4 people, good river views, very friendly, self service drinks, price negotiable out of season, rec; **D-E** *Ban Tammila*, 8/1 Sai Klang Rd (N end of town), T 791234, restaurant, cheaper rooms are very basic with mosquito net and shared bathroom, more expensive have own bathrooms, bungalows with river views. Attractive rambling garden along the river side, good food, friendly and helpful although some recent visitors have said that it is over-priced; **D-E** *Chiang Khong Hotel*, 68/1 Sai Khong Rd, T 791182, F 655647, some a/c, Chiang Khong's original hotel and although it is reasonably maintained this place was designed before 'character' and 'atmosphere' figured in Thai architectural philosophy (some would say they still don't). It is plain, rather bare, and functional, but reasonable value; **D-F** *Orchid Garden Guest House*, 62 Ban Wiang Kaew Soi 2 (about 80m off the main Sai Klang Rd), a friendly little guesthouse that opened in 1996. It is run by young Thais and has a laid back, slightly hip feel, some bungalows with attached bathrooms, rooms in main house with shared facilities (upstairs is best), and some dormitory beds, quiet, and although it does not have the river close by, peaceful and relaxing – the dormitory beds are also the cheapest available.

● **Places to eat** In theory, Chiang Khong would be a great place to eat river fish, but the range

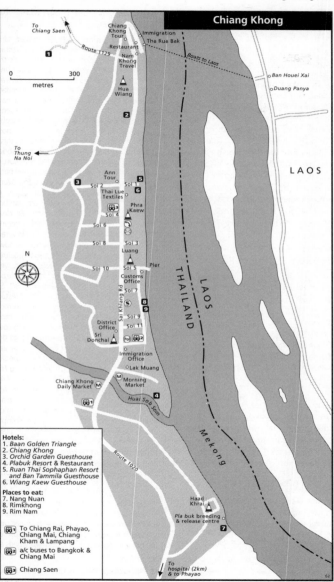

Chiang Khong

To Chiang Saen

Route 1129

Chiang Khong Tour
Restaurant
Nam Khong Travel
Immigration
Tha Rua Bak

Boats to Laos

Ban Houei Xai
Duang Panya

1

0   300
metres

Hua Wiang

2

LAOS

To Thung Na Noi

Ann Tour
Soi 2
Thai Lue Textiles
Soi 1
5
6
3
Soi 4
Phra Kaew
Soi 6
Soi 8
Soi 3
Luang
Soi 10
Soi 5
Pier
Customs Office
Soi 7
8
9
Soi 9
District Office
Soi 11
Sri Donchai
Pol
2
Immigration Office
Lak Muang

N

Sai Khlang Rd

THAILAND
LAOS

Chiang Khong Daily Market
M
M
Morning Market

1
Huai Sob Som
4

Route 1020

Mekong

Haad Khrai
Pla buk breeding & release centre
7

To hospital (2km) & to Phayao

Hotels:
1. *Baan Golden Triangle*
2. *Chiang Khong*
3. *Orchid Garden Guesthouse*
4. *Plabuk Resort & Restaurant*
5. *Ruan Thai Sophaphan Resort and Ban Tammila Guesthouse*
6. *Wiang Kaew Guesthouse*

Places to eat:
7. *Nang Nuan*
8. *Rimkhong*
9. *Rim Nam*

1 To Chiang Rai, Phayao, Chiang Mai, Chiang Kham & Lampang
2 a/c buses to Bangkok & Chiang Mai
3 Chiang Saen

is rather disappointing. However, the position of the riverside restaurants compensates to some degree. In town, along the main road, there are a number of noodle and rice stalls. The more interesting places are along the river road or down one of the sois leading to the Mekong. *Rimkhong* in the centre of town serves probably the best fish, although *Rim Naam*, next door, is good value. *Ruan Thai Saphaphan Resort* is also worth considering: very comfortable with wicker chairs, cold beer, a great view and good food. South of town, *Nang Nuan* is highly rec by locals.

● **Banks & money changers** Thai Farmers, 416 Sai Khong Rd; **Siam Commercial**, Sai Khong Rd, opp the district office, has a currency exchange service.

● **Post & telecommunications Area code**: 053. **Post Office**: on main road next to the army post. **Telephone Office**: in Post Office for international calls.

● **Shopping** Chiang Khong is not the obvious place to come shopping, but there is one decent place selling traditional textiles, wood carvings, handicrafts and other things – *Thai Lue Textiles*, on the main road, just N of Wat Phra Kaew.

● **Transport** 137 km from Chiang Rai, 55 km from Chiang Saen. **Local** Chiang Khong is small enough to explore on foot, but the town does have a rather quaint line in underpowered motorized rickshaws which struggle gamely up anything which is not billiard table-flat. Tour companies provide cars with drivers for around ฿1,200/day. Bicycles and motorbikes were not available for hire on our last visit. **Road Bus**: hourly connections with Chiang Rai 3 hrs. A/c and non-a/c connections with Bangkok and Chiang Mai (6¹/₂ hrs) as well as Lampang and Phayao. A/c buses leave from the office on the main road nr Wat Phra Kaew. Non a/c buses depart from the bus station just over the Huai Sob Som on the S edge of town. Non-a/c buses for Chiang Saen leave from 0600 and take the attractive river road following the Mekong and the Thai-Lao border (2 hrs). **Songthaew**: regular connections with Chiang Saen and from there on to Sop Ruak, Mae Sai and Chiang Rai. Songthaews leave from the bus station on the southern edge of town but can be flagged down as they make their way N through Chiang Khong. **Boat** Boats can be chartered to make the journey to/from Chiang Saen (about ฿150/head).

International connections to Laos It is possible for foreigners to cross into Laos from Chiang Khong, across the Mekong to Ban Houei Xai. Visas can be obtained in Chiang Khong from one of the travel agencies which are mushrooming as travel to Laos becomes easier (see above for details). Long-tailed boats ferry passengers across the Mekong to Ban Houei Xai from Tha Rua Bak (฿20).

UBON RATCHATHANI

The 'Royal City of the Lotus' is an important provincial capital on the Mun River. Like a number of other towns in the NE, Ubon was a US Airforce base during the Vietnam War and as a result houses a good selection of Western-style hotels as well as bars and massage parlours. The money that filtered into the town during the war meant that it became one of the richest in the region: this can still be seen reflected in the impressive, although slowly decaying, public buildings. Like Udon Thani, there is still a small community of ex-GIs who have married local women and are living out their days in this corner of Thailand. With Bangkok and surrounds booming, some of the wealth is filtering back to the NE and can be seen in cities like Ubon: extravagant parties, Mercedes cars and lavish restaurants.

Places of interest

There is a good archaeological, historical and cultural **museum** (the Ubon branch of the National Museum in Bangkok) on Khuan Thani Rd housed in a *panya*-style building erected in 1918. The collection includes prehistoric artefacts collected in the province as well as pieces from the historic period including Khmer artefacts, and cultural pieces such as local textiles and musical instruments. Open 0900-1600 Wed-Sun. Admission ฿20.

Wat Phrathat Nong Bua is 500m W off Chayangkun Rd travelling N to Nakhon Phanom, not far past the army base. It is a large white angular chedi which is said to be a copy of the Mahabodhi stupa in Bodhgaya, India. It is certainly unusual in the Thai context. Jataka reliefs and cloaked standing Buddhas in various stances are depicted on the out-side of the chedi. Take town bus No 2 or 3 or go by tuk-tuk.

Wat Thungsrimuang, on Luang Rd and named after the field (or *thung*) by

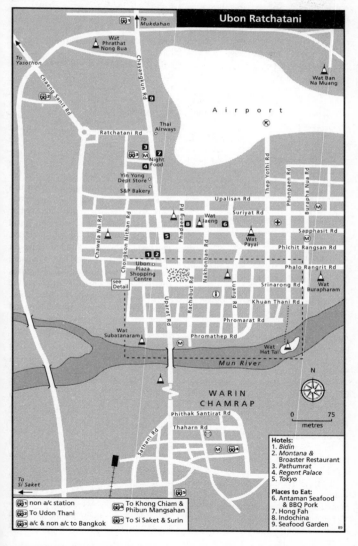

Ubon Ratchatani

Hotels:
1. *Bidin*
2. *Montana &
   Broaster Restaurant*
3. *Pathumrat*
4. *Regent Palace*
5. *Tokyo*

Places to Eat:
6. Antaman Seafood
   & BBQ Pork
7. Hong Fah
8. Indochina
9. Seafood Garden

🚌1 non a/c station
🚌2 To Udon Thani
🚌3 a/c & non a/c to Bangkok
🚌4 To Khong Chiam &
    Phibun Mangsahan
🚌5 To Si Saket & Surin

the provincial hall, is a short walk from the TAT office. The wat is notable for its red-stained wooden *hor trai* (or library) on stilts, in the middle of a stagnant pond. The library contains Buddhist texts and rare examples of Isan literature, but is usually locked. The monastery was built during the reign of Rama III (1824-1851) and there is a fine late Ayutthayan-style bot, graciously decaying. The bot features murals depicting Northeastern country life and episodes from the life of the Buddha, but is usually firmly locked. The viharn, built more recently, contains garish and rather crude murals – and is usually open. Such is life.

Wat Subatanaram, at the W end of Phromathep Rd, is pleasantly situated overlooking the Mun River. It was built in 1853 and supports monks of the Dharmayuthi sect. It is significant for its collection of lintels which surround the bot, commemorating the dead. One of the sandstone lintels is Khmer and is said to date from the 7th century. Also here is a massive, suspended wooden gong, said to be the largest in the country.

Hat Wat Tai is a large sandbank in the middle of the Mun River, linked by a rope footbridge to Phonpaen Rd. The residents of Ubon come here for picnics. Foodstalls set up in the evening and on weekends and it is possible to swim here. Take bus No 1, then walk S along Phonpaen Rd.

There is a bustling **fruit and vegetable market** between the river and Phromathep Rd, E of the bridge.

Excursions

Warin Chamrap is a busy town 3 km S of Ubon, over the Mun River. The main reasons to come here are either to catch a public bus from one of the two bus terminals in the town or to visit the train station. However, in so far as development has been concentrated in Ubon, Warin still possesses some architectural charm including a number of gently decaying wood, brick and stucco shophouses. There is also a good mixed market near the main bus station (the *bor kor sor*). **Getting there**: town bus Nos 1, 2, 3, 6 and 7 all link Warin with Ubon.

Kaeng Sapu are a series of rapids on the Mun River 1 km outside the district town of Phibunmangsahan and about 45 km from Ubon, They do not compare with the rapids at Kaeng Tana National Park (see below) but are much easier to reach. Inner tubes can be hired to float downriver and there is a small market with foodstalls and poor quality handicrafts. **Wat Sarakaew** is close by with a viharn showing some colonial influences. **Getting there**: take town bus Nos 1, 3 or 6 to Warin Chamrap. From here buses run regularly to Phibunmangsahan, 1 hr (฿12). The rapids are 1 km from town; either walk or take a saamlor.

Pha Taem is a sandstone cliff overlooking the Mekong River in Khong Chiam district 98 km from Ubon (along Route 2112 and then onto Route 2368). The Mekong at this point cuts through a wide and deep gorge and the views from the cliff top across the river to Laos are spectacular. Ochre prehistoric paintings, about 3,000 years old, of figures, turtles, elephants, fish and geometric forms stretch for some 400m along a cliff set high above the Mekong. A trail leads down and then along the face of the cliff past three groups of paintings now protected (or, as the sign puts it, "decidedly fenced") by rather unsightly barbed wire. Two viewing towers allow the images to be viewed at eye level. Two km before the turn off for Pha Taem is **Sao Chaliang** an area of strange, heavily eroded sandstone rock formations. Getting there: rather difficult to reach on public transport. First take an Ubon town bus to Warin Chamrap (No 1, 3 or 6), and from there to Khong Chiam via Phibun Mangsahan (where accommodation is available, see below). There are also some direct buses to Khong Chiam from Ubon. From Khong Chiam charter a tuk-tuk for the last 20 km to the cliff (ø150 return). *Chongmek Travellers* and *Takerng Tour* organize boat trips there (see Tours) or hire a motorbike or car (see Local transport).

Kaeng Tana National Park, on the Mun River, lies about 75 km to the E of Ubon, off Route 217 where the park office is located. Alternatively the park can be reached via Route 2222 which affords excellent views of the Kaeng Tana – a series of rapids. The rapids are 2 km off Route 2222. The park covers 8,000 ha and was gazetted in 1981. The Kaeng Tana – the Tana rapids – after which the park is named, are found at a point where the Mun River squeezes through a rocky outcrop before flowing into the Mekong. In the dry season the rocks present an almost lunar landscape of giant ossified bones, jumbled together into a heap of eroded boulders. It is possible to chicken leap across the river to midstream. The controversial Pak Mun Dam, completed in 1994 and designed to generate hydropower and irrigate land can be seen from the rapids. During the dry season it is possible to swim here although the current is usually too strong for safe bathing in the wet season. **Accommodation** Bungalow accommodation available. Getting there: easiest on a tour (see Tours) or by private car/motorcycle (see Local transport).

Kaeng Tana Rapids

There is no easy way to reach the rapids on public transport. However, the nearest town is Khong Chiam. To get to Khong Chiam take town bus Nos 1, 3 or 6 to Warin Chamrap. From Warin, buses run to Khong Chiam, and from there motorcycle taxis may be available to Kaeng Tana. Accommodation is available in Khong Chiam.

Tours

Takerng Tour organize tours to the Kaeng Tana Rapids and Pha Taem (approx ø1,000 pp). *Chongmek Travellers* organize tours along the Mekong River, taking in a Blu village and the Pha Taem cave paintings, with a night in a fishing village. ø1,340 pp, minimum three people for trip. Tours to Prasat Phra Viharn are also now available from companies in Ubon – assuming the monument is open; see the entry above for latest information. This also goes for the State Railways of Thailand who offer a weekend trip to Prasat Phra Viharn leaving at 0925 on Sat and returning 0535 on Mon, including accommodation in Ubon and all transport, T 2256964 or visit the advance booking office at Hualamphong Station, Bangkok.

Festivals

Jul: *Candle Festival* (movable, for 5 days from the first day of the Buddhist Lent or *Khao Phansa*). Enormous sculpted beeswax candles are made by villagers from all over the province and are ceremoniously paraded through the streets before being presented to the monks. The festival seems to have been introduced during the reign of Rama I. The Buddha is said to have remarked that the monk Anurudha, in one of his previous lives, led his people out of darkness using a candle – the festival celebrates the feat and is also associated with learning and enlightenment. Candles are given to the monks so that they have light to read the sacred texts during the Buddhist Lent.

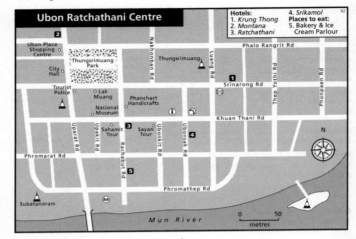

Ubon Ratchathani Centre

Hotels:
1. *Krung Thong*
2. *Montana*
3. *Ratchathani*
4. *Srikamol*

Places to eat:
5. Bakery & Ice Cream Parlour

Local information
● Accommodation

20-30% discounts off the quoted rate available at many hotels. Though Ubon has reasonable mid-range accommodation, there are no good places in the budget category.

A-B *Pathumrat*, 337 Chayangkun Rd, T 241501, F 242313, N of town centre, nr the market bus station, a/c, restaurant, pool, built during the Vietnam war to meet US military demand, it still exudes 70s kitsch, some rooms have been modernized, and there is also a rather sterile new wing, but the *hong kao* – old rooms – have character and atmosphere; **A-B** *Regent Palace*, 265-71 Chayangkun Rd, T 255529, F 241804, a/c, restaurant, newest hotel in town but poorly maintained rooms are already looking worn and jaded; **A-B** *Tohsang Ubon*, 251 Phalo Chai Rd, T 241925, F 244814, a/c, large modern hotel with around 95 rm, comfortable rooms, situated to the S of town.

B *Montana Hotel*, Uparat Rd, a/c, new hotel which opened in mid-1996, 40 rm and friendly staff on a pre-opening visit, central location close to town square, room rate incl breakfast; **B** *Srikamol*, 26 Ubonsak Rd, T 255804, F 243792, a/c, restaurant, ugly towerblock, featureless rooms.

C-D *Racha*, 149/21 Chayangkun Rd, T 254155, some a/c, hot water in a/c rooms, plain and basic, fairly clean and friendly people; **C-D** *Ratchathani*, 229 Khuan Thani Rd,

T 244388, F 243561, some a/c, featureless block in the centre of town nr the TAT office, all rooms with TV and hot water, clean and generally well-run, rooms are competitively priced.

D *Bodin*, 14 Palochai Rd, T 255777; **D** *Krung Thong*, 24 Srinarong Rd, T 241609, a/c, restaurant; **D** *Pathumrat Guesthouse*, 337 Chayangkun (attached to the more lavish *Pathumrat*), a/c, stuck away round the back of the hotel, clean, dark rooms; **D-E** *Suriyat*, 47/1-4 Suriyat Rd, T 241144, some a/c, grubby.

E *Tokyo*, 178 Upparat Rd, T 241739, some a/c, small rooms, range of rooms from very bad to average, rooms in the back are quieter, small sign makes it easy to miss.

F *Homsa-ard*, 30 Suriyat Rd, Sa-ard means 'clean' but it isn't.

● Places to eat

◆◆◆◆-◆◆◆*Hong Fah Restaurant*, Chayangkun Rd (opp the bus station), expensive but excellent Chinese food in sophisticated a/c restaurant; ◆◆◆◆-◆◆◆*Seafood Garden*, Chayangkun Rd (about 1 km N of the bus station on the opp side of the road), large seafood restaurant, BBQ fish and prawn specialities, a/c room but tables on roof are by far the best in the evening; ◆◆◆-◆◆*Antaman Seafood*, Sapphasit Rd (opp the Caltex garage, not far from Wat Jaeng), BBQ seafood incl *gung pao* (prawns), *maengda* (horseshoe crabs), sea and riverfish and crabs; ◆◆*Indochina Restaurant*, Sapphasit Rd (not far from Wat

Jaeng), Vietnamese food in basic restaurant, good value; **Phon**, Yutthaphan Rd, opp fire station, Thai and Chinese, rec; **S and P Bakery Shoppe**, 207 Chayangkun Rd, pastries, ice cream and pizzas in pristine a/c western-style surroundings, a little piece of Bangkok in Ubon; **Broaster Chicken and Pizza**, Uparat Rd, the name says it all really, new, brash a/c restaurant selling fried chicken, pizzas and fries, etc; **No Name Restaurant**, Sapphasit Rd (not far from Wat Jaeng), a rather grubby looking place serving delicious *muhan* or BBQ suckling pig. Three Chinese restaurants on Khuan Thani Rd, close to Ratchathani Hotel eg *Rim Mun 2*, rec.

Foodstalls: Ubon has a profusion of foodstalls. A good range can be found on Chayangkun Rd, just S of the *Pathumrat Hotel*, incl stalls selling *kanom* (sweets and pastries), seafood dishes and fruit drinks.

● **Bars**
10 Pub, Khuan Thani Rd, opp National Museum; *Ziggy Pub*, Upakit Rd.

● **Airline offices**
Thai, 292/9 Chayangkun Rd, T 254431.

● **Banks & money changers**
Bangkok, 88 Chayangkun Rd; Thai Farmers, 356/9 Phromathep Rd; Siam Commercial, Chayangkun Rd; Thai Military, 130 Chayangkun Rd.

● **Hospitals & medical services**
Hospital: Sapphasit Rd, T 254906.

● **Post & telecommunications**
Area code: 045.
Post Office: corner of Srinarong and Luang Rd; telephone office at the back of the Post Office.

● **Shopping**
Baskets: on Luang Rd, nr the intersection with Khuan Thai Rd is a short strip of shops specializing in basketwork.

Department Stores: Ubon Plaza, Uparat Rd, a/c department store and supermarket selling all necessities; *Ying Yong Department Store*, 143 Chayangkun Rd.

Handicrafts: *Phanchart*, 158 Rachabut Rd – selection of antiques and northeastern handicrafts including an excellent range of matmii silk.

Silk: Ketkaew, 132 Rachabut Rd.

● **Sports**
Golf: Golf course at the airport.

● **Tour companies & travel agents**
Chongmek Travellers, Srikamol Hotel, 26 Ubonsak Rd, T 255804; *Takerng Tour*, 425 Phromathep Rd, T 255777.

● **Tourist offices**
TAT, 264/1 Khuan Thani Rd, T 243770. Open: Mon-Sun, 0830-1630. Provides a map of Ubon with bus routes and other handouts. Areas of responsibility are Ubon Ratchathani, Si Saket and Yasothon.

● **Useful addresses**
Immigration: Phibun Mangsahan Rd, T 441108.
Tourist Police: Corner of Srinarong and Uparat Rds, T 243770.

● **Transport**
629 km from Bangkok, 311 km from Korat, 270 km from Nakhon Phanom, 167 km from Mukdahan, 99 km from Yasothon 45 km from Phibun Mangsahan, 89 km from Chongmek.

Local Car and motorbike hire: drivers of cars often wait on Rachabut Rd and nr the TAT office. A car and driver for the day, including petrol, will cost about ฿800. *Watana*, 39/8 Suriyat Rd (฿250 for a motorbike, ฿1,000-1,200 for a car). **Town bus**: town buses follow 13 routes across town; pick up a useful map marking bus routes from the TAT office (fare ฿2-3). **Saamlors and tuk-tuks** also available.

Air Airport on the N side of town. **Transport to town**: it is just about possible to walk into town with cool weather, a following breeze and light bags. A taxi service is available: ฿70 to the town centre, ฿120 to the railway station at Warin Chamrap. Bigger hotels pick up guests gratis. Regular daily connections with Bangkok 1 hr (฿1,400).

Train The station is S of the river along the road towards Warin Chamrap. Town bus Nos 2 and 6 run into town. Regular connections with Bangkok's Hualamphong station 10 hrs, and all stations in between.

Road Bus: BKS station for non-a/c buses is some distance N of town not far from Wat Nong Bua, at the end of Chayangkun Rd. Get there by town bus 2 or 3. The station for a/c and non-a/c buses to Bangkok is at the back of the market on Chayangkun Rd, S of the *Pathumrat Hotel*. Regular connections with Bangkok's Northern bus terminal 8 hrs, Nakhon Phanom 5½-7 hrs, and less frequently with other Northeastern towns – for example, there are two bus companies who service Surin regularly, 4 hrs; a/c and non-a/c tour buses to Bangkok also leave from Khuan Thani Rd, opp the TAT Office; *Sahamit Tour* on Khuan Thani Rd nr the National Museum, run buses to Udon Thani via Mukdahan, That Phanom and Nakhon Phanom; *Sayan Tour* nr the *Ratchathani Hotel*, run buses to Udon Thani via Yasothon, Roiet, Mahasarakhan and Khon Kaen.

International connections with Laos: it is possible to enter Laos E of Ubon at Chongmek. To get to Chongmek, take a bus from the station in Warin Chamrap (see map) to Phibun Mangsahan, 1 hr (₿12), about 45 km. From Phibun Mangsahan there are converted trucks (large songthaews) to the border town of Chongmek, 44 km away (1½ hrs, ₿13). There is a large Thai-Lao market here selling food, baskets, clothes and basic manufactured goods as welll as some 'antiques' and wild animal trans-shipment point for logs from Laos: a timber yard faces the market. The border customs posts are pretty relaxed although ensure that your Lao visa is endorsed permitting entry to Laos at this point. After passing through the Lao border post (exchange facilities available for Thai baht and US$ cash), there are trucks and share taxis waiting to whisk (well, trundle) passsengers to Muang Kao, 1½ hrs (600 kip). From Muang Kao there are long-tail boats across the Mekong to Pakse (200 kip), and at the 'port' in Pakse tuk-tuks wait to ferry passengers onward.

UDON THANI

Udon is a busy town with seemingly the greatest concentration of pedal saamlors in Thailand. This makes for hazardous driving. The N quarter of the town contains government offices, with large, tree-filled compounds. Elsewhere the atmosphere is frenetic (or as close to frenetic as it is possible to get in this part of Thailand). The neatly kept palm-fringed roundabouts provide a tropical Riviera feel amidst the bustle; Udon has a reputation of being one of Thailand's cleanest provincial capitals.

Like Khon Kaen, Udon was a boom town during the Vietnam War, so it retains reminders of that time, with massage parlours, bars, coffee shops and fully air-conditioned hotels. It is said

that about 60 former US servicemen have married Thais and settled here. There is even an Udon branch of the US Veterans of Foreign Wars Association, along with a relay station of VoA (Voice of America) so the US-Udon link lives on. Most tourists only stay here because of its proximity to the outstanding prehistoric site at Ban Chiang.

Excursions

Ban Chiang lies 50 km E of Udon, and represents one of the most important archaeological sites to be uncovered in Southeast Asia since WW2. The site was accidentally discovered by an American anthropology student, Stephen Young, in 1966. While walking in the village fields he fell over the root of a kapok tree and into history: all around him, protruding from the ground, were potsherds. Appreciating that his find might be significant, he sent the potsherds for analysis to the Fine Arts Department in Bangkok and then later to the University of Pennsylvania. Rumours of his finds spread and much of the area was then ransacked by the villagers, who sold the pieces they unearthed to collectors in Bangkok and abroad. Organized excavations only really commenced during the 1970's, when a Thai archaeologist, Pisit Charoenwongsa, and Chester Gorman, from Pennsylvania, arrived to investigate the site (Gorman tragically died of cancer at the age of only 43 in 1981). Even though their task was compromised by the random digging of villagers and others, they still managed to unearth 18 tonnes of material in two years including 5,000 bags of sherds and 123 burials.

There are two burial pits at *Wat Pho Si Nai*, on the edge of the village of Ban Chiang. They have been left open for visitors to gain an idea of the process of excavation and the distribution of the finds – the first 'on site' museum in Thailand. At the other side of the village is a new, and excellent, orthodox *museum*. The Ban Chiang story is retold

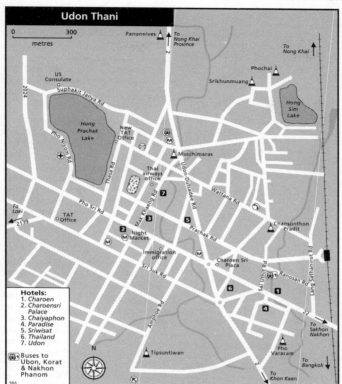

with clarity, displaying excellent models and many of the finds (the exhibition was put together with the help of the Smithsonian, Washington DC and toured the US between 1982 and 1986). Admission ฿20. Open 1000-1600 Wed-Sun. To cash in on the visitors to the site (tour buses now come here) the villagers of Ban Chiang, prevented from selling artefacts openly, market a range of handicrafts instead in shops around the museum.

Getting there: Ban Chiang is 56 km E of Udon Thani; after 50 km turn left onto Route 2225 (signposted to the Ban Chiang Museum). The village is another 6 km along this road. Buses run direct to the village from the Udon bus station. Alternatively take a bus going along Route 22 to Sakhon Nakhon and ask to be let off at Ban Chiang (just after the 50 km marker). Tuk-tuk drivers hang around the junction to take visitors to the site ฿10 one-way.

Erawan Cave (Tham Erawan, 'Elephant Cave') is found 40 km W of Udon, about 2 km off Route 210 on the left-hand side of the road. The cave (as usual, linked to a wat, Wat Tham Erawan) is larger and more impressive than the usual selection of holes in the ground that pass as caves in Thailand. **Getting there:** by bus en route to Loei.

Local information
● Accommodation

With the opening of the Friendship Bridge, Udon has become a mini boom town. Land speculation is rife, two new 'luxury' hotels have opened, another is under construction (reportedly to be named the *Ban Chiang*) and more are mooted.

A-B *Imperial Charoensri*, Prachak Rd (next to the main shopping complex), T 343555, F 343550, a/c, a new hotel with over 250 rm which opened in 1995, excellent Chinese restaurant and heavily discounted as the hotel builds up its reputation; **A-B** *Napalai*, 572 Pracha-Raksa Rd, T 347444, F 347447, a/c, restaurant, pool, opened in 1995 2 km out of the city centre, good service and amenities, wonderful pool, excellent value.

B *Charoen*, 549 Pho Sri Rd, T 248155, F 246126, a/c, restaurant, pool, Western-style, comfortable, good value, with newly opened wing offering high level of comfort – at a higher price. For many years the best hotel in town, it has recently been eclipsed by two newer places (see above).

C *Charoensri Palace*, 60 Pho Sri Rd, T 242611, F 222601, a/c, restaurant; **C** *Udon*, 81-89 Mak Khaeng Rd, T 248160, F 242782, a/c, central with 90 rm, noisy and a little dishevelled, but friendly; **C-E** *Chaiyaphon*, 209-211 Mak Khaeng Rd, T 221913, some a/c.

D-E *King*, 57 Pho Sri Rd, T 221634, some a/c; **D-E** *Paradise*, 44/29 Pho Sri Rd, T 221956, some a/c, usefully located nr the bus station, but little else to particularly rec it; **D-E** *Sawaddiphap*, 264/3 Prachak Rd; **D-E** *Thailand*, 4/1-6 Surakhon Rd, T 221951, some a/c.

E-F *Srisawat*, 123 Prachak Rd, rather seedy place with just 28 rm, and noisy – but more atmospheric than most.

● Places to eat

Fresh-baked 'baguettes' are available in Udon Thani; the bakeries here are some of the best in the country. Local specialities incl shredded pork or *muu yong* and preserved meats. ••*Charoen Hotel*, 549 Pho Sri Rd, expat hang out with surprisingly good Thai food, Thai and International; *Chao Wang*, 1 Udon Thani Rd; *Kluai Mai*, 58 Mak Khaeng Rd, Thai; *Seun Hia*, 54 Mak Khaeng Rd, Chinese; *Thanoo Thong*, 5 Mukkhamontri Rd.

● Airline offices

Thai, 60 Mak Khaeng Rd, T 246697.

● Banks & money changers

Bangkok Bank, Pho Sri Rd; Krung Thai, 216 Mak Khaeng Rd; Thai Farmers, 236 Pho Sri Rd.

● Embassies & consulates

US Consulate, 35/6 Suphakit Janya Rd, T 244270 (northern section of town).

● Hospital & medical services

Pho Niyom Rd, T 222572.

● Post & telecommunications

Area code: 042.

Post Office: Wattananuvong Rd (nr the Provincial Governor's Office).

● Tour companies & travel agents

Most tour companies can arrange visas for Laos, but they are more expensive than in Bangkok. In 1996 the going rate was ฿2,500 for a 7-day wait. The express 2-day service cost ฿3,500.

Kannika Tour, 36/9 Srisatha Rd, T 241378, F 241378 (tours in the NE and to Laos, Cambodia and Vietnam); *Aranya Tour*, 105 Mak Khaeng Rd, T 243182 (will also arrange visas for Indochina); *Toy Ting*, 55/1-5 Thahaan Rd, T 244771.

● Tourist offices

TAT (temporary office), c/o Provisional Education Office, Phosi Rd, T 241968. Areas of responsibility are Udon Thani, Nong Khai and Loei. Open Mon-Sun, 0830-1630. A permanent office will open 'soon' at the northern end of Thesa Rd (see map). The move does not appear to be imminent, though.

● Useful addresses

Immigration: Pho Sri Rd, T 222889.
Police: Sri Suk Rd, T 222285.

● Transport

560 km from Bangkok, 117 km from Khon Kaen, 306 km from Korat.

Local Car rental: VIP Car Rent, 824 Pho Sri Rd, T 223758; Parada Car Rent, 78/1 Mak Khaeng Rd, T 244147.

Air Airport 2 km out of town off Route 2 S to Khon Kaen. Regular connections with Bangkok 1 hr, twice daily Mon-Thur and Sat, 3 times daily on Fri and Sun.

Train Station is off Lang Sathanirotfai Rd. Regular connections with Bangkok's Hualamphong station 10 hrs and all stops en route – Ayutthaya, Saraburi, Korat, Khon Kaen and on to Nong Khai.

Road Bus: Udon has 2 bus stations; BKS '2' is on the N edge of town about 2 km from the centre; buses also stop, however, at the more central BKS '1' on Sai Uthit Rd, just off Pho Sri Rd. Passengers can get to/from BKS 2 by yellow town buses which run into the centre. Regular connections with Bangkok's Northern bus terminal 11-12 hrs and with Nong Khai, Khon Kaen, Korat, Loei and other Northeastern towns as well as with Phitsanulok where there are bus connections to other Central Plains and Northern region destinations.

NONG KHAI

Nong Khai is situated at the end of Route 2, the Friendship Highway, and on the banks of the mighty Mekong River which forms the border between Thailand and Laos. It is also a railhead, lying at the end of the line NE from Bangkok. From here, while supping on a cold beer, you can look across to Tha Deua in Laos and imagine the enormous and rare *pla buk* catfish (*Pangasianodon gigas*), weighing up to 340 kg, foraging on the river bed.

Nong Khai is fast loosing its provincial flavour as neighbouring Laos opens up – with some trepidation – to tourists and investors. The Australian-financed Friendship Bridge at Tambon Meechai 2 km from town, the first bridge across the lower reaches of the Mekong River, was officially opened on 8 April 1994. To cope with the expected surge in arrivals, three major new hotels have opened, the *Nong Khai Holiday Inn*, the *Nong Khai Grand Thani* and the *Jommanee*. Even the riverfront road – Rim Khong Rd – is going to be redeveloped into a 'promenade' for tourists.

The influence of the French presence in Indochina can be seen reflected in the **architecture** of Meechai Rd which runs parallel with the river. In addition to the rather dubious excitement of being on the frontier with Laos – not too far away at Ban Rom Klao the Thai and Lao armies fought a vicious minor battle during the late 1980s – Nong Khai is also a charming, quiet and laidback riverside

town: the sort of place where jaded travellers get 'stuck' for several days doing nothing but enjoying the romantic atmosphere of the place. Should that be too sedentary, there are a number of (admittedly largely unremarkable) wats to visit. Notable is the important teaching wat, **Wat Sisaket** and, towards the E of town past the bus station, **Wat Pho Chai** with its Lao-style viharn and venerated solid gold Buddha, looted from Vientiane by the future Rama I. The bot contains murals showing how the image is reputed to have got to Nong Khai. A third religious building – or rather what remains of it – is **Phrathat Nong Khai**, locally better known as **Phrathat Klang Nam** (Phrathat in the Middle of the River), because of its position submerged close to the centre of the Mekong's course. In Henri Mouhot's account of his trip up the middle and upper reaches of the Mekong in 1860 he wrote of this *that* when he remarked on arrival in 'Nong Kay' that a "Buddhist tat or pyramidal landmark ... has been washed away from the shore, and now lies half submerged, like a wrecked ship". The *that* is only visible during the dry season, when it emerges from the muddy river and is promptly bedecked with pennants. To see the *that*, walk (or take a saamlor) E along Meechai Rd (downriver) for about 2.5 km from the town centre, and turn off, left, down Soi Paa Phrao 3. The *that* should be visible from the riverbank, at the end of the Soi. On the riverfront road, Rim Khong Rd, there is a daily **market** where goods from Laos and beyond are on sale. Nong Khai also happens to be the logical place to start or end a tour of the Thai towns which line the Mekong River.

Excursions

Wat Phrathat Bang Phuan is 22 km SW of Nong Khai. Travel S down Route 2 towards Udon and turn right after 12 km onto Route 211 towards Si Chiang Mai. The wat is another 10 km along this road

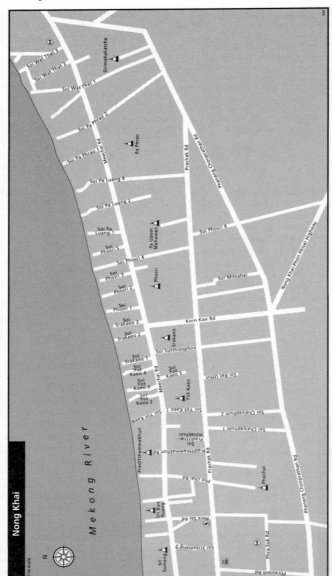

Nong Khai

Not to scale

N

Mekong River

Soi Wat That 3
Soi Wat That 2
Soi Wat That 1
Sirimahatatcha
Soi Pa Phrao 2
Meechai Rd
Pa Phrao
Prachak Rd
Soi Pa Phrao 1
Phanang Choniprathan Rd
Soi Pa Luang 4
Soi Pa Luang 2
Soi Pa Luang
Pa Udom Mahawan
Soi Phosri 4
Soi Phosri 5
Soi Phosri 4
Soi Phosri 3
Phosri
Soi Mitsahai
Soi Phosri 2
Soi Phosri 1
Soi Srakaeo 3
Korn Kan Rd
Soi Srakaeo 2
Srakaeo
Soi Srakaeo 1
Soi Sutthisophon
Meechai Rd
Soi Yot Kaeo 4
Soi Yot Kaeo 5
Soi Yot Kaeo 3
Yot Kaeo
Soi Rat Uthit
Soi Yot Kaeo 2
Soi Yot Kaeo 1
Soi Chaiyaphum 2
Soi Yot Kaeo
Soi Chaiyaphum 1
Praditthammakhun Rd
Soi Praditha-mmakhun
Nong Khai-Phon Phisai Highway
Pho Chai Rd
Prachak Rd
Phochai
Sri Bun Ruang
Phra Sai Rd
Phanang Choniprathan Rd
Sri Sumang
Soi Srisumang 2
Phra Sok Rd
Phraseom Rd

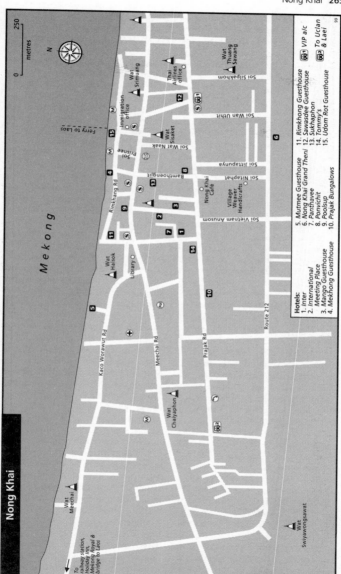

Nong Khai

Mekong

Ferry to Laos

To railway station, Holiday Inn, Mekong Royal & bridge to Laos

Keo Worawut Rd

Meechai Rd

Prajak Rd

Rimkhang Rd

Bamthoengjit

Sol Pohsee

Sol Wat Naak

Sol Wan Uthit

Sol Jittaraphun

Sol Jittananya

Sol Nitaphet

Sol Vietnam Ansoum

Sol Silpakhom

Route 212

Wat Meechai

Wat Haisok

Wat Chaiyaphon

Wat Swiyawongsawat

Wat Srimuang

Wat Wat Sisaket

Wat Thuang Sawang

Library

Immigration office

Thai Airlines office

Nong Khai Café

Village Weaver Handicrafts

To Uclan & Laei

0 — 250 metres

N

VIP a/c

Hotels:
1. Inter
2. International
3. Mango Guesthouse
4. Mekong Guesthouse
5. Mutmee Guesthouse
6. Nong Khai Grand Theni
7. Panthavee
8. Ponvichit
9. Poolsup
10. Prajak Bungalows
11. Rimkhong Guesthouse
12. Sawasdee Guesthouse
13. Sukhaphon
14. Tommy's
15. Udom Rot Guesthouse

and is well signposted now that it has become a national historical sight. The wat contains an Indian-style stupa, similar (it is presumed) to the original Phra Pathom Chedi in Nakhon Pathom. Its exact date of construction is unknown, but it is believed to date from the early centuries AD. A newer chedi was built on the sight in 1559, which toppled over in 1970. In 1978 it was restored. As a result, the unrestored Lao chedis in this same compound are now of greater historical interest. The site is really only worth visiting en route to/from Udon or Nong Khai, and it doesn't begin to compare with other historical sights in the NE. However, with a rumoured 29 relics of the Buddha's chest enshrined here, it has considerable religious importance. Getting there: songthaew or bus running towards Si Chiang Mai and state your destination. Alternatively, catch a bus going S on Route 2 and get off at the junction with Route 211; then catch a bus or songthaew W from here.

Phu Phra Bat Historical Park encompasses an area of 650 ha in the Phu Phan hills and has been a site of almost continuous human habitation since prehistoric times. It was clearly felt to be endowed with considerable religious significance. There are prehistoric cave paintings, Dvaravati boundary stones (7th-10th centuries), Lopburi Bodhisattvas (10th-13th centuries), Lang Chan Buddha images (14th-18th centuries), and a stupa built in 1920 to shelter a Buddha footprint. The terrain consists of rocky outcrops, bare sandy soil, and savanna forest, and it is easy to imagine why people for thousands of years have regarded the area as a magical place. The problem is that it is difficult to get to except by private car or motorcycle, but it is worth it for the peace. Open 0830-1700 Mon-Sun. A new reception centre has been built with a historical exhibition and a small café for drinks and simple food. Guides are also available here. To see all the main sites allow at least 3 hrs. The park is just about equidistant from Nong Khai and Udon Thani – almost 70 km. Getting there: catch a songthaew or bus to Ban Phu (there is a very simple hotel here should visitors need to sleep over), the town where Routes 2020 and 2021 meet, a journey of about 2½ hrs. From there (it is signposted), the park is another 15 km by songthaew towards Ban Tiu (quicker to take a motorcycle taxi from here).

Wat Phutthamamakasama-khom or, rather more simply, **Wat Khaek** ('Indian' Wat) was established in the late 1970s and lies 4.5 km E of Nong Khai on Route 212 to Beung Kan. The wat promotes a strange mixture of Buddhist and Hindu beliefs, and is dominated by a vast array of strange brick and cement statues. Some are clearly of Buddhist and Hindu inspiration; others are rather harder to interpret: eg a life-size elephant being attacked by a large pack of dogs, four in a jeep, and some wearing sunglasses. This represents a Thai proverb; a man who is confident he has done no wrong need not worry about malicious rumour "as an elephant does not care about barking dogs" (hence the apparent nonchalence of the elephant). The 'Life and Death' grouping is especially interesting. The group are set within a walled enclosure, reached along a tunnel (symbolizing the birth process); at the end of the tunnel the visitor is confronted by a carved rock, topped with a lingam. Around the enclosure are arranged an assortment of figures: a baby, a business woman, soldier, beggar ... the series concludes with two couples holding hands, one pair skeletonized and standing next to a coffin on a pyre. The meaning here seems pretty clear – dust to dust, and no loitering. Other figures in Wat Khaek include a giant 7-headed naga, an enormously corpulent Chinese, with some statues over 30m high. The figures are arranged in a garden and music blares out from an equally large concrete encrusted PA system. Very weird to the uninitiated (there is a similar wat and collection of statues outside Vientiane in Laos). Even tour buses visit the wat, so well-known has its strange brand of Buddhism become. **Getting there:** songthaew heading towards Beung Kan (Route 212) or by tuk-tuk. Turn right after the 4 km marker, just past the St Paul Nongkhai School (signpost to Sala Kaeou), and it is 500m off the main road.

Tours to Laos

Several companies and guesthouses organize visas for Laos which are now being processed in 24 hrs. Previously it took 4 days and passports had to be couriered down to Bangkok. Agents that will arrange visas include: *Pam Tour*; *International Meeting Place* (a guesthouse); *Frontier Guesthouse* and *Udom Rot Restaurant*.

Festivals

Mar: *Nong Khai Show* (2nd week).
May: *Rocket Festival*, or *ngarn bang fai* (2nd week).
Jul: *Candle Festival* (the beginning of the Buddhist Lent or Phansa) (see page 257).
Oct: *Boat races* on the Mekong (movable). Naga-prowed canoes with up to 40 oarsmen race along the river with a great deal of cheering and drinking from the onlookers that line the bank.

Local information
● **Accommodation**

With the opening of the new bridge, large hotels have opened in Nong Khai providing (almost) Bangkok-level opulence. Also, guesthouses in Nong Khai are of a high standard.

A+ *Holiday Inn Mekong Royal Nongkhai*, 222 Jomanee Rd (W of railway station, out of town), T 420024, F 421280, B 2713125, a/c, restaurant, pool, tennis, on the outskirts of town, 8-storeyed block with nearly 200 rm overlooking Mekong with all facilities, best in town.

A *Nongkhai Grand Thani*, 589 Muu 5 Nong Khai Poanpisai Rd, T 420033, F 420044, B 2376809, 2 km E of town on Route 212, a/c, restaurant, pool, disco, 'luxury' hotel opened 1992, high-rise block on edge of town, all facilities.

C-E *Phanthavee* (and across the road the *Phanthavee Bungalows*), 1241 Haisok Rd, T 411569, some a/c, management is brusque and unfriendly; rooms are clean but otherwise unremarkable.

D-E *Prajak Bungalows*, 1178 Prajak Rd, T 411116, a quiet place with passable rooms.

E *Frontier Guesthouse*, same entrance as *Mut-Mee Guesthouse*, Kaeo Worawut Rd, shared bathrooms, friendly place, organize visas for Laos; **E** *International Meeting Place*, 1117 Soi Chuanjit, F 412644, run by a convivial Australian, clean small rooms in attractive wooden house, beer (ice cold) available in industrial quantities, rec; **E** *Mango Guesthouse*, Soi Watsri Chomchuen, shared bathrooms, clean rooms, friendly and quiet; **E** *Poolsup*, 843 Meechai Rd, T 411031, Chinese style hotel with perhaps the most hideous chair in the world in the 'foyer'; but don't be put off, the rooms are OK and the proprietress is charming – try her cool rainwater; **E** *Rimkhong Guesthouse*, Rimkhong Rd, shared bathrooms, clean rooms with fans, friendly staff, wooden house with river views; **E** *Vientiane Guesthouse*, Meechai Rd Soi Wat Naak, nr the Post Office, T 411393, clean wooden rooms, quiet, rec; **E-F** *Naina*, Phochai Rd, opp Tommy's and a slight improvement, concrete building with mattresses on the floor, shared bathroom, fan, very clean, friendly, quiet – apart from the construction of a new road along the river; **E-F** *Sawasdee Guesthouse*, 402 Meechai Rd, T 412602, F420259, some a/c, old wooden house with inner courtyard, clean rooms and immaculate bathrooms, help-yourself coffee, friendly, good source of information, fan, hot water; **E-F** *Sukhaphon*, 823 Bamtoengjit Rd, T 411894, old wooden hotel, worth staying here if the more popular guesthouses are full, rooms at the back are quieter.

F *Mekhong Guesthouse*, 519 Rim Khong, T 412320, clean basic wooden rooms, on the river with a good verandah and information, but noisy from the road and the restaurant next door, noisy; rec; **F** *Mut-Mee Guesthouse*, 1111/4 Kaeo Worawut Rd, pricey restaurant, large but rather damp rooms, nice garden by the river with hammocks, very friendly management, information on Laos, bikes for rent, rec; **F** *Tommy's Guesthouse*, Phochai Rd, E side of town, very basic, mattress on the floor, mosquito nets, fans, shared bathroom, wooden house.

● **Places to eat**
Thai: ✦✦✦-✦*Banya Pochona*, 295 Rim Khong Rd, Chinese, Thai and Laos food, fish dishes particularly good; ✦✦*Indochine*, 189/1 Meechai Rd, also serves Vietnamese, rec; ✦✦*Khun Daeng*, 521 Rim Khong Rd (just W from *Udom Rot* and the Immigration office), views over the Mekong River, seafood and Isan specialities which locals claim are excellent; ✦✦*Udom Rot*, 193 Rim Khong Rd, views over the Mekong River, Thai, seafood; ✦*Open air café* at intersection of Meechai and Haisok Rd. Tukata Bakery and restaurant, Meechai Rd, good cheap food.

● **Bars**
Arthit's Pub, Prajak Rd, a little further on from the **Thai** office (live music).

● **Airline offices**
Thai, 453 Prachak Rd, T 411530.

● **Banks & money changers**
Bangkok, 374 Sisaket Rd; **Krung Thai**, 102 Meechai Rd; **Thai Farmers**, 929 Meechai Rd.

● **Embassies & consulates**
A new Lao consulate is rumoured to be opening in Nong Khai.

● **Hospital & medical services**
Meechai Rd, T 411504.

● **Post & telecommunications**
Area code: 042.
Post Office: Meechai Rd (opp Soi Prisnee).

● **Shopping**
The best area to browse is down Rim Khong Rd which (as the name suggests) runs along the river bank. Here Northeastern and Lao handicrafts are sold together with Chinese, Soviet and East European goods. It is possible to come away with a (former) Soviet military watch, an Isan 'axe' pillow, and 'French' sandalwood soap made in Laos. For better quality handicrafts visit *Village Weaver Handicrafts* on Prajak Rd, a short distance on from the bus station, or at their showroom on Soi Jittapunya.

Books: excellent bookshop and book exchange nr the *Mut-Mee Guesthouse*.

● **Tour companies & travel agents**
With the opening of the Friendship Bridge to Laos in Apr 1994, tour operators have multiplied and there are now more than 10, most of whom will arrange visas for Laos. *Udorn Business Travel* (Nongkhai branch), 447/10 Haisok Rd, T 411393. *Pam Tour*, 1112/1 Haisok Rd.

● **Useful addresses**
Immigration: Sisaket Rd, T 411154.
Police: Meechai Rd, T 411020.

● **Transport**
620 km from Bangkok, 55 km from Udon Thani, 204 km from Loei.

Local Bicycle hire: from *Mut-Mee* Guesthouse ฿40/day. **Motorcycle hire**: from the *International Meeting Place*, 1117 Soi Chuanjit (฿200/day).

Train Station is 3 km from town, W on Kaeo Worawut Rd. Regular connections with Bangkok's Hualamphong station 11 hrs and all stops NE – Ayutthaya, Saraburi, Korat, Khon Kaen and Udon.

Road Bus: BKS is on the E side of town on Praserm Rd, off Prajak Rd. Regular connections with Bangkok's Northern bus terminal 9-10 hrs and Khon Kaen, Udon Thani and other Northeastern towns. Note that tuk-tuk drivers have taken to hounding farangs and charging exorbitant rates. Don't pay more than ฿10. VIP buses for Bangkok leave from 745 Prajak Rd. A/c buses from the corner of Haisok and Prajak rds. A/c buses also depart from the BKS station. **NB** There are lots of sharks about.

International connections with Laos The Friendship Bridge over the Mekong River at Tambon Meechai 2 km from town opened in 1994 and now offers the first road link across the Mekong. The Bridge is open from 0800-1800 Mon-Sun. Tourist visas are now being issued in Nong Khai. Processing occurs in a single day. Contact one of the travel agents/tour companies listed on page 267.

NAKHON PHANOM

Nakhon Phanom is an unexciting ramshackle place. Should the world be about to end, Nakhon Phanom would be among the last places to know. It does, however, have one plus point: it is situated on the Mekong River with the mountains of Laos as a backdrop. Across the river is the Lao town of ThaKhek and foreigners are permitted to enter Laos at this point. Like Nong Khai, sipping a beer or eating catfish curry overlooking the river does have a strange romantic appeal. But, most people only visit Nakhon Phanom en route to Phra That Phanom Chedi which is 50 km to the S and is the NE's

Nakhon Phanom

0   200
metres
(approx)

Golf
Course

To
Airport &
Sakhon Nakhon

By Pass Rd

Langlailarlang Rd

Aphibarn Bancha Rd

Salaklang Rd

Sunthorn Vichit Rd

TAT
office

Rachathun Rd

Luk Sua Rd

Fuang Nakhon Rd

Bamrung Muang Rd

Thamrong Prasit Rd

Immigration
office

Clocktower

Ruamjit
Rd

Pier   Thakhek

Poankaew Rd

Sri
Thep

Phosri

Pier

Thutsanapathun Rd

LAOS

Mekong

To
That Phanom
& Mukdahan

Hotels:
1. First
2. Grand
3. Mae Nam Khong
   Grand View
4. Nakhon Phanom
5. River Inn
6. Srithep

North
South
Local Terminal

---

most revered religious building (see That Phanom, below). Nakhon Phanom is the closest town with adequate hotels to the wat. Nakhon Phanom's limited sights include **Wat Sri Thep** on Srithep Road and **Wat Mahathat** (with a lotus-bud chedi), at the S end of Sunthon Vichit Rd. The former monastery has some exuberant murals depicting episodes from the Buddha's life (the jataka tales). Or simply wander along the river front past handicraft shops and a Chinese temple. There is a morning market on the river.

Excursions

Wat That Phanom, the Northeast's holiest religious site, lies 50 km S of town. Getting there: regular buses from the station near the market (∅20).

Renu Nakhon is a weaving centre 6.5 km off the main highway (Route 212), on the way to That Phanom. Getting there: by bus from the station near the market.

Wat Phrathat Narai Chengweng (Phrathat Naweng) is a Khmer prang dating from the 11th or 12th century. In spite of being reconstructed in what appears to be a remarkably haphazard fashion (surely the Khmers, master builders, would have cut stone that fitted?) this small sanctuary is very satisfying. Lying in a peaceful wat compound, it displays finely carved lintels: the E lintel (above the entrance to the sanctuary) shows Siva dancing; the N face, Vishnu reclining on a naga. The wat is 88 km W of Nakhon Phanom on Route 22, at the junction with Route 223 (it is signposted). Walk through a green archway, and the wat is 500m along a dirt track. There is a good, cheap Thai restaurant on the other side of the road from the wat, beyond the intersection on the way to Udon Thani (about 200m). Getting there: take a bus travelling towards Sakhon Nakhon from the bus station near the market.

Festivals

Oct: *Ok Phansa* (9-13th, end of Buddhist Lent) four day celebrations with *long-boat races*, and the launching of illuminated boats onto the Mekong.

Local information
● **Accommodation**

Because few travellers stop here, guesthouse/cheap hotel accommodation is poor. Few places cater to the vicarious needs of the traveller.

A-B *Nam Khong Grand View*, 527 Sunthorn Vichit Rd, T 513564, F 511071, a/c, restaurant, pool, new hotel with 114 rm, best in town.

B-C *Nakhon Phanom*, 403 Aphibarn Bancha Rd, T 511455, F 511071, a/c, restaurant, pool, rather shabby, best rooms in the new wing.

C-D *River Inn*, 137 Sunthorn Vichit Rd, T 511305, some a/c, restaurant, nice position overlooking river, but overpriced and shabby, noisy rooms on the road side; **C-D** *Sri Thep*, 708/11 Srithep Rd, T 511437, F 511346, some a/c, nothing special, rooms in the new wing a tad smarter.

D-E *First*, 370 Srithep Rd, T 511253, some a/c, rooms are rather mixed in terms of quality and cleanliness from acceptable to grubby; **D-E** *Grand Hotel*, Si Thap Rd, T 511526, some a/c, the best of the bunch in this category; **D-E** *Lucky*, 131 Aphibarn Bancha Rd, T 511274.

E *Chakkawan*, 676/12-13 Aphibarn Bancha Rd, T 511298.

● **Places to eat**

There are numerous restaurants along the river road and they all serve the same broad range of dishes. Mekong catfish cooked in a variety of ways – curried, stir fried, deep fried, in soups – is a local speciality.

Ban Suan, 405 Sunthorn Vichit Rd; *Golden Giant Catfish*, Sunthorn Vichit Rd; *NKP Bakery*, by *Nakhon Phanom Hotel*; *Sri Nakhon*, 544/4 Thamrong Prasit Rd.

● **Banks & money changers**

Bangkok, Srithep Rd; Thai Farmers, 439 Aphibarn Bancha Rd.

● **Hospitals & medical services**

Sunthorn Vichit Rd, T 511422.

● **Post & telecommunications**
Area code: 042.
Post Office: Sunthorn Vichit Rd (N end).
Telephone office: off Fuang Nakhon Rd.

● **Shopping**

Souvenir and handicraft shops on the riverfront (Sunthorn Vichit Rd) eg *Tida*.

● **Sports**

Snooker: *Nakhon Phanom Hotel*, Aphibarn Bancha Rd.

● **Tourist offices**

TAT, corner of Salaklang and Suthorn Vichit roads. Areas of responsibility are Nakhon Phanom, Sakhon Nakhon and Mukdahan.

● **Useful addresses**

Immigration: Sunthorn Vichit Rd, T 51147.
Police: Sunthorn Vichit Rd (N end) 3.

● **Transport**

735 km from Bangkok, 242 km from Udon and 296 km from Nong Khai.

Local Bus: the station for local buses and songthaews is nr the market, opp the *Nakhon Phanom Hotel*. **Songthaews:** to That Phanom leave from the local bus station.

Road Bus: there are 2 bus terminals only 200m or so apart. The larger southern bus terminal, for places S of Nakhon Phanom is at the W end of Fuang Nakhon Rd. The northern bus terminal is nr the intersection of Fuang Nakhon and Aphibarn Bancha rds. Regular connections with Khon Kaen, Ubon, Bangkok, 13 hrs and Nong Khai via Sakhon Nakhon. If you wish to take the more interesting route which follows the Mekong, then take a bus to Beung Kan and change. Tour buses running S to Ubon leave twice a day at 0700 and 1400 near the *Windsor Hotel*, 4½ hrs.

International connections with Laos Foreigners can cross the Mekong to Thakhek using the ferry service linking the two settlements.

MUKDAHAN

Mukdahan is the capital of Thailand's newest province created in 1982. The town's greatest claim to fame is as the hometown of one of Thailand's best-known leaders – Field Marshal Sarit Thanarat. Although Mukdahan is changing fast as one of the gateways to an emerging Laos, until recently many of the villages aroundabouts were cut off from the outside world during the wet season. There are still a few old-style wooden houses – but they are fast disappearing.

The town is situated on the Mekong River, and lies directly opposite the important Lao town of Savannakhet. It is like a quiet version of Nong Khai. For the best views of the river and surrounding countryside, climb **Phu Manorom**, a small hill 5 km S of town. Take Route 2034 S towards Don Tan and after 2 km turn right. The summit is another 3 km from the turn-off.

Because of its location, Mukdahan has become an important trading centre with goods from Laos – gems, timber, cattle and agricultural commodities – being exchanged for Thai consumer goods. There is a Lao and Thai **market**, held daily, along the river road running S from **Wat Si Mongkhon Tai** which is situated opposite the pier where boats from Laos land. It is best to get to the market in the morning. Along with Thai consumer goods, Lao silk and cotton cloth (see Shopping, below), good French bread, china, 'axe' cushions and baskets are also sold. Near the pier and opposite Wat Si Mongkhon Tai is a Bodhi tree (*Ficus religiosa*). Traditional soothsayer often offer their advice here. The pier and riverside road is a good place to watch Mukdahan life go – slowly – by.

Wat Sri Sumong on Samran Chai Khong Rd, the river road, is interesting for the colonial architectural elements reflected in the bot or ordination hall: the arches over the windows and the verandah. Between the bot and the more orthodox viharn is a small example of the distinctive Lao, lotus bud chedi. A little further N on the river road, **Wat Yod Kaew Sriwichai** also has Lao lotus bud chedis and a large, gold Buddha in the mudra of spinning the Wheel of Law.

Excursions

Phu Pha Thoep National Park (also known as Mukdahan National Park) lies 15 km S of Mukdahan, off Route 2034.

The park was gazetted in 1984 and covers a modest 54 sq km. The principal forest type here is dry dipterocarp savanna forest and there are a succession of oddly-shaped rock outcrops easily accessible from park headquarters. The environment almost feels prehistoric, and fossils and finger paintings have been found amidst the boulders. Cut into the cliff face which rises above the headquarters is a cave packed with Buddha images deposited here by villagers. **Accommodation** No bungalows, but camping is permitted. **Getting there**: catch a songthaew travelling S towards Don Tan; the turning for the park is between the 14 and 15 km markers and it is a 2 km walk from there to the park headquarters.

Wat Phu Daan Tae contains a massive sitting Buddha made of brick and concrete, surrounded by acolytes. It can be seen clearly from Route 212, running S towards Ubon, about 50 km from town. **Getting there**: only worth stopping for the seriously committed. Take a bus running S towards Ubon.

Tours

There are four small tour offices opposite Wat Si Mongkhon Tai, at the N end of Samran Chai Khong Rd – *TAR Tour*, *Mukdahan Tour (Thailand)*, *Sompong Tour* and *Sakonpasa Department Store*. They are mainly oriented towards Thai tourists travelling to Laos and Vietnam. In 1994 they would only organize tours for foreigners *if they already had a visa* for the country concerned. However, in recent months entry regulations for Laos have eased, and it may be possible to secure a visa through one of these four companies in Mukdahan. Obtaining a visa in Bangkok – *stamped with the correct point of entry* – is the safest bet. Day tours to Laos cost ฿370-470, a 4 day/3 night tour to Vietnam ฿18,000, and a 3 day/2 night tour to Laos ฿12,500.

Local information
● **Accommodation**
A *Indochina Intercontinental*, Samut Sakdarak Rd, T 611893, 1 km S of town centre,

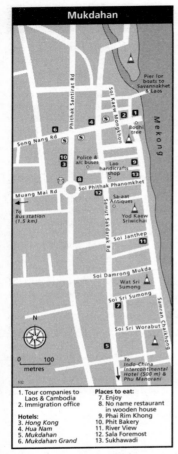

Mukdahan

1. Tour companies to Laos & Cambodia
2. Immigration office

Hotels:
3. Hong Kong
4. Hua Nam
5. Mukdahan
6. Mukdahan Grand

Places to eat:
7. Enjoy
8. No name restaurant in wooden house
9. Phai Rim Khong
10. Phit Bakery
11. River View
12. Sala Foremost
13. Sukhawadi

a/c, restaurant, new hotel with 154 rm; **A** *Mukdahan Grand*, 78 Song Nang Sathit, T 612020, F 612021, a/c, restaurant, new hotel with 200 rm, comparatively plush but in a distinctly provincial manner as evidenced in the local crooners, *Zubano Karaoke Bar* and *MG Snooker Club* – and some people would say all the more charming for it. Arguably the best hotel in town, though.

B-C *Mukdahan*, 8/8 Samut Sakdarak Rd, T 611619, ½ km S of the town centre, some a/c, 4-storey hotel, quite new but already frayed at the edges, a/c rooms have hot water and TV but no ambience, coffee shop with live music.

C-E *Hua Nam*, 36 Samut Sakdarak Rd, T 611137, some a/c, central location on corner with Song Nang Sathit Rd, looks from the outside like a regular Chinese-style hotel, but rooms are large, clean and well maintained, a/c rooms with TVs and hot water, set around courtyard so relatively quiet despite central crossroads location, rec.

D-E *Hong Kong*, 161/1-2 Phithak Santirat Rd, T 611123, some a/c, Chinese-style hotel, quite well maintained, a/c rooms have hot water, central; **D-E** *Sansuk Bungalow*, 2 Phithak Santirat Rd, T 611294, some a/c, nr the centre of town, clean rooms with friendly management, the best of the cheaper accommodation.

● **Places to eat**
The best places to eat are along the river. Tables are set out on the pavement overlooking the Mekong and Laos. In the evening, with fairy light lit trees, and a gentle breeze, there can be few more attractive places to eat and drink. Riverside restaurants incl the *River View*, *Sukhawadi* and *Phai Rim Khong*. ♦♦♦–♦♦*Enjoy Restaurant*, 7/1 Samut Sakdarak Rd, bright and cheerful restaurant with Lao specialities, a few Vietnamese dishes and river fish and prawns; ♦♦*Phai Rim Khong* (*Riverside*), Samran Chai Khong Rd, a riverside restaurant to the S of town, serving good Thai dishes in attractive location with good views; ♦♦*River View*, Samran Chai Khong Rd, chalet-style restaurant with tables overlooking Mekong, average Thai and Lao food, spectacular setting; ♦♦*Sukhawadi*, Samran Chai Khong, Mekong fish is best, but other Thai dishes available, great position on the river; ♦*Foremost*, 74/1 Samut Sakdarak Rd, breakfast, ice cream and coffee in a/c room; ♦*Night market*, Song Nang Sathit Rd (W end nr the bus station). The best place for cheap Isan dishes and also for Vietnamese stall food. ♦*No Name Restaurant*, Phithak Santirat Rd (on roundabout), excellent cheap Thai dishes served from old wooden house; ♦*Phit Bakery*, 709 Phithak Santirat, good breakfasts, coffee, cakes and ice creams, friendly, rec.

● **Banks & money changers**
Bangkok Bank, Song Nang Sathit Rd; Thai Farmers Bank, Song Nang Sathit Rd.

● **Post & telecommunications**
Area code: 042.

Post Office: Phithak Santirat Rd (on the round-about).

● **Shopping**

Antiques: *Sa-aat*, 77 Samut Sakdarak Rd, small collection of antiques for sale including Chinese ceramics, old irons, Buddhist alms bowls and amulets.

Handicrafts: Mukdahan is a good place to buy Lao/Isan handicrafts like baskets, axe cushions and textiles. Cloth is usually sold by the *phun*; a sarong length is normally two *phun*, so when asking the price do not be surprised if the whole piece costs twice (or more) than the amount quoted. Cotton cloth is normally ¢100/*phun*; silk costs several times more. The textiles with the elephant motif are distinctively Lao, although much of the cloth is now woven in Thailand, especially around Nong Khai. Textiles and other handicrafts can be bought in the daily riverside market (see Places of interest, above). There are also permanent shops on Samut Sakdarak Rd.

● **Useful addresses**

Immigration: Samran Chai Khong Rd, T 611074.

● **Transport**

50 km S of That Phanom, 170 km N of Ubon.

Road Bus: the bus terminal (*bor kor sor*) for non-a/c and *some* a/c buses is at the W end of Song Nang Sathit Rd, about 2 km from the town centre (a ¢10 motor saamlor ride). Buses from here to Ubon, Nakhon Phanom and That Phanom, and some other NE towns, as well as Bangkok. A/c tour buses leave from close to Bangkok Bank on Song Nang Sathit Rd. Connections with Bangkok's northern bus terminal 12 hrs, N to That Phanom and Nakhon Phanom 2 hrs, and S to Ubon Ratchathani 3 hrs. Tour buses leave from *Sahamit Tours*, offices on Samut Sakdarak Rd, also close to the town centre.

International connections to Laos Ferries to Savannakhet, Laos leave from the pier near Wat Si Mongkhon Tai. Foreigners can cross from Thailand to Laos here. A second bridge across the Mekong (the first being nr Nong Khai) has been agreed and construction should commence shortly.

THAILAND – INFORMATION FOR TRAVELLERS

BEFORE TRAVELLING

ENTRY REQUIREMENTS

● **Visas**

All tourists must possess passports valid for at least 6 months longer than their intended stay in Thailand.

30 day visa exemptions No visa is required for tourists arriving by air, holding a confirmed onward air ticket and who intend to stay for up to 30 days (not extendable). (Until 1995 tourists were only permitted to stay for 14 days.) Visitors are fined ¢100/day each day they exceed the 30 day limit. The same applies to tourists who arrive via the Thai-Malaysian border by sea, rail or road. This applies to nationals of the following countries: Algeria, Argentina, Australia, Austria, Bahrain, Belgium, Brazil, Brunei, Canada, Denmark, Djibouti, Egypt, Fiji, Finland, France, Germany, Greece, Iceland, Indonesia, Ireland, Israel, Italy, Japan, Kenya, Kuwait, Luxembourg, Malaysia, Mauritania, Mexico, Morocco, Myanmar (Burma), Netherlands, New Zealand, Oman, Papua New Guinea, Philippines, Portugal, Qatar, Republic of Korea, Saudi Arabia, Senegal, Singapore, Slovenia, South Africa, Spain, Sweden, Switzerland, Tunisia, Turkey, UAE, UK, USA, Vanuatu, Western Samoa, Yemen. Malaysian nationals arriving by road from Malaysia do not need evidence of onward journey.

Visas on arrival There is now a new visa booth at Don Muang (Bangkok) Airport itself, at customs control. Visitors without visas can have one issued here and there is even a photo booth to provide passport snaps (one photograph required). However, the desk only provides tourist visas valid for 15 days (¢300), which nationals of many countries do not require in any case (see above). The facility is only useful for nationals of those countries which are not exempted from having an entry visa. These number 76 in total. Applicants must also have an outbound (return) ticket. There are similar desks at Chiang Mai, Phuket and Hat Yai airports.

3 month visa exemptions Nationals from South Korea, New Zealand, Sweden, Denmark, Norway and Finland visiting as a tourist do not require a visa for visits of up to 3 months, and those from Hong Kong for a visit of up to 15 days.

Tourist visas These are valid for 90 days from date of entry (single entry); **transit visas** for 30 days (single entry). **Visa extensions** are obtainable from the Immigration Department in Bangkok (see below) for ฿500. The process used to be interminable, but the system is now much improved and relatively painless. Extensions can also be issued in other towns, such as Koh Samui and Chiang Mai. Applicants must bring two photocopies of their passport ID page and the page on which their tourist visa is stamped, together with three passport photographs. It is also advisable to dress neatly. It may be easier to leave the country and then re-enter having obtained a new tourist visa. Visas are issued by all Thai embassies and consulates.

Passport control at Don Muang Airport during peak arrival periods (usually 1200-1400) can be choked with visitors – be prepared for a wait of an hour or more before reaching the arrivals hall.

90-day non-immigrant visas These are also issued in the applicant's home country (about US$30). A letter from the applicant's company or organization guaranteeing their repatriation should be submitted at the same time.

In the UK there is now a visa information line, operating 24 hrs a day, T 01891 600 150.

● **Procedure for lost or stolen passport**
1. File a report with the local police.

2. Take the report to your local embassy or consulate and apply for a new travel document or passport. (If there is no representation, visit the Passport Division of the Ministry of Foreign Affairs.)

3. Take the new passport plus the police report to Section 4, Subdivision 4, Immigration Bureau, room 311 (3rd floor), Old Building, Soi Suan Plu, Sathorn Tai Rd, Bangkok, T 2873911, for a new visa stamp.

● **Immigration Department**
Soi Suan Plu, Thanon Sathorn Tai, Bangkok 10120, T 2873101. Open: 0930-1630 Mon-Fri, 0830-1200 Sat (tourists only).

● **Vaccinations**
No vaccinations required, unless coming from an infected area (if visitors have been in a yellow fever infected area in the 10 days before arrival, and do not have a vaccination certi-

cate, they will be vaccinated and kept in quarantine for 6 days, or deported. See health section below for details.

● **Representation overseas**
Australia, 111 Empire Circuit, Yarralumla, Canberra, ACT 2600, T (06) 2731149, 2732937; **Austria**, Weimarer Strasse 68, 1180 Vienna, T (0222) 3103423; **Belgium**, Square du Val de la Cambre 2, 1050 Brussels, T 2 6406810; **Canada**, 180 Island Park Drive, Ottawa, Ontario, K1Y 0A2, T (613) 722 4444; **Denmark**, Norgesmindevej 18, 2900 Hellerup, Copenhagen, T (31) 6250101; **France**, 8 Rue Greuze, 75116 Paris, T 47043222; **Germany**, Uberstrasse 65, 5300 Bonn 2, T (0228) 355065; **Italy**, Via Nomentana, 132, 00162 Rome, T (396) 8320729; **Japan**, 3-14-6, Kami-Osaki, Shinagawa-ku, Tokyo 141, T (03) 3441-1386; **Laos**, Route Phonekheng, PO Box 128, Vientiane, T 2508; **Malaysia**, 206 Jl Ampang, 50450 Kuala Lumpur, T (03) 2488222; **Myanmar**, 91, Pyay Rd, Rangoon, T 21713; **Nepal**, Jyoti Kendra Building, Thapathali, PO Box 3333, Kathmandu, T 213910; **Netherlands**, 1 Buitenrustweg, 2517 KD, The Hague, T (070) 3452088; **New Zealand**, 2 Cook St, PO Box 17-226, Karori, T 768618; **Norway**, Munkedamsveien 59B, 0270 Oslo 2, T (02) 832517-8; **Spain**, Calle del Segre, 29, 20 A, 28002 Madrid, T (341) 5632903; **Sweden**, Sandhamnsgatan 36 (5th Floor), PO Box 27065, 10251 Stockholm, T (08) 6672160; **Switzerland**, Eigerstrasse 60 (3rd Floor), 3007 Bern, T (031) 462281; **UK**, 29-30 Queens Gate, London, SW7 5JB, T 0171 589 0173; **USA**, 2300 Kalorama Rd NW, Washington, DC 20008, T (202) 4837200.

HEALTH

Vaccinations: no vaccinations are required, but cholera immunization and a tetanus booster are advisable. A gamma globulin injection (against hepatitis) is also recommended. There is a vaccination clinic in the Science Division of the Thai Red Cross Society, at the corner of Rama IV and Henri Dunant rds, Bangkok, T 2520161.

● **Medical facilities**
For full listing of hospitals, check the Yellow Pages, or listings under Useful addresses in each town. Hospitals in Bangkok are of a reasonable (Western) standard.

● **Food and water**
Tap water is not recommended for drinking.

Cut fruit or uncooked vegetables from roadside stalls may not always be clean.

● **Travelling with children**

(For more information and a check-list, see the Rounding Up section.) Disposable nappies are now widely available in Thailand, although they are expensive. Powdered milks and a good range of powdered foods are on sale in most supermarkets. Bottled water is available everywhere. Fruit is a good source of nutrition and is also widely available. Anti-malarials are recommended (quarter to half dosage by some doctors) if travelling outside the main cities and tourist destinations although opinions – as on most issues connected with malaria – seem to differ. Check with your doctor or telephone your country's centre for tropical diseases.

MONEY

● **ATMs (cash dispensers)**

American Express can be used at Bangkok Bank, JCB at Siam Commercial Bank, Master Card at Siam Commercial, Visa at Bangkok Bank.

● **Credit cards**

Major credit cards such as American Express, Visa, Diners Club, Carte Blanche, Master Charge/Access are accepted in leading hotels, restaurants, department stores and several large stores for tourists. Visitors may have some problems upcountry where the use of credit cards is less common. Generally, Visa and Mastercard are more widely accepted than American Express; the Bangkok Bank takes Amex, but several banks accept Visa and Mastercard. Amex's higher commission also puts off many shopkeepers. **Notification of credit card loss:** American Express, IBM Bldg, Phahon-yothin Rd, T 2730022; Diners Club, Dusit Thani Bldg, Rama IV Rd, T 2332645, 2335775; JCB T 2561361, 2561351; Visa and Master Card, Thai Farmers Bank Bldg, Phahonyothin Rd, T 2701801-10.

● **Cost of living**

Visitors staying in first class hotels and eating in hotel restaurants will probably spend a minimum of ฿1500/day. Tourists staying in cheaper air-conditioned accommodation, and eating in local restaurants will probably spend about ฿500-750/day. A backpacker, staying in fan-cooled guesthouses and eating cheaply, might expect to be able to live on ฿200/day. In Bangkok, expect to pay 20-30% more.

● **Currency**

The unit of Thai currency is the **baht** (฿), which is divided into 100 **satang**. Notes in circulation include ฿20 (green), ฿50 (blue), ฿100 (red), ฿500 (purple) and new ฿1,000 (orange and grey). Coins include 25 satang and 50 satang, and ฿1, ฿5, and ฿10. The two smaller coins are gradually disappearing from circulation and the 25 satang coin, equivalent to the princely sum of US$0.001 (1 cent), is rare.

● **Exchange rates**

It is best to change money at banks or money changers which give better rates than hotels. First class hotels have 24 hrs money changers. There is a charge of ฿13/cheque when changing TCs (passport required). Indonesian Rupiah and Nepalese Rupees cannot be exchanged for Thai currency.

Exchange rates: Jan 1997

Currency	Baht
US$	25
£	41
DM	16
¥	0.23
Malaysian $	10
Singapore $	18
Hong Kong $	3.3
Swiss Franc	19
Dutch Guilder	15
French Franc	4.8
Lire	0.016
Australian $	20
New Zealand $	18

GETTING THERE

AIR

The majority of visitors arrive in Thailand through Bangkok's Don Muang airport. There are also international chartered flights to Chiang Mai in the N and to Phuket in the S (see below). More than 35 airlines and charter companies fly to Bangkok, and Thailand is easily accessible from Europe, North America, Australasia and the Middle East as well as from other Asian countries. **Thai International** is the national airline.

● **Links with Indochina and Myanmar (Burma)**

Bangkok is a transport hub for air connections with Yangon – (Rangoon, Myanmar/Burma), Vientiane (Laos), Hanoi and Ho Chi Minh City/Saigon (Vietnam), and Phnom Penh (Cambodia). Partly as a result it also has a concentration of tour companies specializing in Indochina/Myanmar and is a good place to arrange a visa.

TRAIN

Regular rail services link Singapore and Bangkok, via Kuala Lumpur, Butterworth and the major southern Thai towns. Express a/c trains take two days from Singapore, 34 hrs from Kuala Lumpur, 24 hrs from Butterworth (opp Penang). The *Magic Arrow Express* leaves Singapore on Sun, Tues and Thur, Bangkok-Singapore (฿899-1,965), Bangkok-Kuala Lumpur (฿659-1,432) and to Ipoh (฿530-1,145). An additional train from Butterworth departs at 1340, arriving Bangkok 0835 the next day. The train from Bangkok to Butterworth departs 1515, arriving Butterworth 1225 (฿457-1,147). All tickets should be booked in advance. The most luxurious way to journey by train to Thailand is aboard the *Eastern & Oriental (E&O) Express*. The a/c train of 22 carriages including a salon car, dining car, bar and observation deck and carrying just 132 passengers runs once a week from Singapore to Bangkok and back. Luxurious carriages, fine wines and food designed for European rather than Asian sensibilities make this not just a mode of transport but an experience. The journey takes 43 hrs with stops in Kuala Lumpur, Butterworth and Padang Besar. But such luxury is expensive: US$1,130-2,950. For information call Bangkok 2514862; London (0171) 9286000; US (800) 5242420; Singapore (065) 2272068.

ROAD

The main road access is to and from Malaysia. The principal land border crossings into Malaysia are nr Betong in Yala Province and from Sungei Golok in Narathiwat Province. In Apr 1994 the Friendship Bridge linking Nong Khai with Laos opened – and became the first bridge across the Mekong River. To cross into Laos here foreigners need to obtain a visa in Bangkok – although a consulate is due to open in Nong Khai.

BOAT

No regular, scheduled cruise liners sail to Thailand any longer but it is sometimes possible to enter Thailand on a freighter, arriving at Khlong Toey Port. The *Bangkok Post* publishes a weekly shipping post with details on ships leaving the kingdom.

CUSTOMS

● **Duty free allowance**
250 gr of cigars or cigarettes (or 200 cigarettes) and 1 litre of wine or spirits. One still camera with five rolls of film or one movie camera with three rolls of 8mm or 16mm film.

● **Currency regulations**
Non-residents can bring in up to ฿2,000 pp and unlimited foreign currency although amounts exceeding US$10,000 must be declared. Maximum amount permitted to take out of the country is ฿50,000 pp.

● **Prohibited items**
All narcotics; obscene literature, pornography; fire arms (except with a permit from the Police Department or local registration office).

Some species of plants and animals are prohibited, for more information contact the Royal Forestry Department, Phahonyothin Rd, Bangkok, T 5792776. Permission of entry for animals by air is obtainable at the airport. An application must be made to the Department of Livestock Development, Bangkok, T 2515136 for entry by sea. Vaccination certificates are required; dogs and cats need rabies certificates.

Arranging visas for Indochina and Myanmar

	LENGTH OF VISA	WORKING DAYS TO ARRANGE	COST
Vietnam	4 weeks	4 days	฿1,100-1,300
Laos	2 weeks	7 days	฿1,300-1,600
Cambodia	4 weeks	7 days	฿500-800
Myanmar (Burma)	4 weeks	2 days	฿300-500

NB Above details were collected in Oct 1996

ON ARRIVAL

● **Airport information**

Don Muang airport lies 25 km N of Bangkok. There are two international terminals (adjoining one another) and one domestic terminal. Terminal 1 serves Asia, and Terminal 2 the rest of the world. A 0.5 km-long covered walkway links the domestic and international terminals. Facilities include: banks and currency exchange, post office, left luggage (฿20/item/day – max 4 months), hotel booking agency, airport information, airport clinic, lost and found baggage service, duty-free shops, restaurants and bars including a whole slate of newly-opened fast food outlets – Burger King, Svensson's, Pizza Hut and Upper Crust. **NB** Food is expensive here – cheap food is available across the footbridge at the railway station. The *Airport Hotel* is linked to the international terminal by a walkway. It provides a 'ministay' service for passengers who wish to 'freshen-up' and take a room for up to 3 hrs between 0800 and 1800 (฿400 T 5661020/1). **International flight information**: T 5351386 for departures, T 5351301 for arrivals. **Domestic flight information**: T 5351253. The new domestic terminal has a hotel booking counter, post office, currency exchange counters, restaurant and bookshop. An elevated a/c walkway connects the international and domestic terminals; a shuttle bus is sometimes available, beware – taxis grossly overcharge for a drive of under 1 km.

Airport accommodation: A *Amari Airport*, 333 Chert Wudthakas Rd, T 5661020, F 5661941, a/c, restaurants, pool, connected to airport by foot-bridge; rooms look onto attractive gardens, useful hotel for transit passengersm short-term stays for wash and eat available; A *Rama Gardens*, 9/9 Vibhavadi Rangsit Rd, Bangkaen (7 km from the airport), T 561002, F 5611025, a/c, restaurants, two attractive, large pools, out of town on road to airport, inconvenient for most except those merely stopping-over for a few hours, but spacious grounds with fitness centre, tennis, squash, golf, putting.

Transport to town By taxi: official taxi booking service in the arrivals hall. There are two desks. One for the more expensive official airport taxis (newer, more luxurious vehicles); one for public taxis. The former cost ฿400 downtown; ฿300 to the northern bus terminal; ฿450 to the southern bus terminal; ฿1,500

to Pattaya. Note that airport flunkies sometimes try to direct passengers to this more expensive 'limousine' service: walk through the barriers to the public taxi desk. A public taxi to downtown should cost about half these prices – roughly ฿150-200 with ฿50 extra if using the new elevated expressway. Note that there are both metered and unmetered public taxis; the fare for the latter will be quoted when you state your destination at the desk. If taking a metered taxi, the coupon from the booking desk will quote no fare – ensure that the meter is used or you may find that the trip costs ฿300 instead of ฿200, keep hold of your coupon – some taxi drivers try to pocket it – as it details the obligations of taxi drivers. **Warning** There have been cases of visitors being robbed in unofficial taxis. To tell whether your vehicle is a registered taxi, check the colour of the number plate. Official aiport limousines have green plates, public taxis have yellow plates – and a white plate means the vehicle is not registered as a taxi. The sedan service into town costs ฿500-650. Cars are newer, more comfortable and better maintained than the average city taxi. It takes 30 mins to 1 hr to central Bangkok, depending on the time of day and the state of the traffic. The new elevated expressway reduces journey time to 20 mins – ask the taxi driver to take this route if you wish to save time but note that there is a toll fee – ฿20 and ฿30 for the two sections of this elevated road. Also note that there have been some complaints about taxi drivers at the domestic terminal forming a cartel, refusing to use their meters and charging a fixed rate considerably above the meter rate.

By bus: until 1996 buses were the cheapest but also the slowest way into town. But in Apr a new a/c airport bus service was introduced – ฿70 to Silom Rd (service A1), Sanaam Luang (service A2) (most convenient for Khaosan road guesthouses) and Phra Khanong (service A3). The service operates every 15 mins, 0500-2300. **Stops are as follows**: Silom service **(A1)**: Don Muang Tollway, Din Daeng, Pratunam, Lumpini Park, Silom. **Sanaam Luang service (A2)**: Don Muang Tollway, Din Daeng, Victory Monument, Phayathai, Phetburi, Lan Luang, Democracy Monument, Sanaam Luang. **Phra Khanong service (A3)**: Don Muang Tollway, Din Daeng, Sukhumit, Ekamai, Phra Khanong. While hotel stops are: **Silom service (A1)**: *Century, Indra, Anoma, Grand Hyatt, Erawan, Regent, Dusit Thani*, and *Narai* hotels. **Sanaam Luang service (A2)**: Victory

Monument, *Siam City Hotel*, Soi King Phet, Saphan Khao, *Majestic* and *Rattanakosin* hotels. **Phra Khanong service (A3)**: Amari Building, *Ambassador* and *Delta Grand Pacific* hotels, Bang Chan Glass House, *Novotel*, Soi Ekkamai (Sukhumuit). **NB** Return buses have slightly different stops.

Although many visitors will see ฿70 as money well spent there will still be the hardened few who will opt for the regular bus service, which is just as cheap and slow as it ever was, 1½-3 hrs (depending on time of day) (฿7-15). The bus stop is 50m N of the arrivals hall. Buses are crowded during rush-hours and there is little room for luggage. Bus 59 goes to Khaosan Rd, bus 29 goes to Bangkok's Hualamphong railway station, via the Northern bus terminal and Siam Square. A/c bus 10 goes to Samsen Rd and Silom Rd via the Northern bus terminal, a/c bus 4 goes to Silom Rd, a/c bus 13 goes to Sukhumvit Rd and the Eastern bus terminal, a/c bus 29 goes to the Northern bus terminal, Siam Square and Hualamphong railway station. **By minibus**: ฿100 to major hotels, ฿60 shuttle bus to the *Asia Hotel* on Phayathai Rd. ฿50-80 to Khaosan Rd, depending on the time of day. Direct buses to Pattaya at 0900, 1200 and 1700, ฿180. **By train**: the station is on the other side of the N-S highway from the airport. Regular trains into Bangkok's Hualamphong station, ฿5 for ordinary fares, 3rd clas (the cheapest option). But only 6 ordinary trains per day. For 'rapid' and 'express' a supplementary charge of ฿20-50 is levied. The State Railways of Thailand runs an 'Airport Express' 5 times a day (but not on Sat and Sun), with a/c shuttle bus from Don Muang station to airport terminal, 35 mins (฿100). **Hotel pick-up services**: many of the more expensive hotels operate airport pick-up services if informed of your arrival ahead of time.

● **Airport tax**

Payable on departure – ฿250 for international flights, ฿30 for domestic flights.

● **Clothing**

In towns and at religious sights, it is courteous to avoid wearing shorts and singlets (or sleeveless shirts). Visitors who are inappropriately dressed may not be allowed into temples. Thais always look neat and clean. *Mai rieb-roi* means 'not neat' and is considered a great insult. Beach resorts are a law unto themselves – casual clothes are the norm, although nudity is still very much frowned upon by Thais. In the most expensive restaurants in Bangkok diners may well be expected to wear a jacket and tie.

● **Conduct**

Thais are generally very understanding of the foibles and habits of foreigners (*farangs*) and will forgive and forget most indiscretions. However, there are a number of 'dos and don'ts' which are worth observing:

Common greeting *Wai*: hands are held together as if in prayer, and the higher the wai, the more respectful the greeting. By watching Thai's wai it is possible to ascertain their relative seniority. Again, foreigners are not expected to conform to this custom – a simple wai at chest to chin height is all that is required. When *farangs* and Thais do business it is common to shake hands.

Heads, heart and feet Try not to openly point your feet at anyone – feet are viewed as spiritually the lowest part of the body. At the same time, never touch anyone's head which is the holiest, as well as the highest, part. Among Thais, the personal characteristic of *jai yen* is very highly regarded; literally, this means to have a 'cool heart'. It embodies calmness, having an even temper and not displaying emotion. Although foreigners generally receive special dispensation, and are not expected to conform to Thai customs (all *farang* are thought to have 'hot hearts'), it is important to try and keep calm in any disagreement – losing one's temper leads to loss of face and subsequent loss of respect.

The monarchy Never criticize any member of the royal family or the institution itself. The monarchy is held in very high esteem.

Monastery (*wat*) etiquette Remove shoes on entering, do not climb over Buddha images or have pictures taken in front of one. Wear modest clothing – women should not expose their shoulders or wear dresses that are too short (see below, clothing). Females should never hand anything directly to monks, or venture into the monks' quarters.

Smoking Prohibited on domestic flights, public buses and in cinemas.

Further reading A useful book delving deeper into the do's and don'ts of living in Thailand is Robert and Nanthapa Cooper's *Culture shock: Thailand*, Time Books International: Singapore (1990). It is available from most bookshops.

● **Emergencies**
Police 191, 123; **Tourist Police** 195; **Fire** 199;
Ambulance 2522171-5. **Tourist Police head office**: Unico House, Ploenchit Soi Lang Suan, Bangkok, T 6521721-6. **Tourist Assistance Centre**, Rachdamnern Nok Ave, Bangkok, T 2828129.

● **Hours of business**
Banks: 0830-1530 Mon-Fri. **Currency exchange services**: 0830-2200 Mon-Sun in Bangkok and Pattaya, 0830-1930 in Phuket and 0830-1630 Mon-Fri in other towns. **Government offices**: 0830-1200, 1300-1630 Mon-Fri. **Tourist offices**: 0830-1630 Mon-Sun. **Shops**: 0830-1700, larger shops: 1000-1900 or 2100.

● **Official time**
7 hrs ahead of GMT.

● **Tipping**
Generally unnecessary. A 10% service charge is now expected on room, food and drinks bills in the smarter hotels as well as a tip for any personal service. Increasingly, the more expensive restaurants add a 10% service charge; others expect a small tip.

● **Voltage**
220 volts (50 cycles) throughout Thailand. Most first and tourist class hotels have outlets for shavers and hair dryers. Adaptors are recommended, as almost all sockets are two pronged.

WHERE TO STAY

As a premier tourist destination and one of the world's fastest-growing economies, Thailand has a large selection of hotels – including some of the very best in the world. However, outside the tourist centres, there is still an absence of adequate 'Western style' accommodation. Most 'Thai' hotels are distinctly lacking in character and are poorly maintained. Due to the popularity of the country with backpackers, there are also a large number of small guesthouses, geared to Westerners serving Western food and catering to the foibles of foreigners.

● **Hotels**
Hotels are listed under eight categories, according to the *average* price of a double/twin room for one night. It should be noted that many hotels will have a range of rooms, some with air-conditioning (a/c) and attached bathroom facilities, others with just a fan and shared facilities. A service charge of 10% and

government tax of 11% will usually be added to the bill in the more expensive hotels (categories B-L). Ask whether the quoted price includes tax when checking-in. **NB** During the off-season, hotels in tourist destinations may halve their room rates so it is always worthwhile bargaining.

FOOD AND DRINK

FOOD

Thai cuisine is an intermingling of Tai, Chinese, and to a lesser extent, Indian cuisines. This helps to explain why restaurants produce dishes which must be some of the (spicy) hottest in the world, as well as some which are rather bland. Despite these various influences, Thai cooking is distinctive. Thais have managed to combine the best of each tradition, adapting elements to suit their own preferences. Remarkably, considering how ubiquitous it is in Thai cooking, the chilli pepper is a New World fruit and was not introduced into Thailand until the late 16th century (along with the pineapple and papaya).

When a Thai asks another Thai whether he has eaten he will ask, literally, whether he has 'eaten rice' (*kin khaaw*). Similarly, the accompanying dishes are referred to as food 'with the rice'. A Thai meal is based around rice, and many wealthy Bangkokians own farms upcountry where they cultivate their favourite variety. A meal usually consists (along with the rice) of a soup like *tom yam kung* (prawn soup), *kaeng* (a curry) and *krueng kieng* (a number of side dishes). Generally, Thai food is chilli-hot, and aromatic herbs and grasses (like lemon grass) are used to give a distinctive flavour. *Nam pla* (fish sauce) and *nam prik* (nam pla, chillies, garlic, sugar, shrimps and lime juice) are two condiments that are taken with almost all meals. Food is eaten with a spoon and fork, and dishes are usually served all at once; it is unimportant to a Thai that food be hot. Try the open-air foodstalls to be found in every town which are frequented by middle-class Thais as well as the poor and where a meal costs only ฿15-20. Many small restaurants have no menus. Away from the main tourist spots, 'Western' breakfasts are commonly unavailable, so be prepared to eat Thai-style (noodle or rice soup or fried rice). Finally, due to Thailand's large Chinese population (or at least Thais with Chinese roots), there are also many Chinese-style restaurants whose cuisine is variously 'Thai-ified'.

Tourist centres also provide good European, American and Japanese food at reasonable prices. Bangkok boasts some superb restaurants. Less expensive Western fastfood restaurants can also be found – McDonalds, Pizza Hut, Kentucky Fried Chicken and others.

DRINK

● Drinking water

Water in smaller restaurants can be risky, so many people recommend that visitors drink bottled water (widely available) or **hot tea**.

● Soft drinks

Coffee is also now consumed throughout Thailand (usually served with coffeemate or *creamer*). In stalls and restaurants, coffee come with a glass of Chinese tea. Soft drinks are widely available. Many roadside stalls prepare **fresh fruit juices** in liquidizers (*bun*) while hotels produce all the usual cocktails.

● Alcohol

Spirits Major brands of spirits are served in most hotels and bars, although not always off the tourist path. The most popular spirit among Thais is *Mekhong* – **local cane whisky** – which can be drunk straight or with mixers. It can seem rather sweet to the Western palate but it is the cheapest form of alcohol.

Beer The most popular local beer is *Singha* beer brewed by Boon Rowd. It's alcohol content is high of 6% must be partly to blame. Among expatriates, the most popular Thai beer is the more expensive *Kloster* brand (similar to a light German beer) with an alcohol content of 5.7%. *Singha* introduced a light beer called *Singha Gold* a few years ago which is quite similar to *Kloster*. *Amarit* is a third, rather less widely available, brand but popular with foreigners. Two new 'local' beers (in the sense that they are locally brewed) to enter the fray are *Heineken* and *Carlsberg*. The beer is sweeter and lighter than *Singha* and *Kloster* but still strong with an alcohol content of 6%. Yet another new local beer, although it appears to have only a very small segment of the market (as yet), and is hard to find is: *Bier Chang* or *Elephant Beer*. Beer is relatively expensive in Thai terms as it is heavily taxed by the government. In a café, expect to pay ฿30-50 for a small beer, in a coffee shop or bar ฿40-65, and in a hotel bar or restaurant, more than ฿60.

Wine Thais are fast developing a penchant for wines. Imported wines are expensive by international standards and Thai wines are pretty ghastly – overall. An exception is *Chateau de Loei* which is produced in the northeastern province of Loei by Chaijudh Karnasuta with the expert assistance of French wine maker.

GETTING AROUND

AIR

Thai Airways is the national flag carrier and is also by far the largest domestic airline. Planes are maintained to a high standard.

Thai flies to 8 destinations in the N – Chiang Mai, Chiang Rai, Lampang, Mae Hong Son, Mae Sot, Nan, Phitsanulok and Phrae; 6 in the NE – Khon Kaen, Loei, Nakhon Ratchasima, Sakhon Nakhon, Ubon Ratchathani and Udon Thani; and 6 in the S – Hat Yai, Nakhon Si Thammarat, Narathiwat, Phuket, Surat Thani and Trang. **Head office for Thai** is 89 Vibhavadi Rangsit Rd, T 5130121 but it is better to book flights through one of the local offices or a travel agent displaying the Thai logo. **Bangkok Airways**, flies from Bangkok to Koh Samui, Hua Hin and Pattaya (U-Tapao), and from Koh Samui to Phuket; prices are competitive. An airport recently opened at Sawangkhalok near Sukhothai and Bangkok Airways operates flights between Bangkok and Chiang Mai via Sukhothai. There are also plans to add Chiang Rai, Loei, Udon Thani, Hat Yai and Ranong to their domestic routes, and Luang Prabang in Laos to their international connections.

TRAIN

The State Railway of Thailand is efficient, clean and comfortable, with four main routes to the N, NE, E and S. It is safer than bus travel but can take longer. The choice is 1st class a/c compartments, 2nd class sleepers, 2nd class a/c sit-ups with reclining chairs and 3rd class sit-ups. Travelling 3rd class is often the cheapest way to travel long distance. 1st and 2nd class is more expensive than the bus but infinitely more comfortable. Express trains are known as *rot duan*, special express trains as *rot duan phiset* and rapid trains as *rot raew*. Express and rapid trains are faster as they make fewer stops; there is a surcharge for the service. Reservations for sleepers should be made in advance at Bangkok's Hualamphong station. It is advisable to book the bottom sleeper, as lights are bright on top (in 2nd class compartments). It still may be difficult to get a seat at certain times of year, such as during festivals (like Songkran in Apr).

It is possible to pick up timetables at Hualamphong station (from the information booth in the main concourse): there are two types – the 'condensed' timetable (by region) showing all rapid routes and complete, separate timetables for all classes. Some travel agencies book tickets. The advance booking office is at Hualamphong station, T 2237010. A queue-by-ticket arrangement works efficiently, and waits are not long. If you change a reservation the charge is ¢10. If travelling N or S during the day, it is a good idea to get a seat on the side of the carriage out of the sun.

An alternative to the usual overland tour of Thailand is to book a berth on the *Andaman Princess*. This large cruise ship sails to Koh Tao and back (3 days/2 nights). Passengers can snorkle at Koh Tao and the level of service and safety is very high. Large numbers of young, middle class Thais make the journey and there is lots of entertainment. Around ¢5,000 for a single berth. Contact: *Siam Cruise*, 33/10-11 Sukhumvit Soi Chaiyod (Soi 11), T 2554563, F 2558961.

BUS

Private and state-run buses leave Bangkok for

State railways of Thailand: sample routes and fares

Route	Hours	Distance (km)	Fare (baht)* 1st Class	2nd Class	3rd Class
Bangkok north to:					
Phitsanulok	5-6 hrs	389	324	159	69
Chiang Mai	11-13 hrs	751	593	281	121
Bangkok north-east to:					
Korat	5 hrs	264	230	115	50
Ubon Ratchathani	10 hrs	575	460	221	95
Khon Kaen	8 hrs	450	368	179	77
Nong Khai	11 hrs	624	497	238	103
Surin	8 hrs	420	346	169	73
Si Saket	9½ hrs	515	416	201	87
Udon Thani	9½ hrs	569	457	219	95

* mid-1996 fares quoted. Supplementary charges not included: ¢50 for express train, ¢30 for rapid train, ¢70 for special express, ¢70 for a/c, ¢100-320 for a berth depending on class.

Buses of Thailand: sample routes and fares

Route	Distance	Approx hrs by a/c bus*	VIP+	Fare** a/c	Non-a/c
Bangkok north to:					
Ayutthaya	75 km	1.30	-	38	16
Phitsanulok	368 km	5.30	230	163	72/89
Chiang Mai	713 km	9.45	470	304	135/169
Chiang Rai	849 km	11.50	525	358	189/199
Chiang Khong	875 km	12.45	-	371	206
Bangkok north-east to:					
Korat	256 km	4-5	-	115	64
Surin	451 km	6.40	-	195	108
Udon Thani	561 km	8.45	-	241	134
Ubon Ratchathani	679 km	10	400	290	161
Khon Kaen	444 km	7	295	193	107
Nong Khai	614 km	9	405	263	146

* slower by non-a/c bus ** 1995/96 fares quoted; note that fares may have increased.
+VIP coaches have fewer seats (just 8 rows) and seats that can recline further; VIP coaches are not available on all routes and most travel only on over-night journeys.

every town in Thailand; it is an extensive network and an inexpensive way to travel. The government bus company is called *Bor Kor Sor* (an abbreviation of *Borisat Khon Song*), and every town in Thailand will have a BKS terminal. There are small stop-in-every-town local buses plus the faster long distance buses (*rot duan* – express – or *rot air* – a/c). Standard a/c buses come in two grades: *chan nung* (1st class) and *chan song* (2nd class). *Chan song* have more seats and less elbow and leg room. The local buses are slower and cramped. The seats at the very back are reserved for monks (why, is a mystery), so be ready to move if necessary. For longer/overnight journeys a/c deluxe (sometimes known as *rot tour*) or VIP buses provide stewardess service, with food and drink supplied en route, and more leg room (plus constant Thai music or videos). Many fares include meals at roadside restaurants, so keep hold of your ticket. **NB** The overnight a/c buses are very cold.

● **Private tour buses**
Many tour companies operate bus services in Thailand; travel agents in Bangkok will supply information. These buses are normally more comfortable than the state buses but are more expensive. Overnight trips usually involve a meal stop (incl in price of ticket) and stewardess service for drinks and snacks. They often leave from outside the company office which may not be located at the central bus station.

● **Motorbike taxi**
These are becoming increasingly popular, and are the cheapest, quickest and most dangerous way to get from 'A' to 'B'. Riders wear coloured vests (sometimes numbered) and tend to congregate at important intersections or outside, eg shopping centres. Agree a price before boarding – expect to pay ฿10-20.

● **Saamlor ('three wheels')**
These come in the form of pedal or motorized machines. Saamlor drivers abound and will descend on travellers in any town. Fares should be bargained and agreed before setting off. The motorized saamlor is known affectionately as the *tuk-tuk* (because of the noise it makes).

● **Songthaew ('two rows')**
Songthaews are pick-up trucks fitted with two benches and can be found in many up-country towns. They normally run fixed routes, with set fares, but can often be hired and used as a taxi service (agree a price before setting out). To stop a songthaew use the electric buzzers or tap the side of the vehicle with a coin.

● **Taxi**
Standard taxis can be found in some Thai towns. This is the most expensive form of public motorized transport, and many now have the added luxury of air-conditioning. In Bangkok almost all taxis have meters. If unmetered, agree a price before setting off, and always bargain. In the S of Thailand, long-distance share taxis are common.

● **Postal services**
Local postal charges: ฿1 (postcard) and ฿2 (letter, 20 g). **International postal charges**: Europe and Australasia – ฿9 (postcard), ฿12.50 (letter, 10 g); US – ฿9 (postcard), ฿14.50 (letter, 10 g). Airletters cost ฿8.50. Poste Restante: correspondents should write the family name in capital letters and underline it, to avoid confusion.

Outside Bangkok, most post offices are open from 0800-1630 Mon-Fri and only the larger ones will be open on Sat.

Fax services: now widely available in most towns. Postal and telex/fax services are available in most large hotels.

● **Telephone services**
From Bangkok there is direct dialling to most countries. Outside Bangkok, it is best to go to a local telephone exchange for 'phoning outside the country.

Codes: local area codes vary according to province, they are listed under "Post & telecommunications" in each town; the code can also be found at the front of the telephone directory.

Directory inquiries: domestic long distance including Malaysia and Vientiane (Laos) – 101, Greater Bangkok BMA – 183, international calls T 2350030-5, although hotel operators will invariably help make the call if asked.

Callboxes cost ฿1. All telephone numbers marked in the text with a prefix 'B' mean that they are Bangkok numbers.

ENTERTAINMENT

● **Newspapers**
Until recently there were two major English language daily papers – the *Bangkok Post* and the *Nation Review* (known as *The Nation*). They provide good international news coverage and are Thailand's best known broadsheets.

● **Television and radio**
Five TV channels, with English language sound

track available on FM. Channel 3 – 105.5 MHz, Channel 7 – 103.5 MHz, Channel 9 – 107 MHz and Channel 11 – 88 MHz. The *Bangkok Post* stars programmes where English soundtrack is available on FM. Shortwave radio can receive the BBC World Service, Voice of America, Radio Moscow, see page 308.

HOLIDAYS AND FESTIVALS

Festivals with month only are movable; a booklet of holidays and festivals is available from most TAT offices.

Jan: *New Year's Day* (1st: public holiday).

Feb: *Magha Puja* (full-moon: public holiday) Buddhist holy day, celebrates the occasion when the Buddha's disciples miraculously gathered together to hear him preach. Culminates in a candle-lit procession around the temple *bot* (or ordination hall). The faithful make offerings and gain merit. *Chinese New Year* (movable, end of Jan/beginning of Feb) celebrated by Thailand's large Chinese population. The festival extends over 15 days; spirits are appeased, and offerings are made to the ancestors and to the spirits. Good wishes and lucky money are exchanged, and Chinese-run shops and businesses shut down.

Apr: *Chakri Day* (6th: public holiday) commemorates the founding of the present Chakri Dynasty. *Songkran* (movable: public holiday) marks the beginning of the Buddhist New Year and is particularly big in the N (Chiang Mai, Lampang, Lamphun and Chiang Rai). It is a 3 to 5 day celebration, with parades, dancing and folk entertainment. The first day represents the last chance for a 'spring clean'. Rubbish is burnt, in the belief that old and dirty things will cause misfortune in the coming year. The wat is the focal point. Revered Buddha images are carried through the streets, accompanied by singers and dancers. The second day is the main water-throwing day (originally an act of homage to ancestors and family elders). Young people pay respect by pouring scented water over the elders heads. The older generation sprinkle water over Buddha images. Gifts are given. This uninhibited water-throwing continues for all 3 days (although it is now banned in Bangkok). On the third day birds, fish and turtles are all released, to gain merit and in remembrance of departed souls.

May: *Coronation Day* (5th: public holiday) commemorates the present King Bhumibol's crowning in 1950. *Ploughing Ceremony* (movable: public holiday) performed by the King at Sanaam Luang near the Grand Palace in Bangkok. Brahmanic in origin, it traditionally marks the auspicious date when farmers could begin preparing their riceland. Impressive bulls decorated with flowers pull a sacred gold plough.

Jun: *Visakha Puja* (full-moon: public holiday) holiest of all Buddhist days, it marks the Buddha's birth, enlightenment and death. Candle-lit processions are held at most temples.

Aug: *The Queen's Birthday* (12th: public holiday). *Asalha Puja and Khao Phansa* (full-moon: public holiday) – commemorates the Buddha's first sermon to his disciples and marks the beginning of the Buddhist Lent. Monks reside in their monasteries for the 3 month Buddhist Rains Retreat to study and meditate, and young men temporarily become monks. Ordination ceremonies all over the country and villagers give white cotton robes to the monks to wear during the Lent ritual bathing.

Oct: *Ok Phansa* (3 lunar months after Asalha Puja) marks the end of the Buddhist Lent and the beginning of Krathin, when gifts – usually a new set of cotton robes – are offered to the monks. Particularly venerated monks are sometimes given silk robes as a sign of respect and esteem. Krathin itself is celebrated over two days. It marks the end of the monks' retreat and the re-entry of novices into secular society. Processions and fairs are held all over the country; villagers wear their best clothes and food, money, pillows and bed linen are offered to the monks of the local wat. *Chulalongkorn Day* (23rd: public holiday) honours King Chulalongkorn (1868-1910), perhaps Thailand's most beloved and revered king.

Nov: *Loi Krathong* (full-moon) a *krathong* is a small model boat made to contain a candle, incense and flowers. The festival comes at the end of the rainy season and honours the goddess of water. The little boats are pushed out onto canals, lakes and rivers. Sadly, few krathongs are now made of leaves: polystyrene has taken over and the morning after Loi Krathong lakes and river banks are littered with the wrecks of the night's festivities. **NB** The 'quaint' candles in flower pots sold in many shops at this time, are in fact large firecrackers.

Dec: *The King's Birthday* (5th: public holiday). Flags and portraits of the King are erected all over Bangkok, especially down Rachdamnern Ave and around the Grand Palace. *Constitution Day* (10th: public holiday). *New Year's Eve* (31st: public holiday).

NB Regional and local festivals are noted in appropriate sections.

Information for travellers

BEFORE TRAVELLING

Regulations for tourists and business people are in a constant state of flux. The information below was collated shortly prior to publication, but visitors must be ready for the possibility that new or altered regulations have come into force since then. Over the last few years though, the trend has been towards greater openness. Individual travel on public transport is possible, entry and exit regulations have been eased, and many more private hotels, guesthouses and tour companies have opened.

ENTRY REQUIREMENTS

● **Tourist visas**

As the Lao government is gradually making independent travel easier, it is likely that it will soon be possible to obtain a tourist visa in the usual way – from a Lao embassy or consulate. It is therefore worth checking with your home country Lao embassy or consulate (if there is one) beforehand.

Bangkok, Thailand: most people visiting Laos travel through Thailand and, as a result, Bangkok is the best place to arrange a visa. For many years the embassy in Bangkok would not issue visas to independent travellers and it was necessary to go through a tour/travel agent instead. Recently, however, the embassy has begun issuing 2-week visas costing ฿1,500 (normal) or ฿2,500 (express) (US$60 and US$100 respectively). Even so, many visitors find it is more convenient to use the services of one of the many travel agents in Bangkok. Most are located in those areas of the city where guesthouses are concentrated (in

particular Banglamphu, see page 236). Prices have been decreasing over the last few years and currently stand at about ฿1,600-฿2,000 or US$75 for a 15-day visa. The process takes about 3 working days, although it is possible to pay extra for an 'express' service. The 15-day visa can then be immediately extended in Vientiane for a further 15 days by visiting the sponsoring agency that supported the application. (Every travel agent in Bangkok must have a representative in Vientiane. The name should be written, but probably in Lao, on the visa.) To extend a visa costs US$3 a day. Note that some tour companies in Bangkok insist that you also buy a certain minimum amount of services – transport, accommodation, etc.

A cheaper alternative (US$30 or ฿750) is to ask a sponsoring agency in Vientiane to arrange a visa for you (this is effectively what the travel agents in Bangkok do). 30-day visitors' visas are available in this manner. The sponsoring agency will then telex confirmation through to the Lao Embassy in Bangkok which is then empowered to issue a visa. *Lipco*, T 215635, near Vientiane's Wattay airport (manager Bounneua Douang-pasenth) charges ฿500 and takes about 10 days to arrange a visa in this way. Other hotels and tour companies do the same eg: *Douang Deuane Hotel*, Vientiane, F (856-21) 222300 (but you must stay here too). Some visitors have also reported success arranging a visa through the Ministry of Foreign Affairs in Vientiane for little more than US$10, but this takes 10 weeks. The difficulty and danger with this approach is that it depends on a reliable contact in Vientiane and most visitors do not have such a contact.

Nong Khai, Thailand: visas can also be obtained from travel agents in Nong Khai, the Thai provincial capital near the new Friendship Bridge over the Mekong in Northeast Thailand. The cost is slightly higher than that charged by travel agents in Bangkok. One reliable set up is *The Meeting Place*, 117 Soi Chuenchitt, T/F (042) 421223, run by an Australian couple, although there are now many other tour and travel agents in the town doing much the same. The travel agent accompanies client to immigration on the border and visas are issued on the spot, ₿2,500. A Lao consulate is due to open in Nong Khai. See page 268 for crossing the border here.

Phnom Penh, Cambodia: it used to be quick and cheap getting visas from Cambodia. On the last check, it was costing US$40 and taking 2 weeks.

Yangon (Rangoon), Myanmar (Burma): visas are issued by the Lao embassy in Yangon (Rangoon) for US$25, available the next day, but note that these cannot be extended (see below).

Hanoi, Vietnam: visas available from the embassy at 40 Quang Trang but expensive at US$100 (open 0830-1100, 1430-1600). Transit and tourist visas available from Lao consulates in Ho Chi Minh City (Saigon) and Danang, but again comparatively pricey at US$25.

Mengla, China: 7-day visas are issued at the border near the Chinese town of Mengla. The nearest Lao settlement is Boten (see page 291 for details on crossing the border here).

● **Transit visas**
Usually valid for 7 days and can be obtained by tourists with a confirmed onward airline ticket. These are available from Lao embassies in Bangkok, Hanoi, Phnom Penh, Beijing, and Yangon (Rangoon) and from Lao consulates in Kunming (China), Ho Chi Minh City (Saigon, Vietnam) and Danang (Vietnam). As with regular tourist visas you can pay extra for an 'express' service. **NB** Transit visas are only valid for the Vientiane prefecture (municipal area) and cannot be extended. Those who overstay are fined when they leave the country.

● **Business and visitors' visas**
Business and visitors' visas valid for 30 days may be obtained from Laos' embassies and consulates, although the Lao Embassy in Bangkok often operates as an intermediary. The visa must be approved in Vientiane and requires a formal request from a business or governmental organization in Laos. Approval for issuing the visa is telexed to the appropriate embassy from Vientiane. The business requesting the visa should let the recipient of the visa know the number of the approval-telex sent from Vientiane, as this speeds up the process. A business visa allows travel throughout Laos, with multiple entries and exits. Business visas are renewable in Vientiane.

Visas on arrival Towards the end of 1996 there was some speculation that the Lao government would introduce a system of issuing visas on arrival in the country, possibly in 1997.

Visa restrictions on points of entry and exit Visas used to state the entry and exit points where the visa was to be used. This requirement was lifted at the beginning of 1996 and visas now permit visitors to enter and leave the country at any border post open to foreigners.

Visa extension Visas can be extended in Laos for a further 15 days at the cost of US$3/day. To do this, visit the sponsoring agency in Vientiane that supported your application. (Every travel agent in Bangkok must have a representative in Vientiane. The name should be written, but probably in Lao, on the visa.) Visitors have also reported that it is possible to extend visas by visiting the Immigration office in the Ministry of the Interior opposite the Morning Market in Vientiane or simply going to Lao Tourism in the capital. The cost is reportedly cheaper at US$1/day and takes 2 days to arrange. Note that visas issued in Yangon (Myanmar/Burma) cannot be extended (at present). Some travel agents in Vientiane take a slightly different approach to visa 'extension' and arrange for visitors to leave the country via the Friendship Bridge and then re-enter so that they can be issued with a new visa.

Visas for Thailand With recent changes to Thailand's visa regulations it is no longer necessary for nationals of most countries to obtain a visa in Vientiane before entering the Kingdom. If crossing by land, visas are issued at the Friendship Bridge. However, 3 month visas are available from the Thai Embassy on Thanon Phon Kheng in Vientiane for ₿300 and take about 3 days to process.

Passport photographs It is useful to take several passport photographs with you; they are sometimes used for permits to visit outlying areas.

Registering arrival and departure In most

towns in the N of the country it is necessary to register your arrival and departure: in effect, signing in and signing out. This is usually done at the airport with little hassle and the payment of a fee which ranges between 100 and 500 kip (for some reason, it varies between towns). For visitors with a tourist visa this is all that is required (note, though, that the need to register your arrival may not be obvious and failure to do so can result in a hefty fine). People with a **visitor** or **business** visa must **also** have their arrival card stamped at the local police station before they leave, for a fee of 500 kip. This is often done by hotels. Note that this signing in/signing out system does not operate in towns and cities S of Vientiane and may be suspended countrywide as security improves.

● **Vaccinations**

No vaccinations are required unless coming from an infected area; see page 288 for further details.

● **Entry/exit points**

The main port of entry, other than Vientiane's Wattay airport, is **Tha Deua** which can be reached by boat from Nong Khai in Thailand or via the Mittaphab Bridge. Visitors can also enter Laos at Thakhek, Savannakhet, Chongmek and Ban Houei Xai (all to/from Thailand), Lao Bao (from Vietnam) and Boten (from China). (See **Getting there** page 290.)

TOURS

Because visas still need to be secured through an approved travel or tour agent, many visitors to Laos arrive on a tour (but see the Visa section for ways to avoid booking a tour). In the past, tours allowed little flexibility in terms of accommodation, itinerary or mode of transport. This has changed and most outfits allow customers to customize their package (including choice of accommodation) depending on budget.

There are a number of Thai-based companies operating tours to Laos including Diethelm Travel, Kian Gwan Bldg II, 140/1 Witthayu Rd, Bangkok, T 2559150, F 2560248. See also under useful addresses on page 309. There are also a growing number of overseas companies including Laos on their itineraries. Among these are Explore Worldwide, Aldershot, T 01252 344161, F 01252 343170 (with offices

in Eire, Australia, New Zealand, USA and Canada); Images of Asia, London, T 0181 995 8280; Regent Holidays, Bristol, T 0117 921 1711, F 0117 925 4866, Email 106041,1470@compuserve.com; and Silk Steps, Bristol, T 0117 940 2800, F 0117 940 6900, Email 100677,3446@compuserve.com.

● **Tourist information**

Until independent privately-owned tour operators were permitted to set up shop in 1991, there was a tourist information vacuum in Laos. The official government-run **National Tourism Authority of Lao** is not renowned for its skills in information dissemination. The best source of up-to-date information is from recent travellers, whose comments and advice is documented in scrap books in Nong Khai guesthouses. At the speed with which events are moving in Laos, these sources become outdated very quickly. Certain tour agencies in Bangkok also keep bulletin boards of up-to-date records and travellers' tips, although these informal sources are becoming less useful as travelling becomes easier and information on travelling is more widely available.

There is a local telephone directory, called *How to Call Us and Our Friends*, which lists the telephone numbers of expats living in Vientiane as well as aid agencies and embassies.

The Womens International Group (WIG) produce the *Vientiane Guide*; very useful and full of up-to-date information and good maps. Another useful book is the *Guide to Wats in Vientiane*. There are state produced maps of Vientiane, Luang Prabang, Pakse, Savannakhet and other major towns (major is used advisedly) available but these are often in limited supply. Local maps and guides mentioned above are available at the *Lane Xang Hotel* shop, *Lani's Hotel* and *Raintree books*, all in Vientiane. For information on other maps of Laos, see page 306 Rounding Up.

WHEN TO GO

● **Best time to visit**

In the relatively cool and dry winter months from Nov to Mar. Temperatures in upland areas like the Plain of Jars and the Bolovens Plateau can drop to below freezing in winter. From Apr onwards, temperatures can exceed 40°C in many lowland areas. See page 23 for more details on climate. For monthly temperature graphs for various cities of the country see page 89 (Vientiane), page 118 (Luang Prabang), page 173 (Savannakhet) and page 188 (Pakse).

● **Clothing**

Informal, lightweight clothing is all that is needed, although a sweater is vital for the highlands in the winter months. An umbrella is useful during the rainy season. Sleeveless shirts and singlets, shorts and short skirts are generally frowned upon. When visiting monasteries (wats) women should keep their shoulders covered. In general, 'scruffy' travellers are frowned upon. One of the main reasons why tourism remains tightly controlled in Laos is because of the perceived corrosive effects that badly dressed tourists will have on Lao culture. The assumption is that scruffy dress is a reflection of character.

HEALTH

See the health section beginning on page 314 Rounding Up for more detailed advice on health and staying healthy.

● **Vaccinations**

No innoculations are required except a cholera vaccination if coming from an infected area. It is advisable to take full precautions before travelling to Laos. Hospitals are few and far between and medical facilities are poor. Tetanus, polio, hepatitis, rabies, typhoid and cholera injections are recommended.

● Staying healthy

It is inadvisable to tangle with dogs as **rabies** is rife in Laos and if you are planning to visit rural areas it is advisable to have an anti-rabies jab. **Malaria:** malaria pills are **strongly** advised if travelling outside Vientiane; about a third of the population contracts malaria at some stage in their lives. As a precaution wear long sleeved shirts and trousers, particularly at dusk, and use insect repellent, a mosquito net, coils etc. Contact your doctor concerning the latest advice on malaria prophylactics.

● Food and water

Urban areas have access to safe water, but all water should be boiled or sterilized before drinking. Cheap bottled water is widely available – as are fizzy drinks. Less than a third of rural areas have safe water. Do not swim in stagnant water for risk of bilharzia. Restaurant food is, on the whole, hygienically prepared, and as long as street stall snacks have been well cooked, they are usually fine.

● Medical facilities

Medical services are restricted by a lack of trained personnel and facilities and standards are poor – particularly at district and rural level. There is only one doctor to every 4,545 people. Emergency treatment is available at the Mahosot Hospital and Clinique Settathirath in Vientiane but better facilities are available in Thailand. The Australian and Swedish embassies have clinics – both charge a small fee – for smaller problems. Emergency evacuation to Udon Thani (Thailand) can be arranged at short notice. It is wise to carry a first aid pack in case of emergency. Pharmacies are usually poorly stocked.

Travelling with children: you will need to bring all essentials. Disposable nappies (diapers) are now available in Vientiane.

MONEY

● Currency

The kip is the currency unit: US$1 = 720 kip, ฿ = 37 (late 1996). Denominations in notes used to start at the diminutive – and useless – 1 kip (even in Laos 1 kip, which equals a majestic one tenth of a US cent, can't buy a great deal). 10 and 20 kip notes have also become useless objects of veneration, although you may be handed them at the post office which appears to be their last repository. More commonly used notes are 50, 100, 500 and the newish 1,000 kip note. Most people get by using just the 100, 500 and 1,000; there are no coins in circulation. As the highest

denomination note in normal circulation is worth not much more than US$1, pockets tend to bulge with huge wads of kip.

It is getting much easier to change currency and TCs in Laos. **Le Banque pour Commerce Exterieur Lao,** the **Lao Mai Bank,** and the **Phak Thai Bank** change most major international currencies (cash) and TCs denominated in US$, pounds sterling and French francs. Note that some banks charge a hefty commission of US$2 per TC, so it is sensible to take TCs in larger denominations. While banks will change TCs and cash denominated in most major currencies into kip, some will only change US$ into Thai baht, or into US$ cash. (In other words, some banks will not change pounds sterling and French Francs into Thai baht or US$ – just kip.) It is easier to carry US dollars cash in small denominations or Thai baht when travelling, changing them as you go (most shops and restaurants will give you kip for US dollars or baht). Since the government scrapped its multi-tier exchange rates there has been no black market, and everyone knows the bank rate.

More expensive items eg, tours, car hire, hotels, etc tend to be quoted in dollars (or baht) while smaller purchases are quoted in kip. Thai baht is readily accepted in most towns but it is advisable to carry kip in rural areas (buses, for example, will usually only accept kip). It is quite normal to be quoted a price in kip, US dollars and baht. Nor is it unheard of to pay for a meal in three different currencies and certainly to be handed a bill quoting, for good measure, the total in kip, baht and $.

The kip is non-convertible, so once you leave Laos any remaining notes are useless. It is illegal to enter the country with more than 100,000 baht (US$4,000) without prior clearance.

● Credit cards

Now that Laos has reformed its banking laws and welcomed foreign investment, so payment by credit card is becoming easier – although beyond the larger hotels in Vientiane and Luang Prabang do not expect to be able to get by on plastic. American Express, Visa, Mastercard/Access, Bangkok Bank and MBF cards are accepted in a limited number of more upmarket establishments. **Le Banque pour Commerce Exterieur Lao** will advance cash on credit cards but only after they have telexed Bangkok for clearance. They charge for the cost of this extra administration.

● **Currency regulation**

There are no restrictions on the import or export of foreign currencies other than Thai baht: a maximum of ₿100,000 can be brought into Laos. The Lao kip is a non-convertible currency, but inside Laos it is now as much in demand as US dollars and baht.

GETTING THERE

AIR

● **From Thailand**

Bangkok is the main gateway to Vientiane. If you want to visit Bangkok as well as Laos, the best way is to include the Bangkok-Vientiane sector on your long-haul ticket. This is a cheaper option than purchasing tickets separately in Bangkok. There are daily flights between Vientiane and Bangkok operated by **Thai Airways** and **Lao Aviation**. Both charge the same fare (US$105 one way, US$210 return) and now that Lao Aviation have retired their Antonov 24 turboprops and replaced them with Boeing 737s on this sector, there is little to choose between the airlines. International flights can be paid for using credit cards: Amex and Visa only. At the beginning of 1995, Lao Aviation began a twice-weekly service between **Chiang Mai**, in Northern Thailand, and Vientiane. It is likely that a new international service between Luang Prabang and Chiang Mai will open in 1997, probably operated by **Thai**.

The preferred route out of Laos for many expats is via the Thai city of Udon Thani in Northeast Thailand. This is because the domestic air fare from Udon to Bangkok is half that of the international fare between Vientiane and Bangkok. To get to Udon, take the Mittaphab (Friendship) Bridge across the Mekong and then a taxi or bus to Udon, just over 50 km S. **Thai** operates 2 flights a day, each way, between Bangkok and Udon. There is a wide range of hotels and guesthouses in Udon. See page 262 for more information on Udon Thani.

● **From Vietnam and Cambodia**

There are 4 return flights a week between **Vientiane and Hanoi** operated by **Lao Aviation** and **Vietnam Airlines**, and flights to and from **Ho Chi Minh** (Saigon) once a week.

The **Vientiane-Phnom Penh** route has 2 return flights a week, which drops in on Saigon en route.

● **From China**

China Southern Airlines flies between Vientiane and **Kunming** and **Guangzhou** (Canton) once a week. **Lao Aviation** has one connection a week each with Kunming and Xishuang Banna.

Overland connections with Laos

As Laos has eased overland access for foreigners, so the number of access points has multiplied. This table is designed to help make sense of border crossings and provide cross references to the relevant sections of text. In mid-1996 there were two overland crossings open between Laos and Vietnam, one between Laos and China, and four between Laos and Thailand. The border with Cambodia was closed. Two additional border crossings with Vietnam are expected to open in 1997/1998 (see table).

Border crossings with Thailand (North to South)

Ban Houei Xai – Chiang Khong (see pages 168 and 254)
Vientiane/Tha Deua – Nong Khai (see pages 113, 291 and 268)
Thakhek – Nakhon Phanom (see pages 172 and 270)
Savannakhet – Mukdahan (see page 177 and 273)
Pakse – Chongmek/Ubon Ratchathani (see pages 193 and 260)

Border crossings with Vietnam (North to South)

Muang Khua – Deo Tay Chang/Dien Bien Phu (should open in 1998)
Savannakhet/Xiepong – Lao Bao (Route 9) (see page 177)
Xieng Khoung/Phonsavanh – Nong Het (should open in 1997/1998) (Route 7)

Border crossings with China

Boten – Mengla

● **From Myanmar (Burma)**

There is one connection a week between Yangon (Rangoon) and Vientiane.

● **From Singapore**

Silk Air have 2 flights a week between Singapore and Vientiane.

NB With the reduction of trade with, and aid from, the CIS, Lao Aviation has found it difficult to stock enough spare parts to keep its ageing Antonovs in the air on the few routes it does operate. Services may be curtailed as planes are regularly grounded. **Thai Airways** is the agent for **Lao Aviation** in Bangkok: 491/17 Ground Flr, Silom Plaza, Silom Rd, Bangkok, T 2369822. Tickets bought in Bangkok on Lao Aviation are **not** refundable in Laos.

Lao Aviation's office in Chiang Mai (Thailand) is at 240 Phrapoklao Rd, T 418258, F 418260. In Hanoi, Vietnam: Vietnam Veterans Tourism Services Co Ltd, 41 Quang Trung St, T/F 8229951. In Ho Chi Minh City (Saigon), Vietnam: 93A Pasteur Rd, Quan 1, T/F 8226990. In Phnom Penh, Cambodia: 58B Sihanouk St, Khana Tonle Basak, T/F 426563. In Kunming, China and Yangon/Rangoon, Myanmar/Burma the agents for Lao Aviation are China Yunnan Airlines (T 3121-220, F 3168437) and Myanmar Airlines (T 84566, F 89583) respectively.

● **New Lao Aviation routes**

At the end of 1996, Lao Aviation had the following routes/flights in the pipeline: Vientiane-Yangon (more departures); Vientiane-Singapore; Vientiane-Kunming (more departures); Vientiane-Hong Kong; Vientiane-Taipei (Republic of China); and Vientiane-Xishuang Banna (more departures).

ROAD

The **Thai-Lao Mittaphab (Friendship) Bridge** opened in 1994 (see page 90). Crossing the border at Tha Deua is very easy, open Mon-Sun 0800-1730. Immigration and customs are on both sides of the bridge and a bus transports visitors across (฿20 from Thailand, ฿10 from Laos). Tuk-tuks wait at both customs houses to take visitors either on to Vientiane, 15 mins (฿60) or to Nong Khai in Thailand (฿20). Note that it is necessary to bargain particularly assiduously on the Thai side of the frontier. Buses and taxis from Vientiane leave from the Morning Market. **NB** Do not travel with anybody else's belongings.

The most popular crossing point between Vietnam and Laos is at **Lao Bao**, NW of Hué in Vietnam and E of Savannakhet in Laos, situated in the Annamite chain of mountains which forms a spine separating Laos and Vietnam. (For more information on this crossing point, see page 178, Xepon.) It is important to have your Vietnamese visa stamped with Lao Bao as an exit point (do this when applying for the visa). For some reason, if the Lao visa is acquired in Phnom Penh, then they may not endorse a Lao Bao exit point. To change exit point costs US\$15 in Hanoi (visit *Vietnam Tourism*), US\$20 in Danang and US\$8 in Saigon/Ho Chi Minh City. Hué immigration will not change an exit point. From the border, entering Laos, the last bus to Savannakhet leaves at 1500, arriving 2400, with no food stops.

BOAT

There is an official border post on the Mekong River at the Thai town of **Nong Khai** with a crossing to **Tha Deua** (25 km from Vientiane) but this is only open for locals; tourists must use the bridge. There are regular ferries from 0800-1700, Mon-Fri and 0800-1200, Sat, across the Mekong at **Thakhek** to **Nakhon Phanom** (Thailand) (฿20).

Ferries run between Hua Wiang, 2 km N of **Chiang Khong** (Thailand) and **Ban Houei Xai** (฿20).

Regular ferries between **Savannakhet** and **Mukdahan** (Thailand) between 0830-1700, Mon-Fri, 0830-1230 Sat (฿30).

It is possible to cross the Mekong (100 kip) to **Chongmek** (Thailand) from **Pakse** (see page 193 for details).

From **Cambodia**, the entry point is at **Muang Saen**, across the Mekong River from **Phumi Khampong Sralan** but this crossing is not currently open to foreigners.

From **China** the frontier is close to the Lao town of **Boten**. The nearest Chinese town is **Mengla**. (To get to Mengla, take a bus from Jinghong, 6 hrs and 25 yuan.) From Mengla there are frequent buses to the border (Shaoyong) from 0730, 8 yuan. At the frontier it is possible to change remaining yuan into Lao kip. There are no money changing facilities on the Lao side of the border although *Vieng Champa Tour* will convert US\$ cash at a poor rate of exchange. Around midday buses arrive to take new arrivals on to towns like Luang Namtha and Udom Xai (Muang Xai).

CUSTOMS

● Duty free allowance
500 cigarettes, 2 bottles of wine and a bottle of liquor. There is a small but well-stocked duty-free shop on the Lao side at Tha Duea – and at Wattay Airport.

● Export restrictions
Laos has a strictly enforced ban on the export of antiquities and all Buddha images. The last person to try stealing a Buddha caused the government to close the country to tourists for a year.

ON ARRIVAL

● Airport information
Wattay International Airport is about 6 km from Vientiane. This is what airports used to be like when Comets and Constellations ruled the skyways. Decrepit to the point of charm there isn't a moving walkway or computer in sight. Foreign exchange desk (no exchange of kip to US$ or Thai baht), duty free shop, gift shop, post office, snack bar and VIP salon open for arrivals and departures. Flight information: T 212066.

Transport to town **By bus**: local buses operate from Luang Prabang Rd outside the airport every 45 mins (200 kip). **By taxi**: fares payable in US$, baht or kip: 1-2,000 kip to centre of town (bargain). **By tuk-tuk**: around 1,000 kip to the town centre; it may be necessary to walk out onto the main road to catch one (they usually wait near the airport entrance).

● Airport tax
US$5 on departure for international flights; 300 kip on domestic departures.

● Conduct
Wats Lao monks are said to be not as disciplined as Thai monks – probably owing to the effects of 15 years of Communism – but Buddhism is undergoing a resurgence. If talking to a monk your head should be lower than his. Avoid visiting a wat around 1100 as this is when the monks have their morning meal. It is considerate to ask the abbot's permission to enter the *sim* and shoes should be removed on entry. When sitting down, feet should point away from the altar and main image. Arms and legs should be fully covered when visiting wats. A small donation is often appropriate (kneel when putting it into the box).

Forms of address Lao people are addressed by their first name, not their family name, even when a title is used.

Greeting The *nop* or *wai* – with hands together and head bowed, as if in prayer – remains the traditional form of greeting. Shaking hands, though, is very widespread – more so than in neighbouring Thailand. This can be put down to the influence of the French during the colonial period. Thailand was never colonized.

In private homes Remove shoes. When seated on the floor you should tuck your feet behind you. Do not pat children on the head, as it is the most sacred part of the body.

Eating etiquette In Laos, who eats when is important. At a meal, a guest should not begin eating until his host has invited him or her to do so. Nor should the guest continue eating after everyone else has finished. At a family gathering, the eating order is dictated by age: mother and father take the first food, and then each child in order of their descending age. It is also customary for guests to leave a small amount of food on their plate; to do otherwise would imply that the guest was still hungry and that the host had not provided sufficient food for the meal.

General Pointing with the index finger is considered rude.

● Emergencies
Ambulance: T 195. **Fire brigade**: T 190. **Police**: T 191.

● Hours of business
Government offices: 0800-1700 Mon-Fri but often closed for 2 hrs at lunchtime (usually 1200-1400). **Banks**: 0800-1200, 1400-1500 Mon-Fri; some banks also open on Sat mornings. **Shops**: 0900-1700 Mon-Sat and some on Sun.

● Official time
7 hrs ahead of GMT.

● Photographs
Sensitivity pays when taking photographs. Be very wary in areas that have (or could have) military importance – such as airports, where all photography is prohibited. Also be careful when photographing official functions and parades without permission. Always ask permission before photographing in a monastery.

● Safety
Crime rates are very low but it is advisable to take obvious precautions. Most areas of Laos are safe although vehicles on the roads in the N are periodically ambushed by bandits. In Nov 1995 anti-government Hmong tribesmen attacked a convoy on the main Vientiane-Luang Prabang road, injuring two French tourists and

killing four Laotians. On 30 June 1996 a vehicle from a Swedish aid agency was attacked by bandits (probably Hmong) on the same highway. 2½ months later on 11 September 1996 a van carrying a group of employees of Sodetour was also attacked on the same road near Kasi. Four were killed, including the company's owner and manager Claude Vincent, and one seriously injured. Other routes prone to attack include the road between Luang Prabang and Xieng Khouang. Check with locals for latest information on the state of banditry on the roads of the country.

The Golden Triangle area is unsafe because of the opium trade and foreigners can be mistaken for spies. Xieng Khouang province, the Bolovens Plateau, Xam Neua, and areas along the Ho Chi Minh Trail are littered with *bombis* – small anti-personnel mines and bomblets from cluster bomb units. There are also many large unexploded bombs; in many villages they have been left lying around. They are very unstable so **DO NOT TOUCH**. Five to 10 people are still killed or injured every month in Laos by inadvertently stepping on ordnance, or hitting 'pineapple' bomblets with hoes.

● **Shopping**

Best buys from Laos are minority or hilltribe artefacts and textiles.

Antique textiles from N Laos sell from US$40 upwards. It is hard to find 'antique' textiles in good condition as old *pha sin* (sarongs) are worn over new ones for work or bathing and so wear out quickly. Carol Cassidy in Vientiane (see page 111) has revived high quality traditional weaving and her weavers are producing work of an exceptionally high quality. Prices, though, can run into thousands of US$ for these museum quality pieces.

A wide variety of modern materials are sometimes used to make the *pha sin*, the Lao sarong, and *pha baeng*, or shawl, worn by Lao women. The latter became high-fashion in Bangkok in the early 1990s, after the Thai princess Mahachakri Sirindhorn took to wearing them on her return from Laos. The bridal *sin* is a popular buy; it is usually plain with a single motif repeated over most of the material, but with an elaborate border. Gold and silver thread, *tdinjok*, is often woven into the border pattern. Lao weavers have been isolated from external influences and have maintained many of their original patterns and styles. Most of the materials are sold in weaving villages or are available from markets in the main towns. For more background on Lao textiles see page 51.

Making **silverware** is a traditional craft in Laos – most of it is in the form of jewellery and small silver pots (though they may not be made of silver). Luang Prabang is reputed to produce the best silverware (see page 139) but this may just reflect received wisdom rather than reality. The finest silversmiths, with one or two exceptions, work out of Vientiane. Chunky antique 'tribal' jewellery, bangles, pendants, belts and earrings, are often sold in markets in the main towns, or antique shops in Vientiane.

Craftsmen in Laos are still producing **wood carvings** for temples and coffins. Designs are usually traditional, with a religious theme. Craftsmen produce carved panels and statues for tourists, which are available in outlets in Vientiane.

● **Student cards**

International Student Identity Cards (ISIC) are useful. They sometimes permit free admission to museums and sights, at other times a substantial discount on the entrance charge.

● **Tipping**

It is not common practice, even in hotels but it is normal to tip guides.

● **Voltage**

220 volts, 50 cycles in the main towns. 110 volts in the country. 2 pin sockets are common so adaptors are required. For sensitive equipment it is advisable to use a voltage regulator. Blackouts are common outside Vientiane and many smaller towns are not connected to the national grid and only have power during the evening and early night.

● **Weights and measures**

Metric along with local systems of measurement.

WHERE TO STAY

● **Accommodation**

Rooms in Laos are rarely luxurious and standards vary enormously – you can end up paying double what you would pay in Bangkok. However the hotel industry is expanding rapidly: many older buildings are under renovation, and new hotels are springing up – some in conjunction with Thai companies. Only the *Tai-pan, Royal, Novotel* and *Lane Xang* in Vientiane and the *Villa Santi, Phou Vao* and *L'Hotel Souvannaphoum* in Luang Prabang come into the 1st class bracket. Of these only

Hotel classifications

A US$50-100 (70,000-140,000 kip)
First class: business services, sports facilities (gym, swimming pool etc), Asian and Western restaurants, bars, and discotheques. Only hotels in Vientiane and a couple in Luang Prabang could be said to meet these requirements although there are charming, well run and very comfortable smaller hotels elsewhere.

B US$25-50 (17,500-35,000 kip)
Tourist class: all rooms will have air-conditioning and an attached bathroom, perhaps a swimming pool, restaurant, 24-hr coffee shop/room service and cable films.

C US$15-25 (10,500-17,500 kip)
Economy: air-conditioning, attached bathrooms. Restaurant and room service.

D US$8-15 (5,600-10,500 kip)
Budget: no air-conditioning, attached bathroom. Bed linen and towels, and there may be a restaurant.

E US$4-8 (2,800-5,600 kip)
Guesthouse: fan-cooled rooms, shared bathroom facilities. 'Squat' toilets. Bed linen but no towels. Rooms will probably be small, facilities few.

F US$<4 (<2,800 kip) -
Guesthouse: fan-cooled rooms, usually with shared bathroom facilities. Squat toilets. Variable standards of cleanliness.

the *Novotel* could be said to approach international standards in terms of the range of facilities on offer. *Sodetour* (the Vientiane-based travel and tour company) now runs some beautifully renovated colonial houses and chalets in the S. There is a reasonable choice of hotels of different standards and prices in Vientiane, Luang Prabang and Pakse.

The majority of hotels have fans and attached bathrooms, although more are providing a/c where there is a stable electricity supply; others are installing their own generators. Smaller provincial towns have only a handful of hotels and guesthouses – some of them quaint French colonial villas. In rural villages people's homes are enthusiastically transformed into bed and breakfasts on demand. Tourism infrastructure still has a long way to go before it approaches international standards. Expect to pay upwards of US$15 for a basic air-conditioned double room with attached bathroom in a Western-style hotel.

Note that while mid-range hotels offer reasonably good value for money compared with Thailand, guesthouses at the lower end of the market can seem overpriced. As independent tourism expands this is likely to change rapidly. For the present, though, hotels outside the main tourist destinations are thin on the ground and some provincial capitals will only have one place to stay – and that will be geared largely to visiting officials.

FOOD AND DRINK

FOOD

Expect to pay between US$2-10/head for a meal in main towns and less outside. By eating Lao food in local restaurants it is possible to pay US$1 or less for a meal.

● **Cuisine**

There are many similarities between Lao and Thai food, although it is slightly less influenced by Chinese cuisine. Lao dishes are distinguished by the use of aromatic herbs (including marijuana) and spices such as lemon grass, chillies, ginger and tamarind. Coconut fat is used sparingly. Food takes a long time to prepare and does not keep well, which goes some way to explaining why many restaurants do not offer local dishes, or if they do, they demand advance warning. The best places to try Lao food is often from roadside stalls or in the markets.

The staple Lao foods are **glutinous rice** (*kao niao*) and fermented fish or *pa dek*, often laced with liberal spoons of *nam pa*, or fish sauce. *Nam pa*, or **fish sauce**, like *nam plaa* in Thailand, *nuoc mam* in Vietnam, and *ngan-pyaye* in Myanmar (Burma), is an essential element of Laotian gastronomic life. No meal would be complete without a small dish of *nam pa*, and it is spooned onto almost any savoury dish. To make *nam pa*, freshwater fish are packed into containers and steeped in brine. (Elsewhere, fish sauce is made mostly from small saltwater fish species, but because Laos is landlocked, freshwater fish are used in their place.) The resulting brown liquid – essentially the by-products of slowly putrifying fish – is drained off and bottled. *Pa dek* is *nam pa* with knobs on – or rather *nam pa* with small chunks of fermented fish added, often with rice husks too. It tends to be used in cooking rather than as a condiment and is usually kept in an earthenware pot – often outside as the aroma is so strong!

Restaurant classifications

♦♦♦♦ Over US$15 (10,500 kip) for a meal. A 3-course meal in a restaurant with pleasant decor. Beers, wines and spirits available.

♦♦♦ US$5-15 (3,500-10,500 kip) for a meal. Two courses, reasonable surroundings.

♦♦ US$2-5 (1,400-3,500 kip) for a meal, probably only a single course, surroundings spartan but adequate.

♦ Under US$2 (under 1,400 kip). Single course, often makeshift surroundings such as a street kiosk with simple benches and tables.

Being a landlocked country, most of the fish is fresh from the Mekong. Mutton (goat) is practically unheard of and beef (water buffalo) expensive, so most of the dishes are variations on two themes: fish and bird. There is also a health and technological reason for this: without refrigerators, anyone slaughtering a cow, pig or water buffalo needs to be sure there are enough buyers to purchase all the meat in one day. Outside big towns there is neither the demand nor refridgerators to warrant such a slaughter – except when there is a festival and other significant events, like a wedding. But the Lao cookbook does not stop at chickens and turkeys (there are thousands of turkeys in Luang Prabang, thanks to an esoteric aid project which farm them). The rule of thumb is that if it has wings and feathers, it's edible. In some areas, such as Luang Prabang, the province's birds have long-since been eaten. In the S, where the forests have not (yet) been denuded, wild foods are more plentiful and it is not unusual to see pangolin, deer and turtle on the menu.

The most common vegetables are aubergines, tomatoes, cucumbers and lettuce, often cooked together, puréed and eaten with sticky rice. Soups are eaten at the middle or end of a meal but never at the beginning. They are usually a mixture of fish and meat infused with aromatic herbs. One would have thought, in a place like Laos, that fruit would be on every menu. But, perhaps because familiarity breeds contempt, many restaurants will have no fruit of any kind – even at breakfast and particularly in places not geared to foreigners.

Laap, also meaning 'luck' in Lao, is a traditional ceremonial dish made from (traditionally) raw fish or meat crushed into a paste, marinated in lemon juice and mixed with

chopped mint. It is said to be similiar to Mexican *cerviche*. It is called *laap sin* if it has a meat base and *laap pa* if it's fish based. Beware of *laap* in cheap street restaurants – sometimes it is concocted from raw offal and served cold; this should be consumed with great caution. *Phanaeng kai* is stuffed chicken with pork, peanuts and coconut milk with a dash of cinnamon. *Kai ping* is grilled chicken eaten with sticky rice.

Soups – there are several different types – include *keng no mai* (bamboo shoot soup), *keng khi lek* (vegetable and buffalo skin), *ken chut* (without pimentos) *keng kalami* (cabbage soup with fish or pork), *kenghet bot* (mushroom soup).

The Lao are partial to **sweets**: sticky rice with coconut milk and black beans (which can be bought in bamboo tubes in the markets) and grilled bananas are favourites.

There is a well-ingrained **Vietnamese** culinary tradition and **Chinese** food is never hard to find. *Feu*, Vietnamese noodle soup, is itself an import from China but masquerades in Laos as a Lao dish. It is usually served with a plate of raw vegetables. Most restaurants outside the main towns do not have menus but will nearly always serve *feu* and *laap* or local specialities. Indeed their generic name is *raan khai feu* – restaurants that sell *feu*.

The French in Laos left a legacy of sophisticated cuisine. **French** food is widely available, with street cafés serving delectable fresh *croissants, baguettes, pain au chocolat* and a selection of sticky pastries, which can be washed down with a powerful cup of Lao coffee. The Lao however have a habit of eating *baguette* sandwiches with fish sauce sprinkled on top – these are available in Vientiane, Savannakhet and Pakse. Menus in many of Vientiane's restaurants still have a distinctly French flavour to them – frogs' legs included. Vintage Bordeaux and Burgundies occasionally emerge from the cellars of restaurants too – although most of the fine vintages have now been consumed. Hotels in main towns often provide international menus and continental breakfasts. Even in small towns it is easy enough to create a continental breakfast: baguettes are widely available, wild honey can usually be tracked down, and fresh Bolovens' coffee is abundant (although tragically 'Nescafé' seems to be making insidious inroads). Some people recommend taking a jar of jam or peanut butter to spread on the baguettes. The Lao prefer theirs either with 'paté' – more like spam – or with thick and sweetened condensed milk. It may be significant that while the French left to their former colonies in Southeast Asia, the art of baking and great coffee, the British bestowed such practical things as railways and roads. Perhaps this says something about their respective national characters.

The best Lao cookbook is Phia Sing's *Traditional recipes of Laos* (Prospect Books: Totnes, Devon, UK, 1995).

DRINK

● Beer

Imported beer, wines and spirits can be found in hotels, restaurants, bars and nightclubs but are not particularly cheap. *Beer Lao* (standard and '33' export brew) is a light lager (although the alcohol content is 5%) best served ice-cold. In towns without power it is normal to add ice. *Beer Lao* also has the advantage of being reasonably priced: from about US$1 for a large bottle, depending on the restaurant or bar. Chinese beer is cheaper still and can be found in the northern provinces. French wines can be purchased (at a price) in some supermarkets and quite a few restaurants.

The local brew is rice wine and is traditionally drunk from a clay jug with long straws. The white variety is called *lau-lao* – 'Lao alcohol' – and is made from fermented sticky rice. Red lau-lao – or *fanthong* – is fermented with herbs. Bottled lau-lao is also widely available – *Sticky Rice* brand is the best; always ensure that the screw-top bottles are sealed.

● Soft drinks and bottled water

Soft drinks are expensive – they are imported from Thailand. A can of coke in a stall costs about 600 kip, a bottle some 300 kip. *Nam saa*, weak Chinese tea, is always served with strong coffee and is free. There is now local fresh milk production, so milk and yoghurt are available. **Bottled water** is widely available and produced locally, so it is cheap (about 200 kip for about 1 litre).

● Bars and discos

Most larger towns have bars and 'discos'. But a Lao disco is usually a place where live rather than recorded music is played. In 1996 the government tried to crack down on what was felt to be Thai cultural imperialism and stipulated that bands had to play at least 70% Lao music (as opposed to Thai or Western). They also banned karaoke bars for the same sort of reason: moral depravity. This latter edict seemed to be only weakly enforced in smaller towns and may well have been lifted by the time this book is on the shelves.

GETTING AROUND

PRACTICALITIES

Very few bus/truck/tuk-tuk or taxi drivers understand any foreign languages (except Thai). In order to travel to a particular destination, it is a great advantage to have the name written out in Lao. Map reading is out of the question, and many people will not know road names. However, they will know where all the sights of interest are – eg thats, markets, monuments, waterfalls, etc.

In the N of Laos, it is still important to get your passport stamped in and out of any given town. Failure to do so can result in a hefty fine. In the S, this is no longer necessary. It is probably only a matter of time before this becomes unnecessary throughout the country.

AIR

Many of the major towns are serviced by **Lao Aviation**. Tickets can be purchased from their office in Vientiane. Note that on domestic flights it is not possible to pay with credit cards. (Lao Aviation accept Visa and Amex on their international routes.) Some of Lao Aviation's aeroplanes leave a great deal to be desired; many have bald tyres and one wonders how they still fly. However, it is still the quickest and most convenient form of travel. The purchase of new ATRs (French-built) which service the more popular domestic routes and 737s on the Bangkok-Vientiane route has improved matters. For business travellers, there is an Australian helicopter charter service based at Wattay airport. **Lao Aviation**, at least on its domestic routes, seems to operate on the rather charming principle of *c'est la vie*. Planes are overbooked, underbooked, leave 30 mins early, 2 hrs late, or not at all. Some passengers have even been ticketed (in Lao) to towns they had no wish or intention of visiting – presumably on the basis that they might like the places. As a tourist this can be amusing, even enchanting; as a businessman or woman it can, though, be slightly frustrating.

From Vientiane to (return):

Phonsavanh/Xieng Khouang	US$74
Luang NamTha	US$160
Savannakhet	US$122
Salavan	US$182
Pakse	US$190
Luang Prabang	US$92

If travelling on a series of internal flights it is

Know your plates

PLATE COLOUR	COLOUR OF NUMBER	CATEGORY
Yellow	Red	Private
Yellow	Blue	Resident expat
White	Blue	Diplomat
Blue	White	Ministry, NGO
Red	White	Military
Black	White	Commercial, state enterprise
Black	Yellow	Commercial, private enterprise

necessary to have each leg of the journey reconfirmed. Lao Aviation will only give the departure time for the next leg, requiring that passengers have this checked and written in at each break in the journey. Many hotels will undertake this tiresome task for their guests. For further details on routes see the timetable and route map on pages 324-326.

BUS/TRUCK

It is now possible to travel to most areas of the country by bus, truck or songthaew (converted pick-up truck). The only stretches of road to avoid are the road from Luang Prabang to Phonsavanh (Xieng Khouang) and from Vang Vieng to Luang Prabang. Both have been plagued by bandits ambushing vehicles and the latter stretch (Vientiane-Luang Prabang) is particularly risky (see **Safety**, page 292).

Though it may be possible to travel by road to many areas of the country this is not to imply that road travel is a breeze. Many roads are unsealed, buses are overloaded and break-downs are frequent. One of the most common phrases to be heard is *rot taay* – 'dead' vehicle. For some connections you may need to wait days and journeys can vary enormously in the length of time they take, depending on the weather conditions. During the rainy season (Jun-Dec) expect journey times to be even longer than those listed in the table on page 323; indeed some roads may be closed altogether. Travellers can often negotiate a price if travelling by truck and it seems to be quite easy to hitch. Note that something like 40% of government expenditure is on transport and communications – and much of that on road construction and improvement. Roads are being upgraded and new vehicles slowly introduced so, in theory, journey times should only get shorter. For further details on bus times and fares see the box on page 323.

CAR HIRE

Car hire is anything from US$40-80/day, depending on the vehicle, with first 150 km free, then US$10 every 100 km after that. Price includes a driver. *Jo Rumble (Asia Vehicle Rental)*, T 217493 or 314927 in Vientiane, seems reliable.

OTHER LAND TRANSPORT

● **Bicycle and motorcycle hire**
Bicycles are available in many towns and a cheap way to see the sights. Chinese bikes tend to be better than Thai ones. Many guesthouses have bikes for rent. There are a small number of motorcycles available too.

● **Tuk-tuk/saamlor/trishaw**
Saamlors (literally 'three wheels') or trishaws can be hired in most towns, although they are becoming increasingly rare in Vientiane. Negotiate the price before boarding – it may be helpful to get someone to write your destination down. Outside Vientiane a short trip around town should cost about 200-400 kip depending on the town, the distance, and your bargaining prowess. The majority of motorized three-wheelers known as 'jumbos' or tuk-tuks (a name derived from the noise they make) are large motorbike taxis with two bench seats in the back although Thai-style tuk-tuks are becoming increasingly numerous.

● **Taxi**
Taxis are available, but they are unwilling to travel any distance on an unsealed road.

● **Hitchhiking**
This is well worth trying and unlike Thailand, for example, drivers are likely to stop. At some border crossings it is the only way to secure transport although in such instances it is usual to pay for the journey. Note, though, that there are very few vehicles in Laos and almost no

private cars – expect to hitch on lorries. Reports from travellers indicate that hitching is comparatively productive.

BOAT

It is possible to take river boats up and down the Mekong and its main tributaries. The Mekong is navigable from Ban Houei Xai on the border with Thailand downriver to S of Pakse. En route boats stop at Luang Prabang, Vientiane, Thakhek and Savannakhet as well as other smaller towns and villages. But there is no scheduled service and departures may be limited during the dry season. Boats leave at the last minute, and speaking Lao is definitely an advantage here. Boats are basic but cheap: 27,000 kip for the 'fast' boat between Ban Houei Xai and Luang Prabang; another 47,250 kip from Luang Prabang to Vientiane. Take food and drink and expect somewhat crowded conditions aboard. Prices vary according to size of boat and length of journey. Downriver from Luang Prabang to Vientiane takes 4 days, travelling up to 10 hrs a day. There are plenty of boats available from Luang Prabang, travelling up or down river. The most common riverboats are the *hua houa leim*, with no decks, the hold being enclosed by side panels and a flat roof; note that metal boats get very hot.

COMMUNICATIONS

● Language

Lao is the national language but there are many local dialects. French is spoken by government officials and hotel staff, and many educated people over 40. Most government officials and many shopkeepers have some command of English.

Lao is closely related to Thai and, in a sense, is becoming more so as the years pass. Though there are important differences between the languages, they are mutually intelligible – just about (see Language box, page 311). To many Thais, Lao is a rather basic version of their own more sophisticated language – they often describe it as 'primitive'. Of course the Lao vehemently reject, and resent, such a view and it represents, in microcosm the 'big-brother-little brother' relationship that exists between the two countries and peoples. (It is not accidental that the Lao of the poverty-stricken NE of Thailand are often regarded as country bumpkins in Bangkok.) Today, though, many Lao watch Thai TV, their antennae aimed to receive transmissions from the west. As a result Thai expressions are becoming more common and familiarity with Thai is spreading. Even written Thai is more in evidence. As Thailand dominates mainland Southeast Asia in economic terms (they are the largest investor in Laos) this linguistic imperialism is seen by Thailand's critics as just another facet of a wide ranging Thai cultural colonization of Laos.

Dictionaries and teach yourself Lao books Perhaps the best Lao-English/English-Lao dictionary is by Russell Marcus and published by Charles E Tuttle Co in the US but it costs US$20 or so. Klaus Werner's *Learning and speaking Lao* is also useful and cheaper (about US$12) and then there is the locally produced *Learning Lao for everyone* by Phone Bouaravong which comes with tapes too. *Raintree Books*, Pang Kham Rd, Vientiane, stocks a reasonable selection of dictionaries and 'teach yourself' books.

● Postal services

International service: the outbound service is inexpensive but long-term foreign residents cast aspersions on its reliability; they prefer to have mail hand-delivered by people going to Bangkok. A postcard to Europe costs 300 kip, an airletter 400 kip. A 20g letter to Asia costs 380 kip, 440 kip to Europe, 480 kip to Africa, 520 kip to North America. Contents of outgoing parcels must be examined by an official before being sealed. In-going mail should use the official title, **Lao PDR**. EMS or Express Mail Service is available from main post offices in larger towns.

A telephone and **fax service** is available at the International Service Centre, Settathirath, Vientiane, international telephone service open 24 hrs a day, fax service open daily 0730-2130 and faxes are received 24 hrs a day. Mark incoming faxes with receiver's telephone number and recipient will be informed immediately. **International operator**: T 170.

Poste restante: there is a poste restante at the central post office in Vientiane.

TNT Express Worldwide operate from Laos. Their office in Vientiane is on Lane Xang Ave, next to the Thai Farmers Bank, T 222250.

● Telephone services

Local: all towns are now linked by phone and many places have fax facilities, particularly guesthouses and hotels. Call 178 in Vientiane for town codes.

International: possible from most big towns. Operator: 16.

ENTERTAINMENT

● Newspapers

Vientiane Times is a weekly paper, costing 700 kip, which started in 1994. It provides querky pieces of information and shouldn't have any Pulitzer Prize hopefuls too worried about its razor sharp investigative reporting. The April 1996 issue, for example, had, as its lead story 'First Lao telephone directory – a milestone for communications'. *Discover Laos* is a monthly publication. *Newsweek* is available. The *Bangkok Post* (costing over ฿20) is the most recent addition to newstands which previously stocked only government-controlled Lao language newspapers and *Pravda* in Russian and French. The Lao Government *Khao San Pathet Lao News Bulletin* is produced daily in English and French and yields journalistic treats such as "Sayaboury province exceeds radish production forecast" and "Message of solidarity to Havana". They can be found blowing around hotel lobbies.

● Radio

The Lao National Radio broadcasts news in English. The BBC World Service can be picked up on shortwave on 11.955 MHz and 11.750 (25m band); 9.740 MHz (30m band); 7.145 MHz (41m band); 6.195 MHz (48m band) and 3.195 MHz (76m band). Voice of America also broadcasts (see page 308). Every day in many of the cities and towns loudspeakers blare out broadcasts of the municipal radio station. These days, socialist slogans have been replaced with commercials for soft drinks, washing powder and toothpaste.

● Television

This is becoming more popular as more towns and villages get electricity. Even Vientiane's poorest communities sport forests of aluminium antennae orientated to receive signals from across the Mekong. (Thai broadcasts can be received in the Mekong basin – ie where most of the population centres are to be found – but not in mountainous areas, which includes Luang Prabang.) The national TV station broadcasts in Lao but there is a distinct preference for Thai soaps and game shows. Thailand's Channel 5 gives English sub-titles to overseas news. Many homes have VCRs imported from Thailand, and some upmarket hotels also subscribe to Asia's Star TV (which transmits news as well as sports, music, film and general channels).

HOLIDAYS AND FESTIVALS

Being of festive inclination, the Lao celebrate New Year 4 times a year: the international New Year in Jan, Chinese New Year in Jan/Feb, Lao New Year (Pimai) in Apr and Hmong New Year in Dec. The Lao Buddhist year follows the lunar calendar, so many of the festivals are movable. The first month begins around the full moon in Dec, although Lao New Year is celebrated in Apr. There are also many local festivals (see relevant sections).

The **baci** ceremony is a uniquely Lao *boun* (festival) and celebrates any auspicious occasion – marriage, birth, achievement or the end of an arduous journey for instance. The ceremony dates from pre-Buddhist times and is therefore animist in origin. It is centred around the *phakhouan*, a designer-tree made from banana leaves and flowers (or, today, some artificial concoction of plastic) and surrounded by symbolic foods. The most common symbolic foods are eggs and rice – symbolizing fertility and fecundity. The *mophone* hosts the ceremony and recites memorized prayers, usually in Pali, and ties cotton threads (*sai sin*) around the wrists of guests symbolizing good health, prosperity and happiness. For maximum effect, these strings must have 3 knots in them. It is unlucky to take them off before at least 3 days have elapsed and custom dictates that they never be cut. Many people wear them until, frayed and worn, they fall through sheer decrepitude. All this is accompanied by a *ramvong* (traditional circle dance) which is accompanied by traditional instruments – flutes, clarinets, xylophones with bamboo crosspieces, drums, cymbals and the *kaen*, a hand-held pipe organ that is to Laos what the bagpipes are to Scotland.

Jan *New Year's Day* (1st: public holiday) celebrated by private *baci* throughout the country. *Pathet Lao Day* (6th: public holiday) parades in main towns. *Army Day* (20th: public holiday). *Boun Pha Vet* (movable) to celebrate King Vessanthara's reincarnation as a Buddha. Sermons, processions, dance, theatre. Popular time for ordination.

Feb *Magha Puja* (movable) celebrates the end of Buddha's time in the monastery and the prediction of his death. It is principally celebrated in Vientiane and at Wat Phou, near Champassak. *Chinese New Year* (movable, Jan/Feb) celebrated by Chinese and Vietnamese communities. Many Chinese and Vietnamese businesses shut down for 3 days.

Calendar

The **Gregorian calendar** is the official calendar for administration, but many traditional villages still follow the lunar calendar. The **Lao calendar** is a mixture of Sino-Vietnamese and Thai-Khmer. It is based on the movement of the sun and moon and is different to the Buddhist calendar used in Thailand. New Year is in December, but is celebrated in April when the auspices are more favourable. As in China, each year is named after an animal. Weeks are structured on the waxing and waning of the moon and days are named accordingly.

Mar *Women's Day* (8th: public holiday). *People's Party Day* (22nd: public holiday). *Boun Khoun Khao* (movable) harvest festival, local celebration centred around the wats.

Apr *Boun Pimai* (13th-15th: public holiday) to celebrate Lao New Year. The first month of the Lao New Year is actually Dec but festivities are delayed until Apr when days are longer than nights. By Apr it's also hotting up, so having hosepipes levelled at you and buckets of water dumped on you is more pleasurable. The festival also serves to invite the rains. Pimai is one of the most important annual festivals, particularly in Luang Prabang (see page 102). Statues of the Buddha (in the 'calling for rain' posture) are ceremonially doused in water, which is poured along an intricately decorated trench (*hang song nam pha*). The small stupas of sand, decorated with streamers, in wat compounds are symbolic requests for health and happiness over the next year. It is celebrated with traditional Lao folksinging (*mor lam*) and the circle dance (*ramwong*). There is usually a 3-day holiday. Similar festivals are celebrated in Thailand, Cambodia and Burma.

May *Labour Day* (1st: public holiday) parades in Vientiane. *Visakha Puja* (movable) to celebrate the birth, enlightenment and death of the Buddha, celebrated in local wats. *Boun Bang Fai* (movable) or the rocket festival, is a Buddhist rain-making festival. Large bamboo rockets are built and decorated by monks and carried in procession before being blasted skywards. The higher a rocket goes, the bigger its builder's ego gets. Designers of failed rockets are thrown in the mud. The festival lasts 2 days.

Jun *Children's Day* (1st: public holiday).

Jun/Jul *Khao Phansa* (movable) is the start of Buddhist Lent and is a time of retreat and fasting for monks. These are the most usual months for ordination and for men to enter the monkhood for short periods before they marry. The festival starts with the full moon in Jun/Jul and continues until the full moon in Oct. It all ends with the *Kathin* ceremony in Oct when monks receive gifts.

Aug *Lao Issara* (13th: public holiday), *Free Lao Day*. *Liberation Day* (23rd: public holiday). *Ho Khao Padap Dinh* (movable) is a celebration of the dead.

Sep *Boun Ok Phansa* (movable) is the end of Buddhist Lent and the faithful take offerings to the temple. It is in the '9th month' in Luang Prabang and the '11th month' in Vientiane, and marks the end of the rainy season. Boat races take place on the Mekong River with crews of 50 or more men and women. On the night before the race small decorated rafts are set afloat on the river.

Oct *Freedom from the French Day* (12th: public holiday) which is only really celebrated in Vientiane.

Nov *Boun That Luang* (movable), is celebrated in all Laos' *thats*, although most enthusiastically and colourfully in Vientiane (see page 102). As well as religious rituals, most celebrations include local fairs, processions, beauty pageants and other festivities.

Dec *Hmong New Year* (movable). *Independence Day* (2nd: public holiday), military parades, dancing, music.

NB This list is not exhaustive, but does include the most important festivals. There are many Chinese, Vietnamese and ethnic minority festivals which are celebrated in Laos and there are many regional variations.

Will you help us?

Our authors explore and research tirelessly to bring you the most complete and up-to-date package of information possible. Yet the contributions we receive from our readers are also **vital** to the success of our Handbooks. There are many thousands of you out there making delightful (and sometimes alarming!) discoveries every day.

So important is this resource that we make a special offer to every reader who contacts us with information on places, experiences, people, hotels, restaurants, well-informed warnings or any other features which could enhance the enjoyment of our travellers everywhere. When writing to us, please give the edition and page number of the Handbook you are using.

So please take a few minutes to get in touch with us - we can benefit, you can benefit and all our other readers can benefit too!

Please write to us at:

Footprint Handbooks,
6 Riverside Court, Lower Bristol Road, Bath BA2 3DZ England
Fax: +44 (0)1225 469461 E Mail travellers@footprint.cix.co.uk

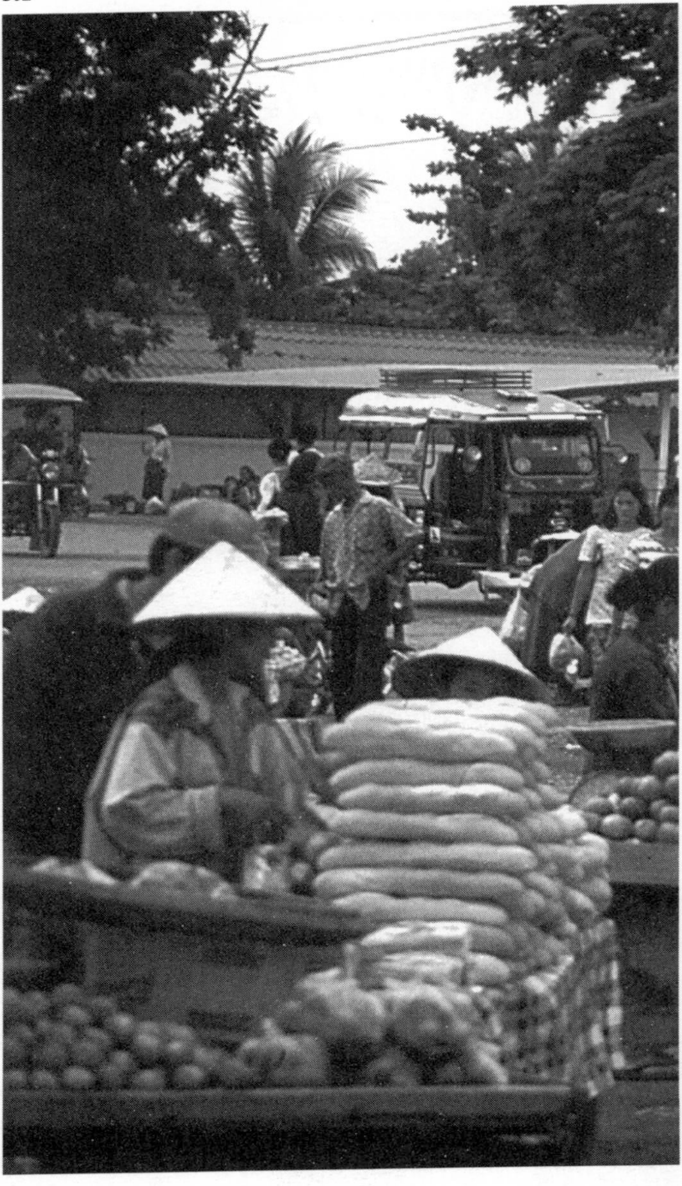

Rounding up

ACKNOWLEDGEMENTS

Natasha Lopez, USA; Eric Lammers, USA; Ponschab Martin, Austria; Toby Chadwick, UK; Pierre Mainetti, Laos; Mary Wall, USA; Robert Robbins, USA; Tapani Mäntysaari, Finland; David Steinke, Germany; Andrea Fiedler, Germany; Pilou Grenié, France; Steve McBride, Northern Ireland; Florian Kubo, Germany; Denise Heywood, UK.

READING AND LISTENING

MAGAZINES

Asiaweek (weekly). A lightweight *Far Eastern Economic Review*, rather like a regional *Time* magazine in style.

The Far Eastern Economic Review (weekly). Authoritative Hong Kong-based regional magazine; their correspondents based in each country provide knowledgeable, in-depth analysis particularly on economics and politics, sometimes in rather a turgid style (although a change of editor has meant some lightening in style).

BOOKS

Cambridge History of Southeast Asia (1992). Two volume edited study, long and expensive with contributions from most of the leading historians of the region. A thematic and regional approach is taken, not

a country one, although the history is fairly conventional. Published by Cambridge University Press: Cambridge.

Dingwall, Alastair (1994) *Traveller's literary companion to South-east Asia*, In Print: Brighton. Experts on Southeast Asian language and literature select extracts from novels and other books by western and regional writers. The extracts are annoyingly brief, but it gives a good overview of what is available.

Dumarçay, Jacques (1991) *The palaces of South-East Asia: architecture and customs*, OUP: Singapore. A broad summary of palace art and architecture in both mainland and island Southeast Asia.

Fraser-Lu, Sylvia (1988) *Handwoven textiles of South-East Asia*, OUP: Singapore. Well-illustrated, large-format book with informative text.

Higham, Charles (1989) *The archaeology of mainland Southeast Asia from 10,000 BC to the fall of Angkor*, Cambridge University Press: Cambridge. Best summary of changing views of the archaeology of the mainland.

Keyes, Charles F (1977) *The golden peninsula: culture and adaptation in mainland Southeast Asia*, Macmillan: New York. Academic, yet readable summary of the threads of continuity and change in Southeast Asia's culture.

King, Ben F and Dickinson, EC (1975) *A field guide to the birds of South-East Asia*, Collins: London. Best regional guide to the birds of the region.

Miettinen, Jukko O (1992) *Classical dance and theatre in South-East Asia*, OUP, Singapore. Expensive, but accessible survey of dance and theatre, mostly focusing on Indonesia, Thailand and Burma.

Osborne, Milton (1979) *Southeast Asia: an introductory history*, Allen & Unwin: Sydney. Good introductory history, clearly written, published in a portable paperback edition.

Rawson, Philip (1967) *The art of South-east Asia*, Thames & Hudson: London. Portable general art history of Cambodia, Vietnam, Thailand, Laos, Burma, Java and Bali; by necessity, rather superficial.

Reid, Anthony (1988) *Southeast Asia in the age of commerce 1450-1680: the lands below the winds*, Yale University Press: New Haven. Perhaps the best history of everyday life in Southeast Asia, looking at such themes as physical well-being, material culture and social organization.

Reid, Anthony (1993) *Southeast Asia in the age of commerce 1450-1680: expansion and crisis*, Yale University Press: New Haven. Volume 2 in this excellent history of the region.

Rigg, Jonathan (1997) *Southeast Asia: the human landscape of modernization and development*, London: Routledge. A book which covers both the market and former command economies (ie Myanmar, Vietnam, Laos and Cambodia) of the region. It focuses on how people in the region have responded to the challenges and tensions of modernization.

SarDesai, DR (1989) *Southeast Asia: past and present*, Macmillan: London. Skilful but at times frustratingly thin history of the region from the 1st century to the withdrawal of US forces from Vietnam.

Savage, Victor R (1984) *Western impressions of nature and landscape in Southeast Asia*, Singapore University Press: Singapore. Based on a geography PhD thesis, the book is a mine of quotations and observations from western travellers.

Sesser, Stan (1993) *The lands of charm and cruelty: travels in Southeast Asia*, Pica-dor: Basingstoke. A series of collected narratives first published in the *New Yorker* including essays on Singapore, Laos, Cambodia, Burma and Borneo. Finely observed and thoughtful, the book is an excellent travel companion. The chapter on Laos is as good an introduction as you are likely to find.

Steinberg, DJ et al (1987) *In search of Southeast Asia: a modern history*, University of Hawaii Press: Honolulu. The best standard history of the region; it skilfully examines and assesses general processes of change and their impacts from the arrival of the Europeans in the region.

Wallace, Alfred Russel (1869) *The Malay Archipelago: the land of the orang-utan and the bird of paradise; a narrative of travel with studies of man and nature*, Macmillan: London. A classic of natural history writing, recounting Wallace's 8 years in the archipelago and now reprinted.

Waterson, Roxana (1990) *The living house: an anthropology of architecture in South-East Asia*, OUP: Singapore. Illustrated, academic book on Southeast Asian architecture, fascinating material for those interested in such things.

Young, Gavin (1991) *In search of Conrad*, Hutchinson: London. This well-known travel writer retraces the steps of Conrad; part travel-book, part fantasy, it is worth reading but not up to the standard of his other books.

BOOKS ON LAOS

History

Manich Jumsai, ML (1971) *A new history of Laos*, Bangkok: Chalermnit Books. This history is very standard in approach and un-critical in terms of the material that is recounted. There are some good stories here, but it should not be taken at face value. It is widely available in Bangkok and relatively cheap.

Stuart-Fox, Martin and Kooyman, Mary (1992) *Historical Dictionary of Laos*, New York: The Scarecrow Press. Takes, as the name suggests, a dictionary approach to Laos' history which is fine if you are looking up a fact or two, but doesn't really lend itself to telling a narrative.

Toye, Hugh (1968) *Laos – Buffer State or*

Battleground, London: Oxford University Press.

Laos and the Indochina War

Castle, Timothy (1993) *A war in the shadow of Vietnam: US military aid to the Royal Lao government 1955-1975*, New York: Columbia University Press.

Grant Evans & Kelvin Rowley (1990) *Red Brotherhood at War, Vietnam Cambodia & Laos since 1975*, Verso.

Grant Evans (1983) *Yellow Rainmakers: Are Chemical Weapons Being Used in Southeast Asia*, Verso.

McCoy, Alfred W. (1991) *The Politics of Heroin: CIA Complicity in the Global Drugs Trade*, Lawrence Hill/Chicago Review Press. Originally published at the beginning of the 1970s, it is the classic study of the politics of drugs in mainland Southeast Asia.

Parker, James (1995) *Codename Mule: fighting the secret war in Laos for the CIA*, Annapolis, Maryland: Naval Institute Press. Another book to add to the growing list that recount the personal stories of the Americans fighting in Laos. Much of it deals with the fighting on the Plain of Jars.

Robbins, Christopher (1979), *Air America: the story of the CIS's secret airlines*, New York: Putnam Books. The earlier of Robbins' two books on the secret war. Made into a film of the same name with Mel Gibson in the starring role.

Robbins, Christopher (1989) *The Ravens: pilots of the secret war of Laos*, New York: Bantam Press. The best known and the most thrilling read of all the books on America's secret war in Laos. The story it tells seems almost incredible.

Warner, Roger (1995) *Back fire: the CIA's secret war in Laos and its link to the war in Vietnam*, New York: Simon and Schuster. The best of the more recent books recounting the experiences of US servicemen in Laos.

Travel and geography

De Carne, Louis (1872) *Travels in Indochina and the Chinese Empire*, London: Chapman Hall. Recounts De Carne's experiences in Laos in 1872, some years before the country was colonized by the French.

Hoskins, John (1991) *The Mekong*, Bangkok: Post Publishing. A large format coffee-table book with good photographs and a modest text. Widely available in Bangkok.

Mouhot, Henri (1986) *Travels in Indochina*, Bangkok: White Lotus. An account of Laos by France's most famous explorer of Southeast Asia. He tried to discover a 'back door' into China by travelling up the Mekong, but died of Malaria in Luang Prabang in 1860. The book has been republished by White Lotus and is easily available in Bangkok; there is also a more expensive reprint available from OUP (Kuala Lumpur).

Economics, politics and development

Dommen, Arthur J (1985) *Laos: keystone of Indochina*, Boulder: Westview Press. Rather out of date now in terms of the economic picture that is painted, but a reasonable overview.

Grant Evans (1990) *Lao Peasants under Socialism*, New Haven: Yale University Press. The definitive account of farmers in modern Laos. A new edition has been published by Silkworm Books in Chiang Mai (Thailand), updated to take into account economic changes brought about by the New Economic Mechanism.

Evans, Grant (1997) (edit) *Laos: culture and society*, Chiang Mai, Thailand: Silkworm Books. A book due to be published in 1997; should provide the most comprehensive account of Laos' culture(s) and society. The editor, Grant Evans, is one of the world's foremost scholars of Laos.

Håkangård, Agneta (1992), *Road 13: A Socio-economic Study of Villagers, Transport and Use of Road 13 S, Lao P.D.R.*, Development Studies Unit, Department of Social Anthropology, Stockholm University. A shortish monography examining how road 13, the main N-S highway is affecting people's lives along the route. Only for the really interested.

Ivarsson, Soren, Svensson, Thommy and Tonnesson, Stein (1995), *The Quest for Balance in a Changing Laos: A Political Analysis*, Nordic Institute of Asian Studies (NIAS) report no. 25, NIAS, Copenhagen. A study which examines the question of Laos' role and place within the wider region and its quest for 'equi-distance' between the powers of the area.

Stuart-Fox, Martin (1982) (edit) *Contem-*

porary Laos, St Lucia: Queensland University Press. A useful over-view of Laos up to 1980. By dint of its publication date, though, it cannot cover important events since the LPDR effectively gave up its attempt to build a revolutionary state.

Stuart-Fox, Martin (1986) *Laos – Politics, Economics and Society*, London: Francis Pinter. Out of date now in terms of the economic picture that is painted, but a good single volume summary of the country providing broad-brush historical and cultural background too.

Stuart-Fox, Martin (1996) *Buddhist kingdom, Marxist state: the making of modern Laos*, Bangkok: White Lotus. Really a collection of Stuart-Fox's various papers published over the years and brought up-to-date. Possibly the single best volume to take. It is particularly good on recent history – from the emergence to the victory of the Pathet Lao in 1975 and developments since then. Widely available in Bangkok.

Trankell, I-B (1993) *On the road in Laos: an anthropological study of road construction and rural communities*, Uppsala Research Reports in Cultural Anthropology, No 12, Uppsala University, Uppsala. A research monograph; like Håkangård's volume; really only for the very interested.

Zasloff, J J and Unger, L (1991) (edits) *Laos: Beyond the Revolution*, Macmillan, Basingstoke. Edited volume with a mixed collection of papers; some of the economics/politics chapters are already rather dated.

Art Connors, Mary, *Lao Textiles and traditions*, Oxford University Press.

Food

Phia Sing (1995) *Traditional recipes of Laos*, Totnes, Devon, UK: Prospect Books. The best Lao cookbook available. The recipes were collected by the chief chef at the Royal Palace in Luang Prabang, Phia Sing, who recorded them in the 1960s. They have been translated into English and made West-friendly by replacing some of the more esoteric ingredients.

Newsletters

Indochina Newsletter (monthly) from Asia Resource Centre, c/o 2161 Massachusetts Ave, Cambridge, MA02140, USA.

MAPS OF LAOS

Regional maps

Bartholomew Southeast Asia (1:5,800,000); Nelles Southeast Asia (1:4,000,000); Hildebrand Thailand, Burma, Malaysia and Singapore (1:2,800,000).

Country maps

Nelles Vietnam, Laos and Cambodia (1:1,500,000); Bartholomew Vietnam, Laos and Cambodia (1:2,000,000); International Travel Map Laos.

Locally available maps

It is sometimes possible to get hold of sheet maps at a scale of 1:100,000 last updated at the beginning of the 1980s and based on French-produced originals. Rather easier to find is a five-sheet country set at a scale of 1:1,000,000. Both are produced by the Service Geographique National. There is also a series of locally produced town maps which covers the major settlements of Vientiane, Luang Prabang, Thakhek, Savannakhet and Pakse. Perhaps the best map of Vientiane is the colourful *Map of Vientiane* produced by the Women's International Group.

Other maps

Tactical Pilotage Charts (TPC, US Airforce) (1:500,000); Operational Navigational Charts (ONC, US Airforce) (1:500,000). Both of these are particularly good at showing relief features (useful for planning treks); less good on roads, towns and facilities.

THE INTERNET

Listed below are Internet addresses which access information on Asia generally, the Southeast Asian region, or Laos. **Newsgroups** tend to be informal talking shops offering information from hotels and sights through to wide-ranging discussions on just about any topic. **Mailing Lists** have a more academic clientele, and probably are not worth plugging into unless you have a specific interest in the subject concerned. **Web sites** offer a whole range of information on a vast variety of topics. Below is only a selection.

Newsgroups on USENET with a Southeast Asian focus

Newsgroups are discussion fora on the USENET. Not every computer linked to the Internet has access to USENET – your computer needs Net News and a News reader. Newsgroups are informal fora for discussion; they are occasionally irreverent, usually interesting.

● Asia general

alt.asian.movies
alt.buddha.short.fat.guy
rec.travel.asia
soc.religion.eastern
talk.religion.buddhism

● Southeast Asia

soc.culture.asean

Mailing lists

These are discussion groups with a more academic content; some may be moderate – ie the content of messages is checked by an editor. Mailing lists communicate using E-mail. The focus of the groups is in square brackets.

● Asia general

actmus-1@ubvm.bitnet
[Asian Contemporary Music Discussion Group]
apex-1@uheevm.bitnet
[Asia-Pacific Exchange]
buddha-1@ulkyvm.bitnet
[Buddhist Academic Discussion Forum]

● Southeast Asia

seanet-1@nusvm.bitnet
[Southeast Asian Studies List]
seasia-1@msu.bitnet
[Southeast Asia Discussion List]

Southeast Asia on the World Wide Web – Web sites

Web sites are on the World Wide Web. They can now be browsed using a graphical mouse-based hypertext system. The two in use are Mosaic and the newer, Netscape. They allow the user to browse through the WWW easily. Note, however, that images (especially) take time to download and if on the Web during the time of the day when the US is alive and kicking expect to spend a very long time twiddling your thumbs. The subject of the web site is in brackets after the address.

● Asia general

http://none.coolware.com/infoasia/
[run by Infoasia which is a commercial firm that helps US and European firms get into Asia]
http://www.city.net/regions/asia
[pointer to information on Asian countries]
http://www.branch.com:80/silkroute/
[information on hotels, travel, news and business in Asia]
http://www.singapore.com/pata
[Pacific Asia Travel Association – stacks of info on travel in the Pacific Asian region including stats, markets, products etc]

● Southeast Asia

http://www.pactoc.net.au/index/resindex.htm
    [Pacific talk homepage with lots of topics and links]
http://libweb.library.wise.edu/guides/SEAsia/library.htm
[the 'Gateway to Southeast Asia', lots of links]
http://emailhost.ait.ac.th/asia/asia.html
[clickable map of mainland Southeast Asia with pointer to sources of other information on the region]
http://www.leidenuniv.nl/pun/ubhtm/mjkintro.htm
[library of 100 slides of Thailand (Phimai, Chiang Mai, Lamphun) and other mainland Southeast Asian countries]

● Laos

http://www.monash.edu.au/ftp/pub/ban e_lao/laoweb/laoVL.htm
[The Laos vitual library with maps, publications, travel material, art and culture, hill peoples and more]

Terms

E-mail = Electronic mail
WWW = World Wide Web or, simply, the Web
HTML = Hypertext Markup Language
URL = Uniform Resource Locators

Sources: the above was collated from *Internet news* published in the *IIAS Newsletter* [International Institute for Asian Studies Newsletter], Summer 1995; *IIAS Newsletter*, Spring 1996 and *Asian Studies Newsletter*, June/July 1996.

SHORT WAVE RADIO

British Broadcasting Corporation (BBC, London) *Southeast Asian service* 3915, 6195, 9570, 9740, 11750, 11955, 15360; *Singapore service* 88.9MHz; *East Asian service* 5995, 6195, 7180, 9740, 11715, 11750, 11945, 11955, 15140, 15280, 15360, 17830, 21715.

Voice of America (VoA, Washington) *Southeast Asian service* 1143, 1575, 7120, 9760, 9770, 15185, 15425; *Indonesian service* 6110, 11760, 15425.

Radio Beijing *Southeast Asian service (English)* 11600, 11660.

Radio Japan (Tokyo) *Southeast Asian service (English)* 11815, 17810, 21610.

Radio

The BBC World Service's *Dateline East Asia* provides probably the best news and views on Asia. Also with a strong Asia focus are the broadcasts of the ABC (Australian Broadcasting Corporation).

Useful addresses

EMBASSIES AND CONSULATES

Australia
1 Dalman Crescent, O'Malley, Canberra, T 2864535, F 2901910

Cambodia
15-17 Thanon Keomani, T 26441, F 85523

China
N23 Haigeng Rd, Rm 501, Kunming, T 4141678, F 2420344. 11 Sanlifun Dongsijie, Beijing (Peking), T 5321224

France
74 Raymond Poincare, T 45537047, F 47275789

Germany
Am Lessing 6, 5330, Koenigwinter, Bonn T 02223, F 3065

India
Friends Colony (East), New Delhi, T 634013

Indonesia
Jn. KintmaniRaja, Keningan Timur, Jakarta, T 5202673

Japan
3-21, 3-Chome, Nishi Azabu, Minato-ku, To-kyo, T 54112291, F 54112293

Malaysia
Jl Bellamy, 50460 Kuala Lumpur, T 2483895, F 2420344; **Myanmar (Burma)**: A1 Diplo-matic Headquarters, Taw Win Rd, Yangon (Rangoon)

Thailand
502/1-3 Ramkhamhaeng Soi 39 (Pracha-Uthit Rd), T 2131203, F 5396678

USA
United Nations, New York, T 8322734, F 7500039. 2222 S St, Washington, T 6670058

Vietnam
22 Tran Binh Trong, Hanoi, T 252271; 181 Hai Ba Trung, Ho Chi Minh City (Saigon), T 299272

SPECIALIST TOUR OPERATORS

THAILAND BASED COMPANIES

Those operating 'individual tours' to Laos, organize short, cheap packages to Vien-tiane for 1-2 nights to gain entry. Then travellers are left on their own to organize the rest of their stay in Laos. The problem is that these companies shut down as fast as they open up. In Oct 1996 visas for Laos were costing ฿1,300-1,600.

Asian Holiday Tour
294/8 Phayathai Rd, Bangkok, T 2155749

Asian Lines Travel
755 Silom Rd, Bangkok, T 2331510, F 2334885

Banglamphu Tour Service
17 Khaosan Rd, Bangkok, T 2813122, F 2803642

Cham Siam
288 Surawong Rd, Bangkok, T 2555570

Dee Jai Tours
2nd flr, 491/29 Silom Plaza Bldg, Silom Rd, Bangkok, T 2341685, F 2374231

Diethelm Travel
Kian Gwan Bldg II, 140/1 Witthayu Rd, Bang-kok, T 2559150, F 2560248

Dior Tours
146-158 Khaosan Rd, Bangkok, T 2829142

East-West
46-1 Sukhumvit Soi Nana Nua, Bangkok, T 2530681

Exotissimo
21/17 Sukhumvit Soi 4, Bangkok, T 2535240, F 2547683, and 755 Silom Rd, Bangkok, T 2359196, F 2834885

Fortune Tours
9 Captain Bush Lane, Charoen Krung 30, Bangkok, T 2371050

Inter Companion Group
86/4 Rambutri Rd, Banglamphu, Bangkok, T 2829400, F 2827316

Kannika Tour
36/39 Srisatta Rd, Udon Thani, T (042) 241378

M K Ways
18/4 Sathorn Tai Soi 3 (Saint Louis), Bangkok, T 2122532, F 2545583

Magic Tours
59/63 Moon Muang Rd, Chiang Mai, T 214572, F 214749

MSK Travel Service
128 Sukhumvit Rd

Pawana Tour and Travel
72/2 Khaosan Rd, Bangkok, T 2678018, F 2800370

Also try **Pangkaj Travel**
625 Sukhumvit Soi 22, Bangkok 10110, T 2582440, F 2591261

S I Tours
288/2 Silom Rd, Bangkok, T 2332631

Siam Wings
173/1-3 Surawong Rd, Bangkok, T 2534757, F 2366808

Skyline Travel Service
491/39-40 Silom Plaza (2nd Flr), Silom Rd, Bangkok, T 2331864, F 2366585

Spangle Tours
205/1 Sathorn Tai Rd, Bangkok, T 2121583, F 2867732

Thai Indochina
4th flr, 79 Pan Rd, Silom, Bangkok, T 2335369, F 2364389

Thai-Indochina Supply Co
4th flr, 79 Pan Rd, Silom, Bangkok, T 2335369, F 2364389

Thai Travel Service
119/4 Surawong Rd, Bangkok, T 2349360

Top Thailand Tour
61 Khaosan Rd, Bangkok, T 2802251, F 2823337

Tour East
Rajapark Bldg, 10th flr, 163 Asoke Rd, Bangkok, T 2593160, F 2583236

Transindo
9th flr Thasos Bldg, 1675 Chan Rd, Bangkok, T 2873241, F 2873246

Vista Travel
244/4 Khaosan Rd, Bangkok, T 2800348

Western Union
branch in the foyer of Atlanta Hotel, 78 Sukhumvit Soi 2, Bangkok, T 2552151.

Note for tour companies based in towns outside Bangkok see the relevant entries in the Thailand section of this book.

VIENTIANE-BASED COMPANIES

Vientiane has the greatest concentration of tour companies in Laos – although Bangkok has even more. These are listed in the Vientiane section (see page 112). They will arrange visas for those people who also book a tour through them. (Some will arrange a visa without a tour.) There are also companies in the larger towns including Luang Prabang, Thakhek, Savannakhet and Pakse (see the relevant section in each town entry for a listing).

Words and phrases

GREETINGS
Yes/No
men/baw
Thank you/no thank you
kop jai/baw, kop jai
Hello/goodbye
suh-bye-dee/lah-gohn
What is your name? My name is...
Chow seu yang? koi seu....
Excuse me, sorry
ko toat
Can/do you speak English?
Koy pahk pah-sah anhg-geet?
A little, a bit
noi, hoi
Where?
you-sigh?
How much is...?
Tow-dai?
It doesn't matter, never mind
baw penh yang
Pardon?
kow toat?
I don't understand
Kow baw cow-chi
How are you? not very well
Chao suh-bye-dee-baw?   baw suh-bye

THE HOTEL
What is the charge each night?
Kit laka van nuang taw dai?
Is the room air conditioned?
Hong me ai yen baw?
Can I see the room first please?
Koi ko beung hong dea?
Does the room have hot water?
Hong me nam hawn baw?
Does the room have a bathroom?
Me hang ap nam baw?
Can I have the bill please?
Koi ton han bai hap?

TRAVEL
Where is the train station?
Sa ta ni lot phai yu sai?

Where is the bus station?
Sa ta ni lot mee yu sai?
How much to go to...?
Khit la ka taw dai...?
That's expensive
pheng-lie
Will you go for...kip?
Chow ja pai...kip?
What time does the bus/train leave for...?
Lot mea oak jay mong...?
Is it far?
Kai baw?
Turn left/turn right
leo sai/leo qua
Go straight on
pai leuy
River
Xe Se, Houei/Houai
Town
Muang/Mouang
Mountain
phou

RESTAURANTS
Can I see a menu?
Kho beung lay kan arhan?
Can I have...?
Khoy tong kan...?
I am hungry
Koy heo kao
I am thirsty
Koy heo nahm
I want to eat
Koh yahk kin kao
Where is a restaurant?
Lahn ah hai you-sigh?
Breakfast
arhan sao
Lunch
arhan athieng
It costs....kip
Lah-kah ahn-nee...kip

TIME
in the morning   muh-sao

in the afternoon thon-by
in the evening muh-leng
today muh-nee
tomorrow muh-ouhn
yesterday muh van-nee

DAYS
Monday Van Chanh
Tuesday Van Ang Khan
Wednesday Van Pud
Thursday Van Pa Had
Friday Van Sook
Saturday Van Sao
Sunday Van Arthid

NUMBERS
1	nung
2	song
3	sahm
4	see
5	hah
6	hoke
7	chet
8	pet
9	cow
10	sip
11	sip-et
12	sip-song
20	sao
21	sao-et
22	sao-song
30	sahn-sip
100	hoy
101	hoy-nung
150	hoy-hah-sip
200	song-hoy
1,000	phan
10,000	sip-phan
100,000	muun
1,000,000	laan

BASIC VOCABULARY
airport deune yonh
bank had xay
bathroom hong nam
beach heva
beautiful ngam
bicycle loht teep
big nyai
boat quoi loth bath
bus loht-buht
bus station hon kay ya
buy sue
chemist han kay ya
clean sa ard
closed arte
cold jenh
day vanh (or) mua
delicious sehb
dirty soka pox
doctor than mah
eat kinh
embassy Satan Tood

excellent dee leuth
expensive pheng
food ah-han
fruit mak-mai
hospital hong moh
hot (temp) hawn
hotel hong
island koh (or) hath
market ta lath
medicine ya pua payad
open peud
petrol nahm-mahn-eh-sahng
police lam louad
police station poam lam louad
post office hong kana pai sa nee
restaurant han arhane
road tha nonh
room hong
shop hanh
sick (ill) bo sabay
silk mai
small noy
stop yoot
taxi loht doy-sanh
that nahn
this nee, ahn-nee
ticket (air) pee yonh
ticket (bus) pee lot mea
toilet hong nam
town nai mouang
very lai-lai
water nam (or) nah
what men-nyung

FOOD
bai boua lotus leaves for wrapping food
dip raw
fahn small deer
feu noodle soup (Vietnamese)
goong shrimp
guea salt
hao tchao Chinese rice
hawn hot
hed mushroom
het khao white mushroom
hom boua haeng shallot
houa phak pheuk Chinese radish
jaew sauce
kah-fay coffee
kai chicken/egg
kai dao egg, fried
kai dom egg, boiled
kai pa jungle (wild) chicken
kaiy mouse deer
kalee curry
kanom cake
kao rice
kao chao non-gutinous rice
kao jee bread
kao jee sticky rice, mashed and grilled
kao khob rice cakes
kao khoua toasted rice
kao niao sticky or glutinous rice

kao poon   rice vermicelli
kao poon Ciin   transparent 'Chinese' vermicelli
katai   rabbit
kem   salty
keng   soup
kha or **kha ta deng**   galingale
khing   ginger
kop   frog
kua   stir fry
kuai   buffalo
kuay   banana
kung   prawn/shrimp
kung yai   lobster
mahk galambee or **phakkad**   cabbage
mak appen   apple
mak fak kham   pumpkin
mak-fal-ahng   potato
mak feuang   star fruit
mak-huhng   papaya
mak kham   tamarind
mak kheua   aubergine or egg plant
mak kheua khua or **mak len**   tomato
mak khi hout   kaffir lime
mak-kieng   orange
mak maw   melon
mak-mo   watermelon
mak muang   mango
mak-my   fruit
mak-naow   lemon
mak-nuht   pineapple
mak paep   sword bean
mak phao   coconut
mak phet   chillies
mak sa-lee   sweetcorn
mak thua   bean
mak thua beu   French bean
mak thua ngork   beansprout
mak thua nyao   'yard long' bean
me nam   noodle soup (Chinese)
moo   pork/pig
nam   water
nam bolisut   bottled water
nam daan   sugar
nam khon   ice
nam mahk naow   lemon juice
nam mak phao   coconut milk
nam nome   milk
nam pa   fish sauce
nam sa   tea

nam sa hawn   hot tea
nam sa yin   iced tea
no mai   bamboo shoots
no so   pickled bamboo shoots
nok   bird
nok kho   quail
pa   fish
pa dek   fish sauce with fish chunks
pa ling   catfish
pad   stir fry
ped   duck
phak   leaf vegetable/vegetable
phak bong   water spinach or swamp cabbage
phak boua nyai   onion
phak boua sot   spring onion
phak hom ho   mint
phak hom pom   coriander
phak hum   spinach
phak i leut   wrapping food
phak itu Lao   leaf used for sweet basil
phak salat   lettuce
phak si   dill
phak tehng   cucumber
phak thiem   garlic
phet   spicy hot
ping   grill
seen moo   pork
seen nua   beef
sikhai   lemon grass
som   sour
waan   sweet
yin   cold

Street food
kao poun   hot noodle
kayo cuon   spring rolls
nem   deep fried ball of rice and meat
roti   waffle
tam mak hung   green papaya salad (spicy hot)
tom yam   lemon grass soup

Useful phrases
kao leng   dinner
kao sao   breakfast
kao tiang   lunch
lai pawd   too much
saierb   tasty

Health

WITH THE FOLLOWING advice and precautions, you should keep as healthy as you do at home. All of the countries have a tropical climate; nevertheless the acquisition of true tropical disease by the visitor is probably conditioned as much by the rural nature and standard of hygiene of the countries concerned than by the climate. There is an obvious difference in health risks between the business traveller who tends to stay in international class hotels in large cities and the backpacker trekking through rural areas. There are no hard and fast rules to follow; you will often have to make your own judgements on the healthiness or otherwise of your surroundings.

Medical care

The quality of medical care is highly variable. In recently devastated countries such as Cambodia it is at a very low level indeed and away from the main cities in Vietnam and Laos it can be equally poor. In Bangkok, medical care is adequate (and rapidly improving) for most exigencies, although Singapore and Hong Kong offer the best facilities for serious illness. In Indochina doctors may speak French, but the likelihood of finding this and a good standard of care diminishes very rapidly as you move away from the big cities. In some of the countries – and especially in rural areas – there are systems and traditions of medicine wholly different from the Western model and you may be confronted with less orthodox forms of treatment such as herbal medicine and acupuncture. At least you can be sure that local practitioners have a lot of experience with the particular diseases of their region. If you are in a city it may be worthwhile calling on your embassy to provide a list of recommended doctors.

Medicines

If you are a long way away from medical help, a certain amount of self administered medication may be necessary and you will find many of the drugs available have familiar names. However, always check the date stamping (sell-by date) and buy from reputable pharmacists because the shelf life of some items, especially vaccines and antibiotics, is markedly reduced in hot conditions. Unfortunately, many locally produced drugs are not subjected to quality control procedures and so can be unreliable. There have, in addition, been cases of substitution of inert materials for active drugs. With the following precautions and advice you should keep as healthy as usual. Make local enquiries about health risks if you are apprehensive and take the general advice of European, Australian or North American families who have lived or are living in the area.

BEFORE YOU GO

Take out medical insurance. You should also have a dental check-up, obtain a spare glasses prescription and, if you suffer from a long-standing condition, such as diabetes, high blood pressure, heart/lung disease or a nervous disorder, arrange for a check-up with your doctor who can at the same time provide you with a letter explaining details of your medical disorder. Check the current practice for malaria prophylaxis (prevention) for the countries you intend to visit.

Vaccination and immunisation

Smallpox vaccination is no longer required. Neither is cholera vaccination, despite the fact that the disease occurs – but not at present in epidemic form – in some of these countries. Yellow fever vaccination is not required either, although you may be asked for a certificate if you have been in a country affected by yellow fever immediately before travelling to Southeast Asia. The following vaccinations are recommended:

Typhoid (Monovalent) One dose followed by a booster 1 month later. Immunity from this course lasts 2-3 years. An oral preparation is also available.

Poliomyelitis This is a live vaccine generally given orally but a full course consists of three doses with a booster in tropical regions every 3-5 years.

Tetanus One dose should be given, with a booster at 6 weeks and another at 6 months. 10 yearly boosters thereafter are recommended.

Meningitis and Japanese B Encephalitis (JVE) There is an extremely small risk of these rather serious diseases; both are seasonal and vary according to region. Meningitis can occur in epidemic form; JVE is a viral disease transmitted from pigs to man by mosquitos. For details of the vaccinations, consult a travel clinic.

Children should also be properly protected against diphtheria, whooping cough, mumps and measles. Teenage girls, if they have not had the disease, should be given a rubella (German measles) vaccination. Consult your doctor for advice on BCG inoculation against tuberculosis: the disease is still common in the region.

Infectious Hepatitis (Jaundice) This is common throughout Southeast Asia. It seems to be frequently caught by travellers. The main symptoms are stomach pains, lack of appetite, nausea, lassitude and yellowness of the eyes and skin. Medically speaking there are two types: the less serious but more common is *hepatitis A* for which the best protection is careful preparation of food, the avoidance of contaminated drinking water and scrupulous attention to toilet hygiene. Human normal immunoglobulin (gammaglobulin) confers considerable protection against the disease and is particularly useful in epidemics. It should be obtained from a reputable source and is certainly recommended for travellers who intend to travel and live rough. The injection should be given as close as possible to your departure and as the dose depends on the likely time you are to spend in potentially infected areas, the manufacturers' instructions should be followed. A vaccination against hepatitis A has recently become generally available and is safe and effective. Three shots are given over 6 months and confer excellent protection against the disease for up to 10 years. Eventually this vaccine is likely to supersede the use of gammaglobulin.

The other, more serious, version is *hepatitis B* which is acquired as a sexually transmitted disease, from a blood transfusion or an injection with an unclean needle, or possibly by insect bites. The symptoms are the same as hepatitis A but the incubation period is much longer.

You may have had jaundice before or you may have had hepatitis of either type before without becoming jaundiced, in which case it is possible that you could be immune to either hepatitis A or C (or a number of other letters). This can be tested for before you travel. If you are not immune to hepatitis B already, a vaccine is available (3 shots over 6 months) and if you are not immune to hepatitis A already, then you should consider having gammaglobulin or a vaccination.

AIDS

This is increasingly prevalent in Southeast Asia. Thus, it is not wholly confined to the well known high risk sections of the population ie homosexual men, intravenous drug abusers, prostitutes and the children of infected mothers. Heterosexual transmission is probably now the dominant mode of infection and so the main risk to travellers is from casual sex. The same precautions should be taken as when encountering any sexually transmitted disease. In some Southeast Asian countries, Thailand is an example, almost the entire population of female prostitutes is HIV positive and in other parts intravenous drug abuse is common. The disease has not yet had the impact on Vietnam, Laos and Cambodia as it has on Thailand (but see box). The AIDS virus (HIV) can be passed via unsterile needles which have been previously used to inject an HIV positive patient, but the risk of this is very small indeed. It would, however, be sensible to check that needles have been properly sterilized or disposable needles used. The chance of picking up hepatitis B in this way is much more of a danger. Be wary of carrying disposable needles. Customs officials may find them suspicious. The risk of receiving a blood transfusion with blood infected with the HIV virus is greater than from dirty needles because of the amount of fluid exchanged. Supplies of blood for transfusion are supposed to be screened for HIV in all reputable hospitals so the risk should be small. Catching the virus which causes AIDS does not necessarily produce an illness in itself; the only way to be sure if you feel you have been put at risk is to have a blood test for HIV antibodies on your return to a place where there are reliable laboratory facilities. However, the test does not become positive for many weeks.

MALARIA

Malaria is prevalent in Southeast Asia and remains a serious disease and you are advised to protect yourself against mosquito bites as above and to take prophylactic (preventative) drugs. Start taking the tablets a few days before exposure and continue to take them 6 weeks after leaving the malarial zone. Remember to give the drugs to babies and children, pregnant women also.

The subject of malaria prevention is becoming more complex as the malaria parasite becomes immune to some of the older drugs. Nowhere is this more apparent than in Southeast Asia – especially parts of Laos and Cambodia. In particular, there has been an increase in the proportion of cases of falciparum malaria which are resistant to the normally used drugs. It would not be an exaggeration to say that we are near to the situation where some cases of malaria will be untreatable with presently available drugs.

Before you travel you must check with a reputable agency the likelihood and type of malaria in the countries which you intend to visit. Take their advice on prophylaxis but be prepared to receive conflicting advice. Because of the rapidly changing situation in the Southeast Asian region, the names and dosage of the drugs have not been included. But Chloroquine and Proguanil may still be recommended for the areas where malaria is still fully sensitive; while Doxycycline, Mefloquine and Quinghaosu are presently being used in resistant areas. Quinine, Halofantrine and tetracycline drugs remain the mainstay of treatment.

It is still possible to catch malaria even when taking prophylactic drugs, although this is unlikely. If you do develop symptoms (high fever, shivering, severe headache, and sometimes diarrhoea) seek medical advice immediately. The risk of the disease is obviously greater the further you move from the cities into rural areas, with primitive facilities and standing water.

OTHER COMMON PROBLEMS

HEAT AND COLD

Full acclimatization to tropical temperatures takes about 2 weeks and during this period it is normal to feel relatively apathetic, especially if the humidity is high. Drink plenty of water (up to 15 litres a day are required when working physically hard in the tropics). Use salt on your food and avoid extreme exertion. Tepid showers are more cooling than hot or cold ones. Large hats do not cool you down but do prevent sunburn. Remember that, especially in highland areas, there can be a large and sudden drop in temperature between sun and shade and between night and day so dress accordingly. Loose-fitting cotton clothes are best for hot weather. Warm jackets and woollens are often necessary after dark at high altitude.

INTESTINAL UPSETS

Practically nobody escapes intestinal infections, so be prepared for them. Most of the time they are due to the insanitary preparation of food. Do not eat uncooked fish, vegetables or meat (especially pork), fruit without the skin (always peel fruit yourself), or food that is exposed to flies (particularly salads). Tap water may be unsafe, especially in the monsoon seasons and the same goes for stream water or well water. Filtered or bottled water is usually available and safe but you cannot always rely on it. If your hotel has a **central** hot water supply, this is safe to drink after cooling. Ice should be made from boiled water but rarely is, so stand your glass on the ice cubes instead of putting them in the drink. Dirty water should first be strained through a filter bag (available from camping shops) and then boiled or treated. Bringing the water to a rolling boil at sea level is sufficient. In the highlands, you have to boil the water a bit longer to ensure that all the microbes are killed (because water boils at a lower temperature at altitude). Various sterilizing methods can be used and there are proprietary preparations containing chlorine or iodine compounds. Pasteurised or heat-treated milk is now fairly widely available as is ice cream and yoghurt produced by the same methods. Unpasteurised milk products, including cheese, are sources of tuberculosis, brucellosis, listeria and food poisoning germs. You can render fresh milk safe by heating it to 62°C for 30 mins followed by rapid cooling or by boiling. Matured or processed cheeses are safer than fresh varieties.

Fish and shellfish are popular foods in mainland Southeast Asia but can be the source of health problems. Shellfish which are eaten raw will transmit food poisoning or hepatitis if they have been living in contaminated water. Certain fish accumulate toxins in their bodies at certain times of the year, which give rise to illness when they are eaten. The phenomenon known as 'red tide' can also affect fish and shellfish which eat large quantities of tiny sea creatures and thereby become poisonous. The only way to guard against this is to keep as well informed as possible about fish and shellfish quality in the area you are visiting. Most countries impose a ban on fishing in periods when red tide is prevalent, although this is often flouted.

Diarrhoea

Diarrhoea is usually the result of food poisoning, but can occasionally result from contaminated water. There are various causes – viruses, bacteria, protozoa (like amoeba), salmonella and cholera organisms. It may take one of several forms coming on suddenly or rather slowly. It may be accompanied by vomiting or severe abdominal pain, and the passage of blood or mucus (when it is called dysentery).

All kinds of diarrhoea, whether or not accompanied by vomiting, respond favourably to the replacement of water and salts taken as frequent small sips of some kind of rehydration solution. There are proprietary preparations consisting of sachets of oral rehydration electrolyte powder which are dissolved in water, or you can make up your own by adding half a teaspoonful of salt (3.5 grams) and 4 tablespoons of sugar (40 grams) to a litre of boiled water. If it is possible to time the onset of diarrhoea to the minute, then it is probably viral or bacterial and/or the onset of dysentery. The treatment in addition to rehydration is Ciprofloxacin (500 mgs every 12 hrs). The drug is now widely available as are various similar ones.

If the diarrhoea has come on slowly or intermittently, then it is more likely to be protozoal, i.e. caused by amoeba (amoebic dysentery) or giardia, and antibiotics will have no effect. These cases are best treated by a doctor as should any diarrhoea continuing for more than 3 days. If there are severe stomach cramps, the following drugs may help: Loperamide (*Imodium*, *Arret*) and Diphenoxylate with Atropine (*Lomotil*). The drug usually used for giardia or amoeba is Metronidazole (*Flagyl*) or Tinidazole (*Fasigyu*).

The lynchpins of treatment for diarrhoea are rest, fluid and salt replacement, antibiotics such as Ciprofloxacin for the bacterial

Children and babies

Younger travellers are more prone to illness abroad, but that should not put you off taking them. More preparation is necessary than for an adult and perhaps a little more care should be taken when travelling to remote areas where health services are primitive. This is because children can become more rapidly ill than adults (they often recover more quickly however). For more practical advice on travelling with children and babies.

Diarrhoea and vomiting are the most common problems so take the usual precautions, but more intensively. Make sure all basic childhood **vaccinations** are up to date as well as the more exotic ones. Children should be properly protected against diphtheria, whooping cough, mumps and measles. If they have not had the disease, teenage girls should be given rubella (german measles) vaccination. Consult your doctor for advice on BCG inoculation against tuberculosis: the disease is still common in the region. Protection against mosquitos and drug prophylaxis against malaria is essential. Many children take to "foreign" food quite happily. Milk in Southeast Asia may be unavailable outside big cities. Powdered milk may be the answer; breast feeding for babies even better.

Upper respiratory infections such as colds, catarrh and middle ear infections are common – antibiotics could be carried against the possibility. **Outer ear infections** after swimming are also common – antibiotic ear drops will help.

The treatment of **diarrhoea** is the same as for adults except that it should start earlier and be continued with more persistence. Children get dehydrated very quickly in the tropics and can become drowsy and uncooperative unless cajoled to drink water or juice plus salts. Oral rehydration has been a lifesaving technique in children.

Protect children against the sun with a hat and high factor tanning lotion. Severe sunburn at this age may well lead to serious skin cancer in the future.

types, and special diagnostic tests and medical treatment for amoeba and giardia infections. Salmonella infections and cholera can be devastating diseases and it would be wise to get to a hospital as soon as possible if these were suspected. Fasting, peculiar diets and the consumption of large quantities of yoghurt have not been found useful in calming travellers' diarrhoea or in rehabilitating inflamed bowels. Oral rehydration has, especially in children, been a lifesaving technique and as there is some evidence that alcohol and milk might prolong diarrhoea they should probably be avoided during, and immediately after, an attack. There are ways of preventing travellers' diarrhoea for short periods of time when visiting these countries by taking antibiotics but these are ineffective against viruses and, to some extent, against protozoa. This technique should not be used other than in exceptional circumstances.

Some preventatives such as Enterovioform can have serious side effects if taken for long periods.

SUNBURN AND HEAT STROKE

The burning power of the tropical sun is phenomenal, especially in highland areas. Always wear a wide-brimmed hat, and use some form of sun cream or lotion on untanned skin. Normal temperate zone suntan lotions (protection factors up to 7) are not much good. You need to use the types designed specifically for the tropics or for mountaineers or skiers, with a protection factor between 7 and 15 or higher. Glare from the sun can cause conjunctivitis so wear sunglasses, particularly on beaches.

There are several varieties of heat stroke. The most common cause is severe dehydration. Avoid this by drinking lots of non-alcoholic fluid, and adding salt to your food.

INSECTS

These can be a great nuisance. Some, of course, are carriers of serious diseases such as malaria, dengue fever or filariasis and various worm infections. The best way of keeping mosquitos away at night is to sleep off the ground with a mosquito net and to burn mosquito coils containing Pyrethrum. Aerosol sprays or a 'flit gun' may be effective as are insecticidal tablets which are heated on a mat which is plugged into the wall socket (if taking your own, check the voltage of the area you are visiting so that you can take an appliance that will work; similarly, check that your electrical adaptor is suitable for the repellent plug; note that they are widely available in the region).

You can, in addition, use personal insect repellent of which the best contain a high concentration of diethyltoluamide (DET). Liquid is best for arms and face (take care around eyes and make sure you do not dissolve the plastic of your spectacles). Aerosol spray on clothes and ankles deter mites and ticks. Liquid DET suspended in water can be used to impregnate cotton clothes and mosquito nets. The latter are now available in wide mesh form which are lighter to carry and less claustrophobic to sleep under.

If you are bitten, itching may be relieved by cool baths and anti-histamine tables (take care with alcohol or when driving), corticosteroid creams (great care – never use if any hint of septic poisoning) or by judicious scratching. Calamine lotion and cream have limited effectiveness and anti-histamine creams have a tendency to cause skin allergies and are therefore not generally recommended. Bites which become infected (a common problem in the tropics) should be treated with a local antiseptic or antibiotic cream such as Cetrimide, as should infected scratches. Skin infestations with body lice, crabs and scabies are unfortunately easy to pick up. Use gamma benzene hexachloride for lice and benzyl benzoate for scabies. Crotamiton cream alleviates itching and also kills a number of skin parasites. Malathion lotion is good for lice but avoid the highly toxic full strength Malathion which is used as an agricultural insecticide.

SNAKE AND OTHER BITES AND STINGS

If you are unlucky enough to be bitten by a venomous snake, spider, scorpion, centipede or sea creature, try (within limits) to catch or kill the animal for identification. Reactions to be expected are shock, swelling, pain and bruising around the bite, soreness of the regional lymph glands, nausea, vomiting and fever. If in addition any of the following symptoms should follow closely, get the victim to a doctor without delay: numbness, tingling of the face, muscular spasms, convulsions, shortness of breath or haemorrhage. Commercial snake-bite or scorpion-sting kits may be available but these are only useful against the specific type of snake or scorpion for which they are designed. The serum has to be given intravenously so is not much good unless you have had some practice in making injections into veins. If the bite is on a limb, immobilize it and apply a tight bandage between the bite and the body, releasing it for 90 seconds every 15 minutes. Reassurance of the victim is very important because death from snake bite is very rare. Do not slash the bite area and try to suck out the poison because this sort of heroism does more harm than good. Hospitals usually hold stocks of snake-bite serum. The best precaution is not walk in long grass with bare feet, sandals, or in shorts.

When swimming in an area where there are poisonous fish such as stone or scorpion fish (also called by a variety of local names) or sea urchins on rocky coasts, tread carefully or wear plimsolls/trainers. The sting of such fish is intensely painful. This can be relieved by immersing the injured part of the body in water as hot as you can bear for as long as it remains painful. This is not always very practical and you must take care not to scald yourself, but it does work. Avoid spiders and scorpions by keeping your bed away from the wall, look under lavatory seats and inside your shoes in the morning. In the rare event of being bitten, consult a doctor.

OTHER AFFLICTIONS

Remember that **rabies** is endemic in many Southeast Asian countries. If you are bitten by a domestic or wild animal, do not leave things to chance. Scrub the wound with soap and water and/or disinfectant, try to have the animal captured (within limits) or at least determine its ownership where possible and seek medical assistance at once. The course of treatment depends on whether you have already been satisfactorily vaccinated against rabies. If you have (and this is worthwhile if you are spending lengths of time in developing countries) then some further doses of vaccine are all that is required. Human diploid cell vaccine is the best, but expensive: other, older kinds of vaccine such as that derived from duck embryos may be the only types available. These are effective, much cheaper and interchangeable generally with the human derived types. If not already vaccinated then anti-rabies serum (immúnoglobulin) may be required in addition. It is wise to finish the course of treatment whether the animal survives or not.

Dengue fever is present in most of the countries of Southeast Asia. It is a viral disease transmitted by mosquito and causes severe headaches and body pains. Complicated types of dengue known as haemorrhagic fevers occur throughout Asia but usually in persons who have caught the disease a second time. Thus, although it is a very serious type it is rarely caught by visitors. There is no treatment, you must just avoid mosquito bites.

Intestinal worms are common and the more serious ones, such as hook worm can be contracted by walking barefoot on infested earth or beaches.

Influenza and **respiratory diseases** are common, perhaps made worse by polluted cities and rapid temperature and climatic changes – accentuated by air-conditioning.

Prickly heat is a very common itchy rash, best avoided by frequent washing and by wearing loose clothing and is helped by the use of talcum powder, allowing the skin to dry thoroughly after washing.

Athlete's foot and other **fungal infections** are best treated by sunshine and a proprietary preparation such as Tolnaftate.

WHEN YOU RETURN HOME

On returning home, remember to take antimalarial tablets for 6 weeks. If you have had attacks of diarrhoea, it is worth having a stool specimen tested in case you have picked up amoebic dysentery. If you have been living rough, a blood test may also be worthwhile to detect worms and other parasites.

FURTHER HEALTH INFORMATION

Information regarding country-by-country malaria risk can be obtained from the World Health Organization (WHO) or in Britain from the Ross Institute, London School of Hygiene and Tropical Medicine, Keppel Street, London WCIE 7HT which also publishes a highly recommended book: *The preservation of personal health in warm climates*. The Centres for Disease Control (CDC) in Atlanta, Georgia, USA will provide equivalent information. The organization MASTA (Medical Advisory Service for Travellers Abroad) also based at the London School of Hygiene and Tropical Medicine (T 0171 631-4408) will provide up-to-date country-by-country information on health risks. Further information on medical problems overseas can be obtained from the new edition of *Travellers health, how to stay healthy abroad*, edited by Richard Dawood (Oxford University Press, 1992). This revised and updated edition is highly recommended, especially to the intrepid traveller. A more general publication, with hints on health and much more besides, is John Hatt's new edition of *The tropical traveller* (Penguin, 1993).

The above information has been compiled by Dr David Snashall, Senior Lecturer in Occupational Health, United Medical Schools of Guy's and St Thomas' Hospitals and Chief Medical Adviser, Foreign and Commonwealth Office, London.

Fares and timetables

TO	Days	Dep Time	Arr Time	Via
Domestic air routes: timetable				
FROM ATTAPEU (ATU)				
Pakse (PKZ)	3	1025	1100	
	6	0755	0830	
FROM BAN HOUEI XAI (HOE)				
Luang Prabang (LPQ)	1	1040	1215	UDY
	1	1455	1545	
	2,7	1240	1330	
	3	1040	1215	LXG
	3	1425	1515	
	4,6	1125	1215	
	4	1410	1545	UDY
	5	1210	1300	
	6	1340	1515	LXG
FROM LAKSAO (LAK)				
Vientiane (VTE)	2,4	1030	1140	
FROM LUANG PRABANG (LPQ)				
Ban Houei Xai (HOE)	1,3	0930	1020	
	1	1300	1435	UDX
	2,7	1130	1220	
	3	1230	1405	LXG
	4,6	0930	1105	UDX
	4	1300	1350	
	5	1100	1150	

TO	Days	Dep Time	Arr Time	Via
	6	0930	1105	LXG
	6	1230	1320	
Luang NamTha (LXG)	3	0930	1120	HOE
	3	1230	1305	
	6	0930	1005	
	6	1230	1420	HOE
Phonsavanh (Xieng Khouang) (XKH)	3	1510	1545	HOE
	5,7	0900	0935	
Udom Xai (UDY)	1	0930	1120	HOE
	1	1300	1335	
	2,7	1400	1435	
	4	0930	1005	
	4	1300	1450	HOE
	5	1430	1505	
Vientiane (VTE)	1,2,3,4	1600	1640	
	1,3,4,6	0930	1010	
	2,7	1130	1210	
	3	1510	1650	XKH
	5	1100	1140	
	5,7	1800	1840	
	6	1530	1610	

322

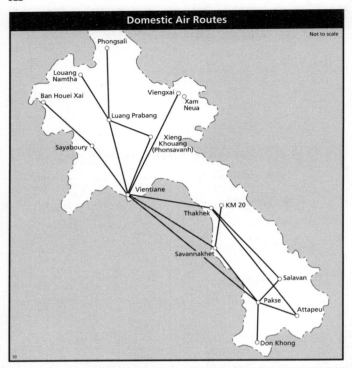

Domestic Air Routes

Not to scale

TO	Days	Dep Time	Arr Time	Via
FROM LUANG NAMTHA (LXG)				
Luang Prabang (LPQ)	3	1140	1215	
	3	1325	1515	HOE
	6	1025	1215	HOE
	6	1440	1515	
Vientiane (VTE)	2,4	1220	1330	
	7	1215	1320	
FROM PAKSE (PKZ)				
Attapeu (ATU)	3	0930	1005	
	6	0700	0735	

TO	Days	Dep Time	Arr Time	Via
Muang Khong (KON)	2	0930	1005	
	2	1025	1100	
	7	0730	0820	
	7	0755	0830	
Savannakhet (ZVK)	1	0930	1020	
	1	1040	1130	
	5	0730	0820	
	5	0840	0930	
Vientiane (VTE)	1,2,3,5,6,7	0850	1010	
	5	1550	1710	

323

FROM PHONSAVANH (XIENG KHOANG) (XKH)

TO	Days	Dep Time	Arr Time	Via
Luang Prabang (LPQ)	3	1415	1450	
	5,7	0955	1030	
Vientiane (VTE)	1,3	1150	1230	
	2,4	1400	1440	
	3	1605	1650	
	5,6	0900	0940	
	5,6	1505	1550	
	7	1500	1540	

FROM SAVANNAKHET (ZVK)

TO	Days	Dep Time	Arr Time	Via
Vientiane (VTE)	1,2,3,4,7	0855	1000	
	5	0825	0930	
	6	1525	1630	

FROM SAYABOURY (ZBY)

TO	Days	Dep Time	Arr Time	Via
Vientiane (VTE)	1,5,6	1235	1320	
	3	1205	1250	

FROM UDOM XAI (UDY)

TO	Days	Dep Time	Arr Time	Via
Luang Prabang (LPQ)	1	1140	1215	
	1	1355	1445	HOE
	2,7	1455	1530	
	4	1025	1215	HOE
	4	1510	1545	
	5	1525	1600	
Vientian (VTE)	3	1310	1430	
	6	1240	1400	

FROM VIENTIANE (VTE)

TO	Days	Dep Time	Arr Time	Via
Laksao (LAK)	2,4	0900	1010	
Luang NamTha (LXG)	2,4	1050	1200	
	7	1050	1155	
Luang Prabang (LPQ)	1,3,4,6	0830	0910	
	1,2,3,4	1500	1540	
	2,7	1030	1110	
	3	1310	1450	XKH
	5	1000	1040	
	5,7	1700	1740	
	6	1430	1510	
Pakse (PKZ)	1,2,3,4,6,7	0700	0820	
	5	1400	1520	
Phonsavanh (Xieng Khouang) (XKH)	1,3	1050	1130	
	2,4	1300	1340	
	3	1310	1355	
	5,6	0800	0840	
	5,6	1400	1445	
	7	1400	1440	
Savannakhet (ZVK)	1,2,3,4,5,7	0730	0835	
	6	1400	1505	
Sayaboury (ZBY)	1,5,6	1130	1215	
	3	1100	1145	
Udon Xai (UDX)	3	1130	1250	
	6	1100	1220	
Xam Neua (SNA)	2,4,7	1200	1310	

FROM XAM NEUA (SNA)

TO	Days	Dep Time	Arr Time	Via
Vientiane (VTE)	2,4,7	1330	1440	

NB1: 1=Mon; 2=Tues; 3=Wed; 4=Thur; 5=Fri; 6=Sat; 7=Sun

NB2: Lao Aviation tend to change their schedule at whim. Times of departure vary from week to week and flights may be cancelled at short notice. One Lao Aviation employee remarked in an unguarded moment that "we never know from one day to the next when or if a plane is going to leave".

1996 Lao Aviation timetable.

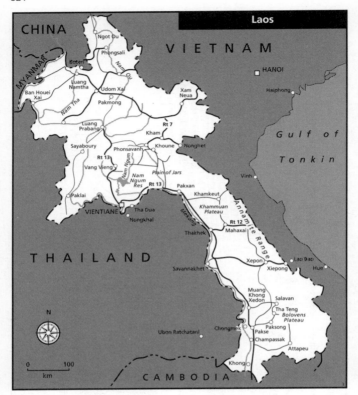

Bus/Truck times and fares (May 1996)

	Distance (km)	Time	Average speed	Fare (kip)	Road conditions
Roads north from Vientiane					
Vientiane to Vang Vieng	160 km	3 hrs	53km/hr	1,500 kip	good, surface road
Vang Vieng to Luang Prabang	260 km	13 hrs	20 km/hr	9,000 kip	upgrading of this road was completed at the end of 1996. The journey time quoted here was before completion. But note that the road is dangerous (see Safety)
Roads south from Vientiane					
Vientiane to Pakxan	155 km	2-3 hrs	62 km/hr	1,300 kip	good surfaced road with new bridges undergoing upgrading and surfacing; due for completion by 1997. Some old bridges still to be replaced
Pakxan to Thakhek	190 km	5-6 hrs	35 km/hr	2,500 kip	
Thakhek to Savannakhet	139 km	3-4 hrs	40 km/hr	1,700 kip	good, surfaced road
Vientiane to Savannakhet	484 km	10-13 hrs	44 km/hr	7,000 kip	
Savannakhet to Vietnamese border	236 km	5 hrs	47 km/hr	2,800 kip	rough road, partly sealed
Savannakhet to Pakse	250 km	6-8 hrs	36 km/hr	4,000 kip	poor road, unsurfaced, but being slowly upgraded
Pakse to Salavan	125 km	3-4 hrs	36 km/hr	1,500 kip	new, surfaced road
Salavan to Sekong	98 km	4 hrs	25 km/hr	1,300 kip	dirt road undergoing improvement
Pakse to Don Khong	130 km	4-5 hrs	29 km/hr	2,200 kip	unsurfaced, laterite

Mid 1996 prices quoted

NB Roads are being improved and new vehicles are appearing. Already there is a noticeable difference in speed between Soviet and newer Japanese buses. Aong with vast differences in road conditions between the wet and dry seasons, the times listed above should be taken as only rough indicators.

Glossary

A

Amitabha
the Buddha of the Past (see Avalokitsvara)

Amulet
protective medallion

Arhat
a person who has perfected himself; images of former monks are sometimes carved into arhat

Avadana
Buddhist narrative, telling of the deeds of saintly souls

Avalokitsvara
also known as Amitabha and Lokeshvara, the name literally means 'World Lord'; he is the compassionate male Bodhisattva, the saviour of Mahayana Buddhism and represents the central force of creation in the universe; usually portrayed with a lotus and water flask

B

Bai sema
boundary stones marking consecrated ground around a Buddhist bot (see page 48)

Ban
village; shortened from muban

Batik
a form of resist dyeing

Bhikku
Buddhist monk

Bodhi
the tree under which the Buddha achieved enlightenment (*Ficus religiosa*)

Bodhisattva
a future Buddha. In Mahayana Buddhism, someone who has attained enlightenment, but who postpones nirvana to help others reach it.

Boun
Lao festival

B

Brahma
the Creator, one of the gods of the Hindu trinity, usually represented with four faces, and often mounted on a hamsa

Brahmin
a Hindu priest

Bun
to make merit

C

Cao Dai
composite religion of south Vietnam

Caryatid
elephants, often used as buttressing decorations

Champa
rival empire of the Khmers, of Hindu culture, based in present day Vietnam

Chao
title for Lao kings

Charn
animist priest who conducts the basi ceremony in Laos

Chat
honorific umbrella or royal multi-tiered parasol

Chedi
from the Sanskrit *cetiya* (Pali, *caitya*) meaning memorial. Usually a religious monument (often bell-shaped) containing relics of the Buddha or other holy remains. Used interchangeably with stupa

Chenla
Chinese name for Cambodia before the Khmer era

D

Deva
a Hindu-derived male god

Devata
a Hindu-derived goddess

Dharma
the Buddhist law

Dipterocarp
family of trees (*Dipterocarpaceae*) characteristic of Southeast Asia's forests

Doi moi
'renovation', Vietnamese perestroika

Dok sofa
literally, 'bucket of flowers'. A frond-like construction which surmounts temple roofs in Laos. Over 10 flowers signifies the wat was built by a king

Dtin sin
Lao decorative border on a tubular skirt

Dvarapala
guardian figure, usually placed at the entrance to a temple

F

Funan
the oldest Indianised state of Indochina and precursor to Chenla

G

Ganesh
elephant-headed son of Siva

Garuda
mythical divine bird, with predatory beak and claws, and human body; the king of birds, enemy of naga and mount of Vishnu

Gautama
the historic Buddha

Geomancy
the art of divination by lines and figures

Gopura
crowned or covered gate, entrance to a religious area

H

Hamsa
sacred goose, Brahma's mount; in Buddhism it represents the flight of the doctrine

Hinayana
'Lesser Vehicle', major Buddhist sect in Southeast Asia, usually termed Theravada Buddhism (see page 64)

Hor kong
a pavilion built on stilts where the temple drum is kept

Hor latsalot
chapel of the funeral cart in a Lao temple

Hor song phra
secondary chapel in a Lao temple

Hor takang
bell tower (see page 48)

Hor tray/trai
library where manuscripts are stored in a Lao or Thai temple (see page 48)

Hor vay
offering temple in a Lao temple complex

I

Ikat
tie-dyeing method of patterning cloth (see page 111)

Indra
the Vedic god of the heavens, weather and war; usually mounted on a 3 headed elephant

J

Jataka(s)
the birth stories of the Buddha; they normally number 547, although an additional 3 were added in Burma for reasons of symmetry in mural painting and sculpture; the last ten are the most important

K

Kala (makara)
literally, 'death' or 'black'; a demon ordered to consume itself; often sculpted with grinning face and bulging eyes over entranceways to act as a door guardian; also known as kirtamukha

Kathin/krathin
a one month period during the eighth lunar month when lay people present new robes and other gifts to monks

Ketumula
flame-like motif above the Buddha head

Kinaree
half-human, half-bird, usually depicted as a heavenly musician

Kirtamukha
see kala

Koutdi
see kuti

Krishna
incarnation of Vishnu

Kuti
living quarters of Buddhist monks in a temple complex

L

Laterite
bright red tropical soil/stone commonly used in construction of Khmer monuments

Linga
phallic symbol and one of the forms of Siva. Embedded in a pedestal shaped to allow drainage of lustral water poured

over it, the linga typically has a succession of cross sections: from square at the base through octagonal to round. These symbolise, in order, the trinity of Brahma, Vishnu and Siva

Lintel
a load-bearing stone spanning a doorway; often heavily carved

Lokeshvara
see Avalokitsvara

M

Mahabharata
a Hindu epic text written about 2,000 years ago

Mahayana
'Greater Vehicle', major Buddhist sect (see page 61)

Maitreya
the future Buddha

Makara
a mythological aquatic reptile, somewhat like a crocodile and sometimes with an elephant's trunk; often found along with the kala framing doorways

Mandala
a focus for meditation; a representation of the cosmos

Mara
personification of evil and tempter of the Buddha

Matmii
Northeastern Thai and Lao cotton ikat

Mat mi
see matmii

Meru
sacred or cosmic mountain at the centre of the world in Hindu-Buddhist cosmology; home of the gods

Mondop
from the sanskrit, *mandapa*. A cube-shaped building, often topped with a cone-like structure, used to contain an object of worship like a footprint of the Buddha

Muang
administrative unit. In Laos, the system, based on local governors, was established by King Samenthai in the 14th century

Muban
village, usually shortened to ban (L)

Mudra
symbolic gesture of the hands of the Buddha (see page 62)

N

Nak
Lao river dragon, a mythical guardian creature (see naga)

Naga
benevolent mythical water serpent, enemy of Garuda (see page 50)

Naga makara
fusion of naga and makara

Nalagiri
the elephant let loose to attack the Buddha, who calmed him

Nandi/nandin
bull, mount of Siva

Nirvana
release from the cycle of suffering in Buddhist belief; 'enlightenment'

Nyak
mythical water serpent (see naga)

P

Pa kama
Lao men's all purpose cloth usually woven with checked pattern

paddy/padi
unhulled rice

Pali
the sacred language of Theravada Buddhism

Parvati
consort of Siva

Pathet Lao
Communist party based in the north-eastern provinces of Laos until they came to power in 1975

Pha biang
shawl worn by women in Laos

Pha sin
tubular piece of cloth, similar to sarong

Phi
spirit (see page 64)

Phra sinh
see pha sin

Pra Lam
Lao version of the Ramayana (see Ramakien)

Pradaksina
pilgrims' clockwise circumambulation of holy structure

Prah
sacred

Prang
form of stupa built in Khmer style, shaped like a corncob

Prasada
stepped pyramid (see prasat)

Prasat
residence of a king or of the gods (sanctuary tower), from the Indian prasada

Q

Quan Am
Chinese goddess (Kuan-yin) of mercy (see page 98)

R

Rama
incarnation of Vishnu, hero of the Indian epic, the *Ramayana*

Ramakien
Lao version of the *Ramayana* (see page 70)

Ramayana
Hindu romantic epic (see page 70)

S

Sakyamuni
the historic Buddha

Sal
the Indian sal tree (*Shorea robusta*), under which the historic Buddha was born

Sangha
the Buddhist order of monks

Sim/sima
main sanctuary and ordination hall in a Lao temple complex, equivalent to the bot in Thailand (see page 48)

Singha
mythical guardian lion

Siva
the Destroyer, one of the three gods of the Hindu trinity; the sacred linga was worshipped as a symbol of Siva

Sofa
see dok sofa

Sravasti
the miracle at Sravasti when the Buddha subdues the heretics in front of a mango tree

Stele
inscribed stone panel

Stucco
plaster, often heavily moulded

Stupa
chedi (see page 50)

T

Tam bun
see bun

Taoism
Chinese religion (see page 57)

Tavatimsa
heaven of the 33 gods at the summit of Mount Meru

Thanon
street

That
shrine housing Buddhist relics, a spire or dome-like edifice commemorating the Buddha's life or the funerary temple for royalty; peculiar to Laos and parts of Northeastern Thailand

Theravada
'Way of the Elders'; major Buddhist sect also known as Hinayana Buddhism ('Lesser Vehicle') (see page 64)

Traiphum
the three worlds of Buddhist cosmology – heaven, hell and earth

Trimurti
the Hindu trinity of gods: Brahma, the Creator, Vishnu the Preserver and Siva the Destroyer

Tripitaka
Theravada Buddhism's Pali canon

U

Ubosoth
see bot

Urna
the dot or curl on the Buddha's forehead, one of the distinctive physical marks of the Enlightened One

Usnisa
the Buddha's top knot or 'wisdom bump', one of the physical marks of the Enlightened One

V

Vahana
'vehicle', a mythical beast, upon which a deva or god rides

Viharn
from Sanskrit *vihara*, an assembly hall in a Buddhist monastery; may contain Buddha images and is similar in style to the bot (see page 48)

Vishnu
the Protector, one of the gods of the Hindu trinity, generally with four arms holding a disc, conch shell, ball and club

Tinted boxes

Index

Illustrations and maps

Map Symbols

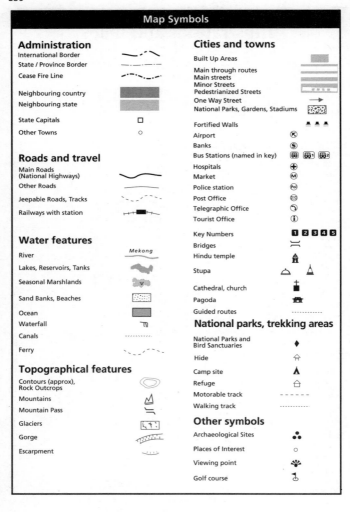

Administration

International Border
State / Province Border
Cease Fire Line

Neighbouring country
Neighbouring state

State Capitals
Other Towns

Roads and travel

Main Roads
(National Highways)
Other Roads
Jeepable Roads, Tracks
Railways with station

Water features

River
Lakes, Reservoirs, Tanks
Seasonal Marshlands
Sand Banks, Beaches
Ocean
Waterfall
Canals
Ferry

Topographical features

Contours (approx),
Rock Outcrops
Mountains
Mountain Pass
Glaciers
Gorge
Escarpment

Cities and towns

Built Up Areas
Main through routes
Main streets
Minor Streets
Pedestrianized Streets
One Way Street
National Parks, Gardens, Stadiums
Fortified Walls
Airport
Banks
Bus Stations (named in key)
Hospitals
Market
Police station
Post Office
Telegraphic Office
Tourist Office

Key Numbers
Bridges
Hindu temple
Stupa
Cathedral, church
Pagoda
Guided routes

National parks, trekking areas

National Parks and
Bird Sanctuaries
Hide
Camp site
Refuge
Motorable track
Walking track

Other symbols

Archaeological Sites
Places of Interest
Viewing point
Golf course

Footprint Handbooks

All of us at Footprint Handbooks hope you have enjoyed reading and travelling with this Handbook, one of the first published in the new Footprint series. Many of you will be familiar with us as Trade & Travel, a name that has served us well for years. For you and for those who have only just discovered the Handbooks, we thought it would be interesting to chronicle the story of our development from the early 1920's.

It all started 75 years ago in 1921, with the publication of the Anglo-South American Handbook. In 1924 the South American Handbook was created. This has been published each year for the last 73 years and is the longest running guidebook in the English language, immortalised by Graham Greene as "the best travel guide in existence".

One of the key strengths of the South American Handbook over the years, has been the extraordinary contact we have had with our readers through their hundreds of letters to us in Bath. From these letters we learnt that you wanted more Handbooks of the same quality to other parts of the world.

In 1989 my brother Patrick and I set about developing a series modelled on the South American Handbook. Our aim was to create the ultimate practical guidebook series for all travellers, providing expert knowledge of far flung places, explaining culture, places and people in a balanced, lively and clear way. The whole idea hinged, of course, on finding writers who were in tune with our thinking. Serendipity stepped in at exactly the right moment: we were able to bring together a talented group of people who know the countries we cover inside out and whose enthusiasm for travelling in them needed to be communicated.

The series started to grow. We felt that the time was right to look again at the identity that had brought us all this way. After much searching we commissioned London designers Newell & Sorrell to look at all the issues. Their solution was a new identity for the Handbooks representing the books in all their aspects, looking after all the good things already achieved and taking us into the new millennium.

The result is Footprint Handbooks: a new name and mark, simple yet assertive, bold, stylish and instantly recognisable. The images we use conjure up the essence of real travel and communicate the qualities of the Handbooks in a straightforward and evocative way.

For us here in Bath, it has been an exciting exercise working through this dramatic change. Already the 'new us' fits like our favourite travelling clothes and we cannot wait to get more and more Footprint Handbooks onto the book shelves and out onto the road.

The Footprint list

Footprint T-shirt

The Footprint T-shirt is available in 100% cotton in various colours.

Mail Order

Footprint Handbooks are available worldwide in good bookstores. They can also be ordered directly from us in Bath (see below for address). Please contact us if you have difficulty finding a title.

The Footprint Handbook website will be coming to keep you up to date with all the latest news from us (http://www.footprint-handbooks.co.uk). For the most up-to-date information and to join our mailing list please contact us at:

Footprint Handbooks
6 Riverside Court
Lower Bristol Road
Bath BA2 3DZ, England
T +44(0)1225 469141
F +44(0)1225 469461
E Mail handbooks@footprint.cix.co.uk